CASS LIBRARY OF AFRICAN STUDIES

GENERAL STUDIES

No. 137

Editorial Adviser: JOHN RALPH WILLIS
Department of History, University of California, Berkeley

The African Slave Trade and its Suppression

The African Slave Trade and its Suppression

A Classified and Annotated
Bibliography of Books,
Pamphlets and Periodical Articles

Peter C. Hogg, B.A., F.L.A.

FRANK CASS : LONDON

First published 1973 in Great Britain by
FRANK CASS AND COMPANY LIMITED
67 Great Russell Street, London WC1B 3BT, England

and in United States of America by
FRANK CASS AND COMPANY LIMITED
c/o International Scholarly Book Services, Inc.
P.O. Box 4347, Portland, Oregon 97208

ISBN 0 7146 2775 5

Library of Congress Catalog Card No. 72 – 90130

*Printed in Great Britain by
The Anchor Press Ltd.,
Tiptree, Essex*

Contents

Acknowledgements

This bibliography is based on one submitted and accepted for Fellowship of the Library Association in 1970. I am indebted to Mr Allan Chapman, F.L.A., who as my supervisor guided the work to a successful conclusion.

I am also grateful to colleagues in the British Museum Library who drew my attention to relevant literature, to a number of librarians in Britain and abroad who were most helpful in answering my enquiries, and above all to my wife for her encouragement and assistance.

I dedicate the work to the memory of Christian Okechukwu Ahakpo and his comrades: *ka onwu ha nwuru awughi na ihi.*

Introduction

As the literature of the African slave trade comprises books, pamphlets and periodical articles in a variety of languages published from the sixteenth century to the present day it is difficult for any individual compiler to assemble bibliographical information about more than a representative selection of the material available. This bibliography can therefore only aspire to serve as a guide to the main categories of printed material on the subject in western languages, and the user should be warned that it has an unavoidable 'bias' towards English-language material. I have excluded manuscripts and kept government publications to a minimum as the latter alone would run into thousands.

Slavery and trade in slaves existed in parts of Africa from the beginning of recorded history. Information on the ancient and medieval slave trade must be pieced together from brief references in classical and Arabic literature. A similar scarcity of sources obtains for the first century or so of European participation in the trade which was begun in a small way by the Portuguese on the Atlantic coast in the 1440s. Only the European colonisation of the Americas created the demand for cheap labour which led to the enormous expansion of the African slave trade between the sixteenth and the nineteenth century. This basic economic function of the trade is the dominant theme of the literature on the subject, whether practical or polemical.

For historical and geographical reasons European literature dealing with the slave trade was always largely concerned with its West African sectors as these constituted one of the vital base lines in the triangular trade between Europe, Africa and the Americas which sustained the Atlantic economic system for three centuries. Not until the European slave trade was being suppressed in the nineteenth century was attention concentrated on the sources of the Muslim slave trade in the Sudan and East Africa.

Although a fair amount of manuscript records survive from the sixteenth century very little information on the slave trade was published in that period apart from accounts of voyages like those of Cà da Mosto and Hawkins. But this century already saw the beginnings of the controversy about the justification of the trade in the works of a few Catholic theologians. The only great markets for slaves in this period were of course the Spanish and Portuguese colonies in tropical America.

In the seventeenth century the Iberian monopoly of the Atlantic slave trade was broken by the new maritime powers of Europe, the Netherlands, England and France, with Denmark and, for a short period, Brandenburg in their wake. All of these states followed the established pattern by acquiring colonies in the New World linked to commercial footholds in West Africa from which slaves could be supplied. This new economic order was reflected in the appearance of geographical and commercial works on Africa by writers of all the new colonial countries. At the same time, however, Protestants joined the Catholics in the sporadic controversy on the slavery issue and by the end of the century several outright attacks on the slave trade had been published, as an omen of the future, by English nonconformists in America.

The eighteenth century is the classical period of the mercantilist European slave trade, marked by further expansion and legal regulation of the system. England gained supremacy in this field, symbolised by her acquisition in 1713 of the 'asiento' contract to supply the Spanish-American colonies with African slaves. An increasing number of books and pamphlets on the African trade resulted from the intensified commercial competition between the European colonial powers and between rival economic groups within these states. At the same time more factual information on the trade was being supplied by traders, missionaries, officials and travellers along the African coast.

The heightened economic competition and the increasing knowledge about the African slave trade caused a growing revulsion in European public opinion against this 'traffic in men'. From the middle of the eighteenth century the new school of rationalists subjected the whole system to a radical critique, while its religious opponents also progressed in the 1760s to moral, legal and economic arguments for its abolition. The leading polemicists in this period were the Americans Benezet and Woolman and the Englishman Granville Sharp, who in 1772 demonstrated by a test case that slavery was not legally sanctioned in England. Simultaneously imaginative literature on African themes developed an antislavery tendency and began to serve as an additional weapon in the abolition controversy.

The growing number of publications devoted at this time to the slavery issue illustrates the increasing momentum of the abolition movement which led to the formation of antislavery societies in New England, Britain and France by 1787–88 and the launching of organised political campaigns for the abolition of the slave trade. The years 1788–92 mark the high tide of the resulting pamphlet warfare. Then the establishment of the revolutionary French republic and the successful slave revolt in Haiti provoked a conservative reaction in Britain where the anti-slave trade campaign soon stalled, while in France the matter appeared to be settled by the abolition of colonial slavery in 1794.

When the nineteenth century opened the slavery question was overshadowed by war in Europe. In 1802, although Denmark withdrew from the slave trade, France actually restored slavery in her colonies and only waited for an opportunity to reopen the slave trade. However, for a combination of economic and moral reasons both Britain and the United States decided in 1807 to end their participation in the slave trade from Africa. From then on it was in their own interest to ensure that their economic rivals—France, Spain, Portugal and the Netherlands —should also cease to resupply their colonies with African slaves. The United States was divided internally on the slavery issue and it was Britain, with her wider imperial interests, that took the lead in the ensuing political struggle.

British abolitionists concerned with the commercial opening up of Africa soon began to attack the 'foreign' slave trade and the defeat of France in 1815 made it possible for Britain within a few years to enforce the abolition of the French slave trade and to negotiate abolition treaties with Spain, Portugal, the Netherlands and many other states. Despite this treaty system, however, the slave trade continued illegally and actually increased in volume during the following decades. With the ending of British colonial slavery in 1834 the abolitionists became more sharply aware of the size of the illicit slave trade. After 1840 the writings of men like Buxton, Madden and Bandinel and the formation of new anti-slavery societies induced the British government to adopt a more active anti-slave trade policy.

British political pressure was now directed mainly against Spain, Portugal and Brazil. These states, together with France and the United States, bitterly resented

Britain's attempt to establish the right of her navy to search their merchant ships at sea and controversy raged for years on the subject. Brazil finally suppressed illegal slave imports in 1851, the civil war ended importation into the United States, and slave smuggling into Spain's Caribbean colonies had finished by 1865 when Britain's Atlantic antislavery patrols were discontinued, leaving only the squadron stationed off East Africa. During the preceding thirty years a surprising amount of literature on the naval blockade had been published, reflecting the importance attached to command of the seas by Britain and the resentment caused by this policy among rival powers.

The new attention paid by abolitionists to the Muslim slave trade in Africa in the nineteenth century is seen in the literature, which focused on northern Africa from about 1840 and on East Africa from about 1870. It is interesting to note the close correlation between the development of European interests in Africa and the changing emphases in the slave trade literature. The concern with North Africa coincided with the political involvement of European powers in the Maghreb and Egypt, while the preoccupation with East Africa paralleled the growth of European strategic and commercial interests in the Indian Ocean area.

From the early 1880s to the end of the century all the major states of western Europe became involved in the competition for territories in Africa. European occupation was commonly justified in the literature of the period in terms of a need to eradicate the Muslim slave trade. This argument was employed with particular insistence by the propagandists of the Congo Free State, in conjunction with the advocates of the Catholic antislavery 'crusade' launched in 1888 by Cardinal Lavigerie. It led to the international antislavery conference held at Brussels in 1889–90 which resulted in agreements on a policy for the military suppression of the 'Arab' slave trade in eastern and central Africa. The ultimate use of this kind of propaganda was made by Italy in 1935 in order to justify her imperial aggression against Abyssinia. The export of slaves from Africa had, in fact, virtually come to an end with the completion of the colonial occupation of Africa around 1900.

The first strictly historical accounts of the African slave trade were, significantly perhaps, written by German scholars between 1779 and 1820. Serious historical research on a wider basis did not emerge until the end of the nineteenth and the beginning of the twentieth century. No major comprehensive history of the subject has yet been produced, though there are a number of useful studies dealing with particular areas and periods. There are still neglected facets, notably the study of the impact of the slave trade within Africa itself. The most detailed historical research has been devoted to two specific aspects, the economic history of the trade and the history of the abolition movement, both seen from the point of view of Europe and America rather than Africa.

Existing bibliographies

The earliest bibliographies on the African slave trade are the *Liste des ouvrages sur la traite et l'esclavage* (Paris, 1790) issued by the Société des Amis des Noirs for the information of the Assemblée Nationale and the bibliography in J. J. Sell, *Versuch einer Geschichte des Negersclavenhandels* (Halle, 1791). The former lists 59 and the latter 104 publications, virtually all 'controversial'. R. Watt, *Bibliotheca britannica* (Edinburgh, 1824), includes about 140 British works on the slave trade. A large number of general bibliographies and catalogues containing material on the subject have been published since then; I can refer here only to the more important ones.

The most comprehensive coverage is to be found in the New York Public

Library's *Dictionary catalog of the Schomburg Collection of Negro Literature & History* (Boston, 1962; with supplement), which contains about a thousand relevant entries among nearly 6000 on the slave trade and slavery. The sections 'Slavery and the slave trade within Africa', 'The African slave trade to America' and 'Slavery and abolition' in M. N. Work, *Bibliography of the negro in Africa and America* (New York, 1928) contain about 380 items; this is a good though somewhat uneven list with the main emphasis on the slave trade to the United States. Another American-orientated bibliography is the New York Public Library's *Dictionary catalog of the history of the Americas* (Boston, 1961) with some 290 items.

Specifically limited in scope is L. J. Ragatz, *A guide for the study of British Caribbean history, 1763–1834, including the abolition and emancipation movements* (Washington, 1932) which contains 490 well annotated entries on the slave trade under the heading 'Abolition and emancipation literature'. Further lists with an explicit emphasis on the British slave trade are to be found in the *Subject catalogue of the Royal Empire Society*, vol. 1 and 3 (London, 1930, 32); J. B. Williams, *A guide to the printed materials for English social and economic history 1750–1850* (New York, 1926); and the *Catalogue of the Goldsmiths' Library of Economic Literature* (vol. 1, Cambridge, 1970).

Among special bibliographies Catalogue 677 of Maggs Brothers Ltd, entitled *Slavery; the history of the slave trade and its abolition* (London, 1939), contains 160 items on the slave trade out of a total of nearly 480, but the League of Nations Library's *List of works relating to slavery catalogued in the Library* (Geneva, 1935) only 45 items out of 315.

Other useful sources are: the *Catalogue of the Colonial Office Library* (London, 1860); the *Catalogue of the Library of Congress: index of subjects* (Washington, 1869); Bibliothèque Nationale, *Catalogue des ouvrages données par M. V. Schoelcher* (Paris, 1884); the *Subject index of the London Library* (London, 1909–55); C. M. Trelles y Govín, *Biblioteca histórica cubana* (Matanzas, 1922–26; annotated); R. A. Peddie, *Subject index of books before 1880* (London, 1933–48); R. Streit, *Bibliotheca missionum*, vol. 15–20 (Münster i. W., 1951–54); and Harvard University Library, *Widener Library shelflist* (Cambridge, Mass., 1965–66).

Apart from the standard national bibliographies the following current bibliographies are essential aids: the *Subject index of modern works added to the Library of the British Museum* (London, 1902–); the *London bibliography of the social sciences* (London, 1931–); *African abstracts* (International African Institute, London, 1950–); the *Library of Congress subject catalog* (Washington, 1951–); the *Índice histórico español* (Barcelona, 1953–); and Centre d'Analyse et de Recherche Documentaires pour l'Afrique Noire, *Bulletin d'information et de liaison* (Paris, 1969–).

Periodical literature is less well covered than books. The basic sources are: W. F. Poole, *Index to periodical literature* (London, 1888–1908); F. Dietrich, *Bibliographie der deutschen Zeitschriftenliteratur/Internationale Bibliographie der Zeitschriftenliteratur* (Leipzig, 1897–); H. W. Wilson Company, *Readers' guide to periodical literature* (Minneapolis, 1905–) and *International index to periodicals/Social sciences & humanities index* (New York, 1916–); Library Association, *The subject index to periodicals/British humanities index* (London, 1919–); and Pan American Union (Columbus Memorial Library), *Index to Latin American periodicals* (Boston, 1962–).

The abolition literature is better represented bibliographically than that of the slave trade itself. Joyce Birt, *Catalogue of a collection of anti-slavery tracts and pamphlets in the possession of the Anti-Slavery Society for the Protection of Human*

Rights (typescript copy, London University Library, 1958) contains 480 titles relating to the slave trade from the period 1767–1855; *William Wilberforce, 1759–1833: a catalogue of the books and pamphlets on William Wilberforce and slavery in the Reference Library of Kingston upon Hull Public Libraries* (Kingston upon Hull, 1959; compiled by Allan Chapman) about 290; D. L. Dumond. *A bibliography of antislavery in America* (Ann Arbor, 1961) about 240 scattered through a single alphabetical sequence of 2400 items; the bibliography on the 'Humanitarian movement' in *The Cambridge history of the British empire*, vol. 2 (Cambridge, 1940), pp. 952–57, about 160; and G. H. Hubbard, *A classified catalogue of the collection of anti-slavery propaganda in the Oberlin College Library* (Oberlin, 1932) about 60 items, now available on microcards.

British parliamentary papers on the slave trade are listed in the *General index to the accounts and papers, reports of commissioners, estimates &c. &c. printed by order of the House of Commons or printed by command 1801–1852* (London, 1938); the *General alphabetical index to the bills, reports, estimates, accounts, and papers, printed by order of the House of Commons, and to the papers presented by command, 1852–1899* (London, 1909); and *A general index to the sessional papers printed by command of the House of Lords or presented by special command* (London, 1860–90), covering the period 1801–1885. Documents relevant to one particular area and period are listed in L. J. Ragatz, *A check-list of House of Commons sessional papers relating to the British West Indies and to the West Indian slave trade and slavery, 1763–1834* (Second edition, London, 1930), and *A check-list of House of Lords sessional papers relating to the British West Indies and to the West Indian slave trade and slavery, 1763–1834* (Second edition, London, 1932). Other useful compilations are the *Catalogue of parliamentary reports, papers, &c., relating to Africa, 1800 to 1899* (London, 1899), published by P. S. King & Son, and the section on 'Slavery and the slave trade' in the 'Select list of parliamentary papers', with the 'Select list of parliamentary debates' (from Hansard 1803–70), in the bibliography to *The Cambridge history of the British empire*, vol. 2 (Cambridge, 1940), pp. 915–19, 922–36.

United States public documents relating to the African slave trade are listed in B. P. Poore, *A descriptive catalogue of the government publications of the United States, September 5, 1774—March 4, 1881* (Washington, 1885) and in A. R. Hasse, *Index to United States documents relating to foreign affairs, 1828–1861* (Washington, 1914–21). There is also a good selection of congressional documents in the bibliography to W. E. B. DuBois, *The suppression of the African slave-trade to the United States of America* (New York, 1896).

Manuscript material on the slave trade is now partially covered bibliographically in the series of *Guides to materials for West African history in European archives* (London, 1962–   ), the *Guide to the sources of the history of Africa* (International Council on Archives, Zug, 1970–   ), and *A guide to manuscripts and documents in the British Isles relating to Africa* . . . Edited by J. D. Pearson (School of Oriental and African Studies, London, 1971).

General notes

The subject arrangement is shown in the list of contents. The order within each section is chronological.

An asterisk before an entry, except for unpublished theses, denotes that I have not located a copy for personal inspection.

In general only the earliest known editions have been included, unless later editions contain significantly new material.

Of translations, with few exceptions, only those into English from other languages are included.

Publishers' names are shown up to 1850, being of greater bibliographical interest and less easily traced before that date. Imaginative literature is listed only up to 1900.

The author index includes names of corporate bodies.

The index to anonymous titles omits anonymous periodical articles. The main antislavery journals are listed in section Q(b).

Common abbreviations, apart from those used for periodical titles, are: bibl. = bibliography; bk. = book; ch. = chapter; col. = column(s); illus. = illustration(s); l. (ll.) = leaf (leaves); n.s. = new series; no. = number; p. (pp.) = page(s); P.P. = Parliamentary Papers (Great Britain); pt. = part(s); ser. = series; vol. = volume(s).

Abbreviations of Periodical Titles

AA	American Anthropologist (Washington)
AESC	Annales. Économies, Sociétés, Civilisations (Paris)
AH	American Heritage (New York)
AHR	American Historical Review (New York)
AJIL	American Journal of International Law (New York)
AL	American Literature (Durham, N. C.)
AM	American Museum (Philadelphia)
AR	African Repository and Colonial Journal (Washington)
ASMR	Anti-Slavery Monthly Reporter (London)
AnR	Annual Register (London)
AtM	Atlantic Monthly (Boston)
BAGS	Bulletin of the American Geographical Society (New York)
BIFAN	Bulletin de l'Institut Français d'Afrique Noire (Paris); Bulletin de l'Institut Fondamental d'Afrique Noire (Dakar)
BIHR	Bulletin of the Institute of Historical Research (London)
BM	Blackwood's Magazine (Edinburgh)
BR	British Review (London)
BrM	Britannic Magazine (London)
CC	Civiltà Cattolica (Rome)
CEA	Cahiers d'Études Africaines (Paris)
CIMM	Century Illustrated Monthly Magazine (New York)
CJ	Chambers's Journal (Edinburgh)
CM	Cornhill Magazine (London)
CMG	Church Missionary Gleaner (London)
CMI	Church Missionary Intelligencer (London)
CO	Christian Observer (London)
CR	Contemporary Review (London)
ColM	Colonial Magazine (London)
CrR	Critical Review (London)
DA	Dissertation Abstracts (Ann Arbor, Mich.)
DBR	De Bow's Review (New Orleans)
DKB	Deutsches Kolonialblatt (Berlin)
DKZ	Deutsche Kolonialzeitung (Frankfurt)
DR	Dublin Review
EHR	English Historical Review (London)
EMLR	European Magazine and London Review (London)
EMM	Evangelisches Missions-Magazin (Basel)
ER	Edinburgh Review
EcHR	Economic History Review (London)
EcR	Eclectic Review (London)
FA	Friend of Africa (London)
FHQ	Florida Historical Quarterly (Tallahassee)
FR	Fortnightly Review (London)

GHM	Göttingisches Historisches Magazin (Hannover)
GHQ	Georgia Historical Quarterly (Savannah)
GM	Gentleman's Magazine (London)
HAHR	Hispanic-American Historical Review (Baltimore)
HMM	Harper's Monthly Magazine (New York)
HT	History Today (London)
IPI	Investigador Portuguez em Inglaterra (London)
JAH	Journal of African History (London)
JAS	Journal of the African Society (London)
JHSN	Journal of the Historical Society of Nigeria (Ibadan)
JMH	Journal of Modern History (Chicago)
JNH	Journal of Negro History (Lancaster, Pa.)
JRGS	Journal of the Royal Geographical Society of London
JSH	Journal of Southern History (Baton Rouge, La.)
LLA	Littell's Living Age (Boston)
MA	Mouvement Antiesclavagiste (Paris)
MAH	Magazine of American History (New York)
MGGW	Mitteilungen der Geographischen Gesellschaft in Wien
MHSC	Massachusetts Historical Society Collections (Boston)
MIFAN	Mémoires de l'Institut Français d'Afrique Noire (Paris); Mémoires de I'Institut Fondamental d'Afrique Noire (Dakar)
MM	Mariner's Mirror (London)
MR	Monthly Review (London)
MVHR	Mississippi Valley Historical Review (Cedar Rapids, Iowa)
McM	Macmillan's Magazine (London)
MoM	Monthly Magazine (London)
NAR	North American Review (New York)
NC	Nineteenth Century (London)
NEK	Neue Evangelische Kirchenzeitung (Berlin)
NEM	New England Magazine (Boston)
NEQ	New England Quarterly (Baltimore)
ÖMO	Österreichische Monatsschrift für den Orient (Vienna)
PA	Présence Africaine (Paris)
PAAS	Proceedings of the American Antiquarian Society (Worcester, Mass.)
PMHB	Pennsylvania Magazine of History and Biography (Philadelphia)
PMLA	Publications of the Modern Language Association of America (Baltimore)
QR	Quarterly Review (London)
RCHG	Revista Chilena de Historia y Geografía (Santiago)
RDHMF	Recueil trimestriel de Documents et travaux inédits pour servir à l'Histoire des Mascareignes Françaises (Saint-Denis)
RDILC	Revue de Droit International et de Legislation Comparée (Bruxelles)
RDM	Revue des Deux Mondes (Paris)
RE	Revue Encyclopédique (Paris)
RFEC	Revue Française de l' Étranger et des Colonies (Paris)
RFHO	Revue Française d'Histoire d'Outre-Mer (Paris)
RH	Revue Historique (Paris)
RHA	Revista Hispano-Americana (Madrid)
RHC	Revue d'Histoire des Colonies (Paris)
RHCF	Revue de l'Histoire des Colonies Françaises (Paris)
RIHGB	Revista do Instituto Historico e Geographico Brasileiro (Rio de Janeiro)

RMFE	Revue Médicale Française et Étrangère (Paris)
SAQ	South Atlantic Quarterly (Durham, N. C.)
SCM	Simmonds's Colonial Magazine (London)
SM	Scots Magazine (Edinburgh)
SNR	Sudan Notes and Records (Khartum)
SuM	Sunday Magazine (London)
TCM	Town and Country Magazine (London)
TNR	Tanganyika Notes and Records (Dar es Salaam)
UM	Universal Magazine of Knowledge and Pleasure (London)
USJ	United Service Journal (London)
USM	United Service Magazine (London)
UZ	Unsere Zeit (Leipzig)
WIG	West-Indische Gids (Amsterdam)
WM	Westermann's Monatshefte (Braunschweig)
WMQ	William and Mary Quarterly (Williamsburg, Va.)
WR	Westminster Review (London)

PART 1:

SLAVE TRADE

A. COLLECTIONS OF EVIDENCE

1   CLARKSON, Thomas
The substance of the evidence of sundry persons on the slave-trade, collected in the course of a tour made in the autumn of the year 1788. James Phillips, London, 1789. vi, 136 pp.

Eyewitness accounts of British participants in the African slave trade collected by Clarkson in preparation for the parliamentary campaign for its abolition.

2   JAMAICA: House of Assembly
Two reports (one presented the 16th of October, the other on the 12th of November, 1788) from the committee of the honourable House of Assembly of Jamaica, appointed to examine into, and report to the House, the allegations and charges contained in the several petitions which have been presented to the British House of Commons, on the subject of the slave-trade, and the treatment of the negroes, &c. &c. &c. Published, by order of the House of Assembly, by Stephen Fuller, Esq; agent for Jamaica. B. White & Son (etc.), London, 1789. 35 pp.

Refutes aspersions against Jamaica slave-holders; with statistics of the slave trade 1764–88.

3   GREAT BRITAIN: House of Commons
Minutes of the evidence taken (in the last session of Parliament) before the Committee of the whole House, to whom the bill for providing certain temporary regulations respecting the transportation of the natives of Africa, in British ships, to the West Indies, and and elsewhere, was committed . . . [London], 1789. 58 pp. (P.P. 1789, XXIV.)

Evidence taken from witnesses in June 1789.

4a   GREAT BRITAIN: House of Commons
Minutes of the evidence taken before a committee of the House of Commons, being a committee of the whole House, to whom it was referred to consider of the circumstances of the slave trade, complained of in several petitions which were presented to the House in the last session of Parliament, relative to the state of the African slave trade. [London,] 1789. 286 pp. (P.P. 1789, XXV.)

Evidence taken in May and June 1789.

4b Minutes of the evidence taken before a committee of the House of Commons, being a select committee, appointed on the 29th day of January 1790, for the purpose of taking the examination of such witnesses as shall be produced on the part of the several petitioners who have petitioned the House of Commons against the abolition of the slave trade. [London,] 1790. 640 pp. (P.P. 1790, XXIX.)

Evidence taken February–April 1790.

4c Minutes of the evidence taken before a committee of the House of Commons, being a select committee, appointed on the 23d day of April 1790, to take the examination of the several witnesses ordered by the House to attend the committee of the whole House, to whom it is referred to consider further of the circumstances of the slave trade. [London,] 1790. 389 pp. (P.P. 1790, XXX.)

Evidence taken in May and June 1790.

4d Minutes of the evidence taken before a committee of the House of Commons, being a select committee, appointed to take the examination of witnesses respecting the African slave trade. [London,] 1791. 281 pp. (P.P. 1790-91, XXXIV.)

Evidence taken in March and April 1791.

5   GREAT BRITAIN: Committee for Trade and Plantations
Report of the Lords of the Committee of Council appointed for the consideration of all matters relating to trade and foreign plantations; submitting to His Majesty's consideration the evidence and information they have collected in consequence of His Majesty's order in Council, dated the 11th of February

1788, concerning the present state of the trade to Africa, and particularly the trade in slaves; and concerning the effects and consequences of this trade, as well in Africa and the West Indies, as to the general commerce of this kingdom. [London,] 1789. 6 pt. map. (P.P. 1789, XXVI.)

Dated 28 March 1789.

6 **GREAT BRITAIN: House of Commons**
Papers received since the date of the report of the Committee for Trade, on the subject of the trade to Africa, and particularly the trade in slaves . . . [London,] 1789. 51 pp. (P.P. 1789, XXVI.)

Includes reports from the British consuls at Tunis and Tangiers.

7 **GREAT BRITAIN: House of Commons**
Abridgment of the minutes of the evidence taken before a committee of the whole House, to whom it was referred to consider of the slave-trade, 1789(–1791). [London, 1789–91.] 4 vol. (82; 246; 157; 163 pp.)

See (4).

8 *ABSTRACT of the evidence contained in the report of the Lords of the Committee of Council, relative to the slave trade, and the treatment of the slaves in the sugar islands: also an abridgment of such of the colonial laws as relate to the treatment of the slaves. [London,] 1790. 83 pp.

See (5).

9 **JAMAICA: House of Assembly**
Report, resolutions, and remonstrance, of the honourable the Council and Assembly of Jamaica, at a joint committee, on the subject of the slave-trade, in a session which began the 20th of October 1789. Published, and presented to the members of both houses of parliament . . . by Stephen Fuller, Esq. agent for Jamaica. B. White & Son (etc.), London, 1790. 23 pp.

Resolutions against abolition of the slave trade, with examinations of some slave traders.

10 **BARBADOS: General Assembly**
Report of a committee of the General Assembly, upon the several heads of enquiry, &c. relative to the slave trade . . . [London,] 1790. 8 pp. (P.P. 1790, XXIX.)

Report submitted to Parliament on the slave trade 1764–88.

11 An ABSTRACT of the evidence delivered before a select committee of the House of Commons in the years 1790, and 1791; on the part of the petitioners for the abolition of the slave-trade. James Phillips, London, 1791. xxvi, 155 pp. map.

Abolitionist evidence on the slave trade and colonial slavery; with a plan of a slave ship.

12 An ABSTRACT of the evidence delivered before a select committee of the House of Commons, in the years 1790 and 1791; on the part of the petitioners for the abolition of the slave trade. Glasgow and Edinburgh Societies, instituted for the Abolition of the Slave trade, Edinburgh, 1791. 128 pp. map.

With a plan of a slave ship.

13 *EXTRACTS from the evidence delivered before a select committee of the House of Commons, in the years 1790 and 1791, on the part of the petitioners for the abolition of the slave-trade . . . L. Wayland, London, 1791. 32 pp.

14 A SUMMARY of the evidence produced before the committee of the Privy Council, and before a committee of the House of Commons, relating to the slave trade. J. Bell, London, 1792. 16 pp.

Edited by Benjamin Vaughan? Evidence favourable to the slave trade and slavery circulated by the West Indian group in answer to the abolitionist 'Summary' (2107).

15 *GREAT BRITAIN: House of Lords
Minutes of the evidence taken at the bar of the House of Lords, upon the order for taking into consideration the . . . trade to Africa, and particularly the trade in slaves . . . [London,] 1792.

16 **JAMAICA: House of Assembly**
Report from the committee of the honourable House of Assembly, appointed to inquire into the state of the colony, as to trade, navigation, and culture, &c. &c. &c. since the report made to the House, on the 23rd of November, 1792. St. Jago de la Vega, 1800. 48 pp.

Report dated 20 Dec. 1799 on the effects on Jamaica of British proposals 1793–99 to abolish or limit the slave trade; with an appendix of economic information.

17 *JAMAICA: House of Assembly
The report from a committee of the House of Assembly of Jamaica, appointed in a session, which began on the 23rd of October, 1804, to inquire into the proceedings of the imperial Parliament of Great Britain and Ireland, relative to the slave trade, &c., &c. London, 1805.

18 GREAT BRITAIN: House of Commons
Extracts from the report of the commissioners appointed for investigating the state of the settlements and governments on the coast of Africa . . . [London,] 1812. 19 pp. (P.P. 1812, X.)

> Includes recommendations on the suppression of the slave trade.

19 ABRÉGÉ des preuves données devant un comité de la Chambre des Communes de la Grande Bretagne, en 1790 et 1791, en faveur de l'abolition de la traite des nègres. Traduit de l'anglois par Jean de Carro. Antoine Strauss, Vienne, 1814. xiv, 186, iv pp. illus.

20 *CLARKSON, Thomas
Resumé du temoignage donné devant un comité de la Chambre des communes de la Grande Bretagne et de l'Irlande, touchant la traite des nègres, adressé . . . aux différentes puissances de la chrétienté. Ad. Egron, Paris, 1814. 32 pp. illus.

> See (2475).

21 JAMAICA: House of Assembly
Further proceedings of the honourable House of Assembly of Jamaica, relative to a bill introduced into the House of Commons, for effectually preventing the unlawful importation of slaves, and holding free persons in slavery, in the British colonies. To which are annexed, examinations, taken upon oath before a committee of that house, for the purpose of disproving the allegations of the said bill. J. M. Richardson; J. Ridgeway, London, 1816. 100 pp.

> Report criticising the bill and disproving allegations of illicit slave trade.

22 GREAT BRITAIN: Foreign Office
Correspondence with the British commissioners at Sierra Leone, the Havannah, Rio de Janeiro, and Surinam, relating to the slave trade. 1822. 1823 . . . London, 1823. vii, 150 pp. (P.P. 1823, IX.)

> Published annually until 1869; continued as 'Correspondence with British representatives abroad' 1872–89.

23 GREAT BRITAIN: House of Commons
Report of the commissioners of inquiry upon the slave trade at Mauritius . . . [London,] 1829. 45 pp. (P.P. 1829, XXV.)

> Describes cases of illegal slave trading since 1810.

24 GREAT BRITAIN: House of Commons
Report from the select committee on the west coast of Africa; together with the minutes of evidence, appendix, and index. [London,] 1842. 2 vol. maps. (P.P. 1842, XI, XII.)

> Includes a great deal of information on the slave trade.

25 GREAT BRITAIN: House of Commons
First (-Fourth) report from the select committee on slave trade; together with the minutes of evidence . . . [London,] 1848. 5 vol. (P.P. 1847–48, XXII.)

> Reports of the committee under William Hutt appointed to investigate means of suppressing the slave trade; evidence was taken April–August 1848.

26 GREAT BRITAIN: House of Commons
First (Second) report from the select committee on the slave trade; together with the minutes of evidence. [London,] 1849. 2 vol. map. (P.P. 1849, XIX.)

> Further evidence taken in May and June 1849. Recommends that the antislavery squadron should be withdrawn.

27 GREAT BRITAIN: House of Lords
Report from the select committee of the House of Lords, appointed to consider the best means which Great Britain can adopt for the final extinction of the African slave-trade; . . . together with the minutes of evidence . . . Session 1849 (1850). [London, 1850.] 2 vol. maps. (P.P. 1850, IX.)

> Recommends that the naval blockade should be maintained and forts and settlements on the African coast extended.

28a PORTUGAL: Ministerio dos Negocios Estrangeiros
Documentos relativos ao apresamento, julgamento e entrega da barca franceza Charles et Georges e em geral ao engajamento de negros, debaixo da denominação de trabalhadores livres nas possessões da Coroa de Portugal na costa oriental e occidental de Africa para as colonias francezas apresentados as Cortes na sessão

legislativa de 1858. (Appendice. Documentos relativos a detenção, no porto do Ibo, da barca franceza Alfred.) Lisboa, 1858. 249, 16, xviii pp.

Selection translated as:

28b The documents relating to the capture and surrender of the Charles et Georges: selection of all the important despatches . . . London, 1859. 59 pp.

> Documents relating to French engagement of 'contract labour' from Mozambique for Réunion 1854–58.

29 GREAT BRITAIN: House of Commons
Report from the select committee on slave trade (east coast of Africa); together with the proceedings of the committee, minutes of evidence, appendix and index . . . [London,] 1871. xxiv, 242 pp. (P.P. 1871, XII.)

30 *TEALL, J. Eastoe
Slavery and the slave-trade, 1889. Facts and memoranda compiled from the slave-trade papers, the statutes at large, and other sources. British and Foreign Anti-Slavery Society, London, 1889. 61 pp.

31 *BRUSSELS SLAVE TRADE CONFERENCE
La traite des esclaves en Afrique.

Renseignements et documents recueillis pour la Conférence de Bruxelles, 1840 à 1889. Bruxelles, 1890. 2 vol. map.

32 *BELGIUM: Département des Affaires Étrangères
Documents relatifs à la répression de la traite des esclaves publiés en exécution des articles LXXXI et suivants de l'acte général de Bruxelles. Année 1892. Bruxelles, 1893. 380 pp.

> Reports on the slave trade and slavery from various countries, published annually until 1914.

33 SPAIN: Archivo de Indias
'Digest of documents in the Archives of the Indies, Seville, Spain, bearing on the negroes in Cuba and especially those employed in the Minas de Cobre.' (JNH, vol. 14, 1929, pp. 60–99.)

> List of documents, largely relating to the Cuban slave trade 1665–1803.

34 DONNAN. Elisabeth
Documents illustrative of the history of the slave trade to America. Washington, 1930–35. 4 vol.

> Unique collection of source material on the Atlantic slave trade, mainly to North America, until 1807.

B. GENERAL ACCOUNTS

(a) CONTEMPORARY ACCOUNTS

35 *DAPPER, Olfert
Naukeurige beschrijvinge der afrikaen-
sche gewesten van Egypten, Barbaryen,
Lybien, Biledulgerid, Negrosland, Guinea, Ethiopien, Abyssinie . . . Getrokken
uyt verscheyde . . . geschriften . . . door
O. Dapper. J. Van Meurs, Amsterdam,
1668. 2 pt. illus, maps.

> General description of Africa, in-
> cluding references to the slave trade
> in various parts. (German edition
> 1670, French edition 1686.)

36 OGILBY, John
Africa: being an accurate description
of the regions of Ægypt, Barbary,
Lybia, and Billedulgerid, the land of
the negroes, Guinee, Æthiopia, and
the Abyssines . . . Collected and translated from most authentick authors
and augmented with later observations . . . by John Ogilby . . . Tho.
Johnson, London, 1670. 767 pp. maps.

> Largely a translation of (35).

37 LA CROIX, Pherotée de
Relation universelle de l'Afrique, an-
cienne et moderne . . . Thomas Amaulry,
Lyon, 1688. 4 vol.

> Based on (35).

38 The HISTORY of Jamaica . . .
T. Lowndes, London, 1774. 3 vol. map.

> By Edward Long. With chapters on
> the slave trade.

39 A SHORT account of the African
slave trade, collected from local knowledge, from the evidence given at the
bar of both Houses of Parliament, and
from tracts written upon that subject.
Ann Smith's Navigation Shop, Liverpool, 1788. 22 pp.

> By Robert Norris. Description and
> defence of the slave trade. (Also
> issued under the author's name.)
> See (165).

40 NORRIS, Robert
A short account of the African slave-

trade . . . A new edition corrected.
W. Lowndes, London, 1789. 41 pp.

> See (39, 165).

41 'NEGROES imported from Africa into
the island of Jamaica, and exported
from thence yearly, between the 2d Sept.
1702, and the 31st Dec. 1778.' (AM,
vol. 9, March 1790, pp. 158–59.)

> Imports amounted to 535,549 and
> exports to 132,115.

42 GREAT BRITAIN: House of Commons
An account of the number of ships, with
their tonnage, which have entered,
in the year 1787 and 1788, in the several
British West India islands from Africa,
with the number of negroes which were
imported on board the same in each
year; and also the negroes imported
from other countries, together with
the number of negroes which were
exported, distinguishing each island . . .
[London, 1790.] (1 p.)

> Total number of slaves imported
> was 44,518 and exported 16,424.

43 AFRICAN INSTITUTION
Apperçu de l'état de la traite des
nègres en Afrique au commencement
de 1818. Extrait du douzième rapport
des directeurs de l'Institution Africaine.
Ellerton & Henderson, Londres, 1818.
43 pp.

44 MEMORANDA respecting the French
slave trade in 1820. Ellerton & Henderson, London, 1820. 44 pp.

> Documents on slaving activities from
> Senegal to Madagascar. See (2554–55).

45 AFRICAN INSTITUTION
Foreign slave trade. Abstract of the
information recently laid on the table
of the House of Commons on the
subject of the slave trade; being a
report made by a committee specially
appointed for the purpose, to the
directors of the African Institution on
the 8th of May, 1821 . . . London, 1821.
180 pp.

> Official documents on the illegal
> slave trade and antislavery measures

1816–20. (Reviewed in: ER, vol. 36, 1822, pp. 34–52.) Translated as: De l'état actuel de la traite des noirs . . . (Londres; Paris, 1821; 208 pp.)

46 FRIENDS, Society of
Information concerning the slave trade. [London, 1821.] 48 pp.

Reports on the slave trade of West and East Africa.

47 'PRESENT state of the slave trade.' (CO, vol. 20, 1821, pp. 289–93, 354–60, 416–23.)

Based on recent reports (44, 45, etc.).

48 STATE of the foreign slave trade . . . C. Baldwin, London, [1821?]. 60 pp.

By S. C. Wilks. Review of recent reports on the illegal slave trade. (First published in: BR, vol. 18, Dec. 1821, pp. 430–87.)

49 *DE la continuation de la traite des noirs, contenant divers renseignements sur l'exercise et l'étendue actuelle de ce commerce coupable. Londres, 1822.

50 *INFORMATION concerning the present state of the slave trade. [Philadelphia?] 1824. 26 pp.

51 FRIENDS, Society of
Statements illustrative of the nature of the slave-trade. To which are subjoined, some particulars respecting the colony at Sierra Leone. Published by a committee appointed by the religious society of Friends, to aid in promoting the total abolition of the slave-trade. Harvey, Darton & Co., London, 1824. 40 pp.

Extracts from documents on the slave trade in recent years.

52 FRIENDS, Society of
A view of the present state of the African slave trade. Published by direction of a meeting representing the religious society of Friends in Pennsylvania, New-Jersey, &c. William Brown, Philadelphia, 1824. 69 pp.

Recent evidence of the continuing slave trade.

53 The FOREIGN slave trade. A brief account of its state, of the treaties which have been entered into, and of the laws enacted for its suppression, from the date of the English abolition act to the present time. John Hatchard & Son; (etc.), London, 1837. 62 pp.

By Joseph Beldam. Describes the slave trade of the last twenty years and the antislavery treaties to 1835.

54 The FOREIGN slave trade. A brief account of its state, and of the treaties and laws relating thereto, continued to the present time. London Anti-Slavery Society; John Hatchard & Son; (etc.), London, 1838. 45 pp.

By Joseph Beldam. Title page headed 'No. II'.

55 BUXTON, Sir Thomas Fowell
The African slave trade. John Murray, London, 1839. xv, 240 pp. map.

Description of the extent of the slave trade, drawing attention to the Muslim trade and the failure of suppression efforts. (Reviewed in: CO, vol. 39, 1839, pp. 235–43; Congregational Magazine, London, n.s., vol. 3, 1839, pp. 722–29, 829–36.) See (2644–45).

56 'SCHETS van den tegenwoordigen toestand des slavenhandels.' (Signed: A.S.R.) (Bijdragen tot de Kennis der Nederlandsche Koloniën, Utrecht, 1844, pp. 18–37, 223–56; 1845, pp. 374–408.)

By A. S. Rueb.

57 *FRIENDS, Society of
An exposition of the African slave trade, from the year 1840 to 1850, inclusive, prepared from official documents, and published by direction of the representatives of the religious Society of Friends, in Pennsylvania, New Jersey, and Delaware. Philadelphia, 1851. 160 pp.

58 'SLAVE-TRADE operations.' (CMI, vol. 7, Nov. 1856, pp. 241–55; illus.)

Account of the slave trade in various parts of Africa.

59 'CUBA and its slave-traffic.' (CMI, vol. 7, Dec. 1856, pp. 265–75; illus.)

60 'The AFRICAN slave trade.' (DBR, vol. 23, July 1857, pp. 47–56.)

On recent slaving in American ships, mostly to Cuba.

61 'The SLAVE trade revived.' (USM, 1860, I, pp. 410–17.)

On some cases of illegal slaving 1856–58.

62 HAMILTON, Archibald
'On the trade with the coloured races of Africa.' (Journal of the Statistical Society of London, vol. 31, 1868, pp. 25–48.)

Estimates slave exports, particularly from West Africa 1848–64.

63 SOUPÉ, Alfred Philibert
'La chasse à l'homme en 1870.' (Revue Contemporaine, Paris, ser. 2, vol. 74, 1870, pp. 641–61.)

    Account of the Muslim slave trade in Africa from the Sahara to East Africa. See (403).

64 'Der SKLAVENHANDEL im ägyptischen Sudan und in Ostafrika.' (Globus, Braunschweig, vol. 22, 1872, pp. 119–21.)

    Description of the slave trade centered on Khartum and Kilwa.

65 COOPER, Joseph
The lost continent: or, slavery and the slave-trade in Africa, 1875 . . . London, 1875. viii, 130 pp. map.

    General description of the slave trade; the only remedy is abolition of slavery in Turkey and Egypt.

66 ROWLEY, Henry
Africa unveiled. London, 1876. 313 pp.

    Ch. 7: 'African slavery and slave trade.'

67 CRUYSSEN, Aldemar Camillo van der
Afrika, naar de beste bronnen. Kortrijk, 1877. 144 pp.

    With a section on the Muslim slave trade based on recent eyewitness accounts.

68 'The SLAVE trade in Africa.' (The Month, London, vol. 30, June 1877, pp. 219–26.)

69 MOREAU D'ANDOY, Alphonse de, *chevalier*
'La traite des noirs en Afrique.' (Revue des Questions Scientifiques, Louvain, Paris, vol. 1, 1877, pp. 562–86.)

    Review article.

70 CZERNY, Franz
'Geschichte und Geographie des Sclavenhandels in Afrika.' (Deutsche Rundschau für Geographie und Statistik, Wien, vol. 2, 1880, pp. 8–13, 62–69.)

    Description of the Muslim slave trade in Africa and of the Brussels conference 1876.

71 ANDREE, Richard
'Sklaverei und Sklavenjagden in Afrika.' (Daheim, Leipzig, vol. 25, 1889, pp. 27–30; map.)

    Notes on the slave trade and abolition efforts.

72 ROHLFS, Gerhard
'Sklaverei und Sklavenhandel.' (WM, vol. 67, 1890, pp. 82–98; illus.)

    Account of the Muslim slave trade in the Sudan and East Africa.

73 JUNG, Emil
'Sklaverei und Sklavenhandel in alter und neuer Zeit.' (Globus, Braunschweig, vol. 58, 1890, pp. 65–68, 90–95, 105–09, 123–26.)

74 JUNG, Emil
'Sklaverei und Sklavenhandel in Afrika.' (Gartenlaube, Leipzig, 1890, pp. 170–72; map.)

    Account of the Muslim slave trade in central Africa.

75 L'ESCLAVAGE en Afrique. Par un ancien diplomate . . . Paris, 1890. vi, 518 pp. map.

    On the slave trade and antislavery crusade.

76 ERMINI, Filippo
La schiavitù moderna. Discorso. Folignano, 1891. 39 pp.

    Notes on the existing slave trade in Africa, based on the accounts of recent explorers and of cardinal Lavigerie.

77 NOYANT, ——, *Abbè*
Les horreurs de l'esclavage, de la sorcellerie, des sacrifices humains et du cannibalisme en Afrique. Paris, 1891. 95 pp.

    Description of the slave trade in various parts of Africa. Europeans must christianise and civilise the continent.

78 *JUNG, M. A.
La chasse à l'homme . . . Nancy, 1894. 32 pp.

    Description of slave raids in Africa and their causes, by a former White Father. (First published in: Bulletin de la Société de Géographie de l'Est, Nancy, vol. 16, 1894, pp. 70–99.)

79 CHATELAIN, Heli
'The internal slave trade of Africa.' (Scientific American, New-York, vol. 76, 1897, pp. 168–69.)

(b) HISTORY

80 SPRENGEL, Matthias Christian
Vom Ursprung des Negerhandels . . . Johann Christian Hendel, Halle, 1779. 71 pp.

    History of the African slave trade from the middle ages.

81 SELL, Johann Jacob
Versuch einer Geschichte des Neger-

sclavenhandels. Johann Jacob Gebauer, Halle, 1791. x, 246 pp. bibl. pp. 226–44.

Historical analysis of the slave trade, with a bibliography of the abolition controversy.

82 HÜNE, Albert
Vollständige historisch-philosophische Darstellung aller Veränderungen des Negersklavenhandels von dessen Ursprunge an bis zu seiner gänzlichen Aufhebung. Johann Friedrich Röwer, Göttingen, 1820. 2 pt.

History of the development and abolition of the slave trade.

83 A REFUTATION of the calumnies circulated against the southern & western states, respecting the institution and existence of slavery among them ... A. E. Miller, Charleston, 1822. 86 pp.

By E. C. Holland. The slave trade to North America was fostered by England and conducted by the northern states.

84 BANDINEL, James
Some account of the trade in slaves from Africa as connected with Europe and America; from the introduction of the trade into modern Europe, down to the present time; especially with reference to the efforts made by the British government for its extinction. Longman, Brown & Co., London, 1842. xv, 323 pp.

Based on British documents, with an account of the antislavery treaties to 1841. (Reviewed in: ER, vol. 79, 1844, pp. 396–406.)

85 'HISTORY of the slave trade.' In: CHAMBERS, W. and CHAMBERS, R. Chambers's miscellany of useful and entertaining tracts, vol. 2 (Edinburgh, 1845), no. 19, pp. 1–32.

86 WALKER, Samuel Abraham
Missions in western Africa, among the Soosoos, Bulloms, &c. ... William Curry, Jun. & Company, Dublin; Longmans, Brown & Co., London, 1845. xix, 572 pp. map.

Introduction, section II: 'History of the slave trade.'

87 OFFICER, Morris
'The African slave trade.' (Evangelical Review, Gettysburg, Pa., vol. 9, July 1857, pp. 32–49.)

Account of the slave trade and its suppression, by a former missionary.

88 *BLAKE, William O.
The history of slavery and the slave trade, ancient and modern ... The African slave trade and the political history of slavery in the United States ... Columbus, Ohio, 1857. 832 pp.

On the slave trade, abolition movement and efforts to suppress the illegal slave trade.

89 *SAWYER, George S.
Southern institutes; or, an inquiry into the origin and early prevalence of slavery and the slave-trade ... Philadelphia, 1858. 393 pp.

90 *CLARK, Rufus Wheelwright
The African slave trade. Boston, [1860]. 102 pp.

91 'SLAVERY and the slave trade.' (Biblical Repertory and Princeton Review, Philadelphia, vol. 34, 1862, pp. 524–48.)

By Charles Hodge. On the history of the British–American slave trade and its abolition.

92 PIM, Bedford
The negro and Jamaica. Read before the Anthropological Society of London. London, 1866. 72 pp.

93 DELGEUR, Louis
'La traite des nègres.' (Bulletin de la Société de Géographie d'Anvers, vol. 1, 1877, pp. 80–103; illus.)

Lecture on the history of the slave trade and the abolition movement.

94 TACHÉ, Henry
'La traite des noirs et l'esclavage des Africains.' (Journal des Économistes, Paris, ser. 4, vol. 7, 1879, pp. 247–69.)

General account of the slave trade in Africa.

95 TOURMAGNE, A., pseud.
Histoire de l'esclavage ancien et moderne. Paris, 1880. iv, 460 pp.

By A. Villard. Includes a section on the modern slave trade of East Africa and the Sudan and the abolition movement.

96 BROWN, Robert
The story of Africa and its explorers. London, 1892–95. 4 vol. illus. maps.

Contains chapters on the slave trade in West Africa, the Nile Valley and East Africa.

97 INGRAM, John Kells
A history of slavery and serfdom. London, 1895. xiv, 285 pp.

98 MERRIMAN-LABOR, A. B. C.
The story of the African slave trade in a nutshell ... Manchester, 1900. 18 pp.

99 **SPEARS, John Randolph**
'The slave trade in America.' (Scribner's Magazine, New York, vol. 28, 1900, pp. 3–15, 303–14, 452–64.)

On the African slave trade and its suppression.

100 ***METCALFE, James Stetson**
'From freedom to slavery.' (Pearson's Magazine, New York, Oct. 1900, pp. 297–305.)

On the Afro-American slave trade.

101 **TILBY, Alexander Wyatt**
Britain in the tropics 1527–1910. London, 1912. viii, 452 pp.

Bk. 2, ch. 3: 'Slavery and the slave trade: 1445–1865.'

102 ***MEERVELDHOVEN, Paschasius van**
Historisch apologetische schets der slavernij. Nijmegen, [1913]. 124 pp.

Ch. 10: 'Negerslavernij en neger-handel.'

103 **MOREL, Edmund Dene**
The black man's burden. Manchester, London, [1920]. x, 241 pp.

Ch. 3: 'The story of the slave trade.'

104 ***BOUMANS, Joseph**
'Slavenhandel in Afrika.' (Het Missie-werk, Den Bosch, vol. 3, 1922, pp. 101–06.)

105 ***CAMERON, Norman Eustace**
The evolution of the negro . . . George-town, Demerara, 1929, 34. 2 vol.

Vol. 2 deals with the African slave trade and slavery.

106 **SELL, Manfred**
'Die schwarze Völkerwanderung.' (Preussische Jahrbücher, Berlin, vol. 224, 1931, pp. 157–81.)

On the demographic effects of the African slave trade to the Americas.

107 **D'AUVERGNE, Edmund Basil Francis**
Human livestock. An account of the share of the English-speaking peoples in the development, maintenance and suppression of slavery and the slave trade. London, 1933. 288 p.

108 ***CARAVACA, Francisco**
Esclavos! El hombre negro instrumento del progreso del blanco. Barcelona, 1933. 168 pp.

109 **MACMUNN, *Sir* George**
Slavery through the ages. London, 1938. xv, 278 pp. illus.

110 **WARD, William Ernest Frank**
Africa and European trade . . . London, 1939. viii, 86 pp.

Ch. 3: 'The slave trade.' (For African schools.)

111 **DU BOIS, William Edward Burghardt**
Black folk then and now. An essay in the history and sociology of the negro race. New York, 1940. ix, 401 pp. maps, bibl. pp. 385–91.

With chapters on the slave trade.

112 **SELL, Manfred**
Die schwarze Völkerwanderung. Der Einbruch des Negers in die Kultur-welt . . . Wien, [1940]. 315 pp. maps.

Nazi view of the slave trade and its racial consequences. (See also an article on the same subject in: WM, vol. 165, 1939, pp. 453–55.)

113 **DELLICOUR, Fernand**
'Une vieille question.' (Institut Royal Colonial Belge, Bulletin des séances, Bruxelles, vol. 12, 1941, pp. 8–26.)

The expansion of the African slave trade was closely linked to the growth of European colonies.

114 **DUCASSE, André**
Les négriers, ou le trafic des esclaves. Paris, 1948. 253 pp. bibl. pp. 247–51.

History of the slave trade, emphasis-ing the French part in it.

115 **RUSSELL, Henry A.**
Human cargoes. A short history of the African slave trade. London, 1948. 103 pp.

General account for African schools.

116 **LETHEM, *Sir* Gordon James**
African slave traffic and West Indian emancipation. A colonial administrator looks back . . . Anti-Slavery Society, London, 1948. 11 pp.

117 ***COMHAIRE, Jean**
'Coup d'oeil sur l'histoire des peuples africains et afro-américains.' (Zaïre, Bruxelles, vol. 7, 1953, pp. 687–706, 1027–51.)

Includes an account of the slave trade.

118 ***BRETAGNE, Christian**
Nègres à vendre. [Givors, Rhône, 1955.] 244 pp.

119 ***SCHMIDT, Alfred Eduard**
Jagd auf schwarzes Elfenbein. Hamburg, 1957. 231 pp.

120 **KI ZERBO, Joseph**
'L'économie de traite en Afrique noire ou le pillage organisé.' (PA, n.s., vol. 11, 1957, pp. 7–31.)

The slave trade had serious demographic effects on Africa.

121 *ONIBONOJE, Gabriel Omotayo
Africa from the rise of Islam to the end
of the slave trade. Ibadan, 1958. 169 pp.

122 DUFFY, James
Portuguese Africa. Cambridge, Mass.,
1959. vi, 389 pp. illus, maps.

Ch. 6: 'The slave trade, slavery, and
contract labor.'

123 JEFFREYS, Mervin David Waldegrave
'Negro influences on Indonesia.' (African Music, Roodepoort, Transvaal,
vol. 2, no. 4, 1961, pp. 10–16.)

Suggests that similarities in African
and Indonesian music are due to the
medieval Arab trade in African
slaves.

124 DAVIDSON, Basil
Black mother. Africa: the years of
trial. London, 1961. 269 pp. bibl. pp.
253–59.

General history of the European
slave trade from Africa. (Also
published in New York 1961 as 'Black
mother; the years of the African
slave trade' and in Boston 1965 as
'The African slave trade: precolonial
history, 1450–1850'.)

125 *ABDEL-MALEK, A.
'Peuples d'Afrique: la traite et la
conquête coloniale.' (Diagrammes,
Monte-Carlo, mai 1961, pp. 48–58.)

126 HÖJER, Signe
Slav stig upp . . . Stockholm, 1961.
247 pp. illus.

Popular work, including chapters on
the African slave trade.

127 CHANG, Hsing-lang
'T'ang shih fei-chou hei-nu shu-ju
Chung-kuo k'ao [On the black slaves
that entered China in the T'ang period].'
In his: Chung-hsi chiao-t'ung shih-liao
hui-pien [The materials for a history
of Sino-foreign relations] (Taipei, 1962),
vol. 3, pp. 48–81.

Discusses the 'k'un-lun' mentioned
in early Chinese texts; references from
A.D. 751–977 onward were to
Africans. (Reprint of 1930 edition;
author's preface to this essay dated
Ch'ing-tao, 1926.)

128 BRUNSCHWIG, Henri
'Histoire, passé et frustration en Afrique
noire.' (AESC, vol. 17, 1962, pp. 873–
84.)

Discounts the slave trade as the main
obstacle to population growth in
Africa.

129 TRAVINSKY, Vladilen Mikhailovich
Kak pogibli millionui negrov. Moskva,
1963. 246 pp. illus.

'How millions of negroes perished.'
Popular history of the African slave
trade and its abolition. (See also his:
Chernuie sud'bui, Leningrad, 1963;
190 pp. illus.)

130 GARÇON, Maurice
'Le commerce du bois d'ébène.' (Revue
de Paris, vol. 70, mai 1963, pp. 1–12.)

Brief account of the African slave
trade.

131 SURET CANALE, Jean
'Contexte et conséquences sociales de
la traite africaine.' (PA, n.s., no. 50,
1964, pp. 127–50.)

The slave trade was one of the main
causes of Africa's backwardness;
its abolition was basically motivated
by economic developments in Europe.

132 *STARKEY, Marion Lena
Striving to make it my home; the story
of Americans from Africa. New York,
[1964]. 256 pp.

133 ANENE, Joseph Christopher
'Slavery and the slave trade.' In: ANENE,
J. C. and BROWN, G. N. Africa in the
nineteenth and twentieth centuries
(Ibadan; London, 1966), pp. 92–109;
maps.

134 KAY, Frederick George
The shameful trade. London, 1967.
218 pp. illus.

135 COLLINS, Robert Oakley
Problems in African history. Edited
by Robert O. Collins. Englewood
Cliffs, N.J., [1968]. ix, 374 pp. maps.

Anthology, including texts on the
slave trade.

136 OSEI, Gabriel Kingsley
Europe's gift to Africa. London, 1968.
120 pp.

An African view of the slave trade and
its effects.

137 ÖSTLING, Sven
Slavhandeln över Atlanten. Stockholm,
1968. 63 pp. illus, maps.

Popular account of the African slave
trade.

138 RICHARDSON, Patrick
Empire & slavery. London, 1968. x,
158 pp. maps.

Includes chapters on the slave trade
and its abolition. (Intended for
schools and colleges.)

139 CLARKE, John Henrik
Slave trade and slavery. Edited by John
Henrik Clarke and Vincent Harding.
New York (etc.), [1970]. xii, 113 pp.
illus.

For schools.

140 RANSFORD, Oliver
The slave trade. The story of trans-
atlantic slavery. London, 1971. x,
292 pp. illus, maps.

Popular account of the African
slave trade, slavery and abolition.

**141 TEAGUE, Michael *and* COWAN,
Zélide**
'An eyeview history of the Atlantic
slave trade. From African barracoon
to the American auction block.' (Art in
America, New York, vol. 59, no. 1,
1971, pp. 58–67; illus.)

On 19th-century illustrations of the
slave trade.

C. WEST AFRICA

(a) CONTEMPORARY ACCOUNTS

142 CAVAZZI, Giovanni Antonio
Istorico descrizione de' tre regni,
Congo, Matamba, et Angola situati
nell' Etiopia inferiore occidentale e
delle missioni apostoliche esercitateui da
religiosi capuccini, accuramente com-
pilata dal P. Gio Antonio Cavazzi da
Montecuccolo . . . e nel presente stile
ridotta dal P. Fortunato Alamandini . . .
Giacomo Monti, Bologna, 1687. 933 pp.

Includes notes on the slave trade to
Brazil in the 1650s.

143 GRÖBEN, Otto Friedrich von der
Guineische Reise-Beschreibung . . .
Simon Reinigern, Marienwerder, 1694.
ii, 134 pp.

On the establishment of Branden-
burgers on the Gold Coast 1683,
with brief references to the slave
trade in West Africa.

144a BOSMAN, Willem
Nauwkeurige beschryving van de guinese
Goud- Tand- en Slave-kust . . . (Deel 2.
Beschrijving van de guinese Goud-
Kust. Waar by gevoegt is, een net
verhael van den slavehandel . . .)
Anthony Schouten, Utrecht, 1704.
280 pp. illus.

Translated as:

144b A new and accurate description of the
coast of Guinea, divided into the Gold,
the Slave, and the Ivory Coasts . . .
With a particular account of the rise,
progress and present condition of all
the European settlements upon that
Coast; and the just measures for improving the several branches of the
Guinea trade . . . (Part 2. A description
of the Gold Coast of Guinea, to which
is added a just representation of the
slave trade . . .) James Knapton; Dan.
Midwinter, London, 1705. 493 pp.
illus, map.

Twenty letters by Bosman, in the
Dutch West India Company's service
on the coast 1688–1702; with two by
David van Nyendael and Jan Snoeck.

Letter 19 describes the slave trade at
Whydah. (Enlarged Dutch edition
1709; English edition reprinted, with
introduction by J. R. Willis and
notes: London, 1967; xvi, 577 pp.)

145 ZUCCHELLI, Antonio
Relazione del viaggio e missione di
Congo nell' Etiopia inferiore occidentale . . . Bartolomeo Giavarina, Venezia,
1712. 438 pp.

Describes attempts by Catholic missionaries to prevent slave trade from
Congo to Protestant nations (ch. 10,
15); the author returned via Brazil
on a slave ship (ch. 20).

146 LABAT, Jean Baptiste
Nouveau voyage aux isles de l'Amér-
ique . . . Pierre-François Giffart,
Paris, 1722. 6 vol. illus, maps.

Includes a chapter on the slave trade
to the French West Indies, based on
Labat's observations as a missionary
1694–1705; as most African slaves
were kidnapped the trade is of
doubtful legitimacy.

147a LABAT, Jean Baptiste
Nouvelle relation de l'Afrique occidentale: contenant une description exacte
du Sénégal & des païs situés entre le
Cap-Blanc & la rivière de Serrelionne,
jusqu'à plus de 300. lieuës en avant
dans les terres . . . Avec l'état ancien et
present des compagnies qui y font le
commerce . . . Theodore le Gras, Paris,
1728. 5 vol. illus, maps.

Translated as:

147b 'Voyages and travels along the western
coast of Africa, from Cape Blanco to
Sierra Leona . . . More particularly, an
account of the rivers Sanaga and
Gambra, and of the French and
English settlements.' *In*: [ASTLEY, T.]
A new general collection of voyages
and travels, vol. 2 (London, 1745), pp.
27–144. map.

Compiled from the notes of La Courbe
(1685–87) and of André Brue (administrator of the French posts in
Senegal 1697–1702 and 1714–20).

The English translation gives only a summary. See (769).

148 BARBOT, Jean
'A description of the coasts of north and south Guinea; and of Ethiopia inferior, vulgarly Angola: being a new and accurate account of the western maritime countries of Africa . . . With a full account of all the European settlements . . . their commerce, and measures for improving the several branches of the Guinea and Angola trade . . .' *In*: CHURCHILL, A. A collection of voyages and travels, vol. 5 (London, 1732), pp. 1–688. illus, maps.

Based on a ms. 'Journal du voyage de Guinée, Cayenne, et illes Antilles de l'Amérique, Aos 1678 et 1679' (Brit. Mus. Add. M.S. 28,788), with added material from Dapper, Bosman, and others. Barbot traded in West Africa for the Compagnie d'Afrique until 1682 but later settled in England. Before publication supplements (pp. 421–688) were added to bring the work up to date, including sections on slaving voyages. See (709–10).

149 GONÇALVES D'ALMADA, André
Relaçaõ, e descripçaõ de Guiné na quel se trata das varias naçoens de negros, que a povoaõ, dos seus costumes, leys, ritos, ceremonias, guerras, armas, trajos, da qualidade dos portos, e do commercio, que nelles se faz . . . Miguel Rodrigues, Lisboa, 1733. 62 pp.

By André Alvares d'Almada. For a better edition, see (188).

150 SNELGRAVE, William
A new account of some parts of Guinea, and the slave-trade, containing:—I. The history of the late conquest of the kingdom of Whidaw by the king of Dahome . . . II. The manner how the negroes become slaves. The numbers of them yearly exported from Guinea to America. The lawfulness of that trade. The mutinies among them on board the ships where the author has been, &c. . . . James, John & Paul Knapton, London, 1734. 288 pp. map.

The author, a slaving captain, traded at Whydah in 1727 and 1730; he complains that the Dahomean conquest has ruined the slave trade there.

151 ATKINS, John
A voyage to Guinea, Brazil, and the West-Indies; in his Majesty's ships the Swallow and Weymouth . . . With remarks on the gold, ivory, and slave-trade . . . Caesar Ward & Richard Chandler, London, 1735. 265 pp.

As naval surgeon on an expedition against the pirates Atkins visited West Africa 1721–22. He deplores the inhumanity of removing slaves from Africa and maintains that the intention of the king of Dahomey in conquering Whydah had been to destroy the export slave trade.

152 MOORE, Francis
Travels into the inland parts of Africa: containing a description of the several nations for the space of six hundred miles up the river Gambia . . . With a particular account of Job ben Solomon, a Pholey, who was in England in the year 1733 . . . J. Stagg, London, 1738. xi, xiii, 305, 86, 23 pp. illus, map.

Detailed description of the slave trade on the Gambia during Moore's time in the service of the Royal African Company, 1730–35.

153 SMITH, William
A new voyage to Guinea . . . John Nourse, London, 1744. iv, 276 pp.

Smith surveyed the Royal African Company's forts in West Africa in 1726; this work was edited from a ms. account left by him, with the addition of extracts from Bosman and others.

154 *RASK, Johannes
En kort og sandfaerdig Rejse-Beskrivelse til og fra Guinea. Trondhiem, 1754. 320 pp.

Includes a description of the Danish slave trade 1709–12.

155 *TILFORLADELIG Efterretning om Negotien paa Kysten Guinea, tilligemed Betænkninger, hvorledes vor Negotie derhen og til Vestindien bedre kunde indrettes. Kiøbenhavn, 1756. 63 pp.

By L. F. Römer. Translated as: Die HANDLUNG verschiedener Völker auf der Küste von Guinea und in Westindien (Kopenhagen, 1758).

156 RÖMER, Ludewig Ferdinand
Tilforladelig Efterretning om Kysten Guinea . . . Ludolph Henrich Lillies Enke, Kiøbenhavn, 1760. 348 pp. illus, map.

With notes on the slave trade, especially at the Danish forts. The preface, by Erik Pontoppidan, defends the slave trade and slavery.

c

(Translated as: Nachrichten von der Küste Guinea, Kopenhagen, 1769.)

157   DEMANET, A. B.
Nouvelle histoire de l'Afrique françoise . . . Veuve Duchesne; Lacombe, Paris, 1767. 2 vol. maps.

Includes a description of the coastal slave trade between Senegal and Sierra Leone about 1764, with information for slave traders.

158a   PROYART, Liévain Bonaventure
Histoire de Loango, Kakongo, et autres royaumes d'Afrique . . . C. P. Berton, N. Crapart, Paris; Bruyset-Ponthus, Lyon, 1776. viii, 390 pp. map.

Translated as:

158b 'History of Loango, Kakongo, and other kingdoms in Africa.' *In*: PINKERTON, J. A general collection of . . . voyages and travels, vol. 16 (London, 1814,) pp. 548–97.

With a chapter on the slave trade.

159   ERASMI, Tage
'Om Guinea.' (Minerva, Kiøbenhavn, vol. 3, 1786, pp. 335–43.)

Outline of an unfinished work on the slave trade, with biographical notes on the author (who served on the Gold Coast 1769–82), signed 'H.B.'

160   ISERT, Paul Erdmann
Reise nach Guinea und den Caribäischen Inseln in Columbien, in Briefen an seine Freunde beschrieben. J. F. Morthorst, Kopenhagen, 1788. 376, lxx pp.

Letters 1783–87 from Christiansborg and the West Indies, including descriptions of the slave trade and a revolt on a Danish slave ship. See (167).

161   MATTHEWS, John
A voyage to the river Sierra-Leone, on the coast of Africa; containing an account of the trade and productions of the country . . . in a series of letters to a friend in England . . . With an additional letter on the subject of the African slave trade . . . B. White & Son; J. Sewell, London, 1788. iv, 183 pp. map.

Letters of a naval lieutenant during a residence at Sierra Leone 1785–87; the last letter, added after his return to England, defends the slave trade. (Reviewed in: GM, May 1788, pp.

433–35; MR, vol. 79, Sept. 1788, pp. 238–41.) See (1923).

162   FALCONBRIDGE, Alexander
An account of the slave trade on the coast of Africa. J. Phillips, London, 1788. 55 pp.

Detailed description, by a former slave ship surgeon, of the methods of the trade and treatment of slaves and crews. (Second edition: J. Phillips, London, 1788; 72 pp.)

163   WADSTRÖM, Carl Bernhard
Observations on the slave trade, and a description of some part of the coast of Guinea, during a voyage, made in 1787, and 1788 . . . James Phillips, London, 1789. ix, 67 pp.

Hostile account of the slave trade by a Swedish abolitionist. (Reviewed in: General Magazine, London, vol. 3, 1789, pp. 348–54.)

164   DESCRIPTION de la Nigritie. Par M.P.D.P. Amsterdam, 1789. viii, 284 pp. maps.

By A. E. Pruneau de Pommegorge, former employee of the French Compagnie des Indes. Account of West Africa, including the slave trade, about 1750.

165   NORRIS, Robert
Memoirs of the reign of Bossa Ahádee, king of Dahomy, an inland country of Guiney. To which are added, the author's journey to Abomey, the capital; and A short account of the African slave trade. W. Lowndes, London, 1789. xvi, 184 pp. map.

Account of visits to Dahomey 1772–75, by a slave trader. The 'short account' (pp. 149–84) is a second edition of (39). (Reviewed in: MR, vol. 80, April 1789, pp. 319–21.) See (40).

166   LAMIRAL, Dominique Harcourt
L'Affrique et le peuple affriquain, considérés sous tous leurs rapports avec notre commerce & nos colonies . . . Dessenne, Paris, 1789. 399 pp. illus, map.

Contains a section on the slave trade in Senegal (pp. 157–265) and an attack on the Société des Amis des Noirs (pp. 368–99); the author served as agent for the Compagnie de la Guyane in Senegal from 1779. See (2009).

167   ISERT, Paul Erdmann
Neue Reise nach Guinea und den

Caribäischen Inseln in Amerika, in den Jahren 1783 bis 1787, nebst Nachrichten von dem Negerhandel in Afrika. Berlin & Leipzig, 1790. 374 pp.

Another edition of (160) with new appendix on the slave trade (pp. 317–74), largely from abolitionist sources.

168 SIERRA LEONE COMPANY
Substance of the report of the court of directors of the Sierra Leone Company to the general court, held at London on Wednesday the 19th October 1791. London, 1791. 61 pp.

Includes a report on the 'State of the slave trade' at Sierra Leone. (Subsequent reports published until 1808.)

169a SIERRA LEONE COMPANY
Substance of the report delivered by the court of directors of the Sierra Leone Company, to the general court of proprietors, on Thursday the 27th March, 1794. London, 1794. 175 pp. map.

Mainly a report on the slave trade as an obstacle to 'civilization'.

Also published as:

169b An account of the colony of Sierra Leone, from its first establishment in 1793. Being the substance of a report delivered to the proprietors. James Phillips, London, 1795. 242 pp. map.

170 DALZEL, Archibald
The history of Dahomey, an inland kingdom of Africa; compiled from authentic memoirs . . . G. & W. Nicol (etc.), London, 1793. xxxi, xxvi, 230 pp. map.

Notes on a visit to Abomey 1772, and on the slave trade, by a governor at Cape Coast; including a reported speech by king 'Adahoonzan' on the abolition efforts in Britain. (Reviewed in: MR, n.s., vol. 18, 1795, pp. 155–62; SM, vol. 57, 1795, pp. 713–15; GM, Jan. 1796, pp. 51–53.)

171 FALCONBRIDGE, Anna Maria
Two voyages to Sierra Leone during the years 1791–2–3, in a series of letters . . . The second edition. London, 1794. 287 pp.

Letters by the wife of an agent of the Sierra Leone Company, including a description of a voyage to Jamaica on a slave ship in 1793 in which she defends the slave trade. See (177).

172 PARK, Mungo
Travels in the interior districts of Africa: performed under the direction and patronage of the African Association, in the years 1795, 1796, and 1797 . . . G. & W. Nicol, London, 1799. xxviii, 372, xcii pp. maps.

Edited by Bryan Edwards. With a chapter on the slave trade and sources of slaves. Park returned from the Niger with a slave caravan to the Gambia and sailed to the West Indies in an American slave ship.

173 GRANDPRÉ, Louis Marie Joseph O'Hier, *comte* **de**
Voyage à la côte occidentale d'Afrique, fait dans les années 1786 et 1787; contenant la description . . . des états du Congo, frequentés par les Européens, et un précis de la traite des noirs, ainsi qu' elle avoit lieu avant la révolution française . . . Dentu, Paris, an IX.–1801. 2 vol. (226; 320 pp.)

Description of slave trade between Mayombe and Ambriz (ch. 4), by an ex-slaver.

174 LABARTHE, Pierre
Voyage au Sénégal, pendant les années 1784 et 1785, d'après les mémoires de Lajaille, ancien officier de la marine française; contenant des recherches sur la géographie, la navigation et le commerce de la côte occidentale d'Afrique, depuis le Cap Blanc jusqu'à la riviere de Sierralione . . . Dentu, Paris, an X [1802]. xii, 262 pp. map.

Compiled on the basis of the papers of G. Lajaille and other documents by Labarthe, an official of the Ministère de la Marine, with notes on the slave trade.

175a DURAND, Jean Baptiste Léonard
Voyage au Sénégal, ou mémoires historiques, philosophiques et politiques sur les découvertes, les établissemens et le commerce des Européens dans les mers de l'Océan atlantique, depuis le Cap-Blanc jusqu'à la riviere de Serre-Lionne inclusivement; suivis de la relation d'un voyage par terre de l'île Saint-Louis à Galam . . . Henri Agasse, Paris, an 10.–1802. 2 vol. illus, maps.

Translated as:

175b A voyage to Senegal; or, historical, philosophical and political memoirs, relative to the discoveries, establishments, and commerce of Europeans in the Atlantic Ocean, from Cape

Blanco to the river of Sierra Leone. To which is added an account of a journey from Isle St. Louis to Galam . . . Richard Phillips, London, 1806. 181 pp. illus, map.

By a French director of trade in Senegal, with notes on the slave trade 1785–88.

176a GOLBÉRY, Sylvain Meinrad Xavier de
Fragmens d'un voyage en Afrique, fait pendant les années 1785, 1786, et 1787, dans les contrées occidentales de ce continent, comprises entre le cap Blanc de Barbarie . . . et le cap de Palmes . . . Treuttel & Würtz, Paris, an X.–1802. 2 vol. illus, maps.

Translated as:

176b Travels in Africa, performed during the years 1785, 1786, and 1787, in the western countries of that continent . . . James Ridgway, London, 1802. 2 vol. illus, maps.

Includes notes on the slave trade in 1785–86, with proposals for its resumption. Africa is so densely populated that it can afford to export a large number of slaves (ch. 26).

177 FALCONBRIDGE, Anna Maria
Narrative of two voyages to the river Sierra Leone, during the years 1791–2–3 . . . Also the present state of the slave trade in the West Indies, and the improbability of its total abolition. The second edition. L. I. Higham, London, 1802. 287 pp.

Another edition of (171).

178 LABARTHE, Pierre
Voyage a la côte de Guinée, ou description des côtes d'Afrique, depuis le cap Tagrin jusqu'au cap de Lopez-Gonzalves. Contenant des instructions relatives à la traite des noirs, d'après des mémoires authentiques . . . Debray (etc.), Paris, an XI.–1803. 310 pp. map.

Twenty 'letters' compiled by Labarthe from reports by Lajaille and other officers of ships visiting West Africa 1784–90.

179 SPILSBURY, Francis B.
Account of a voyage to the western coast of Africa; performed by His Majesty's sloop Favourite, in the year 1805 . . . Richard Phillips, London, 1807. 43 pp. illus.

Includes descriptions of slave traders in the Sierra Leone area.

180 EXPOSÉ des faits relatifs à la traite des nègres dans le voisinage du Sénégal. [London? 1819.] 31 pp.

Information on illegal slave trading 1817–18.

181 ROBERTSON, G. A.
Notes on Africa; particularly those parts which are situated between Cape Verd and the river Congo . . . with hints for the melioration of the whole African population . . . Sherwood, Neely & Jones, London, 1819. xvi, 460 pp. map.

Includes scattered references to the slave trade. (Reviewed in: Anti-Jacobin Review, London, vol. 57, 1820, pp. 417–25.)

182 MONRAD, Hans Christian
Bidrag til en Skildring af Guinea-Kysten og dens Indbyggere, og til en Beskrivelse over de danske Colonier paa denne Kyst, samlede under mit Ophold i Afrika i Aarene 1805 til 1809. Andreas Seidelin, Kiøbenhavn, 1822. xxviii, 382 pp.

With a chapter on the slave trade.

183 WEST-AFRICAN sketches: compiled from the reports of Sir G. R. Collier, Sir Charles Maccarthy, and other official sources. L. B. Seeley & Son, London, 1824. viii, 273 pp.

Contains some notes on the slave trade near the British settlements.

184 GRAY, William
'Miseries of the slave-trade.' (Wesleyan-Methodist Magazine, London, vol. 48, 1825, pp. 602–04.)

Description of a slave caravan in Senegal.

185 'EXTRACTS from the journal of an officer employed on a survey of the western coast of Africa in 1825–6.' (Signed: H.B.R.) (USJ, 1831, I, pp. 457–63; II, pp. 36–42, 185–93, 319–27; III, pp. 52–61, 337–44; 1832, I, pp. 49–56, 324–36.)

Account of a voyage from Cape Town to Sierra Leone, with notes on the slave trade.

186 'ACTUAL state of the slave-trade on the coast of Africa.' (Amulet, London, 1832, pp. 212–50.)

Account of the West African slave trade about 1830, by a British naval officer. (Reprinted in: AR, vol. 8, March 1832, pp. 1–21.)

187a EANNES DE AZURARA, Gomes
Chronica do descobrimento e conquista de Guiné . . . fielmente trasladada
do manuscrito original contemporaneo
. . . J. P. Aillaud, Paris, 1841. xxv,
474 pp.

Translated as:

187b The chronicle of the discovery and
conquest of Guinea . . . London, 1896,
99. 2 vol. maps.

> Describes the beginning of the Portu-
> guese slave trade in West Africa
> 1442–49. (Written about 1460.)

188 ÁLVARES D'ALMADA, André
Tratado breve dos Rios de Guiné do
Cabo-Verde desde o rio do Sanagá até
aos baixos de Sant'Anna . . . 1594 . . .
Porto, 1841. xiv, 108 pp. map.

> Report of 1594 on the coast from
> Senegal to Sierra Leone, with notes
> on the slave trade. See (149). (Re-
> printed from ms. in: BRÁSIO, A.
> Monumenta missionaria africana,
> Lisbon, ser. 2, vol. 3, 1964, pp. 229–
> 378; illus.)

189 *HODGSON, William Brown
The Foulahs of central Africa, and the
African slave trade . . . [New York?]
1843. 24 pp.

190 O'CONNOR, L. Smyth
'Twelve months' service in western
Africa'. (USM, 1845, II, pp. 57–70,
235–44, 424–32, 587–95; III, pp. 196–
210, 505–13; 1846, I, pp. 217–27.)

> Contains information on the slave
> trade and antislavery measures; by
> an army officer.

191 DUNCAN, John
Travels in western Africa in 1845 &
1846, comprising a journey from
Whydah, through the kingdom of
Dahomey, to Adofoodia, in the interior.
Richard Bentley, London, 1847. 2 vol.

> Includes notes on the slave trade,
> the Souza family, and the Dahomean
> king's views on the slave trade.

192 RIDGEWAY, Archibald R.
'Journal of a visit to Dahomey, or, the
snake country. In the months of
March and April, 1847.' (New Monthly
Magazine, London, vol. 81, 1847, pp.
187–98, 299–309, 406–14.)

> The author accompanied a British
> mission to negotiate a treaty against
> the slave trade.

193 *BOUËT-WILLAUMEZ, Louis
Édouard, *comte*
Commerce et traite des noirs aux
côtes occidentales d'Afrique. Paris,
1848. vii, 230 pp. maps.

194 FOX, William
A brief history of the Wesleyan missions
on the western coast of Africa . . . With
some account of the European settlements and of the slave-trade. London,
1851. xx, 624 pp. illus, map.

> Includes chapters on the slave trade,
> historical and contemporary.

195 CASTELNAU, Francis de
Renseignements sur l'Afrique centrale
et sur une nation d'hommes à queue qui
s'y trouverait, d'après le rapport des
nègres du Soudan, esclaves à Bahia.
Paris, 1851. 62 pp. illus, map.

> Interviews with Hausa and other
> slaves in Brazil revealing the slave
> routes to the Gulf of Guinea.

196 'The SLAVE-TRADER Kyetan.' (Nautical Magazine, London, 1852, pp.
549–52.)

> On the trading activities of Caetano
> José Nozolini at Bissao during the
> last 25 years. (Reprinted from:
> Anti-Slavery Reporter, London, n.s.,
> vol. 7, 1852, pp. 114–15.)

197 CARNES, Joshua A.
Journal of a voyage from Boston to
the west coast of Africa: with a full
description of the manner of trading
with the natives on the coast. Boston;
Cleveland, 1852. 479 pp.

> With notes on the slave trade,
> largely quoting earlier sources.

198 WILSON, John Leighton
Western Africa: its history, condition
and prospects. London, 1856. 527 pp.
map.

> Includes a chapter on the slave trade.

199 IRMINGER, Carl Ludvig Christian
'Slavehandelen paa Guinea . . .' (Dansk
Maanedsskrift, Kjøbenhavn, ser. 2,
vol. 1, 1859, pp. 261–72.)

> Reminiscences of the Atlantic slave
> trade before 1848.

200 HUTCHINSON, Thomas Joseph
Ten years' wanderings among the
Ethiopians; with sketches of the man-
ners and customs of the civilized and
uncivilized tribes, from Senegal to
Gaboon. London, 1861. xx, 329 pp.

With notes on the slave trade, slavery and emigration; by the British consul in the Bight of Biafra 1856–61.

201 WADDELL, Hope Masterton
Twenty-nine years in the West Indies and central Africa: a review of missionary work and adventure. 1829–1858. London, 1863. 681 pp.

Includes notes on slavery and the slave trade at Calabar, where the author established a mission in 1846.

202 BURTON, Richard Francis
A mission to Gelele, King of Dahome. With notices of the so called "Amazons," the grand customs, the yearly customs, the human sacrifices, the present state of the slave trade, and the negro's place in nature. London, 1864. 2 vol. illus.

Report of an official visit to Dahomey 1863, with scattered information on the slave trade; the author's racialist views lead him to advocate forced labour emigration to the Americas.

203 GREAT BRITAIN: House of Commons
Report from the Select committee on Africa (western coast); together with the proceedings of the committee, minutes of evidence, and appendix. [London,] 1865. 2 pt. (xviii, 469; v, 92 pp.) maps. (P.P. 1865, V.)

Contains a good deal of evidence on the slave trade.

204 GREAT BRITAIN: Foreign Office
West coast of Africa. Correspondence respecting the slave trade and other matters. From January 1 to December 31, 1869 . . . London, 1870. vi, 98 pp. (P.P. 1870, LXI.)

Headed: 'Class A.' Correspondence for 1870: P.P. 1871, LXII.

205 SCHOELCHER, Victor
L'esclavage au Sénégal en 1880. Paris, 1880. 120 pp.

206 MENDES CASTELLO BRANCO, Garcia
'Relacão da costa d'Africa, da Mina, que é o castello de S. Jorge, até ao Cabo Negro.' In: CORDEIRO, L. Memorias do ultramar (Lisboa, 1881), (no. 1) pp. 26–32.

Account of the trade between the Gold Coast and Angola, from a manuscript of 1621.

207 VOGADO SOTOMAIOR, Manuel
Producções, commercio e governo do Congo e de Angola segundo Manuel Vogado Sotomaior, Antonio Diniz, Bento Banha Cardoso e Antonio Beserra Fajardo. Lisboa, 1881. 26 pp. (Memorias do ultramar. no. 5.)

Edited by L. Cordeiro. Reports of 1620–29, including information on the slave trade.

208 'Das SKLAVENWESEN in Afrika.' (DKB, vol. 1, 1890, pp. 259–61.)

Description of slavery and slave trade in West Africa.

209 URSEL, Hippolyte d', comte
'L'esclavage dans la région du Niger.' (MA, vol. 4, 1892, pp. 72–84; illus.)

Largely extracts from: L. G. Binger, Du Niger au golfe de Guinée (Paris, 1892).

210a PACHECO PEREIRA, Duarte
Esmeraldo de situ orbis . . . Edição annotada por Augusto Epiphanio da Silva Dias. Lisboa, 1905. 173 pp.

Translated as:

210b Esmeraldo de situ orbis . . . London, 1937. xxxv, 193 pp. maps.

Description of the west coast of Africa, including notes on the slave trade, from a manuscript of 1505/8. (First published in: Boletim da Sociedade de Geographia de Lisboa, ser. 21–22, 1903–04.)

211 NEVINSON, Henry Woodd
'The new slave trade.' (HMM, European edition, vol. 50, 1905, pp. 341–50, 535–44, 668–76, 849–58; vol. 51, 1905–06, pp. 114–22, 237–46, 327–37.)

Nevinson visited Angola 1905 to investigate the origin of contract labour for S. Thomé and Principe supplied by Chokwe and Mbundu slavers despite official abolition of the slave trade in 1878.

212 NEVINSON, Henry Woodd
A modern slavery . . . London & New York, 1906. ix, 215 pp. map.

New version of (211).

213 NEVINSON, Henry Woodd
'The Angola slave trade.' (FR, n.s., vol. 82, 1907, pp. 488–97.)

214 BOURNE, Henry Richard Fox
Slave traffic in Portuguese Africa: an account of slave-raiding and slave-trading in Angola and of slavery in

the islands of San Thome and Principe. London, [1908]. 67 pp.

Description of the contract labour system, largely based on Nevinson.

215 STONE, Thora Guinevere
'The journey of Cornelius Hodges in Senegambia, 1689–90.' (EHR, vol. 39, 1924, pp. 89–95.)

With the text of Hodges' report to the Royal African Company on his journey up the Gambia to trade for gold and slaves.

216 OWEN, Nic(hola)s
Journal of a slave-dealer. "A view of some remarkable axcedents in the life of Nics. Owen on the coast of Africa and America from the year 1746 to the year 1757". Edited, with an introduction, by Eveline Martin. London, 1930. 120 pp illus, maps.

Diary of a trader settled in the Sherbro area in the 1750s.

217 ABREU DE BRITO, Domingos de
Um inquérito à vida administrativa e económica de Angola e do Brasil em fins do século XVI . . . Publicação revista e prefaciada por Alfredo de Albuquerque Felner. Coimbra, 1931. xix, 97 pp.

Edition of a manuscript report on Angola and Brazil written 1592, with sections on the slave trade 1575–91.

218 GRACE, Edward
Letters of a West African trader, Edward Grace, 1767–70 . . . [London,] 1950. ii, 40 pp. illus.

Includes references to the slave trade in Senegal.

219 FORDE, Cyril Daryll
Efik traders of Old Calabar. Edited by Daryll Forde. Containing the diary of Antera Duke, an Efik slave-trading chief of the eighteenth century . . . London, 1956. xiii, 166 pp.

Duke's diary covers the years 1785–87.

220 ANDRADE, Francisco d'
'Relation de Francisco d'Andrade sur les îles du Cap-Vert et la côte occidentale d'Afrique (1582).' (BIFAN, ser. B, vol. 29, 1967, pp. 67–87.)

Andrade's report to the king of Spain on the trade of West Africa, including the slave markets between Senegal and Sierra Leone. Edited by Jean Boulègue. (A report on the same area in 1635 is printed in: DOCU-MENTAÇÃO ultramarina portuguesa, Lisboa, vol. 2, 1962, pp. 195–99.)

(b) CONTROVERSY

221 PELLETAN, Jean Gabriel
Mémoire sur la colonie française du Sénégal, avec quelques considérations historiques et politiques sur la traite des nègres, sur leur caractère, et les moyens de faire servir la suppression de cette traite à l'accroissement et à la prospérité de cette colonie . . . Vᵉ Panckoucke, Paris, an IX [1801]. xvi, 118 pp. map.

Advocates transforming slaves in Senegal into 'engagistes'.

222 'ON the progress of the civilization of Africa, as connected with the abolition of the slave trade.' (Signed: Alfred.) (Philanthropist, London, vol. 1, 1811, pp, 117–26.)

By T. Clarkson. Reports British anti-slave trade efforts in West Africa, from Senegambia to the Gold Coast.

223 An INQUIRY into the right and duty of compelling Spain to relinquish her slave trade in northern Africa. J. Butterworth & Son; J. Hatchard, London, 1816. 96 pp.

By James Stephen. Spain refuses to abandon slaving north of the equator, including the Sierra Leone area, but it is the duty of the powers to suppress the slave trade. (Reviewed in: Philanthropist, London, vol. 6, 1816, pp. 53–67.)

224 *ARTHY, Elliot
Africa mercatoria; or, the statesman's, merchant's, and trader's, African intelligencer; giving a full account of the present state of British commerce and barter with the natives of the western coast of Africa . . . and shewing, that a trade considerably more extensive and beneficial may yet be established with those people; and also, by what means that extensive country may be generally colonized, and brought into progressive cultivation, its rude and heathen natives civilized and converted to Christianity and rendered, eventually, a free and independent people. E. Smith & Co., Liverpool; Sherwood, Neely & Jones, London, 1818.

Proposes purchasing slaves for work on British plantations in West Africa, to be emancipated after a period of servitude.

225 *BACON, Ephraim
Abstract of a journal of E. Bacon, assistant agent of the United States, to Africa: with an appendix, containing extracts from proceedings of the Church Missionary Society in England, for the years 1819–20 . . . The whole showing the successful exertions of the British and American governments, in repressing the slave trade. S. Potter & Co., Philadelphia, 1821. 96 pp.

The author was 'assistant agent for the reception of recaptured negroes on the western coast of Africa'.

226 'LIBERIA a means of abolishing the slave trade.' (AR, vol. 3, 1827, pp. 129–36, 161–70.)

Colonies on the West African coast will check the slave trade and establish commercial contact with inland states like the Sokoto empire.

227 JEFFCOTT, John William
Substance of a charge delivered to the grand jury at the general quarter sessions of the peace and general gaol delivery for the colony of Sierra Leone, held at Freetown, on Wednesday the 2nd June, 1830, and subsequent days:— By John William Jeffcott, Esq. His Majesty's chief justice, and judge of the vice-admiralty court . . . M. Tilley, Freetown, 1830. 20 pp.

Address condemning 'anarchy' in the colony, which includes fitting out ships for foreign slave traders. (Reprinted in: P.P. 1831–32, XLVII, no. 364, 'Slave trade, Sierra Leone.')

228 PROEVE over de kust van Guinea; houdende eene poging tot onderzoek, hoe, en in hoeverre, dat land tot eene ware volkplanting zou kunnen gevormd worden. J. Immerzeel, junior, s'Gravenhage, 1831. 154 pp.

The slave trade is the cause of West African backwardness, but abolition will remove its evil effect; the Dutch should establish agricultural colonies on the Gold Coast employing slaves as paid labourers.

229 A LETTER to the committee of the London Anti-Slavery Society, on the present state of the African slave-trade, particularly that which exists in the colony of Sierra Leone: with copious extracts from the documents lately printed by order of the House of Commons, under the head of "Slave trade.—Sierra Leone. 6th April, 1832." Houlston & Son; (etc.), London, 1832. 20 pp.

By W. Naish. The author has resigned from the council of the society because of its lack of concern for the slave trade. See (227, note).

230 McQUEEN, James
A geographical survey of Africa . . . To which is prefixed a letter to Lord John Russell, regarding the slave trade, and the improvement of Africa. B. Fellowes, London, 1840. xciv, xxiv, 303 pp. map.

The antislavery blockade is too expensive, whereas a British settlement at the Niger-Benue confluence will cut off the slave trade in the West African interior.

231 JAMIESON, Robert
An appeal to the government and people of Great Britain, against the proposed Niger expedition: a letter addressed to the Right Hon. Lord John Russell . . . Smith, Elder & Co., London, 1840. viii, 27 pp.

The expedition proposed by Sir Thomas Fowell Buxton is superfluous as the slave trade in the Niger area has already ceased. (The author owned a steam vessel trading on the Niger.) See (233).

232 READ, Paul
Lord John Russell, Sir Thomas Fowell Buxton, and the Niger expedition, or observations on the formation of permanent settlements on the Niger in western Africa . . . James Ridgway, London, 1840. 56 pp.

Commercial expansion should replace the present unsuccessful antislavery efforts; the author had proposed a similar scheme in 1832.

233 STEPHEN, *Sir* George
A letter to the Rt. Hon. Lord John Russell, &c. &c. &c. in reply to Mr Jamieson, on the Niger expedition. Saunders & Otley, London, [1840]. 36 pp.

Jamieson's assertion that the slave trade from the Bights has ended is not true. See (231, 239, 2668).

234 'The NIGER expedition.' (EclR, n.s., vol. 8, Oct. 1840, pp. 456–71.)

Review of recent works for and against the proposed expedition; agricultural settlements in West Africa would only transform 'the slave-hunter to the slave-driver'.

235 'The BRITISH Niger expedition—British policy. President's message.' (AR, vol. 17, Jan. 1841, pp. 21–27.)

The United States should take stronger action against the slave trade.

236 'The EXPEDITION to the Niger—civilization of Africa.' (ER, vol. 72, Jan. 1841, pp. 456–77.)

Review of works on the Niger expedition and colonisation, which will help to exterminate the slave trade by civilising Africa.

237 'REVIVAL of the slave trade in the Bight of Benin.' (FA, no. 3, Feb. 1841, pp. 42–43.)

238 'NEW plan for suppressing the slave trade and obtaining laborers for the British West India colonies.' (AR, vol. 17, May 1841, pp. 145–50.)

Criticises the British plan for African emigration as 'stripping Africa of her laboring population' and threatening the United States.

239 JAMIESON, Robert
A further appeal to the government and people of Great Britain, against the proposed Niger expedition: a letter addressed to the Right Hon. Lord John Russell. Smith Elder, & Co., London, 1841. 31 pp.

Buxton is mistaken about the extent of the slave trade in the Bights; commerce must precede 'civilization'. See (231).

240 RITTER, Carl
'Die Nigerexpedition und ihre Bestimmung.' *In*: BUXTON, T. F. Der afrikanische Sklavenhandel und seine Abhülfe (Leipzig, 1841), pp. ix–lxx.

The main purpose of the Niger expedition is to suppress the slave trade.

241 'The NIGER expedition.' (Signed: W. H.) (Journal of Civilization, London, 1842, pp. 73–76, 133–36, 155–58; map.)

A main objective of the expedition is to promote the civilisation of Africa by stopping the slave trade.

242 SCHÖN, Jacob Friedrich
Journals of the Rev. James Frederick Schön and Mr. Samuel Crowther, who . . . accompanied the expedition up the Niger, in 1841, in behalf of the Church Missionary Society . . . Hatchard & Son (etc.), London, 1842. xxii, 393 pp. map.

Account of the expedition, the purpose of which was to 'arrest the foreign slave trade in its source' and extend British commerce; including notes on the slave trade along the Niger.

243 JAMIESON, Robert
Sequel to appeals made to the government and people of Great Britain, against the Niger expedition before its departure from England . . . Smith, Elder & Co., London, 1843. 32 pp. map.

The African Civilization Society should now confess the error of their plan for agriculture to precede commerce; the palm oil trade has already driven out the slave trade.

244 *MADDEN, Richard Robert
The slave trade and slavery: the influence of British settlements on the west coast of Africa, in relation to both: illustrated by extracts from the letters of Dr. R. R. Madden, in the Morning Chronicle, the United Service Gazette, etc. James Madden, London, 1843. 78 pp.

245 MOUAT, Richard
'A narrative of the Niger expedition.' (SCM, vol. 2, 1844, pp. 138–53, 311–24, 446–65; vol. 3, 1844, pp. 117–26.)

Account of the treaty making at Aboh and Iddah; as the Fulani are the main slave traders, priority should be given to developing trade with them.

246 ISAMBERT, Alfred
'De l'esclavage ou des captifs au Sénégal.' (Abolitioniste Français, Paris, vol. 1, 1844, pp. 337–51.)

Supports the policy of recruiting soldiers from liberated slaves.

247 TRACY, Joseph
Colonization and missions. A historical examination of the state of society in western Africa, as formed by paganism and Muhammedanism, slavery, the slave trade and piracy, and of the remedial influence of colonization and missions. T. R. Marvin, Boston, 1844. 40 pp.

Colonies like Liberia are the cheapest means of suppressing the slave trade.

248 'The SLAVE-TRADE and its remedy.' (CMG, vol. 8, 1848, pp. 52–53.)

Quotes letters from H. Townsend on conditions in Yorubaland.

249 'DAHOMEY and the slave trade—Account of Badagry.' (CMI, vol. 1, 1849, pp. 88–94.)

Extracts from a despatch of a British envoy to Dahomey in 1848 and from a letter by a missionary at Badagri.

250 BERTRAND-BOCANDÉ, E.
'Notes sur la Guinée portugaise ou Sénégambie méridionale.' (Bulletin de la Société de Géographie, Paris, ser. 3, vol. 11, 1849, pp. 265–350; vol. 12, 1849, pp. 57–93; map.)

The final section, 'De la traite des nègres', argues that the slave trade can only be destroyed by other commerce, not by cruisers.

251 HALLEUR, Hermann
Das Leben der Neger West-Afrika's mit Rücksicht auf den Sklavenhandel... Wilhelm Hertz, Berlin, 1850. 46 pp.

Lecture on the barbarities caused in West Africa by the slave trade.

252 HALL, James
'Abolition of the slave trade of Gallinas.' (AR, vol. 26, March 1850, pp. 68–71.)

On slaving in the Sierra Leone area, now suppressed.

253 LANDOR, Henry
The best way to stop the slave trade. Longman, Brown, Green & Longmans, London, 1850. 24 pp.

254 *REMARKS on the colonization of the western coast of Africa, by the free negroes of the United States, and the consequent civilization of Africa and suppression of the slave trade. W. L. Burroughs, New York, 1850. 64 pp.

255 'The WEST-AFRICAN slave-trade.' (CMI, vol. 2, 1851, pp. 73–80; map.)

On the state of the slave trade in the Dahomey area, the African squadron and missions.

256 *FOX, William
The western coast of Africa: comprising suggestions on the best means of exterminating the slave-trade and some account of the success of the gospel. [London,] 1851. 138 pp. map.

257 FORBES, Frederick Edwyn
Dahomey and the Dahomans: being the journals of two missions to the king of Dahomey, and residence at his capital, in the years 1849 and 1850. London, 1851. 2 vol.

Account of a visit by a British naval officer to persuade the king to stop the slave trade; with 'Reflections on the slave trade and the means for its suppression'.

258 'The AFRICAN slave trade.' (Nautical Magazine, London, 1852, pp. 430–36.)

Only negro colonization on the coast can suppress the West African slave trade.

259 *TEIXEIRA DE VASCONCELLOS, Antonio Augusto
Carta acerca do trafico dos escravos na provincia d'Angola, dirigida ao ministro dos negocios da marinha e ultramar. Lisboa, 1853. 15 pp.

260 HUTCHINSON, Thomas Joseph
Narrative of the Niger, Tshadda, & Binuë exploration: including a report on the position and prospects of trade up those rivers . . . London, 1855. xi, 267 pp. map.

The report on trade suggests that the slave trade can only be ended if the African chiefs can be 'taught to use slaves at home for cultivation'.

261 HOWARD, John Garton
Trade with West Africa, by means of native agency. An appeal to Christian merchants in Britain. Thereby to promote the eradication of the slave trade and the propagation of Christianity . . . London, 1855. 16 pp.

262 BAIKIE, William Balfour
Narrative of an exploring voyage up the rivers Kwóra and Bínue (commonly known as the Niger and the Tsádda) in 1854. London, 1856. xvi, 456 pp. map.

Concludes that the only way to check the slave trade is to show the suppliers in the interior that trade in other products would be more profitable.

263 'RENEWAL of the slave-trade.' (CMG, n.s., vol. 7, Dec. 1857, pp. 135–37.)

French 'free emigration' agents and Cuban slavers compete for slaves at Whydah.

264 'LIBERIA and the slave trade.' (AR, vol. 34, Aug. 1858, pp. 225–36.)

Defends the Liberian government from suspicions of conniving at schemes for 'voluntary emigration'.

265 'The RECAPTURED Africans; the benevolent policy of the government towards them: Liberia to be their

home.' (AR, vol. 34, Oct. 1858, pp. 289–300.)

Account of the United States' policy of returning recaptured slaves to Liberia; it could do more in West Africa to stop the slave trade and develop Christianity and commerce. See (757).

266 The WEST-AFRICAN slave-trade: suggestions for its gradual extinction, by a late senior officer of the West-African squadron. London, 1860. 40 pp.

Proposals for ending the slave trade, now conducted mainly from Dahomey and the Congo.

267 WHITE, J. E.
West Africa; viewed in connection with the slave trade, Christianity, and the supply of cotton. London, 1861. 23 pp.

The slave trade continues to Cuba and the United States from Dahomey and the Congo; it can be stopped at source by extending lawful commerce.

268 *BLYDEN, Edward Wilmot
'A chapter in the history of the African slave-trade.' *In his*: Liberia's offering (New York, 1862), pp. 151–67.

Reprinted from: Anglo-African Magazine, New York, vol. 1, June 1859.

269 HEWETT, John Frederick Napier
European settlements on the west coast of Africa; with remarks on the slave-trade and the supply of cotton. London, 1862. viii, 374 pp.

The slave trade can be ended by increasing export farming.

270 ROSS, William Andrew
Letters of An African to "The Times," on the slave trade, and on human sacrifices in Dahomey. London, 1863. 26 pp.

Describes the Dahomean slave trade and suggests containing it with a line of coastal blockhouses.

271 READE, William Winwood
'Black ivory,' *In his*: Savage Africa (London, 1863), pp. 289–99.

The antislavery squadron is ineffective against the Cuban slave trade, but English settlement of the Congo area would entirely end the export of slaves from West Africa.

272 CHINERY, David
West African slavery. The African slave-trade, and the real and practicable means for its suppression. London, 1864. 19 pp.

Instead of Lagos Britain should occupy Whydah and force Spain to stop the Cuban slave trade; the best way to kill it is to develop trade in palm oil and other products.

273 CORTE REAL, José Alberto Homem da Cunha
Resposta á Sociedade Anti-Esclavista de Londres. Lisboa, 1884. 23 pp.

Refutes allegations of slave trade in Portuguese West Africa.

274 SEEGER, ——
'Die Sklaverei im Togolande und der englischen Goldküstenkolonie.' (DKZ, n.s., vol. 5, 1892, pp. 54–56.)

The slave trade continues in the hinterland, largely in the hands of Muslims.

275 BOHNER, Heinrich
'Sklaverei und Sklavenhandel im Kamerun.' (EMM, n.s., vol. 37, 1893, pp. 16–29.)

Describes existing forms of slavery and ways of ending the slave trade.

276 SEIDEL, H.
'Der Sklavenhandel in Togo.' (DKZ, n.s., vol. 12, 1899, p. 123.)

Stories about slave trading are eight years out of date.

277 'The SLAVE trade in Portuguese West Africa.' (Anti-Slavery Reporter, London, ser. 4, vol. 26, 1906, pp. 115–21.)

Largely translated from an article on the Angolan slave trade in the Hamburg 'Fremden Blatt'.

278 *BURTT, Joseph
Report on the conditions of coloured labour on the cocoa plantations of S. Thome and Principe, and the methods of procuring it in Angola. British and Foreign Ant-Slavery Society, London, [1907]. 16 p.

Slaves are recruited for contract labour. Reprinted in (280).

279 *SWAN, Charles Albert
The slavery of to-day; or, the present position of the open sore of Africa. Glasgow, [1909]. 303 pp. illus.

Describes the Angolan labour trade.

280   CADBURY, William Adlington
Labour in Portuguese West Africa . . .
Second edition . . . London, 1910. xii,
187 pp. map.

Includes the report of J. Burtt (278).

281   *CARVALHO, Jeronimo Paiva de
Slavery in West Africa: Portuguese
revelations. Anti-Slavery and Aborigines Protection Society, London, [1912].

282   CADBURY, William Adlington *and*
MOREL, Edmund Dene
'The West African slave traffic. Brit-
ain's duty towards Angola and San
Thomé.' (NC, vol. 72, 1912, pp. 836–
51.)

Until the Angolan government is
reformed, labour recruiting 'cannot
by any possibility be free'.

283   HARRIS, John Hobbis
Portuguese slavery: Britain's dilemma.
London, 1913. 127 pp.

Accuses Portugal of condoning slave
trade in Angola. See (285).

284   ANTI-SLAVERY AND ABORIGINES
PROTECTION SOCIETY
Portuguese slavery: Britain's responsi-
bility. London, [1914]. 20 pp.

285   *FREIRE DE ANDRADE, Alfredo
Augusto
Rapport présenté au ministre des
colonies, à propos du livre Portuguese
slavery du missionaire John Harris.
Lisbonne, 1914. 116 pp.

See (283).

(c) HISTORY

286   'La TRATTA dei negri.' (CC, ser. 6,
vol. 4, 1865, pp. 184–98.)

By V. Steccanella. Account of the
origin of the Portuguese slave trade
in West Africa 1445–95.

287   *GLARDON, Auguste
'La traite des nègres sur la côte occidentale de l'Afrique.' (Bibliothèque
Universelle et Revue Suisse, Genève,
n.s., vol. 47, 1873, pp. 715–35.)

288   BERLIOUX, Étienne Félix
André Brue, ou l'origine de la colonie
française du Sénégal. Paris, 1874.
349 pp. map.

On the organisation of French trade
in Senegal 1697–1724, including the
slave trade; largely based on (147).

289   CORDEIRO, Luciano
Escravos e minas de Africa segundo

diversos. Lisboa, 1881. 28 pp. (Memorias de ultramar. no. 6.)

Contains documents on the Portuguese slave trade, mainly from the
Congo, in the sixteenth century.

290   'A SLAVE-DEALER of 1690.' (CM,
n.s., vol. 14, 1890, pp. 252–66.)

By A. P. Crouch? Description of
Whydah after Bosman (144).

291   DUPONT, Édouard
'La traite à la côte occidentale d'Afrique.' (MA, vol. 2, 1890, pp. 147–52.)

Notes on the history of the slave
trade, particularly in the Congo
area.

292   'Der KRUSTAMM in Westafrika und
die Sklaverei.' (Signed: M.S.) (DKZ,
n.s., vol. 6, 1893, pp. 75–77.)

The Kru people never took part in
the slave trade or allowed the export
of slaves, thus escaping depopulation.

293   CHAZAL, ——
Les Français aux bouches du Niger
avant la révolution. Coulommiers,
[1903]. 60 pp.

On Landolphe and the factory at
Borodo (Benin) 1786–92. See (740).

294   SHAW, Flora Louisa (Mrs Lugard)
A tropical dependency . . . London,
1905. viii, 508 pp. maps.

Historical account of Nigeria, with
chapters on the slave trade and Fulani
slave raiding.

295   MACHAT, Joseph
Documents sur les établissements français de l'Afrique occidentale au XVIIIᵉ
siècle. Paris, 1906, 140 pp. illus, maps.

Includes information on the French
slave trade in Senegal 1763–84.

296   JOHNSTON, *Sir* Harry Hamilton
Liberia. London, 1906. 2 vol.

With two chapters on the slave trade.

297   SPIESS, C.
'Ein Erinnerungsblatt an die Tage des
Sklavenhandels in Westafrika.' (Globus,
Braunschweig, vol. 92, 1907, pp. 205–
08.)

History of the slave trade in the Keta
area.

298   LANG, John
The land of the golden trade (West
Africa) . . . London & Edinburgh, 1910.
ix, 314 pp. maps.

Popular account, with several chapters on the slave trade.

299 CULTRU, Prosper
Histoire du Sénégal du XVe siècle à 1870 . . . Paris, 1910. 376 pp.

Ch. 8: 'La traite au Sénégal.'

300 ARCIN, André
Histoire de la Guinée française. Rivières du Sud, Fouta-Dialo, Région du Sud du Soudan . . . Paris, 1911. ix, 752 pp.

Includes notes on the slave trade before 1815.

301 LARSEN, Kay
De danske i Guinea. København, 1918. 147 pp. illus, maps.

Provides information on the Danish slave trade 1660–1802.

302 FAURE, Claude
'La garnison européenne du Sénégal et le recrutement des premières troupes noires (1779–1858).' (RHCF, vol. 8, 1920, pp. 5–108.)

From 1819 onward the French 'recruited' Senegalese soldiers by purchasing slaves.

303 THULIN, Dieudonné de
'Les Capucins au Congo. L'esclavage et la traite des noirs au Congo (1482–1878).' (Études Franciscaines, Paris, vol. 35, 1923, pp. 615–31.)

By D. Rinchon. A total of 4 million slaves were exported from the Congo 1500–1860.

304 RINCHON, Dieudonné
'Notes sur le marché des esclaves au Congo du XVe au XIXe siècle.' (Congo, Bruxelles, vol. 6, no. 2, 1925, pp. 388–409.)

On the Portuguese slave trade from its origin to the end of the 16th century.

305 GAILLARD, L. J.
'La terrible vengeance du capitaine Landolphe.' (Bulletin du Comité d'Études Historiques et Scientifiques de l'Afrique Occidentale Française, Paris, vol. 9, 1927, pp. 502–11.)

Biographical notes on J. F. Landolphe, whose trading post at Benin was destroyed by the British 1792. See (740).

306 ROUSSIER, Paul
'Documents sur les relations entre la France et le royaume de Ouaire à la côte d'Afrique (1784–1787).' (Bulletin du Comité d'Études Historiques et Scientifiques de l'Afrique Occidentale Française, Paris, vol. 11, 1928, pp. 352–85.)

Notes on Warri and the French slave trade.

307 ROSS, H.
'Some notes on the pirates and slavers active round Sierra Leone and the west coast of Africa, 1680–1723.' (Sierra Leone Studies, Freetown, no. 11, 1928, pp. 16–53.)

308 *RINCHON, Dieudonné
La traite et l'esclavage des Congolais par les Européens; histoire de la déportation de 13 millions 250,000 noirs en Amérique . . . [Bruxelles,] 1929. vi, 306 pp. bibl. pp. 243–80.

309 *WÖLFEL, Dominik Josef
'Los Gomeros vendidos por Pedro de Vera y doña Beatriz de Bobadilla.' (Museo Canario, Las Palmas, vol. 1, 1933, pp. 5–84.)

On late 15th-century slave trade in the Canaries.

310 *ERP, Theodor van
'Slavenhandel en slavernij in Congo.' (Annalen der Missionarissen, Sparrendael, vol. 33, 1933, pp. 28–31, 105–07, 160–61, 197–202, 221–24.)

311 *HERSKOVITS, Melville Jean
'A footnote to the history of negro slaving.' (Opportunity, New York, Vol. 11, 1933, pp. 178–81.)

Memories of the slave trade in Dahomey.

312 HERSKOVITS, Melville Jean
'The significance of West Africa for negro research.' (JNH, vol. 21, 1936, pp. 15–30.)

On the interior slave trade.

313 DENUCÉ, Jean
L'Afrique au XVIe siècle et le commerce anversois . . . Anvers, 1937. 120 pp. illus, map.

Includes accounts of the slave trade in the Congo and Angola.

314 *KNOPS, Petrus
'La traite des noirs sur la côte occidentale de l'Afrique.' (Bulletin de l'Union Missionnaire du Clergé, Bruxelles, vol. 19, 1939, pp. 3–9.)

315 GRAY, Sir John Milner
A history of the Gambia. Cambridge, 1940. x, 508 pp. map.

History of the trading companies during the period of the slave trade and its suppression.

316 BERBAIN, Simone
Le comptoir français de Juda (Ouidah) au XVIIIe siècle. Paris, 1942. 125 pp. illus, maps. bibl. pp. 15–22. (MIFAN, no. 3.)

Title page headed: 'Études sur la traite des noirs au golfe de Guinée.'

317 HARRIS, Jack S.
'Some aspects of slavery in southeastern Nigeria.' (JNH, vol. 27, 1942, pp. 37–54.)

Describes the background to the Igbo slave trade.

318 BOUCHAUD, Joseph
'Les Portugais dans la Baie de Biafra au XVIème siècle.' (Africa, London, vol. 16, 1946, pp. 217–27; map.)

Includes notes on the origin of the Portuguese slave trade in the Benin area around 1500.

319 TORRE Y DEL CERRO, Antonio de la
'Los Canarios de Gomera, vendidos como esclavos en 1489.' (Anuario de Estudios Americanos, Sevilla, vol. 7, 1950, pp. 47–72.)

Contains the text of documents of 1489–1502.

320 BOUVEIGNES, Olivier de
'La traite des esclaves à la côte occidentale d'Afrique au XVIIe siècle.' (Brousse, Léopoldville, no. 2, 1952, pp. 26–38; illus.)

Relates to J. E. J. Capitein.

321a NØRREGAARD, Georg Pedersen
'De danske etablissementer paa Guinea-kysten.' In: BRØNDSTED, J. Vore gamle tropekolonier, vol. 1 (Copenhagen, 1952), pp. 425–619; illus, maps.

Translated as:

321b *Danish settlements in West Africa, 1658–1850 . . . Boston, 1966. xxvii, 287 pp. bibl. pp. 261–71.

Includes an account of the Danish slave trade.

322 DELCOURT, André
La France et les établissements français au Sénégal entre 1713 et 1763 . . . Dakar, 1952. 432 pp. maps. bibl. pp. 27–37. (MIFAN, no. 17.)

Pt. 1 deals with the Compagnie des Indes and private slaving entrepreneurs 1742–53.

323 VERGER, Pierre
'Influence du Brésil au golfe du Benin.' (MIFAN, no. 27, 1952, pp. 11–101.)

On Brazilian slave traders in Dahomey in the 19th century.

324 *VERGER, Pierre
'Cartas de um brasileiro estabelecido no século XIX na Costa dos Escravos.' (Anhembi, São Paulo, vol. 6, 1952, pp. 212–53.)

325 'CAS de conscience sur quelques circonstances du commerce des esclaves en Guinée.' In: CUVELIER, J. Documents sur une mission française au Kakongo 1766–1776 (Bruxelles, 1953), pp. 114–18.

Discusses commercial sharp practices of slave traders.

326 JEFFREYS, Mervin David Waldegrave
'Alt-Kalabar und der Sklavenhandel.' (Paideuma, Frankfurt-am-Main, vol. 6, pt. 1, 1954, pp. 14–24.)

Notes on the slave trade at Calabar 1668–1842 and the development of the 'house' system.

327 HORTON, W. R. G.
'The ohu system of slavery in a northern Ibo village-group.' (Africa, London, vol. 24, 1954, pp. 311–36; map.)

On the role of the Nike slave traders before 1900.

328 FAGE, John Donnelly
An introduction to the history of West Africa. Cambridge, 1955. x, 209 pp. maps.

Includes chapters (rewritten in the 1969 edition) on the slave trade and the abolition campaign.

329 SOUZA, Norberto Francisco de
'Contribution à l'histoire de la famille de Souza.' (Études Dahoméennes, Porto-Novo, no. 13, 1955, pp. 17–21.)

Notes on the slave trader Francisco da Souza (in Dahomey 1788–1849) and his family.

330 WALLACE, Robert
'How the negro came to slavery in America.' (Life. International edition, Denver, Colorado, vol. 21, no. 7, 1956, pp. 32–51; illus.)

On the slave trade from West Africa.

331 ARNOLD, Rosemary
'A port of trade: Whydah on the Guinea coast.' In: POLANYI, K.

Trade and market in the early empires (Glencoe, Ill., 1957), pp. 154–75.

Account of the commercial organisation of Dahomey in the 18th century.

332 *LLOYD, Peter Cutt
'Captain Landolphe and the Compagnie d'Owhere et de Benin.' (Odù, Ibadan, no. 5, 1957, pp. 14–27.)

See (740).

333 SURET-CANALE, Jean
Afrique noire occidentale et centrale . . . Paris, [1958]. 280 pp. maps. bibl. pp. 249–80.

Includes sections on the development of slavery and the social effects of the slave trade in West Africa.

334 RYDER, Alan Frederick Charles
'The re-establishment of Portuguese factories on the Costa da Mina to the mid eighteenth century.' (JHSN, vol. 1, 1958, pp. 157–83.)

Deals with the slave trade 1721–50.

335 OTTENBERG, Simon
'Ibo oracles and intergroup relations.' (Southwestern Journal of Anthropology, Albuquerque, vol. 14, 1958, pp. 295–317; map.)

Describes the Aro trade system developed in response to the overseas slave trade.

336 PRIESTLEY, Margaret A.
'Richard Brew; an eighteenth century trader at Anomabu.' (Transactions of the Historical Society of Ghana, Legon, vol. 4, pt. 1, 1959, pp. 29–46.)

After serving the African Company Brew lived as a private slave dealer at Anomabu 1764–76.

337 JADIN, Louis
'La marine française au Congo au XIXe siècle, avant Stanley.' (Marine Academie van Belgie, Mededelingen, Antwerpen, vol. 12, 1960, pp. 1–25.)

With notes on the slave trade in the Congo area from the 16th to the 19th century.

338 VANSINA, Jan
'Long-distance trade routes in central Africa.' (JAH, vol. 3, 1962, pp. 375–90; map.)

On the development of a trading network inland from Kongo and Angola from the 16th to the 19th century.

339 CHILVER, Elizabeth Millicent
'Nineteenth century trade in the Bamenda grassfields, southern Cameroons.' (Afrika und Übersee, Berlin, vol. 45, 1962, pp. 233–58; map.)

Includes notes on the slave trade northward and to Calabar.

340 ZUCARELLI, François
'Le régime des engagés à temps au Sénégal (1817–1848).' (CEA, vol. 2, 1962, pp. 420–61.)

After 1823 contract labour was provided by purchasing and liberating slaves.

341 LAWRENCE, Arnold Walter
Trade castles & forts of West Africa. London, 1963. 389 pp. illus, map.

Detailed descriptions of the European forts, with references to the slave trade.

342 AKINJOGBIN, Isaac Adeagbo
'Agaja and the conquest of the coastal Aja states 1724–30.' (JHSN, vol. 2, no. 4, 1963, pp. 545–66.)

The object of Dahomey's expansion to the coast was not control of the slave trade, though she became increasingly involved in it after 1730.

343 FYFE, Christopher
'The illegal slave trade.' *In his*: Sierra Leone inheritance (London, 1964), pp. 155–65.

On the trade 1811–64.

344 MORTON-WILLIAMS, Peter
'The Oyo Yoruba and the Atlantic trade, 1670–1830.' (JHSN, vol. 3, no. 1, 1964, pp. 25–45.)

Oyo first traded in slaves through Whydah but changed to Badagri and Porto Novo in the 18th century.

345 POLANYI, Karl
'Sortings and 'ounce trade' in the West African slave trade.' (JAH, vol. 5, 1964, pp. 381–93.)

Artificial trade units were devised to adapt the slave trade to the principle of bartering.

346 RODNEY, Walter
'Portuguese attempts at monopoly on the Upper Guinea coast, 1580–1650.' (JAH, vol. 6, 1965, pp. 307–22.)

Describes the trading relations between Portuguese, Spaniards and African chiefs.

347 **BIRMINGHAM, David**
The Portuguese conquest of Angola. London, New York, 1965. vii, 50 pp. maps.

Largely on the development of the slave trade, particularly 1605–41 and in the 18th century.

348 **EDINBURGH UNIVERSITY: Centre of African Studies**
The transatlantic slave trade from West Africa. [Edinburgh, 1965.] iii, 92 pp.

Report of a seminar held in June 1965, including papers by R. T. Anstey, C. H. Fyfe, J. D. Hargreaves, A. Luttrell and C. D. Rice; largely concerned with Eric Williams' thesis in (1309).

349 **RYDER, Alan Frederick Charles**
'Dutch trade on the Nigerian coast during the seventeenth century.' (JHSN, vol. 3, 1965, pp. 195–210.)

Includes notes on the slave trade in the 1640s.

350 **GRAHAM, James D.**
'The slave trade, depopulation, and human sacrifice in Benin history.' (CEA, vol. 5, 1965, pp. 317–24.)

The slave trade had little effect on Benin; it was conducted mostly through Warri and Lagos.

351 **ROSS, David A.**
'The career of Domingo Martinez in the Bight of Benin 1833–64.' (JAH, vol. 6, 1965, pp. 79–90.)

Illustrates the prosperity and decline of the slave trade at Lagos and Porto Novo about 1840–60.

352 **ABRAMOVA, Svetlana Yur'evna**
Istoriya rabotorgovli na verkhne-gvinei-skom poberezh'e (vtoraya polovina XV—nachalo XIX v.). Moskva, 1966. 193 pp. maps. bibl. pp. 176–92.

History of the slave trade on the Upper Guinea coast, mid-15th to early 19th century.

353 **BIRMINGHAM, David**
Trade and conflict in Angola. The Mbundu and their neighbours under the influence of the Portuguese 1483–1790. Oxford, 1966. xvi, 178 pp. maps.

Ch. 2: 'The opening of the Atlantic slave trade 1483–1565'; ch. 7: 'The expansion of the slave trading system in west central Africa 1683–1790.' (Ph.D. thesis, London, 1964.)

354 **FLINT, John Edgar**
Nigeria and Ghana. Englewood Cliffs, N.J., [1966]. viii, 176 pp.

Ch. 3: 'The European impact and the slave trade.'

355 **RODNEY, Walter**
'African slavery and other forms of social oppression on the Upper Guinea coast in the context of the Atlantic slave-trade.' (JAH, vol. 7, 1966, pp. 431–43.)

West African slavery developed in response to European demand for slaves, not the reverse.

356 **POLANYI, Karl**
Dahomey and the slave trade. An analysis of an archaic economy. Seattle & London, [1966]. xxvi, 204 pp. maps.

The Dahomean slave trade developed in the late 17th century due to the growth of European sugar colonies across the Atlantic.

357 **VERLINDEN, Charles**
'Les débuts de la traite portugaise en Afrique (1433–1448).' In: Miscellanea mediaevalia in memoriam Jan Frederik Niermeyer (Groningen, 1967), pp. 365–78.

Account of the period of Portuguese slave raiding in West Africa, based on (187).

358 **OLIVER, Roland,** editor
The middle ages of African history. London, 1967. 104 pp. maps.

Includes: 'The impact of the Atlantic slave trade on West Africa', by Walter Rodney (pp. 34–40); 'Central Africa and the Atlantic slave trade', by David Birmingham (pp. 56–62).

359 **HANSEN, Thorkild**
Slavernes kyst . . . [Copenhagen,] 1967. 282 pp. illus, map.

Semi-fictional history of the Danish slave trade from Africa, 1673–1802.

360 ***KLEIN, A. Norman**
'Slave trade and state formation in West Africa (with special emphasis on the Ashanti).' In: ASPECTS of African history. Papers delivered at 52nd anniversary meeting of the Association for the Study of Negro Life and History, Greensboro, N.C., October 12–15, 1967.

361 **BOUTILLIER, Jean Louis**
'Les captifs en A.O.F. (1903–1905).' (BIFAN, vol. 30, ser. B, 1968, pp. 513–35.)

Slavery organised for production was an internal factor for economic change in 19th-century West Africa.

362 DAAKU, Kwame Yeboa
'The slave trade and African society.' *In*: RANGER, T. O., *editor*. Emerging themes of African history (Nairobi, 1968), pp. 134–40.

On the political, economic and social effects of the slave trade in West Africa.

363 RIVIÈRE, Claude
'Le long des côtes de Guinée avant la phase coloniale.' (BIFAN, vol. 30, ser. B, 1968, pp. 727–50.)

Contains sections on the slave trade at the rivers Nunez and Pongo in the 18th and 19th centuries.

364 RANDLES, William Graham Lister
'De la traite à la colonisation: les Portugais en Angola.' (AESC, vol. 24, 1969, pp. 289–304; maps.)

Account of Portuguese expansion and slave trade 1575–1880.

365 RODNEY, Walter
West Africa and the Atlantic slave-trade. Nairobi, 1969. 27 pp.

366 FAGE, John Donnelly
'Slavery and the slave trade in the context of West African history.' (JAH, vol. 10, 1969, pp. 393–404.)

Although slavery expanded due to the Atlantic slave trade, the export of slaves was a deliberate choice of African governments and the population loss was not universally damaging. See (4521).

367 STÖBER, Horst
'Der europäische Sklavenhandel und die feudale Produktionsweise an der westafrikanischen Sklavenküste.' (Ethnographisch-Archäologische Zeitschrift, Berlin, vol. 10, 1969, pp. 487–500.)

On the slave trade in the Aja-Yoruba region.

368 HARGREAVES, John Desmond, *editor*
France and West Africa. An anthology of historical documents . . . London, 1969. 278 pp. map.

Includes extracts on the slave trade 1694–1850.

369 PRIESTLEY, Margaret A.
West African trade and coast society. A family study. London, 1969. xv, 210 pp. illus, maps.

On the 18th-century slave trader Richard Brew at Anamobu and his descendants.

370 MASON, Michael
'Population density and 'slave raiding' —the case of the Middle Belt of Nigeria.' (JAH, vol. 10, 1969, pp. 551–64; maps.)

The effects of 19th-century slave raiding in depopulating parts of central Nigeria has been exaggerated. See (374).

371 RODNEY, Walter
A history of the Upper Guinea coast 1545–1800. Oxford, 1970. ix, 283 pp. maps. bibl. pp. 271–78.

Contains chapters on the slave trade 1562–1640 and 1690–1800.

372 MARTIN, Phyllis
'The trade of Loango in the seventeenth and eighteenth centuries.' *In*: GRAY, R. *and* BIRMINGHAM, D. Pre-colonial African trade (London, 1970), pp. 139–61; map.

Describes the organisation of the Loango slave trade in the 18th century.

373 DEBIEN, Gabriel
'Théodore Canot condamné comme négrier en 1834.' (RFHO, vol. 57, 1970, pp. 214–24.)

Canot was convicted of slave trading but resumed the business on the Liberian coast 1836–39.

374 GLEAVE, M. B. *and* PROTHERO, Ralph Mansell
'Population density and 'slave raiding' —a comment.' (JAH, vol. 12, 1971, pp. 319–24.)

Argues that Mason (370) has underestimated the effect of slave raids on the Nigerian Middle Belt; with a reply by Mason: pp. 324–27.

D

D. SUDAN

(a) CONTEMPORARY ACCOUNTS

375 BALDWIN, George
'Memorial relating to the trade in slaves carried on in Egypt, the numbers annually brought into it, and sold; distinguishing those who are natives of Asia from those who are natives of Africa; from what parts they are brought, and whether the male slaves are usually castrated. And further relating to the caravans periodically sent from Egypt into the interior parts of Africa . . .' (EMLR, vol. 17, Feb. 1790, pp. 127–29.)

Report by the British consul at Alexandria 1789; about 5,000 slaves are imported annually from the eastern Sudan, the Fezzan and Abyssinia. (Also printed as: 'Memorial relating to the slave trade in Egypt', in P.P. 1790, XXIX; extract in: SM, vol. 52, Feb. 1790, pp. 71–73.)

376 BROWNE, William George
Travels in Africa, Egypt, and Syria, from the year 1792 to 1798. T. Cadell Junior & O. Rees, London, 1799. xxxviii, 496 pp. maps.

Includes an account of a journey with a slave caravan from Darfur to Assiut 1796.

377 FRANK, Louis
Mémoire sur le commerce des nègres au Kaire, et sur les maladies auxquelles ils sont sujets en y arrivant. Migneret; Brigithe Mathé, Paris, an X, 1802. 52 pp.

Describes the slave trade from Sennar, Darfur and Bornu to Egypt, with notes on diseases (pp. 39–52). Also printed in: INSTITUT D'ÉGYPTE. Mémoires sur l'Égypte, vol. 4 (Paris, an XI–1803), pp. 125–56.

378 LAPANOUSE, Mercure Joseph
'Mémoire sur les caravanes qui arrivent du royaume de Dârfurth en Egypte, avec des détails sur les lieux où elles passent, et sur le commerce qui se fait des esclaves et des autres marchandises précieuses qui viennent de ce pays.—Mémoire sur les caravanes venant du royaume de Sennâar et sur la route qu'elles tiennent, avec des développements sur la nature des divers objets de commerce qu'elles portent . . .' In: INSTITUT D'ÉGYPTE. Mémoires sur l'Égypte, vol. 4 (Paris, an XI–1803), pp. 77–123.

The Darfur caravan sometimes brings 12,000 slaves to Egypt, while only 3–400 are imported annually from Sennar.

379 ADAMS, Robert
The narrative of Robert Adams, a sailor, who was wrecked on the western coast of Africa, in the year 1810, was detained three years in slavery by the Arabs of the great desert, and resided several months in the city of Timbuctoo . . . John Murray, London, 1816. xxxix, 231 pp. map.

Includes notes by Joseph Dupuis on the Saharan slave trade. (The 'Narrative' itself may be spurious.)

380 BURCKHARDT, John Lewis
Travels in Nubia . . . John Murray, London, 1819. xcii, 543 pp. illus, maps.

Describes the slave trade along the Nile in 1814. (Reviewed in: CO, vol. 19, 1820, pp. 456–68; NAR, vol. 40, 1835, pp. 477–510.)

381 LYON, George Francis
A narrative of travels in northern Africa, in the years 1818, 19, and 20 . . . John Murray, London, 1821. xii, 383 pp. map.

Includes accounts of the trans-Saharan slave trade through Murzuk.

382 DENHAM, Dixon
Narrative of travels and discoveries in northern and central Africa, in the years 1822, 1823, and 1824, by Major Denham, Captain Clapperton, and the late Doctor Oudney . . . John Murray, London, 1826. xlviii, 335, 269 pp. illus, maps.

Describes the slave trade between Kano, Bornu and Murzuk. (Republished, with additional documents, by the Hakluyt Society, Cambridge, 1966.)

383a CAILLIÉ, René
Journal d'un voyage à Temboctou et à Jenné, dans l'Afrique centrale . . . Paris, 1830. 3 vol. illus, maps.

Translated as:

383b Travels through central Africa to Timbuctoo; and across the great desert, to Morocco, performed in the years 1824–1828. Henry Colburn & Richard Bentley, London, 1830. 2 vol. illus, maps.

Caillié accompanied a caravan taking slaves from the Niger to Morocco.

384 BOWRING, John
Report on Egypt and Candia. Addressed to the Right Hon. Lord Viscount Palmerston . . . London, 1840. 236 pp. (P.P. 1840, XXI.)

Includes a section on 'Slave-trade and slavery' (pp. 83–103), describing Sudanese slave hunts and Egyptian slave markets.

385 MADDEN, Richard Robert
Egypt and Mohammed Ali. Illustrative of the condition of his slaves and subjects . . . Hamilton, Adams & Co., London, 1841. xvi, 280 pp.

Describes the Sudanese slave trade. (Extract, 'The slave trade in Egypt', in: Journal of Civilization, London, 1842, pp. 236–38.)

386a PALLME, Ignaz
Beschreibung von Kordofan und einigen angränzenden Ländern, nebst einem Ueberblick über . . . die unter der Regierung Mehemed Ali's stattgefundenen Sklavenjagden. J. G. Cotta, Stuttgart & Tübingen, 1843. xii, 220 pp.

Translated as:

386b Travels in Kordofan; embracing a description of that province of Egypt, and of some of the bordering countries . . . as also an account of the slave-hunts taking place under the government of Mehemed Ali. J. Madden, London, 1844. x, 356 pp.

With an account of slave raids in 1838–39.

387 MUHAMMAD IBN 'UMAR, *al Tūnusī*
Voyage au Darfour par le cheykh Mohammed Ebn-Omar el-Tounsy . . . Benjamin Duprat, Paris, 1845. lxxxviii, 491 pp. maps.

Account by a trader who lived in Darfur about 1798–1805, with descriptions of slave raids and the slave trade.

388 SCHOELCHER, Victor
L'Egypte en 1845. Pagnerre, Paris, 1846. 366 pp.

Ch. 9: 'Chasse aux hommes dans le Sennaar et le Kordofan . . .'

389 RICHARDSON, James
Travels in the great desert of Sahara, in the years of 1845 and 1846 . . . Richard Bentley, London, 1848. 2 vol. map.

Includes descriptions of the slave trade in the Fezzan.

390 DAUMAS, Melchior Joseph Eugène, *and* CHANCEL, Ausone de
Le grand désert ou itinéraire d'une caravane du Sahara au pays des nègres (royaume de Haoussa). Napoléon Chaix & Cie, Paris, 1848. xv, 443 pp. map.

Includes notes on the Muslim slave trade; the preface contains a plan to buy Sudanese slaves to work in Algeria. See (439).

391 'The SLAVE markets of Egypt.' (CJ, n.s., vol. 11, 1849, pp. 81–84.)

Eyewitness description of a slave sale.

392 MUHAMMAD IBN 'UMAR, *al Tūnusī*
Voyage au Ouadây par le cheykh Mohammed Ibn-Omar el-Tounsy . . . publié par le Dr Perron et M. Jomard . . . Paris, 1851. lxxv, 756 pp. illus, map.

Includes notes on the slave trade of Wadai in the early years of the 19th century.

393 RICHARDSON, James
Narrative of a mission to central Africa performed in the years 1850–51, under the orders and at the expense of Her Majesty's government. London, 1853. 2 vol.

Contains information on the slave trade.

394 ESCAYRAC DE LAUTURE, Stanislas, *comte* d'
Le désert et le Soudan. Paris, 1853. xvi, 628 pp. maps.

Includes chapters on the slave trade.

395 MUHAMMAD IBN 'UMAR, *al Tūnusī*
Travels of an Arab merchant in Soudan (the black kingdoms of central Africa). I.-Darfur. II.-Wadaï. Abridged from

the French. By Bayle St. John. London, 1854. xvi, 336 pp.

The editor's introduction suggests the possibility of ending the Sudanese slave trade through 'legitimate' commerce under Egyptian rule.

396 TRÉMAUX, Pierre
'Épisode d'un voyage au Soudan oriental et remarques sur l'esclavage.' (Bulletin de la Société de Géographie, Paris, ser. 4, vol. 11, 1856, pp. 153–64.)

Account of a journey along the Blue Nile and of Egyptian slave raids about 1848.

397 HARTMANN, Robert
'Die katholischen Missionen und der Menschenhandel am weissen Flusse.' (Zeitschrift für Allgemeine Erdkunde, Berlin, n.s., vol. 11, 1861, pp. 446–61.)

Account of Catholic missions and the slave trade in the Egyptian Sudan 1847–60.

398 GILBERT, Philippe Louis
'Les négriers et les missions catholiques dans l'Afrique orientale.' (Revue Catholique, Louvain, vol. 20, 1862, pp. 317–29.)

Describes the Catholic missions and the slave trade in the Egyptian Sudan 1848–61.

399 LEJEAN, Guillaume
'Le Haut-Nil et le Soudan. Souvenirs de voyage.' (RDM, vol. 37, 1862, pp. 854–82.)

With notes on the Egyptian slave trade in the Sudan since 1820. See (404).

400 BAKER, Sir Samuel White
The Albert N'yanza, great basin of the Nile, and explorations of the Nile sources. London, 1866. 2 vol. map.

Describes the slaving activities of Sudanese traders on the upper Nile 1863–65.

401 MILLINGEN, Frederick
Slavery in Turkey. The Sultan's harem . . . A paper read before the Anthropological Society of London. London, 1870. 24 pp.

Pt. 1, 'Negro slaves in Turkey', estimates a black population of 30,000 in Constantinople alone, mostly Sudanese females. (First published in: Journal of the Anthropological Society of London, no. 29, April 1870, pp. lxxxv–xcvi.)

402 'Die SKLAVEREI im osmanischen Reiche.' (Signed: A.) (Globus, Braunschweig, vol. 17, 1870, pp. 333–35.)

By Karl Andree?

403a BERLIOUX, Étienne Félix
La traite orientale. Histoire des chasses à l'homme organisées en Afrique depuis quinze ans pour les marchés de l'orient . . . Paris, 1870. xi, 350 pp. map.

Translated as:

403b The slave trade in Africa in 1872. Principally carried on for the supply of Turkey, Egypt, Persia, and Zanzibar . . . London, 1872. viii, 77 pp.

On the slave trade from the Sudan, the Nile basin and East Africa and the markets in Egypt, Zanzibar and Arabia. (The translation is an abridgment. French edition reviewed in (63), English edition in: Bulletin de la Société de Géographie, Paris, ser. 6, vol. 7, 1874, pp. 301–12.)

404 LEJEAN, Guillaume
'La traite des esclaves en Égypte et en Turquie.' (RDM, vol. 88, 1870, pp. 895–913.)

On the Egyptian slave trade since 1862. See (399).

405 HARTMANN, Robert
'Sclavenfang in Afrika.' (Gartenlaube, Leipzig, 1872, pp. 343–46; illus.)

Account of a slave raid on the Dinka of the eastern Sudan.

406 *SOUTHWORTH, Alvan S.
'The Soudan and the valley of the White Nile.' (BAGS, vol. 5, 1873, pp. 95–111.)

407 NACHTIGAL, Gustav
'Zug mit einer Sklavenkarawane in Bagirmi.' (Globus, Braunschweig, vol. 24, 1873, pp. 215–18, 231–33.)

Description of the capture of slaves east of Lake Chad to exchange for horses in Bornu 1872.

408a SCHWEINFURTH, Georg August
Im Herzen von Afrika. Reisen und Entdeckungen im centralen Äquatorial-Afrika während der Jahre 1868 bis 1871. Leipzig, 1874. 2 vol. illus, maps.

Translated as:

408b The heart of Africa. Three years' travels and adventures in the unexplored regions of central Africa. From 1868 to 1871 . . . London, 1873. 2 vol. illus, maps.

Describes the slave trade in the Egyptian Sudan and suggests as a solution the establishment of European protectorates and Chinese immigration.

409 NACHTIGAL, Gustav
'Slave-hunts in central Africa.' (HMM, vol. 48, 1874, pp. 710–17.)

Extracts from Nachtigal's account of slave raids in Baghirmi: 'Sklavenjagden in Central Afrika.' (Kölnischer Zeitung, 20, 28 July 1873.)

410 SOUTHWORTH, Alvan S.
Four thousand miles of African travel: a personal record of a journey up the Nile and through the Soudan to the confines of central Africa, embracing . . . an examination of the slave trade. New York; London, 1875. xi, 381 pp. map.

With chapters on the slave trade of the upper Nile and Abyssinia.

411 'The HEART of Africa and the slave trade.' (ER, vol. 141, 1875, pp. 209–42.)

Review of works by Schweinfurth (408) and Baker (3508), with notes on the slave trade in the Nile valley and its suppression.

412 *COOPER, Joseph
Turkey and Egypt, past and present state in relation to Africa. With an appendix on consular reports concerning slavery and the slave-trade throughout the Ottoman empire by A. Buyacost. London, 1876. iv, 22, 6 pp.

413 CHESSON, Frederick William
Turkey and the slave trade. A statement of facts. London, 1877. 16 pp.

On the Turkish slave trade and European efforts to abolish it 1874–76.

414 REINISCH, Leo
'Zur Sklavenfrage im egyptischen Sudan'. (ÖMO, vol. 6, 1880, pp. 198–99.)

Information on Egyptian slave raids in the eastern Sudan 1879–80.

415 'IETS over den slavenhandel in Soedan en aan de kusten der Roode Zee.' (Tijdschrift van het Aardrijkskundig Genootschap, Amsterdam, vol. 4, 1880, pp. 197–99; map.)

416 'La TRAITE dans le Soudan égyptien.' (Société Belge de Géographie, Bulletin, Bruxelles, vol. 5, 1881, pp. 260–64.)

Translation of a letter to 'The Times'.

417 *PENNAZZI, Luigi
'La via principale della tratta degli schiavi in Egitto.' (Esploratore, Milano, 1881, pp. 65–66.)

418 'DR. Gustav Nachtigal's Reise nach Baghirmi 1872.' (Globus, Braunschweig, vol. 39, 1881, pp. 209–15, 225–31, 241–47, 257–63, 273–79, 289–93, 305–10; illus.)

Account of Nachtigal's journey to Baghirmi, where he witnessed the capture of slaves by its sultan. See (407).

419 'SCLAVENHANDEL in Marokko.' (NEK, 1883, col. 448.)

Report from Morocco on the trans-Saharan slave trade from Timbuktu.

420 HAKE, Alfred Egmont
'Zebehr, slavery, and the Soudan.' (Illustrated London News, vol. 84, 1884, pp. 462–64; illus, port.)

Account of Zubair Pasha's role in the Egyptian Sudan.

421 BOHNDORFF, F.
'F. Bohndorff's Reise nach Dar Abu Dinga.' (Ausland, München, 1884, pp. 541–45, 565–71.)

Description of Zubair Pasha's camps in the Bahr el Arab area 1876–79.

422 SHAW, Flora Louisa
'The story of Zebehr Pasha, as told by himself.' (CR, vol. 52, 1887, pp. 333–49, 568–85, 658–82.)

Zubair's own account of his activities in the Sudan 1857–75.

423 ZUCCHINETTI, Vigilio
Souvenirs de mon sejour chez Emin Pacha el Soudani. Origine de la traite. Cause de la révolte du Soudan . . . Le Caire, 1890. 17 pp.

Address, delivered 1887, on the Egyptian Sudan a decade earlier.

424 BINGER, Louis Gustave
Esclavage, islamisme et christianisme. Paris, 1891. 112 pp.

Notes on slavery and the slave trade in the western Sudan.

425 *GEYER, Franz Xaver
'Negerjagden und Sklavenhandel im Sudan in den letzten Decennien.' (Echo aus Afrika, Salzburg, vol. 4, 1892, pp. 33–36, 53–56.)

426 'La TRAITE des nègres dans le Soudan chez les Mahdistes.' (MA, vol. 5, 1893, pp. 161–64.)

Based on: J. Ohrwalder, Ten years in the Mahdi's camp (London, 1892).

427 GUILLAUMET, Édouard
Le Soudan en 1894. La vérité sur Tombouctou. L'esclavage au Soudan. Paris, 1895. vi, 164 pp. maps.

Pt. 2 describes the slave trade and slavery in the western Sudan.

428 SLATIN, Rudolf Carl
'L'esclavage et la traite des esclaves dans le Soudan.' (MA, vol. 8, 1896, pp. 158–61.)

429 ROBINSON, Charles Henry
Hausaland or fifteen hundred miles through the central Soudan. London, 1896. xv, 304 pp.

Ch. 9: 'Slavery and slave-raiding.'

430 NATHAN, Albert J.
'At the Morocco slave market.' (Missionary Review of the World, New York, n.s., vol. 12, no. 7, 1899, pp. 521–22.)

Account by an American missionary of Sudanese slaves sold at markets in Marrakesh and Fez; condensed from the 'Gospel Messenger', New York. (Translated as 'Auf dem Sklavenmarkt in Marokko' in: EMM, n.s., vol. 43, 1899, pp. 501–04.)

431 *BEDUSCHI, Giuseppe
'Gli orrori della schiavitù. Racconto d'un missionario . . .' (Nigrizia, Verona, vol. 19, 1901, pp. 9–14, 33–35, 44–46, 63–66, 95–98, 125–29, 140–44.)

432 TONKIN, T. J.
'The slave trade in Northern Nigeria.' (Empire Review, London, vol. 1, 1901, pp. 513–25, 648–58; vol. 2, 1902, pp. 68–75, 228–35.)

Account of kidnapping, raids and slave markets in the 1890s. (Abridged as 'The slave-trade in Hausaland' in: Missionary Review of the World, New York, vol, 25, 1902, pp. 456–58.)

433 BENSUSAN, Samuel Levy
'The slave-market at Marrakésh.' (HMM, vol. 108, 1904, pp. 245–53; illus.)

Colourful account of the sale of Sudanese slaves.

434 JACKSON, Henry Cecil
Black ivory and white, or the story of El Zubeir Pasha, slaver and sultan, as told by himself. Translated and put on record by Henry Cecil Jackson. Oxford, 1913. iv, 118 pp.

435 JENNINGS BRAMLEY, W. E.
'Tales of the Wadai slave trade in the nineties. Told by Yunes Bedis of the Majabra to W. E. Jennings Bramley.' (SNR, vol. 23, 1940, pp. 169–83.)

The narrator, from Jalo in Libya, participated with his father in illegal slave trading from Wadai to Egypt via Kufra.

436 MUKHTĀR IBN al-HASAN, called IBN BUTLĀN
'Risālah jāmi'ah li-funūn nāfi'ah fi shira'l-raḳīḳ wa-taḳlīb al-'abīd [A treatise on the art of buying slaves].' In: HARUN, 'Abd al-Salām Muḥammad, editor. Nawādir al-makhṭuṭat, pt. 4 (Cairo, 1954), pp. 351–89.

Advice on the physical selection and characteristics of slaves from Africa (Nubian, Ethiopian, Berber), Asia and Europe; by an 11th-century Christian doctor from Baghdad.

(b) CONTROVERSY

437a*D'GHIES, Hassuna
Lettre adressée à un philantrope anglais, par un voyageur africain, durant son séjour à Londres. Londres, 1822. 25 pp.

Translated as:

437b A letter addressed to James Scarlett, Esq. M.P. and member of the African Institution, on the abolition of the slave trade . . . J. Brettell, London, 1822. 16 pp.

The North African countries must be converted to antislavery before the Saharan slave trade can be abolished; this will only be achieved by introducing 'civilization' and extending commerce, not by force. (The author became foreign minister of Tripoli in 1826.)

438 BAUDE, Jean Jacques, *baron*
'De l'esclavage des noirs dans le nord de l'Afrique.' (Annales Maritimes et Coloniales, Paris, ser. 2, vol. 1, 1838, pp. 927–38.)

Describes the trans-Saharan slave trade and warns against premature abolition of slavery in Algeria which may be 'providential' for the Africans involved.

439 BAUDE, Jean Jacques, *baron*
L'Algérie. Arthus Bertrand, Paris, 1841. 2 vol.

Suggests re-establishing the Saharan slave trade in order to buy Sudanese slaves for 'apprentissage de la liberté' in Algeria; educated negroes may one day return to their countries as 'missionaries' for France, Christianity and liberty (vol. 2, ch. 17).

440 'SLAVE trade in the interior of Africa. Circular of Colonel Warrington.' (FA, no. 21, July 1842, pp. 107–08.)

Includes the text, translated from Arabic, of an anti-slave trade appeal issued by the British consul at Tripoli 26 March 1842.

441 'DE l'esclavage et des captifs en Algérie.' (Abolitioniste Français, Paris, vol. 1, 1844, pp. 351–56.)

Summary of correspondence between the president of the Société de Civilisation de l'Afrique and the Algerian governor general on the slave trade across the Sahara.

442 The PRESENT state of the anti-slavery question in Tunis and Algiers; in a letter addressed to Thomas Clarkson, Esq., president of the British and Foreign Anti-Slavery Society; by a correspondent of the same society. Smith, Elder & Co., London, 1845. 20 pp.

The Bey of Tunis has abolished the slave trade, the first Muslim prince in history to do so, while the French in Algeria are actually planning to re-establish the Saharan slave traffic.

443 CHANCEL, Ausone de
D'une immigration de noirs libres en Algérie . . . Bastide, Alger, 1853. 52 pp.

Proposes buying 100,000 Sudanese from the Tuareg, to be publicly freed and employed as workers in Algeria. See (444).

444 DU PRÉ DE SAINT-MAUR, Jules
Objections contre l'introduction d'engagés noirs en Algérie. Et réponse à une lettre de M. de Chancel auteur du projet. Paris, [1858]. 48 pp.

Reply to (443), opposing the scheme on moral and economic grounds.

445 'The SLAVE-TRADE in Turkey.' (CJ, vol. 9, 1858, pp. 264–66.)

Turkey now depends on Tripoli for its supply of slaves; a couple of cruisers off the coast would stop this trade.

446 'Die SKLAVENJAGDEN der Europäer am Weissen Nil.' (Globus, Hildburghausen, vol. 3, 1863, pp. 214–15.)

European traders are indirectly involved in the Sudanese slave trade.

447 'AUS dem Sudan. 2. Ueber die Sklavenfrage in Mittel-Africa.' (MGGW, vol. 15, 1873, pp. 249–52.)

On the slave trade of the White Nile.

448 MARNO, Ernst
'Die Sclavenfrage in Ostafrica.' (MGGW, vol. 16, 1873, pp. 458–62.)

On the slave trade in the eastern Sudan within Egypt's sphere of influence.

449 MALTZAN, Heinrich, *Freiherr* von
'Menschenhandel in Afrika.' (Gartenlaube, Leipzig, 1873, pp. 519–21.)

Based on a letter from Nachtigal on the slave trade (407).

450 MARNO, Ernst
'Ueber Sclaverei und die jüngsten Vorgänge im ägyptischen Sudan. Die Nilfrage.' (MGGW, vol. 17, 1874, pp. 243–55.)

It is Egypt's task to occupy the upper Nile and eradicate the slave trade.

451 'Der SKLAVENHANDEL im obern Nilgebiet.' (Globus, Braunschweig, vol. 31, 1877, pp. 111–12.)

The Egyptian conquest of Darfur has extended the area of the slave trade.

452 NACHTIGAL, Gustav
'Bagirmi, der Sklavenhandel und die Brüsseler internationale Association zur Erforschung und Erschliessung Inner-Afrikas.' (Deutsche Rundschau, Berlin, vol. 10, 1877, pp. 204–20, 362–85.)

Describes the slave trade of the eastern Sudan and suggests that legitimate trade must be used to supplant it.

453 GUNDERT, Hermann
'Sklavenhandel in Egypten und der Türkei.' (EMM, n.s., vol. 21, 1877, pp. 285–93.)

Description of the slave trade of the Nile basin from recent publications; Gordon now continues Baker's work to suppress it.

454 McCOAN, James Carlile
'Slavery in Egypt.' (Fraser's Magazine, London, n.s., vol. 15, 1877, pp. 563–70.)

Slaving continues only in Darfur and on the White Nile; the government has closed the public markets in Egypt.

455 'WIEDERAUFLEBEN des Sklavenhandels in Egypten.' (ÖMO, vol. 6, 1880, pp. 98–102.)

Letters from Egypt and the Sudan by G. Schweinfurth and others on the illegal slave trade.

456 *BRITISH AND FOREIGN ANTI-SLAVERY SOCIETY
Colonel Gordon and the slave trade in Egypt, the Soudan and equatorial Africa. London, 1880. 11 pp.

457 SCHWEINFURTH, Georg August
'Sklavenhandel in egyptischen Sudan, 1880.' (ÖMO, vol. 6, 1880, pp. 173–75).

Presents evidence that Egyptian officials are still involved in the slave trade.

458 *BRITISH AND FOREIGN ANTI-SLAVERY SOCIETY
Slavery and the slave-trade in Egypt. London, 1881. 12 pp.

459 HANSAL, Martin L.
'Zur Sklavenfrage im Sudan.' (ÖMO, vol. 7, 1881, pp. 102–03.)

Slave trade continues in the Egyptian Sudan.

460 BLACKWOOD, Frederick Temple Hamilton Temple, *Marquis of Dufferin and Ava*
'Le Soudan et la traite.' (Exploration, Paris, vol. 16, pt. 2, 1883, pp. 1–9.)

Suggests antislavery measures, including British naval patrols in the Red Sea.

461 CHURCH MISSIONARY SOCIETY
'The slave trade in Egypt.' (CMI, n.s., vol. 8, 1883, pp. 47–48.)

Memorial to the Foreign Office, Nov. 1883.

462 SCANDALS at Cairo in connection with slavery . . . By an English resident at Cairo. Cairo, 1885. 18 pp.

Describes recent examples of slave trade from the Sudan despite the convention of 1877 for its suppression.

463 BRITISH AND FOREIGN ANTI-SLAVERY SOCIETY
Morocco. Report to the committee of the British and Foreign Anti-Slavery Society, by John V. Crawford . . . and Charles Allen . . . London, 1886. 39 pp.

Includes a section on 'Slavery and the slave trade'.

464 *VICENTINI, Domenico
'La schiavitù in Africa.' (Nigrizia, Verona, vol. 7, 1889, pp. 71–78, 112–20, 149–54, 168–76; vol. 8, 1890, pp. 13–20.)

465 *ALLEMAND-LAVIGERIE, Charles Martial, *Cardinal*
Lettre de Son Eminence le cardinal Lavigerie à M. Keller président du comité de l'Oeuvre antiesclavagiste en France sur l'établissement d'une association pratique pour l'abolition de l'esclavage dans le Sahara et le Soudan. Saint-Cloud, 1890. 42 pp.

466 *'WIE in Dafur die Ghagna geschehen.' (Jahresbericht des Vereins zur Unterstützung der armen Negerkinder, Köln, vol. 41, no. 2, 1894, pp. 76–90.)

On slave raids in Darfur; by F. X. Geyer?

467 SORELA, Luis
'Les causes originelles de l'esclavagisme.' (MA, vol. 6, 1894, pp. 123–26.)

Among the economic causes of the slave trade in the western Sudan is the lack of salt, which could be supplied by Europe via the Niger. (Translated from Revista Antiesclavista Española.)

468 MOCKLER-FERRYMAN, Augustus Ferryman
'Slavery in west central Africa.' (McM, vol. 76, 1897, pp. 190–98.)

Slave raiding in Hausaland must be stopped by the introduction of a cash economy, railways and a new system of trade.

469 ROBINSON, Charles Henry
'The slave trade in the West African hinterland.' (CR, vol. 73, 1898, pp. 698–705.)

The Hausa slave trade can be prevented by extending the railway from Lagos to Kano and by developing general trade.

(c) HISTORY

470 DEHÉRAIN, Henri
Le Soudan égyptien sous Mehemet Ali. Paris, 1898. xii, 384 pp.

With sections on the development of the Egyptian slave trade in the Sudan after 1820.

471 PREISIGKE, Friedrich
'Ein Sklavenkauf des 6. Jahrhunderts.'
(Archiv für Papyrusforschung und
verwandte Gebiete, Leipzig, vol. 3,
1906, pp. 415–24.)

Greek text, with notes, of a late
6th-century Egyptian record of the
sale of a 12-year-old girl from Alwa
in the Sudan.

472 KÜRCHHOFF, Detmar
'Alte und neue Handelsstrassen und
Handelsmittelpunkte in Nordost-
Afrika.' (Geographische Zeitschrift,
Leipzig, vol. 12, 1906, pp. 277–91,
326–39.)

Includes references to the slave
trade of the Nile basin and Libya
in the 19th century.

473 KUMM, Hermann Karl Wilhelm
The Sudan. A short compendium of
facts and figures about the land of
darkness. London, [1907]. xiv, 224 pp.

Ch. 9: 'The open sore of Africa—
slave raiding'.

474 MILLANT, Richard
L'esclavage en Turquie. Société Antiesclavagiste, Paris, 1912. 54 pp. illus.

With a section on 'La traite des
nègres en Afrique' in the 1880s.

475 DOWD, Jerome
'Slavery and the slave trade in Africa.'
(JNH, vol. 2, 1917, pp. 1–20.)

History of the Saharan slave trade.

476 DELAFOSSE, Maurice
'Les débuts des troupes noires en
Maroc.' (Hespéris, Paris, vol. 3, 1923,
pp. 1–12.)

Sudanese slaves were recruited for
the Moroccan army from about 1672
onward.

477 DRIAULT, Édouard
'Mohamed Aly au Soudan (octobre
1838-mars 1839). Mohamed Aly et
la traite des nègres.' (Bulletin de
l'Institut d'Égypte, Le Caire, vol. 9,
1927, pp. 83–87.)

Letter from Muhammad Ali's doctor
Gaetani expressing the hope that
he will abolish slavery.

478 *'Il COMMERCIO schiavista a Cufra
sotto la Senussia.' (Antischiavismo,
Roma, vol. 44, 1932, pp. 237–42.)

479 *QUARANTA DI SAN SEVERINO,
Bernardo
'Khartoum, mercato di avorio e di
schiavi.' (Antischiavismo, Roma, vol.
45, 1933, pp. 355–58.)

480 LOTAR, Léon
'Souvenirs de l'Uélé. Les traitants
nubiens.' (Congo, Bruxelles, vol. 14,
no. 2, 1933, pp. 658–82; vol. 15, no. 1,
1934, pp. 1–12.)

On Sudanese slavers in the Uele
basin 1860–84.

481 PENZER, Norman Mosley
The ḥarēm. An account of the institution as it existed in the palace of the
Turkish sultans with a history of the
grand seraglio from its foundation to
the present time. London, 1936. 276 pp.

Ch. 6: 'The black eunuchs.'

482 OLDEROGGE, Dmitry Alekseevich
'Die Gesellschaftsordnung Songhais im
15. und 16. Jahrhundert.' In: LUKAS, J.
Afrikanistische Studien (Berlin, 1955),
pp. 243–51.

Songhai society was based on slaves
acquired by war or trade.

483 GRAY, John Richard
A history of the southern Sudan
1839–1889. London, 1961. viii, 219 pp.
maps.

Detailed account of the slave trade,
stressing the importance of the Bahr
el-Gazal area.

484 BOAHEN, Albert Adu
'The caravan trade in the nineteenth
century.' (JAH, vol. 3, 1962, pp.
349–59.)

Saharan trade, largely in slaves,
declined during the 19th century,
shifting from central to eastern
routes.

485 McLOUGHLIN, Peter F. M.
'Economic development and the heri-
tage of slavery in the Sudan.' (Africa,
London, vol. 32, 1962, pp. 355–91.)

Notes on the slave trade and its pres-
ent-day effects.

486 WELLARD, James
'The merchandise was human.' (Hori-
zon, New York, vol. 7, no. 1, 1965,
pp. 110–17; map.)

Popular account of the Saharan
slave trade (ch. 6 from his: The
great Sahara, London, 1964).

487 MAŁOWIST, Marian
'Le commerce d'or et d'esclaves au
Soudan occidental.' (Africana Bulletin,
Warszawa, no. 4, 1966, pp. 49–72.)

On the trade from the western Sudan in the 14th–16th centuries.

488 VERLINDEN, Charles
'Esclavage noir en France méridionale et courants de traite en Afrique.' (Annales du Midi, Toulouse, vol. 78, 1966, pp. 335–43.)

African slaves were obtained through Barka *c.* 1300–1490, until Portuguese expansion caused routes to change.

489 YŪSUF FAḌL ḤASAN
The Arabs and the Sudan from the seventh to the early sixteenth century. Edinburgh, [1967]. x, 298 pp. map.

With a section on the slave trade describing the origin of the 'baqt' (tribute) from Nubia, first levied A.D. 652.

490 BAER, Gabriel
'Slavery in nineteenth century Egypt.' (JAH, vol. 8, 1967, pp. 417–44.)

Describes the Sudanese slave trade and its suppression 1820–90.

491 JAMES, W. R.
'A crisis in Uduk history.' (SNR, vol. 49, 1968, pp. 17–44; map.)

Account of slave raids by Arabs and Abyssinians on pagan peoples of the Blue Nile region around 1900.

492 FISHER, Allan George Barnard *and* **FISHER, Humphrey John**
Slavery and Muslim society in Africa. The institution in Saharan and Sudanic Africa and the trans-Saharan trade. London, 1970. xiv, 182 pp. illus, maps.

Study of slavery and the slave trade in the central Sudan.

E. EAST AFRICA

(a) CONTEMPORARY ACCOUNTS

493 NOGUEIRA DE ANDRADE, Jeronimo José
'Descripção do estado em que ficavão os negocios da capitania de Mossambique nos fins de novembre de 1789, com algumas observaçoens e reflexoens sobre as cauzas da decadencia do commercio, e dos estabelecimentos portuguezes na costa oriental da Africa. Escripta no anno de 1790.' (IPI, vol. 11, 1815, pp. 565–74; vol. 12, 1815, pp. 38–47, 184–95, 375–84; vol. 13, 1815, pp. 36–47, 188–96, 328–39, 492–505; vol. 14, 1815, pp. 10–22, 166–72.)

> Includes notes on the slave trade, in particular that of the French, and reveals the commercial importance of Indian traders in Portuguese East Africa.

494 PRIOR, James
Voyage along the eastern coast of Africa, to Mosambique, Johanna, and Quiloa; to St. Helena; to Rio de Janeiro, Bahia, and Pernambuco in Brazil, in the Nisus frigate. Sir R. Phillips & Co., London, 1819. v, 114 pp.

> Includes notes on the slave trade of Mozambique, Kilwa and Zanzibar in 1812–13. (An account of the Zanzibar slave trade in 1811 by Capt. Thomas Smee is printed in: Naval Chronicle, London, vol. 32, 1814, pp. 73–76.)

495 'MAURITIUS.' (ASMR, vol. 3, Aug. 1829, pp. 39–52.)

> On the slave trade in 1822–24.

496 ADAM, William
Paper presented to the General Anti-slavery Convention . . . Slavery in India. [London, 1840?] 12 pp.

> A considerable number of African slaves are imported to British India.

497 GREAT BRITAIN: House of Commons
Mauritius slave trade. Minutes of evidence taken before the select committee appointed, (in the last session of Parliament) to inquire whether the slave trade has prevailed at the Mauritius, and to what extent, and the causes thereof; and to report thereon to the House, together with the minutes of evidence taken before them. 13 May–23 May 1826 . . . [London, 1827.] 89 pp. (P.P. 1826–27, VI.)

498 SLAVERY and the slave trade in British India; with notices of the existence of these evils in the islands of Ceylon, Malacca, and Penang, drawn from official documents. Thomas Ward & Co., London, 1841. viii, 72 pp.

> By John Scoble. Includes a section on 'The external slave trade', mostly from Abyssinia.

499 BRITISH AND FOREIGN ANTI-SLAVERY SOCIETY
A brief view of slavery in British India. London, [1841]. 3 pp.

> With notes on the slave trade from East Africa through Portuguese and other ports.

500 HART, ——, Captain
'Slavery in Sinde'. (USM, 1844, I, pp. 9–18.)

> Karachi is the main entry port for African slaves.

501 'A GENERAL view of the exports and imports of Zanzibar.' (Transactions of the Bombay Geographical Society, vol. 6, 1844, pp. 45–57.)

> By a Mr. Whigham? Includes an account of the slave market at the time of the British naval visit in 1811 (494, note).

502 HARRIS, William Cornwallis
The highlands of Æthiopia. Longman, Brown, Greene, & Longmans, London, 1844. 3 vol.

> Includes chapters on the Abyssinian slave trade in 1841–43.

503 FREIRE F. A. DE CASTRO, Bernardino
'Notice of a caravan journey from the east to the west coast of Africa . . . With remarks by Mr. W. D. Cooley.' (JRGS, vol. 24, 1854, pp. 266–71.)

Letter from the governor of Benguela on the crossing of Africa by Arab slave traders 1851–52.

504 FROBERVILLE, Eugène de
'Notes sur les mœurs, coutumes et traditions des Amakoua, sur le commerce et la traite des esclaves dans l'Afrique orientale.' (Bulletin de la Société de Géographie, Paris, ser. 3, vol. 8, 1847, pp. 311–29.)

Includes notes on the Makua slave trade, the solution for which is African labour 'emigration' to European colonies.

505 *HALL, Sir William Hutcheon
A few remarks relative to the slave-trade on the east coast of Africa: extracted from the voyage of the "Nemesis". London, [1851?]. 15 pp.

Account of slaving in Mozambique and the Comores in 1840.

506 'ASIATIC slave trade.' (DBR, vol. 25, Nov. 1858, pp. 598–600.)

By E. Weiss? Notes on the Muslim slave trade from north eastern Africa.

507 WEISS, Emanuel
'Slave trade in the Red Sea.' (DBR, vol. 27, Dec. 1859, pp. 711–13.)

Account of the slave trade, particularly in Galla children, to Arabia and Egypt.

508 BURTON, Richard Francis
The lake regions of central Africa . . . London, 1860. 2 vol. illus, map.

Vol. 2 contains a section on the East African slave trade.

509 McLEOD, Lyons
Travels in eastern Africa; with the narrative of a residence in Mozambique. London, 1860. 2 vol. maps.

Contains information on the Portuguese slave trade and French 'emigrant labour' system: by the British consul at Mozambique.

510 LIVINGSTONE, David
Narrative of an expedition to the Zambesi and its tributaries; and of the discovery of the lakes Shirwa and Nyassa. 1858–1864. By David and Charles Livingstone. London, 1865. xiv, 608 pp. illus, map.

Includes information about the Portuguese and Arab slave trade and the French 'engagé' system. See (565).

511 WALLER, Horace
'Scenes in an African slave preserve.' (McM, vol. 11, 1865, pp. 426–35.)

Account of the Nyasa area 1861–62 and the new slave trade opened by the Portuguese.

512 'EAST-AFRICAN slave trade. Letter from the Lord Bishop of Mauritius to the right hon. the president of the Church Missionary Society.' (Signed: Vincent W. Mauritius.) (CMI, n.s., vol. 3, 1867, pp. 237–40.)

By V. W. Ryan, Bishop of Mauritius. With extracts from (510), describing the slave trade.

513 LOW, Charles Rathbone
'Massowah and the Red Sea; with notes on the East African slave trade.' (USM, 1867, III, pp. 317–26.)

Account of the coastal slave trade in the 1850s.

514 GREAT BRITAIN: Foreign Office
East coast of Africa. Correspondence respecting the slave trade and other matters. From January 1 to December 31, 1869 . . . London, 1870. v, 103 pp. (P.P. 1870, LXI.)

Correspondence for 1870–72: P.P. 1871, LXII; 1872, LIV; 1873, LXI. (See also: East African slave trade. Draft of a proposed memorial to Government. London, 1870. 20 pp.)

515 GREAT BRITAIN: House of Commons
Report from the select committee on slave trade (east coast of Africa); together with the proceedings of the committee, minutes of evidence, appendix and index . . . [London,] 1871. xxiv, 242 pp. (P.P. 1871, XII.)

The slave trade is mainly conducted through Zanzibar.

516 GREENWELL, Dora
'The East African slave trade.' (CR, vol. 22, 1873, pp. 138–64.)

Review of the slave trade of the Sudan and Zanzibar.

517 'The EAST African slave trade. (Leisure Hour, London, 1873, pp. 168–71.)

Based on evidence from 1867–71.

518 'Der OSTAFRIKANISCHE Sklaven-handel.' (EMM, n.s., vol. 17, 1873, pp. 305–27.)

Review of recent British publications on the slave trade and antislavery squadron.

519 *FLEURIOT DE LANGLE, Alphonse Jean René, *vicomte* de
La traite des esclaves à la côte orientale d'Afrique. Paris, 1873. 44 pp.

Notes on the slave trade and measures to suppress it. (Originally published in: Revue Maritime et Coloniale, Paris, vol. 38, 1873, pp. 785–828.)

520 *NEW, Charles
Life, wanderings, and labours in eastern Africa. With . . . remarks upon East African slavery . . . London, 1873. xii, 525 pp. map.

The slave trade and slavery described by a missionary.

521 *GREAT BRITAIN: Foreign Office
Correspondence relating to slave trade on the east coast of Africa, and Zanzibar. [London,] 1873. 151 pp.

522 'MISSION of Sir Bartle Frere to the east coast of Africa.' (CMI, n.s., vol. 9, Oct. 1873, pp. 296–307, 333–44.)

Extracts from a memorandum by Frere on the slave trade of Egypt and Zanzibar.

523 'BEKÄMPFUNG des Sklavenhandels.' (NEK, 1874, col. 61–63.)

524 GREAT BRITAIN: Foreign Office
Correspondence with British representatives and agents, and reports from naval officers, relative to the East African slave trade. From January 1 to December 31, 1873 . . . London, 1874. iv, 160 pp. (P.P. 1874, LXII.)

525 LIVINGSTONE, David
The last journals of David Livingstone, in central Africa, from 1865 to his death . . . London, 1874. 2 vol. illus, maps.

Contains many references to the East African slave trade. (Reviewed in: CMI, n.s., vol. 11, 1875, pp. 102–12.)

526 LIFE and finding of Dr. Livingstone, containing the original letters written by H. M. Stanley, to the "New York Herald." New and enlarged edition . . . London, [1874]. xxii, 332 pp.

Includes descriptions of the slave trade by Livingstone in letters to the 'New York Herald' and in consular despatches to the Foreign Office 1870–72.

527 *MICHELSEN, A.
'Sklavenhandel Ostafrica's.' (Allgemeine Missions-Zeitschrift, Gütersloh,

vol. 2, 1875, pp. 19–30, 518–27, 537–49; vol. 3, 1876, pp. 335–48, 383–92.)

528 'FORTDAUER des Sklavenhandels in Ostafrika.' (Globus, Braunschweig, vol. 27, 1875, pp. 60–61.)

529 CAMERON, Verney Lovett
Across Africa. London, 1877. 2 vol. illus, map.

Narrative of an expedition across south central Africa 1872–75, with notes on the Arab and Portuguese slave trade. See (591).

530 YOUNG, Edward Daniel
Nyassa; a journal of adventures whilst exploring Lake Nyassa, central Africa, and establishing the settlement of "Livingstonia" . . . Revised by Rev. Horace Waller. London, 1877. xii, 239 pp. maps.

Contains descriptions of the Arab and Portuguese slave trade in 1875–76.

531 ELTON, James Frederick
Travels and researches among the lakes and mountains of eastern & central Africa. From the journals of the late J. Frederic Elton . . . consul at Mozambique . . . London, 1879. xxii, 417 pp. map.

Includes notes on the East African slave trade and its suppression. Extracts published as: 'Elton and the East African coast slave-trade', by E. A. Loftus (London, 1952; 61 pp.)

532 STANLEY, Henry Morton
Address before the Anti-Slavery Society, at Manchester. [Manchester, 1884.] 29 pp.

Account of the slave trade in East Africa and the Congo.

533 BAUMANN, Oscar
'Die Araber an den Stanley-Fällen des Kongo.' (Globus, Braunschweig, vol. 52, 1887, pp. 145–48.)

Description of Tippu Tip's station, destroyed in 1886.

534 BUCHNER, Max
'Meine Sklaven. Ein afrikanisches Stimmungsbild.' (Ausland, Stuttgart, 1887, pp. 781–86.)

On a visit to the Lunda kingdom 1879–80 and the trade in slaves and ivory.

535 'NOTICE sur le pays de la traite.' (MA, vol. 1, 1888, pp. 34–35; map.)

536 KRENZLER, E.
'Sklaverei und Sklavenhandel in Ostafrika.' (Jahresbericht des Württem-
bergischen Vereins für Handelsgeo-
graphie, Stuttgart, vol. 6, 1888, pp.
69–79.)

537 PRUEN, Septimus Tristram
'Slavery in East Africa. Letter from
Dr. Pruen, Mpwapwa.' (CMI, n.s.,
vol. 13, 1888, pp. 661–65.)

Description of slavery and the slave
trade.

538 Le CONGO belge illustré ou l'État
indépendant du Congo (Afrique centrale) sous la souveraineté de S. M.
Léopold II, roi des Belges. Histoire de
sa fondation, géographie, ethnographie,
traite des nègres . . . Ouvrage de vulgarisation . . . par Alexis-M.G. Liège,
1887. vii, 231 pp. illus, map.

By J. B. Gochet. Ch. 2: 'La traite des
nègres dans l'Afrique centrale au
XIXe siècle'.

539 'Der SKLAVENHANDEL in Uganda.'
(Signed: F.) (Globus, Braunschweig,
vol. 54, 1888, pp. 351–52.)

540 BRUCE, Charles
Graphic scenes in African story . . .
Edinburgh, 1888. 255 pp. illus.

Ch. 2: 'The slave trade'. Describes
the East African slave trade as the
'open sore of the world'.

541 'Die ARABER in Mittelafrika.' (Signed:
H.) (DKZ, n.s., vol. 2, 1889, pp. 51–53.)

Arab slavery is not as cruel as generally believed.

542a WISSMANN, Hermann von
Meine zweite Durchquerung Äqua-
torial-Afrikas vom Kongo zum Zambesi
während der Jahre 1886 und 1887.
Frankfurt a.O., [1890]. viii, 261 pp.
illus, maps.

Translated as:

542b My second journey through equatorial
Africa from the Congo to the Zambesi
in the years 1886 and 1887 . . . London,
1891. xiv, 326 pp. illus, map.

With notes on the Arab slave traders
in the southern Congo.

543 GLAVE, E. J.
'The slave-trade in the Congo basin.
By one of Stanley's pioneer officers . . .'
(CIMM, vol. 39, 1890, pp. 824–38;
illus, map.)

Description of slave markets on the
middle Congo in 1883–85. (Reviewed
in: Afrique Explorée et Civilisée,
Genève, vol. 11, 1890, pp. 192–96.)

544 'Das VORDRINGEN der Sklavenhändler in Zentral-Afrika.' (DKZ, n.s.,
vol. 4, 1891, pp. 69–72; map.)

Arab and Mbundu slave traders
threaten the Congo state from the
east and south.

545 PRUEN, Septimus Tristram
The Arab and the African. Experiences
in eastern equatorial Africa during a
residence of three years. London, 1891.
vii, 338 pp.

With chapters on the slave trade and
slavery.

546 'ESCLAVAGISME et antiesclavagisme
au Tanganika.' (MA, vol. 4, 1892, pp.
283–90; map.)

Lists the main groups of Muslim
slavers round Lake Tanganyika.

547 REICHARD, Paul
Deutsch-Ostafrika. Das Land und seine
Bewohner . . . Leipzig, 1892. 524 pp.
illus.

With notes on the slave trade.

548 SIGL, ——, Lt.
'Rapport sur la traite des esclaves
adressé au gouverneur impérial par le
lieutenant Sigl, chef de la station de
Tabora (31 août 1891).' (MA, vol. 5,
1893, pp. 293–96.)

549 JOHNSTON, Harry Hamilton
'La traite des esclaves dans l'Afrique
centrale britannique. Rapport de M. le
commissaire Johnston, sur les trois
premières années de son administration
dans la partie orientale de l'Afrique
centrale britannique. (Extrait.)' (MA,
vol. 7, 1895, pp. 179–88.)

On the Nyasa slave trade 1891–93.

550 MACKENZIE, Donald
A report on slavery and the slave trade
in Zanzibar, Pemba and the protectorates of East Africa; presented
to the . . . British and Foreign Anti-
Slavery Society. London, 1895. 22 pp.
illus.

551 LEMAIRE, Charles François Alexandre
'Les Wamboundous. Les colporteurs
noirs entre l'Atlantique et le Ka-Tanga.'
(Revue de Géographie, Paris, vol. 50,
1902, pp. 499–516; vol. 51, 1903,
pp. 50–68, 134–50.)

Extracts from a diary of a journey to Katanga, with a description of the routes used by the Mbundu, formerly slave traders.

552a BRODE, Heinrich
Tippu Tip. Lebensbild eines zentralafrikanischen Despoten. Nach seinem eigenen Angaben dargestellt. Berlin, 1905. 167 pp.

Translated as:

552b Tippoo Tib. The story of his career in central Africa narrated from his own accounts . . . London, 1907. xx, 254 pp. map.

Biography of East Africa's greatest trader in ivory and slaves, Hamed bin Muhammed bin Juma. See (556).

553 *DARLEY, Henry
Slave trading and slave owning in Abyssinia: being articles by Major Henry Darley and N. A. Dyce Sharp. London, [1922]. 12 pp.

554 DARLEY, Henry
Slaves and ivory. A record of adventure and exploration in the unknown Sudan, and among Abyssinian slave-raiders . . . London, 1926. xvii, 219 pp. illus, maps.

Describes slave raids in southern Ethiopia around 1910.

555 *LANUX, Jean Baptiste de
'Mémoire sur la traitte des esclaves a une partye de la coste de l'est de l'isle de Madagascar.' (RDHMF, oct.–déc. 1932, pp. 79–85.)

Account of the Malagasy slave trade written 1729.

556 HAMED BIN MUHAMMED, *el Murjebi*
Maisha ya Hamed bin Muhammed el Murjebi yaani Tippu Tip. Kwa maneno yake mwenyewe. Historical introduction by Miss Alison Smith . . . [Kampala, 1959.] 171 pp. maps.

Autobiography (in Swahili and English) of Tippu Tib. See (552).

(b) CONTROVERSY

557 CORRESPONDENCE respecting the flagrant existence and unchecked continuance of the abominable slave trade in the isles of France and Bourbon. J. Brettell, London, 1816. 51 pp.

Letters from H. S. Keating and others.

558 MAURICE, ou l'Ile de France. Situation actuelle de cette colonie, et pièces à l'appui de la réclamation des habitans. (Signed: Jouy.) Lacretelle ainé & Compagnie, Paris, 1820. 52 pp.

By V. J. de Jouy. Attacks the British government for accusing the Mauri tians of illegal slave trading.

559 'SLAVE trade at the Mauritius.' (Asiatic Journal, London, vol. 28, 1829, pp. 140–44, 423–26.)

Blames the illegal slave trade until 1822 on the negligence of the governor, Sir Robert Farquhar.

560 TELFAIR, Charles
Some account of slavery at Mauritius, since the British occupation, in 1810; in refutation of anonymous charges promulgated against government and that colony. Jh. Vallet & Vr. Asselin, Port-Louis, 1830. 10, xvi, 262 pp.

Accusation of illegal slave trade, reprinted from: ASMR, vol. 2, Feb. 1829, pp. 430–32, and reply showing this to have been impossible since 1824. (See 2619).

561 TORRES TEXUGO, F.
A letter on the slave trade still carried on along the eastern coast of Africa, called the province of Mosambique . . . Addressed to . . . T. Fowell Buxton, Esquire. J. Hatchard & Son; Smith & Elder, London, 1839. 62, lii pp.

Report on the slave trade from Mozambique to Brazil and Cuba which continues despite the abolition decree of 1836; the appendix contains an account of the Portuguese debate in February 1839 on the slave trade and British antislavery measures.

562 IBBOTSON, Henry
Extracts & remarks from the work of Sir Thomas Fowell Buxton, on "The slave trade and remedy" for central and western Africa, applied to Madagascar and East Africa. [London, 1841.] 16 pp.

Draws attention to the East African slave trade; Madagascar should be made a British colony and a 'Madagascar and East Africa Company' established to combat the trade.

563 'EAST-AFRICAN slave-trade.' (CMG, n.s., vol. 1, April 1851, pp. 150–52; illus.)

Slaving is carried on by Arabs to the Persian Gulf and by Americans to Brazil.

564 LIVINGSTONE, David
'Dr. Livingstone's lecture.' *In*: BRITISH ASSOCIATION FOR THE ADVANCEMENT OF SCIENCE. Bath, 1864. Authorised reprint of the reports in the special daily editions of the "Bath Chronicle" (Bath, 1864), pp. 174–78.

On the author's African travels, with an account of Portuguese and Yao slaving south of Lake Nyasa. (Reprinted as 'Dr. Livingstone on Africa and the slave-trade' in: Anti-Slavery Reporter, London, ser. 3, vol. 12, 1864, pp. 221–25; delivered 19 Sept. 1864.)

565 ALMEIDA E ARAUJO CORRÊA DE LACERDA, José de
Portuguese African territories. Reply to Dr. Livingstone's accusations and misrepresentations. London, 1865. 40 pp.

Denies allegations of slave trading in Mozambique. See (510).

566 *LAVIGNE, Jacques
'La traite dans les parages de Madagascar.' (Annales de la Sainte-Enfance, Paris, vol. 20, 1868, pp. 191–96.)

567 CHURCH MISSIONARY SOCIETY
The slave-trade of East Africa: is it to continue or be suppressed? London, 1868. 32 pp.

By Edward Hutchinson. Amplifies the evidence of (512) and suggests measures to limit and then abolish the Zanzibar slave trade.

568 'EAST-AFRICAN slave-trade.' (CMI, n.s., vol. 5, 1869, pp. 118–22.)

Notes on the slave trade and French 'emigration', with a CMS memorial of February 1869 on suppression of the Zanzibar slave trade.

569 The SLAVE trade of East Africa . . .
Church Missionary Society, London, 1869. 36 pp.

Description based on consular reports, including Livingstone's; recaptured slaves should be settled in the Seychelles. (Reprinted from: CO vol. 69, 1869, pp. 782–92, 850–56.)

570 The EAST African slave trade, and the measures proposed for its extinction, as viewed by residents in Zanzibar. By Captain H. A. Fraser, the Right Rev. Bishop Tozer, and James Christie, M.D. London, 1871. 64 pp.

Edited by E. Steere. Suggested remedies: commercial development and an East African 'Liberia' for recaptured slaves.

571 'The HORRORS of the West African slave trade reviving in East Africa.' (CO, vol. 71, 1871, pp. 710–16.)

Comments on British official reports of 1870 on the slave trade.

572 FRASER, H. A.
A letter to the honourable members of the select committee of the House of Commons appointed to inquire into the question of the slave trade on the east coast of Africa. London, [1872]. 20 pp.

The author defends himself against accusations of employing slave labour at Zanzibar.

573 'EAST African slave-trade.' (CMI, n.s., vol. 8, 1872, pp. 89–96; vol. 9, 1873, pp. 220–24.)

Includes a speech by Frere on the slave trade addressed to Indian merchants and others at Zanzibar.

574 'EAST African slave trade.' (QR, vol. 133, 1872, pp. 521–57.)

By Bishop S. Wilberforce. Extracts from and comments on recent reports.

575 'Der SKLAVENHANDEL in Ostafrika und der Herrscher von Maskat.' (Globus, Braunschweig, vol. 24, 1873, pp. 60–61.)

On measures taken against the Zanzibar slave trade.

576 'FRÖHLICHE Aussichten für Ostafrika.' (EMM, n.s., vol. 17, 1873, pp. 83–96.)

On the efforts to suppress the East African slave trade.

577 'Die SKLAVENHANDEL in Ostafrika und die englische Mission.' (Ausland, Stuttgart, vol. 46, 1873, pp. 371–74.)

Account of British measures to suppress the slave trade and the involvement of Indian merchants in it.

578 'Der OSTAFRIKANISCHE Sklavenhandel.' (Ausland, Stuttgart, vol. 46, 1873, pp. 850–52.)

Discusses Frere's visit to Zanzibar for the suppression of the slave trade.

579 HUTCHINSON, Edward
The slave trade of East Africa. London, 1874. 96 pp. map.

Account of the Zanzibar slave trade and ways to check it; urges settlements for liberated slaves as in West Africa.

580 'EASTERN Africa and the slave trade.' (CMI, n.s., vol. 10, 1874, pp. 321–30.)

Review of recent works on the slave trade and missions.

581 THOUVENIN, P. D.
'L'esclavage à Zanzibar.' (RDM, ser. 3, vol. 5, 1874, pp. 309–38.)

Discusses the slave trade and British measures to suppress it; advocates the building of railways to central Africa for this purpose.

582 'SKLAVEREI und Sklavenhandel.' (NEK, 1874, col. 796–98, 810.)

Refers to Cameron's plan for a railway between Bagamoyo and Ujiji to suppress the slave trade.

583 'The AFRICAN slave trade.' (WR, n.s., vol. 47, 1875, pp. 289–312.)

By J. H. Balfour Browne. Review of recent publications on the slave trade of eastern Africa and efforts to suppress it.

584 COTTERILL, Henry Bernard
African slave-traffic. Edinburgh; London, 1875. 9 pp.

The East African slave trade is increasing and must be stopped by political, missionary and commercial measures.

585 ENGLAND's East African policy. Articles on the relations of England to the Sultan of Zanzibar and on the negotiations of 1873 with general notices concerning East African politics and the suppression of the slave trade. London; Edinburgh, 1875. 62 pp.

Edited by W. E. Malcolm. Discussion of the slave trade; it could be suppressed by introducing commerce and missions, blockading the coast and settling liberated slaves on the mainland.

586 'Der AFRIKANISCHE Sklavenhandel.' (Globus, Braunschweig, vol. 30, 1876, pp. 14–15.)

Notes on the slave trade of the Nyasa area.

587 WALLER, Horace
Paths into the slave preserves of East Africa: being some notes on two recent journeys to Nyassa land performed by Right Rev. Bishop Steere . . . and Mr. E. D. Young. London, [1876]. 40 pp.

588 HUTCHINSON, Edward
The fugitive slave circulars; or, England the protector of the slaves. A letter to Baroness Burdett-Coutts. London, 1876. 35 pp.

Admiralty policy on recaptured slaves is causing concern; Britain should acquire territory in East Africa to resettle them. See (3417)

589 SEWELL, Joseph Stickney
Remarks on slavery in Madagascar, with an address on that subject, delivered at Antananarivo. London, 1876. 39 pp.

Urges measures to end the importation of slaves from Mozambique.

590 ABBADIE, Antoine d'
'Les causes actuelles de l'esclavage en Éthiopie.' (Revue des Questions Scientifiques, Louvain, vol. 2, 1877, pp. 5–30.)

The Ethiopian slave trade is conducted mainly by Muslims; the Christian leaders would co-operate with efforts to suppress it.

591 SOYAUX, Herman
'Colonel Cameron über den Sklavenhandel in Afrika.' (Grenzboten, Leipzig, vol. 36, pt. 2, 1877, pp. 215–21.)

The Portuguese are obstructing suppression of the slave trade. See (529).

592 'SLAVERY in Africa.' (WR, n.s., vol. 51, 1877, pp. 394–423.)

Review of recent works on eastern Africa and the slave trade, which must be suppressed before the area can be developed.

593 *SCHOELCHER, Victor
Restauration de la traite des noirs à Natal. Paris, 1877. 16 pp.

594 COTTERILL, Henry Bernard
'The Nyassa — with notes on the slave trade, and the prospects of commerce and colonisation of that region.' (Journal of the Society of Arts, London, vol. 26, 1878, pp. 678–85.)

Both the Portuguese and Arab slave trade have decreased in an encouraging manner since 1875.

595 HUTCHINSON, Edward
The lost continent; its re-discovery and recovery. London, [1879]. 72 pp.

E

Ch. 5: 'The slave trade. Efforts at recovery'.

596 FISCHER, G.
'Einige Worte über den augenblicklichen Stand der Sklaverei in Ostafrika.' (Zeitschrift der Gesellschaft für Erdkunde zu Berlin, vol. 17, 1882, pp. 70–75.)

Letter from Zanzibar.

597 *BURDO, Alphonse
Les Arabes dans l'Afrique centrale . . Paris, 1883. 48 pp.

598 'SKLAVEREI und Sklavenhandel in Ostafrika.' (NEK, 1883, col. 63.)

German missionaries in Uganda complain that the English exaggerate slavery conditions in East Africa.

599 *STEVENSON, James
The water highways of the interior of Africa with notes on slave hunting and the means of its suppression. Glasgow, 1883. 28 pp. maps.

600 GOODRICH, Laurence C.
'France and the slave trade in Madagascar.' (NC, vol. 14, Aug. 1883, pp. 257–61.)

French predominance will lead to a revival of the Malagasy slave trade.

601 O'NEILL, Henry Edward
The Mozambique and Nyassa slave trade. London, 1885. 24 pp.

Notes on the slave trade and the means of suppressing it through the establishment of missions and trading stations; by the British consul in Mozambique.

602 STROSS, Ludwig
'Sclaverei und Sclavenhandel in Ostafrika und im Rothen Meere.' (ÖMO, vol. 12, 1886, pp. 211–15.)

The slave trade continues, particularly to Jedda.

603 *'EXPORT slave-trade on south-west coast of Madagascar.' (Madagascar Times, Antananarivo, vol. 5, 1886, pp. 24–26, 161, 168; vol. 6, 1887, pp. 114, 119, 126, 275; vol. 7, 1888, pp. 27, 396.)

604 *BRITISH AND FOREIGN ANTI-SLAVERY SOCIETY
A few facts relating to the slave trade in central and eastern Africa . . . London, 1887. 3 pp.

605 DRUMMOND, Henry
Tropical Africa. London, 1888. x, 228 pp. maps.

Ch. 4: 'The heart-disease of Africa, its pathology and cure'. Urges occupation of the East African lake area to 'secure the peace of Africa'.

606 STEVENSON, James
'The Arabs in central Africa.' (Journal of the Manchester Geographical Society, vol. 4, 1888, pp. 72–86; maps.)

More force is needed on Lake Nyasa to safeguard the route to the central African lakes.

607 STEVENSON, James
The Arab in central Africa. Glasgow, 1888. 16 pp. map.

Arab slaving threatens the Scottish missions and the African Lakes Company in the Nyasa–Tanganyika area. (Reissued, with correspondence on Portugal, as: The Arabs in central Africa and at Lake Nyassa, Glasgow, 1888; 16, 5 pp., maps.)

608 'Das AUFTRETEN des Kardinal Lavigerie und die Araberfrage.' (DKZ, n.s., vol. 1, Aug. 1888, pp. 266–68, 274–77; map.)

Describes Lavigerie's 'crusade' and the need for European concerted action against the East African slave trade.

609 CAMERON, Verney Lovett
'Slavery in Africa. The disease and the remedy.' (National Review, London, vol. 12, Oct. 1888, pp. 260–69.)

Suppression of the slave trade should be undertaken by a chartered antislavery society; the author could lead the expedition. (Reprinted separately, London, 1889; 12 pp.)

610 WISSMANN, Hermann von
'On the influence of Arab traders in west central Africa.' (Proceedings of the Royal Geographical Society, London, n.s., vol. 10, 1888, pp. 525–31.)

Recounts the ravages of the slave trade in an area of the upper Congo between the author's visits in 1882 and 1886.

611 TORRENS, William Torrens McCullagh
'The East African slave-trade.' (FR, n.s., vol. 43, 1888, pp. 691–706.)

Describes the slave trade since the 1870's and urges a naval blockade.

612 *SCHNEIDER, ——, Dekan
Die Sklavenfrage in Ostafrika. Vortrag im katholischen Kasino in Stuttgart am 12. Dezember 1888 von Dekan

Schneider, Stadtpfarrer in St. Maria
. . . Stuttgart, 1888. ii, 14 pp.

Published for the benefit of the
Verein zur Unterdrückung der Sklaverei in Ostafrika.

613 'Die ANTISKLAVEREI-BEWEGUNG
und Deutsch-Ostafrika.' (DKZ, n.s.,
vol. 1, Nov. 1888, pp. 349–55.)

Notes on antislavery activities, with a
speech by H. von Wissmann on
'Die Araberfrage und der Sklavenhandel' (30 Oct. 1888).

614 'The ARAB in central Africa.' (Signed:
K.) (CMI, n.s., vol. 13, 1888, pp.
493–508.)

Review of recent works on the East
African slave trade.

615 MENGES, Josef
'Der Sklavenhandel am Roten Meere
und am Golf von Aden.' (DKZ, n.s.,
vol. 1, 1888, pp. 334–36, 343–44; vol.
2, 1889, pp. 1–2.)

Describes the slave trade of the southern Red Sea and suggests that
European cruisers patrol the coasts.

616 DEUTSCHE KOLONIALGESELL-
SCHAFT
'Gegen den Sklavenhandel!' (DKZ,
n.s., vol. 2, 1889, pp. 25–26.)

Appeal (18 Jan. 1889) to Germans
to take up the fight against the slave
trade in East Africa.

617 'Die BEWEGUNG zur Unterdrückung
des Sklavenhandels.' (DKZ, n.s., vol.
2, 1889, pp. 28–29.)

On the plans of the Deutsche Koloni-
algesellschaft to suppress the slave
trade in Africa.

618 'VOM Nyassa-See.' (DKZ, n.s., vol.
2, 1889, pp. 49–50, 81–83; map.)

Lake Nyasa should be the main
base for operations against the slave
trade in East Africa.

619 ALLEMAND-LAVIGERIE, Charles
Martial, *Cardinal*
'L'état actuel de l'Afrique et le congrès
international des sociétés antiesclavagistes . . .' (MA, vol. 1, fév. 1889, pp.
87–97.)

Muslim slave traders are behind
the East African disturbances; a
military expedition must be sent via
the Zambesi and Nyasaland to
Uganda.

620 WISSMANN, Hermann von
'La répression de la traite et l'avenir de
l'Afrique orientale. Discours prononcé
le 26 janvier . . . au Reichstag.' (MA,
vol. 1, fév. 1889, pp. 100–03.)

The East African rebellion must be
crushed so that the ivory and rubber
trade can be extended and German
settlers established.

621 PRESTON, William C.
'Can we kill the slave trade?' (SuM,
1889, pp. 90–97; illus.)

Discusses ways to suppress the slave
trade, including colonisation of the
East African highlands.

622 SEIDEL, H.
'Die Araber in Ost- und Mittelafrika.'
(Globus, Braunschweig, vol. 55, 1889,
pp. 145–50, 168–71; map.)

623 MARBEAU, Édouard
'L'esclavage en Afrique. Le décret
du roi des Belges.' (RFEC, vol. 8,
1889, pp. 577–86.)

On the attempt to stop arms imports
to central Africa.

624 'EAST Africa and the slave trade.'
(Signed: A.M.S.) (Scottish Review,
London, vol. 13, 1889, pp. 161–88.)

Describes the slave trade and measures to suppress it; the coastal
blockade and occupation of the
central lakes area have begun.

625 MARBEAU, Édouard
'L'antiesclavagisme dans l'Afrique équatoriale.' (RFEC, vol. 9, 1889, pp. 271–
82.)

On the slave trade in the Nyasa-
Congo region.

626 BONARDI DU MÉNIL, Jean Ernest,
marquis de
La croisade noire, sa ligne d'opérations,
son organisation stratégique, ses conditions économiques. Paris, 1889. 69 pp.

Plan for an international military
expedition to hold the line of the
East African lakes to cut the slave
routes. (Reprinted from: Le Correspondant, Paris, vol. 155, 1889,
pp. 453–73.)

627 *BAERWINKEL, Richard
Die neueste Antisklavereibewegung und
die evangelische Mission in Ostafrika.
Halle a.S., 1889. 20 pp.

628 WALLER, Horace
'The two ends of the slave-stick.' (CR,
vol. 55, 1889 ,pp. 528–38.)

Plans for suppressing the East African slave trade, quoting a memorandum by F. D. Lugard.

629 DRUMMOND, Henry
'Slavery in Africa.' (Scribner's Magazine, New York & London, vol. 5, June 1889, pp. 660–70; map.)

Depicts the horrors of the East African slave trade and urges young men to become officers in an anti-slavery 'patrol-corps' with African or Indian troops.

630 'Der KONGOSTAAT und die Araber.' (DKZ, n.s., vol. 2, 1889, pp. 268–69.)

The Congo Arabs are connected with East African revolts and the Congo Free State should sever relations with them for its own security.

631 'GEGEN den Sklavenhandel.' (DKZ, n.s., vol. 2, 1889, pp. 351–54.)

Account of an antislavery meeting in Cologne 25 Nov. 1889, with an address by Lt. Giese on the slave trade in German East Africa.

632 LE ROY, Alexandre
'Le congrès de Bruxelles. L'esclavage africain.' (Correspondant, Paris, vol. 157, 1889, pp. 577–97.)

On the East African slave trade and means of suppressing it; by a missionary at Zanzibar.

633 *PAULITSCHKE, Philipp
'Sklaverei im östlichen Afrika.' (Vom Fels zum Meer, Stuttgart, 1889, pp. 1502–12.)

634 HERBERT, Mary Elizabeth, *Baroness Herbert of Lea*
The African slave trade. London, 1890. 16 pp.

Summarizes views on the East African slave trade and recommends the establishment of a military 'Order' to launch a crusade for its suppression. (First published in: Catholic World, New York, vol. 48, 1889, pp. 537–41. An article with the same title appeared in: St. Joseph's Foreign Missionary Advocate, London, vol. 2, 1889–90, pp. 70–72; illus.)

635 STORMS, Émile Pierre Joseph
'L'œuvre antiesclavagiste. Son projet d'opération—son organisation—la participation des gouvernements et des associations particulières dans la sup-

pression de la traite.' (MA, vol. 2, fév. 1890, pp. 63–72.)

Strategic plan to extend military stations along the central African lakes to cut the slave routes. (The author had commanded the Belgian antislavery expedition to Lake Tanganyika 1888.)

636 *GLAVE, E. J.
'La traite africaine entre indigènes.' (Mouvement Géographique, Bruxelles, vol. 7, 1890, pp. 88–89.)

See (543).

637 DUCHESNE, Aug.
'Stanley à Bruxelles. Sa réception à la Société Antiesclavagiste de Belgique—ses idées sur la répression de la traite des nègres.' (MA, vol. 2, avril 1890, pp. 129–40; port.)

Includes a report of a speech by Stanley suggesting action to control the ivory trade in order to check the Congolese slave trade.

638 BOURNICHON, Joseph
L'invasion musulmane en Afrique suivie du reveil de la foi chrétienne dans ces contrées et de la croisade des noirs, entreprise par S.E. le cardinal Lavigerie, archevêque d'Alger et de Carthage. Tours, 1890. 351 pp.

Pt. 5: 'La croisade noire.'

639 'The RED Sea slave-trade. By an eye-witness.' (CJ, ser. 5, vol. 7, 1890, pp. 209–11.)

Describes the slave trade centred on Tajura and proposes an Anglo-Italian blockade.

640 WALLER, Horace
'Ivory, apes, and peacocks;' an African contemplation. London, 1891. 90 pp.

The Arab slave trade in East Africa must be stopped and the legal status of slavery abolished.

641 WISSMANN, Hermann von
'Vertrag des Herrn Reichskommissars Major von Wissmann.' (DKZ, n.s., vol. 4, 1891, pp. 107–08.)

Report of a speech at a conference in Nuremberg in June 1891; Wissmann plans to establish steamers on Lake Victoria and Tanganyika to stop the slave trade.

642 JEPHSON, Arthur Jermy Mounteney
'Opinion d'un compagnon de Stanley sur l'esclavage en Afrique.' (MA, vol. 3, 1891, pp. 437–45; illus.)

On the Zanzibar slave trade from central Africa. (Extract from article in: Scribner's Magazine, New York, vol. 9, 1891, pp. 500–14.)

643 **DUCHESNE, Aug.**
'Les chasseurs d'esclaves dans la région des lacs africains.' (MA, vol. 4, 1892, pp. 52–55.)

Wissmann assisted the slave trade by collaborating with Tippu Tib.

644 **SCHMIDT, Rochus**
'Afrikanische Sklaverei.' (Gegenwart, Berlin, vol. 42, 1892, pp. 227–30.)

Description of the East African slave trade and ways to end it, by a former colonial official at Bagamoyo.

645 *'ESCLAVAGISME et antiesclavagisme au Tanganyka.' (Missions d'Alger, Paris, 1892, pp. 423–31.)

646 *REICHARD, Paul**
'Der Sklavenhandel der Araber in Deutsch-Ostafrika,' (Vom Fels zum Meer, Stuttgart, 1892, pp. 537–42.)

647 **MACKENZIE, George S.**
'British East Africa and the Mombasa railway.' (FR, n.s., vol. 51, 1892, pp. 566–79.)

Building the railway would check the slave trade and save the cost of the antislavery cruisers.

648 'Les ARABES au Congo.' (MA, vol. 5, 1893, pp. 238–43, 270–74, 299–307.)

649 **WALLER, Horace**
Heligoland for Zanzibar, or one island full of free men for two full of slaves. London, 1893. 51 pp.

Britain sanctions the slave trade by using slave porters provided by Arabs; the remedy is abolition of slavery and employment of free labour.

650 **WALLER, Horace**
The slave trade and grievances of native races. Read before the Conference on Church Missions, London, May 30th, 1894. London, [1894]. 6 pp.

The British government has not done enough to end the slave trade to Zanzibar, where slavery still exists.

651 **CHAPAUX, Albert**
Le Congo, historique, diplomatique, physique, politique, économique, humanitaire & colonial. Bruxelles, 1894. ix, 887 pp. maps.

Bk. 6, 'Le Congo humanitaire', describes the slave trade and the

Belgian antislavery movement; the Arabs are the main enemy.

652 **WALLER, Horace**
Slaving and slavery in our British protectorates. London, 1894. 8 pp.

The slave trade continues in Nyasaland and Zanzibar; slavery must be abolished in British territories.

653 **PEASE, Joseph Albert**
How we countenance slavery. London, 1895. 14 pp. map.

The continuation of slavery in the British East African protectorates stimulates the slave trade in the interior, which can only be suppressed by building railways.

654 **LUGARD, Frederick John Dealtry**
'Slavery under the British flag.' (NC, vol. 39, 1896, pp. 335–55.)

Mostly on the East African slave trade and slavery.

655 **WALLER, Horace**
The case of our Zanzibar slaves: why not liberate them? London, 1896. 19 pp.

Illegal slave trading continues and can only be suppressed by the abolition of slavery.

656 **BRITISH AND FOREIGN ANTI-SLAVERY SOCIETY**
Slavery in British protectorates. Memorials of the British and Foreign Anti-Slavery Society, and other documents connected with slavery and the slave-trade in the sultanate of Zanzibar . . . London, 1897. 26 pp.

Notes on anti-slave trade measures since 1861; slavery is the cause of the slave trade and should be abolished.

(c) HISTORY

657 *MADAGASKARA sy ny Masombika, na ny fahorian'ny Malagasy teo aloha sy ny fahorian'ny Masombika ankehitriny izao. (Petite histoire de l'esclavage à Madagascar de 1818 à 1875). Tananarive, 1875. 16 pp.

On the African slaves in Madagascar.

658 *KEPPEL, George Thomas, *Earl of Albemarle***
'Sir Robert Townsend Farquhar and the Malagasy slave trade.' (Antananarivo Annual, Antananarivo, 1891, pp. 319–21.)

Extract from his: Fifty years of my life (London, 1876).

659 SMITH, C. S.
'Slavery.' *In*: ANDERSON-MORS-HEAD, A. E. M. The history of the Universities' Mission to Central Africa, 1859–1896 (London, 1897), pp. 375–432; illus.

Account of the East African slave trade and its suppression.

660 PELTIER, Louis
'La traite à Madagascar au XVIIIe siècle.' (Revue de Madagascar, Paris, vol. 5, pt. 2, 1903, pp. 105–14.)

Extracts from an early 18th-century document on the French slave trade in Madagascar.

661 DEHÉRAIN, Henri
'La traite des esclaves à Madagascar au XVIIe siècle.' (Nature, Paris, vol. 32, pt. 1, 1904, pp. 401–03; illus, map.)

Account of slaving voyages by Dutch and other ships to Madagascar 1663–1706.

662 LYNE, Robert Nunez
Zanzibar in contemporary times. A short history of the southern east in the nineteenth century. London, 1905. xii, 328 pp. maps. bibl. pp. 313–20.

With chapters on the slave trade and its suppression.

663 KEABLE, Robert
'The track of the slave trader.' (Treasury, London, vol. 25, 1915, pp. 110–17; illus.)

Describes an old hiding place for slaves on Zanzibar.

664 BEECH, Mervyn Worcester Howard
'Slavery on the east coast of Africa.' (JAS, vol. 15, 1916, pp. 145–49.)

Most slaves came from central Africa, the majority through Kilwa.

665 FOKEER, A. F.
'The negroes in Mauritius.' (JNH, vol. 7, 1922, pp. 197–205.)

On the slave trade from East Africa 1723–1820.

666 HOLLINGSWORTH, Lawrence William
A short history of the east coast of Africa. London, 1929. viii, 183 pp.

Ch. 10: 'The slave trade and its suppression.'

667 BURTON, William Frederick Padwick
When God changes a man. A true story of this great change in the life of a slave-raider. London, 1929. viii, 124 pp.

The story of a Katangan slave trader, Shalumbo, converted to Christianity.

668 MOORE, Ernst D.
Ivory, scourge of Africa. New York & London, 1931. xviii, 256 pp. illus.

Account of the trade in ivory and slaves conducted by Arabs in eastern Africa.

669 *DECKER, Vincent de
'Sous le signe de la croix. (Des horreurs de la traite aux premières caravanes.)' (Grands Lacs, Louvain, vol. 51, 1935, pp. 523–42.)

On the slave trade in Ruanda.

670 LOTAR, Léon
'Souvenirs de l'Uélé. Les Arabes des Falls dans l'Uélé.' (Congo, Bruxelles, vol. 16, 1935, pt. 1, pp. 641–67; pt. 2, pp. 665–84.)

671 COUPLAND, Reginald
East Africa and its invaders. From the earliest times to the death of Seyyid Said in 1856. Oxford, 1938. vi, 584 pp. maps.

Includes an account of the slave trade and its suppression in the 19th century.

672 JACKSON, Mabel Violet
European powers and south-east Africa. A study of international relations on the south-east coast of Africa, 1796–1856. London, 1942. vi, 284 pp. maps. bibl. pp. 266–76.

Ch. 9: 'Portuguese East Africa and the slave trade (1810–1842).' (Revised edition 1967 with expanded chapter on the slave trade.)

673 BRADY, Cyrus Townsend
Commerce and conquest in East Africa . . . Salem, 1950. xxi, 245 pp. illus.

Includes chapters on the Arab slave trade and its suppression.

674 *DESHAYES, Emile
Marchands d'esclaves.   Leverville (Congo), [c. 1950]. 31 pp. illus.

675 HUNTER, John Alexander
'Tippu Tib—"A sound of guns".' *In*: HUNTER, J. A. *and* MANNIX, D. P. African bush adventures (London, 1954), pp. 11–29; illus.

676 GRAY, *Sir* **John Milner**
'The French at Kilwa, 1776–1784.'
(TNR, no. 44, 1956, pp. 28–49.)

On the slave trade project of J.-V.
Morice.

677 MARSH, Zoë *and* **KINGSNORTH,**
George William
An introduction to the history of East
Africa. Cambridge, 1957. xx, 262 pp.
maps.

Includes chapters on the slave trade
and its abolition.

678 HAMILTON, Genesta Mary, *Lady*
Hamilton
Princes of Zinj. The rulers of Zanzibar.
London, 1957. 272 pp. illus.

Popular work, with chapters on the
British antislave trade treaty of
1845 and on Tippu Tib.

679 PANKHURST, Richard Keir Pethick
An introduction to the economic
history of Ethiopia from early times
to 1800. London, 1961. xvii, 454 pp.

Ch. 31: 'The slave trade.' The appendix includes sections on 'The Habshis
of India' and 'Ibrahim Hannibal'.

680 GRAY, *Sir* **John Milner**
'The French at Kilwa in 1797.' (TNR,
no. 58/59, 1962, pp. 172–73.)

Letters from Kilwa complaining of
the seizure by a French ship of a
dhow bound for Zanzibar with
300 slaves.

681 GRAY, *Sir* **John Milner**
History of Zanzibar from the middle
ages to 1856. London, 1962. 314 pp.
maps. bibl. pp. 281–309.

Ch. 11: 'Seyyid Said and the slave
trade.'

682 HARDYMAN, James Trenchard
'The Madagascar slave-trade to the
Americas (1632–1830).' (Studia, Centro
de Estudos Históricos Ultramarinos,
Lisboa, no. 11, 1963, pp. 501–21.)

683 DE KOCK, Victor
Those in bondage. An account of the
life of the slave at the Cape in the days
of the Dutch East India Company.
Pretoria, 1963, 240 pp. illus.

Ch. 1: 'On board the slavers'; on
the slave trade, mainly from Madagascar, 1658–1795.

684 GRAY, *Sir* **John Milner**
'A French account of Kilwa at the
end of the eighteenth century.' (TNR,
no. 63, 1964, pp. 224–28.)

Includes a description of the slave
trade.

685 PANKHURST, Richard Keir Pethick
'The Ethiopian slave trade in the
nineteenth and early twentieth centuries: a statistical inquiry.' (Journal of
Semitic Studies, Manchester, vol. 9,
1964, pp. 220–28.)

The annual average of slaves exported before 1865 was over 25,000.

686 FREEMAN-GRENVILLE, Greville
Stewart Parker
The French at Kilwa Island. An episode
in eighteenth-century East African
history. Oxford, 1965. xiii, 243 pp.
bibl. pp. 228–32.

Describes the plan of the merchant
Morice to set up a slave trading
post at Kilwa 1776–79.

687 ALPERS, Edward Alter
The East African slave trade. Nairobi,
1967. 27 pp.

The slave trade developed to meet
the demand of the French Indian
Ocean colonies in the 18th century and
of Brazil and Zanzibar after 1810.

688 KELLY, John Barrett
Britain and the Persian Gulf 1795–1880.
Oxford, 1968. xiv, 911 pp. maps. bibl.
pp. 852–66.

Ch. 10: 'The Arab slave trade,
1800–1842'; ch. 13: 'The attack on
the slave trade, 1842–1873.'

689 ABIR, Mordechai
Ethiopia: the era of the princes. The
challenge of Islam and the re-unification
of the Christian empire 1769–1855.
London & Harlow, 1968. xxvi, 208 pp.
maps. bibl. pp. 187–95.

Includes a detailed account of the
slave trade in the early 19th century.

690 BENNETT, Norman Robert
'The East African slave trade.' *In*:
RANGER, T. O., *editor*. Emerging
themes of African history (London,
1968), pp. 141–46.

On the 'Arab-African relationship'
in the 19th century.

691 AKINOLA, G. A.
'The French on the Lindi coast, 1785–
1789.' (TNR, no. 70, 1969, pp. 13–20.)

On J.-V. Morice and the French
slave trade at Kilwa and Mongalo.

692 BENNETT, Norman Robert
'France and Zanzibar.' *In*: McCALL,
D. F., *editor*. Eastern African history
(New York, 1969), pp. 148–75.

On the slave trade 1774–84 and
'labour emigration' in the 1840s.

693 NICHOLLS, Christine Stephanie
The Swahili coast. Politics, diplomacy
and trade on the East African littoral
1798–1856. London, 1971. 419 pp.
maps. bibl. pp. 390–400.

Includes chapters on the Omani
slave trade and its suppression.

F. SLAVING VOYAGES

(a) CONTEMPORARY ACCOUNTS

694a CÀ DA MOSTO, Alvise
'In comenza el libro de la prima nauigatione per locceano a le terre de nigri de la Bassa Ethiopia per commandamento del Illust. Signor Infante Don Hurich fratello de Don Dourth Re de Portogallo.' *In*: FRACANZANO, *da Montalboddo* Paesi nouamente retrouati (Vicentia, 1507), ll. 7–51.

Translated as:

694b 'The voyages of Cadamosto.' *In*: CRONE, G. R. The voyages of Cadamosto and other documents on western Africa in the second half of the fifteenth century (London, 1937), pp. 1–84; maps.

> Accounts of the author's voyages to Senegambia for gold and slaves in 1455 and 1456. See (833).

695 HAWKINS, John
A true declaration of the troublesome voyadge of M. John Haukins to the parties of Guynea and the west Indies, in the yeares of our Lord 1567. and 1568. Lucas Harrison, London, 1569. (28 pp.)

> Narrative of Hawkins' third and last slaving voyage to Sierra Leone and the Caribbean, ending in disaster at San Juan de Ulloa in Mexico.

696 HORTOP, Job
The rare trauailes of Iob Hortop, an Englishman . . . Wherein is declared the dangers he escaped in his voiage to Gynnie, where after hee was set on shoare in a wildernes neere to Panico, hee endured much slauerie and bondage in the Spanish galley. William Wright, London, 1591. (19 pp.)

> The author took part in Hawkins' voyage of 1567 and remained in captivity in Mexico for 23 years.

697 'The FIRST voyage of the right worshipfull and valiant knight Sir Iohn Hawkins, sometimes treasurer of her Maiesties nauie roial, made to the West Indies 1562.—The voyage made by M. Iohn Hawkins Esquire, and afterward knight, captaine of the Iesus of Lubek, one of her Maiesties shippes, and generall of the Salomon, and other two barkes going in his companie, to the coast of Guinea, and the Indies of Noua Hispania, began in An. Dom. 1564.—The third troublesome voyage made with the Iesus of Lubeck, the Minion, and foure other ships, to the parts of Guinea, and the West Indies in the yeeres 1567 and 1568 by M. Iohn Hawkins.' *In*: HAKLUYT, R. The principal navigations, vol. 3 (London, 1600), pp. 500–25.

> The account of the second voyage was written by John Sparke, that of the third by Hawkins himself. These slaving voyages to the Sierra Leone area and the Caribbean were isolated enterprises as far as England is concerned until almost a century later; the method of capturing Africans by force was in the tradition of piracy rather than of commerce, but see (818).

698 ELBÉE, ——, *sieur* d'
'Journal du voyage du sieur Delbée, commissaire général de la Marine, aux Isles, dans la coste de Guynée, pour l'établissement du commerce en ce pays, en l'année 1669. & la présente: avec la description particuliere du royaume d'Ardres; & de ce qui s'est passé entre les François, et le roy de ce pays.' *In*: [CLODORÉ, J. de] Relation de ce qui s'est passé, dans les isles & terre-ferme de l'Amérique (Paris, 1671), vol. 2, pp. 347–73.

> Description of the slave trade at Ardra and the negotiations with its ruler in 1670, by a representative of the Compagnie des Indes Orientales. An English summary, 'A voyage to Ardrah, and travels to the capital Assem, in 1669 and 1670', was published in: [ASTLEY, T.] A new general collection of voyages and travels, vol. 3 (London, 1746), pp. 65–79.

699 A TRUE relation of the inhumane and unparallel'd actions, and barbarous murders of negroes or moors: committed on three Englishmen in Old Calabar in Guiney. Of the wonderful deliverance of the fourth person . . . Together with a short, but true account of . . . the country . . . Thomas Passinger; Benjamin Hurlock, London, 1672. 19 pp.

> Narrative of John Watts, who was left behind at Calabar by a slave ship from London in 1668 and spent several months there.

700 HOFFMAN, Johann Christian
Oost-Indianische Voyage . . . Cassel, 1680. 136 pp.

> Includes an account of an unsuccessful Dutch slaving voyage from Cape Town to Mozambique and Madagascar in 1671–72.

701 DRALSÉ DE GRAND-PIERRE, ——
Relation de divers voyages faits dans l'Afrique, dans l'Amerique & aux Indes Occidentales. La description du royaume de Juda . . . Claude Jombert, Paris, 1718. 352 pp.

> One of the voyages was an expedition to Whydah for slaves 1712–14.

702 VOYAGES aux cotes de Guinée & en Amérique. Par Mr. N***. Etienne Roger, Amsterdam, 1719. 416 pp.

> Includes records of several slaving voyages to Whydah about 1702–12.

703 *JOURNAL d'un voyage sur les costes d'Afrique et aux Indes d'Espagne, avec une description particulière de la rivière de la Plata, de Buenosayres, & autres lieux; commencé en 1702, & fini en 1706. P. Marret, Amsterdam, 1723. 372 pp. map.

> Account of a slaver's voyage.

704 URING, Nathaniel
History of the voyages and travels of Capt. Nathaniel Uring . . . J. Peele, London, 1726. ix, 384; 135 pp. maps.

> Pt. 1 describes slave trading in West Africa about 1701–10

705 DRURY, Robert
Madagascar: or, Robert Drury's journal, during fifteen years captivity on that island . . . Written by himself, digested into order, and now publish'd at the request of friends. W. Meadows (etc.), London, 1729. xvi, 464 pp. map.

> Includes an account of a slaving voyage to Madagascar by Drury in

1719, after his return to England from a long sojourn in the island two years earlier. (Written by Daniel Defoe.)

706 LABAT, Jean Baptiste
Voyage du chevalier des Marchais en Guinée, isles voisines, et à Cayenne, fait en 1725, 1726, & 1727. Contenant une description très exacte & très étendue de ces pais, & du commerce qui s'y fait . . . Saugrain, Paris, 1730. 4 vol. maps.

> Account of a slaving voyage for the Compagnie des Indes to Whydah, based on the notes of Des Marchais; with the text of the French and English assiento treaties of 1701 and 1713. Continues the description in (147) from Sierra Leone to the Cameroons. An English summary of vol. 1 and 2, 'A voyage to Guinea, and the adjacent islands, in 1725', was published in: [ASTLEY, T.] A new general collection of voyages and travels, vol. 2 (London, 1745), pp. 457–63.

707 EVERARD, Robert
'A relation of three years sufferings of Robert Everard upon the island of Assada near Madagascar, in a voyage to India, in the year 1686.' In: CHURCHILL, A. A collection of voyages and travels, vol. 6 (London, 1732), pp. 257–82.

> The author sailed to Madagascar 'for blacks' to be delivered in Sumatra but was left behind and bought as a slave by an Arab.

708 PHILLIPS, Thomas
'A journal of a voyage made in the Hannibal of London, ann. 1693, 1694, from England, to Cape Monseradoe, in Africa; and thence along the coast of Guinea to Whidaw, the island of St. Thomas, and so forward to Barbadoes. With a cursory account of the country, the people, their manners, forts, trades, &c.' In: CHURCHILL, A. A collection of voyages and travels, vol. 6 (London, 1732), pp. 171–239.

> Account of a slaving voyage to Whydah by the captain.

709 BARBOT, Jacques
'An abstract of a voyage to New Calabar river, or Rio Real, in the year 1699. Taken out of the journal of Mr. James Barbot; super-cargo and part-owner . . . in the Albion-Frigate . . .' In: BARBOT, J. A description of the

coasts of north Guinea (London, 1732), pp. 455–66; map.

Account of slave trading at Bonny. See (148).

710 BARBOT, James
'An abstract of a voyage to the Congo river, or the Zair, and to Cabinde, in the year 1700. By James Barbot, junior, supercargo; and John Casseneuve, first mate, in the . . . Don Carlos of London.' *In*: BARBOT, J. A description of the coasts of north and south Guinea (London, 1732), pp. 497–522; map.

Includes notes on the slave trade in Angola.

711 The CASE of James Buchanan, merchant in London, and others, concerned and interested in the ship Scipio, of which Alexander Mackpherson, was master. [London? 1739.] 4 pp.

On a slave ship seized by the French in the West Indies 1736. (Correspondence relating to the case: Calendar of State Papers, Colonial series, vol. 42, London, 1953, pp. 384–85.)

712 BARKER, Robert
The unfortunate shipwright: or cruel captain. Being a faithful narrative of the unparallel'd sufferings of Robert Barker, late carpenter on board the Thetis snow, of Bristol, in a voyage to the coast of Guinea and Antigua. London, [1760]. 40 pp.

Account of a slaving voyage from Bristol to Andoni in the Bight of Biafra 1754–55. See (733).

713 'EXTRACT of a letter from Philadelphia, dated Nov. 11. Being an account of the melancholy disaster that befel the Phœnix, capt. McGacher, in lat. 37 N and long. 72 W. from London, bound to Potowmack, in Maryland, from the coast of Africa, with 332 slaves on board.' (AnR, 1762, vol. 5, 1763, pp. 117–18.)

Describes an emergency and slave revolt at sea.

714 An AUTHENTIC narrative of some remarkable and interesting particulars in the life of ********. Communicated in a series of letters, to the Reverend Mr. Haweis . . . and by him (at the request of friends) now made public. J. Johnson, London, 1764. 208 pp. map.

By John Newton. Religious experiences of a Liverpool slave trader

during voyages to West Africa 1744–55.

715 *PARIS: Parlement
Extrait des registres du Parlement, du 22 juin 1768. [P. G. Simon, Paris, 1768.] 6 pp.

Appeal by officers of the ship 'Roi Guinguin' against sentence by the French Admiralty court in a case of damages for loss of slaves through disease.

716 TOLD, Silas
An account of the life, and dealings of God with Silas Told, late preacher of the Gospel . . . Written by himself. Gilbert & Plummer; T. Scollick, London, 1786. ii, 174 pp.

Includes notes on four slaving voyages from Bristol to Bonny and Calabar about 1727–31.

717 STANFIELD, James Field
Observations on a Guinea voyage. In a series of letters addressed to the Rev. Thomas Clarkson. James Phillips, London, 1788. 36 pp.

A sailor's narrative of a slaving voyage from Liverpool to Benin and the barbarity of the middle passage. See (2024).

718 NEWTON, John
'Treatment of the negro slaves at sea, in a voyage from the coast of Guinea to the West Indies.' (SM, vol. 50, March 1788, pp. 110–12.)

Extract from (1893).

719 GANDY, Harry
'Extract of a letter from Harry Gandy of Bristol, formerly a captain in the African trade, to William Dillwyn of Walthamstow, dated 26th of 7th month 1783.' *In*: BENEZET, A. Some historical account of Guinea (London, 1788), pp. 125–31.

Describes three slaving voyages to the Gambia and Sierra Leone about 1740–62. See (1857).

720 'To the editor of the Repository.' (Signed: A.B.) (Repository, London, no. 11, July 1788, pp. 133–39.)

Notes on the case of the slave ship 'Zong', 1781, with comments supporting the captain, Luke Collingwood.

721 'TO the editor of the Repository.' (Signed: C.D.) (Repository, London, no. 12, Aug. 1788, pp. 189–92.)

Account of the 'Zong' case from (1878), based on notes of the trial belonging to G. Sharp (3998).— The official record of the case (Gregson v. Gilbert, 1783) is printed in: DOUGLAS, S. Reports of cases argued and determined in the Court of King's Bench, vol. 3 (London, 1831), pp. 232–35.

722 'An ACCOUNT of the manner in which slaves are sold in the plantations.' (TCM, July 1789, pp. 300–01.)

Describes the sale of slaves from ships in the west Indies.

723 'An ACCOUNT of the treatment of the sailors, employed in the African trade.' (TCM, Aug. 1789, pp. 345–48.)

By A. Falconbridge. Extract from (162), on the sufferings of seamen; some deserters at Bonny were taken overland to Calabar and sold to an English ship there.

724a SAUGNIER, ——
Relations de plusieurs voyages à la côte d'Afrique, à Maroc, au Sénégal, à Gorée, à Galam, etc. Avec des détails intéressans pour ceux qui se destinent à la traite des nègres, de l'or, de l'ivoire, etc. Tirées des journaux de M. Saugnier . . . Gueffier, Paris, 1791. viii, 341 pp. map.

Translated as:

724b Voyages to the coast of Africa, by Mess. Saugnier and Brisson: containing an account of their shipwreck on board different vessels, and subsequent slavery, and interesting details of the manners of the Arabs of the desert, and of the slave trade, as carried on at Senegal and Galam . . . G. G. J. & J. Robinson, London, 1792. viii, 500 pp. map.

Accounts of two voyages by Saugnier: in 1783, when he was shipwrecked and enslaved for a time, and in 1785, when he purchased slaves, ivory and gold in Senegal; with lists of goods and information on the slave trade.

725 *The TRIAL of Capt. John Kimber for the murder of two female negro slaves on board the Recovery, African slave ship, tried at the Admiralty sessions held at the Old Bailey, June 7, 1792 . . . To which are added observations on the above trial. London, 1792.

726 The TRIAL of Captain John Kimber, for the supposed murder of an African girl, at the Admiralty sessions . . . June 7, 1792, of which he was most honourably acquitted . . . William Lane, London, [1792]. 43 pp.

727 LETTERS to a wife, by the author of Cardiphonia, J. Johnson, London, 1793. 2 vol.

By John Newton. Vol. 1 contains letters written by him during three slaving voyages 1750–55.

728 'TATHAM against Hodgson.' *In*: DURNFORD, C. *and* EAST, E. H. Reports of cases argued and determined in the Court of King's Bench, vol. 6 (London, 1796), pp. 656–59.

Report of a case brought by underwriters against the owners of a Liverpool ship which lost half of its slaves between the Cameroons and Grenada.

729 GREAT BRITAIN: House of Commons
Minutes of evidence respecting the shipping and carrying of slaves. [London,] 1799. 6 pp.

Information from three English slave captains, with a table of the dimensions and cargoes of 49 slave ships.

730 'JOURNAL of a voyage in a slave ship.' (Signed: Leo Africanus.) (CO, vol. 3, 1804, pp. 344–51.)

On a recent passage from Africa to the West Indies, describing conditions on board. Extracts published as: The slave trade delineated, London, 1804 (reviewed in: GM, Dec. 1804, p. 1142).

731 PINCKARD, George
Notes on the West Indies including observations on the island of Barbadoes, and . . . the coast of Guiana . . . Longman, Hurst, Rees & Orme, London, 1806. 3 vol.

Letters of 1796–97, including descriptions of the arrival of slave ships in various parts of the Caribbean. (Reviewed in: CO, vol. 5, 1806, pp. 366–72, 423–29, 507–11.)

732 The TRIAL of Captain Livesley, for cruelty and ill-treatment to Potter Jackson, an African negro, on board the Lord Stanley, a ship in the African trade. Before Lord Ellenborough, in the Court of King's Bench, Guildhall, July 10, 1806. J. Turner, Coventry, [1806?]. 8 pp.

Jackson, a steward on a Liverpool-bound slaver, was awarded damages against the captain.

733 BARKER, Robert
The genuine life of Robert Barker, dictated by himself while in a state of total blindness . . . Galabin & Marchant, London, 1809 [1809–11]. 391 pp.

Includes accounts of the author's voyages on slave ships to Angola in 1751 and to the Bights in 1755. See (712).

734 SLAVE Trade! An account of the murder of a female negro, who was flogged to death by order of an unmerciful captain; and the distress occasioned by the remorse of conscience to the seaman whom he employed to execute his purpose. Shewing the iniquity of the slave trade. A true story. J. Evans & Son; (etc.), London, [c. 1817]. 8 pp.

Printed with Southey's poem 'The sailor who had served in the slave trade', on which it is based.

735 DELANO, Amasa
A narrative of voyages and travels, in the northern and southern hemispheres . . . E. G. House, Boston, 1817. 598 pp.

Ch. 18: 'Particulars of the capture of the Spanish ship Tryal, at the island of St. Maria; with the documents relating to that affair.'—This incident off Chile 1805, in which a ship taken over by Senegalese slaves was recaptured by Delano, provided the material for Melville's 'Benito Cereno' (4382).

736 McLEOD, John
A voyage to Africa with some account of the manners and customs of the Dahomian people. John Murray, London, 1820. iv, 162 pp.

The author was surgeon and factor during a slaving voyage to Whydah in 1803.

737 NETTELBECK, Joachim
Joachim Nettelbeck, Bürger zu Colberg. Eine Lebensbeschreibung, von ihm selbst aufgezeichnet und herausgegeben von J. C. L. Haken. F. A. Brockhaus, Leipzig, 1821–23. 3 vol.

Includes an account of a voyage with a Dutch slaver to West Africa and Surinam in 1772.

738 BUTTERWORTH, William, *pseud.*
Three years adventures, of a minor, in England, Africa, the West Indies, South-Carolina and Georgia. Edwd Baines, Leeds, [1822]. x, 492 pp. port.

By Henry Schroeder. Describes the author's voyage as a boy on a Liverpool slave ship to Old Calabar and Grenada 1785–86.

739 ADAMS, John
Sketches taken during ten voyages to Africa between the years 1786 and 1800; including observations on the country between Cape Palmas and the river Congo . . . with an appendix containing an account of the European trade with the west coast of Africa. Hurst, Robinson & Co., London (etc.), [1822]. v, 119 pp. maps.

Republished 1823, with more material on the slave trade, as 'Remarks on the country extending from Cape Palmas to the river Congo'.

740 LANDOLPHE, Jean François
Mémoires du capitaine Landolphe, contenant l'histoire de ses voyages pendant trente-six ans, aux côtes d'Afrique et aux deux Amériques; rédigés . . . par J. S. Quesné. Arthus Bertrand; Pillet ainé, Paris, 1823. 2 vol.

On slaving voyages to West Africa 1769–92 and the establishment of a factory at Benin.

741 *AFFAIRE de la Vigilante, bâtiment négrier de Nantes. Crapelet, Paris, 1823. 8 pp. illus.

Reviewed in: RE, vol. 19, 1823, pp. 174–75.

742 FRIENDS, Society of
Case of the Vigilante, a ship employed in the slave-trade; with some reflections on that traffic. Harvey, Darton & Co., London, 1823. 13 pp.

Account of a French slaver from Nantes captured in Bonny river in 1822 carrying 345 slaves; with a plan of the ship.

743 PÉRON, ——
Mémoires du capitaine Péron, sur ses voyages aux côtes d'Afrique, en Arabie, à l'île d'Amsterdam, aux îles d'Anjouan et de Mayotte . . . Brissot-Thivars; Bossanges Frères, Paris, 1824. 2 vol.

Includes accounts of a slaving voyage to Angola 1785 (ch. 4) and to the Comores, where slaves were bought for the Île de France, in 1791 (ch. 10).

744 GREAT BRITAIN: Colonial Department
Slaves wrecked in the Portuguese

ship, called The Donna Paula. Return to an address to the honourable House of Commons, dated the 13th of April 1824;—for copy of any information . . . concerning a Portuguese ship, called The Donna Paula; which was wrecked on a shoal in the neighbourhood of Tortola, and the negroes on board of which were afterwards removed to Bahia or Porto Rico; together with an explanation of the circumstances attending the transaction; and of the purposes for which they were so removed. [London,] 1824. 10 pp. map. (P.P. 1824, XXIV.)

The ship was on the way from Malemba to Brazil.

745 MEMOIRS of a West-India planter. Published from an original MS. With a preface and additional details. By the Rev. John Riland. Hamilton, Adams, & Co; J. Nisbet, London, 1827. xxxv, 218 pp.

Includes an account of a voyage on a Liverpool slave ship via Africa to Jamaica in 1801.

746 CROW, Hugh
Memoirs of the late Captain Hugh Crow, of Liverpool; comprising a narrative of his life, together with descriptive sketches of the western coast of Africa; particularly of Bonny. Longman, Rees, Orme, Brown, & Green, London, 1830. xxxiii, 316 pp. illus, map.

Edited by J. S. Walker. Account of slave trading in West Africa 1790–1807.

747 *BROOKE, Henry K.
Book of pirates, containing narratives of the most remarkable piracies and murders, committed on the high seas: together with an account of the capture of the Amistad . . . J. B. Perry (etc.), Philadelphia; N. C. Nafis, New York, 1841. 216 pp. illus.

See (1481).

748 '"The MIDDLE passage".' (Signed: R.) (Journal of Civilization, London, no. 16, 1842, pp. 248–49; illus.)

Describes the horrors of a slave ship.

749 LETTERS from the Virgin Islands: illustrating life and manners in the West Indies. John Van Voorst, London, 1843. x, 286 pp. map.

Letter XVII includes 'Notes of a slaving voyage' from a manuscript

account by Jerrard John Howard, who sailed as surgeon on a Liverpool ship to West Africa and the West Indies 1802–03.

750 *VIDA marítima del día. Original de D.B.V. A. Gaspar, Barcelona, 1844. 320 pp.

Contains sections describing the successful evasion of a British cruiser by a slave ship.

751 GARNERAY, Louis
Voyages, aventures et combats. Souvenirs de ma vie maritime. Schiller aîné, Paris, 1851. 2 vol.

Includes a colourful account (ch. 17–20) of a slaving voyage from Île de France to Zanzibar about 1803, which ended in shipwreck.

752 KENDALL, Edmund Hale
Voyages and travels of Capt. Abel Sampson, in Europe, Asia and Africa . . . Related by himself; written by Edmund Hale Kendall, Esq. Boston, 1852. 91 pp.

Sampson claims to have sailed on an American slave ship to Loango in 1810 (ch. 5).

753 *NEWTON, John
The life of John Newton, once a sailor, afterwards captain of a slave ship, and subsequently rector of St. Mary Woolnoth, London. "An authentic narrative", written by himself; to which some further particulars are added . . . New York, 1854. 116 pp. illus.

See (714).

754 *MAYER, Brantz
Captain Canot; or twenty years of an African slaver; written out from the captain's journals . . . New York, 1854. xvii, 448 pp.

Based on the slaving experiences of Théophile Conneau about 1820–40. Published in London 1855 as 'Revelations of a slave trader'. (Reviewed in: NAR, vol. 80, 1855, pp. 153–70; DBR, vol. 18, 1855, pp. 16–20, 297–305.) See (756).

755 'The SLAVE trade in New York.' (DBR, vol. 18, Feb. 1855, pp. 223–28).

Interview with Captain Smith, a slaver in jail at New York.

756 *CANOT, Theodore
Vingt ans de la vie d'un négrier. Amyot, Paris, [1855?] 2 vol. (520 pp.)

By Théophile Conneau. Original French text of (754).

757 'The CAPTURED Africans at Charleston.' (DBR, vol. 25, Oct. 1858, pp. 456–58.)

Describes the condition of the slaves on a slave ship seized off Cuba and taken to South Carolina; the survivors were sent to Liberia (265).

758 *DRAKE, Richard
Revelations of a slave smuggler: being the autobiography of Capt. Rich'd Drake, an African trader for fifty years—from 1807–1857; during which period he was concerned in the transportation of half a million blacks from African coasts to America. With a preface by his executor, Rev. Henry Byrd West . . . New York, [1860]. xi, 100 pp.

759 'On BOARD a slaver. By one of the trade.' (CJ, vol. 33, 1860, pp. 281–84.)

Voyage of an English sailor on a New York slave ship to Congo and Cuba in 1859.

760 GREAT BRITAIN: Colonial Office
Copy of extracts of despatches from the governor of the Bahamas relating to the wreck of a slaver off the island of Abaco, with copy of extracts of despatches relating to the wreck of a slaver off the Mucaras shoal, in which complaints were made of the violation of British territory by American or Spanish slave traders. [London,] 1861. 30 pp. (P.P. 1861, XL.)

From one of the wrecks 360 Congolese slaves were liberated while the cargo of the other was smuggled over to Cuba.

761 SLAVE-TRADERS in Liverpool. Extracts from the correspondence on the slave-trade, published by command, and presented to Parliament in April 1862, setting forth the case of the slaver "Nightingale," fitted out at Liverpool in October and November 1861. British & Foreign Anti-Slavery Society, London, [1862]. 8 pp.

Official documents on an American ship equipped in England 1860 and captured at Cabinda in April 1861 with 940 slaves.

762 O'CALLAGHAN, Edmund Bailey
Voyages of the slavers St. Jan and Arms of Amsterdam, 1659, 1663; together with additional papers illustrative of the slave trade under the Dutch. Translated from the original manuscripts . . . Albany, N.Y., 1867. xxx, 254 pp.

Journals of slave ships trading between the New Netherlands and Africa, with related documents 1646–65.

763 MANNING, Edward
Six months on a slaver. A true narrative. New York, 1879. 128 pp.

Account of a voyage on an American slave ship to West Africa about 1860.

764 *GARNERAY, Louis
A bord d'un négrier; épisode de la vie maritime tiré des Voyages et aventures de L. Garneray. Tours, 1889. 240 pp.

See (751).

765 HOWE, George
'The last slave-ship.' (Scribner's Magazine, New York, vol. 8, 1890, pp. 113–28.)

The author claims to have sailed as medical officer on an illegal slaving voyage in 1859 between the Congo and Cuba.

766 LA FOSSE, Eustace de
'Voyage à la côte occidentale d'Afrique, en Portugal et en Espagne (1479–1480).' (Revue Hispanique, Paris, vol. 4, 1897, pp. 174–201.)

Account by a Fleming of a voyage to the Gold Coast, where he was captured by the Portuguese; with notes on the slave trade between Sierra Leone and Benin. (Edited from a sixteenth-century manuscript by R. Foulché-Delbosc.)

767 GOUTSBERG, Hendrik and ZOMER, Michiel
'Eerbiedig rapport en journaal gehouden . . . ter g'eerde ordre van't pl. opperhoofd der fortresse de Lijdsaamheijd aan Rio Dela Goa den E. Jan van de Capelle, met's E. Comps: brigantijn schip d'Victoria, ingevolge zijn E. aan ons meede gegevene Instructie van het bevondene en voorgefallene op onse voijagie naer Inhambano ofte Niambani zijnde de baaij van Rio St. Jao Vaz . . . vertrocken pmo: April ende gereverteert 24 Junij 1728.' In: THEAL, G. M. Records of southeastern Africa, vol. 1 (London, 1898), pp. 443–67.

Journal of a voyage for slaves and ivory from Delagoa Bay to Inhambane 1728.

768 RICHARDSON, William
A mariner of England. An account of the career of William Richardson from

cabin boy in the merchant service to warrant officer in the Royal Navy (1780–1819) as told by himself. Edited by Colonel Spencer Childers. London, 1908. xv, 317 pp.

> Ch. 3: '1790–91. Guinea and the slave trade'. (A voyage to the Gold Coast, Bonny and Jamaica.)

769   LA COURBE, Michel Jajolet de
Premier voyage du sieur de La Courbe fait a la coste d'Afrique en 1685 . . . Paris, 1913. lviii, 319 pp. map.

> Account of an inspection and slaving voyage to Senegambia for the Compagnie du Sénégal in 1685–87; probably the basis for the account in Labat (147) of activities attributed to Brue. Published from manuscripts by P. Cultru.

770   NAISH, F. C. Prideaux
'Extracts from a slaver's log.' (MM, vol. 6, 1920, pp. 3–10.)

> On an English slaving voyage under captain Walter Prideaux to the Gold Coast and Jamaica in 1700, during which 212 out of the 452 slaves died.

771   A RHODE ISLAND slaver. Trade book of the sloop Adventure 1773–1774. From the original manuscript . . . with notes and introduction by Prof. Verner W. Crane. Providence, 1922. 10 pp.

> Record kept by Robert Champlin on a voyage to the Gold Coast and Whydah.

772   ROUSSIER, Paul
L'établissement d'Issiny 1687–1702. Voyages de Ducasse, Tibierge et D'Amon à la côte de Guinée publiées pour la première fois et suivis de la Relation du voyage du royaume d'Issiny du P. Godefroy Loyer. Paris, 1935. xxxix, 241 pp.

> The narratives of Du Casse (1687–88) and D'Amon (1698, 1701–02) contain notes on the slave trade in West Africa.

773   RYDER, Alan Frederick Charles
'An early Portuguese trading voyage to the Forcados river.' (JHSN, vol. 1, no. 4, 1959, pp. 294–321.)

> Text of a ship's book for a voyage from S. Thomé to Warri for slaves in 1522. See (776).

774   NEWTON, John
The journal of a slave trader (John Newton) 1750–1754. With Newton's Thoughts upon the African slave trade.

Edited . . . by Bernard Martin and Mark Spurrell. London, 1962. xvii, 121 pp.

> Extracts from the ship's logs kept by Newton during three voyages to the Windward Coast 1750–51, 1752–53 and 1753–54.

775   FREEMAN-GRENVILLE, Greville Stewart Parker
The East African coast. Select documents from the first century to the early nineteenth century. Oxford, 1962. x, 314 pp.

> Includes (no. 5) an account of an Arab voyage in A.D. 922 to Sofala, from which 200 slaves were brought back to Oman; and (no. 38) an account of the slave trade at Kilwa around 1784 by a French slaving captain, J. Crassons de Medeuil.

776   BRÁSIO, António
'Um extraordinário documento quinhentista.' (Studia, Centro de Estudos Históricos Ultramarinos, Lisboa, no. 15, 1965, pp. 155–74.)

> Original Portuguese text of the 'livro de bordo' of the ship 'Samta Maria da Conçeiçà', 1522, first published in English (773). (French translation by R. Mauny in: BIFAN, ser. B, vol. 29, 1967, pp. 512–35.)

(b) HISTORY

777   'Der LETZTE nordamerikanische Sklavenhändler.' (Ausland, Augsburg, vol. 42, 1869, pp. 136–38.)

778   *HOWLAND, J. A.
'The Amistad captives.' (Proceedings of the Worcester Society of Antiquity for 1886, Worcester, Mass., 1887, pp. 61–74.)

779   BALDWIN, Simeon Eben
'The captives of the Amistad.' (Papers of the New Haven Colony Historical Society, New Haven, Conn., vol. 4, 1888, pp. 331–70.)

> Account of the successful revolt by Mende slaves on a Cuban ship and their trial in the United States 1839–41.

780   MOUFFLET, E.
'Voyage d'un navire négrier (1787–88).' (Revue Maritime et Coloniale, Paris, vol. 115, 1892, pp. 250–79.)

> Voyage of a Bordeaux slaver to Mozambique and St. Domingue.

781 FROUDE, James Anthony
English seamen in the sixteenth century . . . London, 1895. 241 pp.

> Ch. 2: 'John Hawkins and the African slave trade.'

782 *METCALFE, James Stetson
'Crowding on a slaver.' (Current Literature, New York, vol. 29, 1900, p. 585.)

783 *BOUTWELL, George Sewall
'Last of the ocean slave-traders.' (NEM, n.s., vol. 23, 1901, p. 263.)

784 'An OLD-TIME slaver.' (McM, vol. 89, 1904, pp. 20–28.)

> Biographical notes on Hugh Crow of Liverpool.

785 'The ADVENTURE of the "Mongovo George".' (GM, vol. 300, 1906, pp. 18–27.)

> On the voyage of a Liverpool slave ship to Loango and New Orleans 1785–86. See (4541).

786 BYERS, Samuel Hawkins Marshall
'The last slave ship'. (HMM, vol. 113, 1906, pp. 742–46.)

> Voyage of the American ship 'Clotilde' to Alabama 1859, based on interviews with survivors. See (814).

787 BRIGGS, Thomas V.
'The cruise of the Caribbee. A chapter of unwritten history.' (HMM, vol. 116, 1907, pp. 16–28.)

> Slaving voyage of an American-built ship in 1852 from Cuba via West Africa to Brazil and back.

788 WALLING, Robert Alfred John
A sea-dog of Devon . . . A life of Sir John Hawkins. London, 1907. xii, 288 pp.

> Popular account, with chapters on his slaving voyages.

789 GAFFAREL, Paul
'Le capitaine Landolphe (1747–1825). Le Jean Bart de la Bourgogne.' In: Le livre d'or de la Bourgogne (Paris, 1907), ser. 1, pp. 1–44.

> Includes notes on the slaving voyages to Benin 1769–92.

790 *ROCHE, Emma Langdon
Historic sketches of the South . . . New York, 1914. iii, 148 pp. illus.

> Includes an account of the voyage of the 'Clotilde' (1859) and the life of the 'Tarkar' slaves imported. See (785, 1559).

791 COOPER, Guy Edward
'Side lights on the slave trade.' (MM, vol. 7, 1921, pp. 34–37.)

> On the case of the 'Zong' (1783), from which 150 slaves were thrown overboard. See (3998).

792 JACKSON, Luther Porter
'Elizabethan seamen and the African slave trade.' (JNH, vol. 9, 1924, pp. 1–17.)

> Largely on the voyages of John Hawkins 1562–68.

793 DOW, George Francis
Slave ships and slaving. Salem, Mass., 1927. xxxv, 349 pp. illus, map.

> Accounts of English and American slaving voyages from the 16th to the 19th century.

794 WILLIAMSON, James Alexander
Sir John Hawkins. The time and the man. Oxford, 1927. xii, 542 pp.

> Appendix contains the text of British Museum Cotton MS., Otho E. VIII, ff. 17–41b, describing Hawkins' third slaving voyage 1567–68.

795 VIGNOLS, Léon
'Une expédition négrière en 1821 d'après son registre de bord.' (RHCF, vol. 16, 1928, pp. 265–324.)

> Account of a French slaving voyage to New Calabar and Cuba.

796 WRIGHT, Irene Aloha
Spanish documents concerning English voyages to the Caribbean 1527–1568. Selected from the Archives of the Indies at Seville . . . London, 1929. x, 167 pp.

> Mostly relating to John Hawkins' slaving voyages.

797 'JOURNAL of an African slaver, 1789–92. With an introductory note by George A. Plimpton'. (PAAS, n.s., vol. 39, 1929, pp. 379–465.)

> Facsimile of account book of the schooner 'Swallow' of South Carolina, trading on the Gold and Slave Coasts.

798 GOSSE, Philip
Sir John Hawkins. London, 1930. xii, 290 pp.

> With chapters on his slaving voyages.

799 FORD, Amelia Clewley
'An eighteenth-century letter from a sea captain to his owner.' (NEQ, vol. 3, 1930, pp. 136–45.)

On a slaving voyage from Boston to West Africa 1734–36.

800 VIGNOLS, Léon
'La campagne négrière de "la Perle" (1755–1757) et sa réussite extraordinaire.' (RH, vol. 163, 1930, pp. 51–78.)

On a slaving voyage from Saint Malo to Angola and Cayenne in which only 4 out of 603 slaves were lost.

801 HAND, Charles Robert
'The Kitty's Amelia, the last Liverpool slaver.' (Transactions of the Historic Society of Lancashire and Cheshire, Liverpool, vol. 82, 1930, pp. 69–80.)

Account of slaving voyages to Africa and the West Indies, based on letters from the ship's owners to the captain 1803–08.

802 WALTON, Perry
'The mysterious case of the long, low, black schooner.' (NEQ, vol. 6, 1933, pp. 353–61.)

On the mutiny of African slaves on the Cuban vessel 'Amistad' in 1839.

803 *RINCHON, Dieudonné
'La campagne négrière de l'"Afriquain" au Congo et son organisation commerciale d'après les documents inédits d'un capitaine gantois.' (Bulletin des Missions, Abbaye Saint-André, vol. 13, 1934, pp. 213–32.)

Based on the papers of P. I. L. van Alstein.

804 *RINCHON, Dieudonné
'La traite des nègres au Congo par un capitaine gantois.' (Bulletin des Missions, Abbaye Saint-André, vol. 14, 1935, pp. 45–54, 255–65.)

805 RINCHON, Dieudonné
'La campagne négrière du "Pompée" (1768–1770). Son organisation commerciale d'après les documents inédits d'un capitaine gantois.' (Études Franciscaines, Paris, vol. 47, 1935, pp. 473–99, 523–46; vol. 48, 1936, pp. 67–93.)

Detailed description of a slaving voyage by P. I. L. van Alstein from Nantes to Loango and St. Domingue.

806 WISH, Harvey
'American slave insurrections before 1861.' (JNH, vol. 22, 1937, pp. 299–320.)

Sect. 1, 'The background of slave ship mutinies', lists cases 1699–1845.

807 WILLIAMSON, James Alexander
The age of Drake. London, 1938. xi, 400 pp. map.

Includes chapters on John Hawkins' voyages.

808 PRANCE, Cyril Rooke
"Knights of the sea" . . . The voyages and adventures of Admiral Sir John Hawkins, maker of history, and his kin. London, 1938. 313 pp.

Defensive account of his slaving activities.

809 HALGAN, Georges
'A bord du navire négrier nantais "Le Mars" vers l'Afrique et vers la Guyane 1791–1793.' (Bulletin de la Société Archéologique et Historique, Nantes, vol. 78, 1938, pp. 52–65.)

Account of a voyage to Old Calabar and Guyana 1792. (Also published separately, Fontenay le Comte, 1939; 16 pp.)

810 *SCHMIDT, Alfred Eduard
Sklavenfahrer und Kuliklipper . . . Berlin, 1938. 244 pp. illus.

811 *'PREMIÈRES relations des Iles avec la côte orientale d'Afrique.' (RDHMF, vol. 4, 1940, pp. 317–98.)

Contains a 'Journal tenu par le Sr De Jean, marchand sur le vaisseau La Vierge de Grâce, pour le commerce à la coste de Soffala 1733' (pp. 329–71); describes the slave trade between East Africa and the Mascarene islands.

812 *'The SAGA of l'Amistad.' (Phylon, Atlanta, Ga., vol. 2, 1941, pp. 1–6; illus.)

813 GREENE, Lorenzo Johnston
'Mutiny on the slave ships.' (Phylon, Atlanta, Ga., vol. 5, 1944, pp. 346–54.)

Account of slave revolts, mostly on New England ships, 1731–1807.

814 HURSTON, Zora Neale
'The last slave ship.' (American Mercury, New York, vol. 58, 1944, pp. 351–58.)

Story of the 'Clotilde' which brought slaves from Dahomey to Alabama in 1859; with notes on Cudjo Lewis, the last survivor. See (785, 1559).

815 *RUKEYSER, Muriel
'The Amistad mutiny.' In: MOON, B. Primer for white folks (New York, 1945), pp. 23–50.

816 RUMEU DE ARMAS, Antonio
Los viajes de John Hawkins a America
(1562–1595). Sevilla, 1947. xix, 484 pp.
maps.

817 NØRREGAARD, Georg Pedersen
'Forliset ved Nicaragua 1710.' (Handels-
og Søfartsmuseet, Helsingør, Aarbog
1948, pp. 69–98; maps.)

> On the wreck of two Danish ships
> carrying 800 slaves from the Gold
> Coast to the West Indies.

818 WILLIAMSON, James Alexander
Hawkins of Plymouth. A new history
of Sir John Hawkins and of the other
members of his family prominent
in Tudor England . . . London, 1949.
xi, 348 pp. illus. maps.

> Suggests that Hawkins' voyages were
> officially sanctioned to create an
> Anglo-Spanish alliance based on 'a
> new mutual interest'; with a chapter
> on the slaving voyage of John
> Lovell 1566–67.

819 SPINNEY, J. D.
'Misadventures of a slaver,' (BM, vol.
270, 1951, pp. 26–37.)

> On the wreck of the Bristol slaver
> 'Princess' off Guinea in 1791, based
> on the captain's manuscript account.

820 MINCHINTON, Walter Edward
'The voyage of the snow Africa.'
(MM, vol. 37, 1951, pp. 187–96.)

> Slaving voyage from Bristol to New
> Calabar and the West Indies 1774–75.

821 BOUGE, Louis Joseph
'Théophile Conneau alias Théodore
Canot, négrier en Afrique, fonction-
naire en Nouvelle-Calédonie, 1804–
1860.' (RHC, vol. 40, 1953, pp. 249–
63.)

> Identifies Canot as the brother of
> Napoleon III's physician Henri Con-
> neau.

822 OWENS, William A.
Slave mutiny. The story of the revolt
on the schooner Amistad. London,
1953. viii, 280 pp. illus.

> Popular account of the famous
> slave mutiny in 1839. (Reviewed in:
> NEQ, vol. 26, 1953, pp. 416–20.)

823 *MOUSNIER, Jehan
Journal de la traite des noirs: Dam
Joulin, Charles Le Breton La Vallée,
Garneray, Mérimée . . . Présenté et
commenté par Jehan Mousnier. Paris,
[1957]. 287 pp.

824 FREUCHEN, Peter
Peter Freuchen's Book of the seven
seas . . . London, 1958. 512 pp.

> Ch. 45: 'Black ivory'; on slaving
> voyages 1752–1858.

825 *MERRIEN, Jean, pseud.
Histoire mondiale des pirates, flibustiers
et négriers . . . Paris, 1959. 487 pp.
illus, maps.

> By R. M. La Poix de Fréminville.

826 UNWIN, Rayner
The defeat of John Hawkins. A bio-
graphy of his third slaving voyage.
London, 1960. 319 pp.

827 COOLEN, Georges
'Négriers dunkerquois.' (Bulletin tri-
mestriel de la Société Académique des
Antiquaires de la Morinie, Saint-
Omer, vol. 19, 1960, pp. 289–323.)

> On a slaving voyage to Malemba and
> St. Domingue 1783–84.

828 MARTIN, Bernard Davis
John Newton and the slave trade . . .
London, 1961. 89 pp. maps.

> The story of Newton's slaving
> voyages retold for schools.

829 DARSEL, Jean
'La courte carrière d'un négrier mor-
laisien . . .' (Bulletin de la Société
Archéologique du Finistère, Brest,
vol. 86, 1961, pp. 79–83.)

> Report on a slave ship from Morlaix
> at Senegal in 1802.

830 *LY, Abdoulaye
Un navire de commerce sur la côte
sénégambienne en 1685. Dakar, 1964.
69 pp. illus.

> Annotated journal of the French
> slave ship 'Amitié'.

831 HENRY, Amand
'Au temps du commerce du "bois
d'ébène". Le périple tragique d'un
négrier.' (Revue du Bas-Poitou et des
Provinces de l'Ouest, Fontenay le
Comte, vol. 76, 1965, pp. 202–14.)

> Account of the voyage of the slaver
> 'Conseil de Flandre' from Ostend to
> Malemba and St. Domingue 1783–84,
> ending in shipwreck.

832 WAX, Darold Duane
'Negro resistance to the early American
slave trade.' (JNH, vol. 51, 1966, pp.
1–15.)

> Examples of revolts on slave ships
> before 1776.

833 BRULEZ, Wilfrid
'Les voyages de Cadamosto et le commerce guinéen au XVᵉ siècle.' (Bulletin de l'Institut Historique Belge de Rome, vol. 39, 1968, pp. 311–26.)

Calculates the profit of the slaving voyages of Cadamosto and Usodimare 1455–56. See (694).

834 HANSEN, Thorkild
Slavernes skibe . . . [Copenhagen,] 1968. 209 pp. illus, maps.

On the Danish Atlantic slave trade.

835 WAX, Darold Duane
'A Philadelphia surgeon on a slaving voyage to Africa, 1749–1751.' (PMHB, vol. 92, 1968, pp. 465–93.)

Based on the diary of William Chancellor, surgeon on a New York slave ship coasting from the Gambia to the Gold Coast.

836 PASQUIER, Roger
'A propos de Théodore Canot, négrier en Afrique.' (RFHO, vol. 55, 1968, pp. 352–54.)

A letter of 1842 shows Conneau as a settler near Cape Mount in Liberia.

837 *WELLS, Tom Henderson
The slave ship Wanderer. Athens, Ga., [1968]. 107 pp. illus, map.

838 MARTIN, Christopher, *pseud.*
The 'Amistad' affair. London (etc.), [1970]. 240 pp.

By E. P. Hoyt. Account of the mutiny and court proceedings 1839–41. See (1481).

G. MEDICAL CONDITIONS

(a) CONTEMPORARY ACCOUNTS

839 AUBREY, T.
The sea surgeon, or the Guinea man's vade mecum. In which is laid down, the method of curing such diseases as usually happen abroad, especially on the coast of Guinea; with the best way of treating negroes, both in health and sickness. Written for the use of young sea surgeons . . . John Clarke, London, 1729. 135 pp.

840 ATKINS, John
The navy-surgeon: or, a practical system of surgery . . . Also an appendix, containing physical observations on the heat, moisture, and density of the air on the coast of Guiney; the colour of the natives; the sicknesses which they and the Europeans trading thither are subject to; with a method of cure. Cæsar Ward & Richard Chandler, London, 1734. x, 257, vii; 28 pp.

> The appendix contains information on the diseases of African slaves, chiefly those bought at Whydah.

841 HUTCHESON, Robert
'Ulcers from dracunculi; by Messieurs Robert Hutcheson and George Forbes, practisers of physick and surgery in the island of Bermuda.' (Medical Essays and Observations, Edinburgh, vol. 5, pt. 2, 1744, pp. 784–87.)

> Describes the treatment for guinea worm of a newly arrived African boy.

842 'A DESCRIPTION of the African distemper called the yaws, with the true method of cure . . .' (Medical Essays and Observations, Edinburgh, vol. 5, pt. 2, 1744, pp. 787–805.)

> On cases treated in the West Indies 1727–33.

843 GALLANDAT, David Henri
'Lettre a l'auteur du Journal de Médecine, sur le dragoneau, ou veine de Médine, & sur l'usage du sublimé corrosif dans cette maladie.' (Journal de Médecine, Chirurgie, Pharmacie, &c., Paris, vol. 12, 1760, pp. 24–28.)

> On cases of guinea worm treated by the author as a surgeon on Dutch slave ships 1752–57.

844 An ESSAY on the more common West-India diseases; and the remedies which that country itself produces. To which are added, some hints on the management, &c. of negroes. By a physician in the West-Indies. T. Becket & P. A. De Hondt, London, 1764. 75 pp.

> By James Grainger. Pt. 1, 'On the choice of negroes', describes the African nations represented and pt. 2 and 3 various diseases.

845 'EASY method of sweetening putrid water, with a hint for remedying some inconveniences attending fire ventilators.' (AnR 1764, vol. 7, 1765, p. 131.)

> The author had made several voyages as captain of a slave ship.

846 HILLARY, William
Observations on the changes of the air and the concomitant epidemical diseases, in the island of Barbadoes. To which is added a treatise on the putrid bilious fever, commonly called the yellow fever; and such other diseases as are indigenous or endemial, in the West India islands, or in the torrid zone. L. Hawes, W. Clarke & R. Collins, London, 1766. 360 pp.

> The treatise enumerates diseases imported from Africa through the slave trade.

847 LIND, James
An essay on diseases incidental to Europeans in hot climates . . . T. Becket & P. A. De Hondt, London, 1768. 348 pp.

> Pt. 2, sect. 3: 'Floating factories recommended': traders in West Africa should live on hulks moored offshore or in rivers.

848 GALLANDAT, David Henri
'Noodige onderrichtingen voor de slaafhandelaaren.' (Verhandelingen uitgegeven door het Zeeuwsch Genootschap

der Wetenschappen te Vlissingen, Middelburg, vol. 1, 1769, pp. 422–60.)

Includes advice for traders on the selection and transport of West African slaves.

849 POUPPÉ DESPORTES, Jean Baptiste
Histoire des maladies de S. Domingue . . . Lejay, Paris, 1770. 3 vol.

Contains a section (vol. 2, pp. 267–74) on the characteristics and diseases of African slaves; scurvy was common among those newly arrived.

850 PERÉ, A.
'Mémoire sur le dragoneau; par M. Peré, ancien chirurgien-major à Saint-Domingue.' (Journal de Médecine, Chirurgie, Pharmacie, &c., Paris, vol. 42, 1774, pp. 121–32.)

On the guinea worm, endemic in West Africa but rare in the Congo.

851 *DAZILLE, Jean Barthélemy
Observations sur les maladies des nègres, leurs causes, leurs traitemens et les moyens de les prévenir . . . Didot le jeune, Paris, 1776. xvi, 316 pp.

Refers to the mortality in the slave trade to the French colonies.

852 SCHOTTE, Johann Peter
A treatise on the synochus atrabiliosa, a contagious fever, which raged at Senegal in the year 1778 . . . J. Murray, London, 1782. 169 pp.

Includes a brief account of the slave trade from Galam and the method used to prevent scurvy during the sea crossing.

853 ATCHISON, Robert
'Observations on the dysentery, as it appears among the negroes on the coast of Guinea.' (Medical Commentaries, Edinburgh, vol. 9, 1785, pp. 268–71.)

Dysentery and fever are the commonest diseases in slave ships, particularly from the Bights; the high mortality is due to overcrowding. By a slave ship surgeon.

854 LÖFLER, Adolph Friedrich
'Chirurgische Wahrnehmungen.' (Archiv der practischen Arzneykunst, Leipzig, vol. 2, 1786, pp. 1–108.)

Includes sections on tropical diseases like guinea worm and yaws in which he refers to his experience in the West African slave trade. (Published

as 'Beyträge zur Wundarzneykunst' in 1788, with an introductory essay on the African slave trade.)

855 HUNTER, John
Observations on the diseases of the army in Jamaica; and on the best means of preserving the health of Europeans, in that climate. G. Nicol, London, 1788. xv, 328 pp.

Includes 'Remarks on some of the diseases of negroes' (pp. 305–14).

856 GREAT BRITAIN: House of Commons
Extracts of such journals of the surgeons employed in ships trading to the coast of Africa, since the 1st of August 1788, as have been transmitted to the Custom House in London, and which relate to the state of the slaves during the time they were on board the ships. —Ordered to be printed 18th June 1789. [London, 1789.] 5 pp.

Information from four journals 1788–89, on the numbers, mortality and diseases of African slaves. See (162, 1956).

857 *SHANNON, Robert
Practical observations on the operation and effects of certain medicines, in the prevention and cure of diseases to which Europeans are subject in hot climates . . . and observations on the diseases and diet of negroes. Vernor & Hood, London, 1794. xlii, 558 pp.

858 ARTHY, Elliot
The seaman's medical advocate: or, an attempt to shew that five thousand seamen are, annually, during war, lost to the British nation, in the West-India merchants' service, and on-board ships of war on the West-India station, through the yellow fever, and other diseases . . . Messrs Richardson; Mr. Egerton, London, 1798. xxv, 248 pp.

The author had served as a surgeon on slave ships 1793–96 and describes the diseases of the crews.

859 *AZEREDO, José Pinto de
Ensaios sobre algumas enfermidades d'Angola . . . Regia Oficina Typografica, Lisboa, 1799. xvi, 149 pp.

Deals with diseases of slaves in Brazil. Republished as: Ensaio sobre as febres d'Angola (Lisboa, 1802).

860 DAVIDSON, George
'Account of the cachexia africana; a disease incidental to negro slaves lately imported into the West-Indies.' (Medi-

cal Repository, New-York, vol. 2, 2nd ed., 1800, pp. 265–67.)

On 'dirt-eating' by exhausted and depressed slaves.

861 WINTERBOTTOM, Thomas Masterman
'Some observations relative to the climate and diseases of Sierra Leone . . .' (Medical Facts and Observations, London, vol. 8, 1800, pp. 56–110.)

Refers to the mortality among European sailors and traders involved in the slave trade.

862 WINTERBOTTOM, Thomas Masterman
An account of the native Africans in the neighbourhood of Sierra Leone; to which is added, an account of the present state of medicine among them. John Hatchard; J. Mawman, London, 1803. 2 vol.

Vol. 2 describes diseases, including references to the slave trade.

863 PRACTICAL rules for the management and medical treatment of negro slaves, in the sugar colonies. By a professional planter. Vernor & Hood, London, 1803. iv, 468 pp.

Attributed to a Dr. Collins. Includes notes on African slaves, their selection and 'seasoning'.

864 ROSS, David
'Minutes of a case of yaws.' (Philadelphia Medical Museum, vol. 1, 1805, pp. 422–24.)

Describes the treatment and cure of an African slave by other Africans in 1770.

865 OLIVEIRA MENDES, Luiz Antonio de
'Discurso academico ao programma: Determinace todos os seus symptomas as doenças agudas, e chronicas, que mais frequentamente accommettem os pretos recem-tirados da Africa: examinando as causas da sua mortandade depois da sua chegada ao Brasil . . .' (Memorias economicas da Academia Real das Sciencias de Lisboa, vol. 4, 1812, pp. 1–64.)

Address delivered 1793; excellent account of the conditions and diseases of African slaves on their way from Angola to Brazil. (Ch. 2: 'Da modo, causas, e principio, por que os pretos da Africa são desapossados da sua apreciavel liberdade.')

866 GRAY, William
'Mr. Gray and Mr. Ellis, on certain diseases of the African slaves.' (Medico-Chirurgical Journal and Review, London, vol. 1, 1816, pp. 373–77.)

Two letters describing cases of dysentery and scurvy on recaptured slave ships at Old Calabar and Sierra Leone in 1815.

867 *THOMSON, James
A treatise on the diseases of negroes, as they occur in the island of Jamaica; with observations on the country remedies. A. Aikman, Jun., Kingston, 1820. viii, 168 pp.

868 GUILLIÉ, Sébastien
'Observations sur une blépharoblénor-rhée contagieuse,' In his: Bibliothèque ophthalmologique, ou recueil d'observations sur les maladies des yeux (Paris, 1820), Vol. 1, pp. 74–80.

Report of an ophthalmic epidemic on the slave ship 'Le Rodeur' during a voyage from Bonny to Guadeloupe in 1819. (Summarized in: MACKENZIE, W. A practical treatise on the diseases of the eye, London, 1830, pp. 350–52.)

869 STORMONT, Charles
Essai sur la topographie médicale de la côte occidentale d'Afrique, et particulièrement sur celle de la colonie de Sierra-Leone; thèse présentée et soutenue à la Faculté de Médecine de Paris . . . Didot le jeune, Paris, 1822. 70 pp.

Contains a description of conditions on slave ships and the effects of overcrowding.

870 AUDOUARD, Mathieu François Maxence
'Relation historique de la fièvre jaune qui a régné au Port-du-Passage en 1823.' (RMFE, vol. 3, 1824, pp. 224–64.)

Yellow fever was brought to Europe by Spanish ships used in the slave trade.

871 AUDOUARD, Mathieu François Maxence
'Mémoire sur l'origine et les causes de la fièvre jaune, considérée comme étant principalement le résultat de l'infection des bâtimens négriers, d'après les observations faites à Barcelone en 1821, et au Port-du-Passage, en 1823.' (RMFE, vol. 3, 1824, pp. 360–408.)

Abolition of the slave trade might eradicate yellow fever.

872 **AUDOUARD, Mathieu François Maxence**
'Considérations hygiéniques sur le typhus nautique, ou fièvre jaune, provenant principalement de l'infection des bâtimens négriers.' (RMFE, vol. 4, 1824, pp. 221–59.)

Includes a 'Précis historique de la traite des noirs et de la fièvre jaune'.

873 **DUPAU, Amédée**
'Note sur la fièvre jaune, considérée comme dépendante de l'infection des vaisseaux négriers . . .' (Journal de la Société de la Morale Chrétienne, Paris, vol. 4, 1825, pp. 54–58.)

Account of yellow fever on slave ships 1821–23.

874 *****AUDOUARD, Mathieu François Maxence**
Recueil de mémoires sur le typhus nautique ou fièvre jaune, provenant principalement de l'infection des bâtimens négriers . . . P. Gueffier, [Paris,] 1825. 7 pt. in 1 vol.

Reprints of articles.

875 **BOYLE, James**
A practical medico-historical account of the western coast of Africa . . . together with the causes, symptoms, and treatment, of the fevers of western Africa . . . S. Highley, London; (etc.), 1831. xvi, vi, 423 pp. maps.

Investigation of sickness on ships of the British navy, with reference to slavers as carriers of disease.

876 *****OLDFIELD, R. A. K.**
'On the diseases of the natives on the banks of the river Niger.' (London Medical and Surgical Journal, vol. 8, 1836, pp. 403–07.)

877 **AUDOUARD, Mathieu François Maxence**
'La traite des noirs considérée comme cause de la fièvre jaune.' (Journal des Connaissances Médico-Chirurgicales, Paris, vol. 6, pt. 1, 1838, pp. 3, 49, 190.)

878 **BLAQUIÈRE, Louis Joseph Étienne**
'Lettre sur la traite des noirs considérée comme cause de la fièvre jaune.' (Journal des Connaissances Médico-Chirurgicales, Paris, vol. 6, pt. 1, 1838, pp. 102–04.)

Letter to the editor in reply to Audouard.

879 *****THÈVENOT, Jean Pierre Ferdinand**
Traité des maladies des Européens dans les pays chauds, et spécialement au Sénégal, ou essai statistique, médical et hygiénique, sur le sol, le climat et les maladies de cette partie de l'Afrique . . . J.-B. Baillière, Paris, 1840. xii, 399 pp.

Medical report on West Africa published by the French navy.

880 **McWILLIAM, James Ormiston**
Medical history of the expedition to the Niger during the years 1841–2 comprising an account of the fever which led to its abrupt termination. John Churchill, London, 1843. viii, 287 pp. illus, map.

The lessons learnt during this expedition brought significant progress in the treatment of malaria.

881 **PRITCHETT, Morris**
Some account of the African remittent fever which occurred on board Her Majesty's steam-ship Wilberforce in the river Niger, and whilst engaged on service on the western coast of Africa: comprising an inquiry into the causes of disease in tropical climates. John Churchill, London, 1843. viii, 184 pp. illus, map.

882 **SIGAUD, Joseph François Xavier**
Du climat et des maladies du Brésil, ou statistique médicale de cet empire. Fortin, Masson & Cie, Paris, 1844. 591 pp.

Sect. 2, ch. 3: 'Des maladies des noirs.' Scurvy, ophthalmia, skin diseases, smallpox, yaws and dysentery are 'les inévitables compagnons' of the slave trade from Africa.

883 **DANIELL, William Freeman**
'Some observations on the medical topography, climate, and diseases, of the Bights of Benin and Biafra, west coast of Africa.' (Friend of the Africans, London, vol. 3, 1845–46, pp. 105–08, 111–13, 138–40.)

Reprinted in (889).

884 **BRYSON, Alexander**
Report on the climate and principal diseases of the African station; compiled from documents in the office of the director-general of the Medical Department, and from other sources, in compliance with the directions of the right honorable the Lords Commissioners of the Admiralty. Under the immediate direction of Sir William Burnett . . . William Clowes & Sons, London, 1847. xv, 266 pp.

Investigation and recommendations on health problems in the antislavery squadron, with a section on 'Diseases most prevalent among captured slaves'.

885 MᶜWILLIAM, James Ormiston
Dr. MᶜWilliam's remarks on Dr. King's "Report on the fever at Boa Vista . . ." John Churchill, London, 1848. 15 pp.

Concludes that the outbreak in the Cape Verds in 1845 was not of local origin but caused by a vessel of the British antislavery squadron. See (893).

886 PYM, Sir William
Observations upon Bulam, vomito-negro, or yellow fever, with a review of "A report upon the diseases of the African coast, by Sir William Burnett and Dr. Bryson," proving its highly contagious powers. John Churchill, London, 1848. xvi, 311 pp.

Deals with mortality in the African squadron. See (888).

887 *DUARTE, José Rodrigues Lima
Ensaio sobre a hygiene da escravatura no Brasil. Laemmert, Rio de Janeiro, 1849.

A doctoral thesis.

888 BRYSON, Alexander
An account of the origin, spread, & decline of the epidemic fevers of Sierra Leone; with observations on Sir William Pym's review of the "Report on the climate and diseases of the African station". Henry Renshaw, London, 1849. x, 174 pp.

On disease in the British West African squadron. See (886).

889 DANIELL, William Freeman
Sketches of the medical topography and native diseases of the Gulf of Guinea, western Africa. Samuel Highley, London, 1849. viii, 200 pp.

Includes references to the slave trade. See (883).

890 *AUDOUARD, Mathieu François Maxence
Fièvre jaune et traite des noirs. Napoléon Chaix & Cie, Paris, 1849. 57 pp.

See (891).

891 DURAND-FARDEL, Maxime
'Des maladies contagieuses et infectieuses à propos d'un mémoire de M. Audouard, intitulé: Fièvre jaune et

traite des noirs.' (RMFE, n.s., 1850, vol. 2, pp. 643–57.)

Expresses doubt about the causal connection between the slave trade and yellow fever. See (890, 892).

892 AUDOUARD, Mathieu François Maxence
'Réponse au mémoire de M. le docteur Durand-Fardel . . . sous ce titre: Des maladies contagieuses et infectieuses à propos d'un autre mémoire sur la fièvre jaune et la traite des noirs.' (RMFE, n.s., 1851, vol. 1, pp. 399–408.)

See (891).

893 KING, Gilbert
The fever at Boa Vista in 1845–6, unconnected with the visit of the "Eclair" to that island. London, 1852. 110 pp.

Reply to (885).

894 AUDOUARD, Mathieu François Maxence
'Étiologie de la fièvre jaune dans ses rapports avec la navigation en général et la traite des noirs en particulier.' (RMFE, n.s., 1853, vol. 2, pp. 656–72.)

Repeats the theory of a connection between slave ships and yellow fever, now raging at New Orleans. (Favourably reviewed in: Bulletin de l'Académie Royale de Médecine de Belgique, Bruxelles, vol. 14, no. 4, 1855, pp. 172–73.)

895 CLARKE, Robert
'Short notes of the prevailing diseases in the colony of Sierra Leone, with a return of the sick Africans sent to hospital in eleven years, and classified medical returns for the years 1853–4 . . .' (Journal of the Statistical Society of London, vol. 19, 1856, pp. 60–81.)

Describes the diseases of the liberated slaves at Sierra Leone 1839–51.

896 CLYMER, George
'Notices on the African station.' (American Journal of the Medical Sciences, Philadelphia, n.s., vol. 38, 1859, pp. 366–89.)

Account of a voyage on a U.S. cruiser from Sierra Leone to Loanda 1856–57.

897 McHENRY, George
Visits to slave-ships. British and Foreign Anti-Slavery Society, London, [1863]. 4 pp.

Describes conditions and sickness on slave ships brought to the quarantine station on St. Helena; by a former surgeon and superintendent of the Liberated African Establishment there. (Dated: Liverpool, May 1862.) See (3270).

(b) HISTORY

898 *JONES, Joseph
'Researches on the relations of the African slave-trade in the West Indies and tropical America to yellow fever.' (Virginia Medical Monthly, Richmond, vol. 2, 1875, pp. 11–26.)

899 CHRISTIE, James
Cholera epidemics in East Africa. An account of the several diffusions of the disease in that country from 1821 till 1872, with an outline of the geography, ethnology, and trade connections of the regions through which the epidemics passed . . . London, 1876. xxiii, 508 pp. maps.

Shows that the epidemics were linked to the caravan routes and slave trade.

900a *PEREIRA, Manoel Victorino
'A filaria de Medina transportada para a America pelos negros d'Africa; provas da sua endemicidade na provincia da Bahia, e da sua introducção no corpo pelo estomago.' (Gazeta Medical da Bahia, ser. 2, vol. 2, 1877, pp. 151–66.)

Translated as:

900b 'Transport de la filaire de Médine en Amérique par les nègres d'Afrique. Preuves de son endémicité dans la province de Bahia, et de son introduction dans le corps humain par l'estomac.' (Archives de Médecine Navale, Paris, vol. 28, 1877, pp. 295–302.)

Guinea worm was introduced to Brazil through the African slave trade. (Extract from the author's doctoral thesis, Bahia, 1876.)

901 *JONES, Joseph
'Observations on the African yaws in insular and continental America.' (New Orleans Medical and Surgical Journal, vol. 5, 1878, pp. 673–93.)

902 PADWICK, H. B.
'Some notes on early attempts at prophylaxis against "coast fever" on the West African station.' (Journal of the Royal Naval Medical Service, London, vol. 8, 1922, pp. 89–98.)

Deals mainly with the period 1830–62, including the Niger expedition 1841.

903 STITT, Edward Rhodes
'Our disease inheritance from slavery.' (United States Naval Medical Bulletin, Washington, vol. 26, 1928, pp. 801–17.)

Lists diseases 'probably introduced from Africa'.

904 ANDEL, Martinus Antonie van
'Geneeskunde en hygiëne op de slavenschepen in de Compagnietijd.' (Nederlandsch Tijdschrift voor Geneeskunde, Haarlem, vol. 75, pt. 1, 1931, pp. 614–37; illus.)

Study of medical conditions on Dutch slave ships of the 17th and 18th century.

905 CARTER, Henry Rose
Yellow fever. An epidemiological and historical study of its place of origin . . . Baltimore, 1931. xii, 308 pp. illus. bibl. pp. 272–89.

Concludes that the disease was imported by slave ships from Africa.

906 DUDLEY, Sheldon Francis
'Yellow fever, as seen by the medical officers of the Royal Navy in the nineteenth century.' (Proceedings of the Royal Society of Medicine, London, United services section, vol. 26, 1933, pp. 443–56.)

Based mainly on material from the West African and West Indian stations.

907 COUTINHO, Ruy
'Alimentação e estudo nutricional do escravo no Brasil.' *In*: ESTUDOS afro-brasileiros (Rio de Janeiro, 1935), pp. 199–213.

Includes references to the African slave trade.

908 *FREITAS, Octávio de
Doenças africanas no Brasil. São Paulo, 1935. 226 pp.

909 SCOTT, Henry Harold
'The slave-trade and disease.' *In his*: A history of tropical medicine (London, 1939), vol. 2, pp. 982–1010.

910 SCOTT, *Sir* Henry Harold
'The influence of the slave-trade in the spread of tropical diseases.' (Transactions of the Royal Society of Tropical Medicine and Hygiene, London, vol. 37, 1943, pp. 169–88; illus.)

Deals with yellow fever, leprosy, yaws, sleeping sickness and other diseases.

911 ASHBURN, Percy Moreau
The ranks of death. A medical history of the conquest of America. New York, [1947]. xix, 298 pp. bibl. pp. 267–86.

Ch. 3, 'Black tragedy', on the medical aspects of the slave trade. In other chapters the author lists diseases carried to the Americas by African slaves, including malaria, yellow fever, intestinal diseases, trachoma and leprosy.

912 NIXON, John Alexander
'Health and sickness in the slave trade.' *In*: PARKINSON, C. N. The trade winds (London, 1948), pp. 273–77.

Describes medical conditions on slave ships in the period 1787–92.

913 SCHOUTE, Dirk
'Scheepschirurgijns-journaal van een slavenschip der Middelburgsche Commercie Compagnie.' (Nederlandsch Tijdschrift voor Geneeskunde, Haarlem, vol. 92, 1948, pp. 3645–62; illus.)

Based on a medical journal kept by P. Couperus during a slaving voyage to West Africa and Berbice 1761–63.

914 *CHICHÉ, Marie-Claire
Hygiène et santé à bord des navires négriers au XVIIIe siècle. Paris, 1957. 95 pp. illus.

Doctoral thesis in medicine based on slave trade records at Nantes.

915 LLOYD, Christopher *and* COULTER, Jack Leonard Sagar
'The West African squadron.' *In*: KEEVIL, J. J. Medicine and the navy 1220–1900, vol. 4 (Edinburgh & London, 1963), pp. 155–72.

On medical conditions in the anti-slavery squadron 1825–65.

916 CURTIN, Philip De Armond
'Epidemiology and the slave trade.' (Political Science Quarterly, New York, vol. 83, 1968, pp. 190–216.)

Medical statistics of the 18th and 19th century.

917 KLEIN, Herbert Sanford
'The trade in African slaves to Rio de Janeiro, 1795–1811; estimates of mortality and patterns of voyages.' (JAH, vol. 10, no. 4, 1969, pp. 533–49.)

Statistical analysis of records of 170,000 slaves, mostly from Angola, showing variations in mortality related to season and length of voyage.

H. LAWS AND OFFICIAL DOCUMENTS

918 *SPAIN: Laws
Assiento que se tomô con Antonio Fernandez Delbas, sobre la renta y prouision general de esclauos negros para las Indias, año de mil y seiscientos y quinze. [Madrid, 1615.] 20 pp.

The fourth 'assiento' issued for the supply of African slaves to the Spanish colonies in America during an eight-year period. See (930).

919 SPAIN: Laws
Assiento y capitulacion que se tomo con Manuel Rodriguez Lamego, sobre la renta y prouision general de esclauos negros que se nauegan a las Indias por tiempo de ocho años, y precio de ciento y viente mil ducados cada año. [Madrid, 1623.] 17 ll.

Contract for importation of 3,500 slaves annually 1622–30 from West Africa to Cartagena or Vera Cruz in Spanish America.

920 GREAT BRITAIN: Laws
An act for the better improvement of the trade to Africa, by establishing a regulated company. [London,] 1708. 7 pp.

The slave trade shall be open to all British subjects as monopoly has harmed the African trade. See (1011).

921 GREAT BRITAIN: Treaties
The assiento, or, contract for allowing to the subjects of Great Britain the liberty of importing negroes into the Spanish America. Sign'd by the Catholick King at Madrid, the twenty sixth day of March, 1713. John Baskett (etc.), London, 1713. 48 pp.

Contract, included in the peace treaty of 1713, for Britain to supply 144,000 African slaves over 30 years to the Spanish colonies. (Text in Spanish and English.) See (1033).

922 *FRANCE: Laws
Le code noir ou édit du roy, servant de règlement pour le gouvernement et l'administration de justice et la police des isles françoises de l'Amérique et pour la discipline et le commerce des nègres et esclaves dans ledit pays. Donné à Versailles au mois de mars 1685. Vve Saugrin, Paris, 1718. 14 pp.

Reprinted in: MOREAU DE SAINT-MÉRY, M. L. E. Loix et constitutions des colonies françoises de l'Amérique sous le vent, vol. 1 (Paris, 1784), pp. 414–24.

923 *FRANCE: Conseil d'État
Arrest du Conseil d'Estat du Roy, qui subroge la Compagnie des Indes aux droits & pretentions appartenant à la Compagnie de Saint Domingue, tant en France qu' à l'Amérique & autres lieux, avec le privilege exclusif de fournir à l'isle de Saint Domingue trente mille negres tirez de l'estranger. Du 10. septembre 1720 . . . [Paris, 1720.]

924 *RHODE ISLAND: Governor and Council
A vindication of the governour and government of His Majesty's colony of Rhode-Island, &c. From the unjust aspersions and calumnies of John Menzies, judge of his Majesty's court of vice-admiralty in the same: relating to the proceedings of said government, in the affair of several slaves, and other goods imported into said colony, from a ship lately lying at Tarpawlin-Cove, &c. [B. Green, Boston, 1721.] 12 pp.

925 *FRANCE: Laws
Arrest pour le payement de gratification de treize livres par teste de nègre que la Compagnie de Sénégal ferait entrer dans les colonies. Paris, 1724. 8 pp.

926 GREAT BRITAIN: Parliament
A bill to enable the South-Sea Company, with the license and consent of the East-India Company, to take in negroes within their limits of trade, and to deliver the same at Buenos Ayres. [London, 1727.] 3 pp.

Permits the assiento company to collect slaves from Madagascar. (Enacted as 13 Geo. I, c.8: The statutes at large, vol. 15, Cambridge, 1765, pp. 384–85.) See (928).

927 *FRANCE: Laws
Le code noir ou edit du roy, servant de reglement pour le gouvernement & l'administration de la justice, police, discipline & le commerce des esclaves negres, dans la province & colonie de la Loüisianne. Donné à Versailles au mois de mars 1724. [Paris, 1727.] 15 pp.

928 *GREAT BRITAIN: Laws
An act to enable the South Sea Company, with the licence and consent of the East India Company, to take in negroes within their limits of trade, and to deliver the same at Buenos Ayres. John Baskett, London, 1727. (5 pp.)

See (926, 1047–49).

929 NETHERLANDS: Staaten Generaal
Nader prolongatie van het octroy voor de Westindische Compagnie en van de eerste prolongatie van dien, voor den tyd van nog dertig jaaren. Gearresteert den 8 Augusty 1730. Jacobus Scheltus,'s Gravenhage, 1730. 20 pp.

930 SPAIN: Treaties
Coleccion de los tratados de paz, alianza, neutralidad, garantia, proteccion, tregua, mediacion, accesion, reglamento de limites, comercio, navegacion, &c. . . . Fielmente sacados . . . por D. Joseph Antonio de Abreu y Bertodano . . . Diego Peralta, Antonio Marin, & Juan de Zuñiga, Madrid, 1740–52. 12 vol.

Contains all the slave trade 'assientos' granted between 1601 and 1696. See (969).

931 FRANCE: Laws
Code noir, ou recueil d'edits, déclarations et arrets concernant les esclaves nègres de l'Amérique, avec un recueil de réglemens, concernant la police des isles françoises de l'Amérique & les engagés. Libraires associez, Paris, 1743. 3 pt.

932 GREAT BRITAIN: Committee for Trade and Plantations
Papers laid before the honourable House of Commons by the Commissioners for Trade and Plantations, pursuant to an address of the House of Lords to His Majesty, the 8th of June 1749. For the better securing, improving, and extending, the trade to Africa. London, 1750. 53 pp.

Memorials from the Royal African Company, merchants of London, Bristol and Liverpool, and West Indian planters, on the African trade.

933 PORTUGAL: Laws
Alvará para que se naõ levem negros dos portos do mar para terras, que naõ sejaõ dos dominios portuguezas. De 14 de outobro de 1751. Miguel Rodrigues, [Lisboa, 1751]. (2 pp.)

Order forbidding slave trade to Brazil from foreign territories.

934 PORTUGAL: Laws
Alvará com força de ley, porque V. Magestade ha por bem que seja livre, e franco, o commercio de Angola, e dos pórtos, e sertoens adjacentes . . . Miguel Rodrigues, [Lisboa, 1758]. (4 pp.)

Order of 11 Jan. 1758 opening the trade of Congo and Angola to Brazilian as well as Portuguese ships.

935 PORTUGAL: Laws
Alvará com força de ley, porque Vossa Magestade ha por bem estabelecer nova fórma para a arrecadação dos direitos dos escravos, e marfim, que sahirem do reino de Angola, e pórtos da sua dependencia, desde 5 de janeiro do anno de 1760. em diante . . . [Lisboa, 1758.] (3 pp.)

Order of 25 Jan. 1758 setting out duties on Angolan slaves and ivory.

936 NETHERLANDS: Staaten Generaal
Nader prolongatie van het octroy voor de Westindische Compagnie voor den tyd van nog dertig jaaren. Gearresteert den 31 December 1761. Isaac Scheltus,'s Gravenhage, 1761. 38 pp.

937 *SPAIN: Laws
Por D. Miguel de Uriarte, vecino de la ciudad del puerto de Santa Maria . . . pliego obligándose a proveer por diez años de esclavos negros diferentes provincias de América . . . [Madrid, 1765.] 19 pp.

Dated 14 June 1765.

938 DENMARK: Laws
Octroy . . . Wir Friderich der Fünfte . . . thun kund hiemit: dass Uns unsere Unterthanen, die Wittwe Gustmeyers u. Bargum, allerunterthänigst vortragen lassen, wie sie gesonnen waren, in Unsere Residenz-Stadt Copenhagen, einen besondern Sclaven-Handel zu errichten . . . [Copenhagen, 1765.] 12 pp.

Order of 18 March 1765 establishing a Danish slaving company; in 1766 it became the Danske Guineiske Handels-Societet and two forts on the Gold Coast were leased to it for twenty years. (Text in German, Danish and French.) See (1100).

939 *DENMARK: Laws
Confirmation paa den Kiøbmand Bargum og Interessentere under 18. Martii 1765 meddeelte Octroy for 20 Aar betreffende det oprettede Societet for at drive Slave Handelen samt det dermed forbundne Sukker–Raffinaderie i Kiøbenhavn. [Copenhagen, 1766.] (8 ll.)

Dated 4 Aug. 1766.

940 FRANCE: Laws
Le code noir, ou recueil des réglemens rendus jusqu'à présent. Concernant le gouvernement, l'administration de la justice, la police, la discipline & le commerce des negres dans les colonies françoises. Et les conseils & compagnies établis à ce sujet. Prault, Paris, 1767. 446 pp.

Laws 1685–1767 regulating the slave trade to the French West Indies.

941 *SPAIN: Laws
Por quanto deseando remediar los perjuicios de mi real hacienda, y el actual asiento general de negros, que corre de cuenta de Españoles, a nombre de Aguirre, Aristegui y Compañía . . . Madrid, 1775. 3 pp.

Dated 18 July 1775.

942 GREAT BRITAIN: Committee for Trade and Plantations
Return from the Commissioners for Trade and Plantations, to the honourable House of Commons, in consequence of the address of the said House to His Majesty, of the 29th day of January 1777; relating to the general state of the trade to Africa; the condition of the forts and settlements there, belonging to the African Company; and in what manner the several sums of money, granted by Parliament for maintaining and supporting the same, have been applied. [London,] 1777. 60 pp.

Warns about the alarming decline of the slave trade.

943 DENMARK: Laws
Kong Christian den Femtes skrevne Befalninger og Anordninger, eller Reskripter for Norge, Island, Ferrøerne og de Indiske Besiddelser, fra . . . 1670 til . . . 1699. Samlede ved Caspar Peter Rothe . . . Kiøbenhavn, 1777, 78. 2 vol.

Includes an accord with Brandenburg on the slave trade to the West Indies (vol. 2, pp. 1031–59) and the 'Octroy for Nikolay Jansen Arff paa den guineiske Handel' 1691 (vol. 2, pp. 1071–84).

944 *LOUISIANA: Laws
Code noir; ou, loi municipale, servant de reglement pour le gouvernement & l'administration de la justice, police, discipline & le commerce des esclaves nègres, dans la province de la Louisianne entreprit . . . en vertu des ordres du roi . . . consignés dans sa lettre faite à Aranjuez le 14 de mai 1777. [Antoine Boudousquié, Nouvelle Orléans, 1778.]

945 *DENMARK: Laws
Octroy for det Kongel. Danske Vestindiske Handels-Selskab paa 25 Aar. Christiansborg Slot den 11 Maji 1778. N. C. Höpffner, Kiöbenhavn, [1778]. 24 pp.

946 DENMARK: Laws
Octroy for det Kongelige Östersöiske og Guineiske Handels-Selskab paa 30 Aar. Fredensborg Slot den 5 Julii 1781. N. C. Höpffner, Kiöbenhavn, [1781]. 40 pp.

Also issued in German. See (4551).

947 FRANCE: Conseil d'État
Arrêt du Conseil d'État du Roi, qui, à compter du 10 novembre prochain, convertit en gratifications & primes d'exemption du demi-droit accordée aux denrées coloniales provenant de la traite des noirs. Du 26 octobre 1784. Imprimerie Royale, Paris, 1784. 8 pp.

948 SPAIN: Laws
Desvelado siempre el paternal amor del Rey nuestro Señor en proporcionar á sus amados vasallos de América todos los medios que conduscan á su mayor prosperidad, y riqueza, regula que uno de los mas útiles, y necesarios á este efecto, es el de facilitarles la introduccion de negres esclavos en aquellos dominios, como únicos brazos en la mayor parte de ellos para la agricultura, y trabajo de las minas, que son los ramos de que depende el comercio . . . [Madrid, 1784.] (3 pp.)

Order of 4 Nov. 1784 reducing import duties on negro slaves in Spanish America.

949 SPAIN: Laws
Deseando el piadoso Real ánimo de S. M. movido de los sentimientos de su grande humanidad, é innata beneficiencia, mitigar, y mejorar la suerte

de los negros esclavos que se conducen
á sus dominios de Indias . . . [Madrid,
1784.] (3 pp.)

Order of 4 Nov. 1784 abolishing the
branding of slaves imported to
Spanish colonies.

950 FRANCE: Conseil d'État
Arrest du Conseil d'État du Roi, portant établissement d'une nouvelle Compagnie des Indes. Du 14 avril 1785.
P. G. Simon & N. H. Nyon, Paris, 1785.
15 pp.

Decree reestablishing a French East
India company, with monopoly of
slave trading in East Africa (§§ 9, 11.)

951 FRANCE: Conseil d'État
Arrêt du Conseil d'État du Roi, qui
ordonne que la gratification accordée au
commerce pour la traite des nègres,
sera restituée à l'adjudicataire des
fermes, avec moitié en sus, par les
armateurs qui l'auront reçue, & qui
n'auront pas importé des noirs aux
colonies. Du 5 juin 1785. Paris, 1785.
3 pp.

Decree to correct abuse of subsidies
granted to slavers 16 Oct. 1784.

952 FRANCE: Conseil d'État
Arrêt du Conseil d'État du Roi, qui
proroge jusqu'au premier août 1789,
la permission accordée par l'arrêt du
28 juin 1783, d'introduire aux Isles du
Vent, dans les ports d'entrepôt, les noirs
de traite étrangère, avec une diminution
de droits à l'entrée . . . & qui porte à
deux cens livres par tête la prime accordée par l'arrêt du conseil du 16 octobre
1784, aux négocians françois sur les
noirs de traite françoise, qui seront
introduits dans les ports des Cayes-Saint-
Louis à Saint-Domingue, pour l'ap-
provisionnement de la partie du sud de
ladite isle, en observant les formalités
prescrites. Du 10 septembre 1786.
N. H. Nyon, Paris, 1787. 8 pp.

Extension of permission for foreigners
to sell slaves in the French West
Indies and of subsidies for French
slave imports to St. Domingue.

953 HOLLAND: Staaten
Resolutie op de objecten in het rapport
van 19 Maart 1787, door Haar Hoog
Mog. Gecommitteerden tot de con-
ferentien met bewindhebberen der West-
Indische Compagnie, uitgebracht. [Am-
sterdam? 1788.] 11 pp.

Criticizes the West India Company's
methods of conducting the slave
trade, which is of primary importance
to the colonies.

954 *FRANCE: Laws
Le code noir, ou recueil des règlements
rendus jusqu'à présent concernant le
gouvernement, l'administration de la
justice, la police, la discipline et le
commerce des nègres dans les colonies
françoises, et les conseils et les compagnies établis à ce sujet. Paris,1788.

The most complete edition of the
'code noir'. See (922).

**955 SAINT DOMINGUE: Conseil Supér-
ieur**
Ordonnance, concernant la liberté du
commerce pour la partie du sud de
Saint-Domingue. Du 9 mai 1789 . . .
Bourdon, Port-au-Prince, [1789]. 8 pp.

Regulations for admission of slaves
and other goods by foreign ships.
See (1115).

956 FRANCE: Conseil d'État
Arrêt du Conseil d'État du Roi, qui
casse & annulle une ordonnance du
gouverneur général de Saint-Domingue,
du 9 mai dernier, laquelle accordait
aux étrangers la liberté du commerce
pour la partie du sud de Saint-Domingue. Du 2 juillet 1789. Versailles, 1789.
4 pp.

Decree annulling the order of 9
May, which was superfluous as
the number of negroes had already
increased in St. Domingue.

957 FRANCE: Conseil d'État
Arrêt du Conseil d'État du Roi, qui
proroge jusqu'au 1er. août 1790, les
dispositions de celui du 10 septembre
1786, concernant les primes accordées à
l'introduction des noirs de traite françoise aux Isles du Vent, à Cayenne &
aux Cayes, dans la partie du sud
Saint-Domingue, ainsi que la liberté
provisoire de l'exportation à l'étranger
des sucres bruts de l'île de Sainte-
Lucie. Du 2 juillet 1789. Versailles, 1789.
3 pp.

Extension for one year of subsidies
to French slave traders.

958 SPAIN: Laws
Real cedula de Su Magestad concediendo libertad para el comercio de
negros con las islas de Cuba, Santo
Domingo, Puerto Rico, y provincia de
Caracas, á Españoles y extrangeros,
baxo las reglas que se expresan. Viuda
de Ibarra, Madrid, 1789. (11 pp.)

Decree of 28 Feb. 1789 establishing free trade in slaves for two years in the Spanish colonies.

959 SPAIN: Laws
Real cedula de Su Magestad concediendo libertad para el comercio de negros con los virreynatos de Santa Fé, Buenos-Ayres, capitania general de Caracas, é islas de Santo Domingo, Cuba, y Puerto-Rico, á Españoles y extrangeros baxo las reglas que se expresan. Lorenzo de San Martin, Madrid, 1791. (15 pp.)

Decree of 24 Nov. 1791 extending the order of 1789 to Buenos Aires, to last until 1797.

960 *SPAIN: Laws
Real orden concediendo varias gracias a los Españoles de Europa y América para que vuelvan a frecuentar las costas de Africa y hagan el comercio de negros. [Madrid? 1793.] (1 p.).

961 *FRANCE: Laws
Decret de la Convention nationale, du 27 juillet 1793, l'an second de la République Française, qui supprime les primes pour la traite des esclaves. Paris, 1793. 2 pp.

962 *FRANCE: Laws
Decret de la Convention nationale, du 19 septembre 1793, l'an second de la République Française, une & indivisible, qui autorise le payement des primes & gratifications accordées au commerce, à l'exception de celles pour la traite des nègres. Paris, 1793. 2 pp.

963 *GREAT BRITAIN: Laws
Abstract of an act for better regulating the manner of carrying slaves, in British vessels, from the coast of Africa. Passed July 12, 1799. London, 1799. 23 pp.

964 *NEW YORK (State): Laws
Laws relative to slaves and the slave-trade. Samuel Stansbury, New York, 1806. 29 pp.

965 *SPAIN: Laws
Real cedula sobre el comprar e introducir negros en las islas y provincias de América. Habana, 1814. 7 pp.

966 PORTUGAL: Laws
'Alvará com força de lei, pelo qual vossa Alteza Real ha por bem regular a arqueação dos navios, empregados na conducção dos negros, que dos portos de Africa se exportão para os do

Brazil . . .' (Portuguez, Londres, vol. 1, 1814, pp, 71–82.)

Order signed 24 Nov. 1813 regulating conditions on slave ships. (Also printed in: IPI, vol. 9, 1814, pp. 234–43.)

967 PORTUGAL: Laws
Collecção chronologica de leis extravagantes, posteriores a' nova compilação das ordenações do reino, publicadas em 1603 . . . Imprensa da Universidade, Coimbra, 1819. 6 vol.

Contains the fundamental 'Alvará' e regimento da ordem, com que se hão de embarcar os negros captivos de Angola para o estado do Brazil' (18 March 1684; vol. 2, pp. 136–45) and those of 1751 and 1758 (933–35). (The law of 1684 is reprinted as 'Ley sobre as arqueações dos navios que carregarem escravos' in: Arquivos de Angola, Luanda, vol. 2, 1936, pp. 313–20.)

968 GREAT BRITAIN: Colonial Department
Jamaica. (Slave trade.) Copy of a dispatch from the Earl of Dartmouth to Sir Basil Keith, governor of Jamaica, with memorials, on the subject of an act passed by the Assembly of Jamaica in 1774, imposing a duty on slaves imported . . . [London,] 1832. 9 pp. (P.P. 1831–32, XLVII.)

Memorials from London, Bristol and Liverpool against the Jamaican duty and instructions to West Indian governors to disallow all similar acts.

969 SPAIN: Treaties
Tratados, conventos y declaraciones de paz y comercio que han hecho con las potentias estrangeras los monarcas españoles de la casa de Borbon. Desde el año de 1700 hasta el dia. Puestos en ordén . . . por Don Alejandre del Cantillo . . . Alegria y Charlain, Madrid, 1843. xxxix, 908 pp.

Includes the text of the asientos of 1701 and 1713 and the treaties with Britain for the abolition of the slave trade 1817 and 1835. See (930).

970 FRANCE: Ministère de la Marine et des Colonies
Instructions générales données de 1763 à 1870 aux gouverneurs et ordonnateurs des établissements français en Afrique occidentale. Recueillies et publiés par Christian Schefer. Paris, 1921, 27. 2 vol.

Pt. 1: 'La période de la traite (1763–1814)' (vol. 1, pp. 1–224).

971 **MELLO, Miguel Antonio de**
'Carta do governador para a Real Junta do Commercio, Agricultura, e Navegação e Fabricas do Reyno de Portugal e seus dominios, propondo medidas mais humanas no tráfico da escravatura.—12 de março de 1799.'

(Arquivos de Angola, Luanda, vol. 2, 1936, pp. 593–602.)

Report from the governor of Luanda on new regulations for the slave trade to Brazil. (Nine other documents concerning the Angolan slave trade 1641–1836 are reprinted in this volume.)

I. ECONOMIC CONTROVERSY

972 COMPANY OF ROYAL ADVEN-
TURERS
The several declarations of the Company
of Royal Adventurers of England
trading into Africa, inviting all His
Majesties native subjects in general to
subscribe, and became sharers in their
joynt-stock. Together with His Royal
Highness James Duke of Yorke and
Albany, &c. and the rest of the said
Royal Companies letter to the Right
Honourable Francis Lord Willoughby
of Parham, &c. intimating the said
companies resolution to furnish His
Majestie's American plantations with
negroes at certain and moderate rates.
As also a list of the Royal Adventurers
of England trading into Africa. [Lon-
don,] 1667. 12 pp.

Scheme to provide 'a competent
and constant supply of Negro-
servants', of which there is a shortage in the American colonies. (Documents dated January and February
1662.)

973 COMPANY OF ROYAL ADVEN-
TURERS
An answer of the Company of Royal
Adventurers of England trading into
Africa, to the petition and paper of
certain heads and particulars thereunto
relating and annexed, exhibited to the
honourable House of Commons by
Sir Paul Painter, Ferdinando Gorges,
Henry Batson, Benjamin Skutt, and
Thomas Knights, on the behalf of
themselves and others concerned in
His Majesties plantations in America.
[London,] 1667. 19 pp.

Complaint of five merchants against
the claim of the new company
to monopolize the trade for slaves;
the colonies will be ruined unless
freedom of trade is restored. The
company replies that it has provided
more and cheaper slaves than the
traders.

974a VEITIA LINAGE, Joseph de
Norte de la contratacion de las Indias
occidentales . . . Iuan Francisco de
Blas, Sevilla, 1672. 264 pp.

Translated as:

974b The Spanish rule of trade to the West-
Indies: containing an account of the
Casa de Contratacion, or India-House
. . . Samuel Crouch, London, 1702.
367 pp.

Describes the laws and regulations
governing trade to Spanish America,
with a chapter on the slave trade
and asientos.

975 SAVARY, Jacques
Le parfait négociant ou instruction
generale pour ce qui regarde le commerce de toute sorte de marchandises . . .
Jean Guignard, Paris, 1675. 2 pt.

Includes a section describing the
African slave trade and defending
it on moral grounds. See (1071).

976 CERTAIN considerations relating to
the Royal African Company of England. In which, the original, growth,
and national advantages of the Guiney
trade, are demonstrated: as also that
the same trade cannot be carried on,
but by a company and joint-stock.
[London,] 1680. 10 pp.

The African trade would be lost
without the Company; the slave trade
is the basis of colonial prosperity.

977 *NEDERLANDSE WEST-INDISCHE
COMPAGNIE
Instructie voor de schippers in den
dienst van de geoctroyeerde West-
Indische Compagnie op den slaef-
handel varende. Barth de Later, Middel-
burgh, [1685].

978 NEDERLANDSE WEST-INDISCHE
COMPAGNIE
Consideration van bewinthebberen der
Generale Geoctroyeerde West-Indische
Compagnie deser landen. Over de
directie van de colonie van Suriname
ende het gouvernement van den Heer
van Sommelsdyck aldaar. [Amsterdam,
1688.] 3 pt.

Collection of documents from 1682–
87 on the Dutch slave trade to
Surinam.

979 PERTINENT en waarachtig verhaal van alle de handelingen en directie van Pedro van Belle, ontrent den slaven-handel, ofte, het assiento de negros, eerst door D. Juan Barosso y Posso, bij zijn overlijden door D. Nicolas Porsio, en daar na door Balthasar Coijmans met den Koning van Spangien aangegaan, zoo in Spangien, de West-Indijes, als op Curaçao . . . Reinier Leers, Rotterdam, 1689. 130, 181 pp.

Account of the contracts for the slave trade to Spanish America 1662–88.

980 *NEDERLANDSE WEST-INDISCHE COMPAGNIE
Notificatie. De bewindhebberen van de Generale Geoctroyeerde West-Ind-ische Compagnie deser landen maken bekent, dat sy goetgevonden hebben op het eylant Curaçao aan te stellen eene opene marct van swarte-slaven, soo wel pieces d'Indias als manquerons . . . Bartholomeus de Later, Middelburg, [1689]. (1 p.)

981 THOMAS, Sir Dalby
An historical account of the rise and growth of the West-India colonies, and of the great advantages they are to England, in respect to trade. Jo Hind-marsh, London, 1690. 53 pp.

An open trade to Africa would pro-vide slaves more cheaply than the Royal African Company.

982 WILKINSON, William
Systema africanum; or a treatise, discovering the intrigues and arbitrary proceedings of the Guiney company, and also how prejudicial they are to the American planters, the woollen, and other English manufacturers: to the visible decay of trade, and consequently greatly impairing the royal revenue, which would be infinitely encreased, provided merchants and mariners were encouraged, who can discover several places not yet known, or traded unto, by the African company . . . London, 1690. 26 pp.

The Royal African Company's trade is too limited; an increased provision of slaves could quadruple production in the American colonies.

983 WILKINSON, William
An answer to the book written by the Guiney Company in their own defence, for the management of the trade in Africa. [London? 1690.] 4 pp.

Arbitrary actions by the company, such as kidnapping, are opening the way for rival nations in West Africa.

984 The CASE between the African Com-pany and the people of England. [London, 1692.] 2 pp.

The company's monopoly of the slave trade has 'crippled' the British colonies; open trade would improve the supply of slaves so that England could get cheaper sugar and undersell other nations.

985 SOME considerations: humbly offered to demonstrate how prejudicial it would be to the English plantations, revenues of the crown, the navigation and general good of this kingdom, that the sole trade for negroes should be granted to a company with a joynt-stock exclusive to all others. [London? 1694?] 2 pp.

The Royal African Company has not conducted the slave trade satis-factorily; the colonies would be best served by free trade to Africa for slaves in areas where the company has no establishments.

986 ROYAL AFRICAN COMPANY
The case of the Royal African Company of England. [London, 1694.] (1 p.)

987 WILKINSON, William
An answer to a paper, lately printed and published by the Affrican-Company . . . [London, 1695.] (2 pp.)

Attacks the company for its monopoly of the slave trade.

988 CARY, John
An essay on the state of England, in relation to its trade, its poor, and its taxes, for carrying on the present war against France. Bristoll, 1695. 178 pp.

Includes a section on the West Indian and African trades; the slave trade, 'the best traffick the kingdom hath', ought not to remain a mono-poly of the Royal African Company. See (1030, 1036).

989 SOME considerations relating to the trade to Guiny. [London, 1695?] (2 pp.)

The Royal African Company is ruining the colonies by not providing the necessary supply of slaves; most of the slaves are purchased where there are no forts.

990   SOME considerations humbly offered, against granting the sole trade to Guiny from Cape Blanco to Cape Lopez, to a company with a joint stock, exclusive of others. [London, 1696.] 2 pp.

991   CONSIDERATIONS on the trade of Africa, humbly offer'd to the honourable House of Commons, in behalf of the bill now before them. (Signed: D. T.) [London, 1698.] 3 pp.

Leaflet written to show that a regulated company is necessary to maintain the forts which protect the slave trade.

992   REASONS humbly offered in behalf of the plantations, against the bill for settling the trade to Affrica. [London? 1698.] (1 p.)

'The welfare and subsistence of the West-Indies entirely depends upon their being furnished plentifully with negroes'; the Royal African Company should be superseded by regulated free traders.

993   CONSIDERATIONS humbly offered to the honourable House of Commons, by the planters, in relation to the bill to settle the trade to Africa. [London, 1698.] (1 p.)

Negro slaves are the basis of colonial production and the slave trade ought to be free in those parts of West Africa, south of the Volta, where there are no forts.

994   REASONS humbly offered by the merchants and traders to Guinny and the West-Indies, against the bill for settling the trade to Affrica. [London, 1698.] (1 p.)

The company had failed to supply the slaves needed in the colonies; free traders could sell them more cheaply.

995   The STATE of the trade to Africa, between 1680 and 1707, as well under the management of an exclusive company, as under that of separate traders, impartially considered, with regard to matter of fact and demonstration; whereby it appears the separate adventurers have improv'd that trade to the benefit of Great Britain at least one million a year. [London, 1708.] 4 pp.

From 1698, when the trade was laid open, the separate traders had carried at least 75,000 slaves to America in the first four years alone, compared with 64,000 transported by the Royal African Company in the period 1680–1707.

996   The CASE of the separate traders to Africa. [London? 1708.] 4 pp.

Since the slave trade was laid open in 1698 it has increased fivefold.

997   The FALSITIES of private traders to Africa discover'd, and the mischiefs they occasion demonstrated: and an account of the settlements on that coast purchased, built, and now possest, by the company. [London, 1708.] 4 pp.

998   The IMPROVEMENT of the African trade farther demonstrated by separate traders, in answer to a scurvilous paper, called The falsities of private traders discovered. [London, 1708.] 4 pp.

999   CONSIDERATIONS upon the trade to Guinea. London, 1708. 30 pp.

The African trade should be laid open to private traders. Ends with a defence of the morality of the slave trade. See (1006).

1000 An ACCOUNT of the number of negroes delivered in to the islands of Barbadoes, Jamaica, and Antego, from the year 1698 to 1708. since the trade was opened, taken from the accounts sent from the respective governours of those islands to the Lords Commissioners of Trade, whereby it appears the African trade is encreas'd to four times more since its being laid open, than it was under an exclusive company. [London, 1709?] 2 pp.

Of 88,000 slaves imported to the three islands 1698–1707 only 17,760 were imported by the Royal African Company and over 70,000 by the separate traders; under the company's monopoly the annual average had been about 5,000 slaves to all colonies.

1001 REFLECTIONS upon the constitution and management of the trade to Africa, through the whole course and progress thereof, from the beginning of the last century, to this time . . . John Morphew, London, 1709. 44; iv, 40; iv, 52 pp.

By Charles Davenant. Account of the development of the English trade with Africa, hostile to the private traders; the improvement of the slave trade is wholly due to the Royal African Company.

1002 SOME remarks on a pamphlet, call'd Reflections, on the constitution and management of the trade to Africa . . . [London,] 1709. 32 pp.

Refutes (1001) with statistics of the slave trade 1698–1707 showing that the open trade has been beneficial to the nation; proposes a new company of 'Adventurers to Africa' open to all.

1003 ROYAL AFRICAN COMPANY
The case of the Royal-African-Company. [London, 1709.] 4 pp.

The slave trade is vital to the colonies and the company must maintain the forts and local alliances in Africa.

1004 A LETTER from the most considerable proprietors of the island of Barbadoes, to the several persons in Great Britain interested in the said island, requesting their application to the honourable House of Commons, for establishing the African trade by a joint-stock. [London? 1709.] 3 pp.

Only a company with a monopoly can ensure a supply of slaves; the separate traders have raised their price.

1005 PROPOSALS for raising a new company for carrying on the trades of Africa and the Spanish West-Indies, under the title of the United Company. Humbly submitted to the consideration of the parliament of Great-Britain. John Morphew, London, 1709. 13 pp.

Suggestions for the improvement of the African trade on a new financial basis; the colonial trade depends on the cheap provision of slaves. See (1006).

1006 ROYAL AFRICAN COMPANY
Remarks on two pamphlets, lately published, in relation to the trades of Africa, and the Spanish-West-Indies. [London, 1709.] 4 pp.

Defends the company against (999) and (1005).

1007 CONSIDERATIONS humbly offer'd to the honourable House of Commons, by the planters, and others, trading to our British plantations, in relation to the African Company's petition, now before this honourable House. [London, 1709?] (1 p.)

Petition against the 10% charge for separate traders which raises the price of slaves.

1008 A MEMORIAL touching the nature and state of the trade to Africa. [London, 1709.] 7 pp.

A privileged company is necessary to ensure a constant supply of slaves for the planters.

1009 SEVERAL arguments proving, that our trade to Africa, cannot be preserved and carried on effectually by any other method, than that of a considerable joint-stock, with exclusive privileges. [London, 1709?] 4 pp.

The Dutch plan to produce sugar with slaves in Africa; this design must be defeated.

1010 A LETTER to a member of parliament concerning the African trade. [London, 1709.] 3 pp.

Opposes the restoration of the Royal African Company's monopoly. See (1015).

1011 SOME considerations on the late act of Parliament, for setling the trade to Africa. [London, 1709?] (1 p.)

The Royal African Company's control of the slave trade should be restored. See (920, 1012).

1012 CONSIDERATIONS on the present trade to Africa, answer'd paragraph by paragraph. [London, 1709.] (1 p.)

Reply to (1011). There is room enough for all on the African coast.

1013 The BARBADOES petition, relating to the African trade. [London, 1710.] 2 pp.

Petition to the Queen signed by 85 settlers; the separate traders have raised prices and imported insufficient slaves compared with the Royal African Company. See (1016).

1014 A TRUE state of the present difference between the Royal African Company, and the separate traders . . . Written by a true lover of his country, and humbly submitted to the wise consideration of both houses of Parliament. London, 1710. 40 pp.

The company's forts are not worth the 10% duty paid by the separate traders who supply most of the slaves to the West Indies; they could be bought more cheaply if the trade were laid open.

1015 SEASONABLE animadversions, on all the papers and pamphlets publish'd by the separate traders to Africa. [London, 1710.] 7 pp.

Reply to (1010) and others.

1016 SOME short and necessary observations proper to be considered in the settlement of the African trade. [London, 1711.] (2 pp.)

Petition to the Queen from planters in Barbados, complaining that prices of slaves have doubled since the trade was laid open. See (1013).

1017 ROYAL AFRICAN COMPANY
Reasons humbly offered for confirming the Royal-African-Company's charter by Parliament, to such persons who are willing to become adventurers in that trade. [London, 1711.] (2 pp.)

1018 REASONS against confirming the charter of the African Company by act of Parliament, humbly offered to consideration. [London, 1711?] (1 p.)

Monopoly in the slave trade is illegal.

1019 REASONS against establishing an African company at London, exclusive to the plantations, and all the outports, and other subjects of Great-Britain. [London? 1711.] 2 pp.

Monopolies are dangerous; the Royal African Company will not be able to supply the colonies and fulfil the assiento. See (1021).

1020 A SHORT and true account of the importance and necessity, of settling the African trade this present session of Parliament; together with a comparative view of the two schemes, proposed to the honourable House of Commons, viz. that for a general joynt-stock; and that for an open trade. [London, 1711.] 4 pp.

Arguments in favour of a company to ensure a steady supply of slaves and keep prices down.

1021 An ANSWER to the Reasons against an African company humbly submitted to the consideration of the patriots of Great-Britain, in this present Parliament assembled. [London, 1711.] 31 pp.

Defends the Royal African Company against the private traders' criticisms (1019).

1022 LETTER from Bristol, touching the trade to Africa, as it relates to the outports of Great Britain. [London, 1711.] 2 pp.

If the Royal African Company's monopoly is restored, Bristol will be excluded from the African trade.

1023 The SEPARATE traders scheme for carrying on the trade to Africa. [London, 1711.] (1 p.)

The Royal African Company should levy duties for upkeep of the forts, but individual traders should be licensed to supply slaves to Spanish America.

1024 An ESSAY upon the trade to Africa, in order to set the merits of that cause in a true light and bring the disputes between the African Company and the separate traders into a narrower compass. [London,] 1711. 48 pp.

By Daniel Defoe. The arguments of both sides are stated, but a privileged company is shown to be the only means of securing the slave trade to Britain.

1025 A TRUE account of the design, and advantages of the south-sea trade: with answers to all the objections rais'd against it. A list of the commodities proper for that trade: and the progress of the subscription towards the South-Sea Company. J. Morphew, London, 1711. 38 pp.

The South Sea Company may help the Royal African Company by selling slaves to the Spanish colonies.

1026 JAMAICA: Council
An address to Her Majesty, from the Governour, Council and Assembly, of the island of Jamaica, against an exclusive trade to Africa. [London, 1712?] (2 pp.)

Petition (June 1711) asserting that the Royal African Company's monopoly of the slave trade may ruin Jamaica.

1027 The DESTRUCTIVE consequences of a regulated trade to Africa, as promoted by the separate traders. [London, 1712?] (2 pp.)

Defence of the Royal African Company.

1028 A PLAIN account of the loss, this nation has sustain'd, by laying open the trade to Africa. [London, 1712.] 2 pp

The separate traders claim to have transported 80,000 slaves in thirteen years but an exclusive company would have made a greater profit for Britain.

1029 A COLLECTION of papers relating to the trade to Africa. [London? 1712.] 62 pp.

Mainly pamphlets of 1708–12, including (996) and (1010), critical of the Royal African Company; stresses the vital importance of the slave trade.

1030 CARY, John
A discourse of the advantages of the African trade to this nation, extracted out of an essay of trade, written by Mr. John Cary, merchant. [London, 1712.] 4 pp.

The section on the African trade extracted from (988).

1031 A LETTER from a West-India merchant to a gentleman at Tunbridg, concerning that part of the French proposals, which relates to North-America, and particularly Newfoundland. With some thoughts on their offers about our trade to Spain and the West-Indies: and an abstract of the assiento. London, 1712. 34 pp.

Summarizes the French assiento of 1702; France may be willing to cede it because of her losses in the slave trade.

1032 The TRADE granted to the South-Sea-Company: considered with relation to Jamaica. In a letter to one of the directors of the South-Sea-Company; by a gentleman who has resided several years in Jamaica. Samuel Crouch, London, 1714. 30 pp.

Criticism of the assiento won in 1713 from the point of view of Jamaica, which has experience of supplying the Spaniards with slaves and is strategically placed; the company should make that island its principal depot for the slave trade.

1033 The ASSIENTO contract consider'd. As also, the advantages and decay of the trade of Jamaica and the plantations, with the causes and consequences thereof. In several letters to a member of parliament. Ferd. Burleigh, London, 1714. 50 pp.

By William Wood. The terms of the assiento are not good enough in view of growing French competition which may ruin the British colonies in the West Indies; the South Sea Company's monopoly will have serious consequences for Jamaica. See (921).

1034 ROYAL AFRICAN COMPANY
The case of the Royal African-Com-

pany and of the plantations. [London], 1714. 3 pp.

Plea for an act to reserve the slave trade exclusively to the company in the interest of Britain and the colonies.

1035 SOME observations, shewing the danger of losing the trade of the sugar colonies. Humbly offer'd to the consideration of the Parliament. By a planter. London, 1714. 15 pp.

By William Cleland. The supply of African labour is vital to the colonies; an exclusive company is needed, as the separate traders have made slaves dearer than before.

1036 CARY, John
An essay towards regulating the trade, and employing the poor, of this kingdom. Tim. Goodwin; Edward Symon, London, 1717. 162 pp.

A new version of (988), with a section on the value of the African slave trade.

1037a MÉMOIRES sur le commerce des Hollandois, dans tous les états et empires du monde . . . Emanuel du Villard, Amsterdam, 1717. xx, 283 pp.

Translated as:

1037b MEMOIRS of the Dutch trade in all the states, empires, and kingdoms of the world . . . The second edition. J. Sackfield (etc.), London, [1718?] xii, 232 pp.

By P. D. Huet. With a chapter on the Dutch West India Company showing the great importance to it of the former slave trade with the Spaniards. (The second French edition, Amsterdam, 1718, incorporates additions in the English and other translations.)

1038 WOOD, William
A survey of trade . . . W. Hinchliffe, London, 1718. xiv, 373 pp.

Includes sections on the African trade and on the assiento, critical of the South Sea Company's monopoly.

1039 SOME matters of fact relating to the present state of the African trade; demonstrating, that there are not wanting any subscriptions, or new projects, for its support. [London, 1720.] 3 pp.

British ships carry about 36,000 slaves yearly to the colonies; African commerce is flourishing as an open trade.

1040 **SAVARY DES BRUSLONS, Jacques**
Dictionnaire universal de commerce . . .
Ouvrage posthume . . . continué . . .
et donné au public, par M. Philemon
Louis Savary . . . Jacques Estienne,
Paris, 1724–30. 3 vol.

Contains information on the slave
trade under 'Assiente', 'Commerce
des costes d'Afrique', 'Compagnies'
and 'Nègres'.

1041 **MORE, Gerald**
Informe en derecho, sobre que la
compañia de el real assiento de la
Gran Bretaña, establecida para la
introduccion de esclavos negros, en
estas Indias, debe declararse libre, y
exempta de la paga de los reales derechos, comprehendidos en el nombre
de alcavala, en todos los puertos, y
demàs lugares de la tierra adentro de
esta America, por lo que toca á las
ropas, y mercaderias de sus navios
annuales, igualmente, como de sus
negros . . . Juan Francisco de Ortega,
Bonilla, Mexico, 1724. 127 ll.

Treatise on the assiento of 1713 and
the South Sea Company.

1042 **HOUSTOUN, James**
Some new and accurate observations
geographical, natural and historical.
Containing a true and impartial account
of the situation, product, and natural
history of the coast of Guinea, so far as
relates to the improvement of that
trade, for the advantage of Great
Britain in general, and the Royal
African Company in particular . . .
Humbly address'd to the honourable
the court of assistants of the Royal
African Company of Great Britain.
J. Peele, London, 1725. 62 pp.

The author, an ex-surgeon in the
service of the company, describes
its West African settlements and
slave trade, 'the hinge on which all
the trade of this globe moves'.

1043 The STATE of the island of Jamaica.
Chiefly in relation to its commerce,
and the conduct of the Spaniards in
the West-Indies. Address'd to a member of parliament. By a person who
resided several years at Jamaica.
(Signed: A---B----.) H. Whitridge, London, 1726. 79 pp.

Spanish captures of British ships,
including slave ships, since 1713
had led to English piracy in reprisal
and a disruption of trade.

1044 *****MENDOÇA CORTE-REAL, Diogo de**
Traduction de la démonstration de la
Compagnie des Indes Occidentales,
contenant les raisons pourquoi les
Portugais ne sont point en droit de
naviguer vers les côtes de la Haute &
Basse-Guinée, &c. et examen et refuta-
tion de toutes ces raisons par Diogo de
Mendoça Corte-Real . . . [Paris?] 1727.
34 pp.

Memoir by the Portuguese envoy
rejecting the Dutch West India
Company's claims in parts of West
Africa not occupied by Portugal,
which had granted a monopoly
of the slave trade to a 'Compagnie
de Corisco' in 1724. See (1045).

1045 *****NEDERLANDSE WEST-INDISCHE
COMPAGNIE**
Wederlegging van de argumenten, en
redenen, dewelke zyn geallegeert door
den Heere Diogo de Mendoça Corte-
Reâl, envoyé extraordinaris van zyn
Majesteit de Konig van Portugaal, in
den Haagh, by zyne Memorie, en
desselfs bylaage, aan haar Hoogh. Mog.
de heeren Staaten Generaal der Vereen-
igde Nederlanden, overgegeven op
den 15. September des jaars 1727 . . .
[Den Haag? 1727?] 36 pp.

Reply to (1044). See (1046).

1046 **MENDOÇA CORTE-REAL, Diogo de**
Examen et reponse a un ecrit publié par la
Compagnie des Indes Occidentales
sous le titre de Refutation des argu-
mens & raisons alleguées par Mr. Diogo
de Mendoça Corte-Real envoié extraordinaire de Portugal à la Haye, dans
son memoire et l'ecrit annexe presenté
à leurs hautes puissances le 15. septembre 1727. &c. [Paris?] 1727. 64 pp.
map.

Contests the Dutch West India
Company's claims in the Gabon
area; with the text of the 'Refutation'
(1045).

1047 SOME observations on the assiento
trade, as it has been exercised by the
South-Sea Company; proving the damage, which will accrue thereby to the
British commerce and plantations in
America, and particularly to Jamaica . . .
By a person who resided several years
at Jamaica. H. Whitridge, London, 1728.
iv, 38 pp.

The South Sea Company, by obtaining
the assiento, has deprived Jamaica
of its former trade in slaves to the
Spanish colonies. See (928).

1048 *An ANSWER to a calumny, with some remarks upon an anonimous pamphlet address'd to His Grace the Duke of Newcastle, entitled: Some observations on the assiento trade, as it has been exercised by the South Sea Company, &c., where by the damage which has or is likely to accrue thereby to the British commerce and plantations, and particularly to Jamaica is also considered. By the factor to the South Sea Company, at whom the calumny was aimed. London, 1728. 2 pt.

By James Houstoun?

1049 A DEFENCE of the Observations on the assiento trade, as it hath been exercised by the South-Sea Company, &c. . . . By the author of the observations on the assiento trade. H. Whitridge London, 1728. vi, 66 pp.

Reply to attacks on (1047) and further criticism of the South Sea Company's conduct of the assiento trade.

1050 GEE, Joshua
The trade and navigation of Great-Britain considered . . . Sam. Buckley, London, 1729. 129, 16 pp.

A mercantilist treatise, with a chapter on the African trade; the private traders provide more and cheaper slaves than the Royal African Company, (The 1767 edition contains a critical note on the act of 1766 to establish 'free ports' in the British West Indies, allowing foreigners to sell slaves there.)

1051 ROYAL AFRICAN COMPANY
The case of the Royal African Company of England. Sam. Aris, London, 1730. 34 pp.

Historical account of the company's achievements since its establishment.

1052 The PARTICULARS of the enquiry into Mr. Benjamin Wooley's conduct; and his being stationed by the Court of Directors of the South-Sea Company, first factor at Porto Bello and Panama. Humbly dedicated to Thomas Waterford, Esq. A. Dodd, London, 1735. 32 pp.

Criticizes Woolley's handling of the asiento slave trade as factor at Havana 1733–34.

1053 TEMPLEMAN, Daniel
The secret history of the late directors of the South-Sea-Company. Containing a particular account of their conduct, with regard to the assiento commerce and other transactions highly injurious to the proprietors, and prejudicial to the King of Spain . . . London, 1735. 62 pp.

1054 FRANCE: Conseil de Commerce
Memorials presented, by the deputies of the Council of Trade in France, to the Royal Council, in 1701 . . . Concerning the commerce of that nation to their American islands, Guinea, the Levant, Spain, England, Holland, and the North . . . In French and English. J. & P. Knapton (etc.), London, 1737. viii, 120 pp.

No. 1: 'A memorial concerning the Guinea Company'; the slave trade is important because it is carried on without cash and provides labour for the colonies.

1055 CONSIDERATIONS on the American trade, before and since the establishment of the South-Sea Company. J. Roberts, London, 1739. 31 pp.

Private trade had been more advantageous than the assiento trade of the South Sea Company. See (1058).

1056 The IMPORTANCE of Jamaica to Great-Britain consider'd . . . In a letter to a gentleman . . . A. Dodd, London, [1740?] 81 pp.

Warns of French competition in the African slave trade and urges Britain to keep Cartagena, recently captured from Spain; the Royal African Company could then sell more slaves at a lower price than before the war.

1057a SAVARY DES BRUSLONS, Jacques
Dictionnaire universel de commerce . . . Nouvelle édition . . . enrichie de beaucoup d'additions . . . Cramer & Frères Philibert, Genève, 1742. 3 vol.

Translated as:

1057b The universal dictionary of trade and commerce, translated . . . with large additions . . . By Malachy Postlethwayt. London, 1751–55. 2 vol. maps.

Vol. 1, pt. 2 of the 1742 edition is devoted entirely to the articles 'Commerce' and 'Compagnie'. See (1104).

1058 A TRUE and impartial account of the rise and progress of the South Sea Company; wherein the assiento contract is particularly considered: proving the great advantages that would have accrued to England by a faithful observance of it on the part of Spain . . . By a gentleman now resident in Jamaica. T. Cooper, London, 1743. 33 pp.

> By James Houstoun. Reply to (1055).

1059   A BRIEF account of the causes that have retarded the progress of the colony of Georgia, in America; attested upon oath . . . London, 1743. 24, 101 pp.

> By Thomas Stephens. Argues the need to introduce black slaves to Georgia as the land granted is useless for want of labour.

1060   The IMPORTANCE of effectually supporting the Royal African Company of England impartially consider'd; shewing, that a free and open trade to Africa, and the support and preservation of the British colonies and plantations in America, depend upon maintaining the forts and settlements, rights and privileges belonging to that corporation, against the encroachments of the French, and all other foreign rivals in that trade . . . In a letter to a member of the House of Commons. M. Cooper, London, 1744. 47 pp. map.

> By Charles Hayes. Foreign control of the African trade would ruin the British colonies, of which 'the negroe trade . . . is the chief and fundamental support'.

1061   REQUESTE van verscheide Hollandsche en Zeeuwsche geinteresseerden in de vaart en handel op de kust van Africa, om daar in gemaintineert te worden volgens het octroi en reglementen, en dat dien handel werde geinterdiceert aan bewindhebberen en bedienden van de Westindische Compagnie, met een berigt van bewindhebberen. [Amsterdam, 1744.] 23 pp.

> Addresses from separate traders to the States-General against the privileges of the Dutch West India company; the octroi of 1730 should not be renewed.

1062   COMMERCIE COMPAGNIE VAN MIDDELBURG
Memorie, uyt namen ende van wegens de directeuren van de Commercie Compagnie der Stad Middelburg, midsgaders de verdere ondergeschreve boekhouders en reeders zoo van Middelburg als Vlissingen met pasport van haar Ho: Mo: navigerende op de kusten van Africa, aan de Ed. Mo: Heeren Staten van Zeeland overgeven . . . wegens de vexes en belemmering haar in den voorsz. handel door de bediende van de W. Indise Compagnie daar te lande wordende aangedaen . . . [Middelburg, 1744.] 28 pp.

> Petition against hindrances inflicted on the Middelburg company in the African slave trade by the West India company.

1063   MEMORIE uyt name ende van wegens d'ondergeschrevene boekhouders en reders, zoo voor haar selve, als vervangende de verdere reders ende geinteresseerdens in de vaart en handel op de kusten van Africa, alle woonagtig binnen de provincie van Holland, overgegeven aan d'Ed: Mog: Heeren Commissarissen van haar Ed: Gr: Mog: de Heeren Staaten van Holland en West-Friesland . . . ten eynde gemainctineerd te werden by de vrye vaart op de kusten van Africa . . . [Amsterdam, 1744.] 25; 46 pp.

> Petition of separate traders for the maintenance of open trade to West Africa, with enclosures on the slave trade.

1064   NEDERLANDSE WEST-INDISCHE COMPAGNIE
Missive van bewindhebberen van de Westindische Compagnie over den handel op de kust van Africa en het permitteeren van den slaavenhandel aan haare bedienden aldaar. [Amsterdam, 1744.] 7 pp.

> Report to the States-General on permits for slave trading given to company servants, in reply to complaints by other traders.

1065   The PRESENT state of the British and French trade to Africa and America consider'd and compar'd . . . E. Comyns, London, 1745. 56 pp.

> With 'Proposals to revive, secure and extend the African trade', suggesting that the Royal African Company should be wound up.

1066   The AFRICAN trade, the great pillar and support of the British plantation trade in America: shewing, that our loss, by being beat out of all the foreign markets for sugar and indigo by the French, has been owing to the neglect of our African trade; which only can supply our colonies with negroes, for the making of sugars, and all other plantation produce: that the support and security of the negroe-trade depends wholly on the due and effectual support of the Royal African Company of England, which has hitherto preserved this invaluable trade to these kingdoms: that the difficulties and discouragements which the said company labours under, threaten the absolute loss of the negroe trade to this nation; and consequently the total ruin of all British plantations in America . . . (Signed: A British merchant.) J. Robinson, London, 1745. 44 pp.

By Malachy Postlethwayt. Urges Parliament to assist the Company in protecting British commerce in West Africa.

1067 DUFRESNE DE FRANCHEVILLE, Joseph
Histoire de la Compagnie des Indes, avec les titres de ses concessions et privilèges . . . De Bure l'aîné, Paris, 1746. 660 pp.

1068 The NATIONAL and private advantages of the African trade considered: being an enquiry, how far it concerns the trading interest of Great Britain, effectually to support and maintain the forts and settlements in Africa; belonging to the Royal African Company of England . . . John & Paul Knapton, London, 1746. 128 pp. map.

By Malachy Postlethwayt. Shows the necessity of the slave trade to the British economy as an 'inexhaustible fund of wealth and naval power.'

1069 SEASONABLE observations on the trade to Africa. In a letter to a member of parliament. London, 1748. 15 pp.

Proposals for reform of the African trade.

1070 ANSWERS to the objections against the proposals of the Royal African Company, for settling the trade to Africa. In a second letter to a member of parliament. (Signed: Philopatris.) [London, 1748.] 4 pp.

1071 SAVARY, Jacques
Le parfait négociant . . . Nouvelle édition, revûe & corrigée . . . Par M. Philemont-Louis Savary . . . Veuve Estienne & Fils, Paris, 1749, 42. 2 vol.

The chapters on the African trade include a new section on the history of the companies 1673–1719. See (975).

1072 A DETECTION of the proceedings and practices of the directors of the Royal African Company of England, from their first establishment by charter in the year 1672, to the present year 1748. With remarks on the use and importance of the British forts and settlements on the coast of Guiney, and the necessity of speedily putting them upon a proper establishment. T. Warner, London, 1749. viii, 51 pp.

The forts are necessary to protect trade but should be handed over by the company, which has mismanaged its affairs, to the Board of Trade or special commissioners. See (1073, 1079).

1073 An ANTIDOTE to expel the poison contained in an anonymous pamphlet, lately published, entitled, A detection of the proceedings and practices of the directors of the Royal African Company of England . . . J. Roberts, London, 1749. 56 pp.

Defence of the Royal African Company against accusations in (1072).

1074 POSTLETHWAYT, Malachy
Considerations on the revival of the Royal-British-assiento; between His Catholick-Majesty, and the honourable the South-Sea Company. With an humble attempt to unite the African-trade to that of the South-Sea Company, by act of Parliament. John & Paul Knapton, London, 1749. vii, 47 pp.

Proposes that the British slave trade should be vested in the South-Sea Company; now that peace is restored, Spain needs to import African slaves again.

1075 The ALARM-BELL: or, considerations on the present dangerous state of the sugar colonies . . . To which are added, queries and answers relating to the African trade. W. Owen, London, 1749. 8 pp.

'Query III. Why are the negroes from the Gold Coast and Whydah the most valuable, and so necessary to the subsistence of sugar-plantations?'

1076 A SHORT view of the dispute between the merchants of London, Bristol, and Leverpool, and the advocates of a new joint-stock company, concerning the regulation of the African trade. London, 1750. 18 pp.

Opposes the formation of a new London-based company; free trade will provide cheaper slaves.

1077 NEDERLANDSE WEST-INDISCHE COMPAGNIE
Missive van de representanten en bewindhebberen van de Westindische Compagnie te Amsterdam, houdende der selver consideratien op eene missive van de hooftparticipanten ter Kaamere Zeeland, rakende de private vaart op de riviere van Ysequebo. [Amsterdam, 1751.] 28 pp.

Address to the States-General on the company's trade between West Africa and Surinam.

1078 COMMERCIE COMPAGNIE VAN MIDDELBURG
Requeste van directeuren van de Commercie-Compagnie te Middelburg en de gesaamentlijke kooplieden te Vlissingen, handel dryvende op de kust van Africa. [Middelburg? 1751.] 38 pp.

Petitions to the States-General (Sept. 1750–July 1751) for the abolition of the privileges of the West India Company.

1079 The DETECTOR detected: or, state of affairs on the Gold Coast, and conduct of the present managers consider'd. With a comparison of the trade in the late company's time—and benefits since received by the open plan for extending the same . . . By J. S. G. last commandant of Commenda, under the Royal African Company. W. Owen, London, 1753. 61 pp.

Answer to (1072), regretting that Postlethwayt's suggestions for company monopoly were ignored; the trade has not improved since the company was abolished.

1080 A GENERAL treatise of naval trade and commerce, as founded on the laws and statutes of this realm . . . The second edition, with many considerable additions . . . Henry Lintot, [London, 1753]. 2 vol.

Includes a chapter on the Royal African Company. (First published 1739.)

1081 *ESSAI sur les intérêts du commerce maritime. Par M. D***. La Haye, 1754. 258 pp.

By P. A. O'Heguerty, comte de Magnières. See (1084).

1082 SOME facts regarding the conduct of the African Committee, and the chief agents and officers by them appointed to have the management of affairs on the Gold Coast and Whydah in Africa. [London, 1755?] 3 pp.

Evidence of illegal actions by employees of the Company of Merchants trading to Africa against English rivals in the slave trade.

1083 CLARKE, William
Observations on the late and present conduct of the French, with regard to their encroachments upon the British colonies in North America . . . To which is added, wrote by another hand; Observations concerning the increase of mankind, peopling of countries, &c. S. Kneeland, Boston, 1755. iv, 47, 15 pp.

The second part, written by Benjamin Franklin 1751, argues that the importation of African slaves has hindered the development of colonial America; free labour is cheaper than slave labour.

1084 'ESSAI sur les intérêts du commerce maritime. Par M. D.' In: HUME, David. Discours politiques, vol. 2 (Amsterdam, 1756), pp. 4–116.

By P. A. O'Heguerty, comte de Magnières. Describes the French slave trade between West Africa and the Caribbean. Reprint of (1081).

1085 POSTLETHWAYT, Malachy
A short state of the progress of the French trade and navegation . . . Humbly inscribed to His Royal Highness William Duke of Cumberland. J. Knapton, London, 1756. 86 pp.

Warns about the growth of French commerce, including that in slaves from West Africa, which will be dangerous to Britain unless checked.

1086 POSTLETHWAYT, Malachy
Britain's commercial interest explained and improved; in a series of dissertations on several important branches of her trade and police . . . D. Browne (etc.), London, 1757. 2 vol.

Includes chapters on the French trade with Africa, reproducing official documents on the Guinea trade 1716–51; and on the English African trade, suggesting that the slave trade be carried on by separate traders but all other trade by the East India Company.

1087 POSTLETHWAYT, Malachy
The importance of the African expedition considered: with copies of memorials, as drawn up originally,

and presented to the Ministry; to induce them to take possession of the French forts and settlements in the river Senagal, as well as all other on the coast of Africa . . . M. Cooper, London, 1758. xxiv, 99 pp.

The African slave trade must be controlled by Britain to deny supplies to the French colonies.

1088 An INQUIRY concerning the trade, commerce, and policy of Jamaica . . . With an appendix, containing, a register of all the ships that have arrived at Jamaica, with the number of negroes they imported, into, and exported from that island for each year, from 1702, to 1749, inclusive . . . T. Kinnersly; G. Woodfal, London, 1759. 92 pp.

1089 REQUESTE van verscheide kooplieden en rheeders te Rotterdam, om by het vernieuwen van het octroy voor de Westindische Compagnie te erlangen voorsiening ontrent eenige pointen tot de commercie op de Westindien specteerende . . . [Amsterdam, 1760.] 3 pp.

Complaint made to the States of Holland 27 March 1760 about the burdensome duties levied by the company from separate traders. See (1090).

1090 NEDERLANDSE WEST-INDISCHE COMPAGNIE
Advis van bewindhebberen van de Westindische Compagnie op de Requeste van verscheide kooplieden en rheeders te Rotterdam . . . [Amsterdam, 1760.] 15 pp.

Report of 6 May 1760 in reply to (1089); the delays of the private slavers are not caused by the duties but by local wars in Africa.

1091 NEDERLANDSE WEST-INDISCHE COMPAGNIE
Advis van bewindhebberen der Westindische Compagnie ter præsidiale Kamer Amsterdam op de Requeste der negotianten, boekhouders, rheeders en fabriquanten, ingeseetenen van Zeeland . . . om ampliatien en veranderingen ten aansien hunner handel by vernieuwing van het octroy voor de Westindische Compagnie; met de voorschreeve Requeste en Memorie selve . . . [Amsterdam, 1760.] 20, 9 pp.

Includes a 'Memorie over de vaart en commercie langs en op de kusten van Africa en America'. (Dated 3 Sept. 1760.)

1092 HOLLAND: Staaten
Rapport over de continuatie van het octroy voor de Westindische Compagnie . . . en op de Requesten van de kooplieden van Rotterdam en Zeeland, alle tot de vaart op de West relatie hebbende. Overgenoomen 1 November 1760. [Amsterdam? 1760.] 6 pp.

The octroi was extended for thirty years in December 1761.

1093 ROTTERDAM: Stad
Memorie van consideratien der Heeren Gedeputeerden der Stad Rotterdam, op het Rapport den 1 November 1760 ter vergadering van haar Edele Groot Mog. uitgebragt, raakende de continuatie van het octroy voor de Westindische Compagnie. [Den Haag? 1760.] 14 pp.

Claim for a reduction of duties and the right of separate traders to trade to Angola; with notes on the economics of slave trading. See (1094).

1094 AMSTERDAM: Stad
Memorie van contra-consideratien en remarques van de Heeren Gedeputeerden der Stad Amsterdam, op de Memorie van consideratien by de Heeren Gedeputeerden der Stad Rotterdam . . . raakende de continuatie van het octroy voor de Westindische Compagnie . . . [Amsterdam? 1761.] 8, 2 pp.

Reply to (1089), dated 9 May 1761. The slave trade has not declined; the number of ships involved in 1760 was greater than any year since 1746.

1095 THOUGHTS on trade in general, our West-Indian in particular, our continental colonies, Canada, Guadaloupe, and the preliminary articles of peace . . . (Signed: Ignotus.) John Wilkie, London, 1763. 86 pp.

The West Indian and African trades are interdependent; Guadaloupe is an important market for slaves.

1096 CONSIDERATIONS on the present peace, as far as it is relative to the colonies, and the African trade. W. Bristow, London, 1763. iv, 68 pp.

The African trade must be reorganised in favour of the British colonies against their defeated French rivals; with arguments 'to remove the prejudices of . . . tender-minded persons against the Negro-trade.'

1097 Le COMMERCE de l'Amérique par Marseille, ou, explication des lettres-patentes du roi, portant reglement pour le commerce qui se fait de Marseille aux iles françoises de l'Amérique, données au mois de février 1719. Et les lettres-patents du roi, pour la liberté du commerce à la Côte de Guinée, données à Paris au mois de janvier 1716. Avec les reglemens que ledit commerce a occasionnés, par un citadin . . . Avignon, 1764. 2 vol. illus, maps.

> By A. Chambon. Includes chapters on the West African slave trade. (Republished as: Le guide du commerce del 'Amérique, Avignon, 1777.) See also (1108).

1098 *GAIGNAT DE L'AULNAIS, C. F.
Le guide du commerce . . . Despilly, Durand & Valade, Paris, [1764]. 444, iv pp.

> Pt. 4 describes the method of trading in slaves between Africa and America.

1099 HIPPISLEY, John
Essays. I. On the populousness of Africa. II. On the trade at the forts on the Gold Coast. III. On the necessity of erecting a fort at Cape Apollonia. T. Lownds, London, 1764. viii, 65 pp.

> Millions of slaves have been exported during the past century but Africa could supply millions more 'to the end of time'; the forts are needed to protect British trade from the Dutch. Moral arguments against the slave trade are irrelevant as 'the impossibility of doing without slaves in the West-Indies will always prevent this traffick being dropped'.

1100 GUSTMEYERS ENKE OG H. F. BARGUM
Plan ueber die Einrichtung eines Sclaven-Handels und einer Zucker-Raffinaderie, unter Direction der Wittwe Gustmeyers & H. F. Bargum in Copenhagen. [Copenhagen, 1765.] 12 pp.

> Scheme dated 9 April 1764 for a company (afterwards Dansk Guineisk Handels-Societet) to carry slaves from Africa to the Danish West Indies and establish a sugar refinery in Copenhagen. (Text in German, Danish and French.) See (938).

1101 NEDERLANDSE WEST-INDISCHE COMPAGNIE
Bericht van den repræsentant van zyne doorluchtige Hoogheid en bewindhebberen van de ge-octroyeerde West-Indische Compagnie ter præsidiaale Kamer Zeeland, op de requeste van zommige borgers en inwoonders der rivieren Essequebo en Demerary, den 19 December 1769 . . . om den vryen invoer van Engelsche en andere vreemde slaven in die colonie &c. . . . [Middelburg, 1770.] 129 pp.

> Opposes the demand of the settlers in Surinam to allow the importation of slaves by foreign traders; with an appendix of documents, 1753–69.

1102 NEDERLANDSE WEST-INDISCHE COMPAGNIE
Berigt van den repræsentant zyner doorlugtige Hoogheid en bewindhebberen der West-Indische Compagnie ter Kamer Zeeland, zoo nopens het rapport van H:H:Mog:Gedeputeerden van den 3 October 1771, belangende den in voer van slaven uit de Engelsche eilanden in de colonie van Essequebo en Demerary, als over het op den 14 daar aan deswegens uitgebragt advis der Heeren Staten van Holland en West-Friesland . . . [Amsterdam? 1771.] 9 pp.

> Reply to demands for the African trade to be opened to all Dutch citizens.

1103 A TREATISE upon the trade from Great-Britain to Africa; humbly recommended to the attention of government. By an African merchant. R. Baldwin, London, 1772. 64, 124 pp.

> By John Peter Demarin. The African trade is 'the main spring of the machine which sets every wheel in motion' in Britain; the legality of the slave trade is upheld against Hargrave and Benezet. The appendix includes articles by 'Mercator', 'West India merchant' and 'Planter' justifying the slave trade. (Reviewed in: MR, vol. 48, Jan. 1773, pp. 42–49.) See (1793).

1104 The UNIVERSAL dictionary of trade and commerce: with large additions and improvements . . . By Malachy Postlethwayt, Esq; the fourth edition. W. Strahan (etc.), London, 1774. 2 vol.

> New edition of (1057b), virtually rewritten by Postlethwayt.

1105 ROBERTS, John
Extracts from an account of the state of the British forts, on the Gold Coast of Africa, taken by Captain Cotton, of his Majesty's ship, Pallas, in May,

and June, 1777. To which are added, observations, by John Roberts, governor of Cape Coast Castle . . . J. Bew, London, 1778. 44 pp.

Attack on the 'African Committee' for mismanaging the important trade in West Africa; less than half as many slaves are now exported as in the time of the Royal African Company.

1106 ROBERTS, John
Cursory observations on the trade to Africa. [London? 1778.] 8 pp.

The committee of merchants have almost destroyed the British slave trade; Parliament should deprive them of the forts in West Africa and vest them in the crown.

1107 *REAL COMPAÑÍA DE LA HABANA
Manifiesto, é informe legal por la Real Compañía de la Habana, en el pleito pendiente en el Supremo Consejo de Indias, con Don Cornelio Copingert, D. Juan Wilmont, y consortes, de nación Ingleses: sobre que se les condene al resarcimiento de daños y perjuicios causados á dicha Real Compañía por la falta de cumplimiento á las contratas que dichos Ingleses celebraron para la introducción de 7400 negros. Joaquin Ibarra, Madrid, 1779. 17 pp.

1108 *TRAITÉ général du commerce de l'Amérique contenant . . . la législation du commerce négrier, les mœurs des esclaves nègres, l'état des marchandises propres au service des esclaves, les précautions à prendre pour les conduire en Amérique . . . Par M.C**, ancien receveur des fermes du roi. M.-M. Rey, Amsterdam; Mossy, Marseille. 1783. 2 vol.

By A. Chambon. New edition of (1097).

1109a ÉMÉRIGON, Balthazard Marie
Traité des assurances et des contrats à la grosse. Jean Mossy, Marseille, 1783. 2 vol.

Translated as:

1109b*An essay on maritime loans . . . with notes . . . By John E. Hall . . . Philip H. Nicklin & Co., Baltimore; (etc.), 1811. 313 pp.

Includes sections on the insurance of slaves for death, revolt or jettison at sea.

1110 DU commerce des colonies, ses principes et ses lois, la paix est le temps de régler & d'agrandir le commerce. [Paris?] 1785. 63 pp.

Attributed to M. R. Hilliard d'Auberteuil. With a chapter 'De la traite des noirs'; if another 40,000 slaves were imported by foreign traders the slave trade could be abolished after five years.

1111 MÉMOIRE sur le commerce étranger avec les colonies françaises de l'Amérique; présenté à la Chambre d'agriculture du Cap, le 17 février 1784. Cuchet, Paris, 1785. 51 pp.

St. Dominigue has lost a million slaves since 1727 through harsh treatment; French merchants' prices are double those of the English, from whom they should learn how to conduct the slave trade.

1112 LETTRES critiques et politiques sur les colonies & le commerce des villes maritimes de France, adressées à G. T. Raynal. Par M.***. Genève, 1785. 14, 292 pp.

By P. U. Dubuisson and J. B. Dubuc. Letter IX: 'De la traite des nègres'; the slave trade is vicious and should be left to foreigners.

1113 RÉFLEXIONS sur la colonie françoise de la Guyane [Paris?] 1788. 52 pp.

The government should pay for about 3,000 African slaves to be introduced annually to populate Guyane until they are numerous enough to reproduce themselves.

1114 DU commerce des colonies. Ph.-D. Pierres, Versailles, [1789]. 43 pp.

Suggests regulation of the slave trade to the French colonies to meet the challenge of British competition.

1115 BARBÉ-MARBOIS, François de, *marquis*
Remontrances de Monsieur de Marbois, intendant de Saint-Domingue, contre l'arrêt d'enregistrement de l'acte intitulé: Ordonnance de M. le gouverneur-général, concernant la liberté du commerce pour la partie du sud de Saint-Domingue. Louis, [Port-au-Prince? 1789.] 11 pp.

The ordinance admitting foreign slavers is illegal (it was annulled 2 July 1789); such competition could ruin the French slave trade. See (955).

1116 LOWE, John
Liberty or death. A tract. By which is vindicated the obvious practicability of

trading to the coasts of Guinea, for its natural products, in lieu of the slave-trade, much more to the interest of the merchants in particular, and the kingdoms of England, Scotland, and Ireland in general. J. Harrop, Manchester, 1789. 56 pp.

Documents of a slaving voyage from Liverpool to Benin showing that abolition of the slave trade would in fact benefit European commerce and Africa.

1117 *DUPRÉ, Joseph
Mémoire sur le commerce en général et celui du Languedoc, dans ses rapports avec les Échelles du Levant, la Compagnie des Indes, les colonies et la traite des noirs. Paris, 1790. 35 pp.

1118 CONSIDÉRATIONS sur les moyens d'augmenter les produits des isles françoises de l'Amérique, par l'introduction des nègres qui leur manquent. [Paris, 1790?] 35 pp.

Foreign traders should be allowed to supply the French colonies with slaves over ten years; it would be glorious for France to take the lead in abolishing the slave trade.

1119 *CASSAN, ——
Considérations sur les rapports qui doivent exister entre les colonies et les metropoles, et particulièrement sur l'état actuel du commerce français dans les Antilles . . . sur les avantages qui résulteront . . . de l'établissement d'un commerce libre . . . sur le danger d'affranchir les nègres dans ce moment. Guillot, Paris, 1790. 127 pp.

1120 PLAN de constitution pour la colonie de Saint-Domingue, suivi d'une dissertation sur le commerce des colonies, relative à ce plan; et de considérations générales sur la navigation et le commerce de France. Par M. Ch. de Ch******, député de Saint-Domingue à l'Assemblée nationale. J. B. N. Crapart, Paris, 1791. 140 pp.

By Charles de Chabanon. To obtain slaves more cheaply additional French trading posts are needed in Africa, and the slave trade should be opened to foreign merchants, e.g. American.

1121 PRÉCIS pour les grands propriétaires des colonies françaises de l'Amérique. Contre les divers écrits des négociants des villes maritimes du royaume. [Paris, 1791?] 8 pp.

The French colonies need at least half a million more slaves but better

treatment of them would in a few years make the slave trade from Guinea unnecessary.

1122 ARNOULD, Ambroise Marie
De la balance du commerce et des rélations commerciales extérieures de la France, dans toutes les parties du globe, particulièrement à la fin du régne de Louis XIV, et au moment de la révolution. Buisson, Paris, 1791. 3 vol.

With notes on the development of the slave trade 1672–1788.

1123 *NUEVA COMPAÑIA DE COMERCIO
Noticia de la Nueva Compañia de Comercio establecida para consignaciones pasivas de negros bozales con la aprobación y autoridad del gobierno y capitanía general de la Havana. Havana, [1792]. 12 pp.

1124 *POLCAÑI, Santiago
Reflexiones sobre el establecimiento de la Nueva Compañía de Comercio para consignaciones pasivas de negros bozales en la Havana . . . [Havana,] 1792. 20 pp.

1125a CUNHA DE AZEREDO COUTINHO, José Joaquim da
Ensaio economico sobre o comercio de Portugal e suas colonias . . . Lisboa, 1794. iii, 153 pp.

Translated as:

1125b An essay on the commerce and products of the Portuguese colonies in South America, especially the Brazils. London, 1807. v, 198 pp.

The slave labour needed in Brazil must be obtained from the Portuguese colonies in Africa. (Second edition 1816 contains further notes on the slave trade.)

1126 A GENERAL and descriptive history of the ancient and present state, of the town of Liverpool . . . together with a circumstantial account of the true causes of its extensive African trade . . . R. Phillips, Liverpool; W. Richardson, London, 1795. vi, 301 pp.

By James Wallace. Section 10 describes the development of the Liverpool trade to Africa from about 1730.

1127 OXHOLM, Peter Lotharius
De Danske Vestindiske Öers Tilstand i Henseende til Population, Cultur og Finance-Forfatning, i Anledning af nogle Breve fra St. Croix, indrykkede i

det Politiske og Physiske Magazin for Marts og April Maaneder 1797 . . . Johan Frederik Schultz, Kiöbenhavn, 1797. 84 pp.

Describes the government loans to planters to buy slaves in the ten years from 1792 until abolition of the trade in 1802 and the effects of British imports on the price and quality of slaves.

1128 LIMOCHEL, F.
La France demandant ses colonies, ou réclamations de l'agriculture, du commerce, des manufactures, des artistes & des ouvriers de tous les départemens: adressées au Corps législatif, au Directoire, & à toutes les autorités constituées de la République françoise. Volland, Paris; Pierre Beaume, Bordeaux, an V [1797]. xii, 99 pp.

Ch. 16: 'De la traite à la côte d'Afrique, du transport des esclaves, & de leur introduction dans les colonies'. The government should supervise a renewed slave trade.

1129 CHARPENTIER-COSSIGNY, Joseph François
Moyens d'amélioration et de restauration, proposés au gouvernement et aux habitans des colonies; ou mélanges politiques, économiques, agricoles, et commerciaux, etc., relatifs aux colonies. Marchant, Paris, an XI–1802. 3 vol.

Regrets the emancipation of slaves in the French colonies in 1794 and prints a 'Mémoire sur la côte orientale d'Afrique' written by the trader Morice in 1777, proposing a slave trading establishment at Kilwa.

1130 BAUDRY DES LOZIÈRES, Louis Nicolas
Second voyage à la Louisiane . . . Charles, Paris, an XI.-1803. 2 vol.

Includes notes on the slave trade in the Congo area, with advice on the trade goods needed to purchase slaves.

1131 RECHERCHES économiques et statistiques sur le département de la Loire Inférieure. Annuaire de l'an XI. (Signed; J.-B.H.) M.me Malassis, Nantes, an XII [1804]. xiv, 511 pp.

By Jean Baptiste Huet de Coetlizan. With a section on the part played by Nantes in the trade to West Africa and the Antilles, mainly in the years 1786–90 when 12,000 slaves were purchased annually.

1132 DICTIONNAIRE universel de commerce, banque, manufactures, douanes, pêche, navigation marchande; des lois et administration du commerce . . . F. Busson; (etc.), Paris, an treizième [1805]. 2 vol.

Contains articles on the slave trade under 'Nègre' and 'Traite des nègres'.

1133 YOUNG, *Sir* William
The West-India common-place book: compiled from parliamentary and official documents; shewing the interest of Great Britain in its sugar colonies . . . Richard Phillips, London, 1807. xxi, 256 pp.

Ch. 1: 'On the African slave trade'. Shows that the Liverpool slave trade doubled 1787–1804 while that of Bristol and London declined.

H

J. ECONOMIC HISTORY

1134a *HUMBOLDT, Alexander, *Freiherr* von
Essai politique sur l'île de Cuba . . .
Gide fils, Paris, 1826. 2 vol. map.

Translated as:

1134b 'Political essay on the island of Cuba.'
In his: Personal narrative of travels
to the equinoctial regions of the New
Continent, during the years 1799–
1804, vol. 7 (London, 1829), ch. 28,
pp. 1–335.

> Contains statistics, and criticisms,
> of the Cuban slave trade. (Reviewed
> in: EcR, ser. 3, vol. 4, 1830, pp.
> 22–37.)

1135 LE PELLETIER DE SAINT-REMY, R.
Saint-Domingue. Étude et solution
nouvelle de la question haïtienne.
Arthur Bertrand, Paris, 1846. 2 vol.

> With a chapter on the slave trade
> before 1790.

1136 The CONQUERORS of the New
World and their bondsmen. Being a
narrative of the principal events which
led to negro slavery in the West Indies
and America. William Pickering, London, 1848, 52. 2 vol.

> By Sir Arthur Helps.

1137 ALBERTI, Christian Carl
'Den danske Slavehandels Historie.'
(Nyt Historisk Tidskrift, Kiøbenhavn,
ser. 2, vol. 3, 1850, pp. 201–44.)

> Account of the Danish slave trade
> 1674–1803.

1138 SLAVERY among the Puritans. A
letter to the Rev. Moses Stuart. (Signed:
Amicus.) Charles C. Little & James
Brown, Boston, 1850. 42 pp.

> The New England slave trade cannot
> be blamed wholly on Britain; the
> colonists took an active part in it.

1139 *AFRICAN slave trade in Jamaica, and
comparative treatment of slaves. Read
before the Maryland Historical Society, October, 1854. [Baltimore,] 1854.
14 pp.

> By Moses Sheppard.

1140 'CARTA de los frailes gerónimos al
Rey manifestando haber hecho algunos pueblos en donde se recogiesan
los indios, dando noticia del estrago
que habia de las viruelas en aquella
isla y en la de Puerto Rico, y pidiendo
para el remedio de la gran perdida de
aquellas islas que pasasen á elles
esclavos negros sin imposiciones.' *In*:
COLECCIÓN de varios documentos
para la historia de la Florida y tierras
adyacentes, vol. 1 (Londres, 1857),
pp. 44–45.

> Letter from Española Feb, 1519,
> signed by fathers Luis de Figueroa
> and Alfonso de Santo Domingo,
> requesting free importation of African
> slaves.

1141 *DUNBAR, Edward Ely
'History of the rise and decline of
commercial slavery in America, with
reference to the future of Mexico.'
In his: The Mexican papers, ser. 1,
no. 5 (New York, 1861), pp. 177–279.

1142 MENDIBURU, Manuel de
'Ojeada sobre la esclavitud bajo el
régimen colonial.' (Revista de Lima,
vol. 5, 1862, pp. 513–30.)

> Includes notes on African slave im-
> ports to Peru, which ended in 1817.

1143 OWEN, Robert Dale
The wrong of slavery, the right of
emancipation and the future of the
African race in the United States.
Philadelphia, 1864. 246 pp.

> Includes chapters on the slave trade
> from Africa.

1144 'La INTRODUZIONE dei negri in
America.' (CC, ser. 6, vol. 5, 1866,
pp. 536–49.)

> By V. Steccanella. On the first African
> slave imports to the Spanish West
> Indies 1502–17.

1145 'I PORTOGHESI e la tratta nel
secolo XVI.' (CC, ser. 6, vol. 6, 1866,
pp. 155–71.)

> By V. Steccanella. Notes on the slave
> trade and Roman Catholic attitudes
> to it.

1146 'Le COMPAGNIE e la tratta.' (CC, ser, 6, vol. 6, 1866, pp. 671–89.)

By V. Steccanella. Notes on the regulated slave trade of the 17th-18th centuries.

1147 ARMAS Y CÉSPEDES, Francisco de
De la esclavitud en Cuba. Madrid, 1866. 479 pp.

With chapters on the slave trade and its abolition.

1148 MARQUES PERDIGÃO MALHEIRO, Agostinho
A escravidão no Brasil. Ensaio historico-juridico-social. Rio de Janeiro, 1866–67. 3 pt.

Pt. 3: 'Africanos.' History of the slave trade to Brazil and its extinction, with an appendix of laws and documents relating to the slave trade, 1682–1852.

1149 WASHBURN, Emory
Slavery as it once prevailed in Massachusetts. A lecture for the Massachusetts Historical Society . . . Boston, 1869. 35 pp.

On slavery and the slave trade before 1780.

1150 *AGUILERA, Francisco Vicente *and* CESPEDES, Ramón
Notes about Cuba . . . [New York, 1872.] 54 pp.

Pt. 1: 'African slave trade.'

1151 *MASON, George Champlin
'The African slave trade in colonial times.' (American Historical Record, Philadelphia, vol. 1, 1873, no. 1, pp. 312–19; no. 8, pp. 338–45.)

Account of the New England slave trade.

1152 SARAIVA, Francisco Justiniano, *Cardinal*
'Nota sobre a origem da escravidão e trafico dos negros.' *In*: Obras completas do cardeal Saraiva, vol. 5 (Lisboa, 1875), pp. 323–47.

Essay written 1829 to show that Portugal merely redirected the medieval slave trade to America.

1153 WILLIAMSON, Joseph
'Slavery in Maine.' (Collections of the Maine Historical Society, Bath, Me, vol. 7, 1876, pp. 207–16.)

Few slaves were imported in the 18th century compared with Massachusetts.

1154 CARVALHO, Antonio Pedro de
Das origens da escravidão moderna em Portugal. Lisboa, 1877. 57 pp.

The Portuguese only extended the slave trade to America.

1155 KIDDER, Frederic
'The slave trade in Massachusetts.' (New-England Historical and Genealogical Register, Boston, vol. 31, 1877, pp. 75–76.)

Letter signed by John Saffin and others showing that a Boston ship was sent to Africa for slaves in 1860.

1156 SACO, José Antonio
Historia de la esclavitud de la raza africana en el Nuevo Mundo y en especial en los paises américo-hispanos. Barcelona, 1879. 442 pp.

Unfinished history of the slave trade to Spanish America until 1789. Supplementary chapters were included in an edition published by Vidal Morales y Morales at Havana in 1892. (Reviewed in: HAHR, vol. 24, 1944, pp. 452–57.)

1157 WILLIAMS, George Washington
History of the negro race in America from 1619 to 1880. Negroes as slaves, as soldiers, and as citizens . . . New York, 1883. 2 vol.

Estimates that over 14,600,000 African slaves were imported until 1860.

1158 LIVERPOOL and slavery: an historical account of the Liverpool–African slave trade . . . Compiled from various sources and authentic documents . . . By a genuine "Dicky Sam". Liverpool, 1884. xii, 137 pp. illus.

1159 PARADA, Alonso de
'Relación del estado en que se hallan las islas Española, Fernandina y Santiago, presentada al Consejo de Indias por el bachiller Alonso de Parada, con propuesta de acudir á su remedio introduciendo negros esclavos.' *In*: COLECCIÓN de documentos inéditos relativos al descubrimiento, conquista y organización de las antiguas posesiones españolas de ultramar, ser. 2, vol. 1 (Madrid, 1885), pp. 428–40.

Document of 1527 requesting the Spanish government to negotiate with Portugal to supply up to 4,800 African slaves, equivalent to the number already in the Caribbean islands.

1160 DEANE, Charles
The connection of Massachusetts with

slavery and the slave trade . . . Worcester, Mass., 1886. 34 pp.

Britain had first introduced African slaves, but Massachusetts participated in the trade. (Also published in: PAAS, vol. 4, 1886, pp. 191–222.)

1161 'A SLAVE-trader's letter-book.' (NAR, vol. 143, 1886, pp. 447–61.)

Extracts of letters by the slave trader C. A. L. Lamar of Savannah 1855–60; possibly a hoax. See (2856).

1162 BROCK, Robert Alonzo
'The fourth charter of the Royal African Company of England, September, 1672, with prefatory note, exhibiting the past relation of Virginia to African slavery.' (Collections of the Virginia Historical Society, Richmond, n.s., vol. 6, 1887, pp. 1–60.)

With the text of the charter and other documents of 1674.

1163 GARNAULT, Émile
Le commerce rochelais au XVIIIe siècle . . . La Rochelle, 1887–1900. 5 vol.

With a chapter on the slave trade and a 'Mémoire de la Commission de commerce de la Rochelle,' 1802, suggesting the re-establishment of a regulated slave trade from Africa.

1164 SANTIAGO DE CUBA: Cabildo
'Carta del Cabildo de Santiago á S.M. refiriendo las arbitrariedades del gobernador Gonzalo de Guzmán y del obispo; encareciendo la necesidad de introducir 700 negros en la isla, por haber muerto de la pestilencia una tercera parte de los indios que había.' In: COLECCIÓN de documentos inéditos relativos al descubrimiento, conquista y organización de las antiguas posesiones españolas de ultramar, ser. 2, vol. 4 (Madrid, 1888), pp. 150–67.

Letter of Sept. 1530 to the king of Spain.

1165 KNAPP, Georg Friedrich
'Der Ursprung der Sklaverei in den Kolonien.' (Archiv für soziale Gesetzgebung und Statistik, Tübingen, vol. 2, 1889, pp. 129–45.)

On the development of the African slave trade to South America in the 16th century.

1166 WEEDEN, William Babcock
'The early African slave-trade in New England.' (PAAS, vol. 5, 1889, pp. 107–28.)

Economics of the 18th century slave trade.

1167 WEEDEN, William Babcock
Economic and social history of New England 1620–1789. Boston & New York, 1890. 2 vol.

Ch. 12: 'The African slave-trade 1708–1764'.

1168 STAKELY, Charles Averett
'Introduction of the negro into the United states. Florida, not Virginia, the first state to receive him.' (MAH, vol. 26, 1891, pp. 349–63.)

African slaves were introduced by the Spaniards in 1565.

1169 BONNASSIEUX, Louis Jean Pierre Marie
Les grandes compagnies de commerce. Étude pour servir à l'histoire de colonisation. Paris, 1892. 562 pp.

Includes the history of the African companies of the Netherlands, England, France, Denmark, Spain, Portugal, and Brandenburg.

1170 BRÉARD, Charles
'Notes sur Saint-Domingue tirées des papiers d'un armateur du Havre (1780–1802).' (Société Normande de Géographie, Rouen, Bulletin, vol. 14, 1892, pp. 168–88.)

Information on the slave trade of Le Havre in the 18th century.

1171 JANVIER, Thomas Allibone
'New York slave-traders.' (HMM, vol. 90, 1895, pp. 293–305; illus.)

Historical notes on the slave trade 1628–1808.

1172 HÄBLER, Konrad
'Die Anfänge der Sclaverei in Amerika.' (Zeitschrift für Social- und Wirtschaftsgeschichte, Weimar, vol. 4, 1896, pp. 176–223.)

On German involvement in the 'asiento' of 1528 and the Spanish American slave trade to 1817.

1173 CAWSTON, George and KEANE, Augustus Henry
The early chartered companies (A.D. 1296–1858). London, New York, 1896. xi, 329 pp.

Ch. 11: 'Summary account of the Guinea (Royal African) and minor chartered companies.'

1174 WILLIAMS, Gomer
History of the Liverpool privateers

and letters of marque with an account of the Liverpool slave trade. London; Liverpool, 1897. xv, 718 pp.

Pt. 2: 'The Liverpool slave trade' (pp. 465–658). (Reviewed in: Athenæum, London, 1898, pp. 81–82.) See (1246).

1175 PEYTRAUD, Lucien Pierre
L'esclavage aux Antilles françaises avant 1789 d'après des documents inédits des Archives coloniales. Paris, 1897. xxii, 472 pp. bibl. pp. xiii–xxii.

Includes chapters on the French slave trade from Africa 1664–1831.

1176 DOORMAN, J. G.
'Die Niederländisch-West-Indische Compagnie an der Goldküste . . .' (Tijdschrift voor Indische Taal-, Land- en Volkenkunde, Batavia, vol. 40, 1898, pp. 388–496; map.)

Includes material on the Dutch slave trade 1625–1791.

1177 'LIVERPOOL: its privateers and its slave-trade.' (CJ, ser. 6, vol. 1, 1898, pp. 241–44.)

1178 *BRANDT, L.
'Massachusetts slave trade.' (NEM, n.s., vol. 21, 1899, pp. 83–96.)

1179 SYLVAIN, Benito
Étude sur le traitement des indigènes dans les colonies d'exploitation . . . Paris, 1899. 347 pp.

Doctoral thesis, including chapters on the slave trade.

1180 SPEARS, John Randolph
The American slave-trade. An account of its origin, growth and suppression . . . New York, 1900. xvii, 232 pp. illus.

Popular work on the slave trade 1619–1862 and its suppression.

1181 *AUGÉARD, Eugène
Étude sur la traite des noirs avant 1790 au point de vue du commerce nantais. Nantes, 1900.

1182 COLLINS, Edward Day
'Studies in the colonial policy of England, 1672–1680: the plantations, the Royal African Company, and the slave trade.' (Annual report of the American Historical Association for the year 1900, Washington, 1901, pp. 139–92.)

On the controversy between the colonies and the company over the supply of slaves.

1183 VERHAEGEN, Pierre
'Le commerce des esclaves en Belgique à la fin du XVIIIᵉ siècle.' (Annales de la Société d'Archéologie de Bruxelles, Bruxelles, vol. 15, 1901, pp. 254–62.)

On slaving voyages to West Africa from Belgium about 1775–80.

1184 KERNKAMP, Gerhard Wilhelm
'Een contract tot slavenhandel von 1657.' (Bijdragen en Mededelingen van het Historisch Genootschap, Amsterdam, vol. 22, 1901, pp. 444–59.)

A contract in Dutch for the Swedish African Company to deliver 600 slaves at Curaçao.

1185 HAMELBERG, J. H. J.
De Nederlanders op de West-Indische eilanden. Amsterdam, 1901, 09. 2 vol. illus.

Includes material on the Curaçao slave trade 1680–1750.

1186 WRIGHT, Richard Robert
'Negro companions of the Spanish explorers.' (AA, n.s., vol. 4, 1902, pp. 217–28.)

With notes on the slave trade to the Caribbean 1501–37.

1187 BALLAGH, James Curtis
A history of slavery in Virginia. Baltimore, 1902. viii, 160 pp. bibl. pp. 149–54.

With a chapter on the slave trade to 1778.

1188 AZEVEDO, Pedro Augusto d'
'Os escravos.' (Archivo Histórico Portuguez, Lisboa, vol. 1, 1903, pp. 289–307.)

On the development of the Afro-Portuguese slave trade 1433–1566.

1189 SCOTT, William Robert
'The constitution and finances of the Royal African Company of England from its foundation till 1720.' (AHR, vol. 8. 1903, pp. 241–59.)

1190 BARKER, Eugene Campbell
'The African slave trade in Texas.' (Quarterly of the Texas State Historical Association, Austin, Texas, vol. 6, 1903, pp. 145–58.)

Some slaves were imported to Louisiana via Texas 1817–56.

1191 SCELLE, Georges
La traite négrière aux Indes de Castille. Contrats et traités d'assiento. Étude de droit public et d'histoire diplomatique . . . Paris, 1906. 2 vol.

History of the Spanish slave trade licences and treaties 1518–1772.

1192 SCELLE, Georges
'Une institution internationale disparue. L'assiento des nègres.' (Revue Générale de Droit International Public, Paris, vol. 13, 1906, pp. 357–97.)

History of the asientos from the 16th century to 1750.

1193 AIMES, Hubert Hillary Suffern
A history of slavery in Cuba 1511 to 1868. New York & London 1907. xi, 298 pp. bibl. pp. 270–91.

1194 DEHÉRAIN, Henri
'L'esclavage au Cap de Bonne-Espérance aux XVIIᵉ et XVIIIᵉ siècles.' (Journal des Savants, Paris, 1907, pp. 488–503; maps.)

The Cape settlement imported slaves 1658-1735 from West Africa, Madagascar and India.

1195 MUIR, John Ramsay Bryce
A history of Liverpool . . . London, 1907. xvi, 372 pp. illus.

Ch. 12: 'The slave trade, 1709–1807.'

1196 WASHINGTON, Booker Talliaferro
The story of the negro. The rise of the race from slavery. New York, 1909. 2 vol.

Brief history of the American slave trade and slavery.

1197 DEHÉRAIN, Henri
Le Cap de Bonne-Espérance au XVIIᵉ siècle. Paris, 1909. 256 pp. maps.

Pt. 2, ch. 6: 'L'esclavage au Cap.'

1198 SCELLE, Georges
'The slave-trade in the Spanish colonies of America: the assiento.' (AJIL, vol. 4, 1910, pp. 612–61.)

History of the Spanish asientos 1595–1750.

1199 *PHILLIPS, Ulrich Bonnell
'The economics of the slave trade, foreign and domestic.' In: The SOUTH in the building of the nation, vol. 5 (Richmond, Va., 1910), pp. 124–29.

1200 MIMS, Stewart Lea
Colbert's West India policy. New Haven, 1912. xiv, 385 pp. bibl. pp. 341–64.

Includes chapters on the West India company 1664–74 and the slave trade.

1201 BEER, George Louis
The old colonial system 1660–1754 . . . New York, 1912. 2 vol.

Only pt. 1 (1660–88) published. Vol. 1, ch. 5: 'The slave-trade and the plantation colonies'.

1202 WÄTJEN, Hermann Julius Eduard
'Der Negerhandel in Westindien und Südamerika bis zur Sklavenemanzipation.' (Hansische Geschichtsblätter, München & Leipzig, 1913, pp. 417–43.)

General account of the slave trade to South America about 1500–1850.

1203 BRAKEL, Simon van
'Eene memorie over den handel der West-Indische Compagnie omstreeks 1670.' (Bijdragen en mededeelingen van het Historisch Genootschap, Amsterdam, vol. 35, 1914, pp. 87–104.)

Contains a memorandum on the Dutch company's trading areas in West Africa and the Caribbean, with notes on the slave trade.

1204 EEKHOF, Albert
'Twee documenten betreffende den slavenhandel in de 17ᵉ eeuw.' (Nederlandsch Archief voor Kerkgeschiedenis, 's-Gravenhage, n.s., vol. 11, 1914, pp. 271–98.)

A contract of 1672 for the Dutch West India company to deliver 3,000 slaves at Curaçao, and instructions of 1685 for a captain to convey 400 slaves from Madagascar to Sumatra.

1205 FORD, Worthington Chauncey
Commerce of Rhode Island 1726–1800. Boston, 1914, 15. 2 vol. (Collections of the Massachusetts Historical Society, ser. 7, vol. 9, 10.)

Correspondence of Rhode Island merchants including material on the slave trade, largely 1767–74. Edited by W. C. Ford and others.

1206 BENJAMINS, Herman Daniël and SNELLEMAN, Joh. F.
Encyclopædie van Nederlandsch West-Indië. 's Gravenhage; Leiden, 1914–17. x, 782 pp. maps.

Sections on the slave trade under 'Compagnie' and 'Slavenhandel' (by S. van Brakel).

1207 ANDREWS, Charles McLean
'Anglo-French commercial rivalry, 1700–1750 . . . ' (AHR, vol. 20, 1915, pp. 539–56.)

On competition in the Atlantic trade.

1208 BUENOS AIRES: Municipalidad
Correspondencia de la ciudad de Buenos Ayres con los reyes de España reunida en el Archivo de Indias de Sevilla, coordenada y publicada por Roberto Levillier . . . Buenos Aires, 1915–18. 3 vol.

Includes documents on the slave trade 1606–80.

1209 MOLINARI, Diego Luis
'Datos para el estudio de la trata de negros en el Río de la Plata.' *In*: FACULTAD DE FILOSOFÍA Y LETRAS, *Buenos Aires*. Documentos para la historia argentina, vol. 7: Comercio de Indias, consulado, comercio de negros y de extranjeros (1791–1809) (Buenos Aires, 1916), pp. ix–xcviii.

Discusses various aspects of the slave trade and its suppression and lists the licences, asientos and laws issued 1493–1809.

1210 PITMAN, Frank Wesley
The development of the British West Indies 1700–1763. New Haven, 1917. xiv, 495 pp. map. bibl. pp. 361–65.

Ch. 3: 'The slave trade'.

1211 WESTERGAARD, Waldemar Christian
The Danish West Indies under company rule (1671–1754) . . . New York, 1917. xxiv, 359 pp. maps. bibl. pp. 263–83.

Ch. 7: 'The slave trade in the Danish West Indies'.

1212 BRAKEL, Simon van
'Bescheiden over den slavenhandel der West-Indische Compagnie . . .' (Economisch-Historisch Jaarboek, 's-Gravenhage, vol. 4, 1918, pp. 47–83.)

Notes and documents on the Dutch slave trade 1662–78.

1213 PHILLIPS, Ulrich Bonnell
American negro slavery. A survey of the supply, employment and control of negro labor as determined by the plantation régime. New York, London, 1918. xi, 529 pp.

1214 ZOOK, George Frederick
The Company of Royal Adventurers trading into Africa . . . Lancaster, Pa., 1919. v, 105 pp. bibl. pp. 97–102.

History of the company 1660–72. (Reprinted from: JNH, vol. 4, 1919, pp. 134–231.) Ph.D. thesis, Cornell University, 1914.

1215 CLEVEN, Nels Andrew Nelson
'Ministerial order of José de Gálvez establishing a uniform duty on the importation of negro slaves into the Indies; and convention between Spain and the United Provinces regulating the return of deserters and fugitives in their American colonies.' (HAHR, vol. 4, 1921, pp. 266–76.)

With the texts of the order, 1784, and the convention, 1791.

1216 WOODSON, Carter Godwin
The negro in our history. Washington, [1922]. xv, 393 pp.

With chapters on the slave trade and the abolition movement. (Later editions revised and enlarged.)

1217 DAVIS, T. R.
'Negro servitude in the United States.' (JNH, vol. 8, 1923, pp. 247–83.)

On the slave trade and slavery in New England.

1218 WRIGHT, Irene Aloha
'The Coymans asiento (1685–1689).' (Bijdragen voor Vaderlandsche Geschiedenis en Oudheidkunde, 's-Gravenhage, ser. 6, vol. 1, 1924, pp. 23–62.)

Concludes that the asiento granted to Coymans & Co. of Amsterdam was lost in 1689 due to growing English influence.

1219 *'DOCUMENTOS para la historia de la esclavitud de los negros en Puerto Rico. Reál cedula declarando la capital asiento de la Compañía de Caracas en 1766.' (Boletín Histórico de Puerto Rico, San Juan, vol. 11, 1924, pp. 79–81.)

The company was granted slaving rights by royal ordinance 31 Oct. 1765, but the trade was discontinued in 1769 as unprofitable.

1220 WEATHERFORD, Willis Duke
The negro from Africa to America. New York, [1925]. 487 pp. bibl. pp. 456–79.

1221 *CARNATHAN, W. J.
'The attempt to reopen the African slave trade in Texas, 1857–1858.' (Proceedings of the sixth annual convention, Southwestern Political and Social Science Association, Austin, Texas, 1925, pp. 134–44.)

1222 *HUDIG DZN., J.
De scheepvaart op West-Afrika en West-Indië in de achttiende eeuw. Amsterdam, 1926. 51 pp.

1223 BROWN, Vera Lee
'The South Sea Company and contra-

band trade.' (AHR, vol. 31, 1926, pp. 662–78.)

On the assiento trade to Spanish America in the 1720s.

1224 MILLIN, Samuel Shannon
Was Waddell Cunningham, Belfast merchant, "a slave-ship projector"? An historic enquiry. (Second edition.) Belfast, 1926. vi, 32 pp.

Clears Cunningham from the allegation that he participated in a slaving project in 1786.

1225 DONNET, Fernand
'Quelques notes sur le commerce des esclaves.' (Bulletin de la Société de Géographie, Anvers, vol. 46, 1926, pp. 6–35.)

On the West African slave trade from the 17th to the 19th century; with the text of a contract of 1769 for the Danish Guinea Company to deliver slaves to the French. (Reprinted separately, Anvers, 1926; 36 pp.)

1226 *MONHEIM, Christian
Étude sur la traite des nègres aux XVIᵉ et XVIIᵉ siècles d'après des documents contemporains. Louvain, 1927. 27 pp.

1227 POSADA, Eduardo
'La esclavitud en Colombia.' (Boletín de Historia y Antigüedades, Bogotá, vol. 16, 1927, pp. 398–403, 526–44, 614–28.)

See (3720).

1228 *TERRY, Roderick
'Some old papers relating to the Newport slave trade.' (Bulletin of the Newport Historical Society, Newport, R.I., no. 62, 1927, pp. 10–34.)

1229 RIDDELL, William Renwick
'The slave in early New York.' (JNH, vol. 13, 1928, pp. 53–86.)

On the slave trade 1623–1734 and negro slavery.

1230 FISHER, Ruth Anna
'Extracts from the records of the African companies, collected by Ruth A. Fisher.' (JNH, vol. 13, 1928, pp. 226–394.)

British documents relating to the West African slave trade, 1678–1780. (Reprinted separately, Washington, [1930?]; 108 pp.)

1231 VIGNOLS, Léon
'El asiento francés (1701–1713) e

inglés (1713–1750) y el comercio francoespañol desde 1700 hasta 1730. Con dos memorias francesas de 1728 sobre estos asuntos.' (Anuario de História del Derecho Español, Madrid, vol. 5, 1928, pp. 266–300.)

1232 AITON, Arthur Scott
'The asiento treaty as reflected in the papers of Lord Shelbourne.' (HAHR, vol. 8, 1928, pp. 167–77.)

On the British slave trade to Spanish America 1727–39.

1233 *MÁRQUEZ DE LA PLATA, Fernando
'Documentos relativos a la introducción de esclavos negros en America.' (RCHG, vol. 57, 1928, pp. 226–49; vol. 58, 1928, pp. 286–304; vol. 59, 1928, pp. 204–14.)

1234 DONNAN, Elizabeth
'The slave trade into South Carolina before the Revolution.' (AHR, vol. 33, 1928, pp. 804–28.)

Deals mainly with the period 1730–74.

1235 TAUSSIG, Charles William
Rum, romance, & rebellion. New York, 1928. xiii, 289 pp. map. bibl. pp. 255–64.

Popular account of the New England trade in rum, sugar and slaves.

1236 *VIGNOLS, Léon
Études négrières de 1774 à 1928 . . . Paris, 1928. 11 pp.

1237 PENSON, Lilian Margery
'The West Indies and the Spanish American trade, 1713–1748.' *In*: The CAMBRIDGE history of the British empire, vol. 1 (Cambridge, 1929), pp. 330–45.

On the assiento and the South Sea Company.

1238 MARTIN, Eveline Christiana
'The English slave trade and the African settlements.' *In*: The CAMBRIDGE history of the British empire, vol. 1 (Cambridge, 1929), pp. 437–59.

Account of the slave trade 1663–1807.

1239 CONNOLLY, James C.
'Slavery in colonial New Jersey and the causes operating against its extension.' (Proceedings of the New Jersey Historical Society, Newark, vol. 14, 1929, pp. 181–202.)

The inflow of white labour and import duties were barriers to African slave importation before 1775.

1240 DONNAN, Elizabeth
'The New England slave trade after the Revolution.' (NEQ, vol. 3, 1930, pp. 251–78.)

On Rhode Island and Massachusetts slave merchants 1783–1808.

1241 DONNAN, Elizabeth
'The early days of the South Sea Company, 1711–1718.' (Journal of Economic and Business History, Cambridge, Mass., vol. 2, 1930, pp. 419–50.)

Describes the problems facing the company from its formation and in the first years of the assiento trade.

1242 *BROWNING, James Blackwell
'Negro companions of the Spanish explorers in the New World.' (Howard University Studies in History, Washington, 1931, no. 11, pp. 3–20.)

1243 *LEUCHSENRING, Emilio Roig de
'La introducción de esclavos africanos. Trato que se daba a los negros esclavos y libres . . . Disposiciones del Cabildo.' *In*: ACTAS capitulares del Ayuntamiento de la Habana, vol. 1 (Habana, 1931), pp. 113–19.

1244 MARTIN, Gaston
Nantes au XVIIIᵉ siècle. L'ère des négriers (1714–1774) d'après des documents inédits. Paris, 1931. 452 pp. illus, maps. bibl. pp. 435–43.

Economic analysis of the slave trade of Nantes.

1245 NETTELS, Curtis
'England and the Spanish–American trade, 1680–1715.' (JMH, vol. 3, 1931, pp. 1–32.)

On the Royal African Company and controversies over the assiento and general trade.

1246 DUMBELL, Stanley
'The profits of the Guinea trade.' (Economic History, London, vol. 2, 1931, pp. 254–57.)

The profit was overestimated by G. Williams (1174).

1247 WENDER, Herbert
'The Southern Commercial Convention at Savannah, 1856.' (GHQ, vol. 15, 1931, pp. 173–91.)

Account of proceedings, including a debate on reopening the African slave trade; a committee was appointed to report on the subject.

1248 AMUNÁTEGUI SOLAR, Domingo
Historia social de Chile. Santiago, 1932. 345 pp.

Includes a section on the slave trade from the 16th century to 1823, originally published in: RCHG, vol. 44, 1922, pp. 25–40.

1249 ESNOUL DE SÉNÉCHAL, L.
'Un manuel du parfait traitant au XVIIIᵉ siècle.' (Mémoires de la Société d'Histoire et d'Archéologie de Bretagne, Rennes, vol. 13, 1932, pp. 197–209.)

Extracts from a document on the West African slave trade, with details of a voyage to Whydah 1755.

1250 *PRESTON, Howard Willis
Rhode Island and the sea . . . Providence, 1932. 140 pp. illus. map.

Includes material on the slave trade.

1251 *MORAES, Evaristo de
A escravidão africana no Brasil (das origens á extincção). São Paulo, 1933. 253 pp.

1252 LA RONCIÈRE, Charles Germain Bourel de
Nègres et négriers. Paris, 1933. 254 pp. bibl. pp. 248–54.

On the French slave trade and anti-slavery movement.

1253 *PROVIDENCE INSTITUTION FOR SAVINGS
The slave trade. Presented by "The Old Stone Bank", Providence, R. I. May 22, 1933. (Providence, 1933.) 10 pp. illus.

On the Rhode Island slave trade.

1254 RAUT, Étienne *and* **LALLEMENT, Léon**
'Vannes autrefois. La traite des nègres.' (Bulletin de la Société Polymathique de Morbihan, Vannes, 1933, pp. 53–74.)

On slave trading from Vannes 1731–64.

1255 L'HONORÉ NABER, Samuel Pierre
'Nota van Pieter Mortamer over het gewest Angola. Een verzuimd hoofdstuk onzer koloniale geschiedenis 1641–1648.' (Bijdragen en Mededeelingen van het Historisch Genootschap, Utrecht, vol. 54, 1933, pp. 1–42.)

A report by the first Dutch governor of Angola on the conquest of the colony and the organisation of the slave trade there, 1643.

1256 NEWTON, Arthur Percival
The European nations in the West
Indies 1493–1688. London, 1933. xviii,
356 pp. maps.

With chapters on the slave trade.

1257 MAC INNES, Charles Malcolm
England and slavery. Bristol, 1934.
224 pp. illus. bibl. pp. 213–18.

Brief history of the English slave
trade and abolition movement.

1258 *BOURCIER, Emmanuel
Le bois d'ébène . . . Paris, [1934]. 221 pp.

On the French slave trade.

1259 QUINLAN, John
'England and the slave-trade.' (The
Month, London, vol. 164, 1934,
pp. 119–26.)

Shows that the slave trade was an
integral part of the mercantilist
economic system.

1260 *MARTIN, Gaston
Négriers et bois d'ébène. Grenoble,
[1934]. 119 pp. illus.

On the French slave trade from Africa.
(Reviewed in: RHCF, vol. 25, 1937,
pp. 187–88.)

1261 *LEMAIRE, Louis
Dunkerque et la traite des noirs au
XVIIIe siècle . . . Dunkerque, 1934.
52 pp.

1262 HUSSEY, Roland Dennis
The Caracas Company, 1728–1784. A
study in the history of Spanish mono-
polistic trade. Cambridge (Mass.), 1934.
x, 358 pp. bibl. pp. 325–46.

Contains notes on the slave trade to
Venezuela 1754–69.

1263 RINCHON, Dieudonné
'Les négriers belges au XVIIIe siècle.'
(Revue de l'AUCAM, Louvain, vol.
9, 1934, pp. 15–20.)

1264 *MENKMAN, W. R.
'Slavenhandel en rechtsbedeeling op
Curacao op het einde der 17e eeuw.'
(WIG, vol. 17, 1935, pp. 11–26.)

1265 BUFFET, Henri François
'Traite des noirs et le commerce de
l'argent au Port-Louis et à Lorient
sous Louis XIV.' (Revue des Études
Historiques, Paris, vol. 102, 1935, pp.
433–50.)

Includes a section on the French
slave trade to Spanish America and
St. Domingue 1684–1713.

1266 LUBBOCK, Basil
Coolie ships and oil sailers . . . Glasgow,
1935. x, 180 pp. illus.

Includes a chapter on English slave
ships and antislavery cruisers.

1267 SEBEZJO, J.
Tratta e schiavismo nella politica ing-
lese dal 1562 al 1928. Roma, 1936.
53 pp.

Account of the English slave trade
and labour conditions written in
defence of the Italian conquest of
Abyssinia.

1268 HATTERSLEY, Alan Frederick
'Slavery at the Cape, 1652–1838.' In:
The CAMBRIDGE history of the
British empire, vol. 8 (Cambridge,
1936), pp. 262–73.

Includes information on slave imports to 1807.

1269 VRIJMAN, L. C.
Slavenhalers en slavenhandel. Amsterdam, 1937. 156 pp.

General history of the African slave
trade, especially that of the Dutch
West India Company.

1270 SIMONSEN, Roberto Cochrane
Historia economica de Brasil 1500–
1820. São Paulo (etc.), 1937. 2 vol. maps.

With a chapter on slavery and the
slave trade.

1271 *COMPAGNIE DES INDES
'Cinq documents relatifs aux premières
traites d'esclaves effectuées au profit
des îles au Sénégal et en Guinée.'
(RDHMF, vol. 3, 1937, pp. 135–48.)

Instructions for the purchase of
West African slaves for the French
Mascarenes, 1729–31.

1272 *COMPAGNIE DES INDES
'Traité fait entre la Compagnie des
Indes et Mr. Gabriel Michel, négociant à Nantes, pour la vente d'une
cargaison de six cents noirs livrables
au Sénégal, pour être transportés de
cette concession aux isles de Bourbon
et de France.—Nantes 25 juillet 1744.'
(RDHMF, vol. 3, 1937, pp. 315–22.)

1273 LEUCHSENRING, Emilio Roig de
'De cómo y por quiénes se realizaba en
Cuba la trata de esclavos africanos
durante los siglos XVIII e XIX.' (Estudios Afrocubanos, La Habana, vol. 1,
1937, pp. 128–38.)

Gives the names of slave traders in a
Havana document of 1778 and in-

formation on slave trading in the early 19th century.

1274 *CAMARGO, Jovelino M. de
'A Inglaterra e o trafico.' *In*: NOVOS estudos afro-brasileiros (Rio de Janeiro, 1937), pp. 171ff.

1275 *MÚRIAS, Manuel
Portugal e o tráfico da escravatura. [Lisboa,] 1938. 28 pp.

1276 HAUSER, Henri
'Naissance, vie et mort d'une institution : le travail servile au Brésil.' (AESC, vol. 10, 1938, pp. 309–18.)

Brief account of slavery and slave trade in Brazilian history.

1277 *WILLIAMS, Wilson E.
Africa and the rise of capitalism, by Wilson E. Williams. Negro disfranchisement in Virginia, by Robert E. Martin. Washington, 1938. viii, 188 pp. (Howard University studies in the social sciences, vol. 1, no. 1.)

Williams argues that the development of England as a capitalist power was based mainly on the slave trade. See (1309).

1278 *RINCHON, Dieudonné
Le trafic négrier, d'après les livres de commerce du capitaine gantois Pierre-Ignace-Liévain van Alstein. L'organisation commerciale de la traite des noirs . . . Paris, 1938. 349 pp. illus, maps.

On slaving from Nantes 1748–93.

1279 *TAUNAY, Affonso de Escragnolle
'Notas sôbre as últimas décadas do tráfico.' (Mensário do Jornal do Comércio, Rio de Janeiro, vol. 3, 1938, pp. 115–19, 181–84, 295–99.)

On the final period of the Brazilian slave trade.

1280 ROSENTHAL, Eric
Stars and stripes in Africa . . . London, 1938. xiii, 306 pp.

Popular work on 'American achievements in Africa', including chapters on the slave trade until 1861.

1281 *ROMERO, Fernando
'El negro en Tierra Firme durante el siglo XVI.' *In*: Actas y trabajos científicas del XXVII° Congreso Internacional de Americanistas (Lima, 1939), vol. 2, pp. 441–61.

1282 HELMER-WULLEN, Hilda von
'Der Sklavenhandel—die historische Grundlage der Negerfrage in Amerika. Statistische Aufzeichnungen von 1492–1807.' (Zeitschrift für Rassenkunde, Stuttgart, vol. 9, 1939, pp. 97–103.)

1283 COLE, Charles Woolsey
Colbert and a century of French mercantilism. New York, 1939. 2 vol. bibl. pp. 591–620.

With sections on the West India company and the slave trade.

1284 DU HALGOUET, Hervé, *vicomte*
Nantes. Ses relations commerciales avec les îles d'Amérique au XVIII° siècle. Ses armateurs. Rennes, 1939. iv, 292 pp. maps.

Includes notes on the slave trade from West Africa.

1285 MAC INNES, Charles Malcolm
A gateway of empire. Bristol, 1939. 456 pp. bibl. pp. 437–43.

On the commerce of Bristol, including chapters on the slave trade.

1286 *ROMERO, Fernando
'La corriente de la trata negrera en Chile.' (Sphinx, Lima, vol. 3, 1939, pp. 87–93.)

1287 *DAM VAN ISSELT, Willem Edmond van
'Slavenhandel tijdens de 2e helft der 17e eeuw.' (Navorscher, Amsterdam, vol. 89, 1940, pp. 14–21.)

1288 WILLIAMS, Eric Eustace
'The golden age of the slave system in Britain.' (JNH, vol. 25, 1940, pp. 60–106.)

While the slave trade and slave-produced sugar were profitable, in the 18th century, public opinion was unmoved by antislavery sentiment.

1289 VIANNA, Luís
'O trabalho do engenho e a reacção do Índio—Estabelecimento de escravatura africana.' *In*: CONGRESSO do Mundo Portugues, Publicações, Lisboa, vol. 10 (Lisboa, 1940), pt. 2, pp. 11–29.

Includes notes on the African slave trade to Brazil from the 16th to the 19th century.

1290 MAIA MENDES, M.
'Escravatura no Brasil (1500–1700)'. *In*: CONGRESSO do Mundo Portugues, Publicações, vol. 10 (Lisboa, 1940), pt. 2, pp. 31–55.

The slave trade from West Africa was an economic necessity to spare the natives of Brazil.

1291 MENKMAN, W. R.
'Nederland in Amerika en West-Afrika.' *In*: HAAN, J. C. de *and* WINTER, P. J. van, Nederlanders over de zeeën (Utrecht, 1940), pp. 9–100.

1292 *KESLER, C. K.
'Uit de eerste dagen van den West-Indischen slavenhandel.' (WIG, vol. 22, 1940, pp. 175–85.)

1293 MARTÍNEZ MONTERO, Homero
'La esclavitud en el Uruguay. Contribución a su estudio histórico-social.' (Revista Nacional, Montevideo, año 3, 1940, pp. 261–73; año 4, 1941, pp. 221–67; año 5, 1942, pp. 403–28.)

On the slave trade in the 18th century, slavery, and abolition of the trade.

1294 TAUNAY, Affonso de Escragnolle
'Subsídios para a história do tráfico africano no Brasil colonial.' (Anais do Terceiro Congresso de História Nacional, 1938; RIHGB, vol. 3, 1941, pp. 523–676.)

Notes on the Portuguese slave trade from Africa and Brazilian slavery, particularly in the 17th and 18th century. (Also published in: Museu Paulista, São Paulo, Annaes, vol. 10, pt. 2, 1941, pp. 5–311.)

1295 *CORBITT, Duvon Clough
'Shipments of slaves from the United States to Cuba, 1789–1807.' (JSH, vol. 7, 1941, pp. 540–49.)

1296 WISH, Harvey
'The revival of the African slave trade in the United States, 1856–1860.' (MVHR, vol. 27, 1941, pp. 569–88.)

Southern pro-slave trade agitation, led by L. W. Spratt, aimed at provoking secession.

1297 *PEREDA VALDÉS, Ildefonso
Negros esclavos y negros libres. Esquema de una sociedad esclavista y aporte del negro en nuestra formación nacional. Montevideo, 1941. 172 pp.

On the slave trade from Africa to Uruguay.

1298 MACKENZIE-GRIEVE, Averil
The last years of the English slave trade. Liverpool 1750–1807. London, 1941. xii, 331 pp.

Popular history of the Liverpool slave trade and its abolition.

1299 KING, James Ferguson
'Evolution of the free slave trade principle in Spanish colonial administration.' (HAHR, vol. 22, 1942, pp. 34–56.)

On the development of a new slave trade policy 1759–1804.

1300 MENKMAN, W. R.
De Nederlanders in het caraibische zeegebied, warin vervat de geschiedenis der Nederlandsche Antillen. Amsterdam, 1942. xii, 291 pp.

Deals with the Dutch slave trade in the 17th and 18th centuries.

1301 *MACEDO, Sérgio D. T. de
Apontamentos para a história do tráfico negreiro no Brasil. Rio de Janeiro, 1942. 127 pp.

1302 GREENE, Lorenzo Johnston
The negro in colonial New England 1620–1776. New York, 1942. 404 pp. bibl. pp. 361–84.

Ch. 1: 'Black merchandise.'

1303 CORBITT, Duvon Clough
'Immigration in Cuba.' (HAHR, vol. 22, 1942, pp. 280–308.)

Includes notes on the slave trade 1770–1840.

1304 WILLIAMS, Eric Eustace
'The British West Indian slave trade after its abolition in 1807.' (JNH, vol. 27, 1942, pp. 175–91.)

1305 *MOLINARI, Diego Luis
La trata de negros. Datos para su estudio en el Río de la Plata. 2ª ed. Buenos Aires, 1944. 633 pp.

See (1209).

1306 *MENKMAN, W. R.
'Nederlandsche en vreemde slavenvaart.' (WIG, vol. 26, 1944, pp. 97–110.)

1307 *MIRAMÓN, Alberto
'Los negreros del Caribe.' (Boletín de Historia y Antigüedades, Bogotá, vol. 31, 1944, pp. 168–87; illus.)

1308 EEGHEN, Christiaan Pieter van
'Over zalf- en hoeden-, over slaven-, over kunst- en boekenhandel in het Amsterdam der 18de eeuw.' (Jaarboek van het Genootschap Amstelodamum, Amsterdam, vol. 40, 1944, pp. 172–97.)

With a section on Dutch slave trade about 1750.

1309 WILLIAMS, Eric Eustace
Capitalism & slavery. Chapel Hill, N.C., 1944. ix, 285 pp. bibl. pp. 262–70.

Study of the relationship between the slave trade and the development of a capitalist economy in Britain in the 18th century. (Based on Ph.D. thesis, Oxford, 1938. Reviewed by F. Tannenbaum in: Political Science Quarterly, Lancaster, Pa., vol. 61, 1946, pp. 247–53.) See (348, 1277, 1446, 3830).

1310 *CORREIA LOPES, Edmundo Armenio
A escravatura. Subsídios para a sua história. Lisboa, 1944. xi, 208 pp.

Includes a section on the Portuguese slave trade from Africa.

1311 ROMERO, Fernando
'The slave trade and the negro in South America.' (HAHR, vol. 24, 1944, pp. 368–86.)

On the distribution of the slave population.

1312 AGUIRRE BELTRÁN, Gonzalo
'The slave trade in Mexico.' (HAHR, vol. 24, 1944, pp. 412–31.)

General history 1518–1817.

1313 *AGUIRRE BELTRÁN, Gonzalo
'Comercio de esclavos en México por 1542.' (Afroamérica, México, vol. 1, 1945, pp. 25–40.)

1314 KING, James Ferguson
'Negro slavery in New Granada.' In: GREATER America. Essays in honor of Herbert Eugene Bolton (Berkeley & Los Angeles, 1945), pp. 295–318.

Includes notes on the African slave trade and asiento system.

1315 DELCOURT, André
'La chambre de commerce de Bordeaux et la traite africaine dans les dernières années de l'ancien régime (1783–1791).' In: COMMISSION de Recherche et de Publication des Documents relatifs à la Vie Économique de la Révolution. Assemblée générale de la commission centrale et des comités départementaux 1939, vol. 2 (Paris, 1945), pp. 425–44.

Study of Bordeaux' involvement in the West African slave trade, at Senegal, Warri and Cabinda.

1316 MAY, Philip S.
'Zephaniah Kingsley, nonconformist (1765–1843).' (FHQ, vol. 23, 1945, pp. 145–59.)

Kingsley was active in the Florida slave trade 1803–21.

1317 TANNENBAUM, Frank
'The destiny of the negro in the western hemisphere.' (Political Science Quarterly, Lancaster, Pa., vol. 61, 1946, pp. 1–41.)

See (1322).

1318 VIANNA, Luís
O negro na Bahia . . . Rio de Janeiro, 1946. 167 pp. illus, maps.

Describes the various phases of the slave trade from Africa.

1319 PETERSEN, Sophie Clausine
Danmarks gamle tropekolonier. København, 1946. 435 pp.

With sections on the Danish slave trade between the Gold Coast and the West Indies to 1802.

1320 MENKMAN, W. R.
De West-Indische Compagnie. Amsterdam, 1947. 186 pp. map.

1321 FRANKLIN, John Hope
From slavery to freedom. A history of American negroes. New York, 1947. xv, 622, xlii pp. bibl. pp. 591–622.

Ch. 4: 'The slave trade'.

1322 TANNENBAUM, Frank
Slave and citizen. The negro in the Americas. New York, 1947. xi, 128, xi pp.

Argues that forced migration was of benefit to the Africans. (Expanded version of 1317.)

1323 *ARIAS ROJAS, Fabio
'Apuntes sobre el origen de la trata de negros.' (Farol, Caracas, sept. 1947, pp. 2–3; illus.)

On the slave trade in Venezuela.

1324 MARTIN, Gaston
Histoire de l'esclavage dans les colonies françaises. Paris, 1948. 318 pp.

History of the French slave trade and its abolition.

1325 *REYNAUD, Jean
'Les négriers ou le trafic des esclaves.' (Revue de la Chambre de Commerce de Marseilles, août 1948, pp. 21–26.)

1326 MAC INNES, Charles Malcolm
'The slave trade.' In: PARKINSON, C. N. The trade winds. A study of British overseas trade during the French wars 1793–1815 (London, 1948), pp. 251–72.

1327 GOULART, Mauricio
Escravidão africana no Brasil (das

origens à extinção do trafico). São Paulo, [1949]. 300 pp. bibl. pp. 281–88.

Includes the history of the Brazilian slave trade and its suppression.

1328   PERRET, André
'René Montaudoin, armateur et négrier nantais (1673–1731).' (Bulletin de la Société Archéologique et Historique de Nantes et de la Loire-Inférieure, Nantes, vol. 88, 1949, pp. 78–94.)

Montaudoin established Nantes as a great slaving port after 1706.

1329   WILLIAMS, Edwin L.
'Negro slavery in Florida.' (FHQ, vol. 28, 1949, pp. 93–110.)

Slave imports were insignificant until the British occupation 1763–83; smuggling continued after annexation by the United States 1821.

1330   DEERR, Noël
The history of sugar. London, 1949, 50. 2 vol. maps.

With chapters on the African slave trade to Brazil and the Caribbean 1520–1858 (imports totalling over 12 million) and its abolition.

1331   ZELINSKY, Wilbur
'The historical geography of the negro population of Latin America.' (JNH, vol. 34, 1949, pp. 153–221).

Describes the distribution of negroes in the Americas 1570–1940.

1332   MARSEILLE: Chambre de Commerce
Histoire du commerce de Marseille publiée . . . sous la direction de Gaston Rambert. Paris, 1949–59. 6 vol.

Vol. 6 (1660–1789), by G. Rambert, includes a section on the slave trade.

1333   SILVA TEIXEIRA, Candido de
'Companhia de Cacheu, Rios e Comercio da Guiné. (Documentos para a sua história.)' (Boletim do Arquivo Histórico Colonial, Lisboa, vol. 1. 1950, pp. 85–521.)

Includes documents on the slave trade 1610–1755.

1334   GOMES, Alfredo
'Achegas para a história do tráfico africano no Brasil—aspectos numéricos.' In: INSTITUTO HISTORICO E GEOGRAFICO BRASILEIRO, IV Congresso de História Nacional, 1949, Anais, vol. 5 (Rio de Janeiro, 1950), pp. 25–78.

Discusses the statistics of the slave trade to Brazil.

1335   ALMEIDA PRADO, João Fernando de
'A Bahia e as suas relações com o Daomé.' In: INSTITUTO HISTORICO E GEOGRAFICO BRASILEIRO, IV Congresso de História Nacional, 1949, Anais, vol. 5 (Rio de Janeiro, 1950), pp. 377–439.

Deals with the Brazilian slave trade in the 18th and 19th century. Translated as 'Les rélations de Bahia (Brésil) avec le Dahomey' in: RHC, vol. 41, 1954, pp. 167–226. See (1361).

1336   WILLIAMS, Eric Eustace
'The negro slave trade in Anglo-Spanish relations.' (Caribbean Historical Review, Port of Spain, no. 1, 1950, pp. 22–45.)

1337   PARKINSON, Bradbury B.
'A slaver's accounts.' (Accounting Research, London, vol. 2, 1951, pp. 144–50.)

Describes the accounting system in Liverpool slaving records, exemplified by a voyage of 1768–69.

1338   HILDEBRAND, Ingegerd
Den svenska kolonin S:t Barthélemy och Västindiska kompaniet fram till 1796. Lund, 1951. vii, 350 pp. map.

On the Swedish West India company (formed 1786) and plans for participation in the slave trade.

1339   DIGGS, Irene
'The negro in the viceroyalty of the Rio de la Plata.' (JNH, vol. 36, 1951, pp. 281–301).

On the slave trade and slavery 1595–1812.

1340   BENNETT, J. Harry, Jr
'The problem of slave labor supply at the Codrington plantations.' (JNH, vol. 36, 1951, pp. 406–41; vol. 37, 1952, pp. 115–41.)

Until 1767 the church estates in Barbados purchased African slaves.

1341   BOXER, Charles Ralph
Salvador de Sá and the struggle for Brazil and Angola 1602–1686. London, 1952. xvi, 444 pp. illus. maps. bibl. pp. 407–23.

Ch. 6, 'Angola, the black mother', shows the importance of the slave trade to the Portuguese.

1342   RICHARDSON, Eudora Ramsay
'A tragic accident.' (SAQ, vol. 51, 1952, pp. 413–18.)

Account of slave imports to the English North American colonies 1618–82.

1343 DELCOURT, André
La France et les établissements français au Sénégal entre 1713 et 1763. Dakar, 1952. 432 pp. maps. bibl. pp. 27–37. (MIFAN, no. 17.)

Includes a chapter on the companies formed for the slave trade in the 1740s.

1344 PARKINSON, Cyril Northcote
The rise of the port of Liverpool. Liverpool, 1952. vii, 163 pp. illus, maps.

Ch. 7: 'The slave trade.'

1345 JOHNSON, Vera M.
'Sidelights on the Liverpool slave trade, 1789–1807.' (MM, vol. 38, 1952, pp. 276–93.)

1346 *LACROIX, Louis
Les derniers négriers; derniers voyages de bois d'ébène, de coolies et de merles du Pacifique. Paris, [1952]. 374 pp. illus, maps.

Pt. 1 on the illegal slave trade in the 19th century. (Reviewed in: RHCF, vol. 39, 1952, pp. 136–37.)

1347 MENKMAN, W. R.
'Slavernij—slavenhandel—emancipatie.' (WIG, vol. 34, 1953, pp. 103–12.)

On the Dutch slave trade and colonial slavery.

1348 HYDE, Francis Edwin
'The nature and profitability of the Liverpool slave trade. By Francis E. Hyde, Bradbury B. Parkinson and Sheila Marriner.' (EcHR, ser. 2, vol. 5, 1953, pp. 368–77.)

Trading accounts of slaving voyages in the second half of the 18th century.

1349 HODSON, J. H.
'The letter book of Robert Bostock, a merchant in the Liverpool slave trade, 1789–1792.' (Liverpool Bulletin, Liverpool, vol. 3, no. 1/2, 1953, pp. 37–59; illus.)

1350 *DÍAZ SOLER, Luis M.
Historia de la esclavitud negra en Puerto Rico (1493–1890) . . . Madrid, [1953]. xv, 432 pp. bibl. pp. 415–32.

Describes the African slave trade 1508–1866.

1351 LY, Abdoulaye
'Sur la politique guinéenne de Louis XIV, conditions et débuts.' (BIFAN, vol. 16, ser. B, 1954, pp. 22–54.)

On the Senegal Company and the slave trade about 1664–77.

1352 COBB, R. C.
'Réclamations d'un négrier d'Honfleur (1794) (Lacoudrais père et fils aîné et Cie).' (Annales de Normandie, Caen, vol. 4, no. 1, 1954, pp. 76–78.)

Letter written by the wife of Lacoudrais to the Comité de Salut Public describing the ruin of the firm after 1791.

1353 CORTES ALONSO, Vicenta
'La conquista de las Islas Canarias a través de las ventas de esclavos en Valencia.' (Anuario de Estudios Atlánticos, Madrid, no. 1, 1955, pp. 479–547.)

Documentary evidence for the sale of Guanche slaves 1489–1511.

1354 THORNTON, Archibald Paton
'The organization of the slave trade in the English West-Indies, 1660–1685.' (WMQ, ser. 3, vol. 12, 1955, pp. 399–409.)

On the African companies and the English colonies.

1355 UNGER, Willem Sybrand
'Iets over den slaefschen handel.' (Tijdschrift voor Geschiedenis, Groningen, vol. 68, 1955, pp. 16–18.)

Notes on the Dutch slave trade.

1356 THORNTON, Archibald Paton
'Spanish slave-ships in the English West Indies, 1660–85.' (HAHR, vol. 35, 1955, pp. 374–85.)

On the organisation of the slave trade.

1357 *RINCHON, Dieudonné
'La traite et les négriers.' (Annales de Nantes, no. 101, 1955, p. 21.)

1358 MAUGAT, Émile
'La traite clandestine à Nantes au XIXᵉ siècle.' (Bulletin de la Société Archéologique et Historique de Nantes etd e la Loire-Inférieure, Nantes, vol. 93, 1955, pp. 162–69.)

On the revival of slave trading at Nantes 1816–30.

1359 *GOUVEIA, Maurilio
História da escravidão . . . Rio de Janeiro, 1955. 423 pp.

With an appendix on the Brazilian slavery laws 1815–55.

1360 CARVALHO NETO, Paulo de
La obra afro-uruguayo del Ildefonso
Pereda Valdés. (Ensayo de crítica de
antropología cultural.) [Montevideo,]
1955. 141 pp.

Critique of some works of Pereda
Valdés, including (1297).

1361 ALMEIDA PRADO, João Fernando de
O Brasil e o colonialismo europeu.
São Paulo, 1956. 484 pp.

Contains 'O inicio do tráfico africano'
(pp. 27–114) and 'A Bahia e as
suas relações com o Daomé' (pp. 115–
226). See (1335).

1362 RINCHON, Dieudonné
Les armements négriers au XVIIIᵉ
siècle d' après la correspondance et la
comptabilité des armateurs et des
capitaines nantais. Bruxelles, 1956.
178 pp. bibl. pp. 148–67.

Based on manuscript records of
slaving firms in Nantes, mainly
relating to the slave trade 1765–91.

1363 FORNELL, Earl Wesley
'Agitation in Texas for reopening the
slave trade.' (Southwestern Historical
Quarterly, Austin, Texas, vol. 60,
1956, pp. 245–59.)

Account of attempts to restore the
African slave trade 1856–59.

1364 UNGER, Willem Sybrand
'Bijdragen tot de geschiedenis van de
Nederlandse slavenhandel . . .' (Economisch-Historisch Jaarboek, 's-Gravenhage, vol. 26, 1956, pp. 133–74; vol.
28, 1961, pp. 3–148.)

Pt. 1: 'Beknopt oversicht van de
Nederlandse slavenhandel in het
algemeen'. Pt. 2: 'De slavenhandel der
Middelburgsche Commercie Compagnie, 1732–1808.'

1365 VERGUIN, J.
'La politique de la Compagnie des
Indes dans la traite des noirs à l'île
Bourbon (1662–1762).' (RH, vol. 216,
1956, pp. 45–48.)

Slaves were bought from Madagascar,
Mozambique and India.

1366 LOGAN, Frenise A.
'The British East India Company and
African slavery in Benkulen, Sumatra,
1687–1792.' (JNH, vol. 41, 1956, pp.
339–48.)

Slaves were brought from Madagascar
and West Africa to the East Indies.

1367 RICHELOT, René
'Robert Surcouf et la traite des noirs
en 1815.' (Bulletin et mémoires de la
Société Archéologique du Département
d'Ille-et-Vilaine, Rennes, vol. 70, 1956,
pp. 95–97.)

On a slave merchant of St. Malo.

1368 DAVIES, Kenneth Gordon
The Royal African Company. London,
1957. ix, 390 pp. maps.

History of the company and its
slave trading to 1713.

1369 *LY, Abdoulaye
'La formation de l'économie sucrière et
le développement du marché d'esclaves
africains dans les îles françaises d'Amérique au XVIIᵉ siècle.' (PA, n.s., no. 13,
1957, pp. 7–22; no. 16, 1957, pp.
112–34.)

On the French sugar plantations and
slave trade 1680–1700. (Reprinted
as pt. 2, ch. 2 of: 1375.)

1370 SPINGARN, Lawrence Perry
'Slavery in the Danish West Indies.'
(American–Scandinavian Review, New
York, vol. 45, 1957, pp. 35–43; illus.)

Brief account of the slave trade,
slavery and abolition in the Virgin
Islands.

1371 *RODRÍGUEZ MOLAS, Ricardo
'El primer libro de entrada de esclavos
negros a Buenos Aires.' (Revista de la
Universidad, La Plata, vol. 2, 1957,
pp. 139–43.)

1372 SAMPAIO GARCIA, Rozendo
'O Português Duarte Lopes e o comércio espanhol de escravos negros.
(Novas achegas à biografia dêste
explorador africano do século XVI.)'
(Revista de História, São Paulo, vol.
14, 1957, pp. 375–85; facsims.)

On a report submitted by Lopes to
the Spanish government in 1589,
with proposals for the slave trade
to America.

1373 VIDALENC, Jean
'La traite des nègres en France au
début de la Révolution (1789–1793).'
(Annales Historiques de la Révolution
Française, Nancy, vol. 29, 1957, pp.
56–69.)

On the West Indian slave trade and
bounty system.

1374 PI-SUNYER, Oriol
'Historical background to the negro in

Mexico.' (JNH, vol. 42, 1957, pp. 237–46.)

On the documentary sources for the slave trade and slavery.

1375 LY, Abdoulaye
La Compagnie du Sénégal. [Paris,] 1958. xv, 310 pp. bibl. pp. 299–310.

See (1369).

1376 CHECKLAND, Sydney George
'Finance for the West Indies, 1780–1815.' (EcHR, ser. 2, vol, 10, 1958, pp. 461–69.)

On the London bankers financing West Indian trade.

1377 STUDER, Elena Fanny Scheuss de
La trata de negros en el Río de la Plata durante el siglo XVIII. Buenos Aires, 1958. 378 pp. illus, maps. bibl. pp. 355–60.

History of the slave trade to Spanish South America, in particular the English asiento. (Reviewed by F. Tannenbaum in: AHR, vol. 65, 1960, pp. 647–48.)

1378 SHERIDAN, Richard Bert
'The commercial and financial organization of the British slave trade, 1750–1807.' (EcHR, ser. 2, vol. 11, 1958, pp. 249–63.)

The city of London was as deeply involved in the slave trade through finance as Liverpool through shipping.

1379 MATIP, Benjamin
Heurts et malheurs des rapports Europe Afrique noire dans l'histoire moderne (du 15e au 18e siècle). Paris, [1959]. 124 pp. map. bibl. pp. 119–21.

Ch. 3, section 2: 'La traite du capital humain africain.'

1380 MELLAFE, Rolando
La introducción de la esclavitud negra en Chile. Tráfico y rutas. Santiago de Chile, 1959. 293 pp. bibl. 265–69.

Analysis of the slave trade to Chile in the 16th and 17th centuries, first via Cartagena, later overland from the River Plate.

1381 *LY, Abdoulaye
L'évolution du commerce français d'Afrique noire dans le dernier quart du XVIIe siècle: la Compagnie du Sénégal de 1673 à 1696. [Paris, 1959.] 310 pp.

1382 HIGH, James
'The African gentleman: a chapter in

the slave trade.' (JNH, vol. 44, 1959, pp. 285–307.)

On the English slave trade before 1783.

1383 MAURO, Frédéric
Le Portugal et l'Atlantique au XVIIe siècle (1570–1670). Étude économique. [Paris,] 1960. lviii, 550 pp. illus, maps. bibl. pp. xi–liv.

With a chapter on the African slave trade.

1384 MARCHAND-THÉBAULT, M. L.
'L'esclavage en Guyane française sous l'ancien régime.' (RFHO, vol. 47, 1960, pp. 5–75.)

Includes information on slave imports 1680–1787.

1385 WADDELL, David Allan Gilmour
'Queen Anne's government and the slave trade.' (Caribbean Quarterly, Port-of-Spain, vol. 6, 1960, pp. 7–10.)

On the Royal African Company's attempts to regain a monopoly of the slave trade 1707–12.

1386 MEYER, Jean
'Le commerce négrier nantais (1774–1792).' (AESC, vol. 15, no. 1, 1960, pp. 120–29.)

The peak period of the Nantes slave trade was 1783–92.

1387 BÉNARD, J. Cl.
'L'armement honfleurais et le commerce des esclaves à la fin du XVIIIe siècle.' (Annales de Normandie, Caen, vol. 10, 1960, pp. 249–64.)

1388 *WILLIAMS, Jack Kenny
'The Southern movement to reopen the African slave trade, 1854–1860: a factor in secession.' (Proceedings of the South Carolina Historical Association, Columbia, S.C., 1960, pp. 23–31.)

1389 *LOWERY, Ralph J.
'The English asiento and the slave trade.' (Negro History Bulletin, Washington, vol. 23, 1960, pp. 128–30.)

1390a*RODRIGUES, José Honório
Brasil e África: outro horizonte; relações e politica brasileiro-africana. Rio de Janeiro, 1961. 359 pp.

Translated as:

1390b Brazil and Africa . . . Berkeley & Los Angeles, 1965. xxii, 382 pp.

Describes the slave trade to Brazil, particularly from Angola and Da-

I

homey, until its suppression in 1856. (Reviewed by Roger Bastide, in: PA, vol. 13, no. 14, 1962, pp. 123–28.)

1391 *ACOSTA SAIGNES, Miguel
'La trata de esclavos en Venezuela.' (Revista de Historia, Caracas, vol. 2, no. 6, 1961, pp. 19–60.)

1392 HARTOG, Johan
'Slavenhandel en slavernij.' *In his*: Curaçao (Oranjestad, Aruba, 1961), pp. 435–66.

Account of the Dutch West Indian slave trade 1639–1821.

1393 *RAY, J. M.
'Newport's golden age.' (Negro History Bulletin, Washington, vol. 25, 1961, pp. 51–57.)

On the Rhode Island slave trade.

1394 JORDAN, Winthrop Donaldson
'The influence of the West Indies on the origins of New England slavery.' (WMQ, ser. 3, vol. 18, 1961, pp. 243–50.)

Slavery was introduced to the mainland colonies from the Caribbean, particularly Barbados.

1395 HARGREAVES, John Desmond
'The slave traffic.' *In*: NATAN, A. Silver renaissance. Essays in eighteenth-century English history (London, 1961), pp. 81–101.

1396 SAMPIO GARCÍA, Rozendo
'Contribuição ao estudo do aprovisionamento de escravos negros na America Espanhola (1580–1640).' (Anais do Museu Paulista, São Paulo, vol. 16, 1962, pp. 1–195.)

Study of the Spanish slave trade during the period of union with Portugal.

1397 *BANGOU, Henri
La Guadeloupe, 1492–1848, ou l'histoire de la colonisation de l'île liée à l'esclavage noir de ses débuts à sa disparition. [Aurillac,] 1962. 351 pp. maps.

1398 MANNIX, Daniel Pratt *and* COWLEY, Malcolm
Black cargoes. A history of the Atlantic slave trade 1518–1865. New York, 1962. 306 pp. illus, maps. bibl. pp. 288–95.

Popular account. Ch. 5, 'The middle passage', first published in: AH, vol. 13, no. 2, 1962, pp. 22–25, 103–07.

1399 FARNIE, D. A.
'The commercial empire of the Atlantic, 1607–1783.' (EcHR, ser. 2, vol. 15, 1962, pp. 205–18.)

Includes a section on British participation in the Atlantic slave trade.

1400 *IANNI, Octavio
As metamorfoses do escravo; apogeu e crise da escravatura no Brasil meridional. São Paulo, [1962]. 312 pp.

1401 WAX, Darold Duane
'Quaker merchants and the slave trade in colonial Pennsylvania.' (PMHB, vol. 86, 1962, pp. 143–59.)

On Quaker involvement in the slave trade 1683–1757.

1402 *CORTES ALONSO, Vicenta
'La trata de esclavos durante los primeros descubrimientos (1489–1516).' (Anuario de Estudios Atlánticos, Madrid, no. 9, 1963, pp. 23–50.)

Study of the slave trade conducted through the 'Casa dos Escravos' at Valencia.

1403 ORTIZ, Fernando
Contrapunteo cubana del tabaco y el azúcar . . . Habana, 1963. xix, 540 pp. illus.

Ch. 14: 'Del inicio de la trata de negros esclavos en América, de su relación con los ingenios de azúcar y del vituperio que cayó sobre Bartolomé de las Casas.'

1404 *OTTE, Enrique *and* RUIZ-BARRU-ECOS, Conchita
'Los Portugueses en la trata de esclavos negros de las postrimerías del siglo XVI.' (Moneda y Crédito, Madrid, vol. 85, 1963, pp. 3–40.)

1405 ANUNCIBAY, Francisco de
'Informe sobre la población indígena de la gubernación de Popayán y sobre la necesidad de importar negros para la explotación de sus minas . . . Año de 1592.' (Anuario Colombiano de Historia Social y de la Cultura, Bogotá, vol. 1, 1963, pp. 197–208.)

Report on the need for black slaves to work Andean mines.

1406 BRITO FIGUEROA, Federico
La estructura económica de Venezuela colonial. Caracas, 1963. 426 pp. bibl. pp. 407–21.

Ch. 4: 'La esclavitud y el comercio de negros'; statistics of the slave trade 1502–1810.

1407 PARRY, John Horace *and* SHERLOCK, Philip Manderson
A short history of the West Indies . . . Second edition. London, 1963. xii, 316 pp.

> Ch. 7: 'The slave trade and the asientos.'

1408 *DUIGNAN, Peter *and* CLENDENEN, Clarence Clemens
The United States and the African slave trade, 1619–1862. [Stanford, Cal.,] 1963. vii, 72 pp. bibl. pp. 63–72.

1409 MAC INNES, Charles Malcolm
Bristol and the slave trade. Bristol, 1963. 19 pp. illus.

1410 EVERAERT, J.
'Les fluctuations du trafic négrier nantais (1763–1792).' (Cahiers de Tunisie, Tunis, vol, 11, no. 43, 1963, pp. 37–62.)

> Statistical analysis showing the Nantes slave trade at its peak 1783–92, developing new markets in southern Africa and concentrating deliveries to St. Domingue.

1411 WELLS, Tom Henderson
'Charles Augustus Lafayette Lamar: gentleman slave trader.' (GHQ, 1963, pp. 158–68.)

> Lamar was involved in the illegal slave trade to the United States until 1858.

1412 MELLAFE, Rolando
La esclavitud en Hispanoamérica. Buenos Aires, 1964. 115 pp. bibl. pp. 103–15.

> Ch. 2: 'Formas y evolución de la trata negrera.'

1413 BRITO FIGUEROA, Federico
'El comercio de esclavos negros y la mano de obra esclavo en la economía colonial venezolana.' (Economía y Ciencias Sociales, Caracas, vol. 6, no. 3, 1964, pp. 5–46.)

> On the slave trade to Venezuela and colonial slavery 1500–1810.

1414 WOLFF, Inge
'Negersklaverei und Negerhandel in Hochperu 1545–1640.' (Jahrbuch für Geschichte von Staat, Wirtschaft und Gesellschaft Lateinamerikas, Köln, vol. 1, 1964, pp. 157–86.)

> On the licences and routes of the slave trade to Peru in the first century after the Spanish conquest.

1415 VERGER, Pierre
Bahia and the West African trade 1549–1851. [Ibadan,] 1964. 39 pp. illus, map.

> Largely on the slave trade.

1416 ESCALANTE, Aquiles
El negro en Colombia. Bogotá, 1964. 196 pp. maps.

> Pt. 1: 'Comercio y transporte de los esclavos.'

1417 CÓRDOVA-BELLO, Eleazar
Compañias holandesas de navegacion, agentes de la colonizacion neerlandesa. Sevilla, 1964. vi, 303 pp.

> Includes the history of the Dutch West India company and the slave trade in the 17th century.

1418 VERGER, Pierre
'Rôle joué par le tabac de Bahia dans la traite des esclaves au Golfe du Bénin.' (CEA, vol. 4, 1964, pp. 349–69.)

> The slave trade from the Dahomey-Lagos area to Bahia 1680–1850 and to Cuba until 1865 brought to them a strong Yoruba element.

1419 WAX, Darold Duane
'Robert Ellis, Philadelphia merchant and slave trader.' (PMHB, vol. 88, 1964, pp. 52–69.)

> Ellis traded in slaves 1719–41.

1420 RINCHON, Dieudonné
Pierre-Ignace-Liévin van Alstein capitaine négrier, Gand 1733—Nantes 1793. Dakar, 1964. 452 pp. (MIFAN, no. 71.) illus, maps.

> Life of a Belgian slave trader based on records of his slaving voyages to West Africa 1749–84. See (4544).

1421 *SEMPAT ASSADOURIAN, Carlos
El tráfico de esclavos en Córdoba, 1588–1610, según las actas de protocolos del Archivo Historico de Córdoba. Córdoba, Argentina, 1965. x, 36 pp.

1422 PEREDA VALDÉS, Ildefonso
El negro en el Uruguay pasado y presente. Montivideo, 1965. 300 pp. illus, map.

> Contains sections on the slave trade.

1423 LANGDON-DAVIES, John
The slave trade & its abolition . . . A collection of contemporary documents compiled and edited by John Langdon-Davies. London, [1965]. (Jackdaw. no. 12.)

> An educational folder.

1424 THOMAS, Hugh
'Slave trade.' (Observer Colour Magazine, London, 17 Oct. 1965, pp. 15–37;
illus, map.)

Account of the Atlantic slave trade.

1425 KELLENBENZ, Hermann
'Die Brandenburger auf St. Thomas.'
(Jahrbuch für Geschichte von Staat,
Wirtschaft und Gesellschaft Latein-
amerikas, Köln, vol. 2, 1965, pp. 196–
217.)

Describes the Brandenburg slave
trade to the West Indies 1686–98.

1426 WAX, Darold Duane
'Negro imports into Pennsylvania,
1720–1766.' (Pennsylvania History, Philadelphia, vol. 32, 1965, pp. 254–87.)

Tables of slave imports show a
sudden increase 1759–65.

1427 TAKAKI, Ronald Toshiyuki
'The movement to reopen the African
slave trade in South Carolina.' (South
Carolina Historical Magazine, Charleston, vol. 66, 1965, pp. 38–54.)

On the Southern controversy over
reviving the slave trade 1854–61.

1428 SEMPAT ASSADOURIAN, Carlos
El tráfico de esclavos en Córdoba de
Angola a Potosí, siglos XVI–XVII.
Córdoba, Argentina, 1966. xi, 60 pp.

1429 *VERGER, Pierre
O fumo da Bahia e o tráfico dos
escravos do gôlfo de Benim. [Salvador,
Brasil, 1966.] 39 pp.

See (1418).

1430 *DUARTE, Abelardo
Três ensaios. Maceió, 1966. 202 pp.

Pt. 2: 'Episódios do contrabando de
Africanos nas Alagoas.' (On the
illegal slave trade to Brazil.)

1431 BERNSTEIN, Barton J.
'Southern politics and attempts to
reopen the African slave trade.' (JNH,
vol. 51, 1966, pp. 16–35.)

Some Southerners used the slave trade
issue in the 1850s to prepare secession
but it was abandoned in 1860 for the
sake of Southern unity.

1432 DIAS, Manuel Nunes
'Fomento ultramarino e mercantilismo:
a Companhia do Grão-Pará e Maranhão (1755–1778).' (Revista de História,
São Paulo, vol. 32, 1966, pp. 359–428;
vol. 33, 1966, pp. 47–120, 367–415;
vol. 34, 1967, pp. 99–148; vol. 35,

1967, pp. 105–66; vol. 36, 1968, pp.
71–113; vol. 37, 1968, pp. 55–83; vol.
38, 1969, pp. 93–126; vol. 39, 1969,
pp. 85–120; vol. 40, 1970, pp. 91–112,
341–63; vol. 41, 1970, pp. 73–94,
347–400; illus, maps, bibl.)

Pt. 4, ch. 2, sect. c (vol. 37): 'As
carregações de mão-de-obra africana';
the slave trade was most lucrative
1756–66.

1433 *FORTUNE, Armando
'Los primeros negros en el istmo de
Panamá.' (Lotería, Panamá, vol. 12,
no. 144, 1967, pp. 56–85.)

On slave imports to Central America
in the 16th century.

1434 LARRAZÁBAL BLANCO, Carlos
Los negros y la esclavitud en Santo
Domingo. Santo Domingo, 1967.
200 pp.

With chapters on the slave trade of
the 16th–19th centuries and the African origins of the slaves.

1435 LAPEYRE, Henry
'Le trafic négrier avec l'Amérique
espagnole.' In: HOMENAJE a Jaime
Vicens Vives, vol. 2 (Barcelona, 1967),
pp. 285–306.

Statistics of slave imports to America
1596–1600 under the asiento granted
to Pedro Gomes Reynel.

1436 ACOSTA SAIGNES, Miguel
Vida de los esclavos negros en Venezuela. Caracas, [1967]. 410 pp. bibl.
pp. 399–410.

Includes chapters on the history of the
Venezuelan slave trade and on the
tribal origins of the slaves.

1437 POPE-HENNESSY, James
Sins of the fathers. A study of the Atlantic slave traders 1441–1807. London,
1967. 296 pp. illus, maps. bibl. pp.
281–85.

A 'selective study', mainly of the 18th
century trade.

1438 AYKROYD, Wallace Ruddell
Sweet malefactor: sugar, slavery and
human society. London, 1967. xv,
160 pp. illus. bibl. pp. 148–54.

Includes chapters on the slave trade
and abolition.

1439 ROTTENBERG, Simon
'The business of slave trading.'
(SAQ, vol. 66, 1967, pp. 409–23.)

On the English 18th century slave trade.

1440 WAX, Darold Duane
'Georgia and the negro before the American revolution.' (GHQ, vol. 51, 1967, pp. 63–77.)

Georgia was founded 1735 without slavery, but after settler protests slave imports were legalised 1750; by 1770 slaves formed nearly half the population.

1441 WAX, Darold Duane
'The demand for slave labour in colonial Pennsylvania.' (Pennsylvania History, Philadelphia, vol. 34, 1967, pp. 331–45.)

The need for slaves in the 18th century was limited by the local economy, white labour, and Quaker influence.

1442 VIEIRA, Hermes
Bandeiras e escravagismo no Brasil. São Paulo, 1967. 156 pp.

Contains sections on the Brazilian slave trade and its abolition.

1443 VERGER, Pierre
'Mouvements de navires entre Bahia et le Golfe de Bénin (XVIIᵉ–XIXᵉ siècles).' (RFHO, vol. 55, 1968, pp. 5–36.)

About 1,200,000 slaves were imported to Bahia 1678–1851, over two-thirds from the Gulf of Benin.

1444 VERGER, Pierre
Flux et reflux de la traite des nègres entre le Golfe de Bénin et Bahia de Todos os Santos du XVIIᵉ au XIXᵉ siècle. Paris, La Haye, 1968. 720 pp. illus, maps. bibl. pp. 19–25.

Detailed history of the slave trade to Bahia 1700–1850.

1445 DANTZIG, Albert van
Het nederlandse aandeel in de slaven-handel. Bussum, 1968. 144 pp. illus, maps.

Good popular history of the Dutch slave trade.

1446 ANSTEY, Roger Thomas
'Capitalism and slavery: a critique.' (EcHR, vol. 21, 1968, pp. 307–20.)

See (1309).

1447 JAKOBSSON, Stig
'Slavhandel och slaveri.' (Svensk Missionstidskrift, Uppsala, vol. 56, no. 1, 1968, pp. 46–53.)

Review of new edition of (1309).

1448 CURTIN, Philip De Armond
The Atlantic slave trade. A census. Madison (Wis.), 1969. xix, 338 pp. maps. bibl. pp. 299–311.

Detailed statistical analysis of the western slave trade estimating the total to be 9½ million slaves landed in Europe and the Americas 1451–1870.

1449 PLATT, Virginia Bever
'The East India Company and the Madagascar slave trade.' (WMQ, ser. 3, vol. 26, 1969, pp. 548–77.)

Malagasy slaves were brought to England's American colonies only 1676–98 and 1716–21, when the company ended the trade.

1450 *CONRAD, Robert Edgar
'The contraband slave trade to Brazil, 1831–1845.' (HAHR, vol. 49, 1969, pp. 617–38.)

1451 *HENDRIX, James Paisley
'The efforts to reopen the African slave trade in Louisiana.' (Louisiana History, New Orleans, 1969, pp. 97–123.)

On the slave trade agitation 1858–59.

1452 WILLIAMS, Eric Eustace
From Columbus to Castro: the history of the Caribbean 1492–1969. London, 1970. 576 pp. illus. bibl. pp. 516–58.

Includes chapters on the slave trade and abolition.

1453 SHUFELDT, Robert Wilson
'Secret history of the slave trade to Cuba written by an American naval officer, Robert Wilson Schufeldt, 1861, edited by Frederick C. Drake.' (JNH, vol. 55, 1970, pp. 218–35.)

Text of a letter describing the illegal slave trade carried on by Americans between the Congo and Cuba.

1454 KLEIN, Herbert Sanford
'North American competition and the characteristics of the African slave trade to Cuba, 1790 to 1794.' (WMQ, ser. 3, vol. 28, 1971, pp. 86–102.)

Havana port records show a rapid growth of United States involvement in the Cuban slave trade during the 1790s.

1455 THOMAS, Hugh
'The slave merchants.' *In his*: Cuba or the pursuit of freedom (London, 1971), pp. 156–67; map.

On the illegal Cuban slave trade in the 19th century.

1456 KLEIN, Martin Allen
'Slavery, the slave trade, and legitimate commerce in late nineteenth-century Africa.' (Études d'Histoire Africaine, Kinshasa, vol. 2, 1971, pp. 5–28.)

European demand for tropical products stimulated the use of slaves within Africa and thus the continuation of slave raiding.

K. BIOGRAPHIES OF SLAVES

1457 BLUETT, Thomas
Some memoirs of the life of Job, son of Solomon the high priest of Boonda in Africa; who was a slave about two years in Maryland; and afterwards being brought to England, was set free, and sent to his native land in the year 1734. Richard Ford, London, 1734. 63 pp.

Ayuba Suleiman Diallo, a Muslim Fulani of Futa Toro (Bondu), was kidnapped in 1730 on the Gambia and sold as a slave but was freed in America and returned to his homeland. See (1460, 1595). (Portrait: GM, 1750, p. 272.)

1458 The ROYAL African: or, memoirs of the young prince of Annamaboe. Comprehending a distinct account of his country and family; his elder brother's voyage to France, and reception there; the manner in which himself was confided by his father to the captain who sold him; his condition while a slave in Barbadoes; the true cause of his being redeemed; his voyage from thence; and reception here in England. Interspers'd throughout with several historical remarks on the commerce of the European nations, whose subjects frequent the coast of Guinea . . . W. Reeve; G. Woodfall & J. Barnes, London, [1750?] 53 pp.

Account of the enslavement of William Ansa Sasraku, son of a Gold Coast caboceer, and his redemption by the Royal African Company. (Portrait: GM, 1750, pp. 272.)

1459 GRONNIOSAW, Ukawsaw
A narrative of the most remarkable particulars in the life of James Albert Ukawsaw Gronniosaw, an African prince, as related by himself. S. Hazard, Bath, [1770?] 49 pp.

Story of a former 'Bournou' slave sold on the Gold Coast at the age of 15; after emancipation in America he settled in England 1762. (Reprinted at Newport, R.I., 1774.)

1460 'CASE of an emancipated slave.' (SM, vol. 34, June 1772, pp. 301–02.)

Letter written in London 1734 by 'Dgiagola, son of Dgiagola, prince of Foat, Africa' (Ayuba Suleiman Diallo) to his former master in Maryland. (Reprinted in: 1774; see 1457.)

1461 'TWO converted negroes to be sent on a mission to Africa.' (SM, vol. 36, Feb. 1774, pp. 62–63.)

Two African freedmen at Newport, R.I., prepare to return to the Gold Coast.

1462 'PETITION of an African slave, to the legislature of Massachusetts.' (Signed: Belinda.) (AM, vol. 1, June 1787, pp. 538–40.)

The 70-year-old petitioner refers to her enslavement in West Africa at the age of 12.

1463 EQUIANO, Olaudah
The interesting narrative of the life of Olaudah Equiano, or Gustavus Vassa, the African. Written by himself. London, [1789]. 2 vol. illus, port.

The author, an Igbo, was kidnapped about 1756 and sold into slavery in the West Indies; he describes his homeland, enslavement and subsequent experiences in America and Europe. (Reviewed in: CrR, vol. 68, 1789, p. 250; MR, vol. 80, 1789, pp. 551–52; GM, Jan. 1790, p. 539; reprinted with an introduction by Paul Edwards, London, 1969; see 1594.)

1464 *SMITH, Venture
A narrative of the life and adventures of Venture, a native of Africa, but resident above sixty years in the United States of America. Related by himself. C. Holt, New-London, Conn. 1798. 32 pp.

Attributed to Elisha Niles.

1465 RUSSISCHE Günstlinge. J. G. Cotta, Tübingen, 1809. viii, 502 pp.

By G. A. W. von Helbig. Includes a brief biographical sketch of 'Abraham

Hannibal', an African slave brought to the court of Peter the Great in 1704.

1466 The NEGRO servant; an authentic narrative of a young negro; shewing how he was made a slave in Africa, carried to Jamaica, and sold to a captain in His Majesty's navy; then taken to America, where he became a Christian; and afterwards brought to England, and baptized. Edinburgh, [1817]. 24 pp.

By Legh Richmond. (First published anonymously, signed 'Simplex', in: Christian Guardian, London, n.s., vol. 1, 1809, pp. 187–90, 310–16; vol. 2, 1810, pp. 17–22.)

1467 MOTT, Abigail
Biographical sketches and interesting anecdotes of persons of colour. Compiled by A. Mott. W. Alexander & Son, York, 1826. xi, 240 pp.

Includes notes on a number of African slaves.

1468 DRUMMOND, António de Meneses Vasconcellos
'Lettres sur l'Afrique ancienne et moderne . . .' (Journal des Voyages, Paris, vol. 32, 1826, pp. 290–324.)

Contains narratives of Hausa slaves recorded in Brazil 1819 by J. B. de Andrada e Silva (pp. 306–22).

1469 'ABDUHL Rahahman, the unfortunate Moorish prince.' (AR, vol. 4, May 1828, pp. 77–81.)

Biographical notes on a Futa Jallon nobleman captured about 1788 and sold as a slave to America; he was freed 1828 but died within a year in Liberia.

1470 *GALLAUDET, Thomas Hopkins
A statement with regard to the Moorish prince, Abduhl Rahhahman . . . Published by order of the committee appointed to solicit subscriptions in New York, to aid in redeeming the family of the prince from slavery. D. Fanshaw, New York, 1828. 8 pp.

See (1469).

1471 *EQUIANO, Olaudah
The life and adventures of Olaudah Equiano, or Gustavus Vassa, the African . . . Abridged by A. Mott. To which are added some remarks on the slave trade . . . S. Wood & Sons, New York, 1829. 36 pp.

1472 JA'FAR IBN 'ABD AL KARĪM
'The story of Ja' far, son of the sultan of Wadai.' (USJ, 1830, I, pp. 435–45, 547–58, 682–92.)

Narrative of a Wadai slave trader who was himself enslaved at Tripoli 1820–26, recorded by J. Barker, British consul at Alexandria.

1473 PRINCE, Mary
The history of Mary Prince, a West Indian slave. Related by herself . . . To which is added, the Narrative of Asa-Asa, a captured African. F. Westley & A. H. Davis, London; Waugh & Innes, Edinburgh, 1831. iv, 44 pp.

Edited by Thomas Pringle. Louis Asa-Asa, a Bassa boy captured and enslaved in 1826, was taken off a French ship, the 'Perle' (2593), in England.

1474 *MEMOIR of Mrs. Chloe Spear, a native of Africa, who was enslaved in childhood and died in Boston, January 3, 1815 . . . aged 65 years. By a lady of Boston. J. Loring, Boston, 1832. iii, 108 pp.

1475 THATCHER, Benjamin Bussey
Memoir of Phillis Wheatley, a native of Africa and a slave. Geo. W. Light, Boston; (etc.), 1834. 36 pp.

The story of an American poetess brought to Boston as a child on a slave ship in 1761.

1476 'ABDUHL Rahhaman.' (Colonizationist and Journal of Freedom, Boston, 1834, pp. 29–31; port.)

Account of the life of an enslaved Futa Jallon nobleman. See (1469).

1477 MADDEN, Richard Robert
A twelvemonth's residence in the West Indies . . . James Cochrane & Co., London, 1835. 2 vol.

Letter XXX contains an autobiographical narrative of a scholar from Timbuktu: 'The history of Abon Becr Sadiki, known in Jamaica by the name of Edward Donlan'. Abu Bakr had been captured by an Ashanti army as a youth about 30 years earlier and sold on the Gold Coast as a slave.

1478 *DWIGHT, Theodore
'On the Sereculeh nation in Nigritia.' (Americˈan Annals of Education and Instruction, Boston, vol. 5, 1835, pp. 451–56.)

Contains a 'Narrative of Lamen Kebe'. See (1509).

1479 RENOUARD, George Cecil
'Routes in North Africa, by Abú Bekr eş şiddík . . .' (JRGS, vol. 6, 1836, pp. 100–13.)

Includes a second autobiographical narrative by Abu Bakr written during his stay in London 1835 on his way home after being manumitted with the help of Dr. Madden. (For further notes on Abu Bakr see: FA, vol. 1, 1841, pp. 64, 151–53; vol. 2, 1842, p. 53.)

1480 WASHINGTON, John
'Some account of Mohammedu-Siseï, a Mandingo, of Nyáni-Marú on the Gambia.' (JRGS, vol. 8, 1838, pp. 448–54.)

Mohamedu had seen Mungo Park pass through his home town in 1805, when he was seventeen; captured during a war in 1810 he was sold to a French slaver which was intercepted by a British warship and taken to the West Indies.

1481 *BARBER, John Warner
A history of the Amistad captives: being a circumstantial account of the capture of the Spanish schooner Amistad, by the Africans on board; their voyage, and capture near Long Island, New York; with biographical sketches of each of the surviving Africans; also, an account of the trials had on their case, before the district and circuit courts of the United States, for the district of Columbia. Compiled from authentic sources, by John W. Barber . . . E. L. & J. W. Barber, New Haven, Ct., 1840. 32 pp. illus, map.

1482 The LIVES of two Ashantee, coast of Guinea, slaves, who were sold in Rio Grand. [Portsmouth? 1840?] (1 p.)

Broadsheet with narrative and verses sold by two ex-slaves from South Carolina.

1483 WRIGHT, Joseph
'Description of a slave war.' In: BEECHAM, J. Ashantee and the Gold Coast (London, 1841), pp. 349–58.

Autobiographical account by an Egba Yoruba of his enslavement about 1825 and recapture at sea by a British warship which landed him at Sierra Leone. Another version is printed in (1593).

1484 CROWTHER, Samuel Ajayi
'Letter of Mr. Samuel Crowther to the Rev. William Jowett, in 1837, then secretary of the Church Missionary Society, detailing the circumstances connected with his being sold as a slave.' In: SCHÖN, J. F. Journals of the Rev. James Frederick Schön and Mr. Samuel Crowther, who . . . accompanied the expedition up the Niger, in 1841 (London, 1842), pp. 371–85.

Account by a Yoruba of his capture as a child at Oshogu in 1821, sale to a ship at Lagos, liberation by a British warship and education at Sierra Leone. (First published anonymously in: Church Missionary Record, London, vol. 8, 1837, pp. 217–24.) See (1590).

1485 HODGSON, William Brown
Notes on northern Africa, the Sahara and Soudan . . . Wiley & Putnam, New York, 1844. 107 pp.

The author, American consul at Algiers, suggests that the slave trade of the Fulani could be stopped if they were converted to Christianity and abolition; he prints a 'Letter of James Hamilton Couper, Esq.' of Georgia, including the story of one of his slaves, "Sali-bul-Ali" (Şāliḥ Bilāli), a Fulani from Massina, captured as a boy and sold to a slave ship on the Gold Coast about 1790.

1486 AVEZAC-MACAYA, Marie Armand Pascal d'
Notice sur le pays et le peuple des Yébous en Afrique. Paris, 1845. 271 pp. (Mémoires de la Société Ethnologique, vol. 2, pt. 2; map, port.)

Description of Ijebu based on information given by a native of Ijebu-Ode, Ochi-Fêkouè Dê (Osifekode), sold as a slave to Brazil in 1820.

1487 McQUEEN, James
'Information obtained from Thomas Wogga, an African.' (JRGS, vol. 15, 1845, pp. 374–76.)

Account of a former slave (perhaps Tiv) shipped from New Calabar about 1815 and liberated at sea by a British warship.

1488 *VIE et mort d'une Ethiopienne décédée au Bon-Pasteur d'Angers le samedi 14 juin 1845. Vve Pignet-Chateau, Angers, [1845].

Pamphlet about Zoava (Camille), an African girl redeemed from slavery by Roman Catholics at Alexandria.

1489 'A LIBERATED African's account of his slavery, and subsequent course.' (CMG, vol. 6, 1846, pp. 16–18, 27–30.)

By M. T. Harding, a Gola recaptive? The author describes his enslavement as a child around 1810 and his life in Sierra Leone. (See also: ibid., vol. 4, 1844, pp. 134–35.)

1490 JOSEPH, John
Life and sufferings of John Joseph, a native of central Africa: who was stolen from his parents at the age of three years, and sold to a Mr. Johnston, a cotton planter, in one of the southern states of North America. Andrew Jack, Edinburgh, 1846. 8 pp.

Story of a young African who escaped to sea from New Orleans in 1843 and was picked up by an English ship.

1491 ARMISTEAD, Wilson
A tribute for the negro: being a vindication of the moral, intellectual, and religious capabilities of the coloured portion of mankind. Illustrated by numerous biographical sketches, facts, anecdotes, etc. . . . William Irwin, Manchester; (etc.), 1848. xxxv, 564 pp. illus.

Pt. 2 consists of 'Biographical sketches of Africans', many of them former slaves.

1492 FROBERVILLE, Eugène de
'Notes sur les Va-Niungue et les Mabsiti, peuples de l'Afrique orientale.' (Bulletin de la Société de Géographie, Paris, ser. 3, vol. 10, 1849, pp. 65–81.)

Information given by two Nyungwe refugees from the Nguni ('Maviti'), who were sold as slaves at Kilimane but were rescued from a Brazilian ship by the British about 1841.

1493 *SLAVERY illustrated in the histories of Zangara and Maquama, two negroes stolen from Africa and sold into slavery. Related by themselves. (Signed: W. A.) William Irwin, Manchester, 1849. 40 pp.

1494 'The SUFFERINGS and deliverance of James Gerber, a twice-liberated African.' (CMG, n.s., vol. 1, 1850, pp. 20–23; illus.)

Gerber, an Egba man, returned home 1843 after fifteen years in Sierra

Leone; in 1848 he was enslaved again but ransomed at Lagos.

1495 'HOW Thomas King became a slave.' (CMG, n.s., vol. 1, 1851, pp. 138–41; illus.)

King was kidnapped as a child in Yorubaland 1825 but was freed and brought to Sierra Leone; in 1850 he was reunited with his mother at Abeokuta.

1496 *ALLINSON, William J.**
Memoir of Quamino Buccau, a pious Methodist. Philadelphia, 1851. 30 pp.

1497 GOOD out of evil; or, the history of Adjai, the African slave boy; an authentic biography of the Rev. S. Crowther . . . By A.F.C. Second edition by the Rev. C. F. Childe. London, 1852. 112 pp.

By A. F. Childe. Story of the slave trade and of Crowther's enslavement and liberation, told for children. (First published 1850.)

1498 The AFRICAN slave boy. A memoir of the Rev. Samuel Crowther, church missionary at Abbeokuta, western Africa . . . London, [1852]. 124 pp.

Reprinted from 'Tracts for the young'.

1499 KOELLE, Sigismund Wilhelm
African native literature. London, 1854. xiv, 434 pp.

Includes 'A biographical sketch of Ali Eisami Gazir', a Kanuri kidnapped by Fulani about 1813 and sold at Porto Novo in 1818 but liberated at sea and sent to Sierra Leone.

1500 *BAQUAQUA, Mahommah Gardo**
Biography of Mahommah G. Baquaqua, a native of Zoogoo, in the interior of Africa (a convert to Christianity) with a description of that part of the world, including the manners and customs of the inhabitants . . . Mahommah's early life, his education, his capture and slavery in western Africa and Brazil, his escape to the United States, from thence to Hayti . . . his reception by the Baptist missionary there, the Rev. W. L. Judd; his conversion to Christianity . . . Written and revised from his own words, by Samuel Moore. Detroit, 1854. 65 pp.

1501 'CUBAN slaves in England.' (Anti-Slavery Reporter, London, ser. 3, vol. 2, 1854, pp. 234–39.)

Narrative of a number of self-emancipated slaves, mostly from Lagos, returning home from Cuba.

1502 ADAMS, Henry Gardiner
God's image in ebony: being a series of biographical sketches, facts, anecdotes, etc., demonstrative of the mental powers and intellectual capacities of the negro race. Edited by H. G. Adams . . . and a concluding chapter of additional evidence, communicated by Wilson Armistead, Esq. London, 1854. xxxi, 168 pp.

Includes accounts of a number of African slaves; ch. 5: 'Olaudah Equiano.'

1503 'The EMANCIPADOS and their fatherland.' (CMI, vol. 6, Dec. 1855, pp. 267–79; illus.)

On Yoruba recaptives in Cuba, including the story of John Baptist Dasalu, an Abeokuta Christian captured by the Dahomeans 1851 and shipped to Cuba 1854 (continued in vol. 7, 1856, pp. 241–44, 265–66).

1504 ERZÄHLUNGEN der drei Neger Mädchen Schiama, Gambra und Asue aus Afrika, welche von dem hochw. Herrn Canonicus Olivieri von Genua, aus der Sclaverei erlöst und in dem wohlehrwürd. Ursuliner-Kloster zu Bruneck vor 2 Jahren eine freundliche Aufnahme fanden. Ihre Rückerinnerungen an die Heimath, ihr Raub und Leiden in der Sclaverei mit vielen interessanten Andeutungen der wilden Sitten und Gebräuche jenes fernen Landes, sind wortgetreu nach ihren mündlichen Mittheilungen wiedergegeben. Bruneck, 1857. 88 pp.

Autobiographies of three Sudanese girls enslaved by Turks and Arabs and taken to Alexandria where they were purchased by an Italian priest and sent to a convent in South Tirol.

1505 'A RECENT incident of the slave trade.' (CMG, n.s., vol. 7, 1857, pp. 112–13.)

The story of a small Sherbro boy kidnapped by Susus but rescued by a British naval patrol.

1506 *NARRATIVE of Dimmock Charlton, a British subject, taken from the brig "Peacock" by the U.S. sloop "Hornet", enslaved while a prisoner of war, and retained forty-five years in bondage. (Signed: Mary L. and Susan H. Cox.) [Philadelphia? 1859.] 15 pp.

The story of an African rescued from a slaver by a British warship but captured by the Americans in 1812 and returned to slavery in Georgia.

1507 DORUGU
'The life and travels of Dorgu, as dictated by himself.' *In*: SCHÖN, J. F. Grammar of the Hausa language (London, 1862), pp. 215–34.

Story of a Hausa boy slave brought to England by H. Barth in 1855. The Hausa version in Schön's Magána Hausa (London, 1886) is translated and annotated by Paul Newman as 'The life and travels of Dorugu' in: KIRK-GREENE, A. H. M. West African travels and adventures (New Haven & London, 1971), pp. 27–130.

1508 *LONGINOV, Mikhail Nikolaevich
'Abram Petrovich Gannibal.' (Russky Arkhiv, Moskva, 1864, vol. 2, pp. 218–32.)

On Abraham Hannibal, Peter the Great's African favourite.

1509 DWIGHT, Theodore
'Condition and character of negroes in Africa.' (Methodist Quarterly Review, New York, vol. 46, 1864, pp. 77–90.)

On some literate African slaves in the United States, including the Soninke Lamine Kebe (enslaved about 1795) and Omar ibn Said; the latter referred to as 'Prince Moro' in: Christian Advocate, Philadelphia, vol. 3, 1825, pp. 306–07.

1510 'The DJUKU slave boy.' (CMG, vol. 16, 1866, pp. 75–76.)

Note on a Jukun boy, purchased by Baikie on the Benue 1853, educated at Sierra Leone and renamed William Carlin, who returned to Iddah as a teacher 1865.

1511 *ADJAÏ, ou le jeune esclave africain. Récit authentique destiné à la jeunesse. Société des Livres Religieux, Toulouse, 1867.

1512 *CALIXTE, le R.P.
Les fleurs du désert, ou vies admirables de trois jeunes éthiopiennes. Tahara, Amna, et Fadalcarim, avec des considérations sur l'œuvre de la régénération de l'Afrique centrale . . . Paris, 1869. 212 pp.

1513a GAUME, Jean Joseph
Suéma, ou la petite esclave africaine enterrée vivante. Histoire contem-

poraine dédiée aux jeunes chrétiennes de l'ancien et du nouveau monde. Paris, 1870. 222 pp.

Translated as :

1513b*'Suema: a tale of African life sixty years ago . . .' (Missionary Annals, Rathmines, vol. 8, 1926, pp. 207–10, 228–30; vol. 9, 1927, pp. 14–15, 32–33, 54–56, 68–69, 95–96, 113–16, 143–47.)

Narrative of a Nyasa girl taken as a slave to Zanzibar, written by a Catholic priest to raise money for the redemption of slave girls.

1514a*SÉGUR, Louis Gaston Adrien de
Aux enfants. Une petite sainte de neuf ans. Notice biographique publiée par Mgr de Ségur. Paris, 1870. 86 pp.

Translated as:

1514b*A little saint of nine years: a biographical notice . . . New York (etc.), 1881. ii, 120 pp.

Story of the African girl Amna (Sister Laurensine Fremiot, 1847–1855).

1515 *Les PETITES fleurs sauvages transplantées à l'ombre de la Vierge immaculée. Histoire de petites négresses sauvées des mains des gélabas. Récits véridiques dediés aux mères chrétiennes et à leurs pieux enfants. Annecy, 1871. xvii, 158 pp.

Narratives of three African girls, Haouah, Suéma and Adroféra Attisa, redeemed from slavery.

1516 'Un DRAME dans le désert. L'esclavage africain et nos relations avec le Soudan.' (Revue Politique Littéraire, Paris, ser. 2, vol. 5, 1873, pp. 493–98.)

Includes a note on a Hausa man, Atman from Hadeija, taken by Tuareg across the Sahara in 1872 and freed by the French at Wargla. The author suggests that the slave trade should be permitted in order to attract commerce to Algeria and obtain black labourers. See (4556).

1517 *NOTICE sur une jeune négresse. Extrait d'une lettre-circulaire du 1er monastère de la Visitation Sainte-Maire d'Annecy, datée du 28 décembre 1875. Annecy, 1876.

Pamphlet about an African girl called Marie, redeemed from slavery.

1518 *NOTICE sur la vie de la jeune sœur négresse Bakita Macca, décédée au monastère de la Visitation de Montéli-

mart . . . Extrait d'une "lettre-circulaire du même monastère", en date du 8 décembre 1878. Riom, 1879.

1519 ADJAI; or, the true story of a little African slave-boy. S.P.C.K., London, [1882]. 16 pp.

On Samuel A. Crowther.

1520 *FARRAGHIT, Emmanuel
'Farraghit, de jonge slaaf. Door J. S., Pr.' (Annalen der Afrikaansche Missiën, Rotterdam, vol. 3, 1886, pp. 3–20.)

Narrative of a Sudanese slave, redeemed by White Fathers in Algeria. Translation from Illustrated Catholic Missions, London, Feb. 1889, reproduced in: 4057, pp. 270–74. (Reprinted in: Maandelijksch Verslag der Afrikaansche Missiën, Mechelen, vol. 19, 1898, pp. 300–18, 327–35.)

1521 MADAN, Arthur Cornwallis
Kiungani; or, story and history from central Africa. Written by boys in the schools of the Universities' Mission to Central Africa. Translated and edited by A. C. Madan. London, 1887. xii, 291 pp. map.

Narratives written in Swahili at Zanzibar 1884 by a dozen freed slaves from different peoples in the area between Lake Nyasa and Uganda.

1522 *SORUR PHARIM DEN, Daniel
'Memorie scritte dal R. P. Daniele Sorur Pharim Dèn.' (Nigrizia, Verona, vol. 5, 1887, pp. 146–53, 170–77; vol. 6, 1888, pp. 56–59, 77–84, 111–19.)

Autobiography of a Dinka redeemed from slavery in Kordofan 1873 who was ordained as a Catholic priest 1887.

1523 SORUR PHARIM DEN, Daniel
'Lettre de Dom Daniel Sorur Dharim Den, prêtre nègre de l'Afrique centrale.' (Annales de la Propagation de la Foi, Lyon, vol. 60, 1888, pp. 51–66.)

Autobiographical narrative.

1524 PAGE, Jesse
Samuel Crowther. The slave boy who became Bishop of the Niger. London, [1889]. 160 pp. illus, map, port.

1525 *ZAPLETAL, Josef
Daniel Sorûr Pharîm Dèn. Die Geschichte eines schwarzen Priesters den kleinen Theilnehmern am Werke der heiligen Kindheit erzählt . . . Neue Ausgabe. Graz, 1889. 36 pp.

1526 *ARIBO, G.
'Das Leben des P. Daniel Sorur Pharim Dên, Neger aus dem Stamme der Dinka in Central-Afrika.' (Echo aus Afrika, Wien, vol. 1, 1890, no. 6, p. 2.)

1527 *'KORTE levensbeschrijvingen van twaalf der vrijgekochte kinderen door de Witte Paters.' (Annalen der Afrikaansche Missiën, Oudenbosch, vol. 6, 1890, pp. 168–71, 182–85, 209–12, 254–55; vol. 7, 1891, pp. 137–41.)

1528 *HALKA, Alexander, *pseud.*
'Das Scapulier des Sclaven. Erzählung aus dem schwarzen Welttheile.' (Echo aus Afrika, Wien, vol. 3, 1891, pp. 7–8, 15–16, 23–24, 30–32.)

By M. T. Ledóchowska.

1529 *CZERMIŃSKI, Marcýn
Pamiętnik miewolnika afrykánskiego. Kraków, 1891. 75 pp.

Memoirs of an African slave.

1530 FURAHANI, Martin
The autobiography of an African slave-boy. Translated from the Swahili . . . and edited by P. L. Jones-Bateman, Archdeacon of Zanzibar. Westminster, 1891. ii, 24 pp.

The narrator, originally Nyamtale from Bunyoro, was captured by Baganda, later sold to the Arabs and rescued by a British cruiser from a dhow near Pemba in 1880.

1531 *CENNI sulla vita della giovanetta africana Amna accolta nel venerando monastero della Visitazione in Pinerolo ed ivi morta nell'aprile 1856. Lettera della Superiora. Seconda edizione. Saluzzo, 1892. 95 pp.

Amna arrived at the convent in 1853, was baptized Giuseppina, but died after two years.

1532 *LEBENDIG begraben. Erlebnisse eines kleinen Negermädchens in den Händen arabischer Sklavenjäger . . . Münster i W., 1893. 63 pp.

By W. Helmes. See (1513).

1533 ALI EFFENDI GIFOON
'Memoirs of a Soudanese soldier (Ali Effendi Gifoon). Dictated in Arabic to and translated by Captain Percy Machell . . .' (CM, n.s., vol. 1, 1896, pp. 30–40, 175–87, 326–38, 484–92.)

The narrator, a Shilluk, was captured about 1859 by Baggara, enrolled in the Egyptian army and served in Mexico 1862–67.

1534 *'AKAL-KASSARA ossia il piccolo schiavo liberato.' (Nigrizia, Verona, vol. 15, 1897, pp. 70–76, 93–96, 108–10, 137–44, 154–55, 170–75, 187–89.)

1535 OKPARABIETOA PEPPLE, David
'Autobiography of David Okparabietoa Pepple.' (Niger and Yoruba Notes, London, vol. 5, Aug. 1898, pp. 13–14.)

Story of an Isuama Igbo kidnapped in childhood and brought to Bonny as a slave about 1860.

1536 *WILKINSON, Thomas Edward, *Bishop for North and Central Europe*
Saat; the native slave-boy of Khartoum. One of Sir Samuel Baker's expedition to the Albert Nyanza. London, 1898. 74 pp.

1537 *FARRAGHIT, Emmanuel
Farraghit le jeune esclave. Malines, [1898?] 48 pp.

Edited by G. Van den Bosch. See (1520).

1538 *ODUSINNA, der befreite Negerknabe. 5. Aufl. Basel, 1900. (Kleine Missions-Traktate. Nr. 2.)

1539 *SORUR PHARIM DEN, Daniel
'Vom afrikanischen Sklaven zum katholischen Priester (Selbstbiographie).' (Stern der Neger, Milan, vol. 3, 1900, pp. 27–34, 52–59, 84–88, 114–19, 133–36, 158–63, 178–85, 275–78.)

1540 *SORUR PHARIM DEN, Daniel
'Il Rev. P. Daniele Sorur, nero della tribù dei Denka, missionario dell'Africa centrale.' (Nigrizia, Verona, vol. 18, 1900, pp. 27–29, 44–45, 74–75.)

1541 'HISTOIRE d'une petite esclave rachetée par les religieuses d'Elmina.' (Annales de la Propagation de la Foi, Lyon, vol. 72, 1900, pp. 40–45; illus.)

Narrative of Adjuah, an Ashanti girl kidnapped about 1892, sold as a slave in Samori's territory and redeemed by the nuns in 1898.

1542 *HESTER, Alfred M.
Story of the slave; paper read before the Monmouth County Historical Association on October 30th, 1902, wherein is given some account of slavery and servitude in New Jersey, with notes concerning slaves and redemptioners in other states. Camden, N. J., 1903. 40 pp.

Includes the narrative of the last survivor of the 500 African slaves landed by the 'Wanderer' in Georgia 1858.

1543 AHUMA, Samuel Richard Brew Attoh
Memoirs of West African celebrities,
Europe, &c. (1700–1850). With special
reference to the Gold Coast. Liverpool,
1905. xx, 260 pp.

Contains material on a number of
former slaves.

1544 PAGE, Jesse
The black bishop, Samuel Adjai Crowther. London, 1908. xv, 440 pp. map.

Ch. 1, 'A little slave boy', includes
Crowther's own narrative of his enslavement and release. (This work
provided material for several popular
booklets on Crowther issued by the
C.M.S. 1913–37.)

1545 MONTGOMERY, Charles J.
'Survivors from the cargo of the negro
slave yacht Wanderer.' (AA, n.s.,
vol. 10, 1908, pp. 611–23.)

Description of some Congolese
brought to the United States as
slaves in 1858.

1546 *FARRAGHIT, Emmanuel
'Emmanuel Farraghit or the story of
a young slave told by himself.' (African
Missions, Quebec, 1909, pp. 25–30,
91–95, 122–27, 156–59.)

1547 CAMPBELL, Dugald
Ten times a slave but freed at last.
Glasgow; London, [1916]. 32 pp. map,
port.

The story of Bwanikwa, a Luba
woman sold to the Yeke in Msiri's
time.

1548 *CAMPBELL, Henry D.
A Congo chattel; the story of an African
slave girl . . . New York, [1917].
213 pp. illus.

1549 EEKHOF, Albert
'De negerpredikant Jacobus Elisa Johannes Capitein. Bijdrage tot de
kennis van onze koloniale kerkgeschiedenis.' (Nederlandsch Archief voor
Kerkgeschiedenis, 's-Gravenhage, n.s.,
vol. 13, 1917 ,pp. 138–74, 209–76;
port.)

Biography of an African from the
Ivory Coast who was bought as a
child and educated in the Netherlands.
See (1721).

1550 HOUGH, F. Harrison
'Gregoire's sketch of Angelo Soliman.'
(JNH, vol. 4, 1919, pp. 281–89.)

On the life of an 18th-century African
(perhaps Mandinka) captured in

childhood and brought as a slave
to Sicily.

1551 *BEDUSCHI, Giuseppe
Il piccolo schiavo. Verona, 1922. 63 pp.

1552 PARRY, Albert
'Abram Hannibal, the favourite of
Peter the Great.' (JNH, vol. 8, 1923,
pp. 359–66.)

Brief account of the tsar's 'Ethiopian'
servant.

1553a *MSATURWA, Wasimira
Wege die ich gegangen bin. Erlebnisse
des Lehrers von Utengule, Deutsch-
Ostafrika. Von ihm selbst erzählt.
Herrnhut, 1923. 40 pp.

Translated as:

1553b Ways I have trodden. The experience
of a teacher in Tanganyika, told by
himself. Translated and abridged . . .
from the German . . . of Frau Elise
Kootz-Kretschmer . . . London, 1932.
32 pp.

The narrator was enslaved as a child
in 1891 but escaped in 1900 to a
mission station.

1554 OMAR IBN SAID
'Autobiography of Omar ibn Said,
slave in North Carolina, 1831.' (AHR,
vol. 30, 1924, pp. 787–95.)

Account written by a Fulani of
Futa Toro captured and sold to
America in 1807.

1555 HEARN, Lafcadio
'The last of the Voudoos.' *In his:*
Miscellanies, vol. 2 (London, 1924),
pp. 201–08.

Obituary of Jean Montanet of New
Orleans, a former slave from Senegal.
(Reprinted from Harper's Weekly,
7 Nov. 1885.)

1556 *O'GORMAN, John Joseph
'Chicaba: the African princess, who
later became Ven. Sister Teresa Juliana
of Saint Dominic.' (Missionary Annals,
Rathmines, Vol. 6, 1924, pp. 208–10,
230–33; vol. 7, 1925, pp. 10–12.)

1557 *KOOTZ, Elise
Grossmutter Narwimba. Was sie erlebte
und was sie erlitt. Herrnhut, 1925.
24 pp.

See (1563).

1558 *WALLIS, Patrick
'Daniel Faragi—catechist. A missionary
tale of African slave days.' (Missionary
Annals, Rathmines, vol. 8, 1926, pp.
132–44.)

1559 HURSTON, Zora Neale
'Cudjo's own story of the last African slaver.' (JNH, vol. 12, 1927, pp. 647–63.)

Interview with Cudjo Lewis, the last survivor of the slaves brought to the United States on the 'Clotilde' in 1859; Lewis himself was captured by the Dahomeans and sold at Whydah. See (814, 1562).

1560 *KOOTZ-KRETSCHMER, Elise
Tatu, das geraubte Muvembakind. Herrnhut, 1927. 18 pp. illus.

1561 KUKU, Aaron
The life of Aaron Kuku of Eweland, born 1860—died 1929. Told by himself. Translated and abridged from the German version of Rev. P. W. Wiegräbe . . . London, 1931. 24 pp.

Kuku, captured by the Ashanti about 1869, escaped to return home and became a chief and a Christian evangelist.

1562 'HONORING Cudjo Lewis: America's last piece of African "black ivory".' (Literary Digest, New York, vol. 111, 21 Nov. 1931, pp. 36–37; port.)

Interview with Lewis, the last survivor of the slaves brought to Alabama on the 'Clotilde'. See (1559).

1563 KOOTZ-KRETSCHMER, Elise
Stories of old times. Being the autobiographies of two women of East Africa. Translated and abridged from the German . . . London, 1932. 32 pp.

Narratives of two former slaves, Chisi-Ndjurisiye Sichayunga (Bisa) and Narwimba (Lambya); the former first published as 'Xisi-Nguririje Sixyajunga erzählt' in the editor's: Die Safwa, vol. 2 (Berlin, 1929), pp. 321–31.

1564 DORUGU
The story of Dorugu. London, [1932]. 30 pp.

Extract from: SCHÖN, J. F. Magána Hausa (London, 1886). See (1507).

1565 SCHÖN, Jacob Friedrich
Hausa tales. Told by Dorugu and others. London, 1932. 24 pp.

Includes stories of the slave trade.

1566 *'VOM Sklaven zum Missionsarzt. Werden und Wirken eines Negerarztes am Tanganjika, Adrian Atiman.' (Afrika-Bote, Trier, vol. 39, 1933, pp. 24–28, 52–56, 79–84, 108–12, 137–40, 165–68, 193–96, 221–24, 248–52, 276–80, 307–08.)

See (1588).

1567 DINSMORE, Charles Allen
'Interesting sketches of the Amistad captives.' (Yale University Library Gazette, New Haven, vol. 9, 1935, pp. 51–55; illus.)

Describes a collection of pencil sketches of Africans, mostly Mende, from the slave ship 'Amistad', drawn about 1840 by W. H. Townsend.

1568 ABŪ BAKR AL-SĪDDĪQ
'Abou Bekir Sadiki, alias Edward Doulan.' (JNH, vol. 21, 1936, pp. 52–55.)

Text of a manuscript account written in Jamaica 1834, edited by Charles H. Wesley.

1569 KILEKWA, Petro
Slave boy to priest. The autobiography of Padre Petro Kilekwa. Translated from the Chinyanja by K. H. Nixon Smith. [London,] 1937. 63 pp. illus, port.

Kilekwa (Chilekwa), of the Bisa tribe, was captured by Angoni about 1883, sold to Swahili slave traders, rescued from an Arab dhow off Muscat by a British warship 1885 and sent to Zanzibar.

1570 SEEBER, Edward Derbyshire
'Phillis Wheatley.' (JNH, vol. 24, 1939, pp. 259–62.)

On the African-born poetess who arrived as a child in Boston 1761.

1571 WILSON, Salim Charles
I was a slave. By Salim C. Wilson (Hatashil Masha Kathish). London, 1939. 256 pp. illus, port.

Reminiscences of a Dinka enslaved by Arabs about 1874 and freed by governor Gordon.

1572 SYPHER, Wylie
'The African prince in London.' (Journal of the History of Ideas, Lancaster, Pa., vol. 2, 1941, pp. 237–47.)

Account of five Africans, including Job ben Solomon and Equiano, who came to London in the eighteenth century.

1573 *BISHOP, Morris
'Cinque, the noble mutineer.' (New Yorker, vol. 17, 20 Dec. 1941, pp. 62 ff.)

On the leader of the 'Amistad' revolt, 1839.

1574 NETTL, Paul
'Angelo Soliman—friend of Mozart.' (Phylon, Atlanta, vol. 7, 1946, pp. 41–46.)

See (1550).

1575 *MACAULAY, Herbert
'The romantic story of the life of a little Yoruba boy named Adjai.' (Nigeria, Ibadan, no. 24, 1946, pp. 169–79.)

On S. A. Crowther.

1576 MIDDLETON, Arthur Pierce
'The strange story of Job Ben Solomon.' (WMQ, ser. 3, vol. 5, 1948, pp. 342–50.)

See (1457).

1577 MYNORS, T. H. B.
'The adventures of a Darfur slave.' (SNR, vol. 30, 1949, pp. 273–75.)

Account of the life of Bakir Ahmed, captured in a slave raid as a child and taken to Nubia.

1578 CALLCOTT, George H.
'Omar ibn Seid, a slave who wrote an autobiography in Arabic.' (JNH, vol. 39, 1954, pp. 58–63.)

1579 *'DR. Adriaan Atiman: een gewezen slaaf, geneesheerkatechist te Karema.' (Signed: N.A.K.) (Nieuw Afrika, Antwerpen, vol. 71, no. 6, 1955, pp. 249–52.)

See (1588).

1580 KIRK-GREENE, Anthony Hamilton Millard
'Abbega and Durogu. An account . . . of two Northern Nigerian students who landed in Britain one hundred years ago.' (West African Review, Liverpool, vol. 27, 1956, pp. 865–69.)

On a Margi and a Hausa boy liberated from slavery and brought to England by H. Barth in 1855. See (1507).

1581 MBOTELA, James Juma
The freeing of the slaves in East Africa. London, 1956. 87 pp. illus.

Translation of a Swahili story based on the reminiscences of the author's father, captured by slave traders in the Lake Nyasa area, freed by a British patrol at sea and settled at Mombasa. (Swahili version: Uhuru wa watumwa, 1934.)

1582 COOK, Fred James
'The slave ship rebellion.' (AH, vol. 8, no. 2, 1957, pp. 60–64, 104–06; illus.)

Account of the revolt of Mende slaves on the 'Amistad' 1839. See (1481).

1583 BARTELS, Francis Lodowic
'Jacobus Eliza Johannes Capitein, 1717–47.' (Transactions of the Historical Society of Ghana, Legon, vol. 4, no. 1, 1959, pp. 3–13.)

See (1549).

1584 LLOYD, Peter Cutt
'Osifakorede of Ijebu.' (Odù, Ibadan, no. 8, 1961, pp. 59–64.)

See (1486).

1585* HAIR, Paul Edward Hedley
'An Ijebu man in Paris 1839.' (Nigeria, Ibadan, no. 68, 1961, pp. 79–82; illus.)

On Osifekunde. See (1486).

1586 HIRN, Sven
'Hannibal och Gamla Finland.' In his: Strövtåg i österled: kulturhistoriska studier (Helsinki, 1963), pp. 48–55; port.

Account of Abram Hannibal's activities as an engineering officer in Russia's Baltic provinces.

1587 NABOKOV, Vladimir
'Abram Gannibal.' In: PUSHKIN, A. Eugene Onegin . . . Translated . . . with a commentary, by Vladimir Nabokov, vol. 3 (London, 1964), pp. 387–447.

Biographical notes on Pushkin's grandfather, concluding that he came from Abyssinia. (First published as 'Pushkin and Gannibal: a footnote' in: Encounter, London, vol. 19, no. 1, 1962, pp. 11–26.)

1588 FOUQUER, Roger
Le docteur Adrien Atiman. Médecin-catéchiste au Tanganyika, sur les traces de Vincent de Paul. Paris, 1964. 166 pp.

Atiman, a Sorko from the Timbuktu area, was sold into slavery as a child, redeemed by White Fathers in North Africa 1876, trained in Malta and sent as a medical missionary to Tanganyika.

1589 ROCHE, Aloysius
Bakhita, Pearl of the Sudan. Langley, [1964]. 95 pp. illus, map, port.

Biography of Josephine Bakhita, born in Darfur, kidnapped as a girl and redeemed by Italian missionaries at Khartum in 1881.

1590 CROWTHER, Samuel Ajayi
'A second narrative of Samuel Ajayi Crowther's early life.' (Bulletin of the Society for African Church History, Aberdeen, vol. 2, no. 1, 1965, pp. 5–14.)

> Text of a letter written by Crowther in 1841, describing his capture by Muslims at the age of thirteen, the route to Lagos and his liberation by a British warship in 1822. See (1484).

1591 MONTEITH, Archibald John
'Archibald John Monteith: native helper and assistant in the Jamaica mission at New Carmel.' (Transactions of the Moravian Historical Society, Nazareth, Pa., vol. 21, pt. 1, 1966, pp. 29–62.)

> Account of an Igbo ex-slave (Aneaso), recorded in 1853 by J. H. Kummer; edited by Vernon H. Nelson.

1592 ABDULBAKI, *Sarkin Burmi*
'Abdulbaki Tanimuddarin Tureta'. *In*: JOHNSTON, H. A. S. A selection of Hausa stories (Oxford, 1966), pp. 144–52.

> Extract from an autobiography of the same title (Zaria, 1954); the author was captured as a youth and kept as a slave among the Tuareg.

1593 CURTIN, Philip De Armond
Africa remembered. Narratives by West Africans from the era of the slave trade. Madison (Wis.), 1967. x, 363 pp. maps.

> Extracts with notes from the biographical accounts of the ex-slaves Ayuba Suleiman Diallo, Olaudah Equiano, Salih Bilali, Abu Bakr al-Siddiq, Ali Eisami Gazirmabe, Osifekunde, Samuel Crowther and Joseph Wright.

1594 EQUIANO, Olaudah
Equiano's travels. His autobiography ... Abridged and edited by Paul Edwards, London, 1967. xviii, 196 pp. illus, maps, port.

> See (1463).

1595 GRANT, William Douglas Beattie
The fortunate slave. An illustration of African slavery in the early eighteenth century. London, 1968. xii, 231 pp. map, port.

> Biography of 'Job, son of Solliman Dgiallo'. See (1457).

1596 EDWARDS, Paul
' "... Written by himself"; a manuscript letter of Olaudah Equiano.' (Notes and Queries, London, n.s., vol. 15, no. 6, 1968, pp. 222–25.)

> A letter of 1792 shows Equiano's fluency in English.

1597 'POSTMARKED 1841.' (AH, vol. 22, no. 1, 1970, p. 111.)

> A letter written from prison by Ka-le, one of the Mende slaves on the 'Amistad', to their defence counsel John Quincy Adams.

K

L. ETHNIC ORIGINS OF SLAVES

1598 **SANDOVAL, Alonso de**
Naturaleza, policia sagrada i profana, costumbres i ritos, disciplina i catechismo evangelico de todos Etiopes. Francisco de Lira, Sevilla, 1627. 334, 81 ll.

> Bk. 1 lists the West African peoples, from Senegal to Angola, known through the slave trade. See (1690).

1599 **BESCHRIJVINGHE** van de volkplantinge Zuriname . . . als ook de slaafsche afrikaansche Mooren . . . Door J. D. Hl. Meindert Injema, Leeuwarden, 1718. 262 pp. illus, map.

> By J. D. Herlein. With a chapter on the origins and transportation of African slaves in Surinam.

1600 **HARTSINCK, Jan Jacob**
Beschryving van Guiana, of de Wildekust, in Zuid-Amerika . . . Waarby komt eene verhandeling over den aart en de gewoontes der negerslaaven . . . Gerrit Tielenburg, Amsterdam, 1770. xii, 962 pp. maps.

> Ch. 25: 'Beschryving der slaaven'; most of the slaves in Surinam come from the Gold Coast and Dahomey.

1601 **OLDENDORP, Christian Georg Andreas**
C. G. A. Oldendorps Geschichte der Mission der evangelischen Brüder auf den caraibischen Inseln S. Thomas, S. Croix und S. Jan. Herausgegeben durch Johann Jakob Bossart. Christian Friedrich Laur, Barby; Weidmanns Erben & Reich, Leipzig, 1777. 1068 pp.

> Includes chapters on the slave trade from West Africa and on the nationalities of the slaves, based on interviews in the West Indies.

1602 'VON den Varietäten und Abarten der Neger.' (Signed: M.) (GHM, vol. 6, 1790, pp. 625–45.)

> By C. Meiners. Description of Africans, based largely on observation of slaves.

1603 **EDWARDS, Bryan**
The history, civil and commercial, of the British colonies in the West Indies. John Stockdale, London, 1793. 2 vol. maps.

> With chapters on the slave trade and tribal origins of the slaves. (Reviewed in: MR, n.s., vol. 14, 1794, pp. 158–70, 292–300; vol. 15, 1794, pp. 63–70, 302–11.) See (2182).

1604 **STEDMAN, John Gabriel**
Narrative of a five years' expedition against the revolted negroes of Surinam, in Guiana, on the Wild Coast of South America; from the year 1772, to 1777 . . . with an account of the Indians of Guiana & negroes of Guinea . . . J. Johnson; J. Edwards, London, 1796. 2 vol. illus, maps.

> Includes sections on the slave trade and the African origins of the slaves in Surinam.

1605 **MOREAU DE SAINT-MÉRY, Médéric Louis Élie**
Description topographique, physique, civile, politique et historique de la partie française de l'île Saint-Domingue . . . Philadelphie, 1797, 98. 2 vol.

> Section 2, 'Des esclaves venu d'Afrique', describes the African nations represented among the slaves of St. Domingue, from Senegal to Mozambique.

1606 **BRIDGES, George Wilson**
The annals of Jamaica. John Murray, London, 1828. 2 vol.

> Concluding chapter: 'The original state of the negroes in their native land.'

1607 **CARMICHAEL, A. C.,** *Mrs*
Domestic manners and social condition of the white, coloured and negro population of the West Indies. Whittaker, Treacher & Co., London, 1833. 2 vol.

> Ch. 12: 'Conversations with native Africans.'

1608 'ON African ethnography.' (FA, no. 6, April 1847, pp. 84–86.)

Account of some African boys brought to Bavaria from Egypt, originating from Darfur and the Dinka and Galla areas.

1609 CLARKE, Robert
Sierra Leone. A description of the manners and customs of the liberated Africans . . . J. Ridgway; Johnson & Co., London, [1843]. iv, 178 pp. illus, map.

Includes notes on various nationalities.

1610 CLARKE, John
Specimens of dialects: short vocabularies of languages: and notes of countries & customs in Africa. Daniel Cameron, Berwick-upon-Tweed, 1848. 104 pp.

Shows the range of African languages (over 350 dialects) represented in the West Indies and among recaptured slaves in West Africa 1830–48.

1611 KOELLE, Sigismund Wilhelm
Polyglotta africana; or a comparative vocabulary of nearly three hundred words and phrases, in more than one hundred distinct African languages. London, 1854. vi, 24, 188 pp. map.

The introduction on the 179 informants, liberated slaves at Sierra Leone, provides information on the slave routes of the Sudan, West and East Africa. See (1667–68, 1672).

1612 CLARKE, Robert
'Sketches of the colony of Sierra Leone and its inhabitants.' (Transactions of the Ethnological Society of London, n.s., vol. 2, 1863, pp. 320–63; illus.)

Describes liberated slaves of several dozen nationalities.

1613 LAST, J. T.
Polyglotta africana orientalis. A comparative collection of two hundred and fifty words and sentences in forty-eight languages and dialects spoken south of the equator . . . London, [1886]. xii, 239 pp. map.

Twenty of the informants, interviewed in East Africa 1879–84, were slaves.

1614 *ORTIZ, Fernando
'Procedencia de los negros de Cuba.' (Cuba y América, New York, vol. 20, no. 6, 1905, pp. 91–92.)

1615 ÉTIENNE, Ignace
'La secte musulmane des Malès du Brésil et leur révolte en 1835.' (Anthropos, Wien, vol. 4, 1909, pp. 99–105, 405–15.)

On Muslim slaves in Bahia, mostly Yoruba. (Longer version: 'Os Malês', RIHGB, vol. 72, 1909, pp. 69–126; illus.)

1616 CLAUDIO, Affonso
'As tribus negras importadas. Estudo ethnographico, sua distribuição regional no Brasil. Os grandes mercados de escravos.' (RIHGB, tomo especial consagrado ao Primeiro Congresso de Historia Nacional, 1914, pt. 2, Rio de Janeiro, 1915, pp. 595–657.)

Includes a chapter on the slave trade and the ethnic origins of the slaves imported to Brazil. (Additional material by Braz do Amaral: ibid., pp. 661–90.)

1617 *ORTIZ, Fernando
Hampa afro-cubana. Los negros esclavos; estudio sociológico y de derecho publico . . . Habana, 1916. viii, 536 pp. illus.

Contains material on the Cuban slave trade and the geographical origins of the Afro-Cubans.

1618 CRUIKSHANK, J. Graham
'Among the 'Aku' (Yoruba) in Canal No. 1, West Bank, Demerara River.' (Timehri, Demerara, ser. 3, vol. 4, 1917, pp. 70–82; illus.)

About 700 Africans (mostly Kongo and Yoruba), introduced as 'immigrants' 1838–51, still lived in British Guiana in 1911.

1619 *DUMONT, Henri
Estudio de antropología y patología de las razas de color de origen africano de la isla de Cuba. Habana, 1922.

Essay written 1876.

1620 LINDBLOM, Karl Gerhard
Afrikanische Relikte und indianische Entlehnungen in der Kultur der Buschneger Surinams. Eine vergleichende ethnographische Studie. Göteborg, 1924. 120 pp. illus.

Ch. 1: 'Ursprung und Transport der Sklaven aus Westafrika.'

1621 *AMARAL, Braz Hermenegildo do
'Os grandes mercados de escravos africanos: as tribus importadas e sua distribuição regional.' (RIHGB, tomo especial, Congresso Internacional de Historia da America, 1922, vol. 5, Rio de Janeiro, 1927, pp. 437–96.)

On the Brazilian slave trade.

1622 HERSKOVITS, Melville Jean
'The New World negro as an anthropological problem.' (Man, London, vol. 31, 1931, pp. 68–69.)

1623 NINA RODRIGUES, Raimundo
Os Africanos no Brasil . . . São Paulo, 1932. 409 pp. illus.

Brazilian slaves were mostly of 'Sudanese' origin in Bahia and Bantu elsewhere.

1624 *HERSKOVITS, Melville Jean
'On the provenience of New World negroes.' (Journal of Social Forces, Chapel Hill, N.C., vol. 12, 1933, pp. 247–62.)

1625 *RAIMUNDO, Jacques
O elemento afro-negro na lingua portuguesa. Rio de Janeiro, 1933. 191 pp. bibl. pp. 181–91.

1626 *MENDONÇA, Renato
A influência africana no português do Brasil . . . Rio de Janeiro, 1933. 138 pp. maps.

1627 ESTUDOS afro-brasileiros. Trabalhos
apresentados ao 1° Congresso Afro-Brasileiro reunido no Recife em 1934 . . . Rio de Janeiro, 1935. 275 pp. map.

1628 *NOVOS estudos afro-brasileiros. Tra-
balhos apresentados ao 1° Congresso Afro-Brasileiro de Recife . . . Rio de Janeiro, 1937. iv, 352 pp. illus.

By Gilberto Freyre and others.

1629 RAMOS, Arthur
As culturas negras no Novo Mundo. Rio de Janeiro, 1937. 399 pp.

With chapters on the slave trade and tribal origins of slaves in South and North America.

1630 *CARNEIRO, Edison
Negros bantús. Notas de etnographía religiosa e folklore. Rio de Janeiro, 1937. 187 pp. illus, map.

On Bantu influence in Brazil.

1631 PUCKETT, Newball Niles
'Names of American negro slaves.' In: STUDIES in the science of society presented to Albert Galloway Keller (New Haven, 1937), pp. 471–94.

Lists African and other names from the 17th–19th century. (Comments by M. D. W. Jeffreys in: AA, vol. 50, 1948, pp. 571–73.)

1632 HERSKOVITS, Melville Jean
'African ethnology and the New World

negro.' (Man, London, vol. 38, 1938, pp. 9–10.)

1633 COELHO DE SENNA, Nelson
Africanos no Brasil . . . Bello Horizonte, 1938 [1940]. 297 pp. bibl. pp. 275–97.

Describes the African tribes and languages brought to Brazil by the slave trade.

1634 HERSKOVITS, Melville Jean
'The ancestry of the American negro.' (American Scholar, New York, vol. 8, 1939, pp. 84–94.)

Most American negroes are of West African origin.

1635 *VIANNA, Luís
'Rumos e cifras do tráfico bahiano.' (Estudos Brasileiros, Rio de Janeiro, vol. 3, 1940, pp. 356–80.)

On the origins of Africans imported to Bahia.

1636 *LATOUR, M. D.
'Boessalsche negers.' (WIG, vol. 22, 1940, pp. 161–65.)

1637 HERSKOVITS, Melville Jean
The myth of the negro past. New York, London, [1941]. xiv, 374 pp. bibl. pp. 341–55.

Contains chapters on the African background of slaves brought to America.

1638 *PIERSON, Donald
'Os Africanos de Bahia.' (Revista do Arquivo Municipal de São Paulo, vol. 7, no. 78, 1941, pp. 39–64.)

1639 PIERSON, Donald
Negroes in Brazil . . . Chicago, 1942. xxviii, 392 pp.

Includes a chapter on the history of the slave trade to Brazil and the African origins of the slaves.

1640a FREYRE, Gilberto
Casa-grande & senzala. Formação da familia brasileira sob o regime de economia patriarcal. 4a edição, definitiva. Rio de Janeiro, 1943. 2 vol. bibl. vol. 2, pp. 715–48.

Translated as:

1640b The masters and the slaves . . . A study
of the development of Brazilian civilisation. New York, 1946. lxxi, 537, xliv pp. bibl. pp. 501–37.

Includes chapters on the African background of slaves in Brazil. (First Brazilian edition 1934.)

1641 **KING, James Ferguson**
'Descriptive data on negro slaves in Spanish importation records and bills of sale.' (JNH, vol. 28, 1943, pp. 204–30.)

On African ethnic origins shown in Caribbean documents of the mid-18th century.

1642 **RAMOS, Arthur**
Introdução à antropologia brasileira. Rio de Janeiro, 1943, 47. 2 vol. illus, maps.

Vol. 1, pt. 2: 'As culturas negras.'

1643 **RAMOS, Arthur**
Las poblaciones del Brasil. México, 1944. 207 pp.

Ch. 12: 'Grupos étnicos del negro.'

1644 **ASHLEY-MONTAGU, Montague Francis**
'The African origins of the American negro and his ethnic composition.' (Scientific Monthly, Washington, vol. 58, 1944, pp. 58–65.)

1645 ***ELIE, Louis E.**
Histoire de Haïti . . . Port-au-Prince, 1944, 45. 2 vol.

Subtitle of vol. 2: 'Les origines du peuple haïtien.'

1646 **AGUIRRE BELTRÁN, Gonzalo**
La población negra de México, 1519–1810. Estudio etnohistórico . . . México, 1946. xi, 347 pp. maps. bibl. pp. 301–19.'

With sections on the economic history of the slave trade and the ethnic origins of the slaves.

1647 **AGUIRRE BELTRÁN, Gonzalo**
'Tribal origins of slaves in Mexico.' (JNH, vol. 31, 1946, pp. 269–352; maps.)

Study of the African origins of Mexican slaves.

1648 **MENDONÇA, Renato**
A influência africana no português do Brasil . . . 3ª edição. Porto, 1948. 285 pp. maps.

Ch. 3: 'O tráfico'; ch. 4: 'Povos negros importados.'

1649 **TURNER, Lorenzo Dow**
Africanisms in the Gullah dialect. Chicago, 1949. xi, 317 pp. maps.

Suggests West African derivations for thousands of words in a negro dialect of South Carolina and Georgia. See (1671).

1650 ***NEIVA, Artur Hehl**
'Proveniência das primeiras levas de escravos africanos.' In: INSTITUTO HISTORICO E GEOGRAFICO BRASILEIRO, IV Congresso de História Nacional, 1949, Anais, vol. 4 (Rio de Janeiro, 1950), pp. 487–523.

1651 **OTT, Carlos**
'O negro bahiano.' (MIFAN, no. 27, 1952, pp. 141–52.)

Most Bahian slaves were of West African origin, after 1830 particularly Yoruba.

1652 **PEREDA VALDÉS, Ildefonso**
'El negro rioplatense. Razas y pueblos africanos trasplantados al continente americano . . .' (MIFAN, no. 27, 1952, pp. 257–61.)

The Uruguayan slave trade increased slightly after 1800, introducing mainly Bantu from Congo and Angola.

1653 **COHEN, Hennig**
'Slave names in colonial south America.' (American Speech, New York, vol. 27, 1952, pp. 102–07.)

On African names in South Carolina 1732–75.

1654 **ROJAS, María Teresa de**
'Algunos datos sobre los negros esclavos y horros en La Habana del siglo XVI.' In: MISCELANEA de estudios dedicados a Fernando Ortiz, vol. 2 (La Habana, 1956), pp. 1273–87.

Includes notes on the African origins of slaves in Cuba about 1550–90.

1655 **RAMOS, Arthur**
O negro na civilização brasileira. Rio de Janeiro, 1956. 246 pp.

Ch. 1: 'O tráfico de escravos no Brasil.'

1656 **DEBIEN, Gabriel**
'Destinées d'esclaves à la Martinique (1746–1778).' (BIFAN, ser. B, vol. 22, 1960, pp. 1–91.)

Contains information on the African origins of slaves.

1657 **LE PAGE, Robert Brock**
Jamaican creole. An historical introduction . . . London, 1960. ix, 182 pp. map.

Ch. 4: 'The slave population.'

1658 ***LACHATAÑERE, Romulo**
'Tipos étnicos africanos que concurrieron en la amalgama cubana.'

(Actas del Folklore, Habana, vol. 1, no. 3, 1961, pp. 5–12.)

1659 *LACHATAÑERE, Romulo
'Nota sobre la formación de la población afrocubana.' (Actas del Folklore, Habana, vol. 1, no. 4, 1961, pp. 3–11.)

1660 *ROMAIN, J. B.
'L'homme haïtien: ses origines ethniques, sa psychologie.' (Revue de la Faculté d'Ethnologie, Port-au-Prince, no. 4, 1961, pp. 3–9.)

1661 *FORTUNE, Armando
'Orígenes extra-africanos y mestisaje étnico del negro panameño a comienzos del siglo XVII.' (Lotería, Panamá, vol. 6, no. 63, 1961, pp. 66–78.)

1662 DEBIEN, Gabriel
'Les origines des esclaves des Antilles.' (BIFAN, ser. B, vol. 23, 1961, pp. 363–87; vol. 25, 1963, pp. 1–38, 215–65; vol. 26, 1964, pp. 166–211, 601–75; vol. 27, 1965, pp. 319–69, 755–99; vol. 29, 1967, pp. 536–58.)

Articles on the African origins of slaves in the French West Indies 1677–1796, written in collaboration with R. Richard, J. Houdaille, R. Massio and M. Delafosse.

1663 ARBOLEDA, José Rafael
'La historia y la antropología del negro en Colombia.' (América Latina, Rio de Janeiro, vol. 5, no. 3, 1962, pp. 3–16.)

Also published in: Universidad de Antioquia, Medellín, vol. 41, 1964, pp. 233–48. (See also his M.A. thesis: The ethnohistory of Colombian negroes, Evanston, Ill., 1950.)

1664 BENOIST, Jean
'Anthropologie physique de la population de l'île de la Tortue (Haïti). Contribution à l'étude de l'origine des noirs des Antilles françaises.' (Bulletin et mémoires de la Société d'Anthropologie de Paris, ser. 11, vol. 3, 1962, pp. 315–35.)

The population investigated is of 'Guinean' type.

1665 JARAMILLO URIBE, Jaime
'Esclavos y señores en la sociedad colombiana del siglo XVII.' (Anuario Colombiano de Historia Social y de la Cultura, Bogotá, vol. 1, 1963, pp. 3–62.)

Includes sections on the slave trade and African origins of Colombian slaves.

1666 CORTES ALONSO, Vicenta
La esclavitud en Valencia durante el reinado de los Reyes Católicos (1479–1516). Valencia, 1964. 546 pp. maps.

Contains documentary evidence of West African slaves imported to Spain.

1667 CURTIN, Philip De Armond *and* **VANSINA, Jan**
'Sources of the nineteenth century Atlantic slave trade.' (JAH, vol. 5, 1964, pp. 185–208; maps.)

On the geographical origins of African slaves, based on (1611). (Comments in: JAH, vol. 6, 1965, pp. 117–20.)

1668 DALBY, David
'Provisional identification of languages in the Polyglotta africana.' (Sierra Leone Language Review, Fourah Bay, no. 3, 1964, pp. 83–90.)

See (1611). (Articles on individual language groups appeared in the Review 1964–67.)

1669 CARVALHO NETO, Paulo de
El negro uruguayo (hasta la abolición). Quito, 1965. 345 pp.

With chapters on the African origins of Uruguayan slaves.

1670 *DEBIEN, Gabriel
'Au sujet des origines ethniques de quelques esclaves des Antilles.' (Notes Africaines, Dakar, no. 106, 1965, p. 58.)

1671 HAIR, Paul Edward Hedley
'Sierra Leone items in the Gullah dialect of American English.' (Sierra Leone Language Review, Fourah Bay, no. 4, 1965, pp. 78–84.)

Turner's identifications (1649) need to be checked by specialists.

1672 HAIR, Paul Edward Hedley
'The enslavement of Koelle's informants.' (JAH, vol. 6, 1965, pp. 193–203.)

Individuals were enslaved through war, kidnapping and sale for debt or crime. See (1611).

1673 HERSKOVITS, Melville Jean
The New World negro. Bloomington, London, 1966. xi, 370 pp.

Section 3, 'Ethnohistory', includes essays on the slave trade and the African origins of American negroes.

1674 *MELÉNDEZ, Ch. Carlos
'Los orígenes de los esclavos africanos en Costa Rica.' *In*: CONGRESSO Internacional de Americanistas, 1964, Actas y memorias, vol. 4 (Sevilla, 1966), pp. 387–91.

1675 *POLLAK-ELTZ, Angelina
'Woher stammen die Neger Südamerikas?' (Umschau in Wissenschaft und Technik, Frankfurt/M., vol. 67, 1967, pp. 244–49.)

1676 PAVY, David
'The provenience of Colombian negroes.' (JNH, vol. 52, 1967, pp. 35–58; maps.)

Shows that the majority of slaves came from coastal West Africa.

1677 PATTERSON, Orlando
The sociology of slavery. An analysis of the origins, development and structure of negro slave society in Jamaica. [London,] 1967. 310 pp. maps.

Ch. 5: 'The tribal origins of the Jamaican slaves.'

1678 SPINAZZOLA, Vittorio
'Islam e schiavitù in Brasile.' (Oriente Moderno, Roma, vol. 47, 1967, pp. 269–85.)

Islam was introduced to Brazil in the late 18th and early 19th century by Malinke, Yoruba and Hausa slaves.

1679 SIGURET, Roseline
'Esclaves d'indigoteries et de caféières au quartier de Jacmel (1757–1791).' (RFHO, vol. 55, 1968, pp. 190–230.)

Includes lists of slaves on St. Domingue plantations, classified by tribal origins.

1680 *COBB, Henry E.
'The African background of the American negro: myth and reality.' (Bulletin of the Southern University and Agricultural and Mechanical College, Baton Rouge, La., vol. 55, 1969, pp. 9–19.)

1681 RODNEY, Walter
'Upper Guinea and the significance of the origins of Africans enslaved in the New World.' (JNH, vol. 54, 1969, pp. 327–45.)

Establishing precise African origins of slaves is relatively meaningless.

1682 HIGGINS, William Robert
'The geographical origins of negro slaves in colonial South Carolina.' (SAQ, vol. 70, no. 1, 1971, pp. 34–47.)

Almost 90% of slaves imported 1735–75 came directly from Africa.

PART 2:

ABOLITION AND SUPPRESSION

M. ABOLITION CONTROVERSY

1683 MERCADO, Thomas de
Tratos y contratos de mercaderes y
tratantes discididos y determínados.
Mathias Gast, Salamanca, 1569. 249 ll.

> Pt. 1, ch. 15: 'Del trato de los negros
> de Cabouerde'; attack on the in-
> justices of the Portuguese slave
> trade, by a Dominican.

1684 LOPEZ, Luis
Instructorium negotiantium duobus con-
tentum libris . . . Sumptibus Claudij
Curlet, Salamanticæ, 1589. 528 pp.

> Bk. 1, ch. 4: 'De emptione manci-
> piorum'; ch. 5: 'De titulis, quibus
> aliqui in seruitutem licite possunt
> venire, & an emptores Æthiopū
> causa negotationis illos emētes, vel
> qui illos aduectos in Hispaniam
> causa seruitij emunt, peccēt cum
> aliqua obligatione restitutionis . . .'

1685 MOLINA, Luis de
De iustitia et iure . . . Sumptibus
Arnoldi Mylij, Moguntiæ, 1602, 03.
2 vol.

> Tract. II, disp. 34–36 describe the
> areas of the Portuguese slave trade
> in Africa and outline the conditions
> under which it is permissible.

1686 REBELLO, Fernando
Opus de obligationibus iustitiæ, relig-
ionis et caritatis . . . Sumptibus Horatii
Cardon, Lugduni, 1608. 889 pp.

> Bk. 1, quest. 10: 'Sítne licita apud nos
> in Lusitania Æthiopum emptio, ac
> possessio?'; quotes recent authors
> on the legality of the African slave
> trade.

1687 *CASTRO Y QUIÑONES, Pedro de,
Archbishop of Sevilla
Instruccion para remediar, y asegurar,
quanto con la divina gracia fuere possible, que ninguno de los negros, que
vienen de Guinea, Angola, y otras
prouincias de aquella costa de Africa,
carezca del sagrado baptismo . . .
Geronymo de Contreras, Lima, 1628.
16 pp.

> Early expression of Catholic concern
> that slaves brought from Africa
> should be baptized.

1688 UDEMANS, Godfried
'Tgeestelyck roer van't coopmans schip,
dat is: trouw bericht hoe dat een
coopman, en coopvaerder, hem selven
dragen moet in syne handelinge in
pays, ende in oorloge, voor God,
ende de menschen, te water ende te
lande, insonderheydt onder de heydenen
in Oost ende West-Indien . . . Den
tweeden druck, verbetert ende vermeer-
dert by den autheur . . . Françoys
Boels, Dordrecht, 1640. 721 pp.

> The 'casus conscientiæ' include one
> on whether Christians may buy
> and sell slaves; these must be chris-
> tianised, but selling them to Catholics
> is 'a cursed and antichristian traffic'
> (pp. 360–66). (First edition 1638.)

1689 FAGUNDEZ, Estevão
De iustitia, & contractibus, & de acqui-
sitione, & translatione dominij, libri
septem . . . Sumpt. Laurentii Anisson
et hæred. G. Boissat, Lugduni, 1641.
663 pp.

> Bk. 2, ch. 2: 'Iudicium de mercatura
> seruorum, maximè Æthiopum, quam
> Lusitani communiter in commerciis
> exercent.'

1690 SANDOVAL, Alonso de
Tomo primero de instauranda Æthio-
pum salute. Historia de Æthiopia,
naturaleça, policia sagrada y profana,
costumbres, ritos, y cathecismo evan-
gelica, de todos Æthiopes cõ que se
restaura la salud de sus almas . . .
Alonso de Paredes, Madrid, 1647.
520 pp.

> New edition of (1598) with sections
> on slavery expanded; the injustice
> and illegalities of the slave trade are
> denounced while slavery is justified
> by reference to scriptural and legal
> opinions.

1691 AVENDAÑO, Diego de
Thesaurus Indicus, seu generalis instruc-
tor pro regimine conscientiæ, in iis
quæ ad Indias spectant. Apud Iacobum
Meursium, Antuerpiæ, 1668. 2 vol.

Pt. 9, ch. 12, par. 8: 'De contractu Æthiopicorum mancipiorum'; quotes Molina and others on the justification of the African slave trade.

1692 BAXTER, Richard
A Christian directory: or, a summ of practical theologie, and cases of conscience . . . Nevill Simmons, London, 1673. 929, 214 pp.

In a section of pt. 2 on the lawfulness of buying slaves, slave traders are condemned but regulated slavery accepted. See (1826, 2000).

1693 GOSPEL family-order, being a short discourse concerning the ordering of families, both of whites, blacks and Indians . . . By G. F. [London,] 1676. 22 pp.

By George Fox, the Quaker leader. Stressed the common humanity of all races, urges masters to give their slaves religious instruction, and suggests that they be released 'after a considerable term of years'.

1694 GODWYN, Morgan
The negro's & Indians advocate, suing for their admission into the Church: or a persuasive to the instructing and baptizing of the negro's and Indians in our plantations . . . London, 1680. 174 pp.

Defends the humanity of the slaves and denounces the slave trade. A 'Supplement' (London, 1681; 12 pp.) replied to arguments against christianising the slaves.

1695 FRIENDLY advice to the gentlemen-planters of the East and West Indies . . . By Philotheos Physiologus. Andrew Sowle, [London,] 1684. 222 pp.

By Thomas Tryon. Pt. 2: 'The negro's complaint of their hard servitude, and the cruelties practised upon them by divers of their masters professing Christianity in the West-Indian plantations'; pt. 3: 'A discourse in way of dialogue, between an Ethiopean or negro-slave and a Christian, that was his master in America'. Criticises the cruelty shown to slaves.

1696 *An EXHORTATION & caution to Friends concerning buying or keeping of negroes, given the 13th day of the 8th month, 1693. [William Bradford, Philadelphia, 1693.] 15 pp.

By George Keith, a Quaker. The first antislavery work printed in America. (Reprinted in: PMBH, vol. 13, 1889, pp. 265–70.)

1697 *The SELLING of Joseph a memorial. Bartholomew Green & John Allen, Boston, 1700. 3 pp.

By Samuel Sewall. Slave owners have no legal title to their African slaves. Reprinted in: (1715), pp. 199–207, and (3615), pp. 83–87. New edition, with commentary by S. Kaplan, Amherst, Mass., 1969; 66 pp.

1698 *SAFFIN, John
A brief and candid answer to a late printed sheet, entituled, The selling of Joseph . . . Boston, 1701. 12 pp.

The earliest defence of slavery published in America. Reprinted in (3615), pp. 251–256.

1699 The ATHENIAN oracle: being an entire collection of all the valuable questions and answers in the old Athenian Mercuries . . . By a member of the Athenian Society. Andrew Bell, London, 1703–04. 3 vol.

Extracts from 1691–96, edited by J. Dunton. The question (vol. 1, pp. 545–48) whether the African slave trade is unlawful, submitted by S. Sewall, is answered by an admission that the trade is unjustifiable. See (1701).

1700 *BENCI, Jorge
Economia christaã dos senhores no governo dos escravos. Deduzida das palavras do capitulo trinta e tres do Ecclesiástico: panis, & disciplina, & opus servo: reduzida a quatro discursos morais . . . Antonio de Rossi, Roma, 1705. xii, 282 pp.

Urges more humane treatment of slaves in Brazil.

1701 *The ATHENIAN oracle, the second edition, printed at London. 1704. Vol. 1, pp. 545 . . . 548. Quest. Whether trading for negros i.e. carrying them out of their country into perpetual slavery, be in it self unlawful, and especially contrary to the great law of Christianity? Samuel Phillips, Boston, Massachusetts, 1705. 4 pp.

The article by S. Sewall extracted from (1699).

1702 The NEGRO christianized. An essay to excite and assist that good work, the instruction of negro-servants in Christianity. B. Green, Boston, 1706. 46 pp.

By Cotton Mather. Urges masters to treat slaves as men and give them religious instruction; baptism will not entitle them to freedom.

1703 A LETTER from a merchant at Jamaica to a member of parliament in London, touching the African trade. To which is added, a speech made by a black of Gardaloupe, at the funeral of a fellow-negro. A. Baldwin, London, 1709. 31 pp.

The slave trade will never thrive unless it is conducted 'with more justice and humanity'; Parliament should improve the condition of colonial slaves.

1704 HEPBURN, John
The American defence of the Christian golden rule, or an essay to prove the unlawfulness of making slaves of men. [Andrew Bradford, Philadelphia, 1714?] 5, 40 pp.

Includes: 'Arguments against making slaves of men. Written by a native of America, September 14, 1713'. See (4122).

1705 GIBSON, Edmund, Bishop of London
Two letters of the Lord Bishop of London: the first, to the masters and mistresses of families in the English plantations abroad; exhorting them to encourage and promote the instruction of their negroes in the Christian faith. The second, to the missionaries there; directing them to distribute the said letter, and exhorting them to give their assistance towards the instruction of the negroes within their several parishes. Joseph Downing, London, 1727. 20 pp.

Attacks masters for putting difficulties in the way of christianising their slaves. See (1707, 1709).

1706 *A BRIEF examination of the practice of the time, by the foregoing and the present dispensation . . . [Philadelphia,] 1729. 74 pp.

By Ralph Sandiford. Protest against negro slavery. See (1708).

1707 A LETTER to the Right Reverend the Lord Bishop of London, from an inhabitant of His Majesty's Leeward-Caribbee-Islands. Containing some considerations on his Lordship's Two letters of May 19, 1727. . . . In which is inserted, A short essay concerning the conversion of the negro slaves in our sugar-colonies: written in the

month of June, 1727, by the same inhabitant. J. Wilford, London, 1730. 103 pp.

By Robert Robertson. The bishop and the British public are completely misinformed about the slave trade and slavery, which are distasteful but 'absolutely necessary to sugar-making'. See (1705).

1708 The MYSTERY of iniquity; in a brief examination of the practice of the times . . . Unto which is added, the injury this trading in slaves doth the commonwealth, humbly offer'd to all of a publick spirit. The second edition, with additions. [London?] 1730. 111 pp.

By Ralph Sandiford. New edition of (1706).

1709 HUMPHREYS, David
An historical account of the incorporated Society for the Propagation of the Gospel in Foreign Parts . . . Joseph Downing, London, 1730. xxxi, 356 pp. maps.

With a chapter on the instruction of negro slaves, including Gibson's letters (1705). See (1747).

1710 FROMAGEAU, Germain
'Esclaves . . . Regles sur le commerce des esclaves en general, & des negres en particulier.' In: LAMET, A. A. de Bussy de and FROMAGEAU, G. Le dictionnaire des cas de conscience, décidés suivant les principes de la morale, les usages de la discipline ecclesiastique, l'autorité des conciles et des canonistes, et la jurisprudence du royaume (Paris, 1733), vol. 1, col. 1437–44.

Article by a doctor of the Sorbonne, dated 1698, answering questions on the legitimacy of slave trading; slaves can be bought and sold only if they have been acquired 'à juste titre'.

1711 *A TESTIMONY against the anti-christian practice of making slaves of men, wherein it is shewed to be contrary to the dispensation of the law and time of the gospel, and very opposite both to grace and nature. (Signed: E— C—) [Boston,] 1733. 24 pp.

By Elihu Coleman. Written 1729–30.

1712 'The SPEECH of Moses Bon Sàam, a free negro, to the revolted slaves in one of the most considerable colonies of the West Indies.' (GM, Jan. 1735, 24 pp. 21–23.)

> Fictitious speech urging slaves to risk their lives for freedom. Reprinted from 'The Prompter', 10 Jan. 1735. (Also printed in: London Magazine, Jan. 1735, pp. 13–15.) See (1714).

1713 'The SPEECH of Caribeus in answer to Moses Bon Saam, in the Prompter, No. 18.' (Signed: M.) (GM, Jan. 1735, pp. 91–93.)

> Attributed to Robert Robertson, minister in Nevis. Advises slaves to submit to their masters.

1714 The SPEECH of Mr John Talbot Campo-bell, a free Christian-negro, to his countrymen in the mountains of Jamaica . . . To which is subjoin'd the speech of Moses Bon Sàam, another free negro. J. Roberts, London, 1736. 88 pp.

> By Robert Robertson. Fictitious speech urging moderation and peace with the whites in Jamaica. See (1712).

1715 *LAY, Benjamin
All slave-keepers that keep the innocent in bondage, apostates pretending to lay claim to the pure & holy Christian religion; of what congregation so ever; but especially in their ministers, by whose example the filthy leprosy and apostacy is spread far and near; it is a notorious sin, which many of the true friends of Christ, and his pure truth, called Quakers, has been for many years and still are concern'd to write and bear testimony against; as a practice so gross & hateful to religion, and destructive to government, beyond what words can set forth, or can be declared of by men or angels, and yet lived in by ministers and magistrates in America . . . [B. Franklin,] Philadelphia, 1737. 271 pp.

> Contains the text of (1697).

1716 WHITEFIELD, George
Three letters from the Reverend Mr. G. Whitefield: viz. Letter I. To a friend in London, concerning Archbishop Tillotson. Letter II. To the same . . . Letter III. To the inhabitants of Maryland, Virginia, North and South Carolina, concerning their negroes. B. Franklin, Philadelphia, 1740. 16 pp.

> Questions the lawfulness of slavery and criticizes the slave holders' cruelty to their slaves.

1717 'A LETTER to the gentleman merchants in the Guinea trade, particularly addressed to the merchants in Bristol and Liverpool.' (Signed: Mercator Honestus.) (GM, July 1740, p. 341.)

> Slave children are born with a 'natural right to liberty'; Guinea traders encourage wars in Africa and West Indian planters treat their slaves shockingly. See (1719).

1718 'The PETITION of the inhabitants of New Inverness, to Gen. Oglethorpe. Jan. 3, 1739.' (GM, Jan. 1741, p. 30.)

> Indicates the danger of introducing more slaves to Georgia instead of English settlers.

1719 'CASE of negroes and planters stated.' (GM, March 1741, pp. 145–47, 186–88.)

> Reply to (1717). Slavery and the slave trade are well established and beneficial. Attributed to Robert Robertson.

1720 JUGLER, Johann Friedrich
Ανδραποδοκαπηλειον. Sive de nundinatione servorum apud veteres liber singularis historico-iuridicus . . . Apud Io. Georg. Loewium, Lipsiæ, 1742. 166 pp.

> Ch. 1: 'De quæstione: an homo iure naturali sit in commercio?'.

1721a *CAPITEIN, Jacobus Elisa Joannes
Dissertatio politico-theologica, de servitute, libertate christianæ non contraria . . . S. Luchtmans & filium, Lugduni Batavorum, 1742. 44 pp.

Translated as:

1721b Staatkundig - godgeleerd onderzoekschrift over de slaverny, als niet strydig tegen de christelyke vryheid . . . Philippus Bonk, Leyden, 1742. 72 pp.

> Thesis written in the Netherlands by an African. See (1549).

1722 An ESSAY concerning slavery, and the danger Jamaica is expos'd to from the too great number of slaves, and the too little care that is taken to manage them. And a proposal to prevent the further importation of negroes into that island. Charles Corbett, London, [1746]. 67 pp.

> By Edward Trelawny. Slavery is contrary to divine and natural law and creates a danger of revolts; if imports to British colonies were stopped, the slaves could be gradually freed.

1723a De L'ESPRIT des loix ou du rapport que les loix doivent avoir avec la constitution de chaque gouvernement, le climat, la religion, le commerce, &c. . . . Barillot, & Fils, Genève, [1748]. 2 vol.

Translated as:

1723b The spirit of the laws . . . With corrections and additions communicated by the author. J. Nourse & P. Vaillant, London, 1750. 2 vol.

> By Charles Louis de Secondat, baron de Montesquieu. Bk. 15 discusses various theories on the origin of slavery and offers ironical arguments for it, including the inferiority of Africans: 'because allowing them to be men, a suspicion would follow that we ourselves are not Christians'. (This section is quoted, in French, in: EMLR, Dec, 1814, pp. 491–92.) See (3849).

1724 FOSTER, James
Discourses on all the principal branches of natural religion and social virtue. London, 1749, 52. 2 vol.

> Vol. 2, ch. 7: 'Of the distinct obligations of masters and servants;' denounces the slave trade as a criminal violation of natural right.

1725 FRIENDS, Society of
An epistle of caution and advice, concerning the buying and keeping of slaves. James Chattin, Philadelphia, 1754. 8 pp.

> Attributed to Anthony Benezet. Exhortation to Quakers not to encourage slavery and slave trade in any manner.

1726 *WOOLMAN, John
Some considerations on the keeping of negroes. Recommended to the professors of Christianity of every denomination. James Chattin, Philadelphia, 1754. 24 pp.

> See (1784).

1727 *MEYNADIER, Jacques
Tentamen philosophico-juridicum de servitute obnoxia . . . A. Van Paddenburg, Trajecti ad Rhenum, 1754. 79 pp.

1728 HUTCHESON, Francis
A system of moral philosophy . . . A. Millar; T. Longman, London, 1755. 2 vol.

> Bk. 3, ch. 3: 'The duties and rights of masters and servants'; enslavement by capture is 'not justifiable even in a just war.' (Published posthumously.)

1729 RIBEIRO ROCHA, Manoel
Ethiope resgatado, empenhado, sustentado, corregido, instruido, e libertado. Discurso theologico-juridico, em que se propoem o modo de comerciar, haver, o possuir validamente, quanto a hum, e outro foro, os pretos cativos africanos, e as principaes obrigaçoes, que correm a quem delles se servir . . . Francisco Luiz Ameno, Lisboa, 1758. 367 pp.

> Treatise on the morality and legality of the slave trade and slavery by a Brazilian priest; slaves should be emancipated when the owners have recovered the cost of their purchase.

1730 *OBSERVATIONS on the inslaving, importing and purchasing of negroes. With some advice thereon extracted from the yearly meeting epistle of London for the present year . . . Christopher Sower, Germantown, 1759. 15 pp.

> By Anthony Benezet. See (1732).

1731 PHILMORE, J.
Two dialogues on the man-trade. J. Waugh; (etc.), London, 1760. 68 pp.

> Condemns slave trade and slavery with most of the arguments used by later abolitionists. See (1734).

1732 OBSERVATIONS on the inslaving, importing and purchasing of negroes; with some advice thereon, extracted from the epistle of the yearly-meeting of the people called Quakers held at London in the year 1748. Second edition. Christopher Sower, Germantown, 1760. 16 pp.

> By Anthony Benezet. Attacks the slave trade as unchristian, unjust, inhumane and therefore offensive to God. See (1730).

1733 WALLACE, George
A system of the principles of the law of Scotland . . . A. Millar, D. Wilson & T. Durham, London; G. Hamilton & J. Balfour, Edinburgh, 1760. xxiv, 592 pp.

> Bk. 3, title 2: 'Of slavery' (pp. 88–98); slavery is unlawful in Scotland and should be abolished in America. (Reviewed in: AnR 1760, vol. 3, 1761, pp. 263–65.)

1734 *A SHORT account of that part of Africa, inhabited by the negroes. With respect to the fertility of the country; the good disposition of many of the natives, and the manner by which the slave trade is carried on. Extracted from several authors, in order to shew the iniquity of that trade, and the falsity of the arguments usually advanced in its vindication. With a quotation from George Wallis's System of the laws, &c. and a large extract from a pamphlet, lately published in London on the subject of the slave trade . . . W. Dunlap, Philadelphia, 1762. 56 pp.

By Anthony Benezet. With extracts from (1731).

1735 A SHORT account of that part of Africa, inhabited by the negroes . . . Extracted from divers authors . . . With quotations from the writings of several persons of note, viz. George Wallis, Francis Hutcheson, and James Foster, and a large extract from a pamphlet lately published in London, on the subject of the slave trade. The second edition, with large additions and amendments. W. Dunlap, Philadelphia, 1762. 80 pp.

By Anthony Benezet.

1736 WOOLMAN, John
Considerations on keeping negroes, recommended to the professors of Christianity, of every denomination. Part second. B. Franklin & D. Hall, Philadelphia, 1762. 52 pp.

See (1784).

1737 ROYER, Alex. Hieron.
De natura et indole servitutis, tum ex jure naturae, tum ex legibus civilibus Hebraeorum, Romanorum, et etiam Belgarum . . . Georg Wishoff, Lugduni Batavorum, 1762. iv, 40 pp.

A dissertation, including a section on slavery in Surinam and the West Indies.

1738 A PLAN for improving the trade at Senegal. Addressed to the Lords Commissioners for Trade and Plantations. R. & J. Dodsley, London, 1763. 26 pp.

Britain should enfranchise the slaves at St. Louis, captured from France, and allow free trade there; free labour is more economic than slave labour. Abolition of the slave trade and slavery would benefit the West Indies.

1739 DISSERTATION sur la traite et le commerce des nègres. [Paris,] 1764. 174 pp.

By J. Bellon de Saint-Quentin. Discusses the justification of the slave trade.

1740 An ESSAY in vindication of the continental colonies of America, from a censure of Mr. Adam Smith, in his Theory of moral sentiments. With some reflexions on slavery in general. By an American. T. Becket & P. A. Hondt, London, 1764. 46 pp.

By Arthur Lee. The author objects to Smith's description, in 1759, of the Africans as heroic and the Americans as 'the refuse of the jails of Europe'; Africans are detestable and dangerous, and negro slavery should be abolished in the interest of the colonies.

1741 *OTIS, James
The rights of the British colonies asserted and proved. Edes & Gill, Boston, 1764. 80 pp.

Refers to Montesquieu's arguments on slavery (1723) and describes the slave trade as 'the most shocking violation of the law of nature', brutalising those involved in it.

1742a NOVA, e curiosa relação de hum abuzo emendado, ou evidencias da razão; expostas a favor dos homens pretos em hum dialogo entre hum letrado, e hum mineiro. Francisco Borges de Sousa, Lisboa, 1764. 8 pp.

Translated as:

1742b 'NEW and curious relation of a grievance redressed or evidences of the right adduced in favour of the black men in a dialogue between a lawyer and a miner.' (Race, London, vol. 5, no. 3, 1963, pp. 39–47.)

Discussion of prejudices against negro slaves in Brazil in the form of a dialogue. (The translation, with notes, is by C. R. Boxer.)

1743 'The SLAVE-TRADE explained and justified.' (Signed: Curiosus.) (SM, Aug. 1765, pp. 399–400.)

Letter (reprinted from the 'London Chronicle') defending the slave trade, African slaves being criminals or prisoners of war.

1744 'TRAITE des negres, (Commerce d'Afrique.)' (Signed: D.J.) *In*: ENCYCLOPEDIE, ou dictionnaire raisonné des sciences, des arts et des métiers, vol. 16

(Neufchastel [=Paris], 1765), pp. 532–33.

> By Louis de Jaucourt. Radical attack on the slave trade and slavery: 'Que les colonies européennes soient donc plutôt détruites, que de faire tant de malheureux!'

1745 BENEZET, Anthony
A caution and warning to Great Britain and her colonies, in a short representation of the calamitous state of the enslaved negroes in the British dominions. Collected from various authors, and submitted to the serious consideration of all, more especially of those in power. Henry Miller, Philadelphia, 1766. 35, 4 pp.

> Written to publicise the iniquity of the slave trade, with quotations from writers on Africa and antislavery authors. (The final section consists of an extract from: 2287.)

1746 *CONSIDERATIONS on slavery. In a letter to a friend. (Signed: A.B.) Edes & Gill, Boston, 1767. 28 pp.

> By Nathaniel Appleton.

1747 A SHORT account of that part of Africa, inhabited by the negroes . . . The third edition. R. Horsfield; (etc.), London, 1768. 80; 45 pp.

> By Anthony Benezet. The second part is an extract from (1709) with the letters. 'Absolute property' in slaves is unchristian; a slave is his master's brother.

1748 THREE tracts respecting the conversion and instruction of the free Indians, and negroe slaves in the colonies. Addressed to the venerable Society for the Propagation of the Gospel in Foreign Parts. [London, 1768?] 41 pp.

> By William Knox. Questions the legality of the slave trade; if the Society does not condemn slaveholding, the slaves must be treated in law as British subjects. With a letter from the Society to Benezet on the subject.

1749 FERMIN, Philippe
Déscription générale, historique, géographique et physique de la colonie de Surinam . . . E. van Harrevelt, Amsterdam, 1769. 2 vol.

> With a chapter on the slave trade and slavery, justifying them on scriptural authority. See (1751).

1750 SHARP, Granville
A representation of the injustice and dangerous tendency of tolerating slavery; or of admitting the least claim of private property in the persons of men, in England . . . Benjamin White; Robert Horsfield, London, 1769. 167 pp.

> Critical study of the status of slavery in English law. See (1755, 1765).

1751 FERMIN, Philippe
Dissertation sur la question s'il est permis d'avoir en sa possession des esclaves, & de s'en servir comme tels, dans les colonies de l'Amerique. Jacques Lekens, Maestricht, 1770. 88 pp.

> Reply to antislavery criticism of his work on Surinam (1749); the slave trade is necessary to the colonies and neither illegitimate nor unjust.

1752 *HENRION DE PANSEY, Pierre Nicolas, *baron*
Mémoire pour un nègre qui réclame sa liberté. J.-T. Hérissant, [Paris,] 1770. 29 pp.

> Supports a negro slave against a merchant.

1753a HISTOIRE philosophique et politique, des établissemens & du commerce des Européens dans les deux Indes. Amsterdam, 1770. 6 vol.

Translated as

1753b A PHILOSOPHICAL and political history of the settlements and trade of the Europeans in the East and West Indies . . . T. Cadell, London, 1776. 4 vol. maps.

> By G. T. F. Raynal. Includes a denunciation of the slave trade answering most of the standard arguments in its favour; it should be abolished, together with slavery, by international agreement. See (1791, 2149).

1754 *TRUMBULL, John
'The Correspondent, No. 8.' (Connecticut Journal and New Haven Post-Boy, 6 July 1770.)

> Ironical essay in pretended defence of the African slave trade. (Reprinted in: 3845, pp. 123–25, and JNH, vol. 14, 1929, pp. 493–95.)

1755 BENEZET, Anthony
Some historical account of Guinea, its situation, produce and the general disposition of its inhabitants. With an inquiry into the rise and progress of

L

the slave-trade, its nature and lamentable effects. Also a re-publication of the sentiments of several authors of note, on this interesting subject; particularly an extract of a treatise, by Granville Sharp. Joseph Crukshank, Philadelphia, 1771. iv, 144; 53 pp.

Account of the West African slave trade, suggesting the abolition of colonial slavery; with an appendix of extracts from (1750) and other antislavery writings. Republished 1784, it provided much of the information for Clarkson's essay of 1785 (1836). See (1778, 1857).

1756 MILLAR, John
Observations concerning the distinction of ranks in society. John Murray, London, 1771. xv, 242 pp.

Ch. 5: 'Of the condition of servants in different parts of the world'; regrets the existence of slavery in British dominions. (Section entitled 'Political consequences of slavery' in 1773 edition.)

1757 'OBSERVATIONS importantes sur l'esclavage des nègres.' (Ephémérides du Citoyen, Paris, vol. 6, 1771, pp. 208–46.)

By P. S. Du Pont de Nemours. Antislavery views in a review article, mainly on Saint-Lambert's 'Ziméo' (4173).

1758 BRITANNIA libera, or a defence of the free state of man in England, against the claim of any man as a slave. Inscribed and submited to the jurisconsulti, and the free people of England. J. Almon, London, 1772. 47 pp.

Attributed to William Bollan, agent for Massachusetts.

1759 CONSIDERATIONS on the negroe cause commonly so called, addressed to the Right Honourable Lord Mansfield, Lord Chief Justice of the Court of King's Bench, &c. By a West Indian. J. Dodsley, London, 1772. 46 pp.

By Samuel Estwick. Legal arguments in the case of Sommersett v. Knowles heard in the Court of King's Bench 1771–72; see: HOWELL, T. B. A complete collection of state trials, vol. 20, (London, 1814), col. 1–82, 1369–86. Slaves are 'property'; the African Sommersett (a slave in Virginia since 1749) was therefore not entitled to a writ of habeas corpus.

1760 HARGRAVE, Francis
An argument in the case of James Sommersett a negro, lately determined by the Court of King's Bench: wherein it is attempted to demonstrate the present unlawfulness of domestic slavery in England. To which is prefixed a state of the case. W. Otridge, London, 1772. 82 pp.

Account of Sommersett v. Knowles, including an attack on slavery and the slave trade, by one of the lawyers involved. (Reviewed in: MR, vol. 47, 1772, pp. 421–26.) See: LOFFT, C. Reports of cases adjudged in the Court of King's Bench (London, 1776), pp. 1–19 ('Somerset against Stewart').

1761 CANDID reflections upon the judgment lately awarded by the Court of King's Bench, in Westminster-Hall, on what is commonly called the negroe-cause, by a planter. T. Lowndes, London, 1772. iv, 76 pp.

By Edward Long. Legal and historical justification of the slave trade and slavery; abolition would ruin the colonies and Britain. See (1759).

1762 'PLEADINGS, and a solemn judgement, on the question, Whether a slave continues to be a slave after coming into Britain?' (SM, vol. 34, June 1772, pp. 297–99.)

Summary of the Sommersett case, followed by 'Some observations upon the slavery of negroes' (pp. 299–301).

1763 'CONSIDERATIONS on a late determination in the Court of King's Bench on the negro cause.' (Signed: A West Indian.) (GM, July 1772, pp. 307–09.)

Slave trade is sanctioned by Parliament and slaves are property. See (1759).

1764 'An ARGUMENT against property in slaves.' (GM, July 1772, pp. 309–10.)

Legal arguments against regarding slaves as chattels.

1765 SHARP, Granville
An appendix to the Representation, (printed in the year 1769,) of the injustice and dangerous tendency of tolerating slavery, or of admitting the least claim of private property in the persons of men in England. Benjamin White; Robert Horsfield, London, 1772. 28 pp.

Additional arguments against slavery occasioned by the Sommersett case; the African slave trade is pernicious. See (1750).

1766 A PLAN for the abolition of slavery in the West Indies. William Griffin, London, 1772. iv, 33 pp.

Attributed to a Mr. Morgan. Published on account of the Sommersett case. African children should be bought, trained in England and sent as free settlers to the American colonies and islands. (Reviewed in: GM, July 1772, pp. 325–26.)

1767 *A MITE cast into the treasury: or, observations on slave-keeping. Joseph Crukshank, Philadelphia, 1772. iv, 24 pp.

By David Cooper.

1768 *SWAN, James
A dissuasion to Great-Britain and the colonies, from the slave trade to Africa. Shewing, the contradiction this trade bears, both to the laws divine and provincial; the disadvantages arising from it, and advantages from abolishing it, both to Europe and Africa, particularly to Britain and the plantations. Also shewing, how to put this trade to Africa on a just and lawful footing. E. Russell, Boston, [1772]. 70 pp.

Slave trading prevents the development of the trade in other commodities from Africa and depopulates the continent. Revised edition published 1773.

1769 THOMPSON, Thomas
The African trade for negro slaves, shewn to be consistent with principles of humanity, and with the laws of revealed religion. Simmons & Kirkby, Canterbury; Robert Baldwin, London, [1772]. 31 pp.

Justification of the slave trade, provided that the slaves are prisoners taken in just wars or criminals; by a missionary. (Reviewed in: MR, vol. 46, May 1772, pp. 541–43.) See (1774).

1770 *An ADDRESS to the inhabitants of the British settlements in America, upon slave-keeping. John Dunlap, Philadelphia, 1773. 30 pp.

By Benjamin Rush. See (1775, 1778).

1771 The APPENDIX: or, some observations on the expediency of the petition of the Africans, living in Boston, &c.

lately presented to the General Assembly of this province. To which is annexed, the petition referred to. Likewise, thoughts on slavery . . . By a lover of constitutional liberty. E. Russell, Boston, [1773]. 15 pp.

Urges the Massachusetts legislature to consider abolition of the slave trade and slavery.

1772 *BRIEF considerations on slavery, and the expediency of its abolition. With some hints on the means whereby it may be gradually effected. Recommended to the serious attention of all, and especially of those entrusted with the power of legislation. Isaac Collins, Burlington, 1773. 16 pp.

Attributed to William Dillwyn. See (1801).

1773 A FORENSIC dispute on the legality of enslaving the Africans, held at the public commencement in Cambridge, New-England, July 21st, 1773. By two candidates for the bachelor's degree. Thomas Leverett, Boston, 1773. 48 pp.

By Theodore Parsons and Eliphalet Pearson. The debate, on whether the slave system increases the happiness of mankind, is left undecided.

1774 *SHARP, Granville
An essay on slavery, proving from Scripture its inconsistency with humanity and religion; in answer to a late publication, entitled, "The African trade for negro slaves shewn to be consistent with principles of humanity, and with the laws of revealed religion" . . . Isaac Collins, Burlington, 1773. 28 pp.

Critical review of (1769), with additional antislavery material by other writers, 'An elegy on the miserable state of an African slave' by William Shenstone, etc. See (1460). Reprinted as appendix to (1793).

1775 *SLAVERY not forbidden by Scripture. Or a defence of the West-India planters from the aspersions thrown out against them by the author of a pamphlet entitled, An address to the inhabitants of the British settlements in America, upon slave-keeping. By a West-Indian. Philadelphia, 1773. iii, 30 pp.

By Richard Nisbet. Answer to (1770). Emancipation would ruin the British colonies; the slaves are not badly treated. See (1779).

1776 CONSIDERATIONS on the negroe cause commonly so called, addressed to the Right Honourable Lord Mansfield . . . The second edition. J. Dodsley, London, 1773. 95 pp.

> By Samuel Estwick. Corrected and enlarged edition of (1759), racialist as well as pro-slavery.

1777 WOOLMAN, John
Serious considerations on various subjects of importance . . . Mary Hinde, London, 1773. 137 pp.

> Contains a section on the miseries of the slave trade and slavery. See (1778).

1778 *PERSONAL slavery established, by the suffrages of custom and right reason. Being a full answer to the gloomy and visionary reveries, of all the fanatical and enthusiastical writers on that subject. John Dunlap, Philadelphia, 1773. 26 pp.

> Polemic against Benezet (1755), Rush (1770) and Woolman (1777), by 'Machiavelus Americanus'.

1779 An ADDRESS to the inhabitants of the British settlements, on the slavery of the negroes in America. The second edition. To which is added, A vindication of the Address, in answer to a pamphlet entitled, "Slavery not forbidden in Scripture; or, a defence of the West India planters". By a Pennsylvanian. John Dunlap, Philadelphia, 1773. 28; 54 pp.

> By Benjamin Rush. Clear arguments for the abolition of slave trade and slavery; the second part is a reply to (1775).

1780 MARTIN, Samuel
An essay upon plantership, humbly inscribed to His Excellency George Thomas, Esq; chief governor of all the Leeward Islands . . . The fifth edition, with many additions; and a preface upon the slavery of negroes in the British colonies. T. Cadell, London, 1773. xvi, xv, 62 pp.

> Second section (xv pp.): 'A preface upon the slavery of negroes, in the British colonies. Shewing, that they are much happier than in their native country, much happier than the subjects of arbitrary governments, and at least as happy as the labourers of Britain.' (Signed: Britannicus.)

1781 WESLEY, John
Thoughts upon slavery. R. Hawes, London, 1774. 53 pp.

Describes the slave trade in West Africa and warns those involved of its injustice. Reissued in later editions, this tract was of importance in showing the antislavery views of the founder of Methodism. (Reviewed in: SM, vol. 36, 1774, pp. 486–88.) See (1783).

1782 WESLEY, John
Thoughts upon slavery. Joseph Crukshank, Philadelphia, 1774. 83 pp.

> Expanded with notes by A. Benezet who included it in two compilations which he edited in 1774: 'A collection of religious tracts' and 'The potent enemies of America laid open'.

1783 A SUPPLEMENT to Mr. Wesley's pamphlet entitled Thoughts upon slavery. H. Reynell, London, 1774. 107 pp.

> Attacks Wesley's tract (1781); slavery is necessary to preserve the British colonies and weaken the Catholic powers.

1784 WOOLMAN, John
The works of John Woolman. In two parts. Joseph Crukshank, Philadelphia, 1774. xiv, 436 pp.

> Includes the 'Considerations' on slavery first published separately in 1754 and 1762. See (1726, 1736).

1785 *PAINE, Thomas
'African slavery in America.' (Postscript to the Pennsylvania Journal and Weekly Advertiser, Philadelphia, 8 March 1775.)

> The slave trade should be abolished. How can Americans complain of being enslaved by Britain while holding slaves themselves? First reprinted in: The writings of Thomas Paine . . . edited by Moncure Daniel Conway, vol. 1 (New York, 1894), pp. 4–9.

1786 *SACY, Claude Louis Michel de
L'esclavage des Américains et des nègres . . . Demonville, Paris, 1775. 12 pp.

1787 *FERGUSON, James
Information for John Wedderburn . . . defender; against Joseph Knight, a negro, pursuer. [Edinburgh? 1775.]

> Defence arguments (4 July 1775) in a case brought by Knight, a former slave in Jamaica, to establish his freedom under Scottish law and to recover wages. See (1788–89, 1799).

1788 *NOTE of authorities quoted on the part of Joseph Knight. [Edinburgh, 1776?]

Dated 20 Feb. 1776. See (1787).

1789 *MACLAURIN, John
Additional information for Joseph Knight, a negro of Africa, pursuer; against John Wedderburn of Ballandean, Esq.; defender . . . [Edinburgh? 1776.] 44 pp.

Prosecution arguments, dated 20 April 1776. See (1787).

1790 *A DIALOGUE, concerning the slavery of the Africans; shewing it to be the duty and interest of the American colonies to emancipate all their African slaves: with an address to the owners of such slaves. Dedicated to the honorable the Continental Congress. Judah P. Spooner, Norwich (Conn.), 1776. 63 pp.

By Samuel Hopkins.

1791 OBSERVATIONS sur plusieurs assertions extraites littéralement de l'Histoire philosophique des etablissements des Européens dans les deux Indes, édition de 1770. Knapen, Amsterdam, 1776. 323 pp.

By Émilien Petit. Contains a defence of the slave trade and slavery (ch. 3, sect. 2) against Raynal (1753).

1792 ANGERS, *Diocese of*
Conférences ecclésiastiques du diocèse d'Angers, sur les états . . . Veuve Desaint, Paris, 1776. 3 vol.

Edited by J. P. Cotelle de la Blandinière. Vol. 3 contains a section 'Du commerce des nègres' (pp. 387–411) which justifies the slave trade on biblical and legal authority.

1793 SHARP, Granville
The just limitation of slavery in the laws of God, compared with the unbounded claims of the African traders and British American slaveholders . . . With a copious appendix: containing, an answer to the Rev. Mr. Thompson's tract in favour of the African slave trade . . . B. White; E. & C. Dilly, London, 1776. 67; 107 pp.

Answer to (1103). The appendix was originally published 1773 (1774).

1794 SHARP, Granville
The law of liberty, or, royal law, by which all mankind will certainly be judged! Earnestly recommended to the serious consideration of all slaveholders and slavedealers. B. White;

E. & C. Dilly, London, 1776. 55 pp.

Scriptural attack on the African slave trade.

1795 SHARP, Granville
The law of passive obedience, or Christian submission to personal injuries: wherein is shewn, that the several texts of Scripture, which command the entire submission of servants or slaves to their masters, cannot authorize the latter to exact an involuntary servitude, nor, in the least degree, justify the claims of modern slaveholders. [B. White; E. & C. Dilly, London, 1776.] 102 pp.

1796 SHARP, Granville
The law of retribution; or, a serious warning to Great Britain and her colonies, founded on unquestionable examples of God's temporal vengeance against tyrants, slave-holders, and oppressors. B. White; E. & C. Dilly, London, 1776. 357 pp.

1797 WOOLMAN, John
A journal of the life, gospel labours and Christian experiences of that faithful minister of Jesus Christ, John Woolman . . . To which are added, his Works, containing his last epistle and other writings. R. Jackson, Dublin, 1776. xv, 434 pp.

The journal describes Woolman's attacks on slavery and the slave trade in America 1754–69.

1798 CONSIDÉRATIONS sur l'état présent de la colonie française de Saint-Domingue. Ouvrage politique et législatif . . . par Mr. H. Dl. Grangé, Paris, 1776, 77. 2 vol.

By M. R. Hilliard-D'Auberteuil. Expresses antislavery views in a chapter on the slave population.

1799 *CULLEN, Robert
Additional information for John Wedderburn . . . defender; against Joseph Knight, a negro, pursuer. [Edinburgh? 1777.]

Dated 6 Feb. 1777. See (1787). Case reported in: MORISON, W. M. The decisions of the Court of Session, vol. 33 (Edinburgh, 1811), pp. 14545–49.

1800 *OBSERVATIONS on the slaves and indented servants, inlisted in the army, and in the navy of the United States . . . The resolve of Congress, for prohibiting the importation of slaves, demonstrates the consistent zeal of our rulers in the

cause of mankind . . . Antibiastes . . .
Styner & Cist, [Philadelphia, 1777].
2 pp.

1801 ESSAYS commercial and political,
on the real and relative interests of
imperial and dependent states, particularly those of Great Britain and her
dependencies . . . To which is added, an
appendix, on the means of emancipating
slaves, without loss to their proprietors.
The Author, Newcastle; J. Johnson,
London, 1777. viii, 147 pp.

The appendix quotes (1772) on a plan
to allow slaves to buy their freedom.

1802 *SERIOUS considerations on several
important subjects; viz. on war and
its inconsistency with the gospel:
observations on slavery. And remarks
on the nature and bad effects of spirituous liquors . . . Joseph Crukshank,
Philadelphia, 1778. 48 pp.

By Anthony Benezet.

1803 *FEBUÉ, ——, Abbé
'Essai philantropique sur l'esclavage
des nègres.' In: MÉMOIRES de la
Société des Philantropes (Berne 1778),
pp. 1-48.

1804 *EHRLEN, Christian Casimir
De servis Æthiopibus Europaeorum
in coloniis Americæ . . . J. H. Heitz,
Argentorati, [1778]. 98 pp.

Thesis published at Strasbourg.

1805 *TONIS, Hendrik Nicolaas
Specimen philosophico-juridicum inaugurale de potestate domini in servos
eorumque prolem . . . A. Van Paddenburg, Trajecti ad Rhenum, 1778, ii,
68 pp.

Utrecht thesis on the legal implica-
tions of slavery.

1806 *EXTRACT from an address in the
Virginia Gazette, of March 19, 1767.
By a respectable member of the community. [Joseph Crukshank, Philadelphia, 1780.] 4 pp.

On slavery.

1807 An EXTRACT from a treatise on the
spirit of prayer . . . With some thoughts
on war: remarks on the nature and
bad effects of the use of spirituous
liquors. And considerations on slavery.
Joseph Crukshank, Philadelphia, 1780.
84 pp.

Last section by Anthony Benezet:
'Thoughts on slavery from different
authors'.

1808 'CRUELTY attending the slave trade as

at present practiced; with a project
for abolishing it.' (Signed; A West
Indian.) (GM, Oct. 1780, pp. 458–
59.)

Deplores the slave trade and colonial
slavery, which could be ended by
cultivation in West Africa as suggested
by the king of Dahomey in 1727.
Supported by letters signed 'Publicus'
(Dec. 1780, p. 564) and 'A.Z.'
(March 1781, pp. 122–23).

1809 *NOTES on the slave trade, &c. [Joseph
Crukshank, Philadelphia, 1780?] 8 pp.

Attributed to Anthony Benezet.

1810 *SHORT observations on slavery, introductory to some extracts from the
writing of the Abbe Raynal on that
important subject. [Joseph Crukshank,
Philadelphia, 1781.] 12 pp.

By Anthony Benezet.

1811 'CONCERNING the condition and
treatment of negroes in the West
Indies.' (Signed: An Englishman.) (GM,
Sept. 1781, pp. 417–18.)

Criticises the African slave trade and
slavery.

1812 SCHWARTZ, Joachim, pseud.
Réflexions sur l'esclavage des nègres.
Par M. Schwartz . . . Société Typo-
graphique, Neufchatel, 1781. xii, 99 pp.

By J. A. N. Caritat, marquis de
Condorcet. Questions the right of a
man to purchase another man.
Possibly misdated. See (1918).

1813 FRIENDS, Society of
The case of our fellow-creatures, the
oppressed Africans, respectfully recommended to the serious consideration
of the legislature of Great-Britain, by
the people called Quakers. J. Phillips,
London, 1783. 16 pp.

By Anthony Benezet. Urges abolition of the African slave trade.

1814 *A SERIOUS address to the rulers of
America, on the inconsistency of
their conduct respecting slavery: form-
ing a contrast between the encroachments of England on American liberty,
and American injustice in tolerating
slavery. (Signed: A farmer.) Isaac
Collins, Trenton (N.J.), 1783. 22 pp.

By David Cooper. Expresses the
hope that the United States will
abolish the slave trade.

1815 *HOPKINS, Samuel
'On the slave trade.' (Newport Mercury,
1 May 1784.)

Proposes laying expense of educating freed slave children on slaveholders after the failure of a motion in the Rhode Island assembly to abolish the trade. Reprinted in: The works of Samuel Hopkins, vol. 2 (Boston, 1852), pp. 745–48.

1816 *A LETTER from ********, in London, to his friend in America, on the subject of the slave-trade; together with some extracts from approved authors of matters of fact, confirming the principles contained in said letter. Samuel Loudon, New-York, 1784. 28 pp.

Attributed to Thomas Day. See (1834).

1817 *CRAWFORD, Charles
Observations upon negro-slavery. Joseph Crukshank, Philadelphia, 1784. 24 pp.

Urges abolition of slave trade and slavery.

1818 *O'KELLY, James
Essay on negro slavery. Philadelphia, 1784.

Abolitionist tract, by a Methodist.

1819 RAMSAY, James
An essay on the treatment and conversion of African slaves in the British sugar colonies. James Phillips, London, 1784. xx, 298 pp.

Moderate criticism of colonial slavery by a clergyman with long experience of the West Indies. Emancipation must be preceded by 'improvement' of the slaves; the slave trade could be replaced by voluntary emigration from Africa. See (1821, 1830).

1820 RAMSAY, James
'The story of Quashi, an African slave . . .' (GM, Aug. 1784, pp. 579–80.)

Extract from (1819).

1821 An ANSWER to the Reverend James Ramsay's Essay, on the treatment and conversion of slaves in the British sugar colonies. By some gentlemen of St. Christopher. Edward L. Low, Basseterre, 1784. ii, 100 pp.

Attack on Ramsay (1819) in defence of slavery and the slave trade. See (1833). (The authors are thought to include J. P. Demarin.)

1822 THOUGHTS on the slavery of the negroes. James Phillips, London, 1784. 32 pp.

By Joseph Woods, member of a Quaker antislavery group formed 1783. Opposes arguments for regulation rather than abolition of the slave trade; it is impossible to distinguish just and unjust enslavement. See (1823). (Second edition, with 'postscript', London, 1785; 39 pp.)

1823 REMARKS on a pamphlet written by the Rev. James Ramsay, M.A. under the title of Thoughts on the slavery of the negroes, in the American colonies. J. P. Bateman, London, 1784. 23 pp.

Wrongly attributes (1822) to Ramsay and accuses him of exaggerating the misery of the slaves.

1824 An INQUIRY into the effects of putting a stop to the African slave trade, and of granting liberty to the slaves in the British sugar colonies. James Phillips, London, 1784. 44 pp.

By James Ramsay. Trade in more profitable African products would increase after abolition of the slave trade. (Reviewed in: MR, vol. 72, June 1785, pp. 437–42.) See (1835, 1842).

1825 FRIENDS, Society of
'The petition of the people called Quakers. To the Commons of Great Britain, in Parliament.' (AnR 1783, vol. 26, 1785, pp. 350–51.)

Address of 16 June 1783 by the London yearly meeting, urging abolition of the slave trade and slavery.

1826 *BAXTER, Richard
Baxter's directions to the slave-holders, revived. First printed in London in the year 1673. To which is subjoined a letter from the worthy Anthony Benezet, late of this city, deceased, to the celebrated Abbe Reynal, with his answer, which were first published in the Brussels Gazette, March 7, 1782. Francis Bailey, Philadelphia, 1785. 16 pp.

See (1692).

1827 'THOUGHTS on the slave trade, with a plan for the better regulating that trade in future.' (Signed: Benevolus.) (Westminster Magazine, London, vol. 13, March 1785, pp. 116–17; May 1785, pp. 249–51.)

Suggestions for improving conditions for the colonial slaves; only small children should be imported in future.

1828 PALEY, William
The principles of moral and political
philosophy. R. Faulder, London, 1785.
vii, xxi, vi, 657 pp.

A chapter on slavery condemns the
African slave trade; colonial slaves
should be gradually emancipated.

1829 *GREGORY, George
Essays historical and moral. J. Johnson,
London, 1785. viii, 349 pp.

Including 'Of slavery and the slave
trade' and 'A short review of the
principal arguments in favour of
the good policy of the slave trade'.
See (1878).

1830 CURSORY remarks upon the Reverend
Mr. Ramsay's Essay on the treatment
and conversion of African slaves in the
sugar colonies. By a friend to the
West India colonies, and their inhabitants. G. & T. Wilkie, London; (etc.),
1785. iv, 168 pp.

By James Tobin. Accuses Ramsay
(1819) of exaggeration. The African
slave trade was not begun by Europeans; English peasants are worse
off than colonial slaves. (Reviewed
in: MR, vol. 73, Oct. 1785, pp. 268–
72.) See (1833, 1852).

1831 *BACKUS, Isaac
Godliness excludes slavery. Benjamin
Edes & Son, Boston, [1785]. 14 pp.

1832 *A DIALOGUE concerning the slavery
of the Africans; shewing it to be the
duty and interest of the American
states to emancipate all their African
slaves. With an address to the owners
of such slaves. Dedicated to the honourable the Continental Congress. To
which is prefixed, the institution of
the Society, in New-York, for promoting the Manumission of Slaves,
and protecting such of them as have
been, or may be, liberated . . . Robert
Hodge, New York, 1785. 72 pp.

By Samuel Hopkins.

1833 RAMSAY, James
A reply to the personal invectives and
objections contained in two answers,
published by certain anonymous persons, to An essay on the treatment and
conversion of African slaves, in the
British colonies. James Phillips, London,
1785. xvi, 107, 5 pp.

Answer to (1821) and (1830). (Reviewed in: MR, vol. 74, Jan. 1786,
pp. 27–33.) See (1842).

1834 DAY, Thomas
Four tracts . . . John Stockdale, London,
1785 [1786]. 129; 110; 154; 40 pp.

Fourth tract: 'Fragment of an original letter on the slavery of the negroes;
written in the year 1776' (dated 1784).
Contends that slavery is unjustifiable.
See (1816).

1835 An APOLOGY for negro slavery: or,
the West-India planters vindicated
from the charge of inhumanity. By
the author of Letters to a young
planter. J. Strachan (etc.), London,
1786. 64 pp.

By Gordon Turnbull. Argues against
(1824) the dangers of abolishing
the slave trade, which is legal and
profitable and has reduced the barbarity of Africa, though the need
for parliamentary regulation is con-
ceded. Answered by (1836–37).

1836 An ESSAY on the slavery and commerce
of the human species, particularly the
African, translated from a Latin
dissertation, which was honoured with
the first prize in the University of
Cambridge, for the year 1785, with
additions. T. Cadell; J. Phillips, London,
1786. xxxi, 256 pp.

By Thomas Clarkson. Historical
account and condemnation of slavery
and the slave trade, with criticism of
(1835). (Subject of dissertation: 'Anne
liceat invitos in servitutem dare.'
Reviewed in: GM, July 1786, pp.
590–91; MR, vol. 75, Nov. 1786,
pp. 364–66.) See (1755, 1839).

1837 SMITH, James S.
A letter from Capt. J. Smith to the
Revd Mr Hill on the state of the negroe
slaves. To which are added an introduction, and remarks on free negroes,
&c. by the editor. J. Phillips, London,
1786. 51 pp.

Letter from a naval officer on the
cruelty to slaves in the colonies,
with notes by the editor, James
Ramsay, on the practicability of
gradual abolition of slavery. See
(1835, 1842).

1838 DISCOURS sur l'esclavage des nègres,
et sur l'idée de leur affranchissement
dans les colonies. Par un colon de
Saint-Domingue. Amsterdam, 1786.
126 pp.

By David Duval de Sanadon. Reply
to writers from Montesquieu and
Raynal who have suggested abolition

of slavery, and defence of the settlers' treatment of slaves.

1839 TURNBULL, Gordon
An apology for negro slavery: or the West-India planters vindicated from the charge of inhumanity. By the author of Letters to a young planter. The second edition, with additions. J. Strachan (etc.), London, 1786. 68 pp.

Contains a new appendix attacking (1836).

1840a BLUMENBACH, Johann Friedrich
'Einige naturhistorische Bemerkungen bey Gelegenheit einer Schweizerreise... Von den Negern.' (Magazin für das neueste aus der Physik und Naturgeschichte, Gotha, vol. 4, 1786, pt. 3, pp. 1–12.)

Translated as:

1840b 'Observations on the bodily conformation and mental capacity of the negroes.' (Philosophical Magazine, London, vol. 3, March 1799, pp. 141–47.)

Gives examples of notable Africans as proof of their equality with Europeans.

1841 SHARP, Granville
Short sketch of temporary regulations (until better shall be proposed) for the intended settlement on the Grain Coast of Africa, near Sierra Leona. H. Baldwin, London, 1786. 88 pp.

Plan for a colony in which slavery will be banned and escaped slaves will be given sanctuary and redeemed. (Reviewed in: GM, Feb, 1787, pp. 162–63.) See (2007).

1842 TOBIN, James
A short rejoinder to the Reverend Mr. Ramsay's Reply: with a word or two on some other publications of the same tendency. G. & T. Wilkie, London; (etc.), 1787. 115 pp.

Answer to (1824, 1833, 1837), with a note on (1836). (Reviewed in: MR, vol. 77, Aug. 1787, pp. 167–68.) See (1845).

1843 BENEZET, Anthony
'Letter on the slave trade, written by Anthony Benezet.' (AM, vol. 1, 1787, pp. 122–23.)

Addressed to Queen Charlotte of Great Britain from Philadelphia, 25 August 1783.

1844 'THOUGHTS on slavery—great injustice of it—inconsistent with the declaration of independence—disgrace-

ful to America...' (AM, vol. 1, March 1787, pp. 238–41.)

1845 RAMSAY, James
A letter to James Tobin, Esq. late member of His Majesty's council in the island of Nevis. James Phillips, London, 1787. viii, 40 pp.

Answer to personal attacks in (1842). See (1882).

1846 'ADDRESS to the heart, on the subject of American slavery.' (AM, vol. 1, June 1787, pp. 540–44.)

Describes life in Africa and the disruptive effect of the slave trade.

1847 DISSERTATION sur les suites de la découverte de l'Amérique... Revue et corrigée pour le concours de l'année 1787... Par un citoyen, ancien syndic de la Chambre du Commerce de Lyon. [Lyons?] 1787. 140 pp.

The African slave trade to the European colonies in America is indefensible except as saving the victims from death. Written 1785. See (1887).

1848 *HOPKINS, Samuel
'The slave trade and slavery.' (Providence Gazette and Country Journal, 13 Oct. 1787.)

Urges abolition of the slave trade to escape divine punishment. Reprinted in: The works of Samuel Hopkins, vol. 2 (Boston, 1852), pp. 613–24.

1849 NICKOLLS, Robert Boucher
A letter to the treasurer of the Society instituted for the purpose of effecting the abolition of the slave trade. James Phillips, London, 1787. 16 pp.

Natural increase should suffice to maintain the West Indian slave population; abolition of the slave trade would oblige planters to care for their slaves; slavery itself could be gradually abolished. See (1885). (Reprinted in: Hibernian Magazine, Dublin, Feb. 1788, pp. 82–85; AM, vol. 3, 1788, pp. 405–10.)

1850 COOPER, Thomas
Letters on the slave trade: first published in Wheeler's Manchester Chronicle; and since re-printed with additions and alterations. C. Wheeler, Manchester, 1787. 36 pp.

Abolitionist. See (1863, 2079).

1851 A SUMMARY view of the slave trade, and of the probable consequences of its abolition. J. Phillips, London, 1787. 14 pp.

By Thomas Clarkson. First publication of the Society for effecting the Abolition of the Slave Trade. Extracts from (1836) on the means of acquiring slaves in Africa, with a synopsis of the author's forthcoming work on the impolicy of the trade (1864). (First part reprinted in: Columbian Magazine, Philadelphia, vol. 1, 1787, pp. 870–72.)

1852   CUGOANO, Ottobah
Thoughts and sentiments on the evil and wicked traffic of the slavery and commerce of the human species, humbly submitted to the inhabitants of Great-Britain. London, 1787. iv, 148 pp.

The author, a Fanti, was kidnapped as a child and sold to the West Indies; he argues the unlawfulness of slavery from Scripture in reply to (1830) and (1835). (Reprinted, with an introduction by Paul Edwards and five letters from Cugoano, London, 1969.)

1853   'LETTERS of a negro.' (Signed: A free negro.) (The Repository, London, no. 2, 16 Jan. 1788, vol. 1, pp. 57–62; no. 3, 1 Feb. 1788, pp. 121–25; no. 9, 1 May 1788, vol. 2, pp. 1–4.)

Defends the character of Africans and refutes arguments justifying the slave trade and slavery. Answered in letters by 'A West Indian' warning against hasty abolition of the slave trade (Feb.–April 1788, vol. 1, pp. 125–38, 309–17, 369–80); replied to by 'L.Y.' (pp. 249–55) and 'Philonomus' (pp. 437–40). See (1856, 1861).

1854   'CONSIDERATIONS on the slave trade . . .' (Signed: Homo sum.) (UM, vol. 82, Feb. 1788, pp. 83–84.)

Welcomes the efforts to abolish the slave trade.

1855   'An ARGUMENT used by some writers in defence of the legality of the slave trade, viz. the mixture of an owran-outang with a female African, by which they think a race of animals may be produced, partaking of the nature of each, refuted.' (Signed: R.) (EMLR, vol. 13, Feb. 1788, pp. 75–76.)

Demolishes a racialist pro-slavery theory.

1856   LETTER of a negro. (Signed: A free negro.) Manchester, 1788. 2 pp.

Broadsheet reproducing the first part of (1853).

1857   BENEZET, Anthony
Some historical account of Guinea, its situation, produce, and the general disposition of its inhabitants. With an inquiry into the rise and progress of the slave trade, its nature and lamentable effects . . . A new edition. J. Phillips, London, 1788. xv, 131 pp.

See (719, 1755).

1858   REMARKS on the slave trade, and the slavery of the negroes. In a series of letters. (Signed: Africanus.) J. Phillips, London; (etc.), 1788. 86 pp.

By William Leigh. Antislavery tract, reviewed in: MR, vol. 78, March 1788, p. 254.

1859a   DISCOURS sur la nécessité d'établir à Paris une société pour concourir, avec celle de Londres, à l'abolition de la traite & de l'esclavage des nègres. Prononcé le 19 février 1788, dans une société de quelques amis, rassemblés à Paris, à la prière du comité de Londres. [Paris, 1788.] 32 pp.

Translated as:

1859b*   An oration, upon the necessity of establishing at Paris, a society to co-operate with those of America and London, toward the abolition of the slave trade and slavery of the negroes. Delivered the 19th of February, 1788, in a society of a few friends, assembled at Paris, at the request of the committee of London. Francis Bailey, Philadelphia, 1788. 159 pp.

By J. P. Brissot. Praises the English and American abolition committees and outlines the policy for a French one. See (1892).

1860   'EXPEDIENCY of a reformation in the treatment of slaves.' (GM, March 1788, pp. 211–12.)

Calls for the abolition of slavery.

1861   HARVEY, S.
Letters in favour of the abolition of slavery. Manchester, 1788. 2 ll.

Reprint of (1856), with a letter to the Manchester Chronicle signed 'S.H.'

1862   A LETTER to Philo Africanus, upon slavery; in answer to his of the 22d of November, in the General Evening Post; together with the opinions of Sir John Strange, and other eminent lawyers upon this subject, with the sentence of Lord Mansfield, in the case of Somerset and Knowles, 1772, with his lordship's explanation of that opinion in 1786. (Signed: Candidus.) W. Brown, London, 1788. 40 pp.

Slave trade is sanctioned by the Bible and a means of civilizing Africa; its abolition would break up the sugar colonies.

1863 COOPER, Thomas
Supplement to Mr. Cooper's Letters on the slave trade. W. Eyres, Warrington, 1788. 50 pp.

Estimates the number of African victims of the slave trade as over 74 million. See (1850).

1864 CLARKSON, Thomas
An essay on the impolicy of the African slave trade . . . J. Phillips, London, 1788. iv, 134 pp.

The slave trade prevents the development of general trade with Africa and causes great mortality among seamen; abolition will not have fatal effects on Britain and her colonies. (Reviewed in: CrR, vol. 66, Sept. 1788, pp. 187–91.)

1865 ADAMS, Thomas Maxwell
A cool address to the people of England, on the slave trade. R. Faulder & J. Stockdale, London, 1788. 43 pp.

Abolition of the slave trade implies abolition of slavery itself, which would ruin the planters and favour France.

1866 'CAUTIONS hinted to the committee on the slave trade.' (Signed: Gustavus.) GM, March 1788, pp. 214–16.)

The abolitionists have exaggerated the cruelty of slavery in their propaganda.

1867 TO the honourable the Commons of Great Britain in Parliament assembled. The humble petition of the undersigned inhabitants of the town and neighbourhood of Manchester . . . [Manchester, 1788.] (1 p.)

Form of petition against the African slave trade.

1868 TO the inhabitants of Manchester. [Manchester, 1788.] (1 p.)

Abolitionist leaflet against a petition in circulation supporting the slave trade.

1869 A LETTER to Granville Sharp, Esq. on the proposed abolition of the slave

trade. J. Debrett, London, 1788. 51 pp.

Reforms are needed in the West Indies but not abolition.

1870 A PROPOSAL for the consideration of those, who interest themselves in the abolition or preservation of the slave-trade. With some observations addressed to the members of the Society for the Propagation of the Gospel. By a clergyman. J. Smart, Wolverhampton (etc.), 1788. 28 pp.

The slave trade is beneficial to the Africans and should be regulated; slavery could be ameliorated and negro missionaries sent to spread civilisation and Christianity in Africa.

1871 'THOUGHTS on the slave trade.' (Signed: B.) (EMLR, vol. 13, April 1788, pp. 256–57.)

Letter opposing abolition.

1872 'ISLE of Wight petition on the slave trade.' (GM, April 1788, pp. 311–12.)

Antislavery petition to Parliament.

1873 TO the honourable the Commons of Great Britain, in Parliament assembled. The humble petition of persons concerned in the manufacturing of neck-yokes, collars, chains, hand-cuffs, leg-bolts, drags, thumb-screws, iron coffins, cats, scourges, and other necessary instruments of torture, for the use of the African slave trade . . . [Manchester, 1788.] (1 p.)

Ironical abolitionist leaflet.

1874 THOUGHTS on the slavery of the negroes, as it affects the British colonies in the West Indies; humbly submitted to the consideration of both houses of Parliament. (Signed: Veritas.) W. Richardson & J. Debrett, [London, 1788]. 43 pp.

Blatant defence of the slave trade and slavery against abolitionist propaganda which is sowing the seed of slave rebellion; suggests sending parliamentary commissioners to the West Indies to investigate conditions there.

1875 *OBSERVATIONS upon the African slave trade, and on the situation of the negroes in the West Indies, with some proposed regulations for a more mild and humane treatment of them . . . By a Jamaica planter. Law (etc.), London, 1788. 56 pp.

Abolition is impracticable except 'by slow degrees'. (Reviewed in:

CrR, vol. 65, April 1788, pp. 319–20; MR, vol. 78, May 1788, pp. 429–30.)

1876 YOUNG, Arthur
'On the abolition of slavery in the West Indies.' (Annals of Agriculture, Bury St. Edmund's, vol. 9, 1788, pp. 88–96.)

Economic arguments to show that slavery is unprofitable, 'the dearest species of labour in the world'.

1877 HALL, Prince
'To the honourable the senate and house of representatives of the commonwealth of Massachusetts, in general court assembled, on the 27th February, 1788. The petition of a great number of blacks, freemen of said common- wealth.' (AM, vol. 3, May 1788, pp. 410–11.)

Includes a condemnation of the Afri- can slave trade.

1878 GREGORY, George
Essays historical and moral . . . Second edition, with considerable additions and alterations. J. Johnson, London, 1788. xix, 410 pp.

Includes essays on the slave trade. See (1829).

1879 *HOLLINGSWORTH, S.
A dissertation on the manners, govern- ments, and spirit of Africa. To which is added, observations on the present applications to Parliament for abolish- ing negroe slavery in the British West Indies . . . William Creech, Edinburgh, 1788. 3, 24, 43 pp.

Urges gradual abolition of the slave trade and slavery, (Reviewed in: MR, vol. 78, May 1788, pp. 430–31.)

1880 'THOUGHTS on the abolition of the African slave trade, considered chiefly in a prudential and political view.' (Signed: Polinus.) (GM, May 1788, pp. 407–09.)

Defends the slave trade; abolition is 'absurd and visionary'.

1881 *'EINIGE Gründe für den Sclavenkauf auf den Küsten von Afrika. Aus dem Wittenbergischen Wochenblatte, mit einigen Anmerkungen.' (Neue histor- ische und geographische Monatsschrift, Halle, no. 8, 1788.)

1882 TOBIN, James
A farewel address to the Rev. Mr. James Ramsay . . . To which is added a letter from the Society for Propa- gating the Gospel, to Mr. Anthony Benezet of Philadelphia: and also a translation of the French King's declara- tion relating to the situation of negroes, &c. in his European dominions. G. & T. Wilkie, London; (etc.), 1788. 39 pp.

Reply to (1845). The letter to Benezet, 1766, declares that the S.P.G. 'cannot condemn the practice of keeping slaves as unlawful'; the French decree of 1777 banished all negroes and mulattoes from metro- politan France.

1883 'REFLECTIONS on the slave trade.' (Signed: Polinus alter.) (GM, July 1788, pp. 598–99.)
Opposes abolition.

1884 NICKOLLS, Robert Boucher
Letter to the treasurer of the Society instituted for the purpose of effecting the abolition of the slave trade . . . A new edition with additions. James Phillips, London, 1788. 35 pp.

1885 *OBSERVATIONS occasioned by the attempts made in England to effect the abolition of the slave trade, shewing the manner in which the negroes are treated in the British colonies in the West Indies; and, also, some particular remarks on a letter addressed to the treasurer of the society for effecting such abolition, from the Reverend Mr. Robert Boucher Nicholls . . . Thomas Strupar & Joseph Preston, Kingston, Jamaica, 1788. xi, 64 pp.

By Gilbert Francklyn. (Another edi- tion: A. Smith's Navigation Shop, Liverpool, 1788; 76 pp.) See (1884, 1904, 1960).

1886 An ADDRESS to the inhabitants in general of Great Britain, and Ireland; relating to a few of the consequences which must naturally result from the abolition of the slave trade. Mrs Egerton Smith, Liverpool; Thomas Evans; John Hamilton Moore, London, 1788. 32 pp.

By Michael Renwick? Abolitionism is a foreign plot to ruin Britain; the slave trade is lawful and particu- larly useful to the country, while liberty would be detrimental to the African slaves.

1887 GENTY, Louis
L'influence de la découverte de l'Amér- ique sur le bonheur du genre-humaine. Nyon, Paris, 1788. x, 352 pp. illus. map.

Contains strong attacks (ch. 4, 7) on the slave trade, urging its abolition and the gradual emancipation of the slaves in the Americas. Written for the same 'concours' as (1847).

1888 CLARKSON, Thomas
An essay on the slavery and commerce of the human species, particularly the African . . . The second edition, revised and considerably enlarged. J. Phillips, London, 1788. xxii, 167 pp.

With added chapters on the history of the slave trade and on the middle passage. See (1961).

1889 NICKOLLS, Robert Boucher
Letter to the treasurer of the Society instituted for the purpose of effecting the abolition of the slave trade . . . A new edition with considerable additions. James Phillips, London, 1788. 58 pp.

With appendix on the economic arguments against slave labour.

1890 BECKFORD, William
Remarks upon the situation of negroes in Jamaica, impartially made from a local experience of nearly thirteen years in that island. T. & J. Egerton, London, 1788. viii, 99 pp.

Opposes immediate abolition of the slave trade as it is required to preserve the slave population; by reforming the treatment of slaves the trade could be ended in fifty years.

**1891 *RÉFLEXIONS d'un cultivateur américain sur le projet d'abolir l'esclavage et la traite des nègres. Ouvrage traduit de l'anglois . . . Londres; Lagrange, Paris, 1788. 99 pp.

Edited by N. F. Jacquemart. Perhaps extracts from Crèvecoeur's Letters from an American farmer (London, 1782).

1892 *CLARKSON, Thomas
An essay on the impolicy of the African slave trade . . . To which is added, An oration, upon the necessity of establishing, at Paris, a society to promote the abolition of the trade and slavery of the negroes. By J. P. Brissot de Warville. Francis Bailey, Philadelphia, 1788. iv, 159 pp.

See (1859, 1864).

1893 NEWTON, John
Thoughts upon the African slave trade. J. Buckland; J. Johnson, London, 1788. 41 pp.

Describes the author's experiences in the West African slave trade,

of which he is now ashamed, and its effects on the sailors and the Africans. Wars were the principal source of slaves. See (2024).

**1894 CONSIDERATIONS on the emancipation of negroes and on the abolition of the slave-trade. By a West-India planter. J. Johnson; J. Debrett, London, 1788. 41 pp.

Slavery cannot be abolished and abolition of the slave trade will only injure the colonies and Britain, though it should be regulated. Answered by (1895–96).

1895 RANDOLPH, Francis
A letter to the Right Honourable William Pitt, Chancellor of the Exchequer, &c. &c. on the proposed abolition of the African slave trade. T. Cadell, London, 1788. 56 pp.

Reply to (1894) and review of other pamphlets. Proposes regulation of the trade and gradual abolition of slavery.

1896 RAMSAY, James
Objections to the abolition of the slave trade, with answers. To which are prefixed, strictures on a late publication, intitled, "Considerations on the emancipation of negroes, and the abolition of the slave trade, by a West India planter". James Phillips, London, 1788. 60 pp.

Deals with 77 objections, mostly political and economic. See (1894, 1901).

**1897 HINTS for a specific plan for an abolition of the slave trade, and for relief of the negroes in the British West Indies. By the translator of Cicero's Orations against Verres. J. Debrett, London, 1788. 32 pp.

By James White. Favours regulation of slavery and proposes a boycott of West Indian sugar to obtain reforms.

**1898 *'EINIGE den Negerhandel betreffende Nachrichten und Schilderungen (aus dem Journal de Paris).' (Hannöverisches Magazin, vol. 26, 1788, no. 99, 104.)

**1899 An ESSAY on the slave trade. G. Nicol, London, 1788. 31 pp.

By Grímr Jónsson Thorkelin, a Danish scholar. Largely notes on medieval European slavery; abolition of the African slave trade is impracticable, but it should be regulated and the slaves freed after a certain period. (Reviewed in: GM, Aug. 1788, pp. 724–25.)

1900   A GENERAL view of the African slave-trade, demonstrating its injustice and impolicy; with hints towards a bill for its abolition. R. Faulder, London, 1788. 39 pp.

By William Roscoe. The slave trade is contrary to religion and the fundamental laws of society as well as uneconomic; it should be abolished by 1800 and slaves in British colonies registered. See (2503).

1901   RAMSAY, James
Objections to the abolition of the slave trade, with answers . . . The second edition, with additions. J. Phillips, London, 1788. 85 pp.

Answers 91 objections. See (1896).

1902   LAFFON DE LADEBAT, André Daniel
Discours sur la nécessité et les moyens de détruire l'esclavage dans les colonies. Lu à la séance publique de l'Académie royale des sciences, belles lettres et arts de Bordeaux, le 26 août 1788. Michel Racle, Bordeaux, 1788. 43 pp.

Attack on the slave trade as a 'crime publique'; slave labour is less productive than free labour.

1903   'SPEECH of an American Quaker on African slavery delivered about the commencement of the late contest.' (AM, vol. 4, Aug. 1788, p. 173.)

Address of 1776 urging Americans to emancipate their slaves consistently with their fight for freedom.

1904   *ANSWER to Observations occasioned by the attempts made in England to effect the abolition of the slave trade. Kingston (Jamaica), 1788.

Reply to (1885) by a Jamaican sugar planter.

1905   *RÉFLEXIONS sur l'abolition de la traite et de l'esclavage des nègres, traduites de l'anglais. Paris, 1788.

Translated by A. G. Griffet de la Beaume.

1906   'UEBER die Rechtmässigkeit des Neger-Handels.' (Signed: M.) (GHM, vol. 2, 1788, pp. 398–416.)

By C. Meiners. Despite African suffering the slave trade has been economically beneficial to mankind.

1907   *WINCHESTER, Elhanan
The reigning abominations, especially the slave trade, considered as causes of lamentations; being the substance of a discourse delivered in Fairfax County, Virginia, December 30, 1774. And now published with several additions. H. Trapp, London, 1788. 32 pp.

1908   HARRIS, Raymund
Scriptural researches on the licitness of the slave-trade, shewing its conformity with the principles of natural and revealed religion, delineated in the sacred writings of the word of God. John Stockdale, London, 1788. 77 pp.

The slave trade is sanctioned by the Bible; abuses do not justify abolition. See (1909–12, 1922).

1909   HUGHES, William
An answer to the Rev. Mr. Harris's "Scriptural researches on the licitness of the slave-trade". T. Cadell, London, 1788. 34 pp.

1910   A SCRIPTURAL refutation of a pamphlet, lately published, by the Rev. Raymund Harris, intitled, "Scriptural researches on the licitness of the slave trade." In four letters from the author to a friend. B. Law, London, 1788. 85 pp.

By William Roscoe.

1911   DANNETT, Henry
A particular examination of Mr. Harris's Scriptural researches on the licitness of the slave trade. T. Payne, London; D. Prince & Cooke, Oxford, 1788. x, 8, 146 pp.

Disproves (1908) on biblical grounds and asserts that the slave trade, necessitating cruelty, is morally wrong.

1912   RAMSAY, James
Examination of the Rev. Mr. Harris's Scriptural researches on the licitness of the slave-trade. James Phillips, London, 1788. 29 pp.

Contains a short list of 'Tracts on the slave trade'.

1913   *The MUTUAL obligations to the exercise of the benevolent affections, as they respect the conduct of all the human race to each other, proved, and applied to the state of the suffering Africans. By Philadelphos. Gardner, London, 1788.

Abolitionist. Reviewed in: MR, vol. 79, Oct. 1788, p. 375

1914 THICKNESSE, Philip
'Thoughts on the slave-trade.' (SM, vol. 50, Oct. 1788, pp. 474–75

Pro-slavery extract from his: Memoirs and anecdotes (London 1788).

1915 'ARGUMENTS for the abolition of the slave-trade.' (Signed: T.A.S.) (GM, Oct. 1788, pp. 858–59.)

This article started a controversy with P. Thicknesse which continued until Feb. 1789 (GM, 1788, pp. 962–63, 1148–49; 1789, pp. 14, 126–27).

1916 *QUESTIONS to be proposed to such gentlemen as have been resident on the coast of Africa, or in the West Indies, or have been in the slave trade. J. Phillips, London, 1788. 16 pp.

See (1956).

1917 McNEILL, Hector
Observations on the treatment of the negroes, in the island of Jamaica, including some account of their temper and character, with remarks on the importation of slaves from the coast of Africa. In a letter to a physician in England. C. G. J. & J. Robinson, London; J. Gore, Liverpool, [1788]. vi, 46 pp.

Slavery is justified and the slave trade necessary to maintain the supply of slaves to the colonies. (Reviewed in: CrR, vol. 66, 1788, pp. 342–43; GM, Dec, 1788, pp. 1093–94.)

1918 SCHWARTZ, Joachim, *pseud.*
Réflexions sur l'esclavage des nègres . . . Nouvelle édition revue & corrigée. Neufchatel; Froullé, Paris, 1788. viii, 86 pp.

By J. A. N. Caritat, marquis de Condorcet. (Reviewed in: MR, vol. 80, 1789, pp. 661–62.) See (1812).

1919 HOLDER, Henry Evans
A short essay on the subject of negro slavery, with particular reference to the island of Barbadoes. Charles Dilly, London, 1788. 45 pp.

Slave trade is justified; the slaves are better off in the West Indies than in Africa.

1920 SLAVERY no oppression; or, some new arguments and opinions against the idea of African liberty. Dedicated to the committee of the company that trade to Africa. Lowndes & Christie, London, [1788.] 36 pp.

To free men slavery would be in-

tolerable, but the unenlightened Africans are better off in the colonies; abolition would mean economic disaster.

1921 MALOUET, Pierre Victor de, *baron*
Mémoire sur l'esclavage des nègres, dans lequel on discute les motifs proposés pour leur affranchissement, ceux qui s'y opposent, & les moyens praticables pour améliorer leur sort. Neufchatel, 1788. 215 pp.

The first part of the work (written 1775) defends French colonial slavery and slave trading as economic necessities. A second part, added by the author after reading (1918), suggests gradual amelioration of slavery leading to a cessation of the trade. See (1949).

1922 HARRIS, Raymund
Scriptural researches on the licitness of the slave-trade . . . the second edition: to which are added, scriptural directions for the proper treatment of slaves, and a review of some scurrilous pamphlets published against the author and his doctrine. H. Hodgson, Liverpool, 1788. ix, 214 pp.

Reply to critics of the first edition (1908). See (1923, 1931, 1935).

1923 AM I not a man? and a brother? With all humility addressed to the British legislature. J. & J. Merrill, Cambridge; (etc.), 1788. 100 pp.

By Peter Peckard, vice chancellor of Cambridge University. Philosophical, moral and religious arguments for the abolition of slavery, with replies to the pro-slavery views of (1922) and (161).

1924 RAMSAY, James
An address on the proposed bill for the abolition of the slave trade. Humbly submitted to the consideration of the legislature. James Phillips, London, 1788. 41 pp.

Economic arguments against the slave trade.

1925 'ESSAY on negro slavery.' (Signed: Othello.) (AM, vol. 4, Nov. 1788, pp. 414–17, 509–12.)

By Benjamin Banneker? Slavery and the African slave trade are repugnant to the principles of the American revolution and ought to be abolished.

1926 'An ADDRESS to my countrymen on slavery and the slave trade.' (Signed:

Philo-Africanus.) (EMLR, vol. 15, Jan. 1789, pp. 24–25.)

Strongly abolitionist.

1927 FROSSARD, Benjamin Sigismond
La cause des esclaves nègres et des habitans de la Guinée, portée au tribunal de la justice, de la religion, de la politique, ou histoire de la traite & de l'esclavage des nègres, preuves de leur illegitimité, moyens de les abolir sans nuir ni aux colonies ni aux colons. Aimé de La Roche, Lyon, 1789. 2 vol.

Dutch edition 1790.

1928 *LIBERAL strictures on freedom and slavery, occasioned by the numerous petitions to Parliament for the abolition of the slave trade. Cadell (etc.), London, 1789. 51 pp.

Abolitionist. Reviewed in: GM, March 1789, p. 240.

1929 *REMARKS on the slave traffic and the negro bondage of our colonies. London, 1789.

By 'Africanus'.

1930 SILFVERHJELM, Jöran Ulrik
'Om slafhandeln. Til Herr de Baville, om uppköper af negrerne, deras öfverförande och ankomst till America.' In his: Samlingar för hjertat och snillet, pt. 1 (Götheborg, 1789), pp. 44–70.

Antislavery essay.

1931 BURGESS, Thomas
Considerations on the abolition of slavery and the slave trade, upon grounds of natural, religious, and political duty. D. Prince & J. Cooke; J. & J. Fletcher, Oxford; Elmsley, White, Payne, Cadell, London, 1789. 166 pp.

Answer to (1922). Abolition of the slave trade would have beneficial effects in Africa and on British commerce. (Reviewed in: CrR, vol. 67, July 1789, pp. 452–54.)

1932 ANDERSON, James
Observations on slavery; particularly with a view to its effects on the British colonies, in the West-Indies. J. Harrop, Manchester, 1789. 38 pp.

Arguments for the gradual abolition of slavery by a Scottish economist.

1933 'FRENCH ideas of the slave trade.' (Signed: Britannus.) (GM, April 1789, p. 291.)

Approves of (1918).

1934 'On SLAVERY and the slave trade.' (Signed: Philo Africanus.) (GM, April 1789, pp. 319–20.)

Biblical quotations against slavery in reply to a recent publication defending it.

1935 SCRIPTURE the friend of freedom; exemplified by a refutation of the arguments offered in defence of slavery, in a tract entitled, Scriptural researches on the licitness of the slave trade. J. Phillips; J. Debrett, London, 1789. vi, 79 pp.

Refutation of (1922), also based on scriptural passages.

1936 'REMARKS on the slave trade.' (AM, vol. 5, May 1789, pp. 429–30; illus.)

Contains an extract from a pamphlet by the Plymouth abolition committee in England and a plan of a slave ship. (Reprinted by the Pennsylvania abolition society, Philadelphia, 1789, as a broadside headed: 'Plan of an African ship's lower deck, with negroes . . .')

1937 LETTRE à MM. les députés des trois ordres, pour les engager à faire nommer par les États-généraux, à l'example des Anglois, une commission chargée d'examiner la cause des noirs. (Signed: Un ami des noirs.) [Paris, 1789.] 51 pp.

1938 A SOLEMN address to the members of the House of Commons, upon the question, this day to be agitated in that House, of the abolition of the slave trade. [London, 1789?] 3 pp.

Opposes abolition.

1939 WEST INDIA COMMITTEE
(Begin.) At a general meeting of the planters, merchants, and others interested in the West-Indies, held at the London-Tavern, May 19, 1789: resolved . . . (Signed: James Allen, secretary.) [London, 1789.] 4 pp.

Nineteen resolutions in favour of the continuation of the African slave trade.

1940 COMMERCIAL reasons for the non-abolition of the slave-trade, in the West-India islands, by a planter and merchant of many years residence in the West-Indies. W. Lane, London, 1789. 20 pp.

Title page headed: 'West-India trade and islands.' Abolition would ruin British trade and the colonies.

1941 *The NEGRO and the free-born Briton compared; or, a vindication of the African slave trade. Proving that it is lawful and right, in a religious, in a political, and in a commercial view . . . London, [1789?]. 57 pp.

Headed: 'Slave trade.'

1942 NOTES on the two reports from the committee of the honourable House of Assembly of Jamaica, appointed to examine into and to report to the House, the allegations and charges contained in the several petitions which have been presented to the British House of Commons, on the subject of the slave trade, and the treatment of the negroes, &c. &c. &c. By a Jamaica planter. James Phillips, London, 1789. 62 pp.

Criticises the reports (2) and the new colonial slave laws.

1943 *DOUBTS concerning the legality of slavery in any part of the British dominions. J. Stockdale, London, 1789. 14 pp.

West Indian slaves can claim freedom as an English birthright. (Reviewed in: CrR, vol. 68, July 1789, p. 72.)

1944 DICKSON, William
Letters on slavery . . . To which are added, addresses to the whites, and to the free negroes of Barbadoes; and accounts of some negroes eminent for their virtues and abilities. J. Phillips; (etc.), London, 1789. x, 190 pp.

Abolition of the slave trade would be a step towards the abolition of slavery; this would not lead to a decline of the colonies. (The author corrected a reviewer in: 'Letter from Mr. Dickson, on the slave trade', GM, July 1789, pp. 621–22.)

1945 *NISBET, Richard
The capacity of negroes for religious and moral improvement, considered; with cursory hints, to proprietors and to government, for the immediate melioration of the condition of slaves in the sugar colonies: to which are subjoined short and practical discourses to negroes, on the plain and obvious principles of religion and morality. James Phillips, London, 1789. 207 pp.

1946 NO abolition; or, an attempt to prove to the conviction of every rational British subject, that the abolition of the British trade with Africa for negroes, would be a measure as unjust as impolitic, fatal to the interests of this nation, ruinous to its sugar colonies, and more or less pernicious in its consequences to every description of the people. In the course of which are inserted important extracts from the report of the right honourable committee of Privy Council. J. Debrett, London, 1789. 52 pp.

Economic arguments against abolition. See (5).

1947 CONSIDERATIONS upon the fatal consequences of abolishing the slave trade, in the present situation of Great Britain. J. Debrett, London, 1789. 36 pp.

Abolition would favour the French at the expense of the British colonies.

1948 *OBSERVATIONS sur la traite des noirs aux côtes d'Afrique. [Paris?] 1789. 18 pp.

1949 RÉPONSE à l'écrit de M. Malouet, sur l'esclavage des nègres. Dans lequel est exprimé le vœu formé par les colons d'avoir des représentans aux États-généraux. Par un membre de la Société des Amis des Noirs. [Paris,] 1789. 99 pp.

Reply to (1921), urging the necessity of abolishing the slave trade in preparation for gradual emancipation.

1950 CLARKSON, Thomas
An essay on the comparative efficiency of regulation or abolition, as applied to the slave trade. Shewing that the latter only can remove the evils to be found in that commerce. James Phillips, London, 1789. xi, 82 pp.

Describes the effects of the trade on Africans and on European seamen and shows that it is economically 'a losing trade'.

1951 RÉCLAMATIONS et observations des colons, sur l'idée de l'abolition de la traite et de l'affranchissement des nègres. Seconde édition. [Paris,] 1789. 52 pp.

By David Duval de Sanadon. The settlers request the États-généraux not to abolish but regulate the slave trade, as slavery is necessary to the colonies. See (1975).

1952 IDÉE de la traite et de l'esclavage des nègres. Philadelphie, 1789. viii, 108, 48 pp.

Extracts from (1888), a 'mémoire' of 1777 on slavery in St. Domingue and (1834).

M

1953 AGENDA d'un député aux États-généraux, contenant, entr'autres choses, plusieurs articles relatifs à la marine & au commerce de mer. [Paris?] 1789. 142 pp.

Includes a brief discussion of the problem of abolition; slave labour is necessary for the plantations but the trade could perhaps be left to foreigners.

1954 BRISSOT, Jacques Pierre
Réflexions sur l'admission, aux États-généraux, des députés de Saint-Domingue. [Paris, 1789.] 36 pp.

France and the colonies have diametrically opposed interests; until the abolition question has been settled, the number of colonial deputies should be limited.

1955 Le MORE-LACK, ou essai sur les moyens les plus doux & les plus équitables d'abolir la traite & l'esclavage des nègres d'Afrique, en conservant aux colonies tous les avantages d'une population agricole. Londres; Paris, 1789. xxxii, 288 pp.

By — Lecointe-Marsillac. Description of the slave trade and slavery, with suggestions for the abolition of the trade and gradual emancipation of the slaves.

1956 COCHRANE, Thomas
Answers to the fifth table of queries, published by the Society in London, instituted for the purpose of effecting the abolition of the slave trade. D. Willison, Edinburgh, 1789. iv, 34 pp.

Information on slave sales and slavery in the West Indies by a doctor, confirming the dangers to health of slaves and sailors. See (1916).

1957 THOUGHTS on civilization, and the gradual abolition of slavery in Africa and the West-Indies. (Signed: A friend to commerce and humanity.) J. Sewell, [London, 1789]. 12 pp.

Slave trade is necessary for the civilisation of Africa and should be regulated by the European nations 'in some general system'.

1958 An INQUIRY into the origin, progress, & present state of slavery: with a plan for the gradual, reasonable, & secure emancipation of slaves. By a member of the Society of Universal Goodwill in London and Norwich. John Murray, London, 1789. 43 pp.

Slaves should be freed after 15–20 years and returned to Africa.

1959 ESSAYS, philosophical, historical, and literary. C. Dilly, London, 1789. iv, 466 pp.

By William Belsham. Essay XXIII: 'On the African slave trade.' It violates the laws of justice and humanity and is not a political necessity; abolition would not ruin the British economy, while regulation would be a disgrace. Published separately 1790 (2033).

1960 FRANCKLYN, Gilbert
Observations, occasioned by the attempts made in England to effect the abolition of the slave trade; shewing the manner in which negroes are treated in the colonies in the West-Indies: and also, some particular remarks on a letter addressed to the treasurer of the society for effecting the abolition, from the Rev. Robert Boucher Nicholls, Dean of Middleham. London, 1789. xx, 87 pp.

Justifies the slave trade and slavery; abolition by Britain would leave the trade to be carried on by her rivals. See (1885).

1961 FRANCKLYN, Gilbert
An answer to the Rev. Mr. Clarkson's Essay on the slavery and commerce of the human species, particularly the African; in a series of letters, from a gentleman in Jamaica, to his friend in London . . . J. Walter; (etc.), London, 1789. xvi, 263 pp.

Clarkson (1888) exaggerated the horrors of the slave trade and slavery, which are perfectly legal.

1962 TRAITE des nègres. A messieurs les députés de l'Assemblée nationale. Baudouin, Paris, 1789. 4 pp.

Urges the Assembly to abolish the slave trade.

1963 LUFFMAN, John
A brief account of the island of Antigua, together with the customs and manners of its inhabitants, as well white as black: as also an accurate statement of the food, cloathing, labor, and punishment, of slaves. In letters to a friend, written in the years 1786, 1787, 1788 . . . The second edition. J. Luffman; James Ridgeway, London, [1789]. 180 pp.

Supports abolition of the slave trade from Africa. See (2024).

1964 LUDWIG, Johann Friedrich
Neueste Nachrichten von Surinam . . .
herausgegeben . . . von M. Philipp
Friedrich Binder. Jena, 1789. xxxii,
260 pp.

Preface by the editor contains a
defence of the slave trade and
slavery against abolitionist critics.

1965 BELIN DE VILLENEUVE, —
Lettre d'un créole de Saint Domingue
à la société établie à Paris sous le
nom d'Amis des Noirs. Paris, 1789.
44 pp.

Slave trade and slavery are both
necessary to the colonial economy
but could be regulated; conditions
in the colonies are preferable to
those in Africa for the slaves.

1966 RÉFLEXIONS sur le sort des noirs dans
nos colonies. [Paris,] 1789. 71 pp.

By Daniel Lescallier. Urges the
Assembly to end the slave trade as a
first step towards abolishing slavery;
both are economically disadvanta-
geous to the colonies as well as
immoral.

1967 ADDRESSE à l'Assemblée nationale.
[Paris, 1789.] 7 pp.

Appeal against abolition of the slave
trade signed by 26 deputies, mostly
from towns involved in it.

1968 DISCOURS à L'Assemblée nationale.
[Paris? 1789.] 124 pp.

By S. A. Sibire, a missionary at
Loango in 1764. With a 'Lettre aux
colonies' (pp. 16–124). Reissued as
(1976).

1969 PRÉCIS sur l'importance des colonies,
et sur la servitude des noirs, suivi
d'observations sur la traite des noirs.
Ph.-D. Pierres, Versailles, [1789]. 50 pp.

By J. F. Begouen. Anti-abolitionist.
See (1975).

1970 ADRESSE à messieurs les députés,
de la part des villes de commerce à
l'occasion de l'affranchissement des
nègres. Beaufleury, Paris, 1789. 7 pp.

Attack on the proposed emancipation
of the slaves which would cause the
loss of the colonies and economic
disaster to France.

1971 QUESNAY DE BEAUREPAIRE, Alexandre Marie
Troisième avis important aux citoyens,
ou le fidèle organe de l'opinion pub-

lique. Baudouin, Versailles, [1789].
11 pp.

French slaves should be liberated and
resettled in Africa.

1972 DE l'état des nègres, relativement à la
prospérité des colonies françoises &
de leur métropole. Discours aux repre-
sentans de la nation. [Paris,] 1789. 32 pp.

The Amis des Noirs are traitors;
abolition would bring economic disaster to France; Britain aims at
'l'empire du monde'.

1973 CHARTON, Louis
Observation de M. Charton à la motion
de M. Moreau de Saint-Méry. [Paris?
1789.] 8 pp.

Opposes emancipation and forecasts a
massacre of French settlers.

1974 ADRESSE à nosseigneurs de l'Assemblée nationale, par les négocians de
Bordeaux. [Bordeaux? 1789?] 12 pp.

Opposes the proposed motion for
abolition of the slave trade, which
would have serious effects on the
colonial economy.

1975 VIEFVILLE DES ESSARS, Jean Louis
de, *baron*
Discours et projet de loi pour l'affranchissement des nègres, ou l'adoucisse-
ment de leur régime, et réponse aux
objections des colons. Paris, [1789].
40 pp.

If abolition of the slave trade has to be
adjourned the National Assembly
should ameliorate the conditions of
slavery. With replies to (1951) and
(1969).

1976 SIBIRE, Sébastien André
L'aristocratie négrière, ou réflexions
philosophiques et historiques sur l'esclavage et l'affranchissement des noirs,
dediées à l'Assemblée nationale. Les-
clapart; Desray, Paris, 1789. 124 pp.

Urges the Assembly to abolish the
slave trade and slavery and appeals
to the settlers not to oppose this;
abolition would make it possible
to extend commerce and Christianity
in Africa. See (1968).

1977 L'ESCLAVAGE des nègres abo'i ou
moyens d'améliorer leur sort. Froullé,
Paris, 1789. 14 pp.

Abolition of the slave trade must be
agreed to by all the colonial powers;
meanwhile France could set an
example by importing labourers who
would be freed after a fixed period.

1978 GRÉGOIRE, Henri Baptiste
Mémoire en faveur des gens de couleur ou sang-mêlés de St. Domingue, & des autres isles françoises de l'Amérique, adressé à l'Assemblée nationale. Belin, Paris, 1789. 52 pp.

The planters' opposition to abolition of the slave trade and to representation of the coloured population could lead to a general revolt. See (1986, 4571).

1979 RAMSAY, James
An address to the publick on the proposed bill for the abolition of the slave trade. J. Phillips, London, 1789. 41 pp.

A reissue of (1924).

1980 REFLECTIONS on the present state of the slaves in the British plantations, and the slave trade from Africa. J. Todd, York; Baldwin, London, 1789. 64 pp.

By M. Kerr. The slave trade and slavery should be regulated. (Reviewed in: MR, vol. 81, Nov. 1789, pp. 464–65.)

1981 An **APPEAL** to candour and common sense, respectfully addressed, to the members of both houses of Parliament, and the community at large. By an individual of little note. [London,] 1789. 12 pp.

Criticism of Wilberforce and other abolitionists, with suggestions for medical regulations on slave ships.

1982 *RÉFLEXIONS sur l'abolition de la traite & la liberté des noirs. L. P. Couret, Orleans, [1789]. 14 pp.

1983 DESCRIPTION of a slave ship. James Phillips, London, 1789. (1 p.)

Plan of the ship 'Brookes', with an extract from (162).

1984 ADRESSE des quatre-vingt-dix électeurs des communes de Bordeaux, à l'Assemblée nationale, au sujet de la révolte des esclaves à la Martinique. Michel Racle, Bordeaux, 1789. 16 pp.

The proposed abolition of the slave trade would be dangerous; emancipation would be unjust to the owners and impolitic.

1985 BRISSOT, Jacques Pierre
Mémoire sur les noirs de l'Amérique septentrionale, lu à l'assemblée de la Société des Amis des Noirs, le 9 février 1789 . . . Bailly; de Senne, Paris, 1789. 56 pp.

Report on a visit to the United States and on measures being taken there to abolish the slave trade and slavery.

1986 OBSERVATIONS d'un habitant des colonies, sur le Mémoire en faveur des gens de couleur, ou sang-mêlés, de Saint-Domingue & des autres isles françoises de l'Amérique, adressé à l'Assemblée nationale, par M. Grégoire . . . (Signed: P.U.C.P.D.D.L.M.) [Paris? 1789.] 68 pp.

The claim made by Grégoire (1978) that other nations intended to stop trading for slaves is misleading. See (4577).

1987 COUP-D'ŒIL sur la question de la traite et de l'esclavage des noirs, considérée dans son rapport avec le droit naturel. Momoro, [Paris, 1790?] 15 pp.

If the rights of man are violated in the slave trade it is by the vendors in Africa; France exploits this violation in the national interest and improves the state of the slaves.

1988 *MAZOIS, Marc
Réponse de M. Marc Mazois, négociant, de Bordeaux, à une lettre d'un ami des noirs insérée dans le Journal de Paris, le 13 janvier 1790. P.G. Calamy, Bordeaux, [1790].

Britain may induce France to abolish the slave trade in order to ruin her and seize her colonies.

1989 OBSERVATIONS pour servir de réponse aux différens faits avancés par les prétendus amis des noirs, et notamment à une lettre du 4 janvier 1790, qui se trouve dans le supplément du Journal de Paris, du 13 dudit mois; par les capitaines du Havre-de-Grace, navigans à la côte d'Afrique. P.-F. Didot jeune, [Paris,] 1790. 13 pp.

The abolitionists have misrepresented the facts about the slave trade, which serves the interests of humanity, and have fomented rebellion by their ideas of liberty.

1990 *MANDAR, Théophile
Observations sur l'esclavage et le commerce des nègres. Pour répondre aux questions insérées dans le Journal de Paris . . . Grand, [Paris, 1790]. 28 pp.

1991 BECKFORD, William
A descriptive account of the island of Jamaica . . . also observations and reflections upon what would probably

be the consequences of an abolition of the slave-trade, and of the emancipation of the slaves. T. & J. Egerton, London, 1790. 2 vol.

Abolition would ruin the colonies and emancipation might lead to a massacre of the whites.

1992 MAGOL, Jean Claude
Discours sur la question relative à la liberté des nègres, prononcé en l'assemblée générale du district des Filles-Saint-Thomas, le février . . . Paris, 1790. 10, 8 pp.

Slavery should be ameliorated but abolition would ruin France; the Amis des Noirs are in the pay of the English, who are conspiring against France. See (1997).

1993 *DUBUC DE MARENTILLE, ——
De l'esclavage des nègres dans les colonies de l'Amérique. Pointe-à-Pitre, 1790.

The slave trade rescues Africans from barbarism.

1994 BOUSELL, John
The standard of the Lord of Hosts exalted; the banner of the Prince of Peace displayed. Being a message unto the King, the ministers of state and the members of both houses of Parliament, to take away the heavy burthen of tithes, and to set at liberty the African slaves. John Dennis; (etc.), London; (etc.), [1790]. 22 pp.

A Quaker exhortation.

1995 *BORDEAUX: Garde Nationale
Adresse à la Garde Nationale Parisienne. G. Calamy, [Bordeaux,] 1790.

Messages from the city of Bordeaux against abolition of the slave trade, sent with a deputation to Paris in February 1790.

1996 MILLY, Louis Lezin de
Discours prononcé le 20 février 1790, par M. de Milly, Américain, citoyen de Paris, avocat en parlement, l'un des commissaires nommés par le district des Filles-Saint-Thomas; pour l'examen de la question relative à la liberté et à l'abolition de la traite des nègres. P. Fr. Didot jeune, Paris, 1790. 38 pp.

Abolition would lead to slave revolts, the loss of the colonies, and the ruin of the French economy.

1997 PARIS: District des Filles-Saint Thomas
Extrait du registre des délibérations

du district des Filles Saint-Thomas. [Paris, 1790.] 6 pp.

Resolutions against abolition of the slave trade and slavery adopted at a meeting 22 Feb. 1790. See (1992).

1998 MOSNERON DE LAUNAY, Jean Baptiste, baron
Discours sur les colonies et la traite des noirs, prononcé le 26 février 1790, par M. Mosneron de L'Aunay, député du commerce de Nantes près l'Assemblée nationale, à la Société des Amis de la Constitution. [Paris, 1790.] 14 pp.

The slave trade must be continued for reasons of state; the abolitionists have exaggerated its harshness and provoked trouble in the colonies.

1999 *GRÉGOIRE, Henri Baptiste
Lettre aux philanthropes, sur les malheurs, les droits et les réclamations des gens de couleur de Saint-Domingue, et des autres îles françoises de l'Amérique . . . Belin (etc.), Paris, 1790. 21 pp.

2000 *BAXTER, Richard
Baxter's directions to slaveholders revived . . . To which is subjoined a letter from the worthy Anthony Benezet, to the celebrated Abbe Raynal. With his answer. F. Bailey, Philadelphia, 1790. 8, 16, 12 pp.

See (1692).

2001 GOUGES, Olympe de
Réponse au champion américain, ou colon très-aisé à connoitre. [Paris, 1790.] 8 pp.

Reply by a female playwright and abolitionist to attacks on her writings.

2002 DUPRÉ, Joseph
Mémoire sur la traite des noirs. Devaux, [Paris, 1790?] 16 pp.

Policy and economic considerations demand continuation of the slave trade; abolition would be ruinous and inhumane.

2003 PETION DE VILLENEUVE, Jérôme
Discours sur la traite des noirs. Desenne; (etc.), Paris, 1790. 80 pp.

Demonstrates that the slave trade is barbarous and uneconomic, being subsidised by the state. With an appendix by M. Carra: 'Observations . . . sur l'abolition de la traite'.

2004 *NÉCESSITÉ de l'abolition immédiate de la traite & de l'abolition graduée de l'esclavage, par une personne qui a habité plusieurs années les colonies. Bailly; Petit, [Paris, 1790].

2005 *L'AMI des colonies aux Amis des des Noirs . . . Monsieur, Paris, 1790. 19 pp.

Opposes abolition of slavery.

2006 *Un MOT sur les noirs, à leurs amis. [Paris? 1790?]

Attack on the Amis des Noirs as unpatriotic.

2007 SMEATHMAN, Henry
'Copy of two letters to Dr. Knowles, on the rice trade of Africa.' (New Jerusalem Magazine, London, vol. 1, 1790, pp. 279–94.)

Plan, proposed in 1783, to establish a settlement near Sierra Leone to supply tropical products by free labour, which would undermine the slave trade to America. See (1841).

2008 PELLERIN, Joseph Michel
Réflexions sur la traite des noirs. Paris, 1790. 15 pp.

Intended speech in the National Assembly by a spokesman for the Bordeaux delegation (1995), attacking the Amis des Noirs and abolition as ruinous for France.

2009 M. LAMIRAL réfuté par lui-même, ou réponse aux opinions de cet auteur, sur l'abolition de la traite des noirs, suivie de quelques idées sur les établissemens libres que la France ne doit point différer de faire au Sénégal. Par un ami des blancs & des noirs. Desenne; Bailli, Paris, 1790. 80 pp.

By F. X. Lanthenas. Lamiral's work (166) was published only to justify the slave trade, but he contradicts himself; abolition would be in the best interest of the French settlers.

2010 DOUBTS on the abolition of the slave trade. By an old member of Parliament. (Signed: Honestus.) John Stockdale, London, 1790. vii, 123 pp.

By John Ranby. Reviewed in: MR, n.s., vol. 1, 1790, pp. 221–22.

2011 *STRICTURES on the slave trade, and their manner of treatment in the West-India islands: in a letter to the Right Honourable William Pitt, in opposition to the exertions now making in the House of Commons, for an abolition thereof, by Mr. Wilberforce. By a gentleman, who resided more than twenty years in Jamaica . . . (Signed: Othello.) W. Richardson, London, 1790. 40 pp.

Reviewed in: CrR, vol. 69, June 1790, p. 707.

2012 *The SLAVE trade indispensable: in answer to the speech of William Wilberforce, Esq., on the 13th of May, 1789. By a West-India merchant. W. Richardson, London, 1790. 77 pp.

By William Innes. Reviewed in: CrR, vol. 69, June 1790, pp. 707–08; GM, July 1790, pp. 638–39. See (2083, 2336).

2013 *MORETON, J. B.
Manners and customs in the West India islands. Containing various particulars respecting the soil, cultivation, produce, trade, officers, inhabitants, &c. &c. . . . Also the treatment of slaves; and the slave-trade. W. Richardson (etc.), London, 1790. 192 pp.

See (2161).

2014 THÉBAUDIÈRES, Pierre André François Viau, *chevalier* **de**
Vues générales sur les moyens de concilier l'intérêt du commerce national avec la prospérité des colonies. Demonville, [Paris, 1790]. 24 pp.

The slave trade should be regulated but not abolished; emancipation of the slaves would lead to the loss of the colonies.

2015 DUBU DE LONGCHAMP, Jean François
Point de la question sur les colonies . . . Seguy-Thiboust, Paris, 1790. 15 pp.

The trade agreement of August 1784, giving foreign merchants access to St. Domingue, should be rescinded and the French slave trade protected by law against English competition.

2016 *CRAWFORD, Charles
Observations upon negro-slavery. A new edition. Eleazer Oswald, Philadelphia, 1790. 125 pp.

2017 'UEBER die Natur der afrikanischen Neger, und die davon abhängende Befreyung, oder Einschränkung der Schwarzen'. (Signed: M.) (GHM, vol. 6, 1790, pp. 385–456.)

By C. Meiners. Africans are not worthy of freedom.

2018 *ATWOOD, Thomas
Observations on the true methods of treatment and usage of the negroe slaves in the British West India islands. And a refutation of the gross misrepresentations calculated to impose on

the nation, on that subject. Mott, London, 1790. 15 pp.

> Reviewed in: MR, n.s., vol. 1, 1790, p. 222.

2019 FRIENDS, Society of
'To the senate and house of representatives of the united states [*sic*]. The address of the people called quakers in annual assembly convened.' (AM, vol. 7, 1790, Appendix II, pp. 26–27.)

> Petition for the abolition of the slave trade from a meeting at Philadelphia 28 Sept.–3 Oct. 1789.

2020 A LETTER to William Wilberforce, Esq; on a fundamental measure for a parliamentary reform . . . and on the folly and fatality of abolishing the slave trade. J. Johnson, London, 1790. 64 pp.

> Conservative opposition to abolition, based on property rights and the political dangers involved.

2021 *CLARKSON, Thomas
Lettre aux auteurs du Journal de Paris. Vve Hérissant, [Paris, 1790]. 4 pp.

> Stresses the difference between African and West Indian slavery.

2022 L'HOMME redevenu homme, ou les Africains à l'Assemblée nationale . . . Par un ancien capitaine d'infanterie. [Paris?] 1790. 16 pp.

> The Assembly has declared that men are born free and equal in rights; the slave trade is therefore a crime and should be abolished.

2023 DUTRÔNE LA COUTURE, Jacques François
Adresse aux François, contre la Société des Amis des Noirs. [Paris, 1790?] 24 pp.

> Slaves are well treated in the French colonies; the Amis are ignorant tools of the British government; the declaration of the rights of man refers only to France; abolition would lead to the secession of the colonies.

2024 ADAIR, James Makittrick
Unanswerable arguments against the abolition of the slave trade. With a defence of the proprietors of the British sugar colonies, against certain malignant charges contained in letters published by a sailor, and by Luffman, Newton, &c. . . . J. P. Bateman, London, [1790]. 375 pp.

> Miscellaneous essays on the West Indies, the treatment of slaves, and

the necessity of the slave trade. See (717, 1893, 1963).

2025 WOODS, Joseph
'Remarks on the slave-trade, occasioned by Bruce's Travels.' (GM, Aug. 1790, pp. 705–08.)

> Quotes the explorer James Bruce on the slave trade (in Abyssinia) and urges its abolition.

2026 *LE GRAND, M.
Observations contre la liberté des nègres et sur la necessité de maintenir la traite. Vve Giraud, Grenoble, 1790. 15 pp.

2027 LETTRE de M.*** à M. Brissot de Warville, président de la Société des Amis des Noirs. Vezard & Le Normant, [Paris, 1790]. 13 pp.

> Reply to a speech by Brissot: the slaves are well off, but more are needed; abolition of the slave trade would be ruinous to France and might provoke the colonies to secede.

2028 RIQUETTI, André Boniface Louis, *vicomte de Mirabeau*
Opinion de M. le vicomte de Mirabeau, député du Limousin, sur la pétition des villes du commerce des colonies, l'esclavage & la traite des noirs. Vezard & Le Normant, [Paris,] 1790. 30 pp.

> Slavery is necessary for the colonies and abolition of the trade would lead to national bankruptcy, but both could be regulated; the Amis des Noirs are enemies of France.

2029 *TRAHISON découverte du comte de Mirabeau. Marat, [Paris, 1790]. 8 pp.

> Attacks Mirabeau for supporting abolition of the slave trade.

2030 DÉNONCIATION de la secte des Amis des Noirs, par les habitans des colonies françoises. [Paris? 1790.] 1 p.

> The abolitionists are subversive enemies of France, the colonies, and the human race. Published by the settlers of the Club de Massiac.

2031 DÉCOUVERTE d'une conspiration contre les intérêts de la France. [Paris? 1790.] 22 pp.

> By L. M. de Gouy? Violent attack on Brissot and the Amis des Noirs as criminal revolutionaries instigated by Britain. Answered by (2032). See (4579).

2032 IL est encore des aristocrates, ou réponse à l'infame auteur d'un écrit intitulé: Decouverte d'une conspiration contre les intérêts de la France. [Paris, 1790.] 15 pp.

Defence of the Amis des Noirs, who hope to prevent a slave revolt by abolishing the slave trade. The planters are an aristocracy more odious than the old French nobility. See (2031).

2033a An ESSAY on the African slave trade. C. Dilly, London, 1790. 20 pp.

Reissued as:

2033b REMARKS on the African slave trade. C. Dilly, London, 1790. 20 pp.

By William Belsham. Extract from (1959).

2034 'HISTORISCHE Nachrichten über die wahre Beschaffenheit des Sclaven-Handels, und der Knechtschaft der Neger in West-Indien.' (Signed: M.) (GHM, vol. 6, 1790, pp. 645–79.)

By C. Meiners. Defence of the African slave trade and slavery.

2035 DESCRIPTION d'un navire négrier. [Paris? 1790?] 15 pp.

Plan of the English ship 'Brookes', with extracts from (162) and (1864).

2036 A LETTER from W. K. Esq. to W. Wilberforce, Esq. J. Debrett, London, 1790. 24 pp.

By William Knox. The slave trade should be regulated, not abolished; Africans are better off in the West Indies than peasants in Britain.

2037 LABORIE, —— de, *chevalier*
Propositions soumises à l'examen du Comité de marine de l'Assemblée nationale. L. M. Cellot, Paris, 1790. 30 pp.

Slave labour is uneconomic; gradual emancipation would lead to the cessation of the slave trade; European labour should be employed in the colonies.

2038 OBSERVATIONS on the project for abolishing the slave trade, and on the reasonableness of attempting some practicable mode of relieving the negroes. J. Debrett, London, 1790. 72 pp.

By John Baker Holroyd, Earl of Sheffield. Immediate abolition would present economic and political dangers; encouragement of slave breeding could eventually replace imports. (Second edition, with additions, 1791; 72 pp.)

2039 MÉMOIRE sur l'esclavage des nègres, contenant réponse à divers écrits qui ont été publiés en leur faveur; par M. DL.DMFY. Garnery, Paris, 1790. 64 pp.

The slave trade is of benefit to the Africans; abolition would ruin France and the colonies, to which slaves are a necessity.

2040 A LETTER to Wm. Wilberforce, Esq. by Philo-Africanus. J. Debrett, London, 1790. 62 pp.

Attributed to G. Ellis. Ironical argument against abolition in the form of a conversation with a West Indian settler in a London coffeehouse; Wilberforce has exaggerated the suffering of the slaves.

2041 *PONS, François Raimond Joseph
Observations sur la situation politique de Saint-Domingue . . . Quillau, Paris, 1790. 8, xvi, 101 pp.

Defence of the slave trade.

2042 SAINT CYRAN, Paul Edme Crublier de
Réfutation du projet des Amis des Noirs, sur la suppression de la traite des nègres & sur l'abolition de l'esclavage dans nos colonies. Devaux, [Paris,] 1790. 51 pp.

Even if France abolished the slave trade, England and other nations might not; emancipation would cause a slave revolt and the loss of the colonies.

2043 BRISSOT, Jacques Pierre
Lettre de J. P. Brissot à M. Barnave, sur ses rapports concernant les colonies, les décrets qui ont suivis, leurs conséquences fatales; sur sa conduite dans le cours de la révolution; sur la caractère des vrais démocrates; sur les bases de la constitution, les obstacles qui s'opposent à son achèvement, la nécessité de le terminer promptement, etc. Desenne (etc.), Paris, 1790. 104 pp.

Attack on Barnave's colonial policy; in deciding against abolition of the slave trade he was influenced by supporters of the status quo against the abolitionists.

2044 'IMPORTANT observations on the commerce in slaves.' (UM, vol. 87, Dec. 1790, pp. 275–76.)

Opposes abolition, drawing attention to the age-old Muslim slave trade from eastern Africa described by James Bruce in Abyssinia (2025).

2045 *REMARKS on the advertisement of the Committee for the Abolition of the Slave Trade, inserted in the public papers. Egerton, London, 1790. 112 pp.

Anti-abolitionist. (Reviewed in: CrR, n.s., vol. 1, Jan. 1791, p. 109; MR, n.s., vol. 4, Feb. 1791, pp. 221–22.)

2046 BEATTIE, James
Elements of moral science. T. Cadell, London; William Creech, Edinburgh, 1790, 93. 2 vol.

Pt. 3 contains a section 'Of slavery— particularly that of the negroes', in which various arguments against abolition are answered. (Written 1778.)

2047 'DEAN Prideaux on the slave trade.' (Signed: B.) (GM, Jan. 1791, p. 17.)

Excerpts from a work by Humphrey Prideaux showing that slavery is not condemned by the Bible. See (2057).

2048 GOUY, Louis Marthe de
Première et dernière lettre de Louis-Marthe de Gouy, député à l'Assemblée nationale, à Jean Pierre Brissot, auteur d'un journal intitulé: Le Patriote Français. [Paris, 1791.] (2 pp.)

Attack on Brissot and the Amis des Noirs as responsible for the slave revolt in Saint Domingue. See (2050).

2049 GOUY, Louis Marthe de
Fragment d'une lettre de Louis-Marthe de Gouy, député à l'Assemblée nationale, adressée à ses commettans; ou seconde fustigation de Jean-Pierre Brissot. [Paris? 1791.] 12 pp.

Further attack on Brissot and the 'Négrophiles'. See (2050).

2050 BRISSOT, Jacques Pierre
Réplique de J. P. Brissot, à la première et dernière lettre de Louis-Marthe Gouy, défenseur de la traite des noirs et de l'esclavage. Belin; (etc.), Paris, 1791. 54 pp.

Reply to arguments against abolition by de Gouy (2048–49) and earlier pro-slavery writers, with a passionate defence of the abolitionist cause from accusations of demagoguery and subversion.

2051 *DANA, James
The African slave trade. A discourse delivered in the city of New-Haven, September 9, 1790, before the Connecticut Society for the Promotion of Freedom . . . Thomas & Samuel Green, New-Haven, 1791. 33 pp.

2052 *PERFIDIE du système des Amis des Noirs. [Nantes, 1791.] 15 pp.

Attributed to Rousseau des Mélotries; dated 23 Feb. 1791. The citizens of Nantes demand a ban on the abolitionists.

2053 The PETITION of the synod of Merse and Tiviotdale. [Glasgow? 1791.] 8 pp.

Petition to the House of Commons for abolition of the slave trade, dated Kelso, 27 April 1789; together with a 'Resolution of the Society established at Glasgow, as published in their Advertiser on Friday the 18th of February, 1791, with list of subscribers'.

2054 *A FEW words on the nature of the slave trade, and the measures which ought to be adopted. Walter, London, 1791. 60 pp.

Abolition must be gradual. (Reviewed in: MR, n.s., vol. 4, March 1791, p. 339; GM, March 1791, pp. 247–49.)

2055 DILLON, Arthur
Motifs de la motion faite à l'Assemblée nationale, le 4 mars 1791. [Baudouin, Paris, 1791.] 3 pp.

Justification of the author's speech against the Amis des Noirs; it had been made from a sense of patriotic duty. See (3052–53).

2056 DUBU DE LONGCHAMP, Jean François
Mémoire et accusation contre M. Brissot de Warville, consors, fauteurs & adhérens. Paris, 1791. 26 pp.

Brissot is an anti-white traitor in English pay; negro slaves will be needed in Saint Domingue when the revolt is over.

2057 GEMSEGE, Paul
'Slave trade not justified by Scripture.' (GM, March 1791, pp. 205–06.)

Reply to (2047); it was wrong to quote Prideaux in support of 'so infamous a traffic'.

2058 LE DANGER de la liberté des nègres. Philadelphie, [1791]. 10 pp.

If the slaves are freed the colonies will secede; the declaration of rights only applied to Frenchmen; Africans have a right to sell slaves and the colonists to buy them.

2059 PEPIN, Silvain
Adresse d'un patriote français à l'Assemblée nationale sur la traite des noirs. Valleyre, [Paris,] 1791. 14 pp.

France should lead Europe in abolishing the slave trade, after which her slaves could be gradually emancipated.

2060 REMARKS upon the evidence given by Thomas Irving, Esq. inspector general of the exports and imports of Great Britain, before the select committee appointed to take the examination of witnesses on the slave-trade. London, 1791. 16 pp.

Irving underestimated the value of the colonies and recommended abolition, but cultivation must be extended; the slave trade is therefore a necessity.

2061 OBSERVATIONS on the evidence given before the committee of the Privy Council and House of Commons in support of the bill for abolishing the slave trade. John Stockdale, London, 1791. viii, 310 pp.

By John Ranby. Critical comments on evidence given by abolitionist witnesses, including extracts.

2062 A COUNTRY gentleman's reasons for voting against Mr. Wilberforce's motion for a bill to prohibit the importation of African negroes into the colonies. J. Debrett, London, 1791. 28 pp.

By William Knox? See (2118).

2063 *The SLAVE trade prohibited by common sense and reason. London 1791.

Abolitionist.

2064 CONSIDÉRATIONS politiques sur les esclaves des colonies françoises de l'Amérique, et sur leurs gens de couleur libres. Moutard, Paris, 1791. 20 pp.

By M. L. E. Moreau de Saint-Méry? Abolition would oblige the colonists to get slaves from other nations; if force were used the colonies would secede.

2065 MOREAU DE SAINT-MÉRY, Médéric Louis Élie
Considérations présentées aux vrais amis du repos et du bonheur de la France, à l'occasion des nouveaux mouvemens de quelques soi-disant amis-des-noirs. Paris, 1791. 74 pp.

The Amis des Noirs have caused the colonial revolts; abolition of the slave trade would not benefit Africa; the British have merely regulated their own trade.

2066 L'ASSEMBLÉE des noirs, asiégée hieur au soir par le peuple, Rue Royale. L. L. Giraud, [Paris, 1791]. 7 pp.

Malicious description of a mob attack on the Amis des Noirs in Paris.

2067 *SWIFT, Zephaniah
An oration on domestic slavery. Delivered at the North Meeting-House in Hartford, on the 12th day of May, A.D. 1791. At the meeting of the Connecticut Society for the Promotion of Freedom, and the Relief of Persons unlawfully holden in Bondage. Hudson & Goodwin, Hartford, 1791. 23 pp.

2068 CLARKSON, Thomas
Letters on the slave-trade, and the state of the natives in those parts of Africa, which are contiguous to Fort St. Louis and Goree . . . James Phillips, London, 1791. vii, 81 pp.

Answers to questions from Frenchmen, with arguments against the slave trade. (Reviewed in: MR, n.s., vol. 8, May 1792, pp. 89–93.)

2069 REFLECTIONS on the slave trade, with remarks on the policy of its abolition. In a letter to a clergyman in the county of Suffolk. By G. C. P. Bury; J. H. Riley, Sudbury; (etc.), 1791. 56 pp.

Rejects arguments in favour of the slave trade; it should be replaced by sending convicts to the West Indies. (Reviewed in: MR, n.s., vol. 6, Oct. 1791, pp. 223–26; GM, Dec. 1791, pp. 1124–26.)

2070 GOUY, Louis Marthe de
Louis-Marthe de Gouy, député à l'Assemblée nationale, à ses commettans. [Paris, 1791.] 46 pp.

Account of the pamphlet war between the Amis des Noirs and the 'colons' since 1790 on the colonial question. See (2074).

2071 'An EXPOSTULATORY address to the people of England on the late memorable decision against the abolition of the slave trade.' (Signed: Junius.) (GM, June 1791, pp. 537–38.)

Condemns Parliament for failing to pass the abolition bill.

2072 FRANKLIN, Benjamin
'On the slave trade.' (AM, June 1791, vol. 9, pp. 336–37.)

> Ironical defence of the slave trade in a purported speech by an Algerian in 1687. First published anonymously in a letter signed 'Historicus' in the Federal Gazette in March 1790; also in: SM, vol. 55, June 1793, pp. 266–67; Hibernian Magazine, Dublin, Aug. 1793, pp. 102–04. (Reprinted in Franklin's Works, vol. 2, Boston, 1806, pp. 459–63.)

2073 'A LETTER on the slave trade from the honourable Mr. C. lately member of parliament for the county of Derby, to the Rev. Dr. B. of Grosvenor-street.' (Submitted by: Leo Africanus.) (GM, Aug. 1791, pp. 707–13.)

> By Nathaniel Curzon? The slave trade is 'the scourge of Africa, and the disgrace of Europe'.

2074 GOUY, Louis Marthe de
Confession d'un député dans ses derniers momens; ou liste des péchés politiques de Louis-Marthe de Gouy, dénoncés à la tribune de l'Assemblée nationale, par plusieurs honorables calomniateurs; avoués, imprimés, publiés et distribués par le coupable . . . [Paris,] 1791. 18, 46 pp.

> Recounts the author's battle with the Amis des Noirs since 1789 over abolition of the slave trade and slavery and other matters; with another issue of (2070).

2075 STOCKDALE, Percival
A letter from Percival Stockdale to Granville Sharp Esq. suggested to the author by the present insurrection of the negroes, in the island of St. Domingo. L. Pennington, Durham; (etc.), [1791]. xi, 28 pp.

> The revolt is justified by the oppression which the negroes suffered in the slave trade and slavery.

2076 *An AUTHENTICK account of the slave trade, and of the colonial slavery. Collected from the evidence delivered before a select committee of the House of Commons, in the years 1790 and 1791. On the part of the petitioners for the abolition of the slave trade . . . W. Cruttwell, Sherborne, [1791?]. 105 pp.

2077a An ADDRESS to the people of Great Britain, on the consumption of West-India produce. I. Phillips; M. Gurney, [London, 1791]. 12 pp.

Reissued as:

2077b An ADDRESS to the people of Great Britain, on the propriety of abstaining from West India sugar and rum . . . The sixth edition, with additions. M. Gurney (etc.), [London,] 1791. (12 pp.)

> By William Fox. Advocates a boycott of slave-grown products until the slave trade is abolished and emancipation begun. See (2078, 2105, 2110).

2078 *A SHORT account of the African slave trade, and An address to the people of Great Britain, on the propriety of abstaining from West India sugar and rum . . . T. Clout, Sevenoaks; (etc.), 1791. 16 pp.

> The 'Address' is by William Fox. See (2077).

2079 CONSIDERATIONS on the slave trade; and the consumption of West Indian produce. Darton & Harvey; (etc.), London, 1791. 16 pp.

> Extracts from (1850) and 'anti-saccharine' appeal.

2080 *REMARKABLE extracts and observations on the slave trade, with some considerations on the consumption of West India produce. Darton & Harvey; (etc.), London, 1791. 12 pp.

> Abolitionist. See (2089).

2081 *VIRTUE triumphant: or, the victory of the planters in Parliament. Ridgway, London, 1791. 22 pp.

> Ironical attack on the members of parliament who rejected the abolition bill in April 1791. (Reviewed in: MR, n.s., vol. 6, Oct, 1791, p. 226.)

2082 *MALLET, Philip
Remarks on a speech made to the National Assembly of France by the deputies from the general assembly of the French part of St. Domingo, with observations on the evidence delivered before a select committee of the House of Commons, in 1790 and 1791, on the part of the petitioners for the abolition of the slave-trade . . . London, 1791.

> Reviewed in: GM, Aug. 1792, p. 741. ('A rhapsody on the abolition of the slave trade.') See (11–13, 2352).

2083 *The SLAVE trade indispensable: in answer to the speeches of William Wilberforce, Esq. By a West India merchant. Debrett, London, 1791.

By W. Innes. Economic arguments against abolition. (Reviewed in: EMLR, vol. 21, Jan. 1792, pp. 34–36.) See (2012).

2084 *HILLIES, Richard
A vindication of the Address to the people of Great Britain on the use of West India produce, with some observations and facts relative to the situation of the slaves. London, 1791.

See (2077).

2085 DU MORIER, Joseph Pierre
Sur les troubles des colonies, et l'unique moyen d'assurer la tranquillité, la prospérité et la fidélité de ces dépendances de l'empire; en réfutation des deux discours de M. Brissot, des 1er. et 3 décembre 1791. Didot jeune, Paris, 1791. 60 pp.

Abolitionist agitation has caused the colonial revolts.

2086 PÉTITION à l'Assemblée nationale, et avis au peuple françois, en faveur des blancs et des noirs. [Paris, 1791.] 5 pp.

The slave trade must be transformed into 'engagement'; Africans could work off their purchase cost and return home with trade goods or engage for another period.

2087 PÉTITION ampliative, en faveur des blancs et des noirs, et projet d'un traité important pour les colonies et pour l'état. [Paris, 1791.] 12 pp.

By C. A. de Brie-Serrant. The disaster in St. Domingue makes the abolition of slavery and transformation of the slave trade into 'enrôlement' urgent; the government should acquire territory in Africa to which the 'engagés' could return.

2088 CORMIER, ——
Mémoire sur la situation de Saint-Domingue. Migneret, [Paris, 1792]. 72 pp.

The Amis des Noirs, incited by the English, are responsible for the slave revolt; the slave trade is vital to the colonies and can only be abolished in agreement with the colonial legislatures.

2089 *A VINDICATION of the use of sugar, the produce of the West India Islands.

In answer to a pamphlet entitled Remarkable extracts . . . The second edition. T. Boosey, London, 1792. iv, 22 pp.

By Henry Clutterbuck? See (2080). Reviewed in: MR, n.s., vol. 7, Jan. 1792, pp. 107–08.

2090 *A LETTER on the greater necessity of an abolition of the African slave trade; in consequence of the insurrection of St. Domingo, &c. By a gentleman long resident in Jamaica. Extracted from the Universal Museum, no. 3, just published. Prefaced by a short address to the publick. By W. M. Bath, 1792. 8 pp.

2091 *PALEY, William
Recollections of a speech, upon the slave trade; delivered in Carlisle, on Thursday the 9th of February, 1792. F. Jollie, Carlisle, 1792. 16 pp.

By an anonymous reporter. See (2278).

2092 *GISBORNE, Thomas
On slavery and the slave trade. London, 1792. 23 pp.

Unauthorized reprint of a chapter from the second edition of Gisborne's 'Principles of moral philosophy investigated'. See (2179).

2093 A SECOND address to the people of Great Britain containing a new, and most powerful argument to abstain from the use of West India sugar. By an eye witness to the facts related . . . J. Evans, London; (etc.), 1792. 11 pp.

By Andrew Burn. Reasons for boycotting sugar include the discovery of a slave's corpse in a barrel of molasses. (Answered by a letter, supposedly 'written by a little boy', in: EMLR, vol. 21, March 1792, pp. 185–86.) See (2116).

2094 *PETITION of the planters, merchants, mortgagees, annuitants, and others concerned in the West India colonies to the honourable the House of Commons of Great Britain, in Parliament assembled. London, 1792.

Appeal against abolition of the slave trade, 29 March 1792.

2095 The DUTY of abstaining from the use of West India produce, a speech, delivered at Coach-Maker's Hall, Jan. 12, 1792. (Signed: W. A.) T. W. Hawkins, London, [1792]. 23 pp.

By William Allen. Englishmen have a moral duty to boycott colonial produce until the slave trade is abolished and measures are taken for the abolition of slavery.

2096 GOUY, Louis Marthe de
Idées sommaires sur la restauration de Saint-Domingue, présentées à la nation, au Roi et à la colonie. Boulard, Paris, 1792. iv, 88 pp.

France profits from the slave trade, and slavery is necessary to the colonies; the Amis des Noirs should be suppressed.

2097 'INSURRECTION of the negroes in St. Domingo.' (Signed: Q.) (GM, Feb. 1792, pp. 125–29.)

Recommends a study of the revolt in St. Domingue to show the fatal influence of the French abolitionists. See (2100).

2098 An ADDRESS to Her Royal Highness the Dutchess of York, against the use of sugar. [London,] 1792. 22 pp.

The duchess could set an example, by abstaining from sugar, to bring about the abolition of the slave trade and slavery.

2099 A LETTER to the members of parliament who have presented petitions to the honourable House of Commons for the abolition of the slave trade. By a West-India merchant. J. Sewell (etc.), London, 1792. 84 pp.

Attributed to William Innes. Pro-slavery attack on abolitionist publicity methods and the anti-sugar campaign.

2100 'ANSWER to the St. Domingo representation.' (GM, March 1792, pp. 226–28.)

Attack on the slave trade in reply to (2097).

2101 'DISPASSIONATE remarks on the slave trade.' (GM, March 1792, pp. 228–31.)

Four letters, three criticising clergymen in the archdeaconry of Leicester for signing petitions for the abolition of the slave trade and one (by T. Greaves) supporting abolition.

2102 FULLER, Stephen
Petition of Stephen Fuller, Esquire, agent for Jamaica, to the House of Commons, 30th March 1792. [London, 1792.] 3 pp.

Contains a resolution of the Jamaica Assembly (4 Nov. 1791) against abolition of the slave trade.

2103 A SUMMARY view of the evidence delivered before a committee of the House of Commons, relating to the slave trade . . . By the author of the Address to the people of Great Britain. M. Gurney, London, 1792. 12 pp.

Abolitionist summary, by William Fox.

2104 A SUBJECT for conversation and reflection at the tea table. [London? 1792?] (3 pp.)

Abolitionist leaflet, with two poems by W. Cowper, 'Reflections' and the 'Complaint' (4226).

2105 STRICTURES on An address to the people of Great Britain, on the propriety of abstaining from West-India sugar and rum . . . Second edition. T. Boosey, London, 1792, 10 pp.

The public has been deluded over slavery, considering the distress of the poor in England. See (2077).

2106 *THOUGHTS on the abolition of the slave trade. By an inhabitant of Lynn. [London?] 1792. 10 pp.

2107 A SUMMARY of the evidence produced before a committee of the House of Commons, relating to the slave trade. The sixth edition. By the author of the Address to the people of Great Britain . . . M. Gurney, London, 1792. (8 pp.)

By William Fox. Abolitionist arguments. See (14).

2108 *HALL, P. W.
Thoughts and inquiry on the principles and tenur of the revealed and supreme law, shewing the utter inconsistency and injustice of our penal statutes, and the illicit traffic and practice of modern slavery . . . With some grounds of a plan for abolishing the same. To which is added a letter to a clergyman on the same subject . . . J. Ridgway, London, 1792. xvi, 304 pp.

2109 BONNEMAIN, Antoine Jean Thomas
Régéneration des colonies, ou moyens de restituer graduellement aux hommes leur état politique, et d'assurer la prosperité des nations; et moyens pour rétablir promptement l'ordre dans les colonies françaises. Cercle Social; Girod & Tessier, Paris, 1792. 111 pp.

The slave trade is horrible and un-economic; it should be abolished immediately followed by gradual emancipation.

2110   An ADDRESS to the people of Great Britain, (respectfully offered to the people of Ireland) on the utility of refraining from the use of West India sugar & rum . . . The sixth edition. W. Sleater, [Dublin,] 1792. 12 pp.

By William Fox. Reprint of (2077b).

2111   *THOUGHTS on the present high price of sugars: proving it to have arisen from the rumour of the slave bill, and from that cause only: and demonstrating the folly, futility, and absurdity of attempting an importation from the East Indies. Dedicated (without permission) to William Wilberforce Esq. By an old trader. Debrett, London, 1792. 92 pp.

Abolition of the slave trade will raise the price of sugar enormously. (Reviewed in: MR, n.s., vol. 8, May 1792, pp. 101–02.)

2112   *A PLAIN man's thoughts on the present price of sugar . . . J. Debrett, London, 1792. 22 pp.

The 'antisaccharites' should be consistent and do without all products of slave labour. (Reviewed in: MR, n.s., vol. 8, May 1792, pp. 103–04.)

2113   'SLAVE trade prohibited in Scripture.' (Signed: R.) (GM, May 1792, p. 416.)

Answer to an earlier letter (p. 228) quoting the Old Testament in defence of slavery. See (2126).

2114   *The TEST of humanity; addressed to Englishmen. By a native of Africa. Scatcherd, London, 1792.

2115   YOUNG, Arthur
'Abolition of the slave trade.' (Annals of Agriculture, Bury St. Edmund's, vol. 17, 1792, pp. 523–27.)

Labour-saving devices should be introduced in the West Indies before abolishing the slave trade.

2116   A SECOND address to the people of Great Britain: containing a new, and most powerful argument to abstain from the use of West India sugar. By an eye witness to the facts related. The second edition, enlarged. (Signed: Andrew Burn.) M. Gurney, London, 1792. 12 pp.

See (2093).

2117   FOOT, Jesse
A defence of the planters in the West-Indies; comprised in four arguments on comparative humanity, on comparative slavery, on the African slave trade, and on the condition of negroes in the West-Indies. J. Debrett, London, 1792. iv, 101 pp.

The slave trade was initiated by Britain, not the planters; natural increase of the slaves may make abolition possible in fifteen years' time. (Reviewed in: MR, n.s., June 1792, pp. 217–18; GM, Oct. 1792, pp. 921–23.)

2118   A COUNTRY gentleman's reasons for voting against Mr. Wilberforce's motion for a bill to prohibit the importation of African negroes into the colonies. J. Debrett, London, 1792. 78 pp.

By William Knox? Regulation would be better than prohibition of the slave trade; parliamentary evidence shows that the condition of the Africans is improved by their removal to the colonies. See (2062).

2119   FARTHER reasons of a country gentleman for opposing Mr. Wilberforce's motion on the 15th day of May last, for prohibiting British subjects trading to Africa to procure negroes for the British colonies. J. Debrett, London, 1792. 24 pp.

By William Knox? The abolitionists are spreading false propaganda and putting the interests of Africans before those of British subjects; the settlers might be forced to secede by an attack on their property.

2120   An ADDRESS to the right reverend the prelates of England and Wales, on the subject of the slave trade. J. Parsons; Ridgway, London, 1792. 15 pp.

By George Harrison. Urges the bishops to do their Christian duty and oppose the slave trade in the House of Lords. See (2180).

2121   CONSIDERATIONS addressed to professors of Christianity of every denomination, on the impropriety of consuming West-India sugar and rum, as produced by the oppressive labour of slaves. W. Porter, Dublin, 1792. 12 pp.

Refusal to use colonial products will help to end the slave trade. (Second edition, corrected: M. Gurney, London, 1792; 8 pp.)

2122 **SCATTERGOOD, John**
An antidote to popular frenzy, particularly to the present rage for the abolition of the slave-trade; with a view to the probable consequences, both present and remote. H. Gardner; (etc.), London; G. Jermyn, Ipswich, 1792. 28 pp.

Criticism of the 'antisaccharists'; abolition would ruin sugar production and lead to migration of negroes into Britain.

2123 An INQUIRY into the causes of the insurrection of the negroes in the island of St. Domingo. To which are added, observations of M. Garran–Coulon on the same subject, read in his absence by M. Guadet, before the National Assembly, 29th Feb. 1792. J. Johnson, London, 1792. 39 pp.

By William Roscoe. The revolt was not caused by efforts to abolish the slave trade but by the inaction of the National Assembly; Garran-Coulon blames the planters, who are opposed to liberty and plan to secede. See (2195).

2124 The AFRICAN slave trade: or a short view of the evidence, relative to that subject, produced before the House of Commons, interspersed with such remarks as naturally flowed from it. All meant to evince the sound policy and moral obligation of its immediate and entire abolition: as also, of adopting such measures as may ascertain liberty to the present slaves in due time. J. Guthrie, Edinburgh, 1792. 206 pp.

By Niel Douglas. Describes the cruelty of the slave trade and colonial slavery; with an appendix containing a summary of the House of Commons debate in April 1792 and various abolitionist documents.

2125 'OM Negerhandelen. Til Herr Secretaire Kirstein.' (Minerva, Kiøbenhavn, Junii 1792, pp. 311–78.)

By C. H. Pram. Summary of recent abolitionist works on the slave trade.

2126 'THOUGHTS on the slave trade.' (Signed: P.P.P.) (GM, July 1792, pp. 627–28.)

Reply to (2113); the Bible allows perpetual bondage for heathen slaves.

2127 *REDHEAD, Henry
A letter to Bache Heathcote, Esq. on the fatal consequences of abolishing the slave-trade, both to England, and her American colonies. J. Stockdale, London, 1792. 80 pp.

Reviewed in: MR, n.s., vol. 8, Aug. 1792, p. 447; GM, Sept, 1792, p. 841.

2128 *STONE, Francis
Thoughts in favour of the abolition of the slave trade, and the emancipation of the negroes, respectfully inscribed to the honourable House of Commons . . . C. Stalker, London, [1792]. 35 pp.

Reviewed in: MR, n.s., vol. 8, Aug. 1792, p. 447.

2129 *The INTERIM; or, thoughts on the traffic of West India slaves; and on some other slaves, not less worthy of compassion; with an address to Mr. Wilberforce. By Homo. Gardner (etc.), London, 1792. 33 pp.

Reviewed in: MR, n.s., vol. 8, Aug. 1792, pp. 447–48.

2130 *REASONS for not signing the petition; or, the abolition scheme taken into cool and candid consideration. By a private disinterested person, independent and unconnected with any sect or party. Evans, London, 1792. 48 pp.

Reviewed in: MR, n.s., vol. 8, Aug. 1792, p. 448.

2131 **GISBORNE, Thomas**
Remarks on the late decision of the House of Commons respecting the abolition of the slave trade. The second edition. B. White & Sons, London, 1792. 49 pp.

Summary of the Commons debate of 2 April 1792, with reasons for immediate abolition. See (2179, 2188).

2132 ARGUMENTS from Scripture, for and against the African slave trade, as stated in a series of letters, lately published in the Glasgow Courier. Glasgow, 1792. 27 pp.

Correspondence between 'Senex' and 'A friend to mankind' (Niel Douglas?), with an extract from (2131) showing that the trade is not sanctioned by the Bible.

2133 *FUGITIVE thoughts on the African slave trade, interspersed with cursory remarks on the manners, customs, and commerce, of the African and American Indians . . . Liverpool, 1792. vi, 66 pp.

Pro-slavery.

2134 *An ESSAY on the abolition, not only of the African slave trade, but of slavery in the British West Indies. T. Becket, London, 1792. 49 pp.

> By John Gray. Suggests introducing Indian labourers to the colonies. (Reviewed in: GM, Aug. 1793, pp. 746–47.)

2135 REMARKS on the new sugar-bill, and on the national compacts respecting the sugar-trade and slave-trade. J. Johnson; J. Debrett, London, 1792. 82 pp.

> Parliament has the right to abolish the slave trade but not slavery; 'indented servants' could be sought in Africa, India or China.

2136 NO rum!—No sugar! or, the voice of blood, being half an hour's conversation, between a negro and an English gentleman, shewing the horrible nature of the slave trade, and pointing out an easy and effectual method of terminating it, by an act of the people. L. Wayland, London, 1792. 23 pp.

> 'Mr. English' is persuaded to renounce rum and sugar until the slave trade is abolished and slaves are better treated. See (2246).

2137 BRADBURN, Samuel
An address, to the people called Methodists; concerning the evil of encouraging the slave trade. T. Harper, Manchester, 1792. 24 pp.

> Slave trade and West Indian slavery must be ended; one way to promote this is to abstain from rum and sugar; the author has stopped drinking tea.

2138 PENNINGTON, John Thomas, Baron Muncaster
Historical sketches of the slave trade, and of its effects in Africa. Addressed to the people of Great-Britain. John Stockdale, London, 1792. 100 pp.

> European slave trading has corrupted Africa; Britain ought to take the initiative in abolishing it.

2139 The TRUE state of the question, addressed to the petitioners for the abolition of the slave trade. By a plain man, who signed the petition at Derby. J. Bell, London, 1792. 14 pp.

> The author regrets signing the petition; recent evidence shows that slaves are better off in the West Indies than in Africa. (Circulated by the West India Committee.)

2140 OBSERVATIONS on slavery, and the consumption of the produce of the West India islands: together with an abstract of the evidence given before the committee of Privy Council and the select committee of the House of Commons, respecting the treatment of slaves in the West Indies. T. Boosey, London, [1792]. 61 pp.

> Attack on the sugar boycott and other 'visionary schemes'; slavery is necessary for the West Indian economy.

2141 A VERY new pamphlet indeed! Being the truth: addressed to the people at large. Containing some strictures on the English Jacobins, and the evidence of Lord M'Cartney, and others, before the House of Lords, respecting the slave trade. (Signed: Truth.) London, 1792. 15 pp.

> Attributed to a Major Crewe. The abolitionists are fanatics who have misled most petitioners; the evidence quoted disproves assertions of cruelty; abolition would destroy the African trade and the colonies. See (2142).

2142 OLD truths and established facts, being an answer to A very new pamphlet indeed! (Signed: Vindex.) [London, 1792.] 13 pp.

> By Thomas Paine. So far no evidence in favour of abolition has been given, yet arguments against the slave trade can be found even in that of pro-slavery witnesses. See (2141).

2143 An ABRIDGEMENT of the evidence delivered before a select committee of the House of Commons, in the years 1790 and 1791, on the part of the petitioners for the abolition of the slave-trade. James Phillips, London, 1792. 24 pp.

> By William Fox. Arguments for abolition based on antislavery evidence. See (4).

2144 A SHORT sketch of the evidence, for the abolition of the slave trade, delivered before a committee of the House of Commons. To which is added, a recommendation of the subject to the serious attention of people in general. (Signed: W.B.C.) London, 1792. 23 pp.

> By William Bell Crafton. Summary of (11) in case it is too long for some readers, showing the necessity to end the trade and urging abstention

from West Indian sugar and rum. (Third edition, with additions: M. Gurney, London, 1792; 24 pp.)

2145 A SHORT address to the people of Scotland, on the subject of the slave trade. With a summary view of the evidence delivered before a committee of the House of Commons, on the part of the petitioners for its abolition. Society instituted for the Abolition of the African slave Trade, Edinburgh, 1792. 30 pp.

By a Mr. Houldbrooke. Exhortation to support abolition, with facts extracted from (12).

2146 *A FRIENDLY address to the well-disposed and peaceable inhabitants of this happy island. In a series of letters which appeared in the news-paper of the World, during the months of June, July, and August; to which is added, an essay on the slave-trade, and on libels, &c. &c. By Amicus. Faulder, London, 1792. 203 pp.

Reviewed in: MR, n.s., vol. 9, Nov. 1792, p. 341.

2147 'ON slavery.' (General Magazine, London, vol. 6, Nov., 1792, pp. 477–80.)

Extracts from Adam Smith's 'Wealth of nations' showing that free labour 'comes cheaper in the end, than that performed by slaves'. (Also published as 'Remarks on slavery by Dr. Adam Smith' in: EMLR, vol. 22, Nov, 1792, pp. 323–25.)

2148 An APOLOGY for slavery; or, six cogent arguments against the immediate abolition of the slave trade. J. Johnson; R. Faulder, London, 1792. 47 pp.

By Alexander Geddes. Ironical defence of slavery.

2149 SLAVE trade. A full account of this species of commerce; with arguments against it, spirited and philosophical: by the celebrated philosopher and historian, Abbé Raynal. Translated from the French. T. Cox, Southwark, [1792?]. 45 pp.

Supposititious work, consisting of extracts from (1753) denouncing the African slave trade. (Probably a translation of: RÉFLEXIONS et notices sur la traite des nègres, 1792.)

2150 SUBSTANCE of a speech intended to have been made on Mr. Wilberforce's motion for the abolition of the slave trade, on Tuesday, April 3, 1792 . . .

Second edition, corrected, with notes, and an appendix. J. Owen, London, 1792. 56 pp.

Abolitionists have exaggerated the cruelty to slaves and obtained signatures to petitions by fraud. The appendix contains an account by the Liverpool slaver W. C. Harborne of events in West Africa 1782–89 and the text of the Danish decree of 16 March 1792 (3165) to end the slave trade after 1802. (Distributed by the West India Committee.)

2151 KERSAINT, Armand Guy
Suite des Moyens proposés à l'Assemblée nationale, pour rétablir, la paix et l'ordre, dans les colonies. Cercle Social, Paris, 1792. 48 pp.

Slavery must eventually be abolished; slaves could still be bought in Africa but made free labourers in the colonies.

2152 FROSSARD, Benjamin Sigismond
Benj. Sig. Frossard à la Convention nationale, sur l'abolition de la traite des nègres. Gueffier, [Paris, 1792]. 32 pp.

2153 *MIFFLIN, Warner
A serious expostulation with the members of the House of Representatives of the United States. Daniel Lawrence, Philadelphia, 1793. 16; 8 pp.

Criticises Congress for rejecting antislavery proposals 1792.

2154 *BUCHANAN, George
An oration upon the moral and political evil of slavery. Delivered at a public meeting of the Maryland Society, for promoting the Abolition of Slavery, and the Relief of Free Negroes, and others unlawfully held in Bondage. Baltimore, July 4th, 1791. Philip Edwards, Baltimore, 1793. 20 pp.

Urges abolition of the African slave trade and gradual emancipation. See (3622).

2155 SHARP, Granville
Extract of a letter to a gentleman in Maryland; wherein is demonstrated the extreme wickedness of tolerating the slave trade, in order to favour the illegalities of our colonies . . . James Phillips, London, 1793. 14 pp.

Antislavery arguments on biblical and legal grounds. (Reprinted 1797 and 1806.)

2156 FROSSARD, Benjamin Sigismond
Observations sur l'abolition de la

traite des nègres, présentées à la Convention nationale. Gueffier, [Paris,] 1793. 32 pp.

> Strong plea for the abolition of the slave trade, which would win glory for France.

2157 LETTERS of Alfred to the Right Honourable William Pitt . . . upon the important subject of the slave trade in general; but, referring particularly to his speech, as printed, of the 2d of April, 1792 . . . London, 1793. 74 pp.

> The slave trade is necessary for the support of the West Indies and British commerce, as well as beneficial to Africa. See (2358).

2158 ADRESSE à la Convention nationale, à tous les clubs et sociétés patriotiques, pour les nègres détenus en esclavage dans les colonies françaises de l'Amérique, sous le régime de la République. G.-F. Galletti, Paris, [1793]. 15 pp.

> By J. Labuissonniere and others. Demands liberty for all slaves in the French colonies.

2159 An APPEAL to the candour of both houses of Parliament, with a recapitulation of facts respecting the abolition of the slave trade. In a letter to William Wilberforce, Esq. M.P. By a member of the House of Commons. John Stockdale, London, 1793. 48 pp.

> By Sir George Thomas? Defence of the West Indian planters against the abolitionists, who have misled the British public. Suppressing the foreign slave trade would be impossible. The 'middle passage' should be ameliorated, slavery in the colonies being an improvement for Africans.

2160 *LETTERS concerning the slave trade, and with respect to its intended abolition: by a merchant to his friend on the continent. Liverpool, [1793]. 36 pp.

2161 MORETON, J. B.
West India customs: containing strictures on the soil, cultivation, produce, trade, officers, and inhabitants; with the method of establishing and conducting a sugar plantation. To which is added, the practice of training new slaves . . . A new edition. J. Parsons (etc.), London, 1793. 192 pp.

> Argues in favour of a general treaty prohibiting the slave trade, which would make possible cheaper production of tropical products in

Africa itself and the gradual abolition of colonial slavery. See (2013).

2162 SHARP, Granville
Letter from Granville Sharp. Esq. of London, to the Maryland Society for promoting the abolition of slavery, and the relief of free negroes and others, unlawfully held in bondage. Published by order of the society. Yundt & Patton, Baltimore, 1793. 11 pp.

> British colonial slave laws are utterly inconsistent with the basis of English law.

2163 WEBSTER, Noah
Effects of slavery on morals and industry. Hudson & Goodwin, Hartford (Conn.), 1793. 56 pp.

> Slavery corrupts the characters of both masters and slaves and should be abolished; the United States could get rid of freed slaves by voluntary 'colonization' in Africa.

2164 PAULUS, Pieter
Verhandeling over de vrage: in welken zin kunnen de menschen gezegd worden gelyk te zyn? En welke zyn de regten en pligten, die daaruit voordvloeien? C. Plaat, Haarlem, 1793. viii, 216 pp.

> Essay written for a competition 1791, ending with a strong attack on the slave trade (pp. 187–214), quoting Frossard at length. (French edition 1794.)

2165 *THOUGHTS on modern politics . . . Button, London, 1793. 244 pp.

> Attributed to Niel Douglas. Includes antislavery poems by Marjoribanks and Cowper and abolitionist addresses and petitions.

2166 VERMEULEN, Gysbert André
Specimen juridicum inaugurale, de conditione servorum; praesertim in colonia Surinamensi . . . Th. Koet, Lugduni Batavorum, 1793. 54 pp.

2167 *ESSAY on the effects of slavery on the moral character, &c. of a nation, read before the Connecticut Society for the Promotion of Freedom to Bondmen. Hartford, 1793. 66 pp.

2168 *Die ART wie die Familien getrennet werden. Schlaven-Handel. Tobias Hirte, Philadelphia, 1794. (1 p.) illus.

> Broadsheet on the horrors of the slave trade.

2169 *An ACCURATE account of that horrible and inhuman traffic, the slave trade, shewing the treatment which the slaves experience; the mode of procuring them, &c., with a description of the iron instruments used in this abominable traffic . . . J. Fairburn, London, [1794]. 23 pp. illus.

2170 *DE l'affranchissement des noirs, ou observations sur la loi du 16 pluviôse an II, et sur les moyens à prendre pour le rétablissement des colonies, du commerce et de la marine. [Paris? 1794.] 33 pp.

By — Gros, a former official in St. Domingue.

2171 FOX, William
A defence of the decree of the National Convention of France, for emancipating the slaves in the West Indies. M. Gurney; D. I. Eaton, London, [1794]. 16 pp.

Urges Britain to follow the French example and abolish slavery; the government had only feared the introduction of Africans because of the dangers of revolts.

2172 CHAUMETTE, Pierre Gaspard
Discours prononcé par le citoyen Chaumette, au nom de la commune de Paris, le décadi 30 pluviôse, l'an II de la République Française, une et indivisible, à la fête célébrée à Paris, en rejouissance de l'abolition de l'esclavage. Imprimée par ordre de la Convention nationale. [Paris, 1794.] 22 pp.

2173 OBSERVATIONS on the present war, the projected invasion, and a decree of the National Convention, for the emancipation of the slaves in the French colonies. R. Baldwin; J. Graham, Sunderland; (etc.), [1794]. 61 pp.

By John Hampson. In abolishing slavery the subversive French government has 'done right, though from wrong motives'; Britain should abolish the slave trade and slavery for reasons of justice and self-interest.

2174 *DWIGHT, Theodore
An oration, spoken before the Connecticut Society for the Promotion of Freedom and the Relief of Persons unlawfully holden in Bondage. Convened in Hartford, on the 8th day of May, A.D. 1794. Hudson & Goodwin, Hartford, 1794. 24 pp.

2175 REMARKS on the methods of procuring slaves, with a short account of their treatment in the West-Indies, &c. Darton & Harvey, London, 1794. (1 p.)

Illustrated broadside based on (11).

2176 *CONDEMNATION of the slave trade; being an investigation of its origin and continuation of that inhuman traffic: humbly inscribed to the citizens of the United States. By a friend to humanity New York, 1794. 20 pp.

2177 'ENORMITIES at St. Domingo.— The abolition of the slave trade.' (GM, 1794, supplement, p. 1167.)

Atrocities during the French reconquest of St. Domingue should silence the abolitionists.

2178 A LETTER to the Right Hon. Henry Dundas, on his speech, delivered in the House of Commons, on the twenty-sixth day of February, 1795, on Mr. Wilberforce's motion, for the abolition of the slave trade. (Signed: Howard.) Daniel Isaac Eaton, London, 1795. 16 pp.

Bitter criticism of Dundas' advocacy of continuing the British slave trade.

2179 GISBORNE, Thomas
The principles of moral philosophy investigated and briefly applied to the constitution of civil society . . . The third edition corrected and enlarged. To which is added, a new edition, with an appendix, of Remarks on the late decision of the House of Commons respecting the abolition of the slave trade. B. & J. White, London, 1795. xvi, 367 pp.

Pt. 2, ch. 8: 'On slavery—application of principles which have been established to the African slave trade'; the appendix summarizes the parliamentary debates on the slave trade 1792–95. (The first edition, 1789, merely defined when, 'agreeable to natural justice', an individual may be enslaved.) See (2092, 2131).

2180 *A SECOND address to the right reverend the prelates of England and Wales, on the subject of the slave trade. J. Johnson, London, 1795.

By George Harrison. Reviewed in: GM, vol. 65, Aug. 1795, p. 668. See (2120).

2181 *CONSIDERATIONS on the present crisis of affairs, as it respects the West India colonies, and the probable effects of the French decree for emancipating the negroes, pointing out a remedy for preventing the calamitous consequences in the British islands . . . J. Johnson, London, 1795. 76 pp.

Only abolition of the slave trade can avert disaster in the colonies. (Reviewed in: MR, n.s., vol. 17, Aug. 1795, pp. 453–59.)

2182 PRESTON, William
A letter to Bryan Edwards Esquire, containing observations on some passages of his History of the West Indies. J. Johnson, London, 1795. 39 pp.

Criticises Edwards for supporting the slave trade and slavery. See (1603).

2183 MÉMOIRE sur les colonies, ou moyens de les reconquérir et de les rendre florissantes, sans que la Convention revienne sur ses décrets. Par P. J. D. A. Cl. Forget, Paris, an III [1795]. 36 pp.

The author welcomed the abolition of slavery, but the ex-slaves should be forced to work until they were 'dignes de la liberté'.

2184 MIGNARD, Jacques
La politique anglaise dévoilée, ou les moyens de rendre les colonies à la France . . . Présenté à la Convention nationale, le 24 vendémiaire, l'an 3ᵉ. Moreaux, Paris, an 3 [1795]. iv, 55 pp.

The war is being fought over the colonies; England has a monopoly of the slave trade and furnishes the French colonies with poisoned slaves, thousands of which have died.

2185 TYRANNICAL libertymen. A discourse upon negro-slavery in the United States: composed at ——, in Newhampshire; on the late federal Thanksgiving-Day. Eagle Office, Hanover, N.H., 1795. 16 pp.

Proposes abolition of the slave trade ('the scourge of Africa and the bane of America') and gradual emancipation; freed slaves could return to Africa or form a separate state represented in Congress.

2186 TUCKER, Saint George
A dissertation on slavery: with a proposal for the gradual abolition of it, in the state of Virginia. Mathew Carey, Philadelphia, 1796. 106 pp.

Since 1793 slave trade to foreign countries has been prohibited; by gradually emancipating newborn children, slavery itself could be gradually abolished, but plans to 'colonize' the freed slaves are cruel and dangerous.

2187 *The ABOLITION of the slave trade; peace; and a temperate reform, essen-

tial to the salvation of England. Crosby, London, 1796. 24 pp.

By W. Ward. Reviewed in: MR, n.s., vol. 21, Nov. 1796. p. 334.

2188 GISBORNE, Thomas
Remarks on the decision of the House of Commons respecting the abolition of the slave-trade, on April 2d, 1792. With an appendix relating to the present state of the question. James Phillips, London, 1786. 42 pp.

The slave trade has redoubled since 1792; only abolition can save the colonies from ruin. See (2131).

2189 'ON the slave trade.' (Watchman, Bristol, no. 4, 25 March 1796, pp. 100–09.)

By S. T. Coleridge. Considers and rejects various arguments against abolition and defends the boycott of West Indian sugar and rum. (The 'Lecture on the slave trade' delivered at Bristol 16 June 1795, on which this article was based, is printed in: The collected works of Samuel Taylor Coleridge, vol. 1, London, 1971, pp. 231–51.)

2190 'TO the editor of the Watchman.' (Signed: T.P.) (Watchman, Bristol, no. 5, 2 April 1796, pp. 129–31.)

By Thomas Poole. Letter describing a dream of a future West Indian society after liberation from slavery.

2191 'SLAVE trade.' (Signed: Pompilius Lænas.) (GM, April 1796, p. 291.)

Remarks on the Commons debate on 10 April and the exaggerations of the abolitionists.

2192 MIFFLIN, Warner
The defence of Warner Mifflin against aspersions cast on him on account of his endeavours to promote righteousness, mercy and peace, among mankind. Samuel Sansom, Philadelphia, 1796. 30 pp.

Account of the antislavery and other views of a Virginian Quaker.

2193 *REFLECTIONS on the inconsistency of man, particularly exemplified in the practice of slavery in the United States, John Buel, New York, 1796. 27 pp.

By 'Amyntor' (Jeremy Belknap).

2194 INSTRUCTIONS for the treatment of negroes. &c. &c. &c. Shepperson & Reynolds, London, 1797. vi, 134, 8 pp.

Letters to the manager of a Barbados plantation (first printed 1786), with a section supporting gradual abolition of the African slave trade.

2195 CREUZÉ-DUFRESNE, Michel Pascal
Lettre de Michel-Pascal Creuzé, membre du Conseil des Anciens, à Jean-Philippe Garan, député du Loiret, sur son rapport des troubles de St-Domingue, distribué au Corps législatif en ventôse, an V, dix-huit mois après la clôture des débats. Maret; Desenne, Paris, an cinq [1797]. 66 pp.

Defence of the settlers against certain accusations, amongst others of having been responsible for maintaining the slave trade and slavery. See (2123).

2196 *MILLER, Samuel
A discourse, delivered April 12, 1797, at the request of and before the New-York Society for promoting the Manumission of Slaves, and protecting such of them as have been or may be liberated. By Samuel Miller, A.M. one of the ministers of the United Presbyterian churches in the city of New-York, and member of the said society. T. & J. Swords, New-York, 1797. 36 pp.

2197 FITZPATRICK, Jeremiah
Suggestions on the slave trade, for the consideration of the legislature of Great Britain. J. Stockdale, London, 1797. 62 pp. illus, map.

Slavery should be gradually replaced by indentured labour or 'apprenticeship' with government inspectors supervising the slave trade in West Africa until it is ended. (Reviewed in: EMLR, vol. 31, June 1797, pp. 405–06.)

2198 'SLAVE-TRADE.' *In*: Encyclopædia Britannica, vol. 17 (Edinburgh, 1797), pp. 532–34.

Hostile account of the trade.

2199 *A LETTER to the Right Hon. William Pitt on the additional tax of 2s. 6d. on every hundredweight of sugar; with some observations on the slave trade. Egerton, London, 1797.

2200 *PHILALETHES ELEUTHERUS, *pseud.*
Over den slavenstand . . . Met eenige aanteekeningen en een voorbericht van den uitgever Jan van Geuns. D. du Mortier & Comp., Leyden, 1797.

By Willem de Vos.

2201 DE l'esclavage des nègres, et de l'état actuel de nos colonies. Masson, Paris, 1797. 59 pp.

Defence of the African slave trade and slavery; as attempts to emancipate the slaves in the French colonies captured by the English could lead to new massacres, it may be best to abandon them.

2202 DE la nécessité d'adopter l'esclavage en France; 1°. Comme moyen de prospérité pour nos colonies. 2°. Comme punition pour les coupables. 3°. Comme ressource en faveur des indigens. Baillio (etc.), Paris, 1797. 74 pp.

Part 1 argues the necessity of re-establishing colonial slavery with the slave trade under government control.

2203 RUSHTON, Edward
Expostulatory letter to George Washington, of Mount Vernon, in Virginia, on his continuing to be a proprietor of slaves. Liverpool, 1797. 24 pp.

Condemns President Washington, the liberator of the United States, for setting a bad example as the owner of hundreds of slaves.

2204 *DUPONT DE NEMOURS, Pierre Samuel
Sur l'esclavage des nègres, et sur l'utilité de former des établissemens à la côte d'Afrique pour la culture du sucre par des nègres libres. [Paris, 1798.]

2205 OBSERVATIONS sur le projet de résolution présenté par le représentant du peuple Duplantier, le 24 vendemiaire an 7, sur les créances résultantes de l'achat des noirs. Guerin, Paris, [1798]. 7 pp.

Headed: 'Au Corps législatif'. Critices the proposed law to cancel debts incurred by settlers for buying slaves as most unfair, since buyer and seller were equally culpable (2365).

2206 *SMITH, Elihu Hubbard
A discourse, delivered April 11, 1798, at the request of and before the New-York Society for promoting the manumission of slaves, and protecting such of them as have been or may be liberated . . . T. & J. Swords, New-York, 1798. 30 pp.

2207 MÉMOIRE sur l'esclavage et sur la traite des nègres. Par le M...... de C...... A. Dulau & Co.; (etc.), Londres, 1798. 52 pp.

Abolition of slavery would be a violation of property; the slave trade saves the lives of millions of Africans and its abolition would ruin France.

2208 *LETTERS on liberty and slavery: an answer to a pamphlet, entitled "Negro slavery defended by the word of God". By Philanthropos. Second edition. R. Wilson, New-York, 1798. 24 pp.

By Morgan John Rhees.

2209 CUNHA DE AZEREDO COUTINHO, José Joaquim da, *Bishop of Pernambuco* Analyse sur la justice de commerce du rachat des esclaves de la côte d'Afrique. A. Dulau & Co.; (etc.), Londres, 1798. xvii, 68 pp.

Defends the slave trade. (Portuguese edition: 2438.)

2210 LETTRE à M**** sur la traite des nègres et l'esclavage. T. Baylis, Londres, 1798. 8 pp.

Slave trade and slavery are absolutely necessary for the colonies and it is a waste of time to defend them as the British government will not abolish the slave trade.

2211 ENTWURF zu eine r hictorisch-philosophischen Abhandlung über den Sclavenhandel der Engländer. J. C. Hendel, Halle, 1798. 50 pp.

Defence of the African slave trade against Wilberforce's motions for its abolition; attempts to emancipate the slaves are dangerous.

2212 *STOCKDALE, Percival A letter to . . . the Lord Bishop of Durham on the slave-trade: to which are added observations on the late parliamentary debate on that subject. L. Pennington, Durham, 1799. 41 pp.

2213 ALBIONICUS, *pseud.* 'Hint to the abolitionists.' (GM, vol. 69, April 1799, pp. 300–01.)

Slavery is ordained by God for the descendants of Ham.

2214 *CHAUFEPIÉ, Charles Abraham de Dissertatio juridica de servitute in coloniis americanis tollenda . . . P. den Hengst, Amstelaedami, 1799. 38 pp.

2215 'THOUGHTS on the probable termination of negro slavery in the United States of America.' (Signed: H.L.) (Monthly Magazine, and American Review, New York, vol. 2, Feb. 1800, pp. 81–84.)

Predicts that when the slave trade ceases the slave population will dwindle away within sixty years.

2216 BELU, C. Des colonies et de la traite des nègres. Debray, Paris, an 9 – 1800. 72 pp.

Slavery must be re-established in the colonies; losses due to the revolution must be made good by reopening the slave trade from West Africa.

2217 *RITTER, George A speech, delivered on the 13th. January, 1802, before the Society called the Proficuous judicatory; concerning the advantages that would be derived from a total abolition of slavery. Philadelphia, 1802. 20 pp.

2218 BAUDRY DES LOZIÈRES, Louis Nicolas Les égaremens du nigrophilisme. Migneret, Paris, an X.–1802. xvi, 323 pp.

Discusses the necessity of colonial slavery and the advantages of the slave trade, whose originator was a 'bienfaiteur des Africains'; both should be reintroduced.

2219 BARRÉ SAINT-VENANT, Jean Des colonies modernes sous la zone torride, et particulièrement de celle de Saint-Domingue . . . Brochot, Paris, an X [1802]. xvi, 516 pp.

Pt. 1, ch. 5: 'Avantages de la transplantation des nègres d'Afrique dans les Antilles.'

2220 APERÇU sur les intérêts des colonies françaises avec la République, autant que les circonstances actuelles permettent de les traiter. Baudouin, [Paris, 1802?] 31 pp.

A revival of the slave trade by France, making the new slaves freedmen, would benefit both Africa and the French colonies and set an example to other nations.

2221 ESMANGART, Charles Des colonies françaises et en particulier de l'île de Saint-Domingue. H. Agasse, Paris, an X [1802]. 74 pp.

St. Domingue should be reconquered and put under military rule; the ex-slaves should remain free, but new slaves should be imported and emancipated after seven years of work.

2222 DE la servitude temporaire des noirs, et d'une colonisation de militaires à Saint-Domingue. Par le cit. Fl..........

Annales des Arts et Manufactures, Paris, an X [1802]. 20 pp.

By Gaëtan de Raxis de Flassan. St. Domingue must be reoccupied and the slaves returned at least to a temporary 'enrôlement' for thirty years.

2223 The CRISIS of the sugar colonies; or, an enquiry into the objects and probable effects of the French expedition to the West Indies; and their connection with the colonial interests of the British empire . . . In four letters to the Right Hon. Henry Addington . . . J. Hatchard, London, 1802. vii, 222 pp.

By James Stephen. Britain should oppose the restoration of slavery by France in St. Domingue and should develop the recently captured Trinidad with free negro labourers as 'indentured servants'.

2224 EXAMEN de l'esclavage en général, et particulièrement de l'esclavage des nègres dans les colonies françaises de l'Amérique. Par V.D.C. ancien avocat et colon à Saint-Domingue. Desenne; Maradan, Paris, an XI–1802. 2 vol.

Attributed to C. F. Valentin de Cullion. Argues for the restoration of the slave trade and slavery. (Reviewed in: ER, 1805, pp. 326–50; the reviewer urges immediate abolition of the slave trade.)

2225 *REID, Dennis
An address to every class of British subjects, and particularly to the legislators and colonists of the British empire; in which some observations are offered on the nature and effects of the slave trade, and a new mode of abolition, humbly recommended to the notice of the publick. By Dennis Reid, Esq. of the island of Jamaica. J. Stockdale, London, 1802. 32 pp.

With better treatment the slaves would increase in number, making imports superfluous. (Reviewed in: GM, June 1803, p. 839.)

2226 An ENGLISH country gentleman's address to the Irish members of the Imperial Parliament, on the subject of the slave trade. J. Hatchard, London, 1802. 103 pp.

Attributed to William Knox. Speech intended to have been delivered in a Commons debate, with an appendix of parliamentary evidence on the slave trade.

2227 *A LETTER to William Wilberforce, Esq., M.P., and those who acted with him most zealously for the abolition of the slave trade. London, 1803.

2228 BROUGHAM, Henry Peter
An inquiry into the colonial policy of the European powers. E. Balfour, Manners & Miller; Archibald Constable, Edinburgh, 1803. 2 vol.

The slave trade should be abolished but slavery must be continued in an ameliorated form.

2229 *REFLECTIONS on slavery; with recent evidence of its inhumanity. Occasioned by the melancholy death of Romain, a French negro. By Humanitas. R. Cochran, Philadelphia, 1803. 40 pp.

2230 The OPPORTUNITY; or reasons for an immediate alliance with St. Domingo. By the author of "The crisis of the sugar colonies." J. Hatchard, London, 1804. viii, 156 pp.

By James Stephen. Alliance with Haiti against France would be incompatible with continuation of the slave trade.

2231 *A CONCISE statement of the question regarding the abolition of the slave trade. J. Hatchard; T. N. Longman & O. Rees, London, 1804. 79 pp.

By H. P. Brougham. Economic arguments against continuation of the slave trade. (Reviewed in ER, 1804, pp. 476–86, by F. Jeffrey, who urges abolition immediately, when, due to the war, it would be equivalent to its total cessation; also in: CO, vol. 3, 1804, pp. 306–10.) See (2232).

2232 *APPENDIX to the Concise statement of the question regarding the abolition of the slave trade. J. Hatchard; T. N. Longman & O. Rees, London, 1804. 28 pp.

By H. P. Brougham. Urges immediate abolition. See (2231). (Reviewed in: CO, vol. 3, 1804, pp. 360–62.)

2233 NOTICES on the slave-trade, in reference to the present state of the British isles. London, 1804. 20 pp.

By George Harrison.

2234 CARITAT, Jean Antoine Nicolas Marie, marquis de Condorcet
'Au Corps électoral, contre l'esclavage

des noirs.' *In his*: Œuvres complètes (Brunswick, 1804), vol. 16, pp. 147–54.

Written 3 Feb. 1789 to urge that a committee be appointed to abolish slave trade and slavery.

2235 HUMPHREYS, David
A valedictory discourse, delivered before the Cincinnati of Connecticut, in Hartford, July 4th, 1804, at the dissolution of the society . . . Gilbert & Dean, Boston, 1804. 60 pp.

Includes an attack on slavery, criticizing (2317).

2236 'STATEMENT of the comparative merits of the plans of gradual and immediate abolition of the slave trade.' (SM, vol. 66, July 1804, pp. 513–16.)

Extract from (2231), by H. P. Brougham.

2237 *ARTHY, Elliot
Introductory observations in favour of the African slave trade, intended to point out the necessity for a more candid, connected, and extensive investigation of that great question than has yet been entered into; and to shew the many benefits which . . . have accrued to the British nation and to the Africans . . . the evils which would ensue from its premature abolition; also, the means of lessening the mortality amongst negro slaves, and among seamen employed in that trade. T. Milner, Liverpool, 1804. 89 pp.

2238 A DEFENCE of the slave trade, on the grounds of humanity, policy and justice. J. Highley; J. Budd, London, 1804. 90 pp.

By Robert Bisset. Slave trade is not unchristian; abolition would cause misery to the Africans, as well as destruction of the British West Indies. See (2241, 2258).

2239 *BRANAGAN, Thomas
A preliminary essay, on the oppression of the exiled sons of Africa. Consisting of animadversions on the impolicy and barbarity of the deleterious commerce and subsequent slavery of the human species; to which is added, a desultory letter written to Napoleon Bonaparte, anno domini, 1801. By Thomas Branagan, late slave trader from Africa. John W. Scott, Philadelphia, 1804. 282 pp.

Reprinted New York, 1969.

2240 A LETTER to the Right Hon. William Pitt, containing some new arguments against the abolition of the slave trade. By Britannicus. C. Chapple (etc.), London, 1804. 33 pp.

By Francis Randolph. Commercial reasons for continuing the slave trade. (Reviewed in: CO, vol. 3, June 1804, pp. 362–68.)

2241 'A DEFENCE of the slave trade.' (ER, Oct. 1804, pp. 209–41.)

Critical review by William Wilberforce of (2238).

2242 POLITICAL economy: founded in justice and humanity. In a letter to a friend. By W. T. . . . Samuel Harrison Smith, Washington, 1804. 24 pp.

By William Thornton. Proposes gradual emancipation by engaging slaves on public works for a few years, then freeing them; while slavery exists it will be impossible to stop the slave trade, and the growing number of negroes in the colonies constitutes a danger.

2243 *HORN, John
Some considerations on the African slave trade, and the use of West India produce. January 17, 1805. G. Cooke, [London, 1805].

Broadside by a London Quaker. See (3990).

2244 'OM Negerhandelens Ophævelse i Hensyn til de danske vestindiske Øer.' (Minerva, Kiøbenhavn, Feb. 1805, pp. 189–240.)

Edited by K. L. Rahbek. On the effects of ending the slave trade to the Danish West Indies; if the slave population could be stabilized and agriculture rationalised slavery itself might gradually be abolished.

2245 *BRANAGAN, Thomas
Serious remonstrances, addressed to the citizens of the northern states, and their representatives: being an appeal to their natural feelings & common sense: consisting of speculations and animadversions, on the recent revival of the slave trade, in the American republic: with an investigation relative to the consequent evils resulting to the citizens of the northern states from that event. Interspersed with a simplified plan for colonizing the free negroes of the northern, in conjunction with those who have, or may emigrate from the southern states, in a distant

part of the national territory . . .
Thomas T. Stiles, Philadelphia, 1805.
133 pp.

2246 *CUSHOO: a dialogue between a negro
and an English gentleman, on the
horrors of slavery and the slave trade.
London, [c. 1805?] 12 pp.

Revised version of (2136) omitting
the boycott proposals. (Cottage library
of Christian knowledge, vol. 2, pt.
7.)

2247 *ADDRESSED to the serious consideration of the peers. No slaves, no sugar!
Containing irresistible arguments in
favour of the African trade. By a
Liverpool merchant. London, 1805.

Reviewed in: GM, vol. 75, May
1805, pp. 449–50.

2248 HORRORS of West India slavery.
C. Whittingham, [London, 1805]. 12 pp.

2249 *ALEXANDER, Ann
An address to the inhabitants of Char-
leston, South Carolina. Kimber, Conrad
& Co., Philadelphia, 1805. 7 pp.

On slavery.

2250 ESSAYS on the negro slave trade. No. 1.
W. McDowall, [London, 1805]. 27 pp.

By Robert Bisset. Slaves are indispensable to the West Indies, and
Africa has a surplus to sell; abolition,
originated by 'mischievous agitators
of religious change', would destroy
British naval paramountcy.

2251 SHARP, Granville
Serious reflections on the slave trade
and slavery. Wrote in March, 1797.
W. Calvert, London, 1805. 46 pp.

Urges abolition on legal and religious
grounds.

2252 STRICTURES on the abolition of the
slave trade, addressed principally to
the Christian church. (Signed: J. S.)
Biggs & Co., London, 1805. 26 pp.

By James Sabine. Christians should
pay for abolition, which would
open Africa to missionaries.

2253 FOOT, Jesse
Observations principally upon the
speech of Mr. Wilberforce, on his
motion in the House of Commons,
the 30th of May, 1804, for the abolition
of the slave trade. T. Becket; (etc.),
London, 1805. 116 pp.

Wilberforce's evidence is out of
date; the planters must be consulted

before abolition, urged by fanatics and
incendiaries regardless of the danger
of a slave revolt. See (2258).

2254 *BISSET, Robert
The history of the negro slave trade in
its connection with the commerce and
prosperity of the West Indies, and the
wealth and power of the British empire.
S. Highley, London, 1805. 2 vol.

Defends the slave trade.

2255 The HORRORS of the negro slavery
existing in our West Indian Islands,
irrefragably demonstrated from official
documents recently presented to the
House of Commons. J. Hatchard;
(etc.), London, 1805. 36 pp.

Amelioration of colonial slavery is
impossible unless Parliament first
abolishes the slave trade. (Reviewed
in: ER, Oct. 1805, pp. 244–48.)

2256 *BIØRN, Andreas Riegelsen
Tanker om Slavehandelen. Resultater
efter Iagttagelser og mangeaarige Erfar-
ing . . . Matthias Johan Sebbelow,
Kiøbenhavn, 1806. 24 pp.

Defends the slave trade.

2257 OXHOLM, Peter Lotharius
'Nogle Anmærkninger over en Af-
handling om Negerhandelens Ophævelse udi Maanedsskriftet Minerva af
Februarii 1805.' (Ny Minerva, Kiøbenhavn, May 1806, pp. 129–60.)

The Danish slave trade should be
resumed for a few years to compen-
sate for the lost period 1799–1802,
until the slave population reaches
30,000. See (4585, 4587).

2258 CLARKE, Thomas
A letter to Mr. Cobbett on his opinions
respecting the slave trade. J. Hatchard,
London, 1806. iv, 113 pp.

Urges abolition in answer to William
Cobbett, who had defended the
slave trade in his 'Political Register',
and to (2238) and (2253).

2259 HERON, Robert
A letter to William Wilberforce, Esq.
M.P. on the justice and expediency
of slavery and the slave-trade, and on
the best means to improve the manners
and condition of the negroes in the
West Indies. Jordan & Maxwell,
London, 1806. viii, 152 pp.

Abolition would violate principles
of reason and equity and might
interrupt 'the internal civilization of

Africa'. (Reviewed in: ER, July 1806, pp. 358–65.)

2260 PARRISH, John
Remarks on the slavery of the black people; addressed to the citizens of the United States, particularly to those who are in legislative or executive stations in the general or state governments; and also to such individuals as hold them in bondage. Kimber, Conrad, & Co., Philadelphia, 1806. 66 pp.

2261 The DANGERS of the country. By the author of War in disguise. J. Butterworth; J. Hatchard, London, 1807. iv, 227 pp.

> By James Stephen. Abolition of the slave trade, 'this national sin', is more essential for the salvation of Britain than her armed forces. See (2263).

2262 LETTERS concerning the abolition of the slave-trade and other West-India affairs. By Mercator. C. & W. Galabin, London, 1807. 32 pp.

> By John Gladstone. Abolition may ruin the colonies and cause famine and wars in overpopulated Africa. See (2267).

2263 NEW reasons for abolishing the slave trade; being the last section of a larger work, now first published, entitled "The dangers of the country". By the author of "War in disguise". J. Butterworth; J. Hatchard, London, 1807. 67 pp.

> By James Stephen. See (2261).

2264 SHARP, Granville
"The system of colonial law" compared with the eternal laws of God; and with the indispensable principles of the English constitution. Vernor, Hood, & Sharp (etc.), London, 1807. 20 pp.

> Colonial slave laws are incompatible with English law; slavery is itself the source of the slave trade and should be abolished.

2265 WILBERFORCE, William
A letter on the abolition of the slave trade; addressed to the freeholders and other inhabitants of Yorkshire. T. Cadell & W. Davies; J. Hatchard, London, 1807. iii, 396 pp.

> Describes the effects of the slave trade on Africa, 'a sum of guilt and misery, hitherto unequalled in the annals of the world'; the slave population could be maintained with-

out it. (Favourable reviews in: CO, vol. 6, 1807, pp. 250–66, 315–28; ER, April 1807, pp. 199–206.) See (2454.)

2266 SMITH, William
A letter to William Wilberforce, Esq. M.P. on the proposed abolition of the slave trade, at present under the consideration of Parliament. Longman, Hurst, Rees, & Orme, London, 1807. 48 pp.

> Discussion of parliamentary tactics by one of Wilberforce's oldest supporters.

2267 A LETTER addressed to Mercator, in reply to his letters on the abolition of the slave trade. By a planter. J. Ridgway, London, 1807. 21 pp.

> The slave trade will aggravate overproduction and overpopulation in the colonies; abolition is in the planters' interest. See (2262). Answered by (2271).

2268 'ON the proposed abolition of the slave trade.' (Signed: Benevolus.) (GM, Feb. 1807, pp. 128–30.)

> Outlines a scheme for abolition.

2269 REFLECTIONS on the slave-trade; extracted from a work, entitled A compendious dictionary of the Holy Bible, under the article Slavery. . . . Extracted by R. R. W. Dutton, London, 1807. 12 pp.

> Indignant denunciation of the slave trade.

2270 CLARKSON, Thomas
Three letters (one of which has appeared before) to the planters and slave-merchants, principally on the subject of compensation. Phillips & Fardon, London, 1807. 16 pp.

> Reply to a petition by the planters against abolition (23 January); the slave trade is not of advantage to Britain; they should improve conditions for the slaves instead.

2271 THIRD letter on the abolition of the slave-trade and other West-India affairs. By Mercator. C. & W. Galabin, London, 1807. 22 pp.

> By John Gladstone. The slave trade cannot be abolished by Britain alone; it is not overproduction but trading difficulties that have caused a colonial crisis. See (2267).

2272 CORRY, Joseph
Observations upon the windward coast

of Africa, the religion, character, customs, &c. of the natives; with a system upon which they may be civilized, and a knowledge attained of the interior of this extraordinary quarter of the globe . . . With an appendix, containing a letter to Lord Howick on the most simple and effectual means of abolishing the slave trade. G. & W. Nicol; James Asperne, London, 1807. xiv, 163 pp.

Suggests gradual abolition of the slave trade after settling slaves as labourers in colonies like Sierra Leone and returning them to their homes as 'agents' of civilisation. (Reviewed in: CO, vol. 6, 1807, pp. 806–19.)

2273 RENNY, Robert
A history of Jamaica . . . To which is added, an illustration of the advantages, which are likely to result, from the abolition of the slave trade. J. Cawthorn, London, 1807. xx, 333 pp.

With a chapter on the slave trade and an appendix: 'The propriety and utility of the abolition of the slave trade'.

2274 *A LETTER to Lord Grenville, on the abolition of the slave trade, by Britannicus. J. Cawthorn, London, 1807. 43 pp.

By Francis Randolph? See (2240).

2275 The CLAIM for fresh evidence on the subject of the slave trade considered. Phillips & Fardon, London, 1807. 16 pp.

The pro-slavery demand for new evidence, despite recent books and parliamentary papers on the slave trade, is merely a delaying tactic.

2276 'SLAVERY and its consequences.' (BrM, vol. 12, 1807, pp. 496–97.)

Welcomes the end of the slave trade and hopes that slavery itself will be abolished.

2277 'DEBATE in the General Assembly respecting the clause on the abolition of the slave trade.' (SM, vol. 69, Aug. 1807, pp. 577–78.)

Account of the Church of Scotland Assembly at Edinburgh 23 May 1807.

2278 PALEY, William
'Proceedings at a meeting of the inhabitants of Carlisle, convened by public notice, on Thursday, February 9th, 1792, to petition Parliament for the abolition of the slave trade. The Archdeacon of Carlisle in the chair.' In: MEADLEY, G. W. Memoirs of William Paley (London; Cambridge, 1809), pp. 139–52.

Resolutions of the meeting and speech by Paley on 'this diabolical traffic'. See (2091).

2279 BURKE, Edmund
'A letter to the Right Hon. Henry Dundas . . . With the sketch of a negro code.' In: The works of . . . Edmund Burke, vol. 9 (London, 1812), pp. 276–315.

Letter written 9 April 1792, with draft regulations for the slave trade and West Indian slavery (original, about 1780: B. M. Add. Mss. 37890), to be used should the policy of gradual abolition proposed by Dundas be adopted. See (2354).

N. SERMONS

2280 *GODWYN, Morgan
Trade preferr'd before religion, and
Christ made to give place to Mammon:
represented in a sermon relating to the
plantations. First preached at West-
minster-Abby, and afterwards in divers
churches in London . . . B. Took,
London, 1685, 34 pp.

On the duty of converting slaves to
Christianity,

2281 VIEIRA, Antonio
'Sermam XXVII. com o santissimo
sacramento exposto.' *In his*: Maria
Rosa Mystica, pt. 2 (Lisboa, 1688),
pp. 391–429.

Sermon to a black religious fraternity
in Brazil, condemning the slave trade
and proclaiming the equality of all
Christians. (Vieira's first public sermon to a black congregation in Bahia
1633, is printed in pt. 1, 1686, pp.
484–521.)

2282 HILL, Anthony
Afer baptizatus: or, the negro turn'd
Christian. Being a short and plain
discourse, shewing I. The necessity
of instructing and baptizing slaves in
English plantations. II. The folly of
that vulgar opinion, that slaves do cease
to be slaves when once baptized. Delivered (most of it) in a sermon preach'd
at Stratford-le-Bow in Middlesex, March
the 15th 170½. Charles Broome; Edward Evett, London, 1702. 55 pp.

Slavery is lawful, but negroes are
'of the same common nature with
ourselves'.

2283 FLEETWOOD, William, *Bishop of
St. Asaph*
A sermon preached before the Society
for the Propagation of the Gospel in
Foreign Parts, at the parish church of
St. Mary-le-Bow, on Friday the 16th
of February, 17$\frac{10}{11}$ . . . Joseph Downing,
London, 1711. 42 pp.

Criticises owners who will not
permit their slaves to receive Christian
instruction; Christianity will not
affect the slaves' legal status.

2284 HALES, Stephen
A sermon preached before the Trustees
for establishing the colony of Georgia
in America; and before the Associates
of the late Rev. Dr. Thomas Bray, for
converting the negroes in the British
plantations, and for other good purposes; at their anniversary meeting
in the parish church of St. Brides,
Fleet-Street, on Thursday, March 21,
1734 . . . T. Woodward, London, 1734.
62 pp.

Urges the planters, in their own
interest, to convert their African
slaves.

2285 TWO sermons, preached to a congregation of black slaves, at the parish
church of S.P. in the province of Maryland. By an American pastor. John
Oliver, London, 1749. 79 pp.

By Thomas Bacon. Explains the
Christian duties of the slaves.

2286 BACON, Thomas
Four sermons, upon the great and
indispensible duty of all Christian
masters and mistresses to bring up
their negro slaves in the knowledge and
fear of God. Preached at the parish
church of St Peter in Talbot County in
the province of Maryland. J. Oliver,
London, 1750. 142 pp.

The African slaves are human
beings, but baptism will not entitle
them to freedom.

2287 WARBURTON, William, *Bishop of
Gloucester*
A sermon preached before the incorporated Society for the Propagation
of the Gospel in Foreign Parts; at their
anniversary meeting in the parish
church at St. Mary-le-Bow, on Friday,
February 21, 1766. E. Owen & T.
Harrison, London, 1766. 32, 68 pp.

Contains one of the earliest direct
attacks on the African slave trade
and slavery in England.

2288 *An ORATION, on the beauties of
liberty, or the essential rights of the
Americans. Delivered at the Second

Baptist Church in Boston, upon the last annual thanksgiving, Dec 3ᵈ, 1772 ... The third edition, carefully corrected by the author, in which are many additions . . . and Remarks on the rights and liberties of the Africans, inserted by particular desire. (Signed: A British Bostonian.) E. Russell, Boston, 1773. 78 pp.

Attributed to Isaac Skillman.

2289 *NILES, Nathaniel
Two discourses on liberty. Delivered at the North Church in Newbury-Port, on Lord's-Day, June 5th, 1774, and published at the general desire of the hearers. I. Thomas & H. W. Tinges, Newbury-Port, 1774. 60 pp.

Warns of retribution on the nation for enslaving fellow men.

2290 *HART, Levi
Liberty described and recommended; in a sermon, preached to the corporation of freemen in Farmington, at their meeting on Tuesday, September 20, 1774. Eben. Watson, Hartford, 1775. 23 pp.

Denounces the slave trade as 'a flagrant violation of the law of nature'.

2291 PORTEUS, Beilby, *Bishop of Chester*
A sermon preached before the incorporated Society for the Propagation of the Gospel in Foreign Parts; at their anniversary meeting in the parish church of St. Mary-le-Bow, on Friday, February 21, 1783. T. Harrison & S. Brooke, London, 1783. 91 pp.

Britain has a particular duty to alleviate the misery of the African slaves because of her leading role in the slave trade; newly imported slaves infect the others with 'heathenish principles' from Africa. (Reviewed in: GM, Oct. 1783, pp. 859–60.)

2292 PORTEUS, Beilby, *Bishop of Chester*
Sermons on several subjects . . . The fourth edition, corrected. T. Payne & Son; T. Cadell, London, 1784. xi, 431 pp.

Includes 'The civilization, improvement, and conversion of the negroe-slaves in the British islands recommended', preached 23 February 1783. The British have a special responsibility as they are the main traders 'in that inhuman merchandize of men'.

2293 MASON, William
An occasional discourse, preached in the cathedral of St. Peter in York, January 27, 1788, or the subject of the African slave-trade. A Ward, York; (etc.), 1788. 27 pp.

Antislavery sermon.

2294 AGUTTER, William
The abolition of the slave trade considered in a religious point of view. A sermon preached before the corporation of the city of Oxford, at St. Martin's Church, on Sunday, February 3, 1788. J. F. & C. Rivington; G. Phillips, London, 1788. 29 pp.

Urges universal abolition of slavery.

2295 ROBINSON, Robert
Slavery inconsistent with the spirit of Christianity. A sermon preached at Cambridge, on Sunday, Feb. 10, 1788. J. Archdeacon, Cambridge; (etc.), 1788. 39 pp.

2296 BRADSHAW, Thomas
The slave trade inconsistent with reason and religion. A sermon preached in the parish-church of Tottenham, Middlesex, on Sunday, March 16, 1788. W. Richardson; Henry Gardner, London, 1788. 21 pp.

Deals with the objections to the abolition of slavery.

2297 PECKARD, Peter
Justice and mercy recommended, particularly with reference to the slave trade. A sermon preached before the University of Cambridge. J. & J. Merrill, Cambridge; (etc.), 1788. 44 pp.

Urges gradual abolition of the trade.

2298 PRIESTLEY, Joseph
A sermon on the subject of the slave trade; delivered to a society of Protestant dissenters at the new meeting, in Birmingham; and published at their request. Pearson & Rollason, Birmingham, 1788. xii, 40 pp.

The African slaves deserve our compassion; abolition of slavery is a non-denominational cause for all Christians. Delivered 4 Feb. 1788.

2299 *HUGHES, William
A discourse in favour of the abolition of slavery in the British West Indies. Preached in the parish church of Ware, Herts. T. Cadell, London, 1788.

Reviewed in: MR, vol. 78, March 1788, p. 269.

2300 *A SERMON intended to enforce the reasonableness and duty on Christian as well as political principles of the abolition of the African slave trade. By the Rev. J. M. Johnson, London, 1788.

> Reviewed in: CrR, vol. 65, April 1788, pp. 320–21; MR, vol. 78, May 1788, p. 446.

2301 DORE, James
A sermon on the African slave trade, preached at Maze-Pond, Southwark, Lord's day afternoon, Nov. 30, 1788. J. Buckland (etc.), London, 1788. 24 pp.

> Supports abolition.

2302 *BIDLAKE, John
The slave trade. A sermon, preached at Stonehouse Chapel, on Sunday, December 28, 1788 . . . Plymouth, 1789. 32 pp.

> Reviewed in: GM, March 1789, pp. 239–40.

2303 *HAWKER, Robert
The injustice of the African slave trade proved from principles of natural equity. A sermon preached in the Church of Charles, Plymouth, January 11, 1789. Law (etc.), London, 1789. 28 pp.

> Reviewed in: MR, vol. 80, March 1789, pp. 284–85.

2304 BEATSON, John
Compassion the duty and dignity of man; and cruelty the disgrace of his nature. A sermon occasioned by that branch of British commerce which extends to the human species. Preached to a congregation of Protestant dissenters in Hull, January 21st, 1789. Hull; (etc.), 1789. 64 pp.

2305 *MENDS, Herbert
The injustice and cruelty of the slave trade considered in a sermon preached in Plymouth, on the Lord's Day, February 22, 1789. Plymouth, 1789. 37 pp.

> Reviewed in: GM, April 1789, p. 341; MR, vol. 80, May 1789, p. 469.

2306 'EXTRACTS from a sermon at Bristol on the slave trade.' (GM, June 1789, pp. 498–99.)

> Antislavery sermon (6 May); submitted by 'An enemy to detraction' in reply to a remark that no clergyman had dared to preach against the slave trade in the slaving centres.

2307 *The UNIVERSAL rights of humanity asserted and applied to the state of the suffering Africans. By Philadelphos. Gardner, London, 1789. 49 pp.

> Reviewed in: MR, vol. 81, July 1789, p. 95 ('Another pulpit philippic against the negro slave trade').

2308 EDWARDS, Jonathan
The injustice and impolicy of the slave trade, and of the slavery of the Africans: illustrated in a sermon preached before the Connecticut Society for the promotion of freedom, and for the relief of persons unlawfully holden in bondage, at their annual meeting in New-Haven, September 15, 1791. Thomas & Samuel Green, [New Haven,] 1791. 37 pp.

> Arguments for and against the slave trade discussed to show that it should be ended.

2309 BOOTH, Abraham
Commerce in the human species, and the enslaving of innocent persons, inimical to the laws of Moses and the gospel of Christ. A sermon, preached in Little Prescot Street, Goodman's Fields, January 29, 1792. C. Dilly; T. Knott, London, 1792. 30 pp.

> 'Manstealers' should be put to death.

2310 *CLARK, Thomas
A sermon on the injustice of the slave trade, preached February 12th, 1792, in the parish church of the Holy Trinity, in Kingston-upon-Hull. J. Ferraby, Hull, 1792. 21 pp.

2311 LIDDON, John
Cruelty the natural and inseparable consequence of slavery, and both diametrically opposite to the doctrine and spirit of the Christian religion: represented in a sermon, preached on Sunday, March 11th, 1792, at Hemel-Hempstead, Herts. C. Dilly (etc.), London, 1792. 32 pp.

> Christians should support abolition by petitions and boycott of slave produce.

2312 SOMERVILLE, Thomas
A discourse on our obligation to thanksgiving, for the prospect of the abolition of the African slave-trade. With a prayer. Delivered in the church of Jedburgh on April 15. J. Palmer, Kelso, 1792. 49 pp.

2313 PATTEN, William
On the inhumanity of the slave-trade, and the importance of correcting it. A

sermon, delivered in the Second Congregational Church, Newport, Rhode-Island, August 12, 1792. J. Carter, Providence, 1793. 14 pp.

2314 HOPKINS, Samuel
A discourse upon the slave-trade, and the slavery of the Africans. Delivered in the Baptist meeting-house at Providence, before the Providence Society for abolishing the slave-trade, &c. at their annual meeting, on May 17, 1793. J. Carter, Providence, 1793. 22 pp.

Slave trade and slavery should be abolished and the free slaves be resettled in Africa.

2315 PECKARD, Peter
National crimes the cause of national punishments. A discourse delivered in the cathedral church at Peterborough, on the fast-day, Feb: 25th, 1795. Jacob, Peterborough; (etc.), [1795]. vi, 28 pp.

Britain is being punished because she is defiled, especially by 'the infernal traffic in human blood'.

2316 *BENSON, Joseph
A sermon, preached at the Methodist chapel, in Hull, on Wednesday, the 7th of March, 1798, being the day appointed for a national fast. G. Whitfield, London, 1798. 40 pp.

Condemns the slave trade.

2317 *BECK, John
The doctrine of perpetual bondage reconcilable with the infinite justice of God, a truth plainly asserted in the Jewish and Christian scriptures . . . Seymour & Woolhopter, Savannah, 1800. 24 pp.

Two sermons. See (2235).

2318 PETERS, Charles
Two sermons, preached at Dominica, on the 11th and 13th of April, 1800 . . . To which is added, an appendix . . . containing . . . remarks and strictures . . . on the slave trade, and the condition of slaves in general in our West-Indian colonies. John Hatchard, London, 1802. 82 pp.

Abolition of the slave trade is necessary to stop the source of the evils of slavery in the West Indies.

2319 *McLEOD, Alexander
Negro slavery unjustifiable. A discourse . . . T. & F. Swords, New York, 1802. 42 pp.

Attacks the African slave trade as unchristian, immoral and dangerous.

2320 *WILLIAMS, Peter
An oration on the abolition of the slave trade; delivered in the African Church, in the city of New-York, January 1, 1808 . . . By Peter Williams, Jun., a descendant of Africa. Samuel Wood, New-York, 1808. 26 pp.

2321 *JONES, Absalom
A thanksgiving sermon, preached January 1, 1808, in St. Thomas's, or the African Episcopal Church, Philadelphia: on account of the abolition of the African slave trade, on that day, by the Congress of the United States . . . Fry & Kammerer, Philadelphia, 1808. 22 pp.

2322 MORSE, Jedidiah
A discourse, delivered at the African meeting-house, in Boston, July 14, 1808, in grateful celebration of the abolition of the African slave-trade, by the governments of the United States, Great Britain and Denmark. Lincoln & Edmands, Boston, 1808. 28 pp.

Sermon, with notes on the abolition of the slave trade.

2323 SIPKINS, Henry
An oration on the abolition of the slave trade; delivered in the African church in the city of New-York, January 2, 1809. By Henry Sipkins, a descendant of Africa. John C. Totten, New-York, 1809. 21 pp.

First anniversary of abolition of the U.S. slave trade.

2324 *MILLER, William
A sermon on the abolition of the slave trade; delivered in the African Church, New-York, on the first of January, 1810 . . . John C. Totten, New-York, 1810. 16 pp.

2325 *CARMAN, Adam
An oration delivered at the fourth anniversary of the abolition of the slave trade, in the Methodist Episcopal Church, in Second Street, New York, January 1, 1811. John C. Totten, New York, 1811. 23 pp.

2326 *PARROTT, Russell
An oration on the abolition of the slave trade . . . Delivered on the first of January, 1812, at the African Church of St. Thomas. James Maxwell, Philadelphia, 1812. 10 pp.

2327 *LAWRENCE, George
An oration on the abolition of the slave trade, delivered on the first day of January, 1813, in the African Methodist

Episcopal Church . . . Hardcastle & Van Pelt, New-York, 1813. 16 pp.

2328 GRAY, Thomas
A sermon delivered in Boston, before the African Society, on the 14th day of July, 1818; the anniversary of the abolition of the slave trade . . . Parmenter & Norton, Boston, 1818. 16 pp.

Urges negroes to accept their station in life.

2329 DEAN, Paul
A discourse delivered before the African Society, at their meeting-house, in Boston, Mass. on the abolition of the slave trade by the government of the United States of America, July 14, 1819 . . . Nathaniel Coverly, Boston, 1819. 16 pp.

2330 *GLOUCESTER, Jeremiah
An oration delivered on January 1, 1823, in Bethel Church, on the abolition of the slave trade . . . John Young, Philadelphia, 1823. 16 pp.

2331 *CARROLL, Daniel Lynn
Sermons and addresses on various subjects. Lindsay & Blakiston, Philadelphia, 1846. 372 pp.

Includes 'A permanent remedy for the African slave trade'.

2332 *ALLEMAND-LAVIGERIE, Charles Martial, *Cardinal*
Allocution de Son Eminence le cardinal Lavigerie, archevêque de Carthage & d'Alger, primat d'Afrique, prononcé le jour du vendredi-saint 19 avril 1889 dans la cathédrale d'Alger avant les prières solennelles pour l'abolition de l'esclavage africain sur la passion de Notre Seigneur Jésus-Christ et sur celle de l'Afrique et ordonnance archiépiscopale portant institution de prières publiques pour la suppression de l'esclavage. Alger, 1889. 19 pp.

O. LEGISLATIVE DEBATES AND SPEECHES

2333 SKETCH of the debate which took place in the House of Commons on Friday, May 9, upon the motion of the Chancellor of the Exchequer. [Manchester, 1788.] 4 pp.

Headed: 'Slave trade.' Pitt successfully moved that the slave trade should be investigated.

2334 BEAUFOY, Henry
The speech of Mr. Beaufoy, Tuesday, the 18th June, 1788, in a committee of the whole House, on a bill for regulating the conveyance of negroes from Africa to the West-Indies. To which are added observations on the evidence adduced against the bill. J. Phillips, London, 1789. 37 pp.

Speech in the debate on Dolben's bill to limit the number of slaves carried on each ship; urges abolition of the slave trade.

2335 GREAT BRITAIN: House of Commons
The speeches of Mr. Wilberforce, Lord Penrhyn, Mr. Burke, Sir W. Young, Alderman Newnham, Mr. Dempster, Mr. Martin, Mr. Pitt, Mr. Grenville, Mr. Fox, Mr. Gascoigne, Alderman Sawbridge, Mr. Smith, &c. &c. on a motion for the abolition of the slave trade, in the House of Commons, May the 12th, 1789. To which are added, Mr. Wilberforce's twelve propositions. John Stockdale, London, 1789. 32 pp.

The 'propositions' were reprinted in: AM, vol. 7, 1790, App. II, pp. 23–26. See (2340).

2336 WILBERFORCE, William
The speech of William Wilberforce, Esq. representative for the county of York, on Wednesday the 13th of May, 1789, on the question of the abolition of the slave trade. To which are added, the resolutions then moved, and a short sketch of the speeches of the other members. J. Walter (etc.), London, [1789]. 76 pp.

Attack on the slave trade by Wilberforce, who declares his intention of bringing in a bill for its total abolition. See (2012).

2337 GREAT BRITAIN: House of Commons
Slave trade. House of Commons, Wednesday, May 13, 1789. [London, 1789.] (4 pp.)

Report of the debate, with speeches by Wilberforce and Penrhyn.

2338 *GREAT BRITAIN: House of Commons
Debates in the British House of Commons, Wednesday, May 13, 1789, on the petitions for the abolition of the slave trade. Joseph Crukshank, Philadelphia, 1789. 24 pp.

2339 GREAT BRITAIN: House of Commons
Speeches in Parliament, respecting the abolition of the African slave trade. D. Willison, Edinburgh, 1789. 116 pp.

Speech of Beaufoy 18 June 1788; debate in the Commons 13 May 1789 on Wilberforce's motion for a committee of inquiry; and translation of the letter of the Amis des Noirs to the 'bailliages', 3 Feb. 1789. (Printed for the Society instituted at Edinburgh, for the Purpose of effecting the Abolition of the Slave Trade.)

2340 EDWARDS, Bryan
A speech delivered at a free conference between the honourable the Council and Assembly of Jamaica, held the 19th November, 1789, on the subject of Mr. Wilberforce's propositions in the House of Commons, concerning the slave-trade. Alexander Aikman, Kingston, Jamaica, 1789. 82, xvi pp.

Accepts Wilberforce's account of how slaves were obtained but argues that the slave trade should be abolished only if all European nations concur. See (2335).

2341 PINKNEY, William
Speech of William Pinkney, Esq. in the House of Delegates of Maryland, at their session in November, 1789. Joseph Crukshank, Philadelphia, 1790. 22 pp.

Condemns the slave trade, for which he blames Britain, and urges gradual emancipation.

2342 **FRANCE: Assemblée Nationale Constituante**
Proceedings of the National Assembly of France, upon the proposed abolition of the slave trade in that kingdom. Translated from the journals of the National Assembly. London, 1790. iv, 28 pp.

Speech by Barnave to the Colonial Committee in support of a petition from Le Havre urging the Assembly to declare that it had no intention to abolish the slave trade.

2343 **GREAT BRITAIN: House of Commons**
The debate on a motion for the abolition of the slave-trade, in the House of Commons, on Monday and Tuesday, April 18 and 19, 1791, reported in detail. W. Woodfall, London, 1791. 123 pp.

Speeches by Wilberforce and others; the motion was lost by 163 votes to 88.

2344 *****TARLETON, *Sir* Banastre**
Heads of the speech delivered . . . on the 18th of April, 1791, in a committee of the House of Commons, on a motion made by Mr. Wilberforce, for the abolition of the slave trade. London, 1791. 33 pp.

2345 **GREAT BRITAIN: House of Commons**
Heads of the speeches, delivered on the 18th and 19th April, 1791, in a committee of the House of Commons, on a motion made by Mr. Wilberforce, for the abolition of the slave-trade, with Detector's letters, &c. Liverpool, 1791. 105 pp.

Summary of speeches, with anti-abolition material including six letters by 'Detector' attacking the abolitionists as 'visionaries' who wish to annihilate British commerce to replace it with a trade monopoly of their own.

2346 *****WILBERFORCE, William**
The speech of William Wilberforce, Esq. representative for the county of York, on Monday April 18, 1791, on the question of the abolition of the slave trade. J. Ferraby, Hull, 1791. 42 pp.

2347 *****PITT, William**
The speech . . . in the House of Commons, on Tuesday, the 19th of April, 1791, on the abolition of the slave trade. [Hull, 1791.] 12 pp.

2348 *****FOX, Charles James**
The speech of the Right Hon. Charles James Fox, in the House of Commons, on Tuesday, the 19th of April, 1791. Concerning the abolition of the slave trade. Hull, [1791]. 15 pp.

2349 *****YOUNG, William**
The speech delivered in Parliament on the subject of the slave-trade, April 19, 1791. London, 1791.

2350 **ROUME, Philippe Rose,**
Sur la question des gens de couleur, par M. Roume, créole et commissaire-ordonnateur de l'île de Tabago. Le 11 mai 1791. [Paris, 1791.] 15 pp.

Speech to the Assemblée Nationale. Abolition of the slave trade and emancipation would ruin the colonies, which must be left to legislate for themselves.

2351 **WILBERFORCE, William**
'Correct and authentic copies of the twelve propositions, submitted, on Tuesday evening, by Mr. Wilberforce, to the consideration of the committee, to whom the report of the privy council, various petitions for the abolition of the slave-trade, and other papers relative thereto, had been referred: which propositions were, by consent, ordered to lie on the table.' (AnR 1789, vol. 31, 1792, pp. 268–71.)

See (2335).

2352 **FRANCE: Assemblée Nationale**
A particular account of the commencement and progress of the insurrection of the negroes in St. Domingo, which began in August last: being a translation of the speech made to the National Assembly, the 3d of November, 1791, by the deputies from the General Assembly of the French part of St. Domingo. T. Boosey, [London,] 1792. 36 pp.

Justifies the slave trade and blames the Amis des Noirs for the revolt. Circulated by the West India Committee. (Second edition, with an appendix, published by J. Sewell, London, 1792; iv, 40 pp.) See (2082).

2353 *****SLAVERY inconsistent with justice and good policy. By Philanthropos.
J. Bradford, Lexington, 1792. 43 pp.

Speech by David Rice to the Kentucky constitutional convention, January 1792, in an attempt to get an antislavery article included in the constitution.

2354 **GREAT BRITAIN: House of Commons**
The debate on a motion for the abolition of the slave-trade, in the House of

Commons, on Monday the second of April, 1792, reported in detail. W. Woodfall, London, 1792. 178 pp.

Wilberforce's motion to abolish the slave trade from Africa was amended to 'gradually' by 230 votes to 85.

2355 GREAT BRITAIN: House of Commons
'An account of the important debate in the House of Commons, on Monday April 2, on Mr. Wilberforce's motion for the abolition of the slave trade.' (UM, vol. 90, April 1792, pp. 289–95.)

2356 *GREAT BRITAIN: House of Commons
Clarendon's accurate and copious account of the debates of the House of Commons on Mr. Wilberforce's motion for an abolition of the slave trade, April 2, 1792. C. Cooke, London, 1792. 44 pp.

2357 An APPEAL to the candour and justice of the people of England, in behalf of the West India merchants and planters, founded on plain facts and incontrovertible arguments. J. Debrett, London, 1792. xvi, 118 pp.

Pro-slavery report of the Commons debate on the slave trade on 2 April 1792, edited by Felix McCarthy and distributed by the West India Committee.

2358 PITT, William
The speech of the Right Honourable William Pitt, on a motion for the abolition of the slave trade, in the House of Commons, on Monday the second of April, 1792. James Phillips, London, 1792. 32 pp.

Urges immediate and total abolition as 'an atonement for our long and cruel injustice towards Africa'. See (2157).

2359 BAILLIE, James
The speech of James Baillie, Esq. agent for Grenada, in the House of Commons, on the question for the abolition of the slave trade. On Monday April 2, 1792. W. Woodfall, London, 1792. 8 pp.

Objections to abolition based on the value of the African and West Indian trade to Britain and the legalisation of the slave trade by acts of parliament since the reign of Charles II.

2360 *JAMAICA: House of Assembly
Proceedings of the hon. House of Assembly of Jamaica, on the sugar and slave-trade, in a session which began the 23d of October, 1792 . . .

A. Aikman, St. Jago de la Vega, 1792. 23 pp.

2361 BERTIE, Willoughby, *Earl of Abingdon*
Speech of the Earl of Abingdon, on His Lordship's motion for postponing the further consideration of the question for the abolition of the slave trade; with some strictures on the speech of the Bishop of St. David's. Debrett; Sewel, London, [1793]. 23 pp.

Speech in the House of Lords 11 April 1793.

2362 WADSTRÖM, Carl Bernhard
Addresse au Corps législatif et au Directoire exécutif de la République Française. [Paris, 1795.] 9 pp.

Deplores the attack on the British settlement at Sierra Leone in 1794; this was not an ordinary colony but had been established with the aim of ending the slave trade.

2363 FRANCIS, Philip
Proceedings in the House of Commons on the slave trade, and state of the negroes in the West India islands . . . Caroline Ridgway, London, 1796. 105 pp.

Speeches of Francis in the debates of 18 April 1791, 15 March 1796 and 11 April 1796 on the slave trade and slavery.

2364 DUNDAS, Henry
Speech of the Right Hon. Henry Dundas, delivered in the House of Commons, the 15th of March, 1796, on the farther consideration of the report of the committee, upon the bill for the abolition of the slave trade: with a copy of the bill, and notes illustrative of some passages in the speech. London, 1796. 74 pp.

The bill is 'dangerous and impolitic' as other nations may continue the trade and Britain has no right to abolish it without the concurrence of the colonies.

2365 *MENTOR, Étienne Victor
Corps législatif. Conseil des Cinq-Cents. Discours prononcé par Mentor, sur le projet de résolution tendant à faire annuler les dettes contractées pour l'achat de noirs. Séance du 24 vendémiaire an VII. Impr. Nationale, [Paris,] an VII [1798]. 4 pp.

See (2205).

2366 LAW, Edward
The opening of the case in support of the petitions of the merchants of Lon-

don and Liverpool, against the bill "to prohibit the trading for slaves on the coast of Africa within certain limits". By Edward Law, Esq. at the bar of The House of Lords, on Tuesday, May 28, 1799. [London, 1799.] 20 pp.

Speech by counsel for the petitioners drawing attention to the importance of the slave trade to the colonial economy. See (2367).

2367 DALLAS, Robert
The summing up of the evidence given in support of the petitions of the merchants of London and Liverpool, against the bill "to prohibit the trading for slaves on the coast of Africa within certain limits." By Robert Dallas, Esq. at the bar of the House of Lords, on Friday, June 14, 1799. [London? 1799.] 19 pp.

See (2366).

2368 WILLIAM, *Duke of Clarence*
Substance of the speech of His Royal Highness the Duke of Clarence, in the House of Lords, on the motion for the recommitment of the slave trade limitation bill, on the fifth day of July, 1799. F. & C. Rivington, London, [1799]. 68 pp.

Defence of the slave trade, 'published at the request of the West India merchants and planters, and the mercantile interest of Liverpool'.

2369 FANE, John, *Earl of Westmoreland*
Substance of the speech of the Right Honourable the Earl of Westmoreland, in the House of Lords, on the motion for the recommitment of the slave trade limitation bill, on the fifth day of July, 1799. F. & C. Rivington, London, [1799]. 28 pp.

Defence of the slave trade; the bill for partial abolition is hasty and unwise.

2370 HORSLEY, Samuel, *Bishop of Rochester*
Substance of the Bishop of Rochester's speech in the House of Peers, Friday, July 5, 1799, in the debate upon the second reading of the bill to prohibit the trading in slaves on the coast of Africa, within certain limits. J. Robson, London, 1799. 44 pp.

Political, humanitarian and biblical reasons to support the bill for the abolition of the slave trade north of Cape Palmas.

2371 CAINES, Clement
Letters on the cultivation of the Otaheite cane . . . and also a speech on the slave trade, the most important feature in West Indian cultivation. Robinson, London, 1801. xv, 301 pp.

Speech to the General Assembly of the Leeward Islands opposing the resolutions of 1798 against abolition of the slave trade; it should be abolished immediately, for the benefit of the planters.

2372 'EXTRACTS from a speech on the slave trade, spoken before the Council of the Leeward Islands, March, 1798.' (Literary Magazine, and American Register, Philadelphia, vol. 2, 1804, pp. 45–47.)

By Clement Caines.

2373 YOUNG, *Sir* William
The speech of Sir William Young, Bart. M.P. on Mr. Wilberforce's motion, Feb. 28, 1805, for the second reading of the bill for the abolition of the slave trade. W. & J. Richardson, London, 1805. 30 pp.

Opposes the bill as unlikely to relieve 'the people of Africa', as an outrage to the British colonies and a danger to the prosperity of the United Kingdom; it was defeated by 77 votes to 70.

2374 PITT, William
The speeches of the Right Honourable William Pitt, in the House of Commons. Longman, Hurst, Rees & Orme (etc.), London, 1806. 4 vol.

Vol. 2 includes his speeches in the abolition debates of 19 April 1791, 2 April 1792 and 27 April 1792.

2375 GREAT BRITAIN: Parliament
Substance of the debates on a resolution for abolishing the slave trade, which was moved in the House of Commons on the 10th June, 1806, and in the House of Lords on the 24th June, 1806. With an appendix, containing notes and illustrations. Phillips & Fardon; John Hatchard, London, 1806. xi, 216 pp.

Speeches by Fox, Wilberforce, Grenville and others in the final debates on abolition; carried in the Commons by 114 votes to 15 and in the Lords by 41 votes to 20.

2376 HIBBERT, George
The substance of three speeches in Parliament, on the bill for the abolition

of the slave trade, and on the petition respecting the state of the West-India trade, in February and March, 1807. W. J. & J. Richardson, London, 1807. vii, 138 pp.

Speeches opposing the abolition bill.

2377 SLAVE trade. Kerby, [London, 1807]. (1 p.)

Election broadsheet with extracts from speeches in Parliament 24 Feb. 1807 by Lord Milton and Wilberforce, parliamentary candidates for Yorkshire.

2378 *FANE, John, Earl of Westmoreland
Report of the speech of the Rt. Hon. the Earl of Westmoreland in the House of Lords on the occasion of the amendments made by the Commons to the bill for the abolition of the African slave trade being taken into consideration, Monday, March 23, 1807. London, 1807. 15 pp.

Abolition would have disastrous effects for humanity and the British empire.

2379 PLUMER, Thomas
The speech of Mr. Plumer, at the bar of the House of Lords, on the second reading of the bill for the abolition of the slave-trade, in support of the petition of the West-India planters and merchants against that measure. C. & W. Galabin, London, 1807. 31 pp.

Arguments opposing abolition as a threat to private property and the security of the islands.

2380 GREAT BRITAIN: Parliament
Substance of the debates on the bill for abolishing the slave trade, which was brought into the House of Lords on the 2d January, 1807, and into the House of Commons on the 10th February, 1807, and which was finally passed into a law on the 25th March, 1807. W. Phillips; John Hatchard, London, 1808. iv, 273 pp.

Report of the passage of the bill which finally led to the abolition of the British slave trade. (See also the account in: AnR 1807, vol. 49, 1809, pp. 110–27.)

2381 *GREAT BRITAIN: House of Commons
Substance of the debate in the House of Commons, Friday, June 15, 1810, on the African slave trade. London, 1810. 33 pp.

Reviewed in: CO, vol. 9, 1810, pp. 779–85. Also reported in: Phil-

anthropist, London, vol. 1, 1811, pp. 58–66, 132–36.

2382 HORSLEY, Samuel, Bishop of St. Asaph
The speeches in Parliament of Samuel Horsley . . . late Lord Bishop of St. Asaph. Robert Stephen Rintoul, Dundee, 1813. 2 vol.

Includes his speeches on the slave trade 5 July 1799 and 24 June 1806.

2383a*SPAIN: Cortes
Documentos de que hasta ahora se compone el expediente que principiaron las Cortes extraordinarias sobre el tráfico y esclavitud de los negros. Repullés, Madrid, 1814. 157 pp.

Translated as:

2383b*Recueil de diverses pièces et des discussions qui eurent lieu aux Cortes générales et extraordinaires d'Espagne, en l'année 1811, sur la traite et esclavage des nègres . . . Paris, 1814. viii, 170 pp.

Contains the debates on the slave trade in the Cortes 1811 and 1813 and related documents.

2384 GREAT BRITAIN: House of Commons
'Parlamento inglez. Trafico da escravatura.' (Portuguez, Londres, vol. 1, no. 2, junho 1814, pp. 133–46.)

Speeches of Wilberforce, Grenville and others urging the government to put pressure on the European powers to abolish the slave trade.

2385 ROMILLY, Sir Samuel
'The speech of Sir Samuel Romilly, in the House of Commons, on the twenty-eighth of June, 1814, on that article in the treaty of peace which relates to the slave trade.' (Pamphleteer, London, vol. 4, no. 8, 1814, pp. 407–30.)

2386 GRENVILLE, William Wyndham, Baron Grenville
Substance of the speech of the Right Honourable Lord Grenville, in the House of Lords, on Monday, June 27, 1814, in moving for certain papers relative to the revival of the slave trade. James Ridgway, London, 1814. vii, 77 pp.

Speech on moving an address to the Prince Regent opposing the treaty with France which allowed an extension of the French slave trade for five years.

2387 FOX, Charles James
The speeches of the Right Honourable Charles James Fox, in the House of

Commons. Longman, Hurst, Rees, Orme, & Brown, London, 1815. 6 vol.

Includes a dozen speeches on the abolition of the slave trade 1788–1806.

2388 BURKE, Edmund
The speeches of the Right Honourable Edmund Burke, in the House of Commons, and in Westminster-Hall. Longman, Hurst, Rees, Orme, & Brown; J. Ridgway, London, 1816. 4 vol.

Vol. 3 includes his speeches on the abolition of the slave trade in the debates of 9 May 1788 and 12 May 1789.

2389 *PALLMER, Charles Nicholas
Substance of the speech ... in the House of Commons, June 19, 1816, on the motion of Mr. Wilberforce, for certain papers relating to the West Indies. London, 1816. 44 pp.

Opposes the bill for the registration of slaves in the colonies.

2390 *CONSTANT DE REBECQUE, Benjamin
Opinion prononcée dans la séance du juin 27, 1821. Par M. Benjamin Constant, député de la Sarthe. Paris, 1821.

See (2401).

2391 BROGLIE, Achille Léonce Victor Charles, *duc*
Discours prononcé par M. le duc de Broglie à la Chambre des Pairs le 28 mars 1822, sur la traite des nègres. L.-É. Herhan, [Paris, 1822]. 154 pp.

Describes cases of slave ships captured 1816–21 and proposes measures to suppress the illegal slave trade.

2392 *BROGLIE, Achille Léonce Victor Charles, *duc* de
Cruautés de la traite des nègres, ou relation des horreurs commises sur les nègres à bord des vaisseaux Le Rôdeur et L'Estelle, extraite du Discours de M. le duc de Broglie, prononcé à la Chambre des Pairs, le 28 mars 1822. H. Servier fils, Paris, 1822. 11 pp.

See (868).

2393 *BROGLIE, Achille Léonce Victor Charles, *duc* de
Développement d'une proposition faite à la Chambre des Pairs par M. le duc de Broglie, et relative à l'exécution des lois prohibitives de la traite des noirs ... Paris, 1822. 154 pp.

Headed: 'Chambre des Pairs de France. Session de 1821. Séance du

jeudi 28 mars de 1822.' (Reviewed in: RE, vol. 14, 1822, pp. 152–53.)

2394 GREAT BRITAIN: House of Commons
Address of the honourable the House of Commons to His Majesty, on the subject of the slave trade. Jovis, 27. die Junii, 1822. Westminster, [1822]. 2 pp.

2395 *WILBERFORCE, William
Résumé du discours prononcé dans la Chambre des Communes le 27 juin 1822, sur l'état actuel de la traite des nègres. Londres, 1822.

Speech on a motion to present an address on the slave trade to the king. (Hansard, Parliamentary debates, n.s., vol. 7, London, 1823, col. 1399–1403.)

2396 FOX, Charles James
The speech of the Rt. Hon. Chas. James Fox, in the House of Commons, June 10th, 1806. On a motion preparatory to the introduction of a bill for the abolition of the slave trade. J. Clark, Newcastle, 1824. 8 pp.

2397 CANNING, George
Speech of the Right Hon. George Canning, Secretary of State for Foreign Affairs, &c. &c. &c. on laying before the House of Commons the papers in explanation of the measures adopted by His Majesty's government with a view of ameliorating the condition of the negro slaves in the West Indies, on Wednesday, the 17th of March, 1824 ... Lupton Relfe; Hatchard & Son, London, 1824. 78 pp.

Concludes with a motion to introduce a bill to treat the slave trade as piracy. (Another version published by John Murray, London, 1824; 44 pp.)

2398 *CANNING, George
'Speech of Mr. Canning on bringing in a bill "for the more effectual suppression of the African slave trade" ... ' (Colonial Register, and West India Journal, London, vol. 1, no. 1, 1824, pp. 84–110.)

2399a *ANDRADA E SILVA, José Bonifacio d'
Representação a Assemblea geral constituinte e legislativa do imperio do Brasil sobre a escravatura. Firmin Didot, Paris, 1825. 40 pp.

Translated as:

2399b Memoir addressed to the General, constituent and legislative assembly of the empire of Brazil, on slavery! ... Butterworth (etc.), London, 1826. 60 pp.

Urges abolition of the slave trade and gradual emancipation of the slaves in Brazil; with a draft for an abolition bill. (Written 1823.)

2400 CANNING, George
The speeches of the Right Honourable George Canning . . . James Ridgway, London, 1828. 6 vol.

Vol. 1 includes Canning's speech on Wilberforce's motion for the abolition of the slave trade on 1 March 1799, defeated by 84 votes to 54.

2401 CONSTANT DE REBECQUE, Benjamin
Discours de M. Benjamin Constant à la Chambre des Députés. Ambroise Dupont & Compagnie, Paris, 1828. 2 vol.

Includes: 'Opinion relative à la traite des noirs' (27 June 1821), on French slaving cases 1818–20 and the 'droit de visite mutuelle'; speeches on the slave trade 5 April and 31 July 1822; and 'Sur le projet de loi relatif à la traite des noirs' (13 March 1827), proposing harder penalties for slave trading. See (2390).

2402 BROUGHAM, Henry Peter, *Baron Brougham and Vaux*
Lord Brougham's speech in the House of Lords, Monday, January 29, 1838, upon the slave trade, with an abstract of the discussion which ensued. James Ridgway & Sons, London, 1838. vi, 24 pp.

'Head money' for captured slave ships should be abolished, as it aggravates the misery of the slaves, and payment by the ton be substituted.

2403 BROUGHAM, Henry Peter, *Baron Brougham and Vaux*
Lord Brougham's speech in the House of Lords, on Tuesday, the 20th of February, 1838, for the immediate emancipation of the negro apprentices. Second edition. James Ridgway & Sons, London, 1838. v, 50 pp.

Includes an appeal for the suppression of the 'foreign' slave trade.

2404 BROUGHAM, Henry Peter, *Baron Brougham and Vaux*
Immediate emancipation. The speech of Lord Brougham in the House of Lords, on Tuesday, February 20th, 1838, on slavery and the slave-trade. Prepared from the most full and accurate reports, and corrected by his lordship.

Central Emancipation Committee, London, [1838]. 24 pp.

2405 BROUGHAM, Henry Peter, *Baron Brougham and Vaux*
Lord Brougham's speech in the House of Lords, Tuesday, March 6, 1838, upon the eastern slave trade. James Ridgway & Sons, London, 1838. v, 65 pp.

Attack on an order in council of 1837 extending 'apprenticeship' in Guiana to allow African and Asian labourers to be imported; this was 'disguised slave-trading'. (Reviewed, with 2402–04, in: ER, vol. 67, 1838, pp. 198–201.)

2406 BROUGHAM, Henry Peter, *Baron Brougham and Vaux*
Speeches of Henry Lord Brougham . . . Adam & Charles Black, Edinburgh, 1838. 4 vol.

Vol. 2 contains his speeches on the slave trade 14 June 1810, 29 Jan. 1838 and 6 March 1838.

2407 LUSHINGTON, Stephen Rumbold
The speech of the Right Hon. Stephen Lushington, M.P., against the proposed admission of slave-grown sugar to home consumption in the House of Commons, Thursday, May 7th, 1841. Thomas Curson Hansard, London, 1841. 15 pp.

A reduction of sugar duties will stimulate the slave trade.

2408 LABOUCHERE, Henry
Speech of the Right Hon. Henry Labouchere, in the House of Commons, on Monday, May 10, 1841. Ways and means. Sugar duties, &c. &c. &c. J. Ridgway, London, [1841]. 12 pp.

The slave trade will not be suppressed by cutting off trade with the countries producing sugar by slave labour.

2409 ADAMS, John Quincy
Mr. Adams' speech on war with Great Britain and Mexico: with the speeches of Messrs. Wise and Ingersoll, to which it is in reply. Emancipator Office, Boston, [1842?] 35 pp.

Speeches in the House of Representatives 14 April 1842. Adams opposes war with Britain over the right of search at sea or with Mexico in defence of Texan slave-holders.

2410 BROUGHAM, Henry Peter, *Baron Brougham and Vaux*
'Connexion of British subjects with

the slave trade.' (FA, no. 23, Sept. 1842, pp. 134–39.)

Speech in the House of Lords 2 Aug. 1842.

2411 TEMPLE, Henry John *Viscount Palmerston*
Speech of Viscount Palmerston, in the House of Commons, on Tuesday the 21st of March, 1843, on the treaty of Washington, of the 9th of August, 1842. James Ridgway, London, 1843. 95 pp.

Includes a discussion of the articles relating to the suppression of the illegal slave trade, criticising the government for lacking in firmness.

2412 BROUGHAM, Henry Peter, *Baron Brougham and Vaux*
Lord Brougham's speech upon the Ashburton treaty, delivered in the House of Lords, on Friday, 7th April, 1843. James Ridgway, London, 1843. 70 pp.

Includes comments on the clause relating to the slave trade and right of search.

2413 GIDDINGS, Joshua Reed
Speech of Mr. Giddings, of Ohio, on the motion of Mr. C. T. Ingersoll to print ten thousand copies of the report of the Committee on Foreign Affairs, in favor of paying for the negroes on board the schooner Amistad. Delivered in the House of Representatives, April 18, 1844. Washington, 1844. 11 pp.

Criticises the report as pro-slave trade and opposes 'waste of public money' on it.

2414 TEMPLE, Henry John, *Viscount Palmerston*
Speech of Viscount Palmerston in the House of Commons, on Tuesday, July 16th, 1844, on the slave trade. J. Hatchard & Son, London, 1844. 48 pp.

Describes the illegal slave trade and urges the government to make further efforts to suppress it.

2415 GREAT BRITAIN: House of Commons
'Lord Palmerston on the horrors of the slave trade.' (AR, vol. 20, Dec. 1844, pp. 353–63.)

Speeches by Palmerston and Peel on a motion for the return of statistics on the Atlantic slave trade 1815–43, 16 July 1844. (Reprinted from: British and Foreign Anti-Slavery Reporter, London, vol. 5, 1844, pp. 149–52.)

2416 WILBERFORCE, Samuel, *Bishop of Oxford*
Cheap sugar means cheap slaves. Speech of the Right Reverend the Lord Bishop of Oxford, in the House of Lords, February 7th, 1848, against the admission of slave labour sugar on equal terms with free labour produce; with an appendix illustrative of the impetus given to the slave trade by the bill of 1846 . . . Second edition. James Ridgway, London, 1848. 31 pp.

The antislavery blockade has aggravated the slave trade and benefited Cuba; the appendix includes evidence from the select committees of 1842 and 1848.

2417 *QUEIROZ COUTINHO MATOSO DA CÂMARA, Eusébio de
Questão do trafico. Rio de Janeiro, 1852.

Speech on the suppression of the Brazilian slave trade in the Câmara dos Deputados, 16 July 1852. (Reprinted from: Anais do Parlamento Brasileiro, Rio de Janeiro, 1852, vol. 2, pp. 241–58.)

2418 *GIDDINGS, Joshua Reed
The Amistad claim. History of the case; decision of the judiciary; comity of the various departments of government; construction of treaties; law of nations . . . Speech of Mr. Giddings, of Ohio, in the House of Representatives, Dec. 21, 1853 . . . [Washington, 1854?] 7 pp.

2419 BROUGHAM, Henry Peter, *Baron Brougham and Vaux*
Lord Brougham's speech upon the slave trade. House of Lords, 26th June, 1855. London, 1855. 10 pp.

On a petition from Barbados for the exclusion from Britain of products of Cuba and Porto Rico until Spain takes steps to suppress the slave trade from Africa and abolish slavery there.

2420 *ETHERIDGE, Emerson
Speech of Emerson Etheridge of Tennessee, the revival of the African slave-trade, and the President's message, delivered in the House of Representatives of the United States, Feb. 21, 1857. Washington, 1857. 16 pp.

2421 *LEACH, DeWitt Clinton
The Amistad case. Men not recognised as property by the constitution. Speech of Hon. DeWitt C. Leach, of Michigan. Delivered in the House of Representa-

tives, January 27, 1858. [Washington, 1858.] 8 pp.

2422 *SPRATT, Leonidas W.
Speech upon the foreign slave trade, before the legislature of South Carolina ... Columbia, S. C., 1858. 11 pp.

> Speech delivered 4 Dec. 1858. Spratt was a leader of the agitation to resume the African slave trade 1856–61.

2423 *HAMPTON, Wade
Speech of Hon. Wade Hampton, on the constitutionality of the slave trade laws. Delivered in the Senate of South Carolina, December 10th, 1859. Columbia, 1860. 20 pp.

2424 *WILSON, Henry
The suppression of the slave trade. Speech of Hon. Henry Wilson, of Mass. Delivered in the Senate of the United States, May 21, 1860. Washington, 1860. 8 pp.

2425 PAPERS relating to free labour and the slave trade; with a corrected report of the debate in the House of Commons, on the 26th of February, 1861, upon resolutions proposed by Mr. Cave, the chairman of the West India Committee, for more effectual suppression of the African slave-trade. Robert Barclay, London, 1861. 64 pp.

> Includes notes on the debates on the slave trade of 8 June 1860 and 26 February 1861, and on the immigration of labour to the West Indies.

2426 SPAIN: Senado
'La cuestion del tráfico negrero en el Senado.' (RHA, vol. 4, 1866, pp, 492–506.)

> Extracts from debates on the slave trade to the Spanish Antilles on 18–20 April 1866.

2427 SPAIN: Congreso de los Diputados
'Cuestion del tráfico negrero en el Congreso.' (RHA, vol. 4, 1866, pp. 673–90.)

> Extracts from proceedings of sessions on 6, 7 and 9 July 1866.

2428 GREAT BRITAIN: House of Lords
The slave circular. Speeches of Lords Cardwell and Selborne in the House of Lords, on Tuesday, March 7, 1876 ... Westminster, 1876. 16 pp.

> From a debate on slaves seeking refuge on British warships. (Reported in: Hansard's Parliamentary debates, ser. 3, vol. 227, London, 1876, col. 1506–12, 1533–47.)

2429 SUMNER, Charles
'Final suppression of the slave-trade. Speech in the Senate, on the treaty with Great Britain, April 24, 1862.' *In*: The works of Charles Sumner, vol. 6 (Boston, 1880), pp. 474–86.

2430 BUXTON, Sydney Charles
'Des mesures à prendre par un congrès international des puissances pour la suppression de la traite.' (MA, vol. 1, Aug. 1889, pp. 277–81.)

> Extract from a speech in the House of Commons on the objectives of the forthcoming antislavery conference: it should abolish the legal status of slavery, treat slave trading as piracy, enforce visitations of all ships and prevent arms imports to central Africa.

2431 CHARMES, Francis
'La traite sur mer et l'Acte de la Conférence de Bruxelles. (Rapport de M. F. Charmes au Parlement français.)' (MA, vol. 3, 1891, pp. 264–71; port.)

> Report on the Brussels act 1890 to the Chambre des Députés.

P. SUPPRESSION CONTROVERSY

2432 FARQUHAR, *Sir* Robert Townsend
Suggestions, arising from the abolition of the African slave trade, for supplying the demands of the West India colonies with agricultural labourers. John Stockdale, London, 1807. 66 pp.

> Proposes Chinese immigration to replace the importation of African slaves. See (2135).

2433 LAYMAN, William
Outline of a plan for the better cultivation, security, & defence of the British West Indies: being the original suggestion for providing an effectual substitute for the African slave trade, and preventing the dependance of those colonies on America for supplies. Black, Parry, & Kingsbury, London, 1807. 93 pp.

> The author had several years earlier proposed the introduction of Chinese workmen; immigration of free labour or slave breeding are the only alternatives since the abolition act.

2434 *The MIRROR of misery; or, tyranny exposed, extracted from authentic documents and exemplified by engravings. Wood, New York, 1807. 48 pp.

> On slavery and the slave trade. Reissued 1814 as: 'Slavery, the mirror of misery; or, tyranny exposed'.

2435 GEDACHTEN over den slavenhandel te Suriname. Wallez & Comp., 's Hage, 1807. 36 pp.

2436 YOUNG, Arthur
'Abolition of the slave trade . . .' (Annals of agriculture, Bury St. Edmunds, vol. 45, 1808, pp. 211–12.)

> Welcomes the abolition act as 'an event which is worth a dozen Trafalgars'.

2437 HINTS respecting the means of civilizing Africa. [London, 1808?] 8 pp.

> The abolition act could liberate most of West Africa from the slave trade; Britain should take over all European settlements and consolidate them to prevent a revival.

2438 *CUNHA DE AZEREDO COUTINHO José Joaquim da, *Bishop of Elvas*
Analyse sobre a justiça do comercio do resgate dos escravos da costa da Africa, novamente revista e acrescentada pelo seu autor . . . João Rodrigues Neues, Lisboa, 1808. xv, 114 pp.

> Defence of the African slave trade, originally published 1798 (2209). See (2631).

2439a GRÉGOIRE, Henri Baptiste
De la littérature des nègres, ou recherches sur leurs facultés intellectuelles, leurs qualités morales et leur littérature; suivies de notices sur la vie et les ouvrages des nègres qui se sont distingués dans les sciences, les lettres et les arts. Maradan, Paris, 1808. xvi, 287 pp.

Translated as:

2439b An enquiry concerning the intellectual and moral faculties, and literature of negroes; followed with an account of the life and works of fifteen negroes & mulattoes, distinguished in science, literature and the arts. Thomas Kirk, [New York,] 1810. 253 pp.

> Dedicated to 275 named abolitionists; attacks racialist assumptions by describing the achievements of negroes. See (1840, 2442).

2440 *CUNHA DE AZEREDO COUTINHO, José Joaquim da, *Bishop of Elvas*
Concordância das leis de Portugal e das bullas pontificias, das quaes umas permittem a escravidão dos pretos d'Africa e outras prohibem a escravidão dos Indios do Brasil. J. Rodrigues Neves, Lisboa, 1808. 21 pp.

> Attacks 'French reformers'.

2441 *SIDNEY, Joseph
An oration, commemorative of the abolition of the slave trade in the United States; delivered before the Wilberforce Philanthropic Association in the city of New-York, on the second of January, 1809. J. Seymour, New-York, 1809. 20 pp.

2442 CRI des colons contre un ouvrage de M. l'evêque et senateur Grégoire,

ayant pour titre De la littérature des
nègres, ou réfutation des inculpations
calomnieuses faites aux colons par
l'auteur, et par les autres philosophes
négrophiles, tels que Raynal, Valmont de
Bomare, etc. . . . Dissertation sur l'esclavage. Delaunay, Paris, 1810. 312 pp.

By F. R. de Tussac. Grégoire's
work (2439) was really abolitionist;
African barbarity had not been
caused by the slave trade.

2443 HARRISON, George
Some remarks on a communication
from Wm. Roscoe to the Duke of
Gloucester, dated March 20, 1809, as
stated in the appendix of the third
report of the African Institution . . .
George Ellerton, London, 1810. 11 pp.

Before legitimate commerce can replace the slave trade, Africa must be
prepared through 'social improvement'. (Also printed in: Philanthropist, London, vol. 1, 1811, pp. 176–
80.) See (2445).

2444 *ANTILLON Y MARZO, Isidoro de
Disertacion sobre el orígen de la
esclavitud de los negros, motivos que
la han perpetuado, ventajas que se le
atribuyen y medios que podrían adoptarse para hacer prosperar nuestras
colonias sin la esclavitud de los negros.
Leida en la Real Academia Madrileña,
de Derecho el 2 de abril de 1802.
M. Domingo, Mallorca, 1811. 125 pp.

The African slave trade should be
renounced by Europe and replaced
with colonies between Senegal and
Angola; slavery should be abolished
and replaced with Indian labour
in America.

2445 REPLY to "Some remarks (by George
Harrison) on a communication from
William Roscoe to the Duke of Gloucester, president of the African Institution, dated March 20, 1809." (Signed:
W.R.) M. Galway & Co., Liverpool,
[1811]. 8 pp.

By William Roscoe. The development of trade with Africa should be
a primary object of the Institution,
without excluding 'civilizing' efforts,
to put an end to the slave trade.
(Reprinted from: Philanthropist, London, vol. 1, 1811, pp. 223–28.) See
(2443, 2449).

2446 *HICKS, Elias
Observations on the slavery of the
Africans and their descendants. Recom-
mended to the serious perusal, and

impartial consideration of the citizens
of the United States of America, and
others concerned . . . Samuel Wood,
New York, 1811. 24 pp.

Owners have no moral right to hold
slaves taken by violence in Africa.

2447 *The WEST Indians defended against
the accusations of their calumniators;
or, facts versus prejudices. By a gentleman. (Signed: Edward White.) Mawman, Bath, London, 1811. 40 pp.

By E. S. Byam. Colonial slavery is
better than life in Africa and the
slave trade should be 'applauded
and encouraged'. (Reviewed in: ER,
vol. 19, Nov. 1811, pp. 129–35.)

2448 'ACCOUNT of a society to promote
the civilization of Africa, and of
some attempts to evade the act for the
abolition of the slave trade.' (Philanthropist, London, vol. 1, 1811, pp.
42–58.)

Describes the African Institution,
founded 1807.

2449 HARRISON, George
'Additional remarks intended to further
the purpose of civilization in Africa.'
(Philanthropist, London, vol. 1, 1811,
pp. 291–302.)

Reply to (2445): in combatting the
slave trade one must 'not do evil that
good may come of it'.

2450 'SLAVE Trade Felony Act.' (Philanthropist, London, vol. 1, 1811, pp.
369–75.)

Welcomes the act and reprints a
letter to The Times (signed 'Mercator')
urging more forceful action against
Portuguese and Spanish slave traders.

2451 *GAISFORD, Stephen
An essay on the good effects which
may be derived in the British West
Indies in consequence of the abolition
of the African slave trade; including an
inquiry into the present insular policy
of those colonies . . . R. Baldwin (etc.),
London, 1811. viii, 236 pp.

2452 'SOBRE a impolitica, e injustiça da
falla, e moçaõ, que no dia 10 de julho
fez Mr. Wilberforce na Camara dos
Communs.' (IPI, vol. 7, 1813, pp.
377–91.)

Wilberforce had falsely accused Portugal of increasing her slave trade,
which was allowed by the treaty of
1810.

2453 *PROYECTO relativo al comercio, suerte y servidumbre de los esclavos, inclinado a su transición oportuna a libres, durante el tiempo que debe continuar la introducción en territorios españoles. Cádiz, 1813. 55, 157 pp.

> Contains 'expositions' by F. de Arango and the Marquis de Someruelos against the proposals to abolish the slave trade advanced 1811 by Guridi y Alcocer and Argüelles.

2454 BOSQUEXO del comercio en esclavos: y reflexiones sobre este tráfico considerado moral, politica, y cristianamente. Ellerton & Henderson, London, 1814. viii, 144 pp. illus.

> By José Maria Blanco y Crespo. Description of the slave trade, largely translated from (2265) with arguments from the Spanish abolition controversy in 1811. See (2564).

2455 'ALVARÁ sobre o commercio da escravatura e sua analyse.' (Portuguez, Londres, vol. 1, no. 1, abril 1814, pp. 70–87.)

> Text of the Portuguese slave trade decree of 24 Nov. 1813, with critical notes.

2456 'REVIVAL of the slave trade.' (ER, vol. 23, April 1814, pp. 131–50.)

> Criticises renewed French slave trading.

2457 'MEMORIAL da Casa dos Pares em Parlamento, ao Principe Regente do Reyno Unido, sobre o commercio da escravatura.' (Portuguez, Londres, vol. 1, no. 2, junho 1814, pp. 146–52.)

> Address to the Prince Regent and his reply (3173), with critical notes.

2458 'FRENCH slave trade.' (CO, vol. 13, June 1814, pp. 396–408.)

> By Z. Macaulay. Attack on the treaty allowing France to continue the slave trade for five years.

2459 'ADDRESS to the inhabitants of the British empire on the subject of the slave trade'. (Signed: Alfred.) (SM, vol. 76, July 1814, pp. 510–12.)

> By T. Clarkson? Condemns the permission given to France (in the peace treaty 30 May 1814) to continue the trade and hopes that the congress at Vienna will reverse this. 'Let the voice of the British nation once declare itself, and the African slave trade must universally cease.'

2460 'REVIVAL of the French slave trade.' (CO, vol. 13, July 1814, pp. 463–69.)

2461 'TRAFFICO da escravatura.' (Portuguez, Londres, vol. 1, no. 3, julho 1814, pp. 239–43.)

> Britain should not meddle in Portugal's internal affairs; the government can attempt abolition in Brazil only at the risk of bloody revolution.

2462 GISBORNE, Thomas
The substance of the speech of the Rev. Thomas Gisborne, M.A. on July 13th 1814. At a general meeting of the county of Stafford convened to deliberate on petitions to the two houses of parliament, respecting the abolition of the slave trade . . . T. Cadell & W. Davies, London, 1814. 30 pp.

> Supports a motion asking the government to force France and other European powers to abolish their slave trade at the approaching peace conference.

2463 OBSERVATIONS on the late treaty of peace with France; so far as it relates to the slave trade: in a letter to a friend. (Signed: Liber.) J. Butterworth & Son, London, 1814. 23 pp.

> The permission given to France to revive their slave trade for five years will have terrible effects in Africa; it could be reversed at the coming congress of the powers.

2464 *OBSERVATIONS on that part of the late treaty of peace with France, which relates to the African slave trade . . . Ellerton & Henderson, London, [1814]. 12 pp.

2465 *REMARKS on that article in the late treaty of peace, which permits a French slave trade for five years. Kendal, 1814.

2466 APPEL aux souverains réunis à Paris, pour en obtenir l'abolition de la traite des nègres. Ellerton & Henderson, Londres, [1814]. 7 pp.

> By the Baroness de Staël. Appeal to the allied sovereigns to enforce the abolition of the slave trade by all European states, following the example of Britain.

2467 APPEL aux nations commerçantes et maritimes de l'Europe, ou réflexions rapides et impartiales sur la question de la traite. Poulet, Paris, 1814. 52 pp.

Questions Britain's right to make France abandon the slave trade.

2468 'The SLAVE trade.' (Philanthropist, London, vol. 4, 1814, pp. 278–91.)

Deplores the permission given to France to continue the slave trade for five years; it should be banned on certain parts of the African coast.

2469 HARRISON, George
'Facts interesting to humanity.' (Philanthropist, London, vol. 4, 1814, pp. 291–92.)

Petition to Parliament expressing 'painful regret' for the slave trade clause in the treaty with France.

2470 *SIMONDE DE SISMONDI, Jean Charles Léonard
Nouvelles réflexions sur la traite des nègres. J.-J. Paschoud, Genève, 1814. 46 pp.

Reprinted in (2484).

2471 CONSIDÉRATIONS générales sur les trois classes qui peuplent les colonies françaises, et sur tout ce qui concerne leur administration intérieure. Poulet, Paris, 1814. viii, 424 pp.

Old-fashioned defence of the slave trade as advantageous to the Africans, by a planter from St. Domingue.

2472 DILLON, Henri
Mémoire sur l'esclavage colonial, la necessité des colonies et l'abolition de la traite des nègres. J.-J. Blaise, Paris, 1814. 41 pp.

Defends slavery and the slave trade as necessary to maintain the French colonies.

2473 *CLARKSON, Thomas
Dangers du commerce des esclaves africains; traduite de l'anglais. Paris, 1814. 144 pp.

2474 *NANTES: Chambre de Commerce
Observations de la Chambre de Commerce de Nantes sur la traite des noirs et la restauration de Saint-Domingue. Brun, Nantes, [1814]. 18 pp.

Abolition of the slave trade, demanded by England in its own interest, will ruin the colonies and French commerce.

2475 *PALISOT DE BEAUVOIS, Ambroise Marie François Joseph, *baron*
Refutation d'un écrit intitulé: Résumé du temoignage . . . touchant la traite des nègres, adressé aux différentes

puissances de la chrétienté . . . Blanchard, Paris. 1814. 56 pp.

Defends the slave trade. See (20).

2476 BERQUIN, ——
Sentimens des colons de Saint-Domingue, envers leur monarque et leur patrie. C. L. F. Panckoucke, Paris, 1814. 28 pp.

Loyal addresses to Louis XVIII urging continuation of the French slave trade; England has no right to propose its abolition.

2477 ROBBERDS, John Warden
A speech intended to have been delivered at the public meeting, held the first of July 1814 on the subject of the slave trade, at St. Andrew's Hall Norwich. Stevenson, Matchett & Stevenson, Norwich, 1814. 16 pp.

2478 CARTWRIGHT, John
Letters to Clarkson on African and English freedom. John M'Creery, London, 1814. iv, 32 pp.

2479 'COMMERCIO da escravatura. Extracto do Times do dia 6 d'outubro, respondendo a algumas invectivas, que nos periodicos franceses se fasem ás pertençoens dos Ingleses sobre a absoluta, e geral abolição da escravatura.' (Portuguez, Londres, vol. 1, sept. 1814, pp. 543–48.)

Criticises the 'pharisaical humanity' of the British government in detaining Portuguese slave ships.

2480 REMARKS on the ordonnance issued at Paris, the 29th August 1814; for the re-establishment of the French slave trade, and on the proposition submitted to the Chamber of Deputies by General Desfourneaux, on the subject of St. Domingo: with notices respecting the present state of that island. Extracted from the Christian Observer for September 1814. J. Hatchard, London, 1814. 17 pp.

Reprinted from: CO, vol. 13, 1814, pp. 603–14; France may hope to restore slavery in Haiti with new African slaves. (Reviewed in: EF, vol. 24, 1814, pp. 124–31.)

2481 MALENFANT, ——
Des colonies, et particulièrement de celle de Saint-Domingue; mémoire historique et politique . . . Audibert, Paris, 1814. xii, 334 pp.

Warns against the danger of trying to reimpose slavery in St. Domingue;

the extension of the slave trade should be used to import new slaves who would be freed after nine years of work.

2482 SIMONDE DE SISMONDI, Jean Charles Léonard
De l'intérêt de la France à l'égard de la traite des nègres. J. J. Paschoud, Genève, 1814. 59 pp.

Continuing the slave trade to restore the plantation economy in St. Domingue would drain France of her remaining capital; she should accept the situation and adopt a free trade policy.

2483 HOMO, *pseud.*
'A few suggestions on the slave trade.' (Pamphleteer, London, vol. 4, 1814, pp. 227–31.)

The French treaty should be allowed to stand, in the hope that the congress at Vienna will 'bring the business to a more favourable issue'.

2484 SIMONDE DE SISMONDI, Jean Charles Léonard
De l'intérêt de la France à l'égard de la traite des nègres . . . Troisième édition, contenant de Nouvelles réflexions sur la traite des nègres. J. J. Paschoud, Genève; John Murray, London, 1814. 100 pp.

Restoring the slave trade would be a crime against the Africans.

2485 CONSIDÉRATIONS importantes sur l'abolition générale de la traite des nègres, adressées aux négociateurs des puissances continentales qui doivent assister au congrès de Vienne. Par un Portugais. Ant. Bailleul; Mme. Goullet, Delaunay, Paris, 1814. 31 pp.

Britain's abolition policy aims at ruining the colonies of other nations and gaining a monopoly of Asian and African commerce; she has no right to force immediate abolition on other states.

2486 VASTEY, J. L., *baron de*
Le système colonial dévoilé. P. Roux, Cap-Henry, 1814. viii, 96 pp.

Calls Haitians to rally against their French ex-masters who insist on continuing the slave trade, a 'monstrosity'.

2487 'REVIVAL of the slave trade.' (ER, vol. 24, Nov. 1814, pp. 106–33.)

Review of recent French and English publications.

2488a WILBERFORCE, William
A letter to His Excellency the Prince of Talleyrand Perigord, &c. &c. &c. on the subject of the slave trade. J. Hatchard; Cadell & Davies, London, 1814. 83 pp.

Translated as:

2488b Lettre à son Excellence Monseigneur le Prince de Talleyrand Périgord . . . au sujet de la traite des negres . . . Schulze & Dean, London, 1814. 98 pp.

Urges Talleyrand to use his influence in France to abolish the slave trade although it had been permitted for a further five years. (Reprinted in: Pamphleteer, London, vol. 5, 1815, pp. 353–97.)

2489 'FRENCH slave trade, and present state of Domingo.' (Philanthropist, London, vol. 5, 1815, pp. 37–61.)

Review of (2481) and (2484).

2490 THORPE, Robert
A letter to William Wilberforce, Esq. M.P. vice president of the African Institution, &c. &c. &c. containing remarks on the reports of the Sierra Leone Company, and African Institution: with hints respecting the means by which an universal abolition of the slave trade might be carried into effect. F. C. & J. Rivington, London, 1815. 84 pp.

Criticises the abolitionists for their methods of attacking the foreign slave trade and charges representatives of the old Sierra Leone Company with being involved in it. See (2491, 2494, 2499).

2491 MACAULAY, Zachary
A letter to His Royal Highness the Duke of Gloucester, president of the African Institution . . . occasioned by a pamphlet lately published by Dr. Thorpe . . . entitled "A letter to William Wilberforce, Esq." . . . Second edition, enlarged. John Hatchard, London, 1815. 62, *58 pp.

Reply to Thorpe's allegations (2490) regarding Macaulay's business interests in the Sierra Leone Company and his views on the slave trade and related matters. See (2497, 2533).

2492 'COMMERCIO de escravatura. (Extracto do Morning Chronicle, de 6 de fevereiro.)' (Portuguez, Londres, vol. 2, fev. 1815, pp. 379–81.)

Attack on Thorpe as typifying the hypocrisy of British philanthropists.

2493 'COMMERCIO de escravatura. (Artigo extrahido de Courier, de 25 de fevereiro, 1815.)' (Portuguez, Londres, vol. 2, março 1815, pp. 431–33.)

Account of negotiations at Vienna leading to the slave trade convention of 7 February.

2494 *THORPE, Robert
Preface to the third edition of A letter to William Wilberforce . . . Containing a reply to an attack on this letter by F. Horner, Esq., M.P., in the House of Commons . . . 23rd February, and an answer to the report of a Committee of the African Institution, read and approved by their board of directors. February 28, 1815. F. C. & J. Rivington, London, 1815. xxvii pp.

Horner, a director of the African Institution, had repudiated Thorpe's charges (2490).

2495 *MAZÈRES, F.
Lettre à M. J.-C.-L. Sismonde de Sismondi sur les nègres, la civilisation de l'Afrique, Christophe et le comte de Limonade. Renard, Paris, 1815. 56 pp.

See (2482, 2484).

2496 *An ADDRESS to William Wilberforce, Esq., M.P. With remarks on the result of his attempt to ameliorate the condition of Africans, by the abolition of the slave trade, slavery, the servitude or actual condition of negroes, or those called slaves, in Jamaica; and on the injuries inflicted on and threatened the planters and others, in consequence of this attempt. Inverness, 1815.

2497 THORPE, Robert
Preface to the fourth edition of A letter to William Wilberforce, Esq., M.P. containing a reply to a letter from Zachary Macaulay, Esq. to the Duke of Gloucester. F. C. & J. Rivington, London, 1815. lvi pp.

Repeats his allegations against Macaulay (2491) and the Sierra Leone Company. See (2498).

2498 MACAULAY, Zachary
A letter to His Royal Highness the Duke of Gloucester . . . Second edition, enlarged. John Hatchard, London, 1815. 62, 58 pp.

Reply to (2497); the second part contains a memoir of 1808 on a scheme for ransoming African slaves for indentured labour.

2499 AFRICAN INSTITUTION
Special report of the directors of the African Institution, made at the annual general meeting, on the 12th of April, 1815, respecting the allegations concontained in a pamphlet entitled "A letter to William Wilberforce, Esq. &c. by R. Thorpe, Esq. &c." J. Hatchard, London, 1815. 157 pp.

See (2490, 2502).

2500a DE la traite et de l'esclavage des noirs et des blancs; par un ami des hommes de toutes les couleurs. Adrien Egron, Paris, 1815. 84 pp.

Translated as:

2500b On the slave trade and on the slavery of the blacks and of the whites. By a friend of all colours . . . To which are annexed, prefatory observations and notes; by the translator. Josiah Conder, London, 1815. xi, 89 pp.

By Henri Grégoire. Discusses the history of the abolition movement and old accusations against the abolitionists; the slave traders hope that the slave trade will be prolonged indefinitely, but the powers of Europe should declare it to be piracy.

2501 'NEGOTIATIONS on the slave trade.' (BR, vol. 6, Aug. 1815, pp. 118–56.)

Review article, describing the negotiations at Vienna.

2502 THORPE, Robert
A reply "point by point" to the Special report of the directors of the African Institution. F. C. & J. Rivington, London, 1815. 113 pp.

Elaboration of his accusations against the Institution of supporting the slave trade and slavery in Sierra Leone and of acting illegally against slave traders, settlers and recaptured slaves. See (2499, 2505).

2503 AFRICAN INSTITUTION
Reasons for establishing a registry of slaves in the British colonies: being a report of a committee of the African Institution. J. Hatchard, London, 1815. 118 pp.

By James Stephen. The only way to prevent illicit importation of slaves to the British colonies is to institute a public registry (Also printed in: Pamphleteer, London, vol. 7, no. 13, 1816, pp. 34–85.) See (1900, 2504, 2506, 2510).

2504 'GENERAL registry of slaves.' (ER, vol. 25, Oct. 1815, pp. 315–45.)

Urges support for registration proposed by the African Institution.
See (2503).

2505 THORPE, Robert
Postscript to the Reply "point by
by point;" containing an exposure of
the misrepresentation of the treatment of
the captured negroes at Sierra Leone;
and other matters arising from the
ninth report of the African Institution.
F. C. & J. Rivington, London, 1815.
64 pp.

Reply to the Institution's defence
against his allegations (2490). See
(2511).

2506 A REVIEW of the reasons given for
establishing a registry of slaves in the
British colonies in a report of a committee of the African Institution,
entitled "Reasons," &c. &c. Ellerton &
Henderson: London, [1816]. 32 pp.

Supports the proposal for registration to prevent violations of the
abolition act. (Reprinted from: CO,
vol. 15, Jan. 1816, pp. 28–59.) See
(2503, 2515).

2507 'AFRICAN Institution and the slave
trade.' (Anti-Jacobin Review, London,
vol. 50, 1816, pp. 134–48, 278–86,
329–41, 636–58, 750–84; vol. 51, 1816–
17, pp. 33–50, 146–64, 502–15.)

Review of various works in the
controversy between Thorpe and
the African Institution, taking the
side of the former against the 'fanat-
icism' of the philanthropists.

2508 KOSTER, Henry
Travels in Brazil. Longman, Hurst,
Rees, Orme & Brown, London, 1816.
ix, 501 pp.

Ch. 20: 'Impolicy of the slave trade.'

2509 MATHISON, Gilbert Farquhar
A short review of the reports of the
African Institution, and of the controversy with Dr. Thorpe, with some
reasons against the registry of slaves
in the British colonies. W. Stockdale;
James Asperne, London, 1816. x,
78 pp.

See (2511).

2510 THOUGHTS on the abolition of the
slave trade, and civilization of Africa;
with remarks on the African Institution,
and an examination of the report of
their committee, recommending a general registry of slaves in the British

West India islands. J. M. Richardson;
J. Ridgway, London, 1816. vii, 235 pp.

By Joseph Marryat, agent for Grenada. Abolition acts and the Sierra
Leone settlement have failed to stop
the slave trade, but registration of
slaves is unjustified as there is no
illicit importation to the West Indies.
See (2503, 2512).

2511 MATHISON, Gilbert Farquhar
A short review of the reports of the
African Institution, and of the controversy with Dr. Thorpe, with some
reasons against the registry of slaves
in the British colonies . . . Second edition, with additions and notes. Wm.
Stockdale; James Asperne, London,
1816. 115 pp.

Supports the criticisms of the African
Institution in (2505); the registration
bill aims at emancipation and is
unwarranted and unconstitutional.

2512 An EXPOSURE of some of the numerous mistatements and misrepresentations contained in a pamphlet commonly
known by the name of Mr. Marryatt's
pamphlet, entitled "Thoughts on the
abolition of the slave trade and the
civilization of Africa, with remarks on
the African Institution . . ." John
Hatchard, London, 1816. 65 pp.

Defends the Sierra Leone government and African Institution from
Marryat's accusations; the registry
bill is justified as the best way of
preventing illegal slave trade. See
(2510, 2522).

2513 *PARROTT, Russell
An address on the abolition of the slave-
trade, delivered before the different
African benevolent societies, on the
1st of January, 1816 . . . T. S. Manning,
Philadelphia, 1816. 12 pp.

2514 JORDAN, Gibbs Walker
An examination of the principles of
the slave registry bill, and of the means
of emancipation, proposed by the
authors of the bill. T. Cadell & W.
Davies, London, 1816. 147 pp.

Opposes emancipation as interference
with the political rights of the colonies;
as there is no illicit slave trade the
bill is unnecessary and possibly
unconstitutional. (By the agent for
Barbados).

2515 *VENABLES, Thomas
The reviewer reviewed; or some cursory observations upon an article in

The Christian Observer for January, 1816, respecting the slave registry bill. In a letter to a member of parliament. London, 1816. 32 pp.

Opposes the registration scheme. Reply to (2506).

2516 BRIEF remarks on the slave registry bill; and upon a special report of the African Institution, recommending that measure. J. M. Richardson; J. Ridgeway, London, 1816. 67 pp.

Contraband trade in slaves has not been proved; the colonists must decide about slavery. (Reprinted in: Pamphleteer, London, vol. 17, no. 14, 1816, pp. 545–95.)

2517 OBSERVATIONS on the bill introduced last session, by Mr. Wilberforce, for the more effectually preventing the unlawful importation of slaves, and the holding of free persons in slavery in the British colonies. J. M. Richardson, London, 1816. 28 pp.

The bill suggested by the African Institution would be an infringement of the property rights of the colonists and was uncalled for; the abolitionists should turn their attention to the poor in Britain.

2518 STEPHEN, James
A defence of the bill for the registration of slaves . . . in letters to William Wilberforce Esq. M.P. Letter the first. J. Butterworth & Son; J. Hatchard, London, 1816. 50 pp.

Reply to (2510–11, 2516–17). These are largely 'insidious apologies for the slave trade' rather than arguments against registration. (Reviewed in: Philanthropist, London, vol. 6, 1816, pp. 132–46.) See (2520).

2519 'SLAVE trade.' (Signed: Sierra Leone!) (GM, April, 1816, p. 321.)

British capital may still be involved in the slave trade; there is a press campaign against suppression of the slave trade. See (2521).

2520 STEPHEN, James
A defence of the bill for the registration of slaves . . . Letter the second. J. Butterworth & Son; J. Hatchard, London, 1816. 218 pp.

The danger of slave smuggling is real. (Reviewed in: Philanthropist, London, vol. 6, 1816, pp. 173–99.) See (2518, 2522, 2526, 2533).

2521 'SLAVE registry bill unnecessary.' (Signed: S. D. D.) (GM, May 1816, pp. 390–92.)

Answer to (2519). Illicit slave trade does not exist. See (2532).

2522 MARRYAT, Joseph
More thoughts, occasioned by two publications which the authors call "An exposure of some of the numerous misstatements and misrepresentations contained in a pamphlet, commonly known by the name of Mr. Marryat's pamphlet, entitled Thoughts, &c." and "A defence of the bill for the registration of slaves." J. M. Richardson; J. Ridgway, London, 1816. vii, 143 pp.

Repeats his attacks on the African Institution and Sierra Leone; the proponents of the registry bill (2512, 2518, 2520) are revolutionary fanatics aiming at the abolition of slavery. See (2538).

2523 The INTERFERENCE of the British legislature, in the internal concerns of the West India islands, respecting their slaves, deprecated. By a zealous advocate for the abolition of the slave trade. J. Mawman, London, 1816. 58 pp.

The registry bill would infringe the political rights of the colonies.

2524 *ORDERSON, J. W.
Cursory remarks and plain facts connected with the question produced by the proposed slave registry bill. Hatchard, London, 1816. 35 pp.

2525 REMARKS on the insurrection in Barbados, and the bill for the registration of slaves. Ellerton & Henderson, London, 1816. 15 pp.

The recent revolt was blamed on Wilberforce's bill to prevent illegal slave imports, but the settlers themselves contributed by describing it as emancipationist.

2526 OBSERVATIONS upon the oligarchy, or committee of soi-disant saints, in a letter to the Right Honourable Viscount Sidmouth . . . By an hereditary planter. Edmund Lloyd, London, 1816. 67 pp.

Primarily an attack on (2518, 2520). The African Institution intended the registry bill to prepare for emancipation; the 'saints' are fanatics responsible for the Barbados insurrection and the cost of the antislavery squadron; shortage of labour in the colonies might necessitate renewal of the slave trade.

P

2527 A LETTER to the members of the imperial parliament, referring to the evidence contained in the proceedings of the House of Assembly of Jamaica, and shewing the injurious and unconstitutional tendency of the proposed slave registry bill. By a colonist. J. M. Richardson, London, 1816. 24 pp.

The bill is unjustified and an attack on private property; the African Institution has already caused £900,000 to be spent on indemnifying Portugal for illegal capture of her ships and for abolishing the slave trade.

2528 'The SLAVE trade—since the treaty for its general abolition.' (Signed: A. H.) (GM, July 1816, pp. 27–28; Aug. 1816, pp. 118–19.)

2529 NEGRO emancipation made easy; with reflections on the African Institution, and slave registry bill. By a British planter. Edmund Lloyd, [London,] 1816. 94 pp.

The African Institution has given no proof of illicit slave trade to the West Indies while it allows slavery and the slave trade to continue at Sierra Leone (2490); gradual emancipation is possible if the philanthropists raise the money to buy the slaves and free them.

2530 The PENAL enactments of the slave registry bill examined, in a letter to Charles N. Pallmer, Esq. M.P. J. M. Richardson, London, 1816. 56 pp.

The penalties for not registering slaves are too heavy; the real intent of the bill, justifiable only if illegal slave trade were proved, is to accomplish 'emancipation in disguise'.

2531 'SLAVE trade, and slave registry question,' (BR, vol. 8, Aug. 1816, pp. 218–80.)

Review of recent works supporting registration.

2532 'OBSERVATIONS on the slave registry bill.' (Signed: S. D. D.) (GM, Aug. 1816, pp. 123–26.)

Smuggling does not exist but the bill has led to slave risings. See (2521, 2534).

2533 The EDINBURGH Review and the West Indies; with observations on the pamphlets of Messrs. Stephen, Macaulay, &c. and remarks on the slave registry bill. By a colonist. John Smith & Son, Glasgow; (etc.), 1816. xv, 360 pp.

Attack on the registry bill. The abolitionists aim at emancipation and 'African sovereignty' in the West Indies, which would be fatal. With notes on the slave trade in Africa and the development of commerce with the interior via the Niger and Congo rivers. See (2491, 2518, 2520).

2534 'ON the slave trade, and the registry bill.' (Signed: A. H.) (GM, Sept. 1816, pp. 226–27.)

Reply to (2532).

2535 CHALMERS, George
Proofs and demonstrations how much the projected registry of colonial negroes is unfounded and uncalled for: comprehending, the reports and resolves of the Bahama Assembly, on the principle and detail of the proposed registry: with the examinations, on oath, of the most respectable persons, as to the facts of the case. The whole arranged, and an introduction prefixed, by George Chalmers, F.R.S. S.A. Thomas Egerton, London, 1816. xiii, 55 pp.

Slaves have not been illegally imported; Parliament should not interfere with slavery in the colonies. (Official documents edited by the agent for the Bahamas.) See (2537).

2536 ANTIDOTE to 'West Indian sketches,' drawn from authentic sources. Whitmore & Fenn, London, 1816–17. no. 1–5.

Attacks the 'calumnies' published in the African Institution's series of 'West Indian sketches' (London, 1816–17).

2537 ARGUMENTS in support of the proposed bill for the registration of slaves in the West Indian colonies; being a reply to the work of Mr. Chalmers, entitled Proofs and demonstrations how much the projected registry of colonial negroes is unfounded and uncalled for . . . Extracted from The Philanthropist for Jan. 1817 . . . Bensley & Son, London, 1817. 44 pp.

Defends the proponents of registration against charges of being 'anarchists'; the abolition acts are clearly insufficient to prevent the illegal slave trade. Review of (2535), reprinted from: Philanthropist, London, vol. 6, 1817, pp. 292–327.

2538 STEPHEN, James
The speech of James Stephen, Esq. at

the annual meeting of the African Institution, at Free-Masons' Hall, on the 26th March, 1817 . . . J. Butterworth & Son; J. Hatchard, London, 1817. 56 pp.

Reply to Marryat's attacks on the registry bill and on the African Institution (2510, 2522); opponents of the bill are friends of the slave trade. See (2542).

2539 KENRICK, John
Horrors of slavery, in two parts. Part I. Containing observations, facts, and arguments, extracted from the speeches of Wilberforce, Grenville, Pitt, Burke, Fox, Martin, Whitbread, and other distinguished members of the British parliament. Part II. Containing extracts, chiefly American, compiled from authentic sources; demonstrating that slavery is impolitic, antirepublican, unchristian, and highly criminal; and proposing measures for its complete abolition through the United States. Cummings & Hilliard; Lincoln & Edmands, Boston, 1817. 59 pp.

Speeches against the slave trade extracted from (3584).

2540 'CONSIDERATIONS on the British commerce, with reference particularly to British India, the United States of America, and the slave trade.' (Pamphleteer, London, vol. 11, 1817, pp. 265–75.)

Only free-labour production of tropical crops can supplant the slave trade.

2541 THORPE, Robert
A view of the present increase of the slave trade, the cause of that increase, and suggesting a mode for effecting its total annihilation: with observations on the African Institution and Edinburgh Review, and on the speeches of Messrs. Wilberforce and Brougham, delivered in the House of Commons, 7th July, 1817; also a plan submitted for civilizing Africa, and for introducing free labourers into our colonies in the West Indies. Longman, Hurst, Rees, Orme, & Brown, London, 1818. iv, 128 pp.

The slave trade carried on by other nations must be suppressed; British establishments along the coast of Africa will help to civilise Africa and procure voluntary labour for the West Indies.

2542 MARRYAT, Joseph
More thoughts still on the state of the West India colonies, and the proceedings of the African Institution: with observations on the speech of James Stephen, Esq. at the annual meeting of that society, held on the 26th of March, 1817. J. M. Richardson; Ridgways, London, 1818. 147 pp.

The Institution has falsely denied any responsibility for the Barbados insurrection and that their aim is emancipation; it has aggravated the slave trade by urging the capture of slavers and caused great expense on bounties, court cases and payments to Portugal and Spain for abolishing the slave trade. See (2538).

2543 L'EUROPE châtiée, et l'Afrique vengée, ou raisons pour regarder les calamités du siècle comme des punitions infligées par la providence pour la traite des nègres. Schulze & Dean, Londres, 1818. 124 pp.

Translation of a series of letters in a London newspaper addressed to the sovereigns at the congress of Aix-la-Chapelle, urging 'un pacte grand et perpétuel' to suppress the slave trade, which should be declared piracy. (Reviewed in: Chronique Religieuse, Paris, vol. 2, 1819, pp. 121–32.) See (2547).

2544 'ADDRESS to congregated sovereigns on slave trade.' (CO, vol. 17, Nov. 1818, pp. 714–20.)

Translation of address presented to the congress at Aix-la-Chapelle. See (2556).

2545 WALSH, Robert
An appeal from the judgments of Great Britain respecting the United States of America . . . Mitchell, Ames & White, Philadelphia, 1819. lvi, 512 pp.

Sect. 9: 'Of the existence of negro slavery in the United States, and of the British abolition of the slave trade.' Having forced slavery on the American colonies, Britain's abolition of the slave trade is self-interested and hypocritical. (J. A. Saco's analysis of this work in Revista Bimestre Cubana, June 1832, contains the first discussion of the illegal Cuban slave trade to be published in Havana; see his: Obras, Nueva York, 1853, vol. 2, pp. 349–415.)

2546 HAZLITT, William
'Prince Maurice's parrot; or, French instructions to a British plenipoten-

tiary.' *In his*: Political essays (London, 1819), pp. 71–74.

> Article of Sept. 1814 reprinted; satirical attack on Castlereagh's handling of the French slave trade question.

2547 ROSIERS, Juste Chanlatte de, *comte*
Hayti reconnaissante en réponse à un écrit, imprimé à Londres, et intitulée: L'Europe chatiée, et l'Afrique vengée... Imprimerie Royale, Sans-Souci [Haiti], 1819. 24 pp.

> Europe's troubles are due to its crimes in Africa and America, but Britain's opposition to the slave trade is unprecedented in world history; the abolitionists should now support recognition of Haiti's independence. See (2543).

2548 THORPE, Robert
A commentary on the treaties entered into between His Britannic Majesty and His Most Faithful Majesty, signed at London, the 28th of July, 1817; between His Britannic Majesty, and His Catholic Majesty, signed at Madrid, the 23rd of September, 1817; and between His Britannic Majesty, and His Majesty the King of the Netherlands, signed at The Hague, the 4th of May, 1818. For the purpose of preventing their subjects from engaging in any illicit traffic in slaves. Longman, Hurst, Rees, Orme & Brown; (etc.), London, 1819. 60 pp.

> The treaties still permit and protect the slave trade; the declaration on total abolition of the slave trade at the congress of Vienna should be carried into effect. (Also printed in: Pamphleteer, London, vol. 14, 1819, pp. 417–45.)

2549 ON the practical abolition of the slave trade as intimately blended with the policy and commercial prosperity of Great Britain. Addressed to His Royal Highness the Prince Regent. (Signed: Aristides.) London, 1819. vii, 63 pp.

> Intercepting slave ships at sea is futile; the best way to annihilate the trade is to establish a British military base in the Cape Verd islands.

2550 *AMERICAN COLONIZATION SOCIETY
Memorial of the president and board of managers of the American Colonization Society. February 3, 1820. Referred to the Committee on so much of the President's message as relates to the slave trade. Gales & Seaton, Washington, 1820. 7 pp.

> Published by the House of Representatives.

2551 AFRICAN INSTITUTION
A review of the colonial slave registration acts, in a report of a committee of the board of directors of the African Institution, made on the 22d of February, 1820, and published by order of that board. Hatchard & Son, London, 1820. 139 pp.

> Analysis of the defects of colonial slave laws.

2552 STORY, Joseph
Slavery & the slave trade. From judge Story's charge to the grand jury of the U.S. Circuit Court, in Portsmouth, N. H.—May term 1820. [Portsmouth, N. H., 1820.] 8 pp.

> On the illegal slave trade, in which Americans are still involved.

2553 *STORY, Joseph
A charge delivered to the grand jury of the Circuit Court of the United States, at its first session in Portland, for the judicial district of Maine, May 8, 1820 . . . A. Shirley, Portland, 1820. 21 pp.

> Mostly on the slave trade.

2554 *MORÉNAS, Joseph Elzéar
Pétition contre la traite des noirs qui se fait au Sénégal, présentée à la Chambre des députés le 14 juin 1820. Corréard, Paris, 1820. 14 pp.

> Translated in (44). See (2555, 2560).

2555 *GIUDICELLI, Juge André
Observations sur la traite des noirs, en réponse au rapport de M. Courvoisier sur la pétition de M. Morénas, par M. l'abbé Giudicelly, ancien préfet apostolique du Sénégal et de Gorée. Paris, 1820. 27 pp.

> See (2554). Translation in (44).

2556 ADRESSE à leurs majestès impériales et royales, et à leurs représentans au congrès d'Aix-la-Chapelle. [London? 1820?] 24 pp.

> Urges the European powers to abolish slavery. See (2544, 2580).

2557 COQUEREL, Charles Augustin
'Sur la législation anglaise relative à la traite des noirs, et sur l'état des nègres affranchis.' (RE, vol. 7, 1820, pp. 231–51.)

On the British anti-slave trade measures and cases of evasion.

2558 *O'GAVAN, Juan Bernardo
Observaciones sobre la suerte de los negros del Africa, considerados en su propia patria y transplantados a las Antillas españolas; y reclamación contra el tratado celebrado con los Ingleses el año de 1817. Madrid, 1821. 24 pp.

Apologia for the slave trade by a Cuban. See (2559).

2559 BOWRING, Sir John
Contestacion á las Observaciones de D. Juan Bernardo O'Gavan, sobre la suerte de los negros de Africa, y reclamación contra el tratado celebrado con los Ingleses en 1817. Leon Amarita, London, Madrid, 1821. 31 pp.

Defence of the Anglo-Spanish slave trade treaty of 1817 against proposals to annul it. See (2558).

2560 *MORÉNAS, Joseph Elzéar
Seconde pétition contre la traite des noirs, présentée à la Chambre des députés le 19 mars 1821 et à celle des pairs le 26 . . . Mme Jeunehomme-Cremière, Paris, 1821. 62 pp.

See (2554). Reviewed in: RE, vol. 10, 1821, pp. 607–08.

2561 LETTERS from the Havana, during the year 1820; containing an account of the present state of the island of Cuba, and observations on the slave trade. John Miller, London, 1821. viii, 135 pp.

By Robert Francis Jameson. Abolition of the slave trade would be an advantage to Cuba.

2562 *MEJÍA, Antonio
Copia fiel de la representación al Rey constitucional Sr. D. Fernando 7o., por D. Antonio Mejía como apoderado de algunos comerciantes de esta plaza, sobre los procedimientos de algunos señores ministros de hacienda exigiéndoles derechos de internación por negros esclavos traídos de Africa, después de restablecida la constitución política . . . Habana, 1821. 9 pp.

Petition from Cuban merchants, listing all privileges granted for the slave trade by the Spanish government.

2563 BABEY, C. M.
'Examen de cette question: Dans quelles vues l'Angleterre poursuit-elle, depuis 1807, auprès des puissances continentales, l'abolition de la traite

des noirs d'Afrique?' (RE, vol. 10, 1821, pp. 271–82, 482–94.)

Account of the British abolition movement since 1790, praising Wilberforce and the African Institution.

2564 BOSQUÉJO sobre o commercio em escravos, e reflexões sobre este trafico considerado moral, politica, e christãmente. Ellerton & Henderson, Londres, 1821. vii, 98 pp.

By J. M. Blanco y Crespo. Translation of (2454).

2565 *GIUDICELLI, Juge André
Réponse de M. L'abbé Giudicelly, expréfet apostolique du Sénégal et de Gorée, à une lettre de Son Exc. le baron Portal, ministre de la marine, en date du avril 30, 1821. Mme Jeunehomme-Crémière, Paris, 1821. 20 pp.

See (2555).

2566 'FERNANDO Po—State of the slave trade.' (QR, vol. 26, Oct. 1821, pp. 51–82.)

Review of recent publications, urging stronger antislavery measures by Britain, 'a kind of moral blockade'.

2567 MACIEL DA COSTA, João Severiano, marquez de Queluz
Memoria sobre a necessidade de abolir a introdução dos escravos africanos no Brazil; sobre o modo e condiçõis com que esta abolição se deve fazer; e sobre os meios de remediar a falta de braços que ela pode ocasionar . . . Oferecida aos brasileiros seus compatriotas. Imprensa da Universidade, Coimbra, 1821. 90 pp.

Britain had economic and political motives for abolishing the slave trade, but it is contrary to the interests of Brazil, which is being inundated with African slaves; Brazilian agriculture could be maintained with free and immigrant labour.

2568 McQUEEN, James
A geographical and commercial view of northern central Africa: containing a particular account of the course and termination of the great river Niger in the Atlantic Ocean. William Blackwood, Edinburgh; (etc.), 1821. xix, 288 pp. maps.

Slavery and the slave trade can only be rooted out by permanent conquest and colonisation, which would also provide new markets for Britain.

2569 CLARKSON, Thomas
The cries of Africa, to the inhabitants of Europe; or, a survey of that bloody commerce called the slave-trade. Harvey & Darton; W. Phillips, London, [1822]. iv, 50 pp.

Extracts from Mungo Park, British parliamentary papers, etc. describing the horrors of the slave trade. (Also published in French, Spanish, Portuguese, Dutch, and Swedish.) See (4594).

2570 CROPPER, James
Letters addressed to William Wilberforce, M.P. recommending the encouragement of the cultivation of sugar in our dominions in the East Indies, as the natural and certain means of effecting the total and general abolition of the slave-trade. Longman, Hurst, & Co., London, 1822. vii, 54 pp.

Sugar production by free labour in Bengal would be the surest way to destroy the slave trade. See (2572).

2571 *DISCURSO do Arguelles da provincia do Maranhão a S. Magestade Nacional, e Real em Cortes geraes sobre a opinião publica, liberdade civil, e commercio da escravatura. (Signed: M. P. S.) João Nunes Esteves, Lisboa, 1822. 16 pp.

By Manuel Paixão Santos Zacheo?

2572 FLETCHER, Thomas
Letters in vindication of the rights of the British West India colonies, originally addressed to the editors of the Liverpool Mercury, in answer to Mr. James Cropper's letters to W. Wilberforce, Esq. M.P. Liverpool, 1822. 68 pp.

Denies Cropper's charge of illegal slave trade to the British colonies in letters published in the London press (2570), and defends slavery and West Indian sugar bounties.

2573 FRIENDS, Society of
An address to the inhabitants of Europe on the iniquity of the slave trade; issued by the religious society of Friends, commonly called Quakers, in Great Britain and Ireland. W. Phillips, London, 1822. 15 pp.

By Josiah Forster. Christian condemnation of the slave trade. (Also issued in Dutch, French, German, Spanish, Swedish, Portuguese, Italian and Danish.)

2574 *WILBERFORCE, William
Lettre à l'Empereur Alexandre sur la traite des noirs . . . G. Schulze, London, 1822. 83 pp.

2575 *GRÉGOIRE, Henri Baptiste
Des peines infamantes à infliger aux négriers. Baudouin frères, Paris, 1822. 60 pp.

2576 HARRIS, Thaddeus Mason
A discourse delivered before the African Society in Boston, 15th of July, 1822, on the anniversary celebration of the abolition of the slave trade. Phelps & Farnham, Boston, 1822. 27 pp.

Notes on the slave trade and abolition movement.

2577 A WORD to the sons of Africa. W. Phillips, London, 1822. 15 pp.

Written for circulation in Africa. describing the fate of slaves sold overseas and urging Africans not to sell any more.

2578 'The SLAVE-TRADE.' (QR, vol. 28, Oct. 1822, pp. 161–79.)

Review of official reports on the illegal slave trade.

2579 CROPPER, James
The support of slavery investigated. George Smith, Liverpool; Hatchard & Son; J. & J. Arch, London, 1824. 27 pp.

The illegal slave trade will not be abandoned until Britain proves slavery to be uneconomic.

2580 *CLARKSON, Thomas
Address presented to the sovereigns of Europe and their representatives when they met at Aix-la-Chapelle in 1818. London, 1824.

See (2556).

2581 McQUEEN, James
The West India colonies; the calumnies and misrepresentations circulated against them by the Edinburgh Review, Mr. Clarkson, Mr. Cropper, &c. &c. examined and refuted. Baldwin, Cradock, & Joy, London, 1824. xxvi, 427 pp.

Warns of the economic dangers of emancipation, refutes the allegations of continuing slave trade to the West Indies, and criticises the means adopted to suppress the foreign slave trade.

2582 THE NEGRO'S memorial, or, abolitionist's catechism; by an abolitionist. Hatchard & Co.; J. & A. Arch, London, [1824]. vi, 127 pp.

By Thomas Fisher. Questions and

answers on slavery, the African slave trade and abolition history.

2583 'ABOLITION of the slave trade—and of slavery.' (ER, Oct. 1824, pp. 194–228).

France, Portugal and the Netherlands still condone the slave trade; West Indian slavery should be abolished by Britain.

2584 Un MOT au sujet de la traite des noirs. Lachevardiere Fils, [Paris, 1825]. 8 pp.

French slave trade is a national dishonour.

2585 TRAITE des nègres. Renseignements tendant à prouver la continuation de ce trafic illégal. Crapelet, [Paris, 1825?] 12 pp.

Extracts from English journals on the French slave trade and the British antislavery squadron.

2586 O'SHIELL, Bernard Barnabé
Réponses aux objections élevées contre le système colonial aux Antilles . . . suivies d'un appendice ou l'on démontre les vices et les dangers de l'affranchissement graduel des nègres dans toutes les colonies occidentales, proposé . . . par M. Buxon. Grimbert, Paris, 1825. x, 520 pp.

The slave trade redeems Africans from misery; its abolition should not be forced by Britain on other nations.

2587 BACON, Leonard
A plea for Africa; delivered in New-Haven, July 4th, 1825. New-Haven, 1825. 22 pp.

The civilisation of Africa requires abolition of the slave trade and the 'return of her exiled children' from America.

2588 PRADT, Dominique Georges Frédéric Dufour de
Congrès du Panama. Béchet ainé, Paris, 1825. viii, 95 pp.

Urges the new South American republics to abolish the slave trade before they become 'Africanised'.

2589 JANSON, Edmund
The following considerations on the slave trade and slavery, are submitted to the public, under a conviction of the soundness of the principles on which they are founded, and which have long been advocated. W. Phillips, [London, 1825?] 4 pp.

The slave trade and slavery can be destroyed by developing free-labour production in India.

2590a ANDRADA E SILVA, José Bonifacio de
Representação á Assemblea geral constituinte e legislativa do imperio do Brasil sôbre a escravatura. Paris, 1825. 40 pp.

Translated as:

2590b Memoir addressed to the General, Constituent and Legislative Assembly of the Empire of Brazil, on slavery! . . . Butterworth (etc.), London, 1826. 60 pp.

The slave trade must be abolished immediately as a 'deadly cancer' to Brazil.

2591 *DÍAZ DE ESPADA Y LANDA, Juan José, *Bishop of Havana*
Carta pastoral que el Exelentísimo e Ilustrísimo Señor Obispo diocesano Doctor Don Juan José Díaz de Espada y Landa dirige al venerable Dean y Cabildo de su santa iglesia catedral, a consecuencia de la real orden de 7 de enero del año corriente que prohibo el tráfico de negros en esta isla. Imprenta Fraternal, Habana, 1826. 16 pp.

2592 *MEMÓRIA sôbre a escravatura e projeto de colonização dos Europeus e prêtos da África no império do Brasil. (Signed: J. E. P. da S.) Rio de Janeiro, 1826.

By J. E. Pessoa da Silva. Recommends gradual replacement of the slave trade by immigration to Brazil.

2593 'AFRICAN slave trade.' (EcR, n.s., vol. 26, 1826, pp. 354–64.)

Examples of illegal slave trading, including that of the 'Perle' (1473).

2594 'STATE of the slave-trade.' (QR, vol. 34, Sept, 1826, pp. 579–608.)

Review of official papers, blaming the 'ultra-abolitionists' for making the slave trade worse than before.

2595 BILLIARD, François Jacques Marie Auguste
Abolition de la traite et de l'esclavage, dans les colonies françaises. Mémoire présenté aux deux Chambres. Brière (etc.) Paris; Duchesne (etc.), Rennes, 1827. iv, 122 pp.

Discussion of the problem of abolition, which ought to begin with amelioration of slavery.

2596 A SHORT review of the slave trade and slavery, with considerations on the benefit which would arise from cultivating tropical productions by free labour. Beilby, Knott, & Beilby, Birmingham, 1827. 129 pp.

Attributed to John Sturge. Description of the extent of the slave trade and the means to suppress it; slavery is uneconomic, as shown by Adam Smith and others. (Reviewed: in ER, Oct. 1827, pp. 490–97.)

2597 ANECDOTES of Africans. (Signed: A lover of Africa.) Harvey & Darton, London, 1827. xi, 88 pp.

Extracts on the slave trade and slavery designed to arouse sympathy for the African slaves.

2598 McQUEEN, James
'Civilization of Africa—Sierra Leone.' (EM, vol. 21, March 1827, pp. 315–29, 596–624.)

British anti-slave trade policy is ineffective in view of the prevalence of slavery in Africa.

2599 FERNANDEZ, John
An address to His Majesty's ministers, recommending efficacious means for the most speedy termination of African slavery. London, 1827. 36 pp.

Africa must be civilized before the slave trade can be eradicated; Britain should establish forts with African garrisons on rivers used by slavers, to support the British navy and protect European commerce and settlements.

2600 *SCRIPTURE evidence of the sinfulness of injustice and oppression. Respectfully submitted to professing Christians, in order to call forth their sympathy and exertions on behalf of the much-injured Africans. Harvey & Darton, London, 1828. 26 pp.

By Mary Dudley.

2601 The SLAVE taker, &c; or, an appeal to all who in any way promote the traffic in . . . their fellow-creatures. London, 1828. 8 pp.

By William Naish.

2602 A PLAN for the abolition of slavery, consistently with the interests of all parties concerned. George Sidford, London, 1828. 32 pp.

The slave trade could make the Americas 'another New Guinea'; Europe and America must unite to abolish slavery and suppress the slave trade with a combined fleet, to promote European emigration to America and transport free negroes back to Africa.

2603 HUMPHREY, Heman
Parallel between intemperance and the slave trade. An address delivered at Amherst College, July 4, 1828. J. S. & C. Adams, Amherst, 1828. 40 pp.

2604 MORÉNAS, Joseph Elzéar
Précis historique de la traite des noirs et de l'esclavage colonial, contenant, l'origine de la traite, ses progrès, son état actuel, et un exposé des horreurs produites par le despotisme des colons; ouvrage dans lequel on prouve qu'on a exporté d'Afrique, depuis 1814 jusqu'à présent, plus de 700,000 esclaves, dont un grand nombre sous pavillon français . . . Firmin Didot, Paris, 1828. 423 pp. illus.

Estimates the total number of slaves exported across the Atlantic as over 7 million. (Reviewed in: RE, vol. 39, 1828, pp. 209–11.)

2605 MOSQUERA, Joaquin
Memoria sobre la necesidad de reformar la ley del Congreso constituyente de Colombia, de 21 de julio, de 1821, que sanciona la libertad de los partos, manumision, y abolicion del trafico de esclavos: y bases que podrian adoptarse para la reforma. Tomas Antero, Caracas, 1829. 30 pp.

The slave trade should be reopened but the slaves introduced should be manumitted.

2606 A SKETCH of the African slave trade, and the slavery of the negroes under their Christian masters, in the European colonies. Compiled from various authors of undoubted authority. Harvey & Darton (etc.), London, [1829?] 4 pp.

2607 WHITEFIELD, George
Remarks on the injustice and immorality of slavery. In eight letters. John Stevens, London, 1830. 42 pp.

The African slave trade and slavery must 'stand or fall together'; ch. 6: 'The captor of Africans is a robber, and the purchaser of Africans is a buyer of stolen property'.

2608 *CLARKSON, Thomas
Abolition of the African slave-trade, by the British Parliament. Abridged from Clarkson. Together with a brief view of the present state of the slave-trade and of slavery . . . P. A. Brinsmade, Augusta (Maine), 1830. 2 vol.

See (3584).

2609 A LETTER to the most Honourable the Marquis of Chandos. By a West India planter. James Ridgway; E. Lloyd, London, 1830. 90 pp.

Opposes emancipation but attacks the British government for admitting slave-grown sugar from Latin America after paying millions to suppress the slave trade.

2610 DUNCAN, Henry
Presbyter's letters on the West India question; addressed to the Right Honourable Sir George Murray . . . T. & G. Underwood, London, 1830. 139 pp.

Letter 10: 'Foreign slave trade— its extent and consequences'.

2611 BRIEF observations on the West India question in the Quarterly Review for April, 1831; with remarks on the continuation of the slave trade by the subjects of other nations; with the most effectual and just mode of inducing them to consent to its total abandonment . . . By a West India proprietor. Cunningham & Salmon, London, 1831. 16 pp.

All conquered colonies should be returned to France and Spain on the condition that they abandon the slave trade; this would rid Britain of the enormous expense of the antislavery squadron.

2612 CHRISTENSEN, Balthazar Mathias
'Om Slavehandelen.' (Valkyrien, Kjöbenhavn, 1832, I, pp. 251–58.)

2613 GARRISON, William Lloyd
Thoughts on African colonization: or an impartial exhibition of the doctrines, principles and purposes of the American Colonization Society . . . Garrison & Knapp, Boston, 1832. iv, 160, 76 pp.

The American 'colonization' scheme is racialist and hypocritical; the slave trade can only be abolished by destroying the 'market for slaves'. Answered by (2614).

2614 CAREY, Matthew
Reflections on the causes that led to the formation of the Colonization Society: with a view of its probable results . . . The effects of colonization on the slave trade—with a slight sketch of that nefarious and accursed traffic. Wm. F. Geddes, Philadelphia, 1832. 19 pp. illus.

Defence of colonisation against (2613). The Liberian colony will probably check the slave trade in a large area of West Africa. (Reissued as 'Letters on the Colonization Society'.)

2615 GARRISON, William Lloyd
An address on the progress of the abolition cause; delivered before the African Abolition Freehold Society of Boston, July 16, 1832. Garrison & Knapp, Boston, 1832. 24 pp.

The slave trade still continues despite the abolition acts; slavery itself ought to have been abolished as well.

2616 'TRAITE des noirs.' (Magasin Pittoresque, Paris, vol. 1, 1833, p. 80; illus.)

By É. Charton? Proposes the creation of an official Anglo-French company to purchase African slaves for contract labour in the colonies.

2617 *A SKETCH of the origin and progress of the American Colonization Society, with some notice of the slave trade, and of the interior condition of Africa. By a friend to the cause. P. Canfield, Hartford, 1833. 24 pp.

2618 WHITTLESEY, Elisha
An address delivered before the Tallmadge Colonization Society, on the fourth of July, 1833; by Hon. Elisha Whittlesey, member of Congress . . . Ravenna (Ohio), 1833. 27 pp.

Colonization will civilise Africa and suppress the slave trade.

2619 JEREMIE, John
Recent events at Mauritius . . . S. Bagster, Jun., London, 1835. xi, 260 pp.

The introduction contains a statement by G. Stephen alleging slave trade by Mauritians until 1820. See (560, 2620).

2620 A SHORT appeal to the House of Commons, in answer to the charge brought against the inhabitants of Mauritius, more particularly in a pamphlet, by John Jeremie, Esq. entitled "Recent events at Mauritius." W. Glindon, London, [1835]. 30 pp.

Reply to accusations of illegal slave trade and falsification of the slave registers (2619), which would disentitle the Mauritian settlers to compensation for the freeing of their slaves.

2621 'The FOREIGN slave-trade.' (QR, vol. 55, Dec. 1835, pp. 250–85.)

Review of works on the slave trade and colonial commerce; the removal of sugar duties will aggravate the former.

2622 'DE l'esclavage, de son origine et de ses résultats, chez les peuples anciens et modernes.' (Revue Britannique, Bruxelles, ser. 3, vol. 2, déc. 1835, pt. 2, pp. 387–405.)

All governments should cooperate to suppress the slave trade.

2623 *FREEMAN, Frederick
Yaradee; a plea for Africa, in familiar conversations on the subject of slavery and colonization . . . J. Whetham, Philadelphia, 1836. 360 pp.

The return of American negroes to Africa would help to extirpate the slave trade. (Second edition, 1837, entitled: A plea for Africa.) See (2777).

2624 'FOREIGN slave trade—New treaty with Spain.' (ER, vol. 63, July 1836, pp. 373–95.)

Review of official documents and (3260).

2625 The WAR in Texas: a review of facts and circumstances, showing that this contest is the result of a long premeditated crusade against the government, set on foot by slaveholders, land speculators, &c. with the view of re-establishing, extending, and perpetuating the system of slavery and the slave trade in the republic of Mexico. By a citizen of the United States. Merrihew & Gunn, Philadelphia, 1836. 56 pp.

By Benjamin Lundy. (Second, enlarged edition 1837.)

2626 MÉMOIRE pour les habitans de l'île Maurice, en réponse aux accusations portées contre eux dans le but de les priver de la portion qui leur est attribuée par la commission aux fonds de compensation, sur les £20,000,000 votés par l'acte des 3ᵐᵉ et 4ᵐᵉ années de William IV, chap. 73, comme indemnité aux propriétaires des esclaves affranchis par ledit acte. Par un colon. Cernéen, Port-Louis, 1836. 211 pp.

The slave trade had been declared illegal at Mauritius in 1815 and a public registry had been established, since when the trade had ceased.

2627 *ROBERTS, Thomas
The cruel nature and injurious effects

of the foreign slave trade, represented in a letter addressed to the Right Hon. Lord Brougham and Vaux. John Taylor, Bristol, 1836. 40 pp.

2628 *MONIZ BARRETO, Domingos Alves Branco
Memoria sobre a abolição do comercio da escravatura, offerecida ao Rei D. João VI. Rio de Janeiro, 1837. 48 pp.

Published six years after the author's death.

2629 MEMORIA analytica a'cerca do commercio d'escravos e a'cerca dos malles da escravidão domestica. Por F.L.C.B. Rio de Janeiro, 1837. xi, 142 pp.

By F.L.C. Burlamaqui. Demonstration of the odiousness of the slave trade and its dangerous effects on Brazil; African slaves should be replaced by European immigrants.

2630 SACO, José Antonio
Mi primera pregunta. ¿ La abolicion del comercio de esclavos africanos arruinará ó atrasará la agricultura cubana? Marcelino Calero, Madrid, 1837. 39 pp.

Suppression of the illegal slave trade will not ruin Cuba and must be carried out before it is too late.

2631 *MEMORIA sobre o commercio dos escravos, em que se pretende mostrar que este trafico he, para elles, antes hum bem do que hum mal. Escrita por XXX, natural dos Campos dos Goitacazes. Const. de J. Villeneuve & Comp., Rio de Janeiro, 1838. 13 pp.

By J. J. da Cunha de Azeredo Coutinho. New version of (2438).

2632 McQUEEN, James
A letter to the Right Honourable Lord Glenelg, on the West Indian currency, commerce, African slave trade, &c. &c. B. Fellowes, London, 1838. 52 pp.

On monetary reforms needed for the British colonies to meet the competition from slave economies.

2633 GASPARIN, Agénor Étienne de, comte
Esclavage et traite. Joubert, Paris, 1838. xvi, 261 pp.

The slave trade continues to the Spanish colonies, Brazil and the United States; its suppression is a prerequisite for the abolition of slavery.

2634 *ON the cultivation of the soil of India, with reference to the African slave trade. [London, 1839.] 3 pp.

2635 *FRIENDS, Society of
Extracts and observations on the foreign slave trade. Published by a committee appointed by the yearly meeting of Friends held in Philadelphia in 1839, on the subject of slavery. J. Richards, Philadelphia, 1839. 12 pp.

2636 *REMARKS upon slavery and the slave trade, addressed to the Hon. Henry Clay. (Signed: A slave-holder.) [Paris,] 1839. 23 pp.

Attributed to Morgan Gibbes.

2637 CUNHA BARBOZA, Januario da
'Se a introducção dos escravos africanos no Brasil embaraça a civilisação dos nossos indigenas, dispensando-se-lhes o trabalho, que todo foi confiado a escravos negros. Neste cazo qual he o prejuizo que soffre a lavoura brasileira?' (Revista trimensal de Historia e Geographia, Rio de Janeiro, vol. 1, 1839, pp. 145–52.)

The African slave trade to Brazil saved the Indians but has been an obstacle to civilizing them; free labour is more economical than slavery. (Postscript by José Silvestre Rebello, ibid., pp. 153–58, maintains the opposite: African slavery has promoted the civilisation of the Indians and is potentially profitable.)

2638 MADDEN, Richard Robert
A letter to W. E. Channing, D.D. on the subject of the abuse of the flag of the United States in the island of Cuba, and the advantage taken of its protection in promoting the slave trade. William D. Ticknor, Boston, 1839. 32 pp.

Reveals the involvement of the U.S. consul at Havana (N. P. Trist) and American capital in the slave trade, which has increased steadily since 1820; all Spanish slave ships are built in the U.S.A. See (2643).

2639 JAY, William
A view of the action of the federal government, in behalf of slavery. J. S. Taylor, New-York, 1839. 217 pp.

The U.S. government tolerates the illegal African slave trade because of the political influence of the Southern states. See (2642).

2640 *FRIENDS, Society of
An appeal to the inhabitants of Europe, on slavery and the slave trade: issued on behalf of the religious Society of Friends in Great Britain . . . Harvey & Darton, London, 1839.

Also issued in French, Portuguese and Spanish. (Reprinted in: Irish Friend, Belfast, vol. 2, no. 10, 1839, pp. 73–74.)

2641 'The AFRICAN slave-trade.' (British and Foreign Review, London, vol. 9, 1839, pp. 466–507.)

Review of works by Buxton and others on the slave trade.

2642 JAY, William
A view of the action of the federal government, in behalf of slavery . . . Second edition. American Anti-Slavery Society, New York, 1839. 240 pp.

With a new section: 'Present participation of citizens of the United States in the African slave trade'. See (2639, 2709).

2643 A LETTER to Wm. E. Channing, D.D. in reply to one addressed to him by R. R. Madden, on the abuse of the flag of the United States in the island of Cuba, for promoting the slave trade. By a calm observer. William D. Ticknor, Boston, 1840. 36 pp.

Defence of consul Trist and the U.S. against Madden's allegations (2638).

2644 BUXTON, Sir Thomas Fowell
The remedy; being a sequel to The African slave trade. John Murray, London, 1840. xvi, 278 pp.

Continuation of (55). The remedies for the slave trade are: increased efficiency of the antislavery squadron; treaties with African governments; encouragement of African commerce and agriculture through European settlements, especially on the Niger. See (2645, 2653).

2645 BUXTON, Sir Thomas Fowell
The African slave trade and its remedy. John Murray, London, 1840. viii, 582 pp. map.

See (55) and (2644). Reviewed in: ER, vol. 72, 1840, pp. 179–93; Methodist Magazine, New York, vol. 22, 1840, pp. 428–42. (Reprinted, with an introduction by G. E. Metcalfe, London, 1968.) See (2664–65, 2670).

2646 ALEXANDER, William
Dominion of the prince of peace; with its application to the slave trade and slavery. York, 1840. 54 pp.

The slave trade cannot be suppressed by 'brute force', only by peaceful moral means and the prior abolition of slavery.

2647   JEREMIE, John
A letter to T. Fowell Buxton, Esq. on negro emancipation and African civilization. J. Hatchard & Son; Simpkin, Marshall & Son, London, 1840. 52 pp.

The author (who became governor of Sierra Leone 1840–41) supports Buxton's scheme for agricultural colonies in Africa (2644), adding a proposal to resettle black freedmen, 'the sons of Africa', from America.

2648a SÁ NOGUEIRA DE FIGUEIREDO, Bernardo de, *visconde de Sá da Bandeira*
O trafico da escravatura, e o bill de Lord Palmerston. José Baptista Morando, Lisboa, 1840. 82 pp.

Translated as:

2648b The slave trade, and Lord Palmerston's bill. [London?] 1840. 68 pp.

Refutes accusations made by Palmerston during the debate on the bill for the forcible suppression of the Portuguese slave trade (1839), that Portugal had not fulfilled her anti-slave trade agreements; the bill is a violation of international law and really a pretext for British ambitions.

2649   GREG, William Rathbone
Past and present efforts for the extinction of the African slave trade. Ridgway, London, [1840]. 99 pp.

The current methods of suppressing the slave trade are wrong; it can only be abolished by proving 'the superior cheapness of free labour' in the West Indies through admitting negro and Indian immigration and maintaining protective duties on their sugar and coffee.

2650   INNES, John
Thoughts on the present state of the British West India colonies, and on measures for their improvement, tending to the extinction of the African slave trade. Pelham Richardson, London, 1840. 54 pp.

The government should encourage emigration from Africa to the West Indies; the returning workers would 'civilize' Africa.

2651   ARCHER, Edward Caulfield
Free labour versus slave labour. A letter to the Right Hon. S. Lushington,

M.P. and the opponents of free labour, shewing that in their opposition to emigration from India to the British colonies they are virtually encouraging the slave trade. Smith, Elder & Co., London, 1840. 23 pp.

Emancipation has led to a fall in West Indian production; the costly squadron has not been able to stop the African slave trade; British colonial produce must be protected against slave-grown, and only Indian immigration can lower the costs.

2652   TURNBULL, David
Travels in the West. Cuba; with notices of Porto Rico, and the slave trade. Longman, Orme, Brown, Green & Longmans, London, 1840. xvi, 574 pp. map.

Notes from a visit 1837–39, showing increasing American participation in the slave trade. (Reviewed in: Tait's Edinburgh Magazine, vol. 7, 1840, pp. 211–17.)

2653 'REMEDIES for the slave trade. Fowell Buxton—Turnbull.' (Signed: M.L.) (WR, vol. 34, 1840, pp. 125–65.)

By Macgregor Laird. Review of (2644) and (2652); increased trade and free emigration from Africa would be more effective than the squadron. See (2693).

2654   GURNEY, Joseph John
A winter in the West Indies, described in familiar letters to Henry Clay, of Kentucky. M. Day & Co., New-York, 1840. 203 pp.

Includes a chapter on the Cuban slave trade, in which U.S. capital is involved.

2655 *The EXTINCTION of the slave-trade, and the civilization of Africa: a review of "The African slave-trade, and its remedy", by Sir Thomas Fowell Buxton . . . J. Mason, London, 1840. 26 pp.

Reprinted from: 'Review of Buxton on the slave-trade' (Wesleyan–Methodist Magazine, London, vol. 63, July 1840, pp. 577–94). See (2645).

2656   BUXTON, Sir Thomas Fowell
Abridgement of Sir T. Fowell Buxton's work on the African slave trade and its remedy. With an explanatory preface and an appendix . . . John Murray, London, 1840. 68 pp.

The appendix contains further suggestions for suppressing the slave trade and the prospectus of the African Civilization Society. See (3077).

2657 *BOTELHO, Sebastião Xavier
Escravatura. Bemficios que se podem previr ás nostras possessões de Africa da prohibição d'aquelle trafico. Projecto de uma companhia commercial, que promova e fomente a cultura e civilisação d'aquelles dominios. Obra posthuma . . . offerecida ao corpo de commercio portuguez. José B. Morando, [Lisboa,] 1840. xi, 41 pp.

2658 *FRIENDS, Society of
Memorial of the Society of Friends in Pennsylvania, New Jersey and Delaware, on the African slave trade. Joseph & William Kite, Philadelphia, 1840. 7 pp.

2659 ALEXANDER, George William
Några ord om slafhandeln och slafveriet, tillegnade svenska folket. Lars J. Hjertas Förlag, Stockholm, 1840. 20 pp.

Proves statistically that slavery is uneconomic.

2660 *FORSYTH, John
Address to the people of Georgia. Including—letter of Pope Gregory XVI on slavery and resolutions of the general anti-slavery convention held in London, June 12–23, 1840. [Fredericksburg, Va., 1840.] 8 pp.

See (3084) and (3201).

2661 'EMIGRATION from Africa to the British West Indies.' (ColM, vol. 1, 1840, pp. 325–32.)

Proposed 'free' emigration would be slave trade in disguise.

2662 *BRASAHEMECO, Ananias Dortano, *pseud.*
Rights of Portugal, in reference to Great Britain, and the question of the slave trade. Lisbon, 1840. 2 vol.

By António Barão de Mascarenhas.

2663 SIMS, Thomas
Africa; and her children. R. B. Seeley & W. Burnside, London, 1840. xx, 116 pp.

Describes the slave trade and abolition measures; Christianity will civilise the Africans.

2664 'REMEDIES for the slave trade—Sir T. F. Buxton.' (EcR, n.s., vol. 8, Sept. 1840, pp. 351–68.)

Review of three works presenting different views on abolition (2645, 2652–53).

2665 *REMARKS on the Society for the extinction of the slave trade and the civilization of Africa; and on "The slave trade and its remedy." London, 1840. 16 pp.

By John Sturge. See (2670).

2666 CONVERSE, John Kendrick
The history of slavery, and means of elevating the African race. A discourse delivered before the Vermont Colonization Society, at Montpelier, Oct. 15, 1840. Chauncey Goodrich, Burlington (Vt.), 1840. 24 pp.

The slave trade can only be abolished by establishing more colonies like Liberia.

2667 *CORNISH, Samuel E. *and* **WRIGHT, Theodore S.**
The colonization scheme considered, in its rejection by the colored people— in its tendency to uphold caste—in its unfitness for christianizing and civilizing the aborigines of Africa, and for putting a stop to the African slave trade: in a letter to the Hon. Theodore Frelinghuysen and the Hon. Benjamin F. Butler . . . A. Guest, Newark (N. J.), 1840. 26 pp.

The authors were 'pastors of the colored Presbyterian churches in . . . Newark and New York'.

2668 STEPHEN, *Sir* **George**
A second letter to the Right Hon. Lord John Russell, &c. &c. &c. on the plans of the Society for the Civilization of Africa. Saunders & Otley, London, [1840]. 36 pp.

Reply to criticisms of the African Civilization Society. See (233).

2669 STEPHEN, *Sir* **George**
A third letter to the Right Hon. Lord John Russell, &c. &c. &c. on the plans of the Society for the Civilization of Africa. Saunders & Otley, London, [1840]. 32 pp.

The society's plans will relieve Britain of its 'heavy and perennial expenditure' on suppressing the slave trade.

2670 STURGE, John
Remarks on the Society for the extinction of the slave-trade, and the civilization of Africa; and on "The slave-trade, and its remedy." Hamilton, Adams & Co.; (etc.), London, 1841. 16 pp.

The society supports armed suppression of the slave trade, which has utterly failed judging by Buxton's own book (2645); the trade will not stop until slavery itself is abolished. (Sturge, as a pacifist, had broken with Buxton in 1839 and formed the British and Foreign Anti-Slavery Society.)

2671 *BRECKINRIDGE, Robert Jefferson
Speech of Robert J. Breckinridge, delivered in the Courthouse Yard at Lexington, Ky., on the 12th day of October, 1840 . . . more particularly in regard to the questions of the power of the legislature on the subject of slavery, the importation of slaves, of abolitionism, of British influence, of religious liberty, etc. . . . Second edition. R. J. Matchett, Baltimore, 1841. 32 pp.

2672 PILKINGTON, George
An address to the English residents in the Brazilian empire. Laemmert, Rio de Janeiro, 1841. 21 pp.

> Warns English slave owners of their responsibility for the illegal African slave trade and the danger of a black revolution.

2673 'SLAVE trade.' (American Almanac, Boston, 1841, pp. 76–79.)

> Statistics 1828–37 extracted from (3077) and (2645).

2674 'SUPPRESSION of the slave-trade in Cuba.' (FA, no. 8, June 1841, pp. 113–15.)

2675 CLARKSON, Thomas
'Letter from Thos. Clarkson, Esq., to the secretary of the African Civilization Society.' (FA, no. 8, June 1841, pp. 115–20.)

> Supports Buxton's scheme for 'civilizing' Africa.

2676 'ISLAND of Cuba. Memorial from certain proprietors. To His Excellency the President, Governor and Captain-General.' (FA, no. 8, June 1841, pp. 122–23.)

> The slave trade threatens to create a dangerous black majority and prevents European immigration to Cuba.

2677 MERLIN, María de los Mercédes de Jaruco, *condesa* **de**
Les esclaves dans les colonies espagnoles. Paris, 1841. 40 pp.

> The slave trade must be abolished, but not slavery; the slaves are happier in Cuba than in Africa. (Reprinted from: RDM, vol. 26, 1841, pp. 734–69.)

2678 HAYDON, Benjamin Robert
Description of Haydon's picture of the great meeting of delegates held at the Freemasons' Tavern, June 1840, for the abolition of slavery and the slave trade throughout the world. Thomas Clarkson, president. [London, 1841.] 20 pp. illus.

> Includes a list of delegates and an address by the British and Foreign Anti-Slavery Society.

2679 'THREE modes for suppressing the slave trade.' (AR, vol. 17, Aug. 1841, pp. 241–49.)

> The principal schemes are: naval blockade, abolition of slavery itself, and African colonisation; the latter is the only effective one.

2680 'The SLAVE trade to Cuba.' (FA, no. 11, Sept. 1841, pp. 161–62.)

2681 HAVANA: Ayuntamiento
'Memorial of the municipality of Havana.' (FA, no. 11, Sept. 1841, pp. 169–72.)

> Condemns the slave trade but opposes emancipation.

2682 GURLEY, Ralph Randolph
Letter to the Hon. Henry Clay, president of the American Colonization Society, and Sir Thomas Fowell Buxton, chairman of the general committee of the African Civilization Society, on the colonization and civilization of Africa. With other documents on the same subjects. Wiley & Putnam, London, 1841. x, 66 pp.

> Defence of 'colonization' against British criticism; it is the best method to suppress the slave trade and civilise Africa.

2683 *HAMILTON, W.
Emigration from the west coast of Africa and Sierra Leone, to Trinidad. London, 1841. 23 pp.

2684 'SLAVE-SMUGGLING into the United States.' (FA, no. 12, Oct. 1841, pp. 183–84.)

> On the illegal slave trade in the 1830s.

2685 'SUGAR, slavery, and the slave trade.' (ColM, vol. 6, 1841, pp. 419–23.)

> Reduction of sugar duties would perpetuate the foreign slave trade.

2686 *BELDAM, Joseph
A review of the late proposed measure for reduction of the duties on sugar, so far as it relates to slavery and the slave

trade. Addressed to Sir T. F. Buxton. London, 1841. 79 pp.

2687 *TORRENTE, Mariano
Cuestion importante sobre la esclavitud. Viuda de Jordan & hijos, Madrid, 1841. 94 pp.

Urges respect for the slave trade treaties and emancipation in the Spanish West Indies.

2688 'SIR T. F. Buxton's plan for the extinction of the slave trade.' (Journal of Civilization, London, 1842, pp. 39–40.)

African agriculture should be developed to replace the slave trade with legitimate exports.

2689 *FRIENDS, Society of
Facts and observations relative to the participation of American citizens in the African slave trade. Published by direction of a meeting representing the religious Society of Friends in Pennsylvania, New Jersey, &c. Joseph & William Kite, Philadelphia, 1841. 36 pp.

2690 EMIGRATION to the British West Indies. D. Marples, Liverpool, 1842. 14 pp.

Emigration from West Africa must be resisted as it will undermine efforts to suppress the slave trade.

2691 *ALEXANDER, George William
Observaciones sobre la esclavitud y comercio de esclavos . . . E informe del Dr. Madden sobre la esclavitud en la isla de Cuba. Barcelona, 1841. 68 pp.

2692 ELLSWORTH, Henry Leavitt
Mr. Ellsworth's appeal to the friends of African colonization. Alexander & Barnard, [Washington, 1842]. 14 pp.

Lining the coast of Africa with colonies like Liberia will create perpetual barriers against slave dealers.

2693 *LAIRD, Macgregor
Remedies for the slave trade. London, 1842. 88 pp.

Reprinted from (2653), with additions.

2694 *MOREAU DE JONNÈS, Alexandre
Recherches statistiques sur l'esclavage colonial et sur les moyens de le supprimer . . . Bourgogne, Paris, 1842. 275 pp.

2695 FRIENDS, Society of
An appeal to the professors of Christianity, in the southern states and elsewhere, on the subject of slavery: by the representatives of the yearly meeting

of Friends for New England. Knowles & Vose, Providence (R.I.), 1842. 24 pp.

Extracts from various sources on the African slave trade, which is inseparable from American domestic slavery.

2696 *PEREIRA MARINHO, Joaquim
Memoria contra a facção dos negreiros etc. Gouvêa, Lisboa, 1842. x, 104 pp.

2697 ALEXANDER, George William
Letters on the slave-trade, slavery, and emancipation . . . Charles Gilpin; Duncan & Malcolm, London, 1842. xvi, 176 pp. bibl. pp. vii–xii.

History and present state of the slave trade and abolition movement.

2698 BRITISH AND FOREIGN ANTI-SLAVERY SOCIETY
An epitome of anti-slavery information: or a condensed view of slavery and the slave trade, &c. &c. T. Ward & Co., London, 1842. 20 pp.

2699 BRITISH AND FOREIGN ANTI-SLAVERY SOCIETY
Emigration from Africa to the West Indies. London, 1842. 2 pp.

The proposal to recruit African labourers for the colonies may revive the African slave trade.

2700 JOLLIVET, Adolphe
De la philanthropie anglaise. Ad. Blondeau, Paris, 1842. 49 pp.

The author, a French colonial deputy, attacks the treaties for 'right of search' as an attempt by Britain to gain supremacy at sea while she permits slavery to continue in India.

2701 CLARKSON, Thomas
Not a labourer wanted for Jamaica: to which is added, an account of the newly erected villages by the peasantry there, and their beneficial results; and of the consequences of reopening a new slave-trade, as it relates to Africa, and the honour of the British government in breaking her treaties with foreign powers: in a letter addressed to a member of parliament, appointed to sit on the West India committee. Thomas Ward & Co., London, 1842. 15 pp.

Jamaica is not short of labour; to look for emigrants from Africa would be to institute a 'new slave-trade'.

2702 TREW, J. M.
Africa wasted by Britain, and restored by native agency, in a letter to . . . the

Lord Bishop of London. J. Hatchard & Son, London, 1843. 61 pp.

History of the slave trade and proposal to establish a mission at Fernando Po for the civilisation of Africa.

2703 SCHOELCHER, Victor
Colonies étrangères et Haiti. Résultats de l'émancipation anglaise. Pagnerre, Paris, 1843. 2 vol.

Vol. 1 contains notes on the schemes for immigration of free African labourers to the English colonies, and 'Quelques mots sur la traite et sur son origine'; vol. 2 includes a section on the right of visit, supporting it in principle for the suppression of the slave trade.

2704 WEST INDIA COMMITTEE
Report of the acting committee to the standing committee of West India planters and merchants. Maurice & Co., London, 1843. 82 pp.

Correspondence with the government, urging removal of all obstructions to the transfer to the West Indies of liberated slaves and free Africans; the slave trade can only be destroyed by cheaper free-labour production.

2705 HOWITT, William
A serious address to the members of the Anti-Slavery Society, on its present position and prospects. Written . . . for and in behalf of the advocates of the free labour of British India, as the grand means for the extinction of slavery. Effingham Wilson & Chappel, London, 1843. 15 pp.

After 50 years of antislavery effort the slave trade has increased, and African emigration to the West Indies would be a 'new slave-trade under another name'; free-labour production in India is 'the great remedy for slavery and the slave trade'.

2706 *ADDRESS of the Irish liberator, to the Irish Repeal Association of Cincinnati, Ohio; with the Pope's bull on slavery and the slave trade. New York, 1843. 24 pp.

By Daniel O'Connell.

2707 'Les ESCLAVES noirs.' (Magasin Pittoresque, Paris, vol. 12, 1844, pp. 50–52; illus.)

Describes the Atlantic slave trade and

urges abolition of slavery by France.

2708 *El TRÁFICO de negros, considerado como medio de emancipacion immediata y civilizacion universal. Por un piloto español. Viuda de Mayol, Barcelona, 1844. 68 pp.

2709 JAY, William
A view of the action of the federal government in behalf of slavery. N. Y. S. Anti-Slavery Society, Utica, 1844. 112 pp.

With an appendix, 'The Amistad case', by Joshua Leavitt. See (1481, 2542).

2710 *GEDACHTEN over de emancipatie der negerslaven en de afschaffing van den slavenhandel, waardoor jaarlijks een aantal negers worden vervoerd uit Afrika naar Amerika. W. P. van Stockum, 's Hage, 1844.

2711 READ, William George
Letters of the late Bishop England to the Hon. J. Forsyth, on the subject of domestic slavery: to which are prefixed copies, in Latin and English, of the Pope's apostolic letter, concerning the African slave trade, with some introductory remarks, etc. John Murphy, Baltimore, 1844. 156 pp.

Letters I, II, discuss the apostolic letter 'de nigritarum commercio' (3 Dec. 1839) of Pope Gregory XVI (3201).

2712 BLAIR, William Thomas
On the introduction of slave-grown produce into the British markets. [British and Foreign Anti-Slavery Society, London, 1844]. (2 pp.)

Admission of Cuban and Brazilian sugar on equal terms with British West Indian would increase the slave trade from Africa.

2713 LAIRD, Macgregor
The effect of an alteration in the sugar duties on the condition of the people of England and the negro race considered . . . Second edition. Effingham Wilson, London, 1844. iv, 86 pp.

Equalisation of the sugar duties will benefit England and the Africans, by a new demand for 'free negro labour' in the British colonies which will put an end to the slave trade, rather than encourage it, and thus save the cost of the blockading squadron; the government should arrange such emigration to the West Indies.

2714 McQUEEN, James
'Africa—slave trade—tropical colonies.'
(BM, vol. 55, June 1844, pp. 731–48.)

The only solution to the slave trade
is to employ 'African free labour'
both in the West Indies and in 'free
European settlements' in Africa itself.

2715 'The SLAVE trade and the sugar duties.'
(Signed: W. R. G.) (WR, vol. 41, June
1844, pp. 486–515.)

By W. R. Greg. Review article,
supporting government-sponsored
emigration from Africa to the West
Indies as the best way to suppress the
slave trade and to civilise Africa.

2716 RITCHIE, James Ewing
Thoughts on slavery and cheap sugar, a
letter to the members and friends of
the British and Foreign Anti-Slavery
Society. Aylott & Jones, London,
[1844]. 39 pp.

Attempt to win the society over to
free trade as 'the only thing by which
slavery can be destroyed'.

2717 PROPOSAL for extending commercial
intercourse with Africa, as a means
towards the extinction of slavery and
the introduction of civilization. [Turner
& Rose, Liverpool, 1844.] 1 p.

2718 MERLIN, Maria de los Mercédes de
Jaruco, *condesa* de
La Havana. Amyot, Paris, 1844. 3 vol.

Includes material on the slave trade,
abolition and the right of search.

2719 FRIENDS, Society of
An appeal on the iniquity of slavery
and the slave-trade: issued by the yearly
meeting of the religious society of
Friends, held in London, 1844. Edward
Marsh, London, 1844. 10 pp.

Addressed to rulers and slave-holders.
(Also issued in French, German and
Dutch.)

2720 *QUELQUES mots aux amis de l'humanité sur l'esclavage et la traite des
nègres. Lévêque, Cambrai, [1845]. 8 pp.

By Thomas Clarkson.

2721 SACO, José Antonio
La supresion de tráfico de esclavos
africanos en la isla de Cuba; examinada
con relacion a su agricultura y a su
seguridad. Panckoucke, Paris, 1845.
70 pp.

The slave trade must be ended and
replaced with white immigration.

(Reviewed by Xavier Durrieu in:
RDM, n.s., vol. 9, 1845, pp. 899–
923.) Reprinted in his: Obras (Nueva
York, 1853), vol. 1, pp. 171–232.
See (2757).

2722 *INFORME fiscal sobre fomento de la
población blanca en la isla de Cuba, y
emancipación progresiva de la esclava
. . . Presentado a la superintendencia
general delegada de la real hacienda,
en diciembre de 1844. Por el fiscal de la
misma. J. Martin Alegria, Madrid,
1845. xviii, 195, 328 pp.

By V. Vázquez Queipo. Translated as:
Cuba, ses ressources, son administra-
tion, sa population (Paris, 1851).
See (2736).

2723 SAGRA, Ramón de la
Estudios coloniales con aplicacion a
la isla de Cuba . . . I. De los efectos de
la supresion en el trafico negrero.
D. Dionisio Hidalgo, Madrid, 1845.
88 pp.

Recommends suppression of the
slave trade and abolition of slavery
in Cuba, to be replaced by free white
labour.

2724 DUVIVIER, Franciades Fleurus
Abolition de l'esclavage, civilisation du
centre de l'Afrique. Projet pour y
parvenir. J. Dumaine, Paris, 1845.
48 pp.

African labourers should be obtained for the French colonies, either
voluntarily or by purchase; after ten
years they could return to Africa, be
armed and sent to conquer and
civilise the interior.

2725 *AMERICAN TRACT SOCIETY
The enormity of the slave trade; and
the duty of seeking the moral and
spiritual elevation of the colored race.
Speeches of Wilberforce, and other
documents and records. New York,
[1846]. 144 pp.

Contains speeches of Wilberforce and
Fox 1791, Clarkson's 'Summary
view' (1851), etc.

2726 PALMER, Henry
Letters on the slave trade. Hamilton,
Adams & Co., London; John S.
Crossley, Leicester, 1846. 56 pp.

Abolition of the slave trade and
slavery was wrong; slaves cannot
now escape from the horrors of
Africa while slavery is needed in
the Caribbean.

2727 *WHITMAN, Walt
'Slavers and the slave trade.' (Daily Eagle, Brooklyn, 18 March 1846.)

Article on recent cases of illegal slave trading, urging the use of force against Brazil. (Reprinted in: The uncollected poetry and prose of Walt Whitman, New York, 1921, vol. 1, pp. 106–08.)

2728 *MASSIE, James William
The slave: hunted, transported, and doomed to toil; a tale of Africa. James Lowndes, Manchester, 1846. 176 pp.

2729 The SUGAR duties. Free and slave labour. Smith, Elder & Co., London, 1846. 20 pp.

Advocates 'a well-regulated system of immigration' from Africa to the British West Indies in order to undercut the slave trade to Brazil.

2730 'SLAVE-GROWN sugar.' (Christian Remembrancer, London, n.s., vol. 12, Oct. 1846, pp. 325–76.)

Review article: the African squadron and the sugar duties act 1846 only aggravate the slave trade; Christianity must be allowed to improve the world.

2731 CARROLL, Thomas
'Dr. Carroll on the slave trade. A permanent remedy for the African slave trade.' (AR, vol. 22, Nov. 1846, pp. 329–41.)

Lecture by a former secretary of the New York State Colonization Society; the only solution is the return to Africa of her 'exiled, but now civilized sons'.

2732 *VERSES on the slave trade and the press, suggested by a leading article in "The Times", August 21, 1846. J. Hatchard & Son, London, 1847. 32 pp.

2733 CLARKE, Edward Hyde
Prophetic letters, on the West Indian interest. Simpkin, Marshall & Co., London; (etc.), 1847. 15 pp.

The sugar act of 1846 will encourage the slave trade and harm the British colonies.

2734 THOUGHTS on British Guiana. By a planter. Second edition, revised and corrected . . . Royal Gazette Office, Demerara, 1847. 42 pp.

The only way of saving the West Indies is large-scale immigration from Africa; the planters are willing to pay African chiefs for slaves.

2735 CLAIMS of the West India colonies. Milton Press, [London, 1847]. 22 pp.

By J. C. Colquhoun. Proposes abolition of the slave trade by paying African chiefs to emancipate their slaves; this would open the way for 'unfettered immigration' of free labour to the West Indies.

2736 *SACO, José Antonio
Replica de Don José Antonio Saco a la contestación del Sr. fiscal de la real hacienda de La Habana, Don Vicente Vazquez Queipo en el examen del Informe sobre el fomento de la población blanca, etc., en la isla de Cuba. M. Rivadeneira, Madrid, 1847. 44 pp.

Defence of the author's 'Carta de un cubano', 1845, against criticisms in (2722), with sections on the statistics of the Cuban slave trade. (Reprinted in his: Colección de papeles cientificos, historicos, politicos y de otros ramos sobre la isla de Cuba, vol. 3, La Habana, 1963, pp. 247– 328.)

2737 ABEKEN, Hermann
Amerikanische Negersklaverei und Emancipation . . . Berlin, 1847. 232 pp.

Includes sections on the suppression of the slave trade and its replacement by free labour immigration.

2738 *LEGUAY, Émile
Institut de Notre-Dame de Charité du Bon-Pasteur. Notice sur l'œuvre du rachat des esclaves . . . A. Le Clerc, Paris, 1847. 35 pp.

2739 JAMAICA: Chamber of Commerce
Report of the standing committee of the Chamber of Commerce, Jamaica, upon the present condition of that colony; the causes of its depression; and the remedial measures necessary to restore its prosperity. Cowie, Jolland & Co., London, 1847. 23 pp.

Removal of sugar tariffs and of all restrictions on African labour immigration to the British West Indies is the most effective way of ending the slave trade.

2740 LEFROY, Christopher Edward
Letter to the freeholders of Basingstoke. S. Chandler, Basingstoke, 1847. 14 pp.

Attack on Palmerston for promoting the slave trade by admitting slave-grown sugar; with an extract from a speech by Lord George Bentinck in the House of Lords opposing the sugar bill in July 1846 on the same grounds.

2741 PAIN, Henri
Quelques propositions concernant les intérêts coloniaux, et spécialement de l'émancipation immédiate, avec association et indemnité. Charles Gailmard, Nantes, 1847. 5 pt.

Anti-abolitionists hope to revive the slave trade, but France and England will not abandon their policy of suppression.

2742 PHILLIPS, Edward
'Cannot Europe's colonies flourish without perpetuating the chains of African slavery?' (SCM, vol. 12, Sept. 1847, pp. 6–24.)

Europe should help to civilise Africa, by irrigation works or 'moral enlightenment'.

2743 'The FRIENDS of the African.' (QR, vol. 82, Dec. 1847, pp. 153–75.)

Review article charging the abolitionists with utter failure to suppress the slave trade, at immense expense. See (2745).

2744 WEST INDIA COMMITTEE
Report of the acting committee to the standing committee of West India planters and merchants, at their half-yearly meeting, held at the West India Committee Rooms . . . on the 12th. January, 1848. London, 1848. 41 pp.

All recaptured slaves at Sierra Leone should be settled in the West Indies and ships be provided for emigrants from the Kru country, while steamers should blockade the slave-importing countries; the true remedy for the slave trade lies in competing out slave products.

2745 JOHNSTON, Charles
'The friends of the African.' (SCM, vol. 13, 1848, pp. 292–96, 435–39.)

Reply to (2743) defending the abolitionists; Africa can be civilized by the development of tropical agriculture.

2746 McNEILE, Hugh
Slave labor versus free labor sugar. Speech of the Revd. Dr. McNeile, delivered at a public meeting held at Liverpool, 13th. June, 1848. F. Syrett, London, 1848. 18 pp.

The sugar act of 1846 will lead to a revival of the slave trade and ruin the West Indian estates.

2747 OPMERKINGEN omtrent den Afrikaanschen slavenhandel en de emancipatie in de Brittische koloniën, met aanbeveling van middelen om Afrika te beschaven, den bloei der West-Indiën te herstellen en de slaven in Suriname te emanciperen. Gebr. Belinfante, 's Gravenhage, 1848. 111 pp.

By G. S. de Veer.

2748 ADRES aan Z. M. den Koning ingediend door eenige Christenen, betreffende afschaffing van den slavenhandel en de slavernij. H. Höveker, Amsterdam, 1848. 4 pp.

2749 JAY, Charles
The dawn of African freedom, and the natural extinction of slavery, briefly considered. John Ollivier, London, 1848. 15 pp.

Moral rather than armed force should be used to suppress the slave trade; 'free African immigration' would civilise the Africans and extinguish the trade.

2750 SACO, José Antonio
Ideas sobre la incorporación de Cuba en los Estados-Unidos. Panckoucke, Paris, [1848]. 16 pp.

Suggests that the annexationists wish to reanimate the slave trade under United States protection. See (2757).

2751 'The SLAVE trade.' (AR, vol. 24, Nov. 1848, pp. 343–48.)

Review of US–British diplomatic exchanges on the Brazilian slave trade 1844–46.

2752 CAVE, Stephen
A few words on the encouragement given to slavery and the slave trade, by recent measures, and chiefly by the Sugar Bill of 1846. John Murray, London, 1849. 34 pp.

Slave trade and slavery have increased; it is inconsistent of Britain to chase slavers and pay for slave-grown produce.

2753 *FREE PRODUCE ASSOCIATION OF FRIENDS, Philadelphia
An address to our fellow members of the religious society of Friends on the subject of slavery and the slave-trade in the western world, by Philadelphia Free Produce Association of Friends. Philadelphia, 1849. 16 pp.

2754 **CHRISTY, David**
A lecture on African colonization. Including a brief outline of the slave trade, emancipation, the relation of the republic of Liberia to England, &c. Delivered in the hall of the House of Representatives of the state of Ohio . . . J. A. & U. P. James, Cincinnati, 1849. 56 pp.

Address by an agent of the American Colonization Society, 19 Feb. 1849.

2755 'The SLAVE trade.' (Signed: G.F.P.) (People's Journal, London, vol. 8, 1849, pp. 66–68.)

2756 **MADDEN, Richard Robert**
The island of Cuba: its resources, progress, and prospects, considered in relation especially to the influence of its prosperity on the interests of the British West India colonies. Charles Gilpin, London, 1849. xxiv, 252 pp.

Includes notes on the Cuban slave trade made 1836–39, when the author was British superintendent of liberated slaves at Havana; the appendix contains later information on the trade and its suppression.

2757 IDEAS sobre la incorporacion de Cuba en los Estados Unidos, en contraposicion á las que ha publicado Don José Antonio Saco. 'La Verdad', [New York,] 1849. 28 pp.

By Gaspar Betancourt Cisneros. Discusses Saco's views on the suppression of the slave trade, emancipation and white immigration, which have been frustrated by Spain. See (2750, 2768).

2758 **HUNTLEY, Sir Henry Veel**
Observations upon the free trade policy of England, in connexion with the Sugar Act of 1846, showing the influence of the latter upon the British tropical possessions, and its direct operation to perpetuate the slave-trade. Simpkin, Marshall, & Co., London; Beck, Leamington, 1849. 104 pp.

Quotes evidence to a recent commission showing the dangers of free competition from slave economies to the British West Indies and its effects on the slave trade; the duties should be restored.

2759 *FRIENDS, Society of
Address to sovereigns on the slave trade issued by the yearly meeting of Friends 1849. [London?] 1849. 4 pp.

Also published in French, Dutch, Italian, Swedish, Spanish and Portuguese. See (2788).

2760 *CHRISTY, David
A lecture on African civilization . . . and the relations of American slavery to African civilization . . . J. A. & U. P. James, Cincinnati, 1850. 52 pp.

Delivered in the hall of the House of Representatives of Ohio 19 Jan. 1850.

2761 **FITZ-GERALD, John**
Man stealing by proxy: or, the guilt of our countrymen in upholding slavery & the slave trade, by the purchase of slave grown produce. W. H. Dalton, London, 1850. 23 pp.

Evidence to the parliamentary committee on the slave trade 1849, and defence of a boycott and the African squadron.

2762 **BLYTH, G.**
Means of suppressing the slave trade. Extract of a letter written by the Rev. G. Blyth, lately from Jamaica. [Glasgow? 1850.] (2 pp.)

The antislavery treaties of 1810–35 should be enforced by the British government.

2763 *CHRISTY, David
A lecture on the present relations of free labor to slave labor, in tropical and semi-tropical countries: presenting an outline of the commercial failure of West India emancipation, and its effects upon slavery and the slave trade, together with its final effect upon colonization to Africa. Addressed to the constitutional convention of the state of Ohio, 1850 . . . J. A. & U. P. James, Cincinnati, 1850. 72 pp.

2764 **HOSTMANN, F. W.**
Over de beschaving van negers in Amerika, door kolonisatie met Europeanen, of beschouwingen omtrent de maatschappelijke vereeniging der negers in Afrika, den staat, waarin zij door den zoogenaamden slavenhandel komen, en later door abolitie en emancipatie overgaan. J. C. A. Sulpke, Amsterdam, 1850. 2 vol.

Abolition of the slave trade was a violation of international justice by Britain; it had saved millions of Africans and should be continued in the form of emigration of free labour to Surinam.

2765 STANLEY, Edward Henry
Claims and resources of the West Indian colonies. A letter to the Rt. Hon. W. E. Gladstone, M.P. . . . Third edition. T. & W. Boone, London, 1850. 111 pp.

The sugar tariff removed in 1846 should be restored to save the British colonies; blockading Brazil or Cuba to stop the slave trade is futile.

2766 The JAMAICA movement, for promoting the enforcement of the slave-trade treaties, and the suppression of the slave-trade; with statements of facts, convention, and law: prepared at the request of the Kingston committee. Charles Gilpin, London, 1850. 430 pp.

Edited by David Turnbull. Account of Britain's attempts to suppress the slave trade to Cuba and Brazil in the 1840s, accusing British merchants of being involved in it. (Reviewed in: ColM, vol. 18, 1850, pp. 419–28.) See (2767).

2767 LLOYD, Thomas
A letter to Lord Viscount Palmerston . . . Containing a refutation of Mr. Turnbull's statements that British merchants are implicated in the slave-trade. C. Gilpin, London, [1850]. 31 pp.

Turnbull (2766) has misrepresented the case of a suspected slave ship seized in 1840, of which Lloyd was part-owner.

2768 SACO, José Antonio
Réplica de Don José Antonio Saco á los anexionistas que han impugnado sus Ideas sobre la incorporacion de Cuba en les Estados Unidos. Madrid, 1850. 59 pp.

It would be wrong to revolt because Spain protects the illegal slave trade; the Cubans are guilty themselves and the trade would continue after annexation by the United States. See (2757).

2769 A CRY from the middle passage; or the act of 1846, and its effects on the slave trade. Seeley's, London, 1850. viii, 148, 4 pp.

The 1846 act has increased the slave trade and will perpetuate slavery.

2770 GILBERT, Thomas
Documents and evidence produced on an investigation relative to the treatment of immigrants. Held at San Fernando, Naparima . . . by order of His Excellency, Lord Harris, governor

of the island of Trinidad . . . Alexander Murray, San Fernando, Trinidad, 1850. iv, 52 pp.

On maltreatment of 'captured Africans' (many Yoruba) sent to Trinidad as agricultural labourers.

2771 TURNBULL, David
An address by the chief judge of the Court of Mixed Commission for the suppression of the slave trade; prepared in the commencement of the present year to be read at the Academy of Moral and Political Science at Paris. [London,] 1851. 36 pp.

The European powers should force the Spanish and Brazilian governments to end the slave trade and slavery. (Published posthumously.)

2772 'PRESENT condition of the slave trade.' (Sharpe's London Journal, vol. 14, 1851, pp. 10–15.)

2773 *The CASE of England and Brazil and the slave trade, stated—by a Brazilian merchant—with introduction and notes by an English merchant. N. H. Coates, London, 1851. xii, 40 pp.

2774 TAIT, William
The slave-trade overruled for the salvation of Africa. London, 1851. 43 pp. map.

The slave trade has opened the way for missionaries through the return of ex-slaves and the influence of the antislavery squadron.

2775 *CUESTION negrera de la isla de Cuba, por los editores y colaboradores de La Verdad. New York, 1851. 15 pp.

2776 ROESGEN VON FLOSS, Philippe von
Considérations sur la traite et l'émancipation des esclaves aux Indes-Occidentales. Delft, 1852. vi, 111 pp.

2777 *FREEMAN, Frederick
Africa's redemption the salvation of our country . . . New-York, 1852. 383 pp.

See (2623).

2778 The CASE of the free-labour British colonies, submitted to the British legislature and British nation for an impartial re-hearing. London, 1852. xvi, 155 pp.

The sugar duties act of 1846 stimulated the slave trade; the government should support African labour immigration to the British West Indies.

(Published by the Colonial Sub-Committee of the National Association for the Protection of Industry and Capital throughout the British Empire.)

2779 The UNCLE Tom's Cabin almanack or abolitionist memento, for 1853. London, [1852]. 70 pp. illus.

Includes articles on the slave trade.

2780 FRIENDS, Society of
Narrative of a recent visit to Brazil, by John Candler and Wilson Burgess: to present an address on the slave-trade and slavery . . . London, 1853. 91 pp.

2781 FIVE hundred thousand strokes for freedom. A series of anti-slavery tracts, of which half a million are now first issued by the friends of the negro. (Leeds anti-slavery tracts.) London, 1853. No. 1–82.

Edited by Wilson Armistead. Includes tracts and poems on the slave trade.

2782 DENMAN, Thomas, *Baron Denman*
Uncle Tom's Cabin, Bleak House, slavery and slave trade. Six articles by Lord Denman, reprinted from the "Standard"; with an article containing Facts connected with slavery, by Sir George Stephen, reprinted from the "Northampton Mercury". London, 1853. 51 pp.

Two articles on the slave trade.

2783 LENDRICK, William Edmonstone
Sugar-trade & slave-trade. The West-India question considered. London, 1853. 136 pp.

The sugar act of 1846 encouraged the slave trade, which could be suppressed by a more selective blockade, reduction of duties on free-labour sugar, and promotion of 'free immigration' from Africa.

2784 ARMISTEAD, Wilson
A 'cloud of witnesses' against slavery and oppression. Containing the acts, opinions, and sentiments of individuals and societies in all ages. Selected from various sources, and for the most part chronologically arranged. London, 1853. 154, 6 pp.

Useful compendium of opinions against the slave trade and slavery.

2785 *TENAZA, Ignacio, *pseud.*
Cuba and Africa. The Cuban question considered in relation to the African race. Paris, 1853. 16 pp.

By José Aniceto Iznaga. On the slave trade to Cuba. (Translated from an article entitled 'Africanización de Cuba'.)

2786 TORRENTE, Mariano
Memoria sobre la esclavitud en la isla de Cuba, con observaciones sobre los asertos de la prensa inglesa relativos al trafico de esclavos. Slavery in the island of Cuba, with remarks on the statements of the British press relative to the slave trade. London, 1853. 107, 32 pp.

Regrets abolition of the slave trade but suggests its replacement by African contract labour.

2787 CAREY, Henry Charles
The slave-trade, domestic and foreign: why it exists, and how it may be extinguished. A. Hart, Philadelphia, 1853. 426 pp.

The only solution to the African slave trade is to 'raise the value of man in Africa' by industrialisation there.

2788 FRIENDS, Society of
Proceedings in relation to the presentation of the address of the yearly meeting of the religious society of Friends, on the slave-trade and slavery, to sovereigns and those in authority in the nations of Europe, and in other parts of the world, where the Christian religion is professed. London, 1854. 62 pp.

Address prepared in 1849, with reports on the work of distributing it since then. See (2759).

2789 *LLAMAMIENTO de la isla de Cuba a la nacion española, dirigido al Excmo. é Illmo. Señor Don Baldomero Espartero, duque de la Victoria, presidente del Consejo de ministros, por un hacendado, en diciembre de 1854. Nueva-York, [1855?] 233, lv pp.

By C. F. Madan. Slave trade and slavery are compatible with economic progress and morality.

2790 AMERICAN COLONIZATION SOCIETY
Mémoire joint à une lettre adressée à S.M. l'Empereur au nom de la Société américaine de colonisation, et rédigé par un membre de la Société délégué auprès de toutes les puissances maritimes de l'Europe et de l'Amérique, pour obtenir d'elles qu'elles prennent conjointement les mesures nécessaires pour détruire la traite comme contraire

au droit des gens. (Signed: C.-F. Mercer.) Paris, [1855]. 20 pp.

2791 *SLAVERY indispensable to the civilization of Africa. Baltimore, 1855. 51 pp.

2792 EZQUERRA DEL BAYO, Joaquín
Parangon entre el esclavo y el proletario libre en el siglo XIX. Madrid, 1856. 43 pp.

The British employ recaptured slaves as 'apprentices'; African labour is necessary to Cuba, and the government should maintain the slave trade in a regulated form.

2793 'The SLAVE traffic.' (AR, vol. 32, Aug. 1856, pp. 241–44.)

Presents evidence of American participation in the slave trade.

2794 *SUÁREZ ARGUDÍN, José
Proyecto, ó representacion respetuosa sobre inmigracion africana dirigida al Escmo. Sr. gobernador y capitan general de la isla de Cuba, á fin de que por su conducto, y mereciendo su aprobacion, pueda ser elevada á S.M. Habana, 1856. 13, 5 pp.

2795 BACHILLER Y MORALES, Antonio
'Exàmen del proyecto de inmigracion de aprendices africanos.' (Revista de Jurisprudencia, Habana, vol. 1, 1856, pp. 150–64, 201–06.)

Discusses the disadvantages of importing African labour to Cuba. (The author was a member of a commission of enquiry on the subject.)

2796 *SEWARD, William Henry
Immigrant white free labor, or imported black African slave labor. Speech of Hon. William H. Seward at Oswego, New York, November 3, 1856. [Republican Association of Washington, Washington, 1856.] 7 pp.

2797 'The SOUTHERN Convention at Savannah . . . Debate on the slave trade.' (DBR, vol. 22, Feb. 1857, pp. 216–24.)

Speeches for and against repeal of the foreign slave trade laws of the United States.

2798 CHRISTY, David
Ethiopia; her gloom and glory, as illustrated in the history of the slave trade and slavery, the rise of the republic of Liberia, and the progress of African missions . . . Cincinnati, 1857. 255 pp.

Collection of lectures published separately 1849–53; colonisation is the only practical remedy for the slave trade.

2799 BRIEFE über Brasilien . . . Frankfurt am Main, 1857. vi, 58 pp.

The first letter, 'Sklavenhandel', denies the contention of Charles Reybaud (Le Brésil, 1856) that British policy prolonged the slave trade to Brazil and that the trade has now ended.

2800 FITZHUGH, George
'The middle passage; or, suffering of slave and free immigrants.' (DBR. vol. 22, June 1857, pp. 570–83.)

The slave trade to the United States, if regarded as vital, should be legalised; free immigrants suffer more than slaves.

2801 *BRITISH AND FOREIGN ANTI-SLAVERY SOCIETY
The immigration slave trade. [London, 1857.] 6 pp.

2802 *MILLER, C. W.
Address on re-opening the slave trade, by C. W. Miller, Esq., of South Carolina, to the citizens of Barnwell at Wylde-Moore, August 29, 1857. Columbia, S.C., 1857. 10 pp.

2803 'AFRICAN slave trade. A question of recent history.' (AR, vol. 33, Oct. 1857, pp. 302–07.)

Discusses efforts in the United States to withdraw the antislavery squadron and even to revive the slave trade.

2804 The NEGRO labour question. By a New-York merchant. New-York, 1858. 55 pp.

Proposes that African labour be obtained, 'if need be, by coercion'.

2805 *FRIENDS, Society of
The appeal of the religious society of Friends in Pennsylvania, New Jersey, Delaware, etc. to their fellow-citizens of the United States on behalf of the coloured races. Philadelphia, 1858. 48 pp.

On the New York slave trade.

2806 *MARANA, pseud.
The future of America. Considered . . . in view of . . . re-opening the slave trade. By Marana. . . . Boston, 1858. 70 pp.

2807 *HARPER, Robert G.
An argument against the policy of re-opening the African slave-trade. Atlanta, Ga., 1858. 78 pp.

2808 *ADGER, John Bailey
A review of reports to the legislature of S.C., on the revival of the slave trade ... From the April number of the Southern Presbyterian Review. Colombia, S.C., 1858. 36 pp.

2809 *NOTICE of the Rev. John B. Adger's article on the slave trade ... Charleston, 1858. 28 pp.

2810 LE PELLETIER DE SAINT-REMY, R.
'Les colonies françaises depuis l'abolition de l'esclavage.' (RDM, ser. 2, vol. 28, jan. 1858, pp. 86–117.)

Britain should not prevent France from remedying the labour shortage in her colonies by 'free immigration' from Africa and India, which will put an end to African slavery. (Published separately, Paris, 1858; 45 pp.)

2811 SPRATT, Leonidas W.
'Report on the slave trade, made to the Southern Convention at Montgomery, Alabama, by L. W. Spratt, Esq., chairman of the special committee.' (DBR, vol, 24, June 1858, pp. 473–91.)

Recommends that a committee of the Southern states investigate the reopening of the African slave trade.

2812 'LATE Southern Convention at Montgomery.' (DBR, vol. 24, June 1858, pp. 574–606.)

Includes a section on 'African slave-trade' (pp. 599–603); the issue was referred to the Committee on Business. (Report on the slave trade by W. L. Yancey: DBR, vol. 25, July 1858, pp. 121–22.)

2813 'CUBA and the slave trade.' (USM, 1858, II, pp. 345–54.)

The way to suppress the slave trade is to close the Cuban market and to persuade Africans to develop agriculture for export.

2814 *BRYAN, Edward B.
Letters to the southern people concerning the acts of Congress and the treaties with Great Britain, in relation to the African slave trade. Charleston, S.C., [1858]. 89 pp.

2815 'The SLAVE-TRADE in 1858.' (ER, vol. 108, 1858, pp. 541–86.)

Review of American pro-slavery literature, including proposals to revive the African slave trade. (See also sections on 'Foreign slave trade' in the annual reports of the American Anti-Slavery Society, New York, 1858–61.)

2816 'The REVIVAL of the African slave trade. Southern opinion on this subject.' (AR, vol. 34, Oct. 1858, pp. 303–06.)

Two articles by Southerners opposing the slave trade.

2817 ROBERTS, Percy
'African slavery adapted to the North and Northwest. The practicability, and policy, of introducing African slave labor into the western states and territories.' (DBR, vol. 25, Oct. 1858, pp. 379–95.)

Urges the reopening of the slave trade and reintroduction of slavery in the North to create 'a homogeneous system of labor' and restore harmony in the United States.

2818 COLLINS, John Gunn
An essay in favour of the colonization of the North and North-West Provinces of India, with regard to the question of increased cotton supply, and its bearing on the slave trade. London, [1858?] 39 pp.

British cotton-growing settlements in the Himalayan foothills will lead to the gradual extinction of the American slave trade.

2819 *SPRATT, Leonidas W.
The foreign slave trade. The source of political power—of material progress, of social integrity, and of social emancipation to the South. Charleston, 1858. 31 pp.

Articles reprinted from the 'New Orleans Delta'.

2820 DELONY, Edward
'The South demands more negro labor. To the people of Louisiana.' (DBR, vol. 25, Nov. 1858, pp. 491–506.)

America needs 'more and cheaper slave labor'; as Africa is 'designed' to supply it, the slave trade should be resumed.

2821 HUGHES, Henry
State liberties, or the right to African contract labor. Port Gibson, 1858. 53 pp.

Discusses the author's theory of 'warranteeism' and advocates 'a regulated supply of African labor' which would fall outside federal control. (Reprinted in: DBR, vol. 25, Dec. 1858, pp. 626–53.)

2822 TROY, D. S.
'Is the slave trade piracy? The constitutionality of the act of Congress declaring the slave trade to be piracy.' (DBR, vol. 26, Jan. 1859, pp. 23–28.)

Under the 1787 constitution the slave trade was not illegal; slave traders cannot therefore be punished as pirates.

2823 WALTON, Thomas
'Further views of the advocates of the slave trade.' (DBR, vol. 26, Jan. 1859, pp. 51–66.)

Federal laws prohibiting the slave trade are unconstitutional and should be annulled.

2824 FITZHUGH, George
'The administration and the slave trade.' (DBR, vol. 26, Feb. 1859, pp. 144–48.)

The slave trade is vital for the South and will continue whether legalised or not.

2825 JAMIESON, Robert
Commerce with Africa. The inefficacy of treaties for the suppression of the African slave trade, and their injurious influences on British commercial interests in Africa . . . Revised edition. London, 1859. 47 pp. map.

The attempt to suppress the slave trade by force has failed; the best method of overcoming it is to develop legitimate trade with Africa.

2826 *HUGHES, Henry
A report of the African apprentice system, read at the Southern Commercial Convention, by Henry Hughes. Held at Vicksburg, May 10th, 1859. [Vicksburg, 1859.] 15 pp.

2827 *GRAY, Peter W.
An address of Judge Peter W. Gray, to the citizens of Houston, on the African slave trade. Delivered May 30th, 1859, and published by several gentlemen who heard it. [Houston? 1859.] 28 pp.

2828 La QUESTION de Cuba. Paris, 1859. 63 pp.

By Francisco de Frías y Jacott, conde de Pozos Dulces. The Spanish government, not the Cubans, are responsible for the continuation of the slave trade which threatens Cuba with 'africanisation'.

2829 'SOUTHERN Convention at Vicksburg. Debate on the slave trade—speeches of Mr. Spratt, of South Carolina, and Gov. H. S. Foote, of Mississippi.' (DBR, vol. 27, Aug. 1859, pp. 205–20, 468–71.)

Debate on the report submitted by Spratt advocating revival of the African slave trade; Foote opposes this on political grounds.

2830 'AFRICAN Labor Supply Association.' (DBR, vol. 27, Aug. 1859, pp. 231–35.)

Letter from W. L. Yancey and reply from J. D. B. De Bow explaining the aims of the association, formed to promote the African slave trade in Southern states.

2831 BARRETT, William Garland
Immigration to the British West Indies. Is it the slave-trade revived or not? London, [1859]. 32 pp.

2832 CHANCEL, Ausone de
'Cham et Japhet ou de l'émigration des nègres chez les blancs considérée comme moyen providentiel de régénérer la race nègre et de civiliser l'Afrique intérieure.' (Revue Britannique, Paris, Sept. 1859, pp. 87–141, 343–92.)

African slaves should be redeemed and employed as 'engagés' for no more than ten years. (Also published separately, Paris, 1859; 104 pp.)

2833 FITZHUGH, George
'Missionary failure.' (DBR, vol. 27, Oct. 1859, pp. 382–87.)

Urges missionaries in Africa to support a 'humanely regulated slave trade' as 'the only practical means of converting the heathen'.

2834 HILLER, Oliver Prescott
A chapter on slavery: presenting a sketch of its origin and history, with the reasons for its permission, and the probable manner of its removal. London, 1860. v, 175 pp.

The slave trade was permitted by Providence in order to cultivate America and christianise Africa.

2835 LOVE, William De Loss
'The reopening of the African slave trade.' (New Englander, New Haven, vol. 18, Feb. 1860, pp. 90–124.)

Review article, deploring Southern proposals to resume slave imports.

2836 *SUÁREZ ARGUDÍN, José
Proyecto de inmigración africana, presentado al superior gobierno de esta isla, por los señores Argudín, Cunha Reis y Perdones, marzo de 1860. Habana, 1860. 85 pp.

Proposals on African immigration for Cuba, Puerto Rico and Brazil. (A critical reply by J. J. de Frias, 'Examen del proyecto de colonización africana', written 1861, was published in Revista de Cuba, Havana, vol. 8, 1880.)

2837 NETSCHER, Adriaan David van der Gon
De quaestie van vrijen arbeid en immigratie in de West-Indie . . . 's Gravenhage, 1860. 148 pp.

It is the duty of the European colonial powers to remove restrictions on African emigration to the West Indies, which will undermine African slavery and benefit the colonies.

2838 WILSON, John Leighton
'The foreign slave trade; can it be revived without violating the most sacred principles of honor, humanity, and religion?' (AR, vol. 36, July 1860, pp. 193–203.)

It would be inhuman to renew the African slave trade. (Extract from a pamphlet, Charleston, 1859.)

2839 *SUÁREZ ARGUDÍN, José
Proyecto de inmigración africana. Para las islas de Cuba y Puerto Rico y el imperio del Brasil presentado á los respectivos gobiernos por los sres. Argudín, Cunha Reis y Perdones. Habana, 1860. 600 pp.

The 'proyecto', the negative comment of Frias, and a number of articles supporting the scheme.

2840 JAY, John
The American church and the African slave trade. Mr. Jay's speech in the New York diocesan convention of the Protestant Episcopal Church. On the 27th September, 1860 . . . New York, 1860. 30 pp.

New York has become 'the greatest slave trading mart in the world'; the Church should condemn the slave trade, which is a danger to American missions in West Africa.

2841 'FOREIGN slave-trade.' (Annual report of the American Anti-Slavery Society, 1859–60, New York, 1861, pp. 13–30.)

Includes an account of the case of the slave ship 'Wanderer'.

2842 SPRATT, Leonidas W.
'A protest from South Carolina against a decision of the Southern Congress.

Slave trade in the Southern Congress.' (LLA, vol. 68, March 1861, pp. 801–10.)

Letter, reprinted from Spratt's 'Charleston Mercury' (13 Feb. 1861), criticizing the Confederate decision to prohibit the African slave trade.

2843 *CUNHA REIS, Manuel Basilio da
Memoria general ó sea resumen de las razones justificativas del proyecto de inmigración de brazos libres africanos que para la sustentacion de la riqueza agrícola de la isla de Cuba presentan al gobierno los sres. D. Manuel B. Cunha Reis, D. José Suárez Argudín y D. Luciano Fernandez y Perdones . . . Madrid, 1861. 93 pp.

2844 *The ENORMITY of the slave-trade; and the duty of seeking the moral and spiritual elevation of the colored race. Speeches by Wilberforce, and other documents and records. American Tract Society, New York, [1861]. 144 pp.

2845 WENKSTERN, Otto
An anti-slavery pamphlet. London, 1861. 136 pp.

The antislavery squadron is a costly failure; the British West Indies need 'coolie' immigration to combat Cuban slave production.

2846 'BESCHOUWINGEN over de Afrikanen en hunne geschiktheid als vrije arbeiders voor de West-Indische kolonien.' (Koloniale Jaarboeken, Zutphen, vol. 1, Sept. 1861, pp. 257–85.)

Compared to slavery at home, Africans are better off as 'free emigrant' labourers in the West Indies.

2847 WILDER, ——
'The slave-trade in New York.' (Continental Monthly, New York, vol. 1, 1862, pp. 86–90.)

Many Americans are still engaged in the Atlantic slave trade.

2848 CARLIER, Auguste
De l'esclavage dans ses rapports avec l'Union américaine. Paris, 1862. xv, 495 pp.

The North had profited most from the illegal slave trade; both Confederacy and Union should give formal guarantees to renounce it and make peace.

2849 POEY, Juan
Informes presentados al Excmo. Sr. Capitan general gobernador superior

civil de la isla de Cuba, sobre el proyecto de colonizacion africana, y al Ilmo. Sr. Intendente de hacienda de la propia isla, sobre derechos de los azúcares. Madrid, 1862. 162 pp.

> The first part (printed separately, Habana, 1862; 73 pp.) argues the disadvantages to Cuba of African immigration as suggested since 1855 by Suárez Argudín and others.

2850 *SPRATT, Leonidas W.
'The slave trade in the Southern Congress.' (Southern Literary Messenger, Richmond, Va., vol. 32, June 1862, pp. 409–20.)

> Answered by 'The African slave trade', ibid., vol. 33, Aug. 1862, pp. 105–13.

2851 *REFUTACION al informe emitido por la Real Universidad de la Habana sobre el proyecto de inmigracion africana. (Signed: J. S. A.) Nueva York, 1862. 24 pp.

> By J. Suárez Argudín.

2852a*REPRESENTACIÓN á la Reina de España, sobre la abolición de la esclavitud en las islas de Cuba y Puerto Rico. (Signed: Un habanero.) Filadelfia, 1862. 28 pp.

Translated as:

2852b MEMORIAL to the Queen of Spain, for the abolition of slavery in the islands of Cuba and Puerto Rico. (Signed: A Cuban.) New York, [1862?] 30 pp.

> Attributed to Félix M. Tanco.

2853 BRITISH AND FOREIGN ANTI-SLAVERY SOCIETY
The African slave trade to Cuba. London, [1862]. 4 pp.

2854 BRITISH AND FOREIGN ANTI-SLAVERY SOCIETY
Spain & the African slave-trade. An address to Spaniards; from the committee of the British & Foreign Anti-Slavery Society. 1862. London, [1862]. 6 pp.

> Urges Spaniards to demand that their government should effectively suppress the slave trade. (Also issued in Spanish.)

2855 CAIRNES, John Elliott
The Southern Confederacy and the African slave trade. The correspondence between Professor Cairnes, A.M., and George M'Henry, Esq. . . . Dublin, 1863. xxviii, 61 pp.

Letters to a newspaper (Nov.–Dec. 1862) in which Cairnes charges the South with desiring to reopen the slave trade and McHenry denies this.

2856 *The AFRICAN slave trade. The secret purpose of the insurgents to revive it. No treaty stipulations against the slave trade to be entered into with the European powers. Judah P. Benjamin's intercepted instructions to L. Q. C. Lamar, styled commissioner, etc. C. Sherman, Son & Co., Philadelphia, 1863. 24 pp.

> See (1161).

2857 CAIRNES, John Elliott
The slave power: its character, career and probable designs: being an attempt to explain the real issues involved in the American contest . . . Second edition. Much enlarged . . . London & Cambridge, 1863. xliv, 410 pp.

> Confederates probably intend to revive the African slave trade, which continued until 1860.

2858 HORRORS of the slave-trade. [London, 1863.] 4 pp.

> Extracts from documents on the illegal slave trade 1857–61.

2859 *La CUESTIÓN africana en la isla de Cuba, considerada bajo su doble aspecto de la trata interior y esterior. Por un cubano propietario. Madrid, 1863. 63 pp.

> By Joaquín Santos Suárez.

2860 SARGENT, Fitzwilliam
England, the United States, and the Southern confederacy . . . Second edition, revised and amended. London, 1864. vii, 184 pp.

> Ch. 4, 'The re-opening of the slave-trade', alleges that it was the deliberate intention of the Confederate government to revive the African slave trade.

2861a*FERRER DE COUTO, José
Los negros en sus diversos estados y condiciones; tales como son, como se supone qué son, y como deben ser. Nueva York, 1864. 310 pp.

Translated as:

2861b Enough of war! The question of slavery conclusively and satisfactorily solved, as regards humanity at large and the permanent interests of present owners. New York, 1864. 312 pp.

The slave trade ought to be restored by international agreement as 're-demption of slaves and prisoners' from Africa.

2862 EXPILLY, Charles
La traite, l'émigration et la colonisation au Brésil . . . Paris, 1865. ix. 336 pp.

Reprinted from: Revue du Monde Colonial, Asiatique et Américain, Paris, vol. 12, 1864, pp. 321–57; vol. 13, 1865, pp. 5–35, 173–209, 369–400; vol. 14, 1865, pp. 7–38, 183–208, 366–97; vol. 15, 1865, pp. 204–21, 372–83. The first section deals with the suppression of the slave trade.

2863 SACO, José Antonio
'Introduccion de colonos africanos en Cuba y sus inconvenientes.' (RHA, vol. 2, 1865, pp. 167–72, 207–12, 245–49; vol. 3, 1865, pp. 9–13.)

Opposes projects to replace the slave trade with African immigration to Cuba.

2864 *CUESTIÓN Dulce-Zulueta-Argüelles. [Habana, 1865.] 39 pp.

Argüelles, a Cuban official, was accused of selling 'contraband' slaves captured in 1863 and fled to New York.

2865 GONZÁLEZ OLIVARES, Ignacio
Observaciones sobre la esclavitud en la isla de Cuba. Madrid, 1865. 78 pp.

Defends the slave trade of the past but urges compliance with the aboli-tion laws and gradual emancipation.

2866 CHRISTIE, William Dougal
Notes on Brazilian questions . . . Lon-don & Cambridge, 1865. lxxi, 236 pp.

On the African 'emancipados' and Britain's diplomatic pressure on Bra-zil to abolish the slave trade, advising against repealing the Aberdeen act of 1845; by a former British envoy in Brazil.

2867 BERNAL, Calixto
'El gobierno y la trata de esclavos en las Antillas.' (RHA, vol. 4, 1865, pp. 24–27.)

Welcomes the Spanish decree of 27 Oct. 1865 providing for the return to West Africa of recaptured slaves.

2868 VIZCARRONDO CORONADO, Julio L. de
'El proyecto de ley de 19 de febrero para la represion y castigo del tráfico negrero.' (RHA, vol. 4, 1866, pp. 351–55.)

Spain must make every effort to suppress the slave trade. See (2873).

2869 'EXPOSICION presentada al Senado por varios dueños de ingenios con esc-lavos en la isla de Cuba.' (RHA, vol. 4, 1866, pp. 446–48.)

Petition to the Spanish senate for the suppression of the slave trade, signed 20 March 1866 by various Cuban slave owners. (Reprinted in: 2870.)

2870 APUNTES sobre la cuestion de la reforma política y de la introduccion de africanos en las islas de Cuba y Puerto-Rico. Madrid, 1866. 347 pp.

Collection of documents and articles on colonial reform and on the sup-pression of the slave trade. See (2869).

2871 FIGUERA, Fermin
Estudios sobre la isla de Cuba. La cuestión social. Madrid, 1866. 132 pp.

The Cuban slave trade must be suppressed and replaced by immigra-tion of labourers from the United States, the West Indies or Europe.

2872 *FERNÁNDEZ GOLFÍN Y FERRER, Luis
Breves apuntes sobre las cuestiones más importantes de la isla de Cuba. Barcelona, 1866. 159 pp.

Opposes the slave trade but supports slavery.

2873 *VIZCARRONDO CORONADO, Julio L. de
Proyecto de ley para la represión del tráfico de negros presentado en el Senado por el Sr. ministro de ultramar. Madrid, 1866. 15 pp.

See (2868).

2874 VALIENTE, Porfirio
Réformes dans les îles de Cuba et de Porto-Rico . . . Paris, 1869. xx, 412 pp.

Urges the Spanish government to make slave trading piracy.

2875a*CARSTENSEN, Edward
Propositions sur l'organisation d'une émigration et d'une immigration afri-caines. Paris, 1869. 19 pp.

Translated as:

2875b*Propositions for the organisation of an African emigration and immigration. Copenhagen, 1869. 18 pp.

2876 PETIT, J. de
'La traite orientale et les missions catholiques en Afrique.' (Revue Générale, Bruxelles, n.s., vol. 1, 1873, pp. 673–92; vol. 2, 1873, pp. 53–70, 128–46.)

Account of the East African and Sudanese slave trade and the role of the Catholic missions.

2877 'ZUR Bekämpfung der Sclaverei und des Sclavenhandels.' (NEK, 1873, col. 491–94.)

2878 'The SLAVE trade in Africa.' (London Quarterly Review, vol. 42, April 1874, pp. 71–82.)

Review of works on the slave trade and naval blockade (403, 3301–02).

2879 BAKER, Sir Samuel White
'Slavery and the slave trade.' (McM, vol. 30, 1874, pp. 185–95.)

The slave trade in Africa will be abolished by European civilisation, but the emancipation of slaves in the Muslim countries must be gradual.

2880 'AFRIKA und der Sklavenhandel.' (NEK, 1874, pp. 410–13.)

Recent explorers have revealed the extent of the slave trade in Africa.

2881 *MÉMOIRE sur l'état actuel de la traite des nègres, 1875. Paris, [1875].

A pamphlet.

2882 *AMERICAN MISSIONARY ASSOCIATION
What remains of slavery and the slave trade. The freedmen and Africa. Papers and addresses at the twenty-ninth anniversary of the American Missionary Association . . . New-York, 1875. 32 pp.

2883 CASTILLO, Carlos del
Carta de Cárlos del Castillo al director de "La Independencia" (de Nueva York) con motivo de su artículo editorial de 12 de agosto de 1875, titulado "¡La tea! ¡Y siempre la tea!" Londres, 1875. 86 pp.

Appendix contains anonymous articles 'Esclavitud y tráfico de esclavos' and 'Inglaterra y Cuba', refuting British allegations about Cuban slavery and slave trade.

2884 *Os EXPLORADORES inglezes em Africa e as suas infundadas arguições ao governo portuguez, julgados na Camara dos Senhores Deputados nas sessões de 15 e 16 de fevereiro. Seguido de um artigo do Sr. M. de Buhões sobre as providencias que Portugal tem tomado para acabar com a escravatura e a escravidão. Lisboa, 1877. 72 pp.

2885 'The SLAVE trade in Africa.' (Month, London, vol. 30, 1877, pp. 219–26.)

By H. J. Coleridge.

2886a BANNING, Émile
L'Afrique et la conférence géographique de Bruxelles . . . Bruxelles, 1877. 150 pp. map.

Translated as:

2886b Africa and the Brussels geographical conference . . . London, 1877. xv, 188 pp. map.

With a chapter on the African slave trade and the text of the declarations against it at Vienna 1814 and Verona 1822.

2887 BANNING, Émile
L'Afrique et la conférence géographique de Bruxelles. Deuxième édition, revue et augmenté . . . Bruxelles, 1878. xvi, 224 pp. maps.

Includes further evidence of the slave trade in Africa and the measures being taken to suppress it.

2888 *ALLEMANDE-LAVIGERIE, Charles Martial, Archbishop of Algiers
L'esclavage africain et les missionnaires d'Alger. Allocution prononcée par Mgr l'Archevêque d'Alger en son église cathédrale à l'occasion du départ de dix-huit missionnaires de la Société des Missions d'Alger, pour l'Afrique équatoriale. Alger, 1879. 17 pp.

2889 SALDANHA DA GAMA, Antonio de, conde de Porto Santo
Memoria historica e politica sobre o commercio da escravatura entregue no dia 2 de novembro de 1816 ao Conde Capo d'Istria, ministro do Imperador da Russia. (Mémoire historique et politique sur la traite des nègres.) Lisboa, 1880. 39 pp.

Discussion of Britain's motives for suppressing the slave trade and putting diplomatic pressure on Portugal; commercial and colonial monopoly is the real reason. (Written in 1816).

2890 TEDESCHI, Prospero
La schiavitù. Piacenza, 1882. 160 pp.

Muslim slave trade is a serious barrier to civilisation in Africa, to be overcome only by Christian missions.

2891 *EBEN, W.
Afrika.—De slavenhandel en de aard-rijkskundige conferentie van Brussel. Leuven, 1882. 219 pp. map.

2892 *EBEN, W.
Africa. De slavenhandel en de internationale maatschappij ter beschaving en verkenning van Africa . . . Leuven, 1882. 218 pp. map.

2893 *ROHLFS, Gerhard
'Soppressione della tratta degli schiavi.' (Esploratore, Milano, 1882, p. 363.)

2894 SOCIEDADE DE GEOGRAPHIA DE LISBOA
Stanley's first opinions. Portugal and the slave trade. Lisbon, 1883. 9 pp.

A letter from H. M. Stanley and reply from L. Cordeiro, 1878, on Portuguese attitudes to slavery. (First published 1878; reprinted as 'Portugal and the slave trade' in: Boletim da Sociedade de Geographica de Lisboa, ser. 4, no. 8, 1883, pp. 355–59.)

2895 SOCIEDADE DE GEOGRAPHIA DE LISBOA
Portugal and the Congo: a statement. Prepared by the African Committee of the Lisbon Geographical Society, L. Cordeiro, recording secretary . . . London, 1883. vi, 104 pp. maps.

By Luciano Cordeiro. Demonstrates Portugal's 'claim' to the Congo area and maintains that she was the first to suppress the slave trade in Europe itself; slavery has now been abolished in Portuguese territories.

2896 *SOCIEDADE DE GEOGRAPHIA DE LISBOA
A questão do Zaire. Portugal e a escravatura. Carta da Commissão nacional Africana da Sociedade de Geographia de Lisboa a todos os institutos e sociedades em relação com esta. Lisboa, 1883. 24 pp.

Also issued in French as: La question du Zaire. Le Portugal et la traite des noirs (Lisbonne, 1883; 30 pp.).

2897 WALLER, Horace
The speech . . . on the present slave-trade in Africa, at the annual meeting of the Ladies' Negroes' Friend Society . . . 1883. London, [1883]. 8 pp.

2898 ALLEN, Charles Harris
'Slavery and the slave trade.' (Leisure Hour, London, 1884, pp. 418–21.)

Slave trading remains to be suppressed in central Africa, the Portuguese territories and the Nile basin.

2899 CUST, Robert Needham
'On purchase, redemption, and pawning of negroes.' (Church Work: Mission Life, London, n.s., vol. 12, 1886, pp. 286–91.)

Attacks French Catholic missionaries for the redemption by purchase of African slaves. (Reprinted as 'On purchase of slaves by missionaries of the Church of Rome' in his: Linguistic and oriental essays, ser. 4, London, 1895, pp. 365–69.)

2900 ALLEMAND-LAVIGERIE, Charles Martial, *Cardinal*
L'esclavage africain. Conférence sur l'esclavage dans le Haut Congo faite à Sainte-Gudule de Bruxelles par le cardinal Lavigerie. Bruxelles; Paris, 1888. 35 pp.

Speech describing the Arab slave trade in the eastern Congo and welcoming the formation of a 'Société Nationale Anti-esclavagiste' in Brussels.

2901 ALLEMAND-LAVIGERIE, Charles Martial, *Cardinal*
L'esclavage africain. Conférence faite dans l'église de Saint-Sulpice à Paris. Paris, 1888. 52 pp.

Speech and documents on the misery of the central African slave trade. See (2998).

2902 *MAURI, Egidio, *Bishop of Osimo*
'Sulla schiavitù africana.' (Rosario; memorie dominicane, Ferrara, vol. 6, 1888, pp. 110–16, 129–33, 250–55.)

2903 *CARCERERI, S.
'Gli schiavi africani.' (Bollettino della Società Africana d'Italia, Napoli, vol. 7, 1888, pp. 215–19.)

2904 *VADON, Henri
L'esclavage africain. Conférence en faveur de l'œuvre antiesclavagiste faite dans la cathédrale de Tunis, le 8 avril 1888 . . . Tunis, [1888]. 43 pp.

2905 *'MOHAMMEDANISM and the slave-trade in Africa.' (Science, New York, 1888, pp. 325–26; map.)

2906 ALLEMAND-LAVIGERIE, Charles Martial, *Cardinal*
Lettre de S. Em. le cardinal Lavigerie sur l'esclavage africain à messieurs les directeurs de l'Œuvre de la Propagation de la Foi. Lyon, 1888. 77 pp. maps, port.

Describes the horrors of the slave trade and the projected Œuvre Antiesclavagiste. (Reprinted from: Missions Catholiques, Lyon, vol. 20, 1888, pp. 457–62, 469–75, 481–87, 493–99, 517–22; also published in translation as: Sulla schiavitù africana, Milano, 1889; 64 pp.)

2907 *GOWER, Granville George Leveson, *Earl Granville*
L'esclavage africain. Conférence faite à Londres le 31 juillet 1888. Paris, [1888]. 27 pp.

2908a ALLEMAND-LAVIGERIE, Charles Martial, *Cardinal*
L'esclavage africain. Discours prononcé au meeting tenu à Londres, le 31 juillet 1888 sous la présidence de Lord Granville . . . Paris, 1888. 27 pp.

Translated as:

2908b Slavery in Africa. A speech by Cardinal Lavigerie made at the meeting held in London July 31, 1888. Presided over by Lord Granville, former minister of English foreign affairs. Boston, 1888. 20 pp.

2909 ALLEMAND-LAVIGERIE, Charles Martial, *Cardinal*
Crusade against the slave-trade: oration by Cardinal Lavigerie at a meeting of the Anti-Slavery Society held in the Prince's Hall, London, Tuesday July 31st, 1888. London, 1888. 30 pp.

2910 *'SLAVE trade in Africa.' (BAGS, vol. 20, 1888, pp. 382–85.)

2911 *'AFRIKANISCHER Sklavenhandel eine Frucht des Islam.' (Christliche Welt, Leipzig, vol. 2, 1888, p. 444.)

2912 *ALLEMAND-LAVIGERIE, Charles Martial, *Cardinal*
De slavernij in Afrika. Mij tegen Slavenhandel, Bruxelles, 1888. 32 pp.

2913 CAMERON, Verney Lovett
'Slavery in Africa.' (Good Words, London, vol. 29, 1888, pp. 678–82.)

Account of the extension of the Muslim slave trade since 1840 and appeal for active countermeasures.

2914 *SANTOS SUÁREZ, Joaquín
'Informe de la Junta de Fomento, de Agricultura y Comercio de la Habana, acerca de la ley penal para castigo de los traficantes de negros. 1844.' (Revista Cubana, Havana, vol. 7, 1888.)
Address on a proposed anti-slave

trade law, reprinted with related documents from 1841–44.

2915 *BÜTTNER, Carl Gotthilf
'Afrikanischer Sklavenhandel und die Versuche ihn zu unterdrücken 1888.' (Export, Berlin, vol. 10, 1888, pp. 705–13.)

2916 ALLEMAND-LAVIGERIE, Charles Martial, *Cardinal*

Mémoire en forme de lettre à monsieur le président du Congrès des catholiques allemands de Fribourg sur la création d'une société anti-esclavagiste en Allemagne par le cardinal Lavigerie, primat d'Afrique. Paris, 1888. 45 pp.

Describes the state of slavery, particularly in German East Africa, and urges the formation of a German anti-slavery society.

2917 *HELMES, Walter
Gott will es! Wer bleibt zurück im Kampfe für Christentum und Menschenrechte? Münster i.W., 1888. 36 pp.

2918 *Der SCLAVENHANDEL in Afrika und seine Greuel, beleuchtet nach den Vorträgen des Cardinals Lavigerie und Berichten von Missionaren und Forschern, von Humanus . . . Münster i.W., 1888. 78 pp. port.

By W. Helmes. Account of Lavigerie's campaign against the African slave trade. See (2920, 2932).

2919 *DE MENSCHENONTEERENDE slavenhandel in Afrika in al zijne gruwelijkheid tentoongesteld. Mededelingen getrokken uit de onlangs gehouden redevoeringen van z. em. kardinaal Lavigerie en gestaafd door onwraakbare bewijsstukken van ooggetuigen. Rotterdam, 1888. vi, 58 pp. port.

2920 Los HORRORES de la trata de negros en el África. Por Humanus. Versión castellana aumentada con nuevos é interesantes documentos . . . Madrid, 1888. 129 pp.

Translation of (2918), with an account of European antislavery efforts and a biographical sketch of Lavigerie.

2921 DESCAMPS, Édouard Eugène François, *baron*
'Les grandes initiatives dans la lutte contre l'esclavage.' (MA, vol. 1, déc. 1888, pp. 2–13; fév. 1889, pp. 81–86; illus.)

On Belgian and Catholic action against the slave trade. (First part reprinted separately, Bruxelles, 1888; 12 pp.)

2922 *PIZZOLI, Domenico
Sulla tratta dei negri in Africa. Conferenza tenuta nel tempio della Casa professa al 15 dicembre 1888. Palermo, 1888. 26 pp.

2923 *ALLEMAND-LAVIGERIE, Charles Martial, *Cardinal*
'Brief van Kard. Lavigerie an het Anti-Slavencomité te Keulen.' (Annalen der Afrikaansche Missiën, Oudenbosch, vol. 5, 1888–89, pp. 135–36.)

2924 *PAUL, C.
'Bewegung gegen den Sklavenhandel in Deutschland.' (Christliche Welt, Leipzig, vol. 3, 1889, pp. 10–14.)

2925 PRESTON, William C.
'Slavery in central Africa.' (SuM, 1889, pp. 23–31; illus.)

2926 DELMER, Louis
'La Belgique et l'œuvre antiesclavagiste.' (MA, vol. 1, jan. 1889, pp. 40–56; illus.)

Account of the work of the Société Antiesclavagiste de Belgique.

2927 MÜNZENBERGER, Ernst Franz August
Afrika und der Mohammedanismus. Frankfurt a.M., 1889. 72 pp.

Equates Islam with slavery in Africa.

2928 *WAUTERS, Alphonse Jules
'La traite africaine. Son histoire. Son importance. Le caractère de ses opérations. Ses territoires de chasse. Ses marchés et ses débouchés. Les moyens préconisés pour la combattre et la détruire.' (Mouvement Géographique, Bruxelles, vol. 5, 1889, pp. 73–74, 77–78, 84.)

2929 SPONT, Alfred
La traite africaine. Ses origines et son état actuel. Le mal et ses remèdes. Paris, 1889. 32 pp.

Notes on the slave trade of the Sudan and East Africa; the remedy lies in educating the Africans. (Reprinted from: Revue de Géographie, Paris, vol. 25, 1889, pp. 81–94.)

2930 LACOUR, Jean Antoine Armand
L'esclavage africain. Dunkerque, 1889. 65 pp.

Describes the central African slave trade and urges support for the anti-slavery crusade in France.

2931 *RUFFET, Louis
La traite des nègres et l'esclavage en Afrique. Genève, 1889.

2932 La TRATTA degli schiavi in Africa ed i suoi orrori rilevati sulla scorta dei discorsi del cardinal Lavigerie e dei rapporti di missionari e viaggiatori . . . Roma, 1889. 80 pp.

Translation of (2918), with appendix containing a British report on the slave trade in northern Africa 1888 and a letter from Lavigerie to the Archbishop of Palermo.

2933 ALLEMAND-LAVIGERIE, Charles Martial, *Cardinal*
'L'état actuel de l'Afrique et le congrès international des sociétés antiesclavagistes. Lettre de S.E. le cardinal Lavigerie.' (MA, vol. 1, fév. 1889, pp. 87–97.)

2934 'De SLAVENHANDEL in Afrika.' (Signed: S.v.d.A.) (Studien op Godsdienstig, Wetenschappelijk en Letterkundig Gebied, Utrecht, n.s., vol. 20, 1889, pp. 66–90.)

By S. van den Anker.

2935 *RÖSEL, G.
Der Feldzug gegen die Sklaverei in Afrika, dessen Nothwendigkeit, Ausführbarkeit und Organisation. Trier, 1889. 31 pp.

2936 *SAGET, P.
Die Greuel der Sklaverei in Afrika und ihre Bekämpfung. Aachen, 1889. 29 pp.

2937 *Der SCHWARZE Kreuzzug. Die Greuel der Negersklaverei und die Bestrebungen des Afrikavereins deutscher Katholiken. Paderborn, 1889. 64 pp.

2938 *BALTZ, Johanna
Der Engel der Barmherzigkeit. Lebende Bilder mit verbindende Text. Münster i.W., 1889. 50 pp.

Includes accounts of the slave trade in Africa.

2939 CAMERON, Verney Lovett
'Slavery in its relation to trade in tropical Africa.' (Journal of the Society of Arts, London, vol. 37, March 1889, pp. 299–309.)

Civilized powers must rule the interior of Africa in order to suppress slavery and introduce legitimate trade. (Another address on the subject is printed in: Journal of the Manchester Geographical Society, vol. 4, 1888, pp. 301–06.)

2940 SIMON, Jules
'L'esclavage africain. Discours pro-

noncé au grand amphithéatre de la Sorbonne.' (MA, vol. 1, mars 1889, pp. 113–29; illus.)

On the reasons for and effects of the Muslim slave trade in Africa and the need for a 'crusade' against it.

2941 *THIERNESSE, A.
Les horreurs de l'esclavagisme en Afrique. Liège, 1889. 27 pp.

2942 *LE ROY, Alexandre
'L'esclavage africain.' (Annales Apostoliques, Paris, vol. 4, 1889, pp. 124–42.)

2943 *GÖSER, Johannes Ev.
Wider Sklavenjagd und Sklavenhandel in Afrika! Vortrag von Joh. Ev. Goeser, Stadtpfarrer in Saulgau. Mitglied des deutschen Reichstags . . . Saulgau, 1889. 14, ii pp.

2944 *DESCAMPS, Édouard Eugène François, baron
La part de la Belgique dans le mouvement africain. [Bruxelles? 1889.] 24 pp.

2945 MEAUX, Marie Camille Alfred de, vicomte
'La lutte contre l'esclavage.' (Correspondant, Paris, vol. 154, 1889, pp. 997–1021.)

On the preparations for an antislavery crusade.

2946 MERENSKY, Alexander
'Was sagt der Koran über Sklavenjagden und Sklaverei?' (DKZ, n.s., Vol. 2, April 1889, pp. 132–33.)

The Koran legitimises slave raiding among pagans.

2947 *PIZZOLI, Domenico
L'opera antischiavista del card. Lavigerie. Lettera del parroco D. Pizzoli delegato promotora dell'opera in Sicilia al Sig. Comm. Andrea Guarneri senatore del regno. Palermo, 1889. 20 pp.

2948 *L'UNITÀ del genere umano e la tratta dei negri in Africa. Lettera pastorale al clero ed al popolo dell'archidiocesi di Palermo per la quaresima 1889. Palermo, 1889. 13 pp.

By Cardinal P. G. M. Celesia.

2949 *AGOSTINI, Domenico, Cardinal
Per la emancipazione degli schiavi in Africa. Lettera pastorale di S.E. il cardinale Domenico Agostini patriarca di Venezia. Venezia, 1889. 10 pp.

2950 MARBEAU, Édouard
'Suppression de l'esclavage africain. Projet de conférence internationale.' (RFEC, vol. 8, 1889, pp. 129–38.)

The European powers should meet in Brussels and set up an international antislavery commission, with a fleet of cruisers at its disposal.

2951 *ABBADIE, Antoine d'
'Idee per l'abolizione della schiavitù africana.' (Bollettino della Società Africana d'Italia, Napoli, vol. 8, 1889, pp. 165–73.)

2952 *BRESSI, Salvatore Maria Brunone, Archbishop of Otranto
Sull'abolizione della schiavitù. Articoli riportati dal benemerito giornale "Unità Cattolica" di Torino . . . Scafati, 1889. 23 pp.

2953 *La TRAITE des nègres et la croisade africaine. Choix raisonné de documents relatifs à la question de l'esclavage africain et comprenant la lettre encyclique de Léon XIII sur l'esclavage, le discours du cardinal Lavigerie à Bruxelles . . . les témoignages des grands explorateurs . . . les missionaires françaises, les révélations du livre bleu anglais, etc., ainsi que l'organisation des sociétés antiesclavagistes en Belgique et en Europe, ouvrage de vulgarisation . . . par Alexis–M.G. . . . Liège, 1889. 237 pp. illus, maps.

By Jean Baptiste Gochet. Also published in a Flemish edition. (Reviewed in: Revue des Questions Scientifiques, Bruxelles, vol. 26, 1889, pp. 272–77.)

2954 TORRES CAMPOS, Rafael
'La campaña contra la esclavitud y los deberes de España en Africa.' (Boletín de la Sociedad Geográfica de Madrid, vol. 26, 1889, pp. 271–305.)

Account of the Muslim slave trade and the obligation of Spain to take part in its suppression.

2955 *EBELING, Adolf
Die Sklaverei von den ältesten Zeiten bis auf die Gegenwart . . . Paderborn, 1889. iv, 107 pp.

Includes sections on African slavery and Lavigerie's antislavery campaign.

2956 *Die PRAKTISCHEN Möglichkeiten einer Lösung der afrikanischen Sklavenfrage. Gedanken für Antisklavereikongresse. Von P. Superior der deutschen St. Benediktus-Missionsgesellschaft. St. Ottilien, 1889. 22 pp.

The slave trade can only be exterminated by extending Christianity through 'missionary monasteries' linked by railways and telegraphs.

2957 *WARNECK, Gustav
Die Stellung der evangelischen Mission zur Sklavenfrage. Geschichtlich und theoretisch erörtert. Gütersloh, 1889. 126 pp.

2958 *La BARBARIE africaine et l'action civilisatrice des missions catholiques au Congo et dans l'Afrique équatoriale, contenant, comme préliminaires, un chapitre sur le movement anti-esclavagiste et le discours du cardinal Lavigerie à Londres . . . par Alexis M.G. . . . Liège, 1889. 208 pp. illus.

By J. B. Gochet.

2959 ALLEMAND-LAVIGERIE, Charles Martial, *Cardinal*
Documents sur la fondation de l'Œuvre antiesclavagiste. Saint-Cloud, 1889. lix, 724 pp. maps.

Letters, speeches, conference documents and eyewitness reports on the African slave trade. Lavigerie was charged by the Pope with making propaganda for European military intervention to facilitate missionary work in Africa.—See also: DIN-DINGER, G. 'Missionsschrifttum von und über Kardinal Lavigerie' in: Miscellanea Pietro Fumasoni-Biondi vol. 1 (Roma, 1947), pp. 105–91.

2960 BÉTHUNE, Léon, *baron*
'Les puissances européennes et la traite des nègres depuis la Congrès de Berlin.' (MA, vol. 1, août 1889, pp. 267–76.)

2961 *LE ROY, Alexandre
'Notes sur l'esclavage africain.' (Revue Catholique de l'Alsace, Rixheim, vol. 8, 1889, pp. 555–66, 618–26, 705–12.)

2962 *PRINA, Benedetto
'La schiavitù africana e la Società Antischiavista.' (Annali Francescani, Milano, vol. 20, 1889, pp. 338–42, 365–71.)

2963 LATINI, Silvestro
Leone XIII e la tratta dei negri. Cuneo, 1889. 33 pp.

Only the introduction of Catholicism can end the horrors of the slave trade in central Africa.

2964 *HUNTINGTON, Collis Potter
'The African slave-trade.' (American, Philadelphia, vol. 18, 1889, p. 367.)

2965 SEVIN-DESPLACES, Louis
'La campagne anti-esclavagiste.' (Nouvelle Revue, Paris, vol. 60, sept. 1889, pp. 361–70.)

On the suppression of the Muslim slave trade in Africa.

2966 *LE ROY, Alexandre
Le congrès de Bruxelles. L'esclavage africain . . . Paris, 1889. 23 pp.

2967 PLAUCHUT, Edmond
'Le congrès anti-esclavagiste.' (RDM, ser. 3, vol. 96, 1889, pp. 428–60.)

On the Muslim slave trade in Africa.

2968 *Ein WORT an alle, welche der Anti-sclaverei-Bewegung in Österreich Erfolg wünschen. Wien, 1889.

By Countess Ledóchowska?

2969 *PALADINI, Leone
Proposta di una associazione internazionale europea che si obblighi ad una pace decennale per concorrere all'abolizione della schiavitù in Africa, mediante la costruzione di una ferrovia transsaharica. Roma, 1889. 40 pp.

2970 LUGARD, Frederick John Dealtry
Coercive measures for suppression of the slave trade. London, [1889]. 14 pp.

2971 SHAW, Flora Louisa
'A propos de la Conférence de Bruxelles.' (MA, vol. 2, déc. 1889, pp. 3–6.)

Analyses the diplomatic problems facing the conference in its aim of suppressing the African slave trade.

2972 SCHUTZ, Édouard Henri
'La suppression de l'esclavage au moyen d'un ordre de chevalerie.' (MA, vol. 2, déc. 1889, pp. 6–7.)

Proposes that the antislavery blockade be conducted by a Christian order of privateers financing itself by selling freed slaves as contract labourers.

2973 MOLINARI, Gustave de
'La question de l'esclavage africain et la conférence de Bruxelles.' (Journal des Économistes, Paris, vol. 48, déc. 1889, pp. 321–34.)

On the suppression of the slave trade as background to the Brussels antislavery conference.

2974 *ALLEMAND-LAVIGERIE, Charles Martial, *Cardinal*
'Estensione ed orrori della schiavitù in Africa.' (Nigrizia, Verona, vol. 7, 1889, pp. 19–28; vol. 8, 1890, pp. 49–60, 81–87, 112–20, 138–51, 179–86; vol. 9, 1891, pp. 18–21.)

2975 CLARKE, Richard Henry
'The new crusade of the nineteenth century.' (American Catholic Quarterly

Review, Philadelphia, vol. 15, 1890, pp. 53–72.)

Account of the slave trade in central Africa and Catholic plans for its suppression by force.

2976 *ALLEMAND-LAVIGERIE, Charles Martial, *Cardinal*
Lettre de Son Eminence le cardinal Lavigerie à Monsieur le Président de la Conférence internationale de Bruxelles pour l'esclavage, relativement aux événements récents de l'Ouganda et aux dangers dont menacent l'Afrique les sectes musulmanes et principalement celle des Snoussya. Alger, 1890. 64 pp.

Dated 19 Feb. 1890.

2977 *ALLEMAND-LAVIGERIE, Charles Martial, *Cardinal*
Conférence sur l'esclavage africain faite à Rome dans l'église du "Gesù". Alger, 1890. 47 pp.

Speech delivered 23 Dec. 1888.

2978 *HABIL KLARIN M'TA EL CHOTT, *pseud.*
L'esclavage en Afrique, par le cheikh Si Habil Klarin M'ta el Chott. Paris, 1890.

By Abel Clarin de la Rive.

2979 *ZARAGOZA, José
Liberia; apúntes historicos de su fundación hasta su declaración en estado independiente, con una reseña de los horrores de la trata en el centro de Africa, y algunas consideraciones y documentos importantes sobre los beneficios que reportan á la humanidad las sociedades colonizadoras y antiesclavistas . . . Manila, 1890. 173 pp. maps.

2980 HUTCHINSON, William Nelson
'Are slave raids preventible?' (USM, n.s., vol. 4, March 1890, pp. 513–20.)

Suggests suppressing the slave trade in Africa by means of military 'aëronauts' in navigable balloons.

2981 BOURNICHON, Joseph
L'invasion musulmane en Afrique suivie du réveil de la foi chrétienne dans ces contrées et de la croisade des noirs entreprise par S.E. le cardinal Lavigerie archevêque d'Alger et de Carthage. Tours, 1890. 351 pp. illus, port.

Pt. 5: 'La croisade noire.'

2982 KURTH, Godefroid
La croix et le croissant . . . Deuxième édition. Liège, 1890. 33 pp.

Urges support for Lavigerie's crusade as a campaign against Islam.

2983 *LE ROY, Alexandre
Mehr Licht in die Zustände des dunklen Welttheils. Die Sclaverei und ihre Bekämpfung. Denkschrift gerichtet an den Luzerner Antisclaverei-Congress von P. Alexander Le Roy, Superior der Mission von Mrogoro, Ostafrika . . . Münster i.W., 1890. 28 pp.

2984 *ALLEMAND-LAVIGERIE, Charles Martial, *Cardinal*
Discours sur l'esclavage africain prononcé par S.E. le cardinal Lavigerie à Londres. Paris, 1890. 45 pp.

**2985a*De ANTI-SLAVERNIJ-CONFERENTIE en invoerrechten in den Congo-Staat. Door een koopman. Rotterdam, 1890.

Translated as:

**2985b*The ANTI-SLAVERY conference and import duties in the Congo state. By a trader . . . Liverpool, 1890. 16 pp.

By W. C. Schalkwijk. (Also published in French.)

2986 ALLEMAND-LAVIGERIE, Charles Martial, *Cardinal*
'Lettre de S.E. le cardinal Lavigerie aux comités nationaux de la Société antiesclavagiste.' (MA, vol. 2, août 1890, pp. 268–93.)

On the background to the antislavery movement and the tasks ahead.

2987 *ALLEMAND-LAVIGERIE, Charles Martial, *Cardinal*
Lettre de Son Éminence le cardinal Lavigerie à M. le président du Congrès catholique de Coblentz. Saint-Cloud, [1890]. 12 pp.

Antislavery message to German Catholics.

2988 *ALLEMAND-LAVIGERIE, Charles Martial, *Cardinal*
Lettre de Son Éminence le cardinal Lavigerie à MM. les prèsidents et membres des comités nationaux de la Société antiesclavagiste, à l'occasion de la prochaine réunion d'un congrès libre antiesclavagiste. Alger, 1890. 58 pp.

**2989 *La CONFÉRENCE de Bruxelles et les Pays-Bas, par un ami de la vérité. Anvers, 1890. 24 pp.

Reply to (2985). See (2995).

**2990 'Le CONGRÉS anti-esclavagiste de Paris.' (Afrique Explorée et Civilisée, Genève, 1890, pp. 350–58.)

2991   **BAUMGARTEN, Johannes**
Ostafrika, der Sudan und das Seeen-gebiet. Land und Leute . . . Aufgaben und Kulturerfolge der christlichen Mission, Sklavenhandel. Die Antisklaverei-bewegung, ihre Ziele und ihr Ausgang . . . Gotha, 1890. xvi, 563 pp.

Includes chapters on the slave trade in Africa and an appendix on the antislavery movement.

2992   ***ALLEMAND-LAVIGERIE, Charles Martial, *Cardinal***
Lettre pastorale de Son Éminence le cardinal Lavigerie portant communication à MM. les curés de ces deux diocèses du bref "Catholicae Ecclesiae" adressé par Notre Saint Père le Pape Léon XIII aux evêques du monde chrétien relativement à l'Œuvre anti-sclavagiste et à une quête annuelle en faveur de cette Œuvre. Alger, 1890. 20 pp.

Letter of 8 Dec. on the encyclical of 20 Nov. 1890.

2993   **SLATTERY, John Richard**
'The African slave-trade.' (Catholic World, New York, vol. 50, 1890, pp. 666–77.)

Describes various schemes to suppress the trade and suggests sending American negro priests to Africa as missionaries. Based on (4057).

2994   **WOLSELEY, *Sir* Garnet**
'The anti-slavery congress.' (USM, n.s., vol. 2, Oct. 1890, pp. 1–8.)

The right way to suppress the African slave trade is to stop imports of fire-arms and ammunition.

2995   DE KONGO-VRIJSTAAT en de handel . . . Door een koopman. Rotterdam, 1890. 35 pp.

Reply to (2989), by W. C. Schalkwijk. The Dutch are not opposed to the suppression of the slave trade but commerce should not have to pay for this policy.

2996   ***HALKA, Alexander, *pseud.***
'Das Werk der Antisclaverei. I. Sein Wesen, II. sein Entstehen und III. seine Entwicklung.' (Echo aus Afrika, Wien, vol. 2, 1891, no. 1, pp. 2–4; no. 2, pp. 1–3; no. 3, pp. 2–4; no. 4, pp. 2–5; no. 5, pp. 1–4; no. 6, pp. 1–3; no. 7, pp. 1–3; no. 8, pp. 2–3; no. 9, pp. 1–4; no. 10, pp. 1–6; no. 11, pp. 1–5; no. 12, pp. 2–4.)

By M. T. F. Ledóchowska.

2997   ***KORWIN SZYMANOWSKI, Theodore de***
L'esclavage africain . . . Paris, 1891. 15 pp.

2998   **CHAFIK, Ahmed**
'L'esclavage au point de vue musulman.' (Bulletin de la Société Khédiviale de Géographie, Le Caire, ser. 3, no. 6, mars 1891, pp. 409–66.)

Reply to Lavigerie (2901) in defence of the Muslim position. (Published as: Al-riqq fī'l–Islām, Cairo, 1892.)

2999   **RUFFET, Louis**
'Le devoir des chrétiens évangeliques dans la question de l'esclavage en Afrique.' (Revue Chrétienne, Paris, n.s., vol. 8, 1891, pp. 437–58.)

Report to an Evangelical conference in Florence (10 April 1891), criticizing the Catholic antislavery campaign as a 'marche dans le sang'. (Reprinted separately, Dole, 1891; 24 pp.)

3000   **ALLEMAND-LAVIGERIE, Charles Martial, *Cardinal***
L'esclavage africain. Conférences de Son Éminence le cardinal Lavigerie primat d'Afrique à Paris, à Londres et à Bruxelles illustrées de XII planches . . . Gand, 1891. iv, 16 pp.

Speeches on the slave trade 1888–90.

3001   **LEFÈVRE-PONTALIS, Eugène Amédée**
Conférences antiesclavagistes. Saint-Cloud, [1891]. 32 pp.

Two speeches 1890–91 in praise of Lavigerie's work.

3002   **DEUTSCHE KOLONIALGESELL-SCHAFT**
'Was tun wir Deutsche gegen den Sklavenhandel? Eine Frage an das Gewissen des deutschen Volks.' (Signed: v. C.) (DKZ, n.s., vol. 4, Juni 1891, pp. 91–93.)

Suggests military, economic and missionary efforts to suppress slavery in Africa.

3003   ***ALLEMAND-LAVIGERIE, Charles Martial de, *Cardinal***
Lettre de Son Éminence le cardinal Lavigerie à tous les volontaires qui se sont proposés à l'œuvre antiesclavagiste de France, sur l'Association des Frères Armés ou Pionniers du Sahara. Paris, 1891. 50 pp.

Outlines rules for an anti-slave trade crusading order.

3004 *L'ACTE général de la Conférence de Bruxelles devant les Chambres françaises, réflexions d'un homme politique sur les objections des membres de la commission parlementaire. Saint-Cloud, 1891. 16 pp.

By Émile Banning.

3005 SCHWERIN, Hans Hugold von, *friherre* Slafveri och slafhandel i Afrika. Lund, 1891. 45 pp.

Attacks the sentimentality of anti-slavery ideas; only European trade will develop Africa.

3006 TREE, Lambert 'The treaty of Brussels and our duty.' (Forum, New York, vol. 12, Jan. 1892, pp. 614–20.)

3007 *NETTELBLADT, F. von, *Freiherr* 'Sklaverei und Sklavenhandel in Afrika.' (Monatsschrift für Stadt und Land, Halle, 1892, vol. 1, pp. 184–88; vol. 2, pp. 1272–76.)

3008 *'TRAITE et esclavage dans l'Afrique équatoriale.' (Missions d'Alger, Paris, 1892, pp. 242–50.)

3009 ASMUSSEN, P. 'Sklavenwesen in West- und Ostafrika.' (Deutsche Geographische Blätter, Bremen, vol. 15, 1892, pp. 250–56.)

Slavery can be allowed to continue in Africa but the slave trade must be suppressed.

3010 *SORUR PHARIM DÈN, Daniel Meine Brüder, die Neger in Afrika. Ihr Wesen, ihre Befähigung, ihre jetzige traurige Lage, ihre Hoffnungen. Ein ernstes Wort an Europas Christen von Daniel Sorur Pharim Den, früherer Sklave, jetziger Missionär. Nach dem italienischen Manuskript besorgte und mit einer Vorrede versehene deutsche Ausgabe von Dekan Schneider in Stuttgart . . . Münster i/W., 1892. 96 pp. illus.

Published by W. Helmes. Perhaps a translation of the text printed as 'Le pene dei negri schiavi in Africa' in: Euntes docete, Pontificia Universitas Urbaniana, Roma, vol. 17, 1964, pp. 51–93.

3011 *SCHLAUCH, Lőrincz, *Bishop of Nagy-várad* Due discorsi. I. Sulla tratta degli schiavi in Africa. II. Sulla questione operaja. Budapest, 1892. 81 pp.

3012 STANLEY, Henry Morton 'Slavery and the slave trade in Africa.'

(BMM, vol. 86, March 1893, pp. 613–32; illus.)

Partition of Africa was the first effective blow against the slave trade in the interior; England can help to end it by building a railway to Lake Nyanza. (Reprinted separarately, New York, 1893; 86 pp.)

3013 COUSINS, H. T. 'Slavery in Africa.' (SuM, 1893, pp. 166–72; illus.)

Missionary view of the slave trade.

3014 CHRISTIANITY and the slave trade. By Saladin. London, 1894. 91 pp.

By W. S. Ross. Both Roman Catholics and Protestants bear responsibility for having tolerated the slave trade in the past.

3015 *ALLEN, Charles Harris What is Great Britain doing to suppress slavery and the slave trade? [London? 1894.]

3016 IMBART DE LA TOUR, Joseph Jean Baptiste, *comte*

L'esclavage en Afrique et la croisade noire. Paris, [1894]. iv, 184 pp.

Describes the slave trade in Africa and the movement to suppress it.

3017 *ABBADIE, Antoine d' Sur l'abolition de l'esclavage en Afrique. Paris, 1896. 8 pp.

Reprinted from: Bulletin de la Société des Études Coloniales et Maritimes, Paris, vol. 21, 1896.

3018 PICOT, Georges 'La Société antiesclavagiste, son action générale et son role pratique.' (Réforme Sociale, Paris, vol. 32, 1896, pp. 539–45.)

Account of the work of the French antislavery society, by its vice-president.

3019 CHATELAIN, Heli 'African slavery; its status and the antislavery movement in Europe.' *In*: BOWEN, J. W. E. Africa and the American negro (Atlanta, 1896), pp. 103–12.

Proposes a 'Philafrican Liberators' League' in North America to promote settlements for liberated slaves in Africa.

3020 *GAUTHEY, Léon L'esclavage africain, allocution prononcée à la cathédrale d'Autun le

10 janvier 1897 ... Société Antiesclava-giste de France, Paris, 1897. 16 pp.

3021 CUST, Robert Needham
'Armed opposition to slave-trade.' *In his*: Linguistic and oriental essays, ser. 5, vol. 2 (London, 1898), pp. 761–64.

Article, first published in 1889; the use of force against slavers in Africa, as advocated by Catholics and Presbyterians, will not help the missions.

3022 TOLLI, Filippo
'Il congresso antischiavistico a Parigi nel 1900.' (Rivista Internazionale di Scienze Sociali, Roma, vol. 23, 1900, pp. 21–25.)

3023 DARCY, Jean
'La Société antiesclavagiste de France.' (Correspondant, Paris, vol. 207, 1902, pp. 101–17.)

On the aims of the society in Africa.

3024 DU TEIL, Joseph, *baron*
'L'antiesclavagisme en Afrique, à pro-pos du récent congrès de Rome 22–24 avril 1903.' (Correspondant, Paris, vol. 211, 1903, pp. 1191–1201; map.)

Islam must be combatted and 'villages de liberté' supported in Africa.

(Reprinted as a pamphlet, Paris, 1903; 15 pp.)

3025 DU TEIL, Joseph, *baron*
'Les villages de liberté en Afrique, à propos du concours ouvert par la Société antiesclavagiste de France.' (Réforme Sociale, Paris, vol. 48, 1904, pp. 483–92; illus, map.)

Reprinted as a pamphlet, Paris, 1904; 12 pp.

3026 *DU TEIL, Joseph, *baron*
La Société antiesclavagiste de France et ses villages de liberté en Afrique ... Paris, [1904]. 16 pp. illus, map.

3027 TOLLI, Filippo
'La società antischiavistica italiana in Africa.' (Rivista Internazionale di Scienze Sociali, Roma, vol. 44, 1907, pp. 239–41.)

3028 CAGIGAL, Juan Manuel
'Tráfico de esclavos.' *In his*: Escritos literarios y cientificos (Caracas, 1930), pp. 149–56.

Critique (written Feb. 1839) of the anti-slave trade treaty concluded between Venezuela and Britain 19 May 1837; it is unfavourable and should be renegotiated.

Q. ABOLITION SOCIETIES AND CONFERENCES

(a) PUBLICATIONS AND REPORTS

3029 *SOCIETY FOR THE ABOLITION OF THE SLAVE TRADE
List of the Society, instituted in 1787, for the purpose of effecting the abolition of the slave trade. London, 1787. 93 pp.

Report and list of committee members and subscribers.

3030 PENNSYLVANIA SOCIETY FOR PROMOTING THE ABOLITION OF SLAVERY
The constitution of the Pennsylvania Society, for promoting the Abolition of Slavery, and the Relief of Free Negroes, unlawfully held in Bondage. Begun in the year 1774, and enlarged on the twenty-third of April, 1787. To which are added, the acts of the General Assembly of Pennsylvania, for the gradual abolition of slavery. Joseph James, Philadelphia, 1787. 15 pp.

3031 SOCIETY FOR THE ABOLITION OF THE SLAVE TRADE
'Circular report of the committee for abolishing the slave trade.' (Signed: Granville Sharp.) (GM, vol. 58, Feb. 1788, pp. 161–63.)

Report of 15 Jan. 1788; first issued as a broadsheet.

3032 SOCIETY FOR THE ABOLITION OF THE SLAVE TRADE
'Report of the Society, instituted for the purpose of effecting the Abolition of the Slave Trade.' (Signed: Granville Sharp.) (Annals of Agriculture, Bury St. Edmund's, vol. 9, 1788, pp. 82–87.)

Report of 15 Jan. 1788. (A second report was issued 12 Aug. 1788 and printed in the 'List' for 1788.)

3033 SOCIETY FOR THE ABOLITION OF THE SLAVE TRADE, Manchester
At a general meeting held this day at the Exchange-Tavern . . . (Signed: Thomas Walker, chairman.) [Manchester, 1788.] (1 p.)

Report on the formation of the Society for the Purpose of effecting the Abolition of the Slave Trade, 27 Dec. 1787, and resolutions adopted at a meeting 29 Dec. 1787.

3034 SOCIETY FOR THE ABOLITION OF THE SLAVE TRADE
'Letter to the president, vice-president and committee of the Pennsylvania society for promoting the abolition of slavery, and the relief of free negroes unlawfully held in bondage, from the committee of the London society for promoting the abolition of the slave-trade.' (Signed: Granville Sharp, 28 Feb. 1788.) (AM, vol. 4, Nov. 1788, pp. 413–14.)

Regrets the failure of Congress to abolish the slave trade in 1787 and reports on abolitionist efforts in Britain.

3035 PENNSYLVANIA SOCIETY FOR PROMOTING THE ABOLITION OF SLAVERY
'To the honourable the convention of the United States of America, now assembled in the city of Philadelphia. The memorial of the Pennsylvania society for promoting the abolition of slavery, and the relief of free negroes, unlawfully held in bondage.' (AM, vol. 3, May 1788, pp. 404–05.)

The society expresses distress at the revival of African slave trade after the restoration of peace in 1783 and the involvement of American ships. (Intended for presentation in June 1787 but withheld to avoid antagonising some southern states.)

3036 SOCIÉTÉ DES AMIS DES NOIRS
Réglemens de la Société des Amis des Noirs. [Paris, 1788.] 46 pp.

Rules of the French antislavery society. See (3661).

3037 SOCIÉTÉ DES AMIS DES NOIRS
'Letter from the society established in Paris, on the plan of those in England and America, to effect the abolition of the commerce and slavery of the negroes

—To the committee of the Pennsylvania society for the abolition of slavery, and the relief of free negroes unlawfully held in bondage.' (AM, vol. 4, Nov. 1788, p. 507.)

> Requests assistance for J. P. Brissot during his visit to the United States.

3038 SOCIETY FOR THE ABOLITION OF THE SLAVE TRADE
'Letter to the president, vice-president and committee of the Pennsylvania society for promoting the abolition of slavery, and the relief of free negroes unlawfully held in bondage, from the committee of the London society for promoting the abolition of the slave trade.' (Signed: Granville Sharp, 30 July 1788.) (AM, vol. 4, Dec. 1788, pp. 507–09.)

> Describes the activities of the London society and explains its policy of concentrating on abolition of the slave trade; the cause has been harmed by allegations that it also aims at emancipation.

3039 *SOCIÉTÉ DES AMIS DES NOIRS
La Société des Amis des Noirs à la nation française sur l'abolition de la traite et de l'esclavage des nègres dans les colonies françaises . . . Paris, 1789. 2 ll.

> Dated 3 Feb. 1789.

3040 SOCIÉTÉ DES AMIS DES NOIRS
Tableau des membres de la Société des Amis des Noirs. Année 1789. [Paris, 1789.] 8 pp.

3041 SOCIÉTÉ DES AMIS DES NOIRS
Lettres de la Société des Amis des Noirs, à M. Necker, avec la réponse de ce ministre. [Paris,] 1789. 14 pp.

> Correspondence about statements on the slave trade made by Necker in his opening address to the States General.

3042 *PROVIDENCE SOCIETY FOR ABOLISHING THE SLAVE-TRADE
Constitution of a Society for abolishing the slave trade. With several acts of the legislatures of the states of Massachusetts, Connecticut, and Rhode-Island, for that purpose. John Carter, Providence, 1789. 19 pp.

3043 *MARYLAND SOCIETY FOR PROMOTING THE ABOLITION OF SLAVERY
Constitution of the Maryland Society for promoting the Abolition of Slavery, and the Relief of Free Negroes, and others, unlawfully held in Bondage. William Goddard & James Angell, Baltimore, 1789. 8 pp.

3044 SOCIÉTÉ DES AMIS DES NOIRS
Adresse à l'Assemblée nationale, pour l'abolition de la traite des noirs. Par la Société des Amis des Noirs de Paris. L. Potier de Lille, Paris, 1790. 22 pp.

> Plea for abolition of the slave trade, 5 Feb. 1790.

3045 SOCIÉTÉ DES AMIS NOIRS
Seconde adresse à l'Assemblée nationale, par la Société des Amis des Noirs, établie à Paris. [Paris, 1790.] 7 pp.

> Welcomes the declaration of human rights and urges the Assembly to abolish the slave trade and slavery.

3046 SOCIÉTÉ DES AMIS DES NOIRS
Adresse aux amis de l'humanité; par la Société des Amis des Noirs, sur le plan de ses travaux. Lue au comité, le 4 juin 1790 . . . [Paris, 1790.] 4 pp.

> Outline of methods and work proposed by the society.

3047 SOCIÉTÉ DES AMIS DES NOIRS
Réflexions sur le code noir, et dénonciation d'un crime affreux, commis à Saint-Domingue; addressés à l'Assemblée nationale. Patriote François, Paris, 1790. 15 pp.

> The horrors of slavery would best be removed by abolition of the slave trade.

3048 SOCIETY FOR THE ABOLITION OF THE AFRICAN SLAVE TRADE
Two of the petitions from Scotland, which were presented to the last Parliament, praying the abolition of the African slave trade. Society established at Edinburgh, for effecting the Abolition of the African Slave Trade, Edinburgh, 1790. 15 pp.

> Petitions from the Edinburgh Chambers of Commerce and Manufactures (Feb. 1788) and the Presbytery of Edinburgh (April 1789); with W. Cowper's poem 'The negro's complaint' (4226) and a list of subscribers.

3049 SOCIETY FOR THE ABOLITION OF THE AFRICAN SLAVE TRADE
An address to the inhabitants of Glasgow, Paisley, and the neighbourhood, concerning the African slave trade. By a society in Glasgow. Alex. Adam, Glasgow, 1791. 15 pp.

Urges cooperation with the abolition societies in England.

3050 SOCIÉTÉ DES AMIS DES NOIRS
Adresse de la Société des Amis des Noirs, à l'Assemblée nationale, à toutes les villes de commerce, à toutes les manufactures, aux colonies, à toutes les sociétés des amis de la constitution; adresse dans laquelle on approfondit les relations politiques et commerciales entre la métropole et les colonies, &c. Rédigée par E. Clavière, membre de cette société. Paris, 1791. vii, 128, 20 pp.

Statement of the society's policy on slavery, the slave trade and colonial policy.

3051 SOCIÉTÉ DES AMIS DES NOIRS
Adresse de la Société des Amis des Noirs, à l'Assemblée nationale, à toutes les villes de commerce, à toutes les manufactures, aux colonies, à toutes les sociétés des amis de la constitution . . . Seconde édition, revue et corrigée. Desenne; (etc.), Paris, 1791. xxviii, 318 pp.

Rejects blame for the colonial revolts; the slave trade is incompatible with the Revolution but the society has never demanded immediate abolition of slavery.

3052 SOCIÉTÉ DES AMIS DES NOIRS
Plainte de la Société des Amis des Noirs, contre M. Dillon, à l'Assemblée nationale. [Paris, 1791.] 3 pp.

Dillon had charged the Amis with causing the colonial troubles, being 'sold to foreign powers'; the Assembly should censure him or deprive him of his legal immunity. See (2055).

3053 SOCIÉTÉ DES AMIS DES NOIRS
La Société des Amis des Noirs à Arthur Dillon, député de la Martinique à l'Assemblée nationale. Patriote François, [Paris, 1791]. 11 pp.

Reply to (2055); the settlers of St. Domingue share responsibility for the revolt.

3054 PENNSYLVANIA SOCIETY FOR PROMOTING THE ABOLITION OF SLAVERY
Memorials presented to the Congress of the United States, by the different societies instituted for promoting the abolition of slavery, &c. &c. in the states of Rhode-Island, Connecticut, New-York, Pennsylvania, Maryland, and Virginia . . . Francis Bailey, Philadelphia, 1792. 31 pp.

All memorials ask for abolition of the African slave trade and slavery.

3055 *CONNECTICUT SOCIETY FOR THE PROMOTION OF FREEDOM
The constitution of the Connecticut Society for the Promotion of Freedom, and the Relief of Persons unlawfully held in Bondage, as revised and enlarged on the 13th day of September, 1792. [Thomas & Samuel Green, Hartford, 1792.] 3 pp.

3056 NEW JERSEY SOCIETY FOR PROMOTING THE ABOLITION OF SLAVERY
The constitution of the New-Jersey Society, for promoting the Abolition of Slavery: to which is annexed, extracts from a law of New-Jersey, passed the 2d March, 1786, and supplement to the same, passed the 26th November, 1788. Isaac Neale, Burlington, 1793. 14 pp.

The laws are 'to prevent the importation of slaves'.

3057 AMERICAN CONVENTION FOR PROMOTING THE ABOLITION OF SLAVERY
Address of a convention of delegates from the Abolition Society, to the citizens of the United States. W. Durrell, New-York, [1794]. 7 pp.

Recommends abolition of the African slave trade and slavery.

3058 *AMERICAN CONVENTION FOR PROMOTING THE ABOLITION OF SLAVERY
Minutes of the proceedings of a convention of delegates from the abolition societies established in different parts of the United States, assembled at Philadelphia, on the first day of January, one thousand seven hundred and ninety-four, and continued by adjournment, until the seventh day of the same month inclusive. Zachariah Poulson, Jun., Philadelphia, 1794. 30 pp.

Later reports issued most years until 1839 under slightly varying titles. (Extracts in: JNH, vol. 6, 1921, pp. 200–31, 331–39.)

3059 *VIRGINIA SOCIETY FOR PROMOTING THE ABOLITION OF SLAVERY
The constitution of the Virginia Society, for promoting the Abolition of Slavery, and the Relief of Free Negroes, or others, unlawfully held in Bondage, and other humane purposes . . . [Richmond, 1795.] (1 p.).

3060 SOCIETY FOR THE ABOLITION OF THE SLAVE TRADE
'Abolition of the slave trade.' (GM, Aug. 1795, pp. 635–36.)

Report of 26 June 1795, signed by Granville Sharp; submitted by a critic of the society's methods.

3061 *SOCIÉTÉ DES AMIS DES NOIRS
Lettre de la Société des Amis des Noirs, aux auteurs de la Décade Philosophique. [Paris, 1796?] 8 pp.

3062 SOCIÉTÉ DES AMIS DES NOIRS
Réglement de la Société des Amis des Noirs et des Colonies, adopté dans sa séance tenue à Paris le 30 frimaire an VII. Paris, an VII [1798]. 8 pp.

In resuming its work, the society now has to work for the final abolition of slavery in the French colonies and the destruction of the slave trade throughout the world.

3063 *PENNSYLVANIA SOCIETY FOR PROMOTING THE ABOLITION OF SLAVERY
Constitution and act of incorporation of the Pennsylvania Society for promoting the Abolition of Slavery, and the Relief of Free Negroes, unlawfully held in Bondage. And for improving the condition of the African race. To which are added, the acts of the General Assembly of Pennsylvania for the gradual abolition of slavery, and the acts of Congress of the United States, respecting slaves and the slave-trade . . . J. Ormrod, Philadelphia, 1800. 53 pp.

3064 *DELAWARE SOCIETY FOR PROMOTING THE ABOLITION OF SLAVERY
Constitution of the Delaware Society for promoting the Abolition of Slavery; and for the Relief and Protection of Free Blacks and People of Colour unlawfully held in Bondage or otherwise oppressed. Bonsal & Niles, Wilmington, 1801. 8 pp.

3065 *AMERICAN CONVENTION FOR PROMOTING THE ABOLITION OF SLAVERY
Address of the American Convention for promoting the Abolition of Slavery and improving the Condition of the African Race, assembled at Philadelphia, in January, 1804, to the people of the United States. S. W. Conrad, Philadelphia, 1804. 8 pp.

3066 *AFRICAN INSTITUTION
Report of the committee of the African Institution, read to the general meeting on the 15th July, 1807. Together with the rules and regulations which were then adopted for the government of the society. William Phillips, London, 1807. 88 pp.

Abolition of the slave trade will open the way for the civilisation of Africa by establishing legitimate commerce. Later reports published annually to 1827, varying slightly in title.

3067 *RÉUNION DES CHEVALIERS LIBÉRATEURS DES ESCLAVES
Collection des pièces principales annexées au rapport du président de la Réunion des Chevaliers Libérateurs des Esclaves blancs aussi-bien que des noirs en Afrique. Paris, 1816. 35 pp.

3068 *AMERICAN COLONIZATION SOCIETY
The first annual report of the American Society for Colonizing the Free People of Colour in the United States . . . Davis & Force, Washington, 1818. 28 pp.

The annual reports continue until 1910 with slight variations in title; the earlier reports contain a certain amount of material on the slave trade, particularly in the region of Liberia.

3069 *PENNSYLVANIA SOCIETY FOR PROMOTING THE ABOLITION OF SLAVERY
Constitution and act of incorporation of the Pennsylvania Society for promoting the Abolition of Slavery, and for the Relief of Free Negroes, unlawfully held in Bondage, and for the improving the Condition of the African Race. To which are added abstracts of the laws of the states of Pennsylvania, New York, New Jersey, Delaware and Maryland, and of the acts of Congress, respecting slavery and the slave trade. Hall & Atkinson, Philadelphia, 1820. 31 pp.

3070 FRIENDS, Society of
Report of the meeting for sufferings, to the yearly meeting, 1822, on the abolition of the slave-trade. Harvey, Darton & Co., London, [1822]. 3 pp.

Begins with a 'Report to the yearly meeting, from the committee of the meeting for sufferings, appointed to aid in promoting the total abolition of the slave-trade' (13 May 1822); contains an extract from a letter by governor C. McCarthy¨on the West African slave trade.

3071 FRIENDS, Society of
Report, and other documents, on the subject of the slave trade. London, 1825. 4 pp.

Presented to the London yearly meeting by the meeting for sufferings, from its 'Committee . . . to aid in promoting the total abolition of the slave-trade'.

3072 *SOCIÉTÉ DE LA MORALE CHRÉT-IENNE: Comité pour l'Abolition de la Traite des Nègres
Faits relatifs à la traite des noirs. Crapelet, Paris, 1826. 59 pp.

Reviewed in: RE, vol. 29, 1826, pp. 896–97.

3073 *AMERICAN ANTI-SLAVERY SOC-IETY
Declaration of sentiments of the American Anti-Slavery Society. Adopted at the formation of said society, in Philadelphia, on the 4th day of December, 1833. [New York, 1834?] 4 pp.

3074 *AMERICAN ANTI-SLAVERY SOC-IETY
First annual report of the American Anti-Slavery Society; with the speeches delivered at the anniversary meeting . . . New-York, on the sixth of May, 1834 . . . and the minutes of the meetings of the society for business. Dorr & Butterfield, New-York, 1834. 64 pp.

Later reports published 1835–40, 1855–61. After a split in 1840 a breakaway group formed the American and Foreign Anti-Slavery Society.

3075 *AMERICAN ANTI-SLAVERY SOC-IETY
The declaration of sentiments and constitution of the American Anti-Slavery Society; together with all those parts of the constitution of the United States which are supposed to have any relation to slavery . . . New-York, 1835. 16 pp.

3076 AFRICAN CIVILIZATION SOCIETY
Africa. Queries relative to the state of the slave trade . . . [London, 1839?] 105 pp.

Questions with blank spaces for answers to be returned to the society.

3077 AFRICAN CIVILIZATION SOCIETY
Prospectus of the Society for the Extinction of the Slave Trade and for the Civilization of Africa, instituted June, 1839. [London, 1840.] 14 pp.

The only 'complete cure' for the slave trade is to introduce Christianity to Africa; the Niger expedition and treaty making are supported, but the society cannot participate in colonisation or trade.

3078 BEVAN, William
The moral influence of slavery, the substance of a paper presented to the anti-slavery convention held in London, June, 1840. T. Ward & Co., London, 1840. 11 pp.

3079 BRITISH AND FOREIGN ANTI-SLAVERY SOCIETY
Address from the committee of the British & Foreign Anti-Slavery Society to the women of England. [London, 1840?] 4 pp.

Explains the aims of the Society; the slave trade costs Africa half a million people per year.

3080 AFRICAN CIVILIZATION SOCIETY
Proceedings at the first public meeting of the Society for the Extinction of the Slave Trade, and for the Civilization of Africa, held at Exeter Hall, on Monday, 1st June, 1840 . . . London, 1840. 73 pp.

Speeches of the chairman, Sir T. F. Buxton, and others; with the prospectus and rules.

3081 BRITISH AND FOREIGN ANTI-SLAVERY SOCIETY
Minutes of the proceedings of the general anti-slavery convention, called by the committee of the British and Foreign Anti-Slavery Society, held in London on the 12th of June, 1840, and continued by adjournments to the 23rd of the same month. London, 1840. 32 pp.

Addresses on the continuing slave trade and its suppression.

3082 BRITISH AND FOREIGN ANTI-SLAVERY SOCIETY
The first annual report of the British and Foreign Anti-Slavery Society, for the abolition of slavery and the slave-trade, throughout the world. Presented to the general meeting held in Exeter Hall, on Wednesday, June 24th, 1840 . . . Johnston & Barrett, London, 1840. 31 pp.

Later reports were published until 1908, containing a great deal of material on the continuing slave trade and measures taken to suppress it.

3083   AFRICAN CIVILIZATION SOCIETY
Present state of Africa. [London, 1841?] (2 pp.)

Leaflet supporting Buxton's anti-slavery schemes. See (2645).

3084   BRITISH AND FOREIGN ANTI-SLAVERY SOCIETY
Proceedings of the general anti-slavery convention, called by the committee of the British and Foreign Anti-Slavery Society, and held in London, from Friday, June 12th, to Tuesday, June 23rd, 1840. London, 1841. xi, 597 pp.

3085   AFRICAN CIVILIZATION SOCIETY
Report of the committee of the African Civilization Society to the public meeting of the society held at Exeter Hall, on Tuesday, the 21st of June, 1842. With an appendix. John Murray, London, 1842. 99, cxxxiv pp. map.

The society deplores the losses of the Niger expedition but is determined not to relax its vigilance against the slave trade; the appendix contains recent information about the trade.

3086   BRITISH AND FOREIGN ANTI-SLAVERY SOCIETY
Proceedings of the general anti-slavery convention, called by the committee of the British and Foreign Anti-Slavery Society, and held in London, from Tuesday, June 13th, to Tuesday, June 20th, 1843. By J. F. Johnson, short-hand writer. John Snow, London, [1843]. vii, 360 pp.

3087   *BRITISH AND FOREIGN ANTI-SLAVERY SOCIETY
General anti-slavery convention, 1843. Address of the convention held in London, from the 15th to the 22nd June inclusive, to Christian professors. Johnston & Barrett, London, [1843]. 7 pp.

Signed: Thomas Clarkson, president of the convention.

3088   BRITISH AND FOREIGN ANTI-SLAVERY SOCIETY
The slave-trade and its remedy. (Signed: John Scoble.) [London, 1848.] 8 pp.

Text of memorial presented to the government urging a bill to exclude produce from the Spanish colonies and Brazil until slavery is abolished there.

3089   *BRITISH AND FOREIGN ANTI-SLAVERY SOCIETY
Slavery and the slave-trade. 1849. (Signed: John Scoble.) London, 1849. 8 pp.

3090   *SOCIEDADE CONTRA O TRÁFICO DE AFRICANOS
Systhema de medidas adoptaveis para a progressiva e total extincção do trafico, e da escravatura no Brasil, confeccionado e approvado pela Sociedade contra o Trafico de Africanos, e promotora da Colonisação, e da Civilisação dos Indigenas. Rio de Janeiro, 1852. 28 pp.

3091a   *BRITISH AND FOREIGN ANTI-SLAVERY SOCIETY
Comercio de esclavos en la isla de Cuba. Al Excmo. Sr. General Espartero, duque de la Victoria. New York, 1855. 8 pp.

Also issued as:

3091b   *Cuban slavery and the slave trade.
(Signed: Louis Alexis Chamerovzow.) [London, 1855.]

Address of 2 March 1855 reminding the governor of Cuba of Spanish treaty obligations to suppress the slave trade.

3092   BRITISH AND FOREIGN ANTI-SLAVERY SOCIETY
The slave-trade as it is. Forty thousand annually to Cuba. [London, 1860.] 4 pp.

3093   BRITISH AND FOREIGN ANTI-SLAVERY SOCIETY
The slave trade to Cuba, as set forth in an address to Marshal Espartero, from the committee of the British and Foreign Anti-Slavery Society, on the 2nd March 1855. With additional facts to the present date. London, 1861. 22 pp.

3094   BRITISH AND FOREIGN ANTI-SLAVERY SOCIETY
Special report of the anti-slavery conference, held in Paris, in the Salle Herz, on the twenty-sixth and twenty-seventh August, 1867. London, [1869]. ii, 166 pp.

Conference of French, Spanish, English and American antislavery societies; with papers on the slave trade of East Africa, Liberia, Brazil, Cuba and Puerto Rico.

3095   BRITISH AND FOREIGN ANTI-SLAVERY SOCIETY
The slave trade in 1872. Report of

addresses delivered at a public meeting at the Friends' Meeting House, Bishopsgate St., during the yearly meeting, 1872, by Sir Bartle Frere, G.C.S.I., K.C.B., Horace Waller, M.A., Sir Thomas Fowell Buxton, Bart., Theophilus Waldemeir, etc., etc. London, 1872. 22 pp.

3096 *ASSOCIATION DES DEUX MONDES
Projet d'association, pour le développement de la civilisation et l'extinction de la traite par les chemins de fer en Afrique. Paris, [1879].

3097 SOCIÉTÉ ANTIESCLAVAGISTE DE BELGIQUE
Règlement général. [Bruxelles, 1888.] 4 pp.

The society's aim is to suppress the slave trade and slavery, particularly in the Congo Free State.

3098 *COCHIN, Henry
Discours de M. Henry Cochin sur l'abolition de l'esclavage africain. Lille, 1889. 24 pp.

Address to the Catholic congress at Lille 1888.

3099 *KORUM, Michael Felix, *Bishop of Trier*
Die afrikanische Sklaverei, Reden von Bischof Dr. Korum u. Professor Dr. Mosler. Trier, 1889. 38 pp.

Speeches at antislavery conferences at Liège 16 Dec. and Trier 26 Dec. 1888.

3100 *ALLEMAND-LAVIGERIE, Charles Martial, *Cardinal*
Lettre de Son Éminence le cardinal Lavigerie à MM. les présidents et membres des comités antiesclavagistes pour les inviter à un congrès international de leur œuvre qui se réunira à Lucerne, le 3 août 1889. Saint-Cloud, 1889. 12 pp.

Dated Algiers 25 April 1889.

3101 *CONGRÈS international antiesclavagiste de Lucerne. Alger, [1889]. 11 pp.

Dated 16 June 1889; includes a letter from Lavigerie announcing a competition for a cantata on the abolition of African slavery.

3102 ALLEMAND-LAVIGERIE, Charles Martial, *Cardinal*
Lettre de Son Éminence le cardinal Lavigerie, archevêque de Carthage et d'Alger, à messieurs les présidents des comités centraux de l'Œuvre antiesclavagiste sur les modifications

apportées au programme du congrès antiesclavagiste de Lucerne. Alger, 1889. 8 pp.

Dated 12 July 1889.

3103 *ALLEMAND-LAVIGERIE, Charles Martial, *Cardinal*
Lettre de Son Éminence le cardinal Lavigerie, archevêque de Carthage et d'Alger, à messieurs les présidents des comités centraux de l'Œuvre antiesclavagiste sur la prorogation du congrès antiesclavagiste de Lucerne. Lucerne, [1889]. 2 ll.

Dated 24 July 1889.

3104a*BRUSSELS SLAVE TRADE CONFERENCE
Actes de la conférence de Bruxelles (1889–1890). Bruxelles, 1890. 703 pp.

Translated as:

3104b Translations of protocols and general act of the slave trade conference held at Brussels, 1889–90; with annexed declaration . . . London, [1890]. 191 pp. (P.P. 1890, L.)

3105 ALLEMAND-LAVIGERIE, Charles Martial, *Cardinal*
Allocution prononcé le 21 septembre 1890, par S. Ém. le cardinal Lavigerie dans l'église Saint-Sulpice à Paris pour l'ouverture d'un congrès antiesclavagiste. Œuvre Antiesclavagiste, Paris, 1890. 102 pp.

Speech on the African slave trade. (Printed in: MA, vol. 2, 1890, pp. 312–30; illus.)

3106 *ALLEMAND-LAVIGERIE, Charles Martial, *Cardinal*
Discours sur l'esclavage africain, prononcé par S.É. le cardinal Lavigerie dans l'église de Saint-Sulpice à l'occasion du congrès antiesclavagiste. Paris, 1890. 52 pp.

3107 *SOCIÉTÉ ANTIESCLAVAGISTE DE FRANCE
'Société Anti-esclavagiste de France.' (Missions d'Alger, Paris, 1890, pp. 329–44, 361–415.)

Rules of the society, with material on the anti-slave trade campaign launched by Cardinal Lavigerie.

3108 *DESCAMPS, Édouard Eugène François, *baron*
Discours sur l'Afrique nouvelle, prononcé le jour de l'ouverture du Congrès libre antiesclavagiste. Louvain, 1890. 16 pp.

Speech on the task of extinguishing Muslim slavery in Africa, 22 Sept. 1890. (Reprinted from: MA, vol. 2, 1890, pp. 331–47.)

3109   DUCHESNE, D.
'Le Congrès libre antiesclavagiste de Paris.' (MA, vol. 2, sept. 1890, pp. 354–62.)

Report of proceedings.

3110   URSEL, Hippolyte d', *comte*
'Rapport de monsieur le comte Hippolyte d'Ursel sur le Congrès libre antiesclavagiste de Paris.' (MA, vol. 2, sept. 1890, pp. 371–82.)

Resolutions of the conference.

3111   'Le DOMAINE de la traite et le partage politique de l'Afrique.' (Signed: Alexis-M. G.) (MA, vol. 2, nov. 1890, pp. 440–42; vol. 3, déc. 1890, pp. 31–32; vol. 3, fév. 1891, pp. 81–87; map.)

By J. B. Gochet. Speech at the anti-slavery conference in Paris, 22 Sept. 1890.

3112   BRUSSELS SLAVE TRADE CONFERENCE
Conférence internationale de Bruxelles. 18 novembre 1889–2 juillet 1890. Protocoles et acte final. Paris, 1891. 514 pp.

Published by the Ministère des Affaires Étrangères of France.

3113   *CONGRÈS LIBRE ANTIESCLAVAGISTE, Paris
Documents relatifs au Congrès libre antiesclavagiste tenu à Paris les 21, 22 et 23 septembre, 1890. Œuvre Antiesclavagiste, Paris, [1891]. 210 pp.

3114   BRUSSELS SLAVE TRADE CONFERENCE
Conférence internationale et commission de Bruxelles. Novembre 1890–février 1891. Correspondance diplomatique. Paris, 1891. 164 pp.

Documents on the conference and on the measures taken against the slave trade 1889–91. Published by the Ministère des Affaires Étrangères of France.

3115   DUCHESNE, Aug.
'Les conférences antiesclavagistes libres de Bruxelles. Compte rendu—Rapport sur l'Œuvre antiesclavagiste belge.' (MA, vol. 3, 1891, pp. 161–216.)

Speeches at an antislavery meeting in Brussels, 28–30 April 1891.

3116   DESCAMPS, Édouard Eugène François, *baron*

Discours sur l'avenir de la civilisation en Afrique prononcé à l'assemblée générale du Congrès de Malines le 10 août 1891. Louvain; Bruxelles, 1891. 16 pp.

It is the task of the Belgians to end the curse of slave trading in Africa.

3117   *URSEL, Hippolyte d', *comte*
Rapport sur l'œuvre antiesclavagiste de Belgique, présenté au Congrès de Malines en 1891. Bruxelles, 1891. 16 pp.

Report presented 10 Sept. 1891; reprinted from: MA, vol. 3, 1891, pp. 351–65.

3118   BRUSSELS SLAVE TRADE CONFERENCE
Conférence internationale de Bruxelles. Documents diplomatiques. Juillet-décembre 1891. Paris, 1891. 24 pp.

Published by the Ministère des Affaires Étrangères.

3119   SOCIÉTÉ ANTIESCLAVAGISTE DE BELGIQUE
Les conférences antiesclavagistes libres données au Palais des Académies de Bruxelles les 28, 29, et 30 avril 1891. Bruxelles, 1892. 114 pp. illus.

Speeches on the antislavery movement, slavery and missions in Africa.

3120   SOCIÉTÉ ANTIESCLAVAGISTE DE BELGIQUE
'Les travaux de la Société antiesclavagiste de Belgique pendant l'année 1891–1892.' (MA, vol. 4, 1892, pp.159-68.)

Report on activities in the Congo and Europe.

3121   SORELA, Luis
Memoria presentada al excmo. Sr. D. Antonio Cánovas del Castillo, presidente de la Sociedad Antiesclavista Española, por el delegado general D. Luis Sorela. Madrid, 1892. 21 pp.

Report on the activities of the society 1889–92.

3122   *SOCIÉTÉ ANTIESCLAVAGISTE DE BELGIQUE
Manifeste de la Société antiesclavagiste de Belgique. Bruxelles, 1893. 15 pp.

3123   *SOCIÉTÉ DES PIONNIERS AFRICAINS
Statuts de la société. Paris, [1893].

Rules of the Société des Pionniers Africains pour l'Abolition de l'Esclavage et la Civilisation du Soudan Français, founded by M. A. Jung, former director of the Frères Armés du Sahara.

3124 SORELA, Luis
Los estados ibero-americanos y la **Liga** Internacional Antiesclavista en el congreso geográfico de Madrid. Documentos referentes á la proposición presentada por el delegado general Don Luis Sorela. Madrid, 1893. 55 pp.

Urges the congress and the Spanish antislavery society to call for support for the 'Liga' from the Latin American states.

3125 *CONGRÈS INTERNATIONAL ANTIESCLAVAGISTE, Paris
Congrès international antiesclavagiste tenu à Paris les 6, 7, 8 août 1900. Compte rendu des séances. Société Antiesclavagiste de France, Paris, 1900. 202 pp.

An account by H. Dehérain, 'Der internationale Antisklaverei-Kongress', is printed in: DKZ, n.s., vol. 13, 1900, pp. 391–92.

3126 *LEDÓCHOWSKA, Marya Teresa Franciszka, *Gräfin*
Die Antisclaverei-Bewegung und die St. Petrus Claver-Sodalität. Ansprache der General-Leiterin der St. Petrus Claver-Sodalität, Gräfin M. Theresia Ledóchowska. Gehalten in der III. Festversammlung des I. österr. Antisclaverei-Congresses zu Wien am 22. November 1900. Maria Sorg bei Salzburg, [1901]. 6 ll.

3127 *CONGRÈS INTERNATIONAL ANTIESCLAVAGISTE, Paris
Congrès international antiesclavagiste, tenu à Paris du 6 au 8 août 1900. Procès-verbaux sommaires. Paris, 1901. 12 pp.

Published by the Ministère du Commerce of France.

3128 *ÖSTERREICHISCHER ANTISKLAVEREI-CONGRESS
Bericht über den I. österreichischen Antisklaverei-Congress in Wien. Herausgegeben von der St. Petrus Claver-Sodalität für die afrikanische Missionsthätigkeit. Salzburg, 1901. 120 pp.

3129 *CONGRESSO ANTISCHIAVISTA ITALIANO
Atti del primo Congresso antischiavista italiano tenuto in Roma nei giorni 22–23–24 aprile 1903. San Vito al Tagliamento, 1903. 107 pp.

3130 ALEXANDER, Joseph Gundry
'The Rome anti-slavery congress.' (Anti-Slavery Reporter, London, ser. 4, vol. 28, 1908, pp. 3–8.)

Report of a conference 3–5 Dec. 1907; the Italian antislavery society is 'almost wholly devoted to Tripoli'.

(b) ABOLITION JOURNALS

3131 *Analyses des papiers anglois. no. 1–102. Paris, 1787–88.

By the comte de Mirabeau. Served as an organ for the Société des Amis des Noirs.

3132 Journal de la Société de la Morale Chrétienne. vol. 1–12. Paris, 1822–30.

Contains reports on the slave trade by the 'Comité pour l'Abolition de la Traite des Nègres' of the society.

3133 The Anti-Slavery Magazine, and Recorder of the Progress of Christianity in the Countries connected with Slavery. no. 1–12. Jan.–Dec. 1824. Derby, 1824. viii, 200 pp.

3134 The Humming Bird. vol. 1, no. 1–12. Dec. 1824–Nov. 1825. Leicester, 1824–25.

3135 The African Repository and Colonial Journal. vol. 1–68. March 1825–Jan. 1892. Washington, 1825–92.

Published by the American Colonization Society; title varies. (Preceded by the 'African Intelligencer', 1820–25.)

3136 Anti-Slavery Monthly Reporter. no. 1–72. June 1825–Dec. 1830. London, 1825–30.

Published by the Society for the Abolition of Slavery throughout the British Dominions. (Continued as 'The Anti-Slavery Reporter', 1831–36, and 'The British Emancipator', 1837–40.)

3137 *The African Observer . . . vol. 1, no. 1; April 1827–March 1828. Philadelphia, 1827–28. 384 pp.

Edited by Enoch Lewis.

3138 The Abolitionist. vol. 1, no. 1–4. Aug. 1834–May 1835. [London, 1834–35.] 208 pp.

Published by the British and Foreign Society for the Universal Abolition of Negro Slavery and the slave trade.

3139 The Slave's Friend. vol. 1–4. New York, 1836–39.

Published for the American Anti-Slavery Society.

3140   Slavery in America: with notices of the present state of slavery and the slave trade throughout the world. Conducted by the Rev. Thomas Price, D.D. no. 1–14. July 1836–August, 1837. London, 1836–37. viii, 320 pp.

3141   The British and Foreign Anti-Slavery Reporter. vol. 1–6. London, 1840–45.

Published by the British and Foreign Anti-Slavery Society. (Continued as 'The Anti-Slavery Reporter', 1846–1909.)

3142   *Institut d' Afrique. Annales. vol. 1–27. Jan. 1841–avril 1867. Paris, 1841–67.

Monthly journal concerned with African slavery.

3143   The Friend of Africa. no. 1–28. Jan. 1841–Feb. 1843. London, 1841–43.

Published by the Society for the Extinction of the Slave Trade and for the Civilization of Africa.

3144   The Friend of the African. no. 1–36. June 1843–May 1846. London, 1843–46.

From no. 11 (April 1844) called 'The Friend of the Africans'.

3145   L'Abolitioniste Français. vol. 1–7. Paris, 1844–50.

Published by the Société Française pour l'Abolition de l'Esclavage.

3146   The Colonial Intelligencer, or, Aborigines' Friend. London, 1847–54.

Published by the Aborigines' Protection Society. (Continued as 'The Aborigines' Friend and Colonial Intelligencer', 1855–58, 'Colonial Intelligencer and Aborigines' Friend', 1859–67, and 'Transactions of the Aborigines' Protection Society', 1874–1909.)

3147   *The Anti-Slavery Advocate. vol. 1–3. Oct. 1852–May 1863. London, 1852–63.

Published by the Anglo-American Anti-Slavery Association.

3148   L'Afrique Explorée et Civilisée. Journal mensuel. vol. 1–15. Genève, 1879–94.

3149   Le Mouvement Antiesclavagiste. Revue mensuelle internationale illustrée. vol. 1–14. Bruxelles, 1888–1902.

3150   *Bollettino del Comitato Centrale Antischiavista di Palermo per la Sicilia. Palermo, 1888–90.

Monthly 1888–89, bi-monthly from 1890. (Continued as 'Bollettino della Società Antischiavista d'Italia', 1891–1924.)

3151   *Bulletin de la Société Antiesclavagiste de France. no. 1–27. Paris, 1888–93.

Continued as 'Société Antiesclavagiste de France. Revue trimestrielle', 1895–1909, and 'L'Afrique Libre', 1910–14.

3152   *Gott will es! Monatsschrift für alle Förderer und Freunde der Bewegung gegen die afrikanische Sclaverei insbesondere für die Mitglieder des Afrika-Vereins deutscher Katholiken. Münster i.W., 1889–1915.

Monthly journal founded Jan. 1889 by W. Helmes. Published at München-Gladbach 1891–98, with the subtitle 'Katholische Zeitschrift für die Antisklaverei-Bewegung deutscher Zunge'.

3153   *Bulletin de la Société Anti-esclavagiste Suisse. no. 1, mars 1889– . Genève, 1889– .

3154   *Antisclaverei-Monats-Revue. Revue antisclavagiste mensuelle. Wien, 1889– .

Published from Sept. 1889 as a bilingual journal.

3155   France Noire. Bulletin mensuel de la Société Française des Pionniers Africains. vol. 1–vol. 4, no. 39. Paris, 1894–97.

R. LAWS AND OFFICIAL DOCUMENTS

3156 *PENNSYLVANIA: Laws
An act for the gradual abolition of slavery. [Philadelphia, *c.* 1785.] 16 pp.

> Pennsylvania was the first American state to legislate against slavery, by this act of 1 March 1780 (signed by Thomas Paine as clerk to the General Assembly); also contains 'Rules for the regulation of the Society for the Relief of Free Negroes unlawfully held in Bondage'.

3157 VIRGINIA: Laws
'An act to prevent the further importation of slaves into this commonwealth.' (AM, vol. 2, 1787, p. 502.)

> Dated Richmond, October 1786.

3158 RHODE ISLAND: Laws
'An act to prevent the slave trade, and to encourage the abolition of slavery.' (AM, vol. 2, 1787, pp. 502–03.)

> Dated October 1787.

3159 PENNSYLVANIA: Assembly
'Report on slave trade from committee of Pennsylvania assembly.' (GM, June 1788. p. 545.)

> Report on legislation to end the African slave trade and gradually abolish slavery.

3160 CONNECTICUT: Laws
'An act to prevent the slave trade, passed by the general assembly of the state of Connecticut, October, 1788.' (AM, vol. 4, 1788, pp. 512–13.)

3161 BARBADOS: General Assembly
'Report and resolution of a committee of the General Assembly of Barbadoes, upon the several heads of enquiry, &c. relative to the slave trade.' (SM, vol. 52, Feb. 1790, p. 73.)

> Slaves imported 1764–88 total about 45,000.

3162 *RHODE ISLAND: Laws
An act to incorporate certain persons by the name of the Providence Society for promoting the Abolition of Slavery, for the Relief of Persons unlawfully held in Bondage, and for improving the Conditions of the African Race. J. Carter, [Providence, 1790]. 4 pp.

3163 *FRANCE: Laws
Loi portant que tout homme est libre en France & que quelle que soit sa couleur, il y jouit de tous les droits de citoyen, s'il a les qualités prescrites par la Constitution. Donnée à Paris le 16 octobre 1791. Impr. Royale, Paris, 1791. 2 pp.

3164 GREAT BRITAIN: House of Commons
Report from the committee of the whole House, to whom it was referred to consider further measures to be taken for the abolition of the slave trade carried on by British subjects, for the purpose of procuring slaves from Africa . . . [London, 1792.] 3 pp. (P.P. 1791, IX.)

> Resolutions for gradual abolition of the slave trade.

3165 *DENMARK: Laws
Forordning om Neger-Handelen. Christiansborg Slot den 16de Martii 1792. P.M. Høpffner, Kiøbenhavn, [1792]. 2 ll.

> Denmark was the first European state to order the abolition of the slave trade, after a ten-year extension 1792–1802. See (2150, note).

3166 KIRSTEIN, Ernst Philip
'Udtog af Forestillingen til Kongen angaaende Negerhandelens Afskaffelse.' (Minerva, Kiøbenhavn, April 1792, pp. 43–86.)

> Summary of the report of a special commission on the gradual abolition of the Danish slave trade, by one of its members; with the text of the resulting royal order of 16 March 1792.

3167 *UNITED STATES OF AMERICA: Congress
Report of the committee to whom was referred the several petitions of the Quakers of New England, of the Providence Society for the Abolition of the Slave Trade, and the petitions from the delegates of the several societies for the same purpose, in convention

assembled in Philadelphia, January, 1794. [Childs & Swaine, Philadelphia, 1794.] 1 l.

3168 FRANCE: Conseil des Cinq Cents
Rapport fait par J.-P.-F. Duplantier, député du département de la Gironde, au nom d'une commission spéciale, sur la pétition de divers particuliers, relativement aux créances résultantes de l'achat des noirs. Séance du 24 vendémiaire an 7. Imprimerie Nationale, Paris, an 7 [1798]. 7 pp.

3169 FRANCE: Convention Nationale
Décret de la Convention Nationale, du 16 ième. jour de pluviôse, an second de la République Française une et indivisible, qui abolit l'esclavage des nègres dans les colonies. Société des Amis des Noirs et des Colonies, [Paris, 1799]. 3 pp.

Published on the fifth anniversary of the abolition of French colonial slavery in 1794.

3170 GREAT BRITAIN: Laws
'An act for the abolition of the slave trade.' *In*: The STATUTES of the United Kingdom of Great Britain and Ireland, vol. 47 (London, 1807), pp. 140–48.

The act (47 Geo. III. c. 36; 25 March 1807) abolishing the British slave trade from 1 May 1807.

3171 GREAT BRITAIN: Laws
Abstract of the acts of Parliament for abolishing the slave trade, and of the orders in council founded on them. African Institution, London, 1810. 43 pp.

Acts and orders in council 1806–08.

3172 *HAVANA: Ayuntamiento
Representación de la ciudad de la Habana á las Cortes, el 20 de julio de 1811, con motivo de las proposiciones hechos por D. José Miguel Guridi Alcocer y D. Agustín Argüelles, sobre el tráfico y esclavitud de los negros, extendida por el alferez mayor de la ciudad, D. Francisco de Arango, por encargo del Ayuntamiento, Consulado y Sociedad Patriótica de la Habana. Cádiz, [1811].

Protest to the Córtes at Cadiz, opposing the abolition proposals of Guridi (26 March 1811) and Argüelles. (Written by Arango and dated 20 July 1811.)

3173 GREAT BRITAIN: House of Commons
'The humble addresses of the House of Commons to His Royal Highness the Prince Regent, on the African slave trade: with His Royal Highness's answers.' (GM, vol. 84, 1814, pp. 161–63.)

Urges the government to obtain prohibition of the slave trade by France and other European powers.

3174 PORTUGAL: Plenipotentiaries
'Exposição apresentada ao Congresso, pelos plenipotenciarios de Portugal, sobre a pretenção da Inglaterra á abolição immediata de trafico da escravatura.' (Portuguez, Londres, vol. 3, julho 1815, pp. 265–68.)

Memorandum of 14 Dec. 1814 presented to the Congress of Vienna protesting against British actions involving Portuguese slave ships. (Also in: IPI, vol. 13, 1815, pp. 261–64.)

3175 PORTUGAL: Treaties
'Convenção entre os muito altos, e muito poderosos Senhores o Principe Regente de Portugal, e el Rey do Reino Unido da Grande Bretanha e Irlanda, para terminar as questoens e indemnizar as perdas dos vassallos portuguezes no trafico de escravos de Africa. Feita em Vienna pelos plenipotenciarios de uma e outra corte, em 21 de janeiro, de 1815, e ratificada por ambas.' (Portuguez, Londres, vol. 4, dez. 1815, pp. 123–28.)

Convention to indemnify Portuguese slave traders, ratified at Rio de Janeiro 8 June 1815. (Text in Portuguese and English; also in: IPI, vol. 14, 1815, pp. 200–04.)

3176 PORTUGAL: Treaties
'Tratado da abolição do trafico de escravos em todos os lugares da costa de Africa ao norte do equador, entre os muito altos, e muito poderosos Senhores o Principe Regente de Portugal, e el Rey do Reino Unido da Grande Bretanha e Irlanda: feito em Vienna pelos plenipotenciarios de uma e outra corte, em 23 de janeiro de 1815, e ratificado por ambas.' (Portuguez, Londres, vol. 4, dez. 1815, pp. 128–38.)

Treaty to abolish the Portuguese slave trade north of the equator, ratified at Rio de Janeiro 8 June 1815. (Text in Portuguese and English; also in: IPI, vol. 14, 1815, pp. 204–12.)

3177 UNITED STATES OF AMERICA: Laws
'An act to prohibit the importation of

slaves into any port or place within the jurisdiction of the United States, from and after the first day of January, in the year of our Lord, one thousand eight hundred and eight.' *In*: LAWS of the United States of America, from . . . 1789, to . . . 1815, vol. 5 (Philadelphia; Washington City, 1816), pp. 94–99.

Act of 2 March 1807 abolishing the slave trade; extended by acts of 1818, 1819 and 1820.

3178 VIENNA CONGRESS
'Declaration relative to the slave trade.' (AnR 1815, vol. 57, 1816, pp. 358–60.)

Denunciation of the African slave trade, signed 8 Feb. 1815.

3179 SPAIN: Treaties
Tratado entre S.M. el Rey de España y de las Indias, y S.M. el Rey del Reino Unido de la Gran Bretaña e Irlanda. Para la abolicion del tráfico de negros, concluido y firmado en Madrid en 23 de setiembre de 1817. Madrid, 1817. 81 pp.

Treaty extracted from Spain to abolish the slave trade by 1820; with instructions for naval officers and regulations for mixed commission courts. (Text in Spanish and English; also in: P.P. 1818, XVIII, no. 1.)

3180 *SPAIN: Laws
Real cedula para la abolición del tráfico de negros, concluido y firmado en Madrid en 29 de septiembre de 1817. Madrid, [1817]. 4 pp.

Another abolition order of 19 Dec. 1817 is reprinted as 'Real cédula que prohibió el tráfico de esclavos negros entre las costas de Africa y los dominios españolas' in: Revista del Archivo Nacional, Bogotá, no. 19, 1939, pp. 188–91.

3181 MARTENS, Georg Friedrich von
Nouveau recueil de traités . . . depuis 1808 jusqu'à présent . . . Dieterich, Gottingue, 1817–42. 22 vol.

Includes the treaties for the abolition of the slave trade between Great Britain and various other states 1815–39. (Completed by F. Murhard and others in 55 vol., 1843–1908.)

3182 GREAT BRITAIN: Treaties
Treaty between His Britannic Majesty and His Majesty the King of the Netherlands. Signed at the Hague, the 4th of May 1818 . . . London, 1818. 22 pp. (P.P. 1818, XVIII.)

Text in English and French.

3183 PORTUGAL: Laws
'Alvará com força de lei, em que se estabelecem penas para os que fizerem commercio prohibido de escravos.' (IPI, vol. 22, julho 1818, pp. 233–39.)

Law of 26 Jan. 1818 on penalties for slave trading north of the equator. (Also in: Correio Braziliense, Londres, vol. 21, 1818, pp. 137–42.)

3184 GREAT BRITAIN: Treaties
Convention between His Britannic Majesty and His Most Faithful Majesty. Signed at London, the 28th of July 1817 . . . London, 1818. 31 pp. (P.P. 1818, XVIII.)

Defines the Portuguese dominions, establishes mixed commission courts and settles further compensation. (Text in English and Portuguese; the latter also printed in: IPI, vol. 21, 1818, pp. 86–94.)

3185 LUNAN, John
An abstract of the laws of Jamaica relating to slaves. From 33 Charles II. to 59 George III. inclusive. With the slave law at length, also, an appendix, containing an abstract of the acts of Parliament relating to the abolition of the slave-trade. Saint Jago de la Vega Gazette, [Spanish Town,] 1819. xv, 192 pp.

3186 *UNITED STATES OF AMERICA: House of Representatives
Extracts from documents in the Departments of State, of the Treasury, and of the Navy, in relation to the illicit introduction of slaves into the United States. E. De Krafft, Washington, 1819. 14 pp.

Referred to the committee on the 1819 slave trade bill.

3187 SURINAM: Mixed Commission Court
Proces ordre—of vorm van procedeeren voor het gemengd geregtshof in Suriname, tot weering van den slaven handel [Paramaribo, 1822.] (8 pp.)

With English text: 'Mode of process— or form of procedure for the mixed court at Surinam, for the prevention of the slave-trade.'

3188 UNITED STATES OF AMERICA: Laws
Laws of the United States, relative to the slave-trade. Davis & Force, Washington, 1823. 43 pp.

Text of acts 1794–1820.

3189 GREAT BRITAIN: Foreign Office
Correspondence with foreign powers, relative to the slave trade. 1822. 1823. London, 1823. viii, 165 pp. (P.P. 1823, XIX.)

Continued annually, under varying titles, 1824–69, 1872–73, 1878–89.

3190 UNITED STATES OF AMERICA: Department of State
'Suppression of the slave trade. Negociations for the suppression of the slave trade.' (Niles' Weekly Register, Baltimore, vol. 26, 1824, pp. 346–62.)

Correspondence between the U.S. and British governments January-June 1823.

3191 GREAT BRITAIN: Laws
An act for the more effectual suppression of the African slave trade. [31st March 1824.] George Eyre & Andrew Strahan, London, 1824. (2 pp.)

Law providing for slave trade to be treated as piracy (4 Geo. IV. c. 17).

3192 GREAT BRITAIN: Foreign Office
British and foreign state papers . . . London, 1825–1900. 93 vol.

Contains acts, treaties and official correspondence relating to the slave trade. (Vol. 1 was published in 1841.)

3193 UNITED STATES OF AMERICA: Department of State
'Negotiations on the slave trade.' (Niles' Weekly Register, Baltimore, vol. 29, 1826, pp. 313–15.)

Correspondence between the U.S. and British governments June-August 1823.

3194 GREAT BRITAIN: Treaties
A complete collection of the treaties and conventions, and reciprocal regulations, at present subsisting between Great Britain & foreign powers, and of the laws, decrees, and orders in council, concerning the same; so far as they relate to commerce and navigation, to the repression and abolition of the slave trade, and to the privileges and interests of the subjects of the high contracting parties. Compiled . . . by Lewis Hertslet. Henry Butterworth, London, 1827–1925. 31 vol.

Supersedes an edition in 2 vol. compiled by L. Hertslet and published in 1820. (Completed by Edward Hertslet and others. From 1898 published by H.M.S.O.)

3195 *SPAIN: Laws
Condiciones con que se reparten los negros que se emancipan, por el gobierno, pertenecientes a diferentes buques españoles apresados por otros de S.M.B. conforme el artículo 7o. del reglamento paro comisiones mistas establecidas en esta plaza, en cumplimiento del tratado de 1817, para la abolición del tráfico de esclavos. Habana, 1829. 4 pp.

3196 GREAT BRITAIN: Treaties
Treaty between His Majesty and the Queen of Spain, during the minority of her daughter Donna Isabella the Second, Queen of Spain, for the abolition of the slave trade, signed at Madrid, June 28, 1835 . . . London, 1836. 23 pp. (P.P. 1836, L.)

Text in English and Spanish.

3197 *PORTUGAL: Laws
'Decreto abolindo o tráfico da escravatura nos dominios portugueses . . .' In: COLLECÇÃO de leis e outros documentos officiaes, ser. 6 (Lisboa, 1837), pp. 221–26.

Decree of 10 Dec. 1836; reprinted in: Arquivos de Angola, Luanda, vol. 2, 1936, pp. 685–94.

3198 *TWO SICILIES: Treaties
Ferdinando II., per la grazia di Dio Re del regno delle Due Sicilie . . . a dimostrare vie più il nostro abborrimento per l'inumano traffico de' negri, ci siamo determinate di accedere alla seguente convenzione stipulata tra le reali corti di Francia e d'Inghilterra. [Napoli, 1839.] 31 pp.

Sicily's accession to the Anglo-French slave trade treaties of 1831 and 1833, signed 14 Feb. 1838. (Text in French and Italian.)

3199 PORTUGAL: Ministerio dos Negocios Estrangeiros
Documentos officaes relativos á negociação do tractado entre Portugal e a Gram Bretanha para a suppressão do trafico da escravatura mandados imprimir por ordem da Camara dos Senadores. Lisboa, 1839. iv, 144, 82 pp.

Draft treaties and notes exchanged with Britain 1836–39; the Anglo-Portuguese treaty to end the slave trade was finally concluded in 1842.

3200 MASSACHUSETTS: Senate
Report and resolves on the subject of the foreign slave trade. [Boston, 1839.] 16 pp. (Documents printed by order of

the Senate of the Commonwealth of Massachusetts. 1839. no. 35.)

Report of a special committee on memorials urging more effective measures to suppress the slave trade and protect the growing commerce with West Africa.

3201 ROME, Church of (*Pope Gregory XVI*) Sanctissimi Domini nostri Gregorii divina providentia Papæ XVI litteræ apostolicæ de nigritarum commercio non exercendo. Typis Reverendæ Cameræ Apostolicæ, Romae, 1839. v pp.

Apostolical letter ('In supremo apostolatus') of 3 Dec. 1839 against the slave trade. See (2660, 2711).

3202 GREAT BRITAIN: Foreign Office Documentos ácerca do trafico da escravatura extrahidos dos papeis relativos a Portugal apresentados ao Parlamento britanico. Lisboa, 1840. 104 pp.

Diplomatic correspondence 1834–39 on the slave trade.

3203 *UNITED STATES OF AMERICA: House of Representatives Africans taken in the Amistad. Congressional document, containing the correspondence, &c. in relation to the captured Africans. Anti-Slavery Depository, New York, 1840. 48 pp.

Reprint of: House Executive document no. 185, 26 Cong., 1 sess.

3204 FRANCE: Treaties 'Ordonnance du Roi qui prescrit la publication de la convention conclue, le 29 août 1840, entre la France et la république d'Haïti, dans le but d'assurer la répression de la traite des noirs. Au Palais de Neuilly, le 10 juillet 1841.' (Annales Maritimes et Coloniales, Paris, ser. 2, vol. 26, 1841, pt. 1, pp. 893–98.)

3205 GREAT BRITAIN: Treaties Treaty between Her Majesty and the Republick of Texas, for the suppression of the African slave trade. Signed at London, November 16, 1840. London, 1842. 12 pp. (P.P. 1842, XLV.)

3206 GREAT BRITAIN: Treaties Treaty between Great Britain, Austria, France, Prussia, and Russia, for the suppression of the African slave trade. Signed at London, December 20, 1841. London, [1842]. 24 pp. (P.P. 1842, XLV.)

The 'quintuple treaty'. See (3328, 3444, 3914).

3207 *GREAT BRITAIN: Treaties 'Traité des Anglais avec Radama Ier au sujet des esclaves.' (Revue Coloniale, Paris, vol. 4, 1844, pp. 254–56.)

Antislavery convention and additional articles between Britain and Madagascar, 1817–23.

3208 GREAT BRITAIN: Treaties Treaties, conventions, and engagements, for the suppression of the slave trade. T. R. Harrison, London, 1844. iv, 631 pp.

Treaties between Britain and various other states, 1815–42.

3209 GREAT BRITAIN: Laws 'An act to amend an act, intituled An act to carry into execution a convention between His Majesty and the Emperor of Brazil, for the regulation and final abolition of the African slave trade.' *In*: The STATUTES of the United Kingdom of Great Britain and Ireland, vol. 85 (London, 1845), pp. 1059–63.

The 'Aberdeen act' (8 & 9 Vict. c. 122; 8 Aug. 1845), providing unilaterally for the continuation of anti-slave trade measures after the expiry of the existing agreement with Brazil.

3210 MARTENS, Karl, *Freiherr* **von and CUSSY, Ferdinand de Cornot,** *baron* **de** Recueil manuel et pratique de traités, conventions et autres actes diplomatiques, sur lesquels sont établis les relations et les rapports existant aujourd'hui entre les divers états souverains du globe, depuis l'année 1760 jusqu'à l'époque actuelle. F. A. Brockhaus, Leipzig, 1846–57. 7 vol.

Vol. 6 includes slave trade treaties signed 1847–49.

3211 GREAT BRITAIN: House of Lords The African slave trade. 1850. Report from the select committee of the House of Lords appointed to consider the best means which Great Britain can adopt for the final extinction of the African slave trade . . . Harrison & Sons, London, 1850. 13 pp.

3212 BRAZIL: Laws 'Lei Nº 581—de 4 de setembro de 1850. Estabelece medidas para a repressão do trafico de Africanos neste Imperio.' *In*: COLLECÇÃO das leis do Imperio do Brasil, 1850, vol. 11, pt. 1 (Rio de Janeiro, 1851), pp. 267–70.

The act which brought the Brazilian slave trade to an end; signed by Eusébio de Queiroz.

3213   GREAT BRITAIN: House of Commons
Report from the select committee on slave trade treaties; together with the proceedings of the committee, minutes of evidence, appendix, and index . . . [London,] 1853. xii, 260 pp. maps. (P.P. 1852–53, XXXIX.)

3214   KEMBALL, Arnold Burrowes
'Paper relative to the measures adopted by the British government, between the years 1820 and 1844, for effecting the suppression of the slave trade in the Persian Gulf . . . To which are appended, copies of the engagements entered into with the British government, between the years 1822 and 1851, by His Highness the Imaum of Muskat, the Arab chiefs of the Persian Gulf, and the government of Persia, for the attainment of the above object.' *In*: SELECTIONS from the records of the Bombay Government, n.s., no. 24 (Bombay, 1856), pp. 635–87.

Report by the British political resident in the Persian Gulf.

3215   *SOUTH CAROLINA: Governor
Message no. I of His Excellency James H. Adams to the Senate and House of Representatives at the session of 1856. Columbia, 1856.

A revival of the African slave trade is necessary to preserve South Carolina's economy.

3216   *SOUTH CAROLINA: House of Representatives
Report of the special committee of the House of Representatives of South Carolina, on so much of the message of His Excellency Gov. Jas. H. Adams, as relates to slavery and the slave trade. Columbia, S.C., 1857. 48 pp.

Favours reopening the African slave trade.

3217   *SOUTH CAROLINA: House of Representatives
Report of the minority of the special committee of seven, to whom was referred so much of his late Excellency's message no. 1, as relates to slavery and the slave trade. (Signed: J. Johnston Pettigrew.) Columbia, S.C., 1857. 40 pp.

Opposes the slave trade. (Reprinted as 'Protest against a renewal of the slave-trade' in: DBR, vol. 25, 1858, pp. 166–85, 289–308.)

3218   *TEXAS: House of Representatives (*Committee on Slaves and Slavery*)
A report and treatise on slavery and the slave trade. Austin, 1857. 81 pp.

Urges repeal of all laws and treaties prohibiting the importation of African slaves.

3219   LOUISIANA: Legislative Council
'Importation of African laborers.' (DBR, vol. 24, May 1858, pp. 421–24.)

Report of a select committee headed by Edward Delony, supporting the revival of the African slave trade.

3220   GREAT BRITAIN: Foreign Office
Regulations for the guidance of the Mixed Courts of Justice established in pursuance of the treaty of the 7th of April 1862, between Her Britannic Majesty and the United States of America, for the suppression of the African slave trade. London, 1863. 30 pp.

3221   SPAIN: Laws
'Real decreto, dictando varias disposiciones encaminadas á la estincion de la trata de negros en las islas de Cuba y Puerto Rico.' *In*: COLECCIÓN legislativa de España, vol. 94 (Madrid, 1865), pp. 720–23.

Decree of 27 Oct. 1865 for the transportation to Fernando Poo of African slaves recaptured in Cuba on a Portuguese ship.

3222   *SPAIN: Laws
Disposiciones sobre la represión y castigo del tráfico negrero, mandadas observar por real decreto de 29 de septiembre de 1866. Madrid, 1866. 27 pp.

3223   *SPAIN: Laws
Reglamento aprobado por S.M. para la aplicación de la ley de 29 de septiembre de 1866 sobre represión y castigo del tráfico negrero. Madrid. Junio 18 de 1867. Habana, 1867. 28 pp.

3224   *SERRANO Y DOMÍNGUEZ, Francisco, *duque de la Torre*
Informe presentado por el capitán general duque de la Torre al ministro de ultramar en mayo de 1867. Madrid, 1868. 32 pp.

Requests action by the Spanish government to suppress the slave trade and abolish slavery in Cuba.

3225   GREAT BRITAIN: Foreign Office
Memorandum on treaties with Zanzibar and Muscat. (Signed: E. Hertslet.) [London,] 1871. 4 pp.

Confidential notes on the slave trade treaties in force.

3226 EGYPT: Treaties
'Convention entre l'Égypte et la Grande-Bretagne pour la suppression du commerce des esclaves, signée à Alexandrie le 4 août 1877.' (Annuaire de l'Institut de Droit International, Gand, vol. 4, 1880, pp. 270–77.)

Text of the convention and related documents.

3227 ROME, Church of (*Pope Leo XIII*)
'Circulaire adressée par le Saint-Père aux évêques du Brésil le 5 mai 1888 pour les féliciter de la suppression de l'esclavage. Bienfaits du christianisme. Traite des nègres dans l'Afrique et le Soudan.' (Analecta Juris Pontificii, Rome, ser. 27, no. 242, 1888, col. 1243–53.)

Latin text of the encyclical 'In plurimis' on slavery.

3228 *PORTUGAL: Ministério da Marinha e do Ultramar
Memoria ácerca da extincção da escravidão e do trafico da escravatura no territorio portugues. Lisboa, 1889. 94 pp.

By A. Vidal de Castilho Barreto e Noronha; defence of Portuguese policy prepared for the Brussels conference. (Also issued as: Mémoire sur l'abolition de l'esclavage et de la traite des noirs sur le territoire portugais, Lisbonne, 1889; 98 pp.)

3229 *BRUSSELS SLAVE TRADE CONFERENCE
La traite des esclaves en Afrique. Actes internationaux et documents relatifs à la législation des pays d'Orient recueillis pour la Conférence de Bruxelles. Bruxelles, 1889. 58 pp.

3230 COQUILHAT, Camille
'Rapport au Roi-Souverain sur les mesures politiques et militaires prises et à prendre pour amener la répression de la traite des esclaves dans les territoires de l'État Indépendant du Congo.' (E.I.C., Bulletin official, Bruxelles, 1889, pp. 210–17.)

Dated 29 Oct. 1889.

3231 *ITALY: Ministero degli Affari Esteri
Tratta degli schiavi (1884–89) . . . Roma, 1889. xix, 240 pp. (Documenti diplomatici. XVI legislatura, sess. 4, no. 15.)

Presented to the Italian parliament by foreign minister Crispi 17 Dec. 1889.

3232 BRUSSELS SLAVE TRADE CONFERENCE
General act of the Brussels Conference, 1889–90; with annexed declaration . . . London, [1890]. 37 pp. (P.P. 1899, L.)

3233 UNITED STATES OF AMERICA: Treaties
General act between the United States of America and other powers for the repression of the African slave trade and the restriction of the importation into, and sale in, a certain defined zone of the African continent, of firearms, ammunition and spirituous liquors. Signed July 2, 1890. [Washington, 1890.] 45 pp.

Reprinted in: AJIL, vol. 3, supplement, 1909, pp. 29–59.

3234 CONGO FREE STATE: Laws
'Législation pénale contre la traite.' (État Indépendant du Congo, Bulletin officiel, Bruxelles, 1891, pp. 144–50.)

Decree against the slave trade, signed by Leopold II on 1 July 1891. (Reprinted as 'Le premier code pénal de la traite sur terre' in: MA, vol. 3, 1891, pp. 289–92.)

3235 *BELGIUM: Parlement
Approbation par les Chambres législatives belges de l'Acte général de la Conférence de Bruxelles du 2 juillet 1890 et la déclaration du même jour. Exposé des motifs et documents. Bruxelles, 1891. 65 pp.

3236 EETVELDE, Edmond van
'La traite des esclaves au Congo. Rapport du Sécretaire d'État au Roi-Souverain, sur les mesures prises par l'État Indépendant du Congo en exécution de l'Acte de Bruxelles.' (MA, vol. 7, 1895, pp. 69–81.)

3237 *EGYPT: Service pour la Répression de la Traite
Convention, décrets et règlements relatifs à la suppression de la traite des esclaves. [Cairo?] 1896. 25 pp.

S. NAVAL BLOCKADE

(a) OFFICIAL DOCUMENTS

3238 GREAT BRITAIN: Admiralty
A. Copies or extracts of all communications received by the Lords Commissioners of the Admiralty, from the naval officers stationed on the coast of Africa, or in the West Indies, since the 1st of January 1820; relative to the state of the slave trade. B. Copies or extracts of all instructions issued by the Lords Commissioners of the Admiralty to naval officers since the 1st of January 1819; relative to the suppression of the slave trade. [London, 1821.] 88 pp. (P.P. 1821, XXII.)

Published under varying titles until 1828. (Later reports of naval officers are included in the volumes of 'Correspondence with the British commissioners' 1848–89.)

3239 GREAT BRITAIN: Admiralty
A return of the numbers of vessels of every class in Her Majesty's service which have been employed on the West African station, in each year since the year 1828 . . . [London, 1842.] 11 pp. (P.P. 1842, XLIV.)

Includes annual expense on the squadron since 1819 and a list of slave ships captured since 1831. Published under varying titles until 1868.

3240 GREAT BRITAIN: Treaties
Treaty between Her Majesty and the United States of America, signed at Washington, August 9, 1842. London, [1843]. 8 pp. (P.P. 1843, LXI.)

The 'Webster-Ashburton treaty'; articles vii-ix provide for joint cruising and diplomatic cooperation.

3241 GREAT BRITAIN: Foreign Office
Correspondence between Great Britain and the United States relative to the treaty lately concluded at Washington. London, [1843]. 19 pp. (P.P. 1847, LXI.)

Letters on the slave trade and seizure of ships.

3242 GREAT BRITAIN: Admiralty
Instructions for the guidance of Her Majesty's naval officers employed in the suppression of the slave trade. London, 1844. vii, 684 pp.

Contains laws and treaties relating to the slave trade. Also printed as: P.P. 1844, L. (iv, 556, iv pp.) See (3256).

3243 GREAT BRITAIN: Foreign Office
Slave trade.—Slave vessels. Returns of cases adjudged under slave trade treaties, and numbers of slaves emancipated in consequence:—Also of the number of slave vessels arrived in transatlantic states since 1814, &c. [London, 1845.] 45 pp. (P.P. 1845, XLIX.)

Detailed lists of court cases 1829–43 and of known slaving voyages 1817–43.

3244 GREAT BRITAIN: Parliament
Minutes of evidence taken before the Duke de Broglie and the Rt. Hon. Stephen Lushington, D.C.L. March 31, April 1, 2, 3, and 4, 1845. London, [1847]. 63 pp. (P.P. 1847, LXVII.)

Hearings of a commission on the right of search.

3245 GREAT BRITAIN: Admiralty
Papers relating to engagements entered into by King Pepple and the chiefs of the Bonny with Her Majesty's naval officers, on the subject of the suppression of the slave trade . . . London, 1848. vi, 36 pp. (P.P. 1847–48, LXIV.)

Correspondence 1839–48, with the text of two engagements signed 1841 and 1844.

3246 GREAT BRITAIN: Foreign Office
Return of all vessels, their names and tonnage, captured (on suspicion of being engaged in slave trade), from 1840 to 1848 both inclusive, specifying the date of capture, the latitude and longitude, and whether with slaves on board or not; and of the number of slaves captured during the same period in each year, with the number of

deaths between the date of capture and adjudication, showing the annual per centage of mortality . . . [London,] 1850. 21 pp. (P.P. 1850, LV.)

Further lists of captured slave ships were published for the years 1849–79.

3247 GREAT BRITAIN: Foreign Office
Papers relative to the reduction of Lagos by Her Majesty's forces on the west coast of Africa. London, [1852]. v, 214 pp. (P.P. 1852, LIV.)

Correspondence 1849–52 on events leading up to the attacks on Lagos in 1851.

3248 GREAT BRITAIN: Foreign Office
Correspondence with the United States government on the question of right of visit. London, [1859]. 72 pp. (P.P. 1857–58, XXXIX.)

3249 GREAT BRITAIN: Treaties
Treaty between Her Majesty and the United States of America, for the suppression of the African slave trade. Signed at Washington, April 7, 1862. London, [1862]. 10 pp. (P.P. 1862, LXI.)

Agreement on the right of search, with instructions for the two navies and regulations for the mixed courts. See (3447).

3250 GREAT BRITAIN: Admiralty
Slave trade instructions, being instructions for the guidance of the commanders of Her Majesty's ships of war employed in the suppression of the slave trade. London, 1865. 142; 207 pp.

The supplement contains treaties and engagements with various states.

3251 GREAT BRITAIN: Admiralty
Instructions for the guidance of naval officers employed in the suppression of the slave trade. London, 1869. 5 pp.

3252 GREAT BRITAIN: Treaties
Convention between Her Majesty and the United States of America, additional to the treaty signed at Washington, April 7, 1862, for the suppression of the African slave trade. Signed at Washington, June 3, 1870. London, [1870]. 4 pp. (P.P. 1870, LXIX.)

Further agreement on procedure in naval operations.

3253 GREAT BRITAIN: Royal Commission on Fugitive Slaves
Report of the commissioners, minutes of the evidence, and appendix . . .

London, 1876. lxxxv, 251 pp. (P.P. 1876, XXVIII.)

Investigation of the international consequences of receiving fugitive slaves on British warships in foreign territorial waters.

3254 GREAT BRITAIN: Admiralty
Correspondence regarding the death of Captain Brownrigg of H.M.S. London, senior naval officer at Zanzibar. [London,] 1881. 39 pp.

Brownrigg was killed in a fight with a slave dhow off Pemba 3 Dec. 1881.

3255 GREAT BRITAIN: Admiralty
Instructions for the guidance of the captains and commanding officers of Her Majesty's ships of war employed in the suppression of the slave trade on the west coast of Africa station in their dealings with the kings and chiefs of uncivilized states. London, 1882. 292 pp.

3256 GREAT BRITAIN: Admiralty
Instructions for the guidance of the captains and commanding officers of Her Majesty's ships of war employed in the suppression of the slave trade. London, 1882. 616 pp.

Reissued 1892 in 2 vol. See (3242).

3257 GREAT BRITAIN: Admiralty
Slave trade: instructions for officers of Her Majesty's Navy employed on detached boat service. [London,] 1892. 109 pp.

(b) WEST AFRICA

3258 'CAPTURE of the Spanish slaver, Marinerito, by the Black Joke.' (USJ, 1832, II, pp. 63–65.)

On the seizure of a slave ship off Calabar in April 1831.

3259 'The LIFE and adventures of the "Black Joke", lately deceased at Sierra-Leone. From authentic sources.' (USJ, 1832, III, pp. 58–62.)

Career of an antislavery vessel 1828–32. See (3453).

3260 LEONARD, Peter
Records of a voyage to the western coast of Africa, in His Majesty's ship Dryad, and of the service on that station for the suppression of the slave trade, in the years 1830, 1831, and 1832. William Tait, Edinburgh (etc.), 1833. iv, 267 pp.

Vivid account by a naval surgeon. (Reviewed in: Tait's Edinburgh Magazine, vol. 2, 1833, pp. 789–99.)

3261 HOLMAN, James
A voyage round the world, including travels in Africa, Asia, Australasia, America, etc. etc. from MDCCCXXVII to MDCCCXXXII. Smith, Elder & Co., London, 1834–35. 4 vol. illus.

Detailed account by a blind author, the first part of the voyage being on the antislavery cruiser H.M.S. Eden from England via Sierra Leone and the Bights to Brazil 1827–28.

3262 RANKIN, F. Harrison
The white man's grave; a visit to Sierra Leone, in 1834. Richard Bentley, London, 1836. 2 vol.

Describes the 'liberated Africans' and the capture of slave ships.

3263 ALEXANDER, *Sir* James Edward
Narrative of a voyage of observation among the colonies of western Africa, in the flag-ship Thalia; and of a campaign in Kaffir-land . . . in 1835. Henry Colburn, London, 1837. 2 vol.

Vol. 1 contains a description of the blockade system.

3264 'DESTRUCTION of slave factories by Captain Denman.' (FA, no. 6, April 1841, pp. 83–84.)

On the action at Gallinas; with the text of a treaty between Denman and King Siaka, 21 Nov. 1840.

3265 'SIERRA Leone and the liberated Africans.' (ColM, vol. 6, 1841, pp. 327–34, 463–69; vol. 7, 1842, pp. 29–43, 214–25, 286–96, 404–12; vol. 8, 1842, pp. 37–44, 220–23.)

See the account of 'Liberated Africans' at Sierra Leone in: KUCZYNSKI, R. R. Demographic survey of the British colonial empire, vol. 1 (London, 1948), pp. 95–150.

3266 'The SLAVER. From the note-book of an officer employed against the slave trade.' (Signed: F.) (USM, 1842, I, pp. 375–80.)

Slaves were recaptured off Brazil and landed in British Guiana.

3267 'NARRATIVE of the Niger expedition. 1841–1842. (Compiled from official documents).' (USM, 1843, III, pp. 223–31, 376–84, 591–98; 1844, I, pp. 227–41.)

The expedition was officially planned as an anti-slave trade measure.

3268 MURRAY, Augustus Charles
'Narrative of a voyage from Accra to Sierra Leone, from August 12th, to January 5th, 1841, in the Dores, a captured slaver, to H.M.B. Dolphin.' (USM, 1845, I, pp. 512–21.)

3269 JOURNAL of an African cruiser: comprising sketches of the Canaries, the Cape de Verds, Liberia, Madeira, Sierra Leone, and other places of interest on the west coast of Africa. By an officer of the U.S. navy. Edited by Nathaniel Hawthorne. Wiley & Putnam, London, 1845. viii, 179 pp.

By Horatio Bridge. Critical account of the cruise of an American squadron 1843–44. (Reviewed in: ColM, vol. 5, pp. 506–07.)

3270 McHENRY, George
'An account of the liberated African establishment at St. Helena.' (SCM. vol. 5, 1845, pp. 172–83, 434–41; vol, 6, 1845, pp. 149–56, 253–66, 428–44; vol. 7, 1846, pp. 16–38, 133–50.)

Description of recaptured slaves and their medical condition, by a surgeon.

3271 KINGSTON, William Henry Giles
'The slavers of the Quorra; an after-dinner reminiscence of the African coast. Narrated by Captain S——, R.N., to William H. G. Kingston.' (USM, 1846, II, pp. 59–76.)

On the capture of Spanish ships in the Niger delta in the 1830s.

3272 SHREEVE, William Whitaker
Sierra Leone: the principal British colony on the western coast of Africa. By William Whitaker Shreeve, six years resident, and late acting first writer to Her Britannic Majesty's commissioners under the slave trade suppression treaties . . . Simmonds & Co., London, 1847. iv, 114 pp.

With a chapter on 'Slave trade' and notes on the mixed commission courts and antislavery squadron.

3273 'SHORT notice of a cruise in the West Indies, with some account of a Spanish slave captain.' (USM, 1847, I, pp. 392–403; II, pp. 29–44, 392–406; III, pp. 12–25, 335–48; 1848, I, pp. 27–38.)

Account of an antislavery patrol 1828; with a biography of Giuseppe Fornaro.

3274 ALLEN, William *and* THOMSON, Thomas Richard Heywood
A narrative of the expedition sent by Her Majesty's government to the river Niger, in 1841. Under the command of Capt. H. D. Trotter . . . Richard Bentley, London, 1848. 2 vol. illus.

Vol. 2, ch. 13: 'The slave question considered'. (Critical review by Charles Dickens, 'The Niger expedition', Examiner, 19 Aug. 1848; reprinted in his: Miscellaneous papers, London, 1908, vol. 1, pp. 117–35.)

3275 BRENT, John Carroll
'Leaves from an African journal.' (Knickerbocker, New-York, vol, 32, 1848, pp. 412–20; vol. 33, 1849, pp. 41–48, 116–27, 206–15, 334–40, 399–409; vol. 34, 1849, pp. 127–33, 226–34, 300–05; vol. 35, 1850, pp. 105–08, 377–84.)

Diary of a cruise with the U.S. West African squadron to Monrovia, Accra and Whydah, Oct. 1848–Feb. 1849.

3276 FORBES, Frederick Edwyn
Six months' service in the African blockade, from April to October, 1848, in command of H.M.S. Bonetta. Richard Bentley, London, 1849. ix, 145 pp. map.

Describes the slave trade on the Windward Coast.

3277 HUNTLEY, *Sir* Henry Veel
Seven years' service on the slave coast of western Africa. Thomas Cautley Newby, London, 1850. 2 vol.

On antislavery cruising in the 1830s. (Reviewed in: WR, vol. 56, 1851, pp. 1–26.)

3278 'The SLAVER.' (CJ, n.s., vol. 18, 1852, pp. 273–75.)

Account of the capture of a Brazilian slave ship off Ambriz in 1850.

3279 FOOTE, Andrew Hull
Africa and the American flag. New York, 1854. 390 pp. illus.

On Liberian colonisation and the U.S. squadron in the suppression of the slave trade; by an American commander on the coast 1850–51.

3280 WILBERFORCE, Edward
Brazil viewed through a naval glass: with notes on slavery and the slave trade. Longman, Brown, Green, & Longmans, London, 1856. x, 236 pp.

Account of antislavery cruising about 1851.

3281 'RECAPTURED slaves at St. Helena.' (CMG, n.s., vol. 9, 1859, pp. 59–60.)

Describes the condition of recently arrived African slaves.

3282 *THOMAS, Charles W.
Adventures and observations on the west coast of Africa, and its islands. Historical and descriptive sketches of Madeira, Canary, Biafra and Cape Verd islands . . . New York, 1860. 479 pp.

Narrative of a cruise from Morocco to Angola 1855–57; by a chaplain of the U.S. African squadron.

3283 AVÉ-LALLEMANT, Robert
'Aus dem brasilianischen Sklavenhandel.' (Daheim, Leipzig, vol. 5, 1869, pp. 633–36, 650–52.)

Eyewitness account of the capture of a Brazilian slave ship in 1837 by H.M.S. Grecian.

3284 'TWO encounters with slavers in 1850.' (Internationale Revue über die gesamten Armeen und Flotten, Hannover, vol. 4, pt. 1, 1885, pp. 88–90.)

Narrative by a British naval officer of the seizure of Brazilian slave ships, one of them a paddle steamer.

3285 HOBART, Augustus Charles
Sketches of my life by the late Admiral Hobart Pasha . . . Second edition. London, 1886. vii, 282 pp.

Ch. 5–6: 'Slave hunting'; on the Brazilian station in the early 1840s.

3286 'EXTRACT from journal of the U.S.S. Cyane, 1820.' (MAH, vol. 30, 1893, pp. 92–95.)

Describes the capture of American slave ships off West Africa; from the journal of Captain Edward Trenchard. See (3432).

3287 HALL, Wilburn
'Capture of the slave-ship "Cora". The last slaver taken by the United States.' (CIMM, vol. 48, 1894, pp. 115–29; illus.)

On a prize with over 700 slaves taken off Angola in 1860 and sailed to New York by the author.

3288 HAY, John Charles Dalrymple
Lines from my log-books. Edinburgh, 1898. 412 pp. illus.

Contains information on the author's service in the British West African squadron 1834–36.

3289   WOOD, J. Taylor
'The capture of a slaver.' (AtM, vol. 86, 1900, pp. 451–63.)

On a prize taken from the Bights to Liberia about 1850 by a U.S. ship in which the author was midshipman.

3290   WOODS, *Sir* Henry Felix
'Extract from "Spunyarn." by Admiral Sir Henry Woods Pasha, K.C.V.O.' (Sierra Leone Studies, Freetown, no. 12, 1928, pp. 14–20.)

From his: Spunyarn. From the strands of a sailor's life afloat and ashore (London, 1924), vol. 1, ch. 2: 'Chasing the slave-traders'; dealing with the service in the West African antislavery squadron 1859.

3291   STODDART, James
'A cruise in a slaver.' (BM, vol. 245, 1939, pp. 186–99.)

Extract from the journal of a British officer, describing the sailing of a prize from the Bights to Sierra Leone about 1835.

(c) EAST AFRICA

3292   'SLAVE trade and the civilization of Africa.' (Philanthropist, London, vol. 3, 1813, pp. 74–79.)

Describes the capture in 1811 of three slave ships on their way from Madagascar to Mauritius.

3293   HILL, Pascoe Grenfell
Fifty days on board a slave-vessel in the Mozambique Channel, in April and May, 1843. John Murray, London, 1844. 115 pp. map.

Describes the suffering of slaves on a captured slave ship taken to Simons-town. (Reviewed by Thomas Hood in: Hood's Magazine, London, vol. 1, 1844, pp. 186–89; also in: CO, vol. 44, 1844, pp. 117–26; CJ, vol. 1, 1844, pp. 152–54; BM, vol. 55, 1844, pp. 425–30.)

3294   BARNARD, Frederick Lamport
A three years' cruize in the Mozambique Channel, for the suppression of the slave trade. Richard Bentley, London, 1848. xii, 319 pp.

Experiences of a naval lieutenant 1843–46. (Reprinted, with an introduction by D. H. Simpson, London, 1969; map.)

3295   HILL, Pascoe Grenfell
A voyage to the slave coasts of West and East Africa. Charles Gilpin, London; James B. Gilpin, Dublin, 1849. 47 pp.

Cruise from Simonstown to Mozambique 1844.

3296   'HOW we got to windward of the slave-dealers.' (CJ, vol. 44, 1867, pp. 109–12.)

Account by C. R. Low of the capture of dhows near Berbera by a schooner from Aden in 1857.

3297   LOW, Charles Rathbone
'A cruise in the Mozambique.' (USM, 1867, II, pp. 517–23.)

Patrol from Simonstown in the 1850s.

3298   DEVEREUX, William Cope
A cruise in the "Gorgon;" or, eighteen months on H.M.S. "Gorgon," engaged in the suppression of the slave trade on the east coast of Africa . . . London, 1869. xv, 421 pp. map.

By the commander of a steamer of the east coast squadron 1861–63. (Reprinted, with an introduction by D. H. Simpson, London, 1968.)

3299   'The SLAVE-TRADE as it now is.' (CJ, vol. 47, 1870, pp. 81–85, 110–12.)

Description of the Zanzibar slave trade and cruising methods by a naval officer.

3300   CHALLICE, John Armstrong
'In pursuit of slavers.' (Dark Blue, London, vol. 4, 1872, pp. 303–07.)

On the capture of slave dhows off Madagascar and East Africa in 1868; by a naval lieutenant.

3301   SULIVAN, George Lydiard
Dhow chasing in Zanzibar waters and on the eastern coast of Africa. Narrative of five years' experiences in the suppression of the slave trade. London, 1873. x, 453 pp. illus, map.

Account of service 1849–50, 1866, 1868–69; with extracts from documents on the slave trade, showing how it tripled in this period. (Reprinted, with an introduction by D. H. Simpson, London, 1967.)

3302   COLOMB, Philip Howard
Slave-catching in the Indian Ocean. A record of naval experiences. London, 1873. vii, 503 pp. illus, map.

Account of the East African slave trade by the captain of the 'Dryad' 1869–70.

3303 'SLAVE catching and dhow chasing.' (CMI, n.s., vol. 9, 1873, pp. 177–88; 252–56.)

Review of (3301–02).

3304 'MY first slaver. A tale of the Zanzibar coast.' (USM, 1880, II, pp. 355–64.)

Describes the capture of a dhow smuggling slaves to Zanzibar in 1873.

3305 'SKLAVENHANDEL in den ostafrikanischen Gewässern.' (DKB, vol. 2, 1891, pp. 292–93.)

Summary of British official report on the naval antislavery patrol in 1890.

3306 STOPFORD, Philip James
'A boat-cruising experience.' (CJ, vol. 94, 1917, pp. 301–03.)

On the capture of a slave dhow off Pemba.

3307 FREER-SMITH, Sir Hamilton Pym
Recollections ancient and modern. London, [1925]. 103 pp.

Includes reminiscences of antislavery patrolling in the Zanzibar area 1871–73.

(d) CONTROVERSY

3308a 'REPREZENTAÇOENS que o corpo do commercio da Bahia dirigio a Sua Alteza Real o Principe Regente Nosso Senhor em que expoem as violencias que lhe tem feito alguns individuos da marinha ingleza.' (IPI, vol. 6, março 1813, pp. 359–75.)

Translated as:

3308b*REPRESENTATIONS of the Brazilian merchants against the insults offered to the Portuguese flag, and against the violent and oppressive capture of several of their vessels by some officers belonging to the English navy; to which is added . . . other interesting pieces . . . J. Darling, London, 1813. xxxii, 96 pp.

Two protests against the arrest of Brazilian slavers near Lagos and Cabinda by British warships, in violation of the 1810 treaty of friendship and alliance.

3309 *RÉMONSTRANCES des négocians du Brésil, contre les insultes faites au pavillon portugais: et contre la saisie violente et tyrannique de plusieurs de leurs navires, par les officiers de la marine anglaise, accompagnées d'autres pièces intéressantes: traduites du portugais et de l'anglais, par F. S. Constancio . . . Madame Goullet, Paris, 1814. xii, 80 pp.

Translation of (3308).

3310 *CONDUCTA injuridica del Juzgado de Presas de las islas de Bahama con respecto al comercio marítimo de Cuba. Habana, 1814. 28 pp.

3311 'IMPORTANT question respecting the practical abolition of the slave trade.' (EMLR, vol. 69, May 1816, p. 392.)

Letter urging an 'adequate naval force' to suppress the trade.

3312 McQUEEN, James
'Civilization of Africa.—Sierra Leone. —Liberated Africans. To R. W. Hay, Esq. Under Secretary of State, &c. &c.' (BM, vol. 20, Dec. 1826, pp. 872–92; vol. 21, March 1827, pp. 315–29; May 1827, pp. 596–624.)

Fernando Po must replace Sierra Leone as headquarters for the British squadron and depot for recaptured slaves.

3313 'The BRITISH naval service, and the treaties on the slave-trade.' (USJ, 1837, I, pp. 21–37.)

Account of the treaty system written for naval officers. See (3314).

3314 'The TREATIES on the slave trade; and the mixed commission court at Sierra Leone.' (Signed: W.S.) (USJ, 1837, I, pp. 380–85.)

Criticism of interpretation of treaties in (3313).

3315 LAIRD, Macgregor *and* OLDFIELD, R. A. K.
Narrative of an expedition into the interior of Africa, by the river Niger, in the steam-vessels Quorra and Alburkah, in 1832, 1833, and 1834. Richard Bentley, London, 1837. 2 vol.

Vol. 2 contains 'Remarks on our commerce with Africa' (probably by Laird) advocating a close blockade to suppress the slave trade.

3316 FAIR, Robert
A letter to the Hon. W. T. Fox Strangways, Under Secretary of State for Foreign Affairs, on the present state of the slave trade in the West Indies,

and on the means of more effectually counteracting it. Ridgway, London, 1838. 47 pp.

Proposals by a naval captain for an antislavery squadron in the West Indies, a new mixed commission court in the Bahamas and improvements in the slave trade treaties.

3317 PRACTICAL remarks on the slave trade of the west coast of Africa, with notes on the Portuguese treaty. Ridgway, London, 1839. 22 pp.

By Joseph Denman. Criticises British antislavery strategy; the cruisers should be increased and concentrated off the African coast.

3318 MODEL of a Spanish slaver. W. B. Brodie & Co., Salisbury, [c. 1840]. 4 pp.

Leaflet by a naval officer for the exhibition of a model of a brig taken off Bonny with 600 slaves.

3319 *JUSTIFICAÇÃO das reclamações apresentadas pelo govêrno brasileiro a S.M. britânica (pelo que respeita às prêsas feitas pelos cruzadores inglêses na costa ocidental da África). Rio de Janeiro, 1840.

Britain's antislave trade policy is hypocritical.

3320 LEEKE, *Sir* Henry
'On the blockade of the west coast of Africa.' (FA, no. 3, Feb. 1841, pp. 47–48.)

Letter dated 7 Sept. 1840 advocating a strict blockade of the Volta-Cameroons area. (The author commanded the ship that rescued S. A. Crowther from a Portuguese slaver in 1822.)

3321 'The INTERNATIONAL law of the slave trade and the maritime right of search.' (Law Magazine, London, vol. 26, 1841, pp. 88–97.)

By John Codman Hurd. Notes on prize law and the right of search, critical of British policy.

3322 'TREATY entered into by the five great powers of Europe for the more effectual suppression of the slave trade.' (FA, no. 15, Jan. 1842, pp. 1–2.)

Leading article welcoming the quintuple treaty (3206).

3323 'The SLAVE trade.' (BM, vol. 51, Feb. 1842, pp. 147–50.)

Attack on American opposition to the right of search.

3324 'MARITIME right of search. The Earl of Aberdeen and Mr. Stevenson.' (ColM, vol. 7, 1842, pp. 145–62.)

Exchange of letters Sept.—Oct. 1841 between the British Foreign Secretary and U.S. envoy, on American slavers and naval visitation.

3325 *An EXAMINATION of the question, now in discussion, between the American and British governments, concerning the right of search By an American. N. Hickman, Baltimore, 1842. 55 pp.

By Lewis Cass. Attack on the British demand for reciprocal right of searching suspected slavers. (French translation published in Paris 1842.) See (3328–29).

3326 'WAR with America. An examination of the instigations and probable effects. By a Kentuckian.' (Great Western Magazine, London, vol. 1, April 1842, pp. 70–97.)

By Duff Green. Warns Britain against pressing antislavery policy to the point of war with the United States; the slave trade issue has been exaggerated for reasons of commercial imperialism. See (3336).

3327 'The RIGHT of search and African slave trade.' (AR, vol. 18, April 1842, pp. 107–20.)

On the U.S.–British controversy over naval visitation 1840–41.

3328 *BERG, Olof
Nordamerikas Stellung zum Quintupel-Tractat vom 20. December 1841. Eine Beleuchtung der Sklaven- und Handelsverhältnisse der Vereinigten Staaten, als Versuch eines Commentars zum Note des Generals Cass . . . Königsberg, 1842. xii, 177 pp.

See (3206, 3325, 3340).

3329 REPLY to an "American's examination" of "right of search:" with observations on some questions at issue between Great Britain and the United States, and on certain positions assumed by the North American government. By an Englishman. John Rodwell, London, 1842. iv, 111, lxii pp.

By Sir William Ouseley. U.S. refusal to accede to the anti-slave trade-treaties is due to pro-slavery interests. See (3325).

3330 'The RIGHT of search.' (FA, no. 19, May 1842, pp. 61–64.)

Hopes that the United States will co-operate with Britain in suppressing the slave trade.

3331 'DECISION of the French ministry relative to the ratification of the treaty of Dec. 20th, 1841.' (FA, no. 20, June 1842, pp. 77–80.)

Deplores the French government's refusal to ratify the quintuple treaty.

3332 *JOLLIVET, Adolphe
Du droit de visite . . . A. Blondeau, Paris, 1842. 53 pp.

3333 HALL, James
'The African trade—right of search—slave trade under the American flag, &c.' (AR, vol. 18, Aug. 1842, pp. 241–53.)

A sufficient naval force should be stationed on the African coast to deter U.S. citizens from participating in the slave trade.

3334 *PETIT DE BARONCOURT, ——
Atteinte à la liberté des mers, du droit de visite maritime accordé à l'Angleterre par les puissances du continent. Amyot, Paris, 1842. 26 pp.

Britain's real motives for suppressing the slave trade are commercial advantages, naval supremacy and colonial monopoly. (Reprinted as appendix in: 3351.)

3335 *SCHAUER DE MARCKOLSHEIM, Louis
Encore le droit de visite. Revue administratif de la marine française . . . Paris, 1842. 120 pp.

3336 'The UNITED States and England. By an American.' (Great Western Magazine, London, vol. 2, Sept. 1842, pp. 1–122; map.)

By Duff Green. The main difficulties in the Ashburton negotiations relate to the slave trade, but not a single slave has been imported to the U.S. for over 30 years. See (3326, 3444).

3337 *WHEATON, Henry
Enquiry into the validity of the British claim to a right of visitation and search of American vessels suspected to be engaged in the African slave-trade. Lea & Blanchard, Philadelphia, 1842. 151 pp.

3338 *ENGLAND opposed to slavery; or some remarks upon "An examination into the real causes of the war against the United States, and an appeal to the other powers of Europe against the purposes of England". B. H. Greene, Boston, 1842. 55 pp.

By G. B. Loring. See (3326).

3339 COMMENTS on Lord Brougham's attack upon General Lewis Cass. By Americanus . . . Argus Office, Harrisburg, Pa., 1843. 13 pp.

Supports the U.S. view on the right of search.

3340 *BERG, Olof
Sklaverei, Seeherrschaft und die preussische Staatszeitung. Ein Nachtrag zu meiner Schrift: "Nordamerikas Stellung zum Quintupel-Tractat am 20. December 1841". Königsberg, 1843. 88 pp.

See (3328).

3341 'The AFRICAN slave trade.' (Dublin University Magazine, vol. 21, 1843, pp. 439–46.)

Review of recent publications, including discussion of the right of search at sea.

3342 'OUR "African squadrons".' (AR, vol. 20, Feb. 1844, pp. 57–63.)

Liberia should be the centre for the U.S. squadron's operations.

3343 *ABOLITION du droit de visite réciproque, et extension de la visite nationale. Paris, 1844.

By —— Dutrône. Pamphlet, suggesting that cruisers carry commissioners from several nations to search their own ships.

3344 GIRARDIN, Alexandre Louis Robert, comte de
Mémoire sur la situation politique et militaire de l'Europe à l'occasion des traités de 1831, 1833 et 1841 sur le droit de visite. Amyot, Paris, 1844. 360 pp.

Hostile discussion of Britain's claims to a naval right of search.

3345 'RIGHT of visit.' (LLA, vol. 2, 1844, pp. 431–32.)

On the difficulties of the blockade if France continues to oppose searching of her ships.

3346 *JOLLIVET, Adolphe
Historique de la traite et du droit de visite. Bruneau, Paris, 1844. 35 pp.

3347 *LAFOND DE LURCY, Gabriel
Un mot sur l'émancipation de l'esclavage, et sur le commerce maritime de la

France, en réponse à M. le Duc de Broglie, au projet du gouvernement et au rapport de M. Mérilhou, à la Chambre des Pairs. Dondey–Dupré, Paris, [1844]. 36 pp.

Attacks British policy.

3348 *Un MOT sur l'abolition de la traite, l'émancipation des noirs et le droit de visite. Par M. L. ....p. J. B. Gaudelet, Le Puy, 1845. 30 pp.

Opposes the right of search as an insult to the French flag.

3349 COLIN, Auguste
'Du droit de visite.' (Revue Indépendante, Paris, vol. 18, 1845, pp. 521–50.)

Proposes an international agreement in Europe to sanction the right of search, 'une nouvelle sainte-alliance'.

3350 'PROSPECTS of slave-trade suppression.' (LLA, vol. 5, 1845, p. 202.)

The French proposal for joint cruising is absurd; the system has failed and should be replaced by 'something rational'. (Reprinted from the Spectator.)

3351 PETIT DE BARONCOURT, ——
De l'émancipation des noirs ou lettres à M. le duc de Broglie sur les dangers de cette mesure suivies de considérations sur le droit de visite . . . Deuxième édition. Amyot, Paris, 1845. xv, 323 pp.

With appendices on the right of visit. See (3334).

3352 INGLATERRA e Brasil. Trafego de escravos. Por um deputado. J. J. da Rocha, Rio de Janeiro, 1845. 273, xviii pp.

By Justiniano José da Rocha. Articles on the 'Aberdeen Bill'; Britain's antislavery policy is dictated by sordid self-interest and disregard for international law.

3353 FOOTE, John
'A few remarks on the slave-trade in the Brazils.' (USM, 1845, II, pp. 378–87, 573–80.)

On the Brazilian slave trade debate and British cruisers, by a Royal Navy commander; antislavery measures should be intensified.

3354 NELSON, Thomas
Remarks on the slavery and slave trade of the Brazils. J. Hatchard & Son, London, 1846. 85 pp.

Contends that the naval blockade is inadequate; boycott of produce would worry Brazil more.

3355 DENMAN, Joseph
West India interests, African emigration, and slave trade. James Bigg & Son, London, 1848. 40 pp.

Plea for firm action against slave traders by a naval captain; the emigration scheme would be slave trade under another name. (First printed privately, Worcester, 1848; 4, 32 pp.)

3356 MATSON, Henry James
Remarks on the slave trade and African squadron . . . Third edition. James Ridgway, London, 1848. 94 pp.

Defence of the squadron by a commander; with his evidence to the parliamentary committee on the slave trade. (The author suppressed the second edition, 1848.)

3357 DENMAN, Thomas, *Lord Denman*
A letter from Lord Denman to Lord Brougham, on the final extinction of the slave-trade. Second edition, corrected. J. Hatchard & Son, London, 1848. xii, 80 pp.

The squadron should not be withdrawn but supplemented with other measures. See (3363).

3358 'The SLAVE-TRADE and the West Indies.' (LLA, vol. 16, 1848, pp. 519–21.)

The squadron should be withdrawn and labour supplied by African emigration until the British colonies are 'fully stocked'. (Reprinted from the Examiner.)

3359 'REVIEW of works on the slave trade.' (CO, vol. 48, Nov. 1848, pp. 752–61.)

Extracts from (25) and (3357) with comments; Britain must employ force against Brazilian slavers.

3360 SMITH, George
The case of our West-African cruisers and West-African settlements fairly considered. J. Hatchard & Son, London, 1848. 71 pp.

Proposes government and missionary measures to increase the effectivity of the blockade.

3361 STEPHEN, *Sir* George
A letter from Sir George Stephen to Sir E. F. Buxton, Bart., M.P. on the proposed revival of the English slave

trade. Simpkin, Marshall, & Co., London, 1849. 16 pp.

Antislavery opinion must rally to prevent parliament from withdrawing the squadron.

3362 ALLEN, William
A plan for the immediate extinction of the slave trade for the relief of the West India colonies, and for the diffusion of civilization and Christianity in Africa, by the co-operation of Mammon with philanthrophy. James Ridgway, London, 1849. 36 pp.

Scheme of a naval officer to replace the blockade by military establishments and the purchase of slaves for indentured labour in the West Indies.

3363 DENMAN, Thomas, *Lord Denman*
A second letter from Lord Denman to Lord Brougham, on the final extinction of the slave trade, with remarks on a late narrative of the Niger expedition in 1841. J. Hatchard & Son, London, 1849. 34 pp.

Comments on a scheme to replace the squadron with settlements in Africa. See (3357).

3364 'REMARKS on the African slave trade and emigration. By one who has served in the preventive squadron.' (USM, 1849, I, pp. 572–80; II, pp. 37–46.)

On the difficulties of the blockade and means of improving the squadron.

3365 FREE trade in negroes. John Ollivier, London, 1849. 51 pp.

Attributed to John Ollivier. Withdrawal of the squadron would lead to increased slave trade; it can only be suppressed by force.

3366 'The PREVENTIVE squadron on the West-African coast.' (CMI, vol. 1, 1849, pp. 171–74.)

Results of the blockade are now appearing in the mission at Abeokuta.

3367 STEPHEN, *Sir* **George**
The Niger trade considered in connection with the African blockade. Simpkin, Marshall & Co., London (etc.), 1849. 71 pp. map.

Review of recent works on West Africa; with a scheme to replace the squadron by treaties, African bases, and voluntary emigration to the West Indies.

3368 'The SLAVE trade and the sugar bill.' (ColM, vol. 16, 1849. pp. 230–41.)

Role of the squadron compared with commerce in displacing the slave trade.

3369 'De UITKOMSTEN van de kruis-eskaders op de westkust van Africa, tot wering van den slavenhandel.' (Verhandelingen en Berigten betrekkelijk het Zeewesen en de Zeevaartkunde, Amsterdam, 1849, pp. 682–91.)

On the controversy over the British antislavery squadron; the volume of the slave trade depends on economic factors, not on the size of the squadron.

3370 RICHARDSON, James
The cruisers: being a letter to the Marquis of Lansdowne . . . in defence of armed coercion for the extinction of the slave trade. Hatchard & Son, London, 1849. 40 pp.

Defence of the squadron against critics in Britain, with consideration of alternative schemes.

3371 'The AFRICAN squadron.' (ColM, vol. 17, 1849, pp. 136–44, 447–56, 481–500; vol. 18, 1850, pp. 3–28, 116–28, 342–51.)

By Joseph Denman. Defence of the cruisers, with review of recent works on the subject.

3372 'AFRICAN coast blockade.' (WR, vol. 52, Jan. 1850, pp. 500–41.)

The cruisers have failed; diplomatic approaches should be made to Brazil.

3373 DENMAN, Joseph
The slave trade, the African squadron, and Mr. Hutt's committee . . . John Mortimer, London, [1850]. 56 pp.

Reprinted from (3371).

3374 THOMSON, Thomas, Richard Heywood
The Brazilian slave trade, and its remedy: showing the futility of repressive force measures. Also, how Africa and our West Indian colonies may be mutually benefited. John Mylrea, Douglas, Isle of Man; Simpkin & Marshall; Houlston & Stoneman, London, 1850. 86 pp.

The blockade has only injured legitimate trade; the remedy is regulated African emigration to Brazil and abolition of slavery. By a naval surgeon with antislavery experience.

3375 ANALYSIS of the evidence given before the select committees upon the slave trade. By a barrister. Partridge & Oakey, London, 1850. 121 pp.

> By Sir George Stephen. Opposes withdrawal of the squadron; 'emigration' would be a modified slave trade. See (25–27).

3376 OUSELEY, *Sir* William Gore
Notes on the slave-trade, with remarks on the measures adopted for its suppression. To which are added: a few general observations on slavery, and the prejudices of race and colour, as affecting the slave-trade; and some suggestions on the means by which it may be checked. John Rodwell, London, 1850. iv, 75 pp.

> The squadron should be kept, combined with colonisation and African emigration to the British West Indies.

3377 DENMAN, Joseph
The African squadron and Mr. Hutt's committee . . . Second edition, enlarged . . . John Mortimer (etc.), London, [1850]. 70 pp.

> See (3373).

3378 CHURCH MISSIONARY SOCIETY
The African squadron. Petition of the committee of the Church Missionary Society, deprecating the diminishing or removal of the squadron . . . [London,] 1850. 11 pp.

> Petition to Parliament; with extracts from evidence to the Lords select committee 1849 and from the Commons debate of March 1850. (Also printed in: CMI, vol. 1, 1850, pp. 267–70.)

3379 STOKES, Robert
Regulated slave trade. Reprinted from the evidence of Robert Stokes, Esq., given before the select committee of the House of Lords in 1849 . . . James Ridgway, London (etc.), 1850. viii, 18 pp.

> The blockade has not led to greater crowding in slave ships.

3380 'The AFRICAN squadron.' (ER, vol. 92, July 1850, pp. 241–62.)

> Review of parliamentary reports on the slave trade 1848–49; removal of the squadron would be disastrous.

3381 YULE, *Sir* Henry
The African squadron vindicated . . .

Second edition. James Ridgway (etc.), London (etc.), 1850. 41 pp.

> Review of recent publications; withdrawal would be a national dishonour.

3382 WILSON, John Leighton
'The slave trade. By . . . an American missionary, resident at the river Gaboon.' (ColM, vol. 19, Sept. 1850, pp. 189–204.)

> Commerce and missions in West Africa owe their existence to the British squadron. See (3385).

3383 'The HOUSE of Lords on the slave trade.' (ColM, vol. 19, Sept. 1850, pp. 230–40.)

> Analysis of the Lords select committee report (27).

3384 'REMARKS on the suppression of the African slave trade.' (USM, 1850, I, pp. 369–84, 545–60.)

> Discusses recent criticism of the anti-slavery squadron but argues that it has checked the slave trade and should be continued.

3385 WILSON, John Leighton
The British squadron on the coast of Africa . . . James Ridgway, London, 1850. 16 pp.

> First published as an article (3382). See (3391).

3386 BRODIE, William
Modern slavery, and the slave trade. A lecture . . . J. Hatchard & Son, London, 1850. 51 pp.

> A clergyman's view of the squadron's importance.

3387 SLAVE trade.—African squadron. Letters from the Rev. Samuel Crowther . . . and the Rev. Henry Townsend . . . John Mortimer, London, 1850. 15 pp.

> Letters from two missionaries on antislavery and missionary successes in the Lagos area. (First published in: ColM, vol. 19, Dec. 1850, pp. 505–17.)

3388 EXTRACTS from the evidence taken before committees of the two houses of parliament relative to the slave trade, with illustrations from collateral sources of information. By a barrister of the Middle Temple. London, 1851. 126 pp.

> Selection defending the squadron and warning of the consequences of its withdrawal. See (25–27).

3389 AFRICAN slave trade—African squadron. A question of great national importance has lately been much agitated, namely, whether the measures in operation for the suppression of the slave trade, should, or should not, be abandoned . . . Circular . . . [London, 1851.] 8 pp.

Reasons why the maintenance of the squadron is essential, with a list of signatories headed by the Archbishop of Canterbury.

3390 'The AFRICAN slave trade.' (ColM, vol. 21, 1851, pp. 26–36, 124–34, 331–40.)

Reasons why the squadron should not be withdrawn, and review of recent works on the subject (3385, 3388).

3391 WILSON, John Leighton
The British squadron on the coast of Africa . . . With notes by Captain H. D. Trotter. London, 1851. 32 pp. map.

See (3385).

3392 'The WEST-AFRICAN slave-trade.' (CMI, vol. 2, April 1851, pp. 73–80; map.)

3393 'The AFRICAN slave trade.' (CO, vol. 51, Aug. 1851, pp. 553–69.)

Defence of the squadron in a review of recent publications (3377, 3381, 3385).

3394 MANSFIELD, J. S.
Remarks on the African squadron. London, 1851. 22 pp.

The cruisers have been effective and worth the expense.

3395 A LETTER to the Right Honourable Lord Denman, on the slave trade; with a plea for its speedy and final extinction. (Signed: E.T.H.) London, 1851. 70 pp.

The squadron is insufficient to stop the slave trade; it should be replaced by colonisation to open up Africa.

3396 'The DESTRUCTION of Lagos and the suppression of the slave-trade.' (ColM, vol. 23, 1852, pp. 258–68.)

The blockade must be followed up by treaties with African governments.

3397 The DESTRUCTION of Lagos. London, 1852, 24 pp.

The occupation of Lagos 1851 struck a death blow to the slave trade, but the squadron must not be reduced.

3398 EARDLEY-WILMOT, Arthur Parry
A letter to the Right Honorable Viscount Palmerston . . . on the present state of the African slave trade, and on the necessity of increasing the African squadron. London, 1853. 16 pp.

Report on the slave trade by a naval commander on active service.

3399 'LAGOS, and missionary operations in the Bight of Benin.' (CMI, vol. 4, Dec. 1853, pp. 267–78; illus, map.)

Warns against reducing the 'repressive force' in West Africa while slave traders still obstruct 'African improvement'.

3400 WILSON, John Leighton
The slave trade:—its present state, and the means of its suppression. Letter from the Rev. John Leighton Wilson, to a friend in England. [Boston, 1854?] 11 pp.

3401 *WILDMAN, Richard
Plain directions to naval officers as to the laws of search, capture, and prize. London, 1854.

3402 LATROBE, John H. B.
'Withdrawal of the African squadron.' (AR, vol. 30, Sept. 1854, pp. 257–66.)

Removing the squadron, as recommended by the Senate foreign affairs committee, will have serious consequences.

3403 BLEBY, Henry
Scenes in the Caribbean Sea: being sketches from a missionary's notebook. London, 1854. iv, 210 pp.

Ch. 8: 'The captured slaver'; ch. 9: 'The slaver wrecked.'

3404 FOOTE, Andrew Hull
'The African squadron—Ashburton treaty . . .' (AR, vol. 31, May 1855, pp. 148–54.)

The United States should not withdraw its squadron while its citizens still participate in the slave trade.

3405 FOOTE, Andrew Hull
The African squadron: Ashburton treaty: consular sea letters . . . Philadelphia, [1855]. 16 pp.

The U.S. squadron should be maintained for joint cruising with the British to end American participation in the slave trade.

3406 'BRAZIL and the slave trade.' (USM, 1856, I, pp. 595–601.)

On the difficulties of the blockade and the danger of withdrawing the cruisers from Brazil.

3407 *BROWN, William Keer
On neutral trade and right of search, five letters, written in 1854 . . . London, 1857. 69 pp.

3408 WHITMAN, James
An inquiry into the right of visit or approach, by ships of war. New York, 1858. 31 pp.

Analysis by a Canadian barrister of Britain's claim to a 'right of visit' as distinct from 'right of search'; no insult to the United States flag is implied.

3409 LAWRENCE, William Beach
Visitation and search; or an historical sketch of the British claim to exercise a maritime police over the vessels of all nations, in peace as well as in war, with an inquiry into the expediency of terminating the eighth article of the Ashburton treaty. Boston, 1858. ix, 218 pp.

Account of the legal and diplomatic controversy over the anti-slave trade treaties from the American point of view.

3410 COXE, Richard Smith
'The African slave fleet and right of search.' (DBR, vol. 25, 1858, pp. 512–45.)

Rejects British accusations against the United States over the slave trade.

3411 'The SLAVE-TRADE during the last two years.' (CMI, vol. 12, 1861, pp. 149–59.)

On the illegal slave trade to Cuba and America and the antislavery patrol.

3412 VENN, Henry
West African colonies. Notices of the British colonies on the west coast of Africa. London, 1865. 39 pp.

The British squadron must not be weakened during the American civil war and should be supplemented by developing the African colonies.

3413 CHOWN, Francis H.
Letters on slavery on the south-east coast of Africa (Zanzibar). Devonport, 1868. 15 pp.

The squadron must be increased to suppress the slave trade; liberated slaves should be settled on the mainland under British protection.

3414 CHALLICE, John Armstrong
Appendix to a scheme for the more effectual suppression of the East African sea transit slave trade. By means of introducing a much-needed and universal system of self-registration, &c., for all legal trading vessels . . . [London,] 1871. 17 pp.

The original registration scheme was submitted in 1869.

3415 CHALLICE, John Armstrong
Addenda to a scheme for the general and effectual suppression of the African sea-transit slave-trade in the East, by means of introducing a much-needed and universal scheme of self-registration, &c., for all legal trading vessels in that part of the world . . . London, 1872. 25 pp.

3416 'Die INSEL Socotra und der ostafrikanische Sklavenhandel.' (Globus, Braunschweig, vol. 23, 1873, p. 30.)

Critical remarks on the suggestion that Socotra should be occupied as a British cruiser station and depot for freed slaves instead of the Seychelles.

3417 TUKE, Henry George
The fugitive slave circulars. A short account of the case of Sommersett the negro, and of Lord Mansfield's celebrated judgment, under which slavery in England received its death-blow. Also of Forbes v. Cochrane, extending the doctrine of Sommersett v. Steuart to slaves on board British public ships, with a note of other cases on the subject . . . with a reference to the slave trade acts of 1873, and a note as to the right of searching slave vessels. London, 1876. v, 90 pp.

Legal criticism of British policy on fugitive slaves in East Africa. See (588, 1759).

3418 WALLER, Horace
'La traite en Afrique.' (Exploration, Paris, vol. 13, 1882, pt. 1, pp. 198–200.)

Letter to The Times on the suppression of the East African maritime slave trade.

3419 *MAGALHÃES MENDONÇA, Antonio Hygino de
Presas e escravatura; memória apresentada no concurso para lente da 8ª.

cadeira do curso da escola naval . . .
Lisboa, 1888. 117 pp.

On prize law with reference to the slave trade.

3420 'Zur OSTAFRIKANISCHEN Küsten-sperre.' (Signed: H.) (DKZ, n.s., vol. 1, Dez. 1888, pp. 435–36; vol. 2, Jan. 1889, pp. 3–4.)

Welcomes the blockade as a turning-point in the struggle to suppress the East African slave trade.

3421 'The SLAVE blockade in East African waters.' (WR, vol. 131, 1889, pp. 160–66.)

Discussion of the legality and effect of blockades with reference to the Anglo-German blockade 1889.

3422 MILES, Victor
'Der Sklavenhandel in Ostafrika und die Küstenblokade.' (UZ, 1889, pt. 1, pp. 266–75; map.)

3423 *DESJARDINS, Arthur
Discours prononcé par M. Desjardins. La traite maritime, le droit de visite, et la conférence de Bruxelles. Paris, 1890. 73 pp.

3424 DESJARDINS, Arthur
'La France, l'esclavage africain et le droit de visite.' (RDM, ser. 3, vol. 107, 1891, pp. 864–903.)

Discusses the right of visit earlier in the century in relation to the decisions of the Brussels conference regarding the Indian Ocean.

3425 ENGELHARDT, Édouard Philippe
'Traite maritime . . . Mémoire et avant projet présenté à l'Institut par M. Éd. Engelhardt, d'accord avec M. de Martens.' (Annuaire de l'Institut de Droit International, Paris, vol. 13, 1894, pp. 36–49.)

Draft law for the suppression of the maritime slave trade.

(e) HISTORY

3426 GUIZOT, François Pierre Guillaume
'Le droit de visite.' In his: Mémoires pour servir à l'histoire de mon temps, vol. 6 (Paris, 1864), pp. 130–241.

On the negotiations with Britain 1840–45 over the right of search.

3427 *KINGSTON, William Henry Giles
Our sailors: or, anecdotes of the engagements and gallant deeds of the British navy during the reign of Her Majesty Queen Victoria. London, 1865. xv, 282 pp.

Includes chapters on the occupation of Lagos 1851 and capture of slave ships 1840–48.

3428 HOPPIN, James Mason
Life of Andrew Hull Foote, Rear-Admiral United States Navy. New York, 1874. x, 411 pp.

Ch. 6–7: 'Cruise of the Perry on the African coast'; account of a U.S. antislavery patrol 1850–51.

3429 SCHUYLER, Eugene
American diplomacy and the further-ance of commerce. London, [1886]. xiv, 469 pp.

Ch. 5: 'The right of search and the slave-trade'.

3430 'The OLD slave-ship.' (CJ, vol. 70, 1893, pp. 558–60.)

Account of slave ships before 1850.

3431 CLOWES, Sir William Laid
The Royal Navy. A history from the earliest times to the present . . . London, 1897–1903. 7 vol.

Ch. 44, 47: Military history 1816–1900, including antislavery opera-tions.

3432 MACLAY, Edgar Stanton
Reminiscences of the old navy. From the journals and private papers of Captain Edward Trenchard, and Rear-Admiral Stephen Decatur Trenchard. New York & London, 1898. x, 362 pp.

Includes an account of the cruise of the 'Cyane' (Capt. E. Trenchard) off West Africa in 1820. See (3286).

3433 MACLAY, Edgar Stanton
A history of the United States navy from 1775 to 1901 . . . New and en-larged edition . . . New York, 1901. 3 vol.

Vol. 2, ch. 4: 'Cruising against slavers' (about 1820–50).

3434 JACKSON, Emily L.
St. Helena: the historic island . . . London, 1903. 343 pp. illus, map.

Includes a chapter 'On slavery and the work of H.M. cruisers on the west coast of Africa' 1840–48.

3435 *SARRIEN, Ferdinand
La traite des nègres et la droit de visite au cours du XIXe siècle dans les rapports de la France et de l'Angleterre. Paris, 1910. 143 pp.

3436 ADAMS, Ephraim Douglass
'Lord Ashburton and the treaty of Washington.' (AHR, vol. 17, 1912, pp. 764–82.)

Account of the negotiations for the treaty of 1842 (3240).

3437 *FONSSAGRIVES, Jean Baptiste
'La répression de la traite sur mer dans le Golfe de Bénin. Mémoires.' (Afrique Libre, Paris, no. 12, 1912, pp. 249–54; no. 13, 1913, pp. 284–96.)

3438 *MAUPASSANT, Jean de
Le droit de visite sous Louis-Philippe. L'affaire du "Marabout" (1841–1852). Bordeaux, 1913. 74 pp.

On a French vessel captured by the British navy; judgment was finally awarded against the captors.

3439 ALDEN, Carroll Storrs
George Hamilton Perkins, Commodore, U.S.N. His life and letters. Boston & New York, 1914. xii, 302 pp. illus.

Ch. 4: 'On the West African coast'; antislavery cruising 1859–61.

3440 CURREY, Edward Hamilton
'Boat actions and river fights. The East African slave trade . . .' (USM, 1915, pp. 659–71.)

Attacks on slave dhows off Pemba 1887–88 described from original reports.

3441 SENIOR, William
'An act of state.' (CM, n.s., vol. 54, 1923, pp. 561–66.)

On Capt. Denman's destruction of the Gallinas barracoons in 1840 and the legal action against him. (See P.P. 1842, XII, pp. 449–60.)

3442 HERRINGTON, Elsie Irene
'British measures for the suppression of the slave trade upon the west coast of Africa, 1807–1833.' (BIHR, vol. 2, 1924, pp. 54–56.)

Summary of M.A. thesis (4438): British diplomatic efforts aimed at the effect rather than the cause of the trade, slavery itself.

3443 VAN ALSTYNE, Richard Warner
'The British right of search and the African slave trade.' (JMH, vol. 2, 1930, pp. 37–47.)

On the controversy with the U.S. government 1858–62.

3444 SIOUSSAT, St. George Leakin
'Duff Green's "England and the United States": with an introductory study of American opposition to the quintuple treaty of 1841.' (PAAS, n.s., vol. 40, 1930, pp. 175–276.)

With the text of Green's work (published anonymously in Paris 1842), which opposed Britain's right of search; British antislavery policy was motivated by fear of American economic rivalry. See (3206, 3336).

3445 MILNE, Alexander Taylor
'The slave trade and Anglo-American relations, 1807–62.' (BIHR, vol. 9, 1931, pp. 126–29.)

Summary of M.A. thesis (4443): the question of cruising and the right of search embittered relations between Britain and the United States.

3446 SOULSBY, Hugh Graham
The right of search and the slave trade in Anglo-American relations 1814–1862. Baltimore, 1933. 185 pp. bibl. pp. 177–81.

History of British naval and diplomatic efforts to end the American slave trade. (Ph.D. thesis, Johns Hopkins University, 1931.)

3447 MILNE, Alexander Taylor
'The Lyons-Seward treaty of 1862.' (AHR, vol. 38, 1933, pp. 511–25.)

Diplomatic history of the Anglo-American treaty for the suppression of the African slave trade. See (3249).

3448 SCOTTER, William Henry
'International rivalry in the Bights of Benin and Biafra, 1815–85.' (BIHR, vol. 12, 1934, pp. 63–66.)

Summary of Ph.D. thesis (4445) on British efforts to suppress the slave trade.

3449 ROSE, John Holland
Man and the sea. Stages in maritime and human progress. Cambridge, 1935. ix, 288 pp.

Ch. 12: 'Steam power and the suppression of the slave trade' (by the British navy).

3450 BARROWS, Edward Morley
The great commodore. The exploits of Matthew Calbraith Perry. Indianapolis, New York, [1935]. 397 pp. illus.

Ch. 10: 'Chasing shadows in a deadly climate'; on the U.S. African squadron under Perry's command 1843–45.

3451 ROSE, John Holland
'The Royal Navy and the suppression

of the West African slave trade (1815–1865).' (MM, vol. 22, 1936, pp. 54–64, 162–71.)

3452 ROSE, John Holland
'The truth about it. The slave trade.' (Seafarer, London, no. 13, 1937, pp. 7–9; no. 14, 1937, pp. 41–43.)

On the suppression of the Atlantic slave trade 1815–65.

3453 MUDDIMAN, Joseph George
'H.M.S. the Black Joke' (Notes and Queries, London, vol. 172, 1937, pp. 200–01

See (3259).

3454 MACKENZIE-GRIEVE, Averil
'The last of the Brazilian slavers, 1851.' (MM, vol. 31, 1945, pp. 2–7; illus.)

Accounts of the capture of the 'Piratenim' (22 July 1851) by Lieut. John Bailey, based on his diary. See (4623).

3455 'GOOD hunting in the Bight. By Shalimar.' (BM, vol. 261, 1947, pp. 202–14.)

Fictionalized account, with an historical introduction, of the capture of a slave ship by a British warship in the Bight of Benin 1830.

3456 LLOYD, Christopher
The navy and the slave trade. The suppression of the African slave trade in the nineteenth century. London, 1949. xii, 314 pp. illus, maps.

Standard work on the British antislavery squadrons. (Reviewed by C. M. MacInnes in: EHR, vol. 66, 1951, pp. 600–02.)

3457 AUBREY, Philip
'Preventive squadron. The Royal Navy and the West African slave trade, 1811–1868.' (BIHR, vol. 23, 1950, pp. 90–91.)

Summary of Julian Corbett Prize Essay 1948: on the conditions of service and achievements of the squadron.

3458 *CARNEIRO, David
A história do incidente Cormoran. Curitiba, 1950.

The British cruiser 'Cormorant' contributed decisively in 1850 to the ending of the Brazilian slave trade.

3459 *JONES, Wilbur Devereux
'The influence of slavery on the Webster-Ashburton negotiations.' (JSH, vol. 22, 1956, pp. 48–58.)

On the U.S.-British discussions for the treaty of 1842 (3240).

3460 STAUDENRAUS, Philip John
'Victims of the African slave trade, a document.' (JNH, vol. 41, 1956, pp. 148–51.)

Letter by S. Sitgreaves 1822, describing the return of recaptured Africans to Liberia.

3461 GRAY, *Sir* John Milner
The British in Mombasa 1824–1826, being the history of Captain Owen's protectorate. London, 1957. viii, 216 pp. illus, maps.

On the unauthorized efforts of W. F. W. Owen to suppress the Indian Ocean slave trade.

3462 BROOKS, George E.
'A. A. Adee's journal of a visit to Liberia in 1827.' (Liberian Studies Journal, Greencastle, Ind., vol. 1, 1958, pp. 56–72.)

Extracts from an account by a surgeon on a U.S. antislavery vessel on patrol off West Africa.

3463 FURNAS, Joseph Chamberlain
'Patrolling the middle passage.' (AH, vol. 9, no. 6, 1958, pp. 4–9, 101–02; illus.)

The U.S. navy was hamstrung by Southern influence before 1860.

3464 WHITRIDGE, Arnold
'The American slave-trade.' (HT, vol. 8, 1958, pp. 462–72; illus.)

On U.S.-British relations over the right of search before 1862.

3465 PEARSALL, A. W. H.
'Sierra Leone and the suppression of the slave trade.' (Sierra Leone Studies, Freetown, no. 12, 1959, pp. 211–29; illus.)

Account of the West African squadron 1819–69, originally with Freetown as its only base.

3466 BOUQUET, Michael R.
'The capture of the 'Sunny South' slaver.' (HT, vol. 10, 1960, pp. 573–78; illus.)

On the seizure of an American ship with 843 slaves off Mozambique in August 1860.

3467 FYFE, Christopher
A history of Sierra Leone. London, 1962. vii, 773 pp. maps.

Contains a good deal of information on the antislavery squadron, mixed commission court and recaptured slaves.

3468   JONES, Wilbur Devereux
'The origins and passage of Lord Aberdeen's act.' (HAHR, vol. 42, 1962, pp. 502–20.)

Diplomatic history of the British act of 1839 to suppress the slave trade to Brazil.

3469   IFEMESIA, Christopher C.
'The 'civilising' mission of 1841; aspects of an episode in Anglo-Nigerian relations.' (JHSN, vol. 2, 1962, pp. 291–310.)

On the Niger expedition 1841–42.

3470   BOYD, Willis D.
'American Colonization Society and the slave recaptives of 1860–1861: an early example of United States-African relations.' (JNH, vol. 47, 1962, pp. 108–26.)

Over 4000 Congolese slaves, liberated by U.S. warships, were sent to Liberia.

3471   BOOTH, Alan Rundlett
'The United States African squadron, 1843–61.' *In*: BUTLER, J. Boston University papers in African history, vol. 1 (1964), pp. 77–177.

On the suppression of the slave trade in its 'American' phase.

3472   MEYER-HEISELBERG, Richard
Notes from Liberated African Department. Extracts from sources on the trans-Atlantic slave trade 1808–1860 from the archives of Fourah Bay College, the University College of Sierra Leone, Freetown, Sierra Leone. Uppsala, 1967. xii, 61 ll.

List of records of recaptured slaves.

3473   MORISON, Samuel Eliot
"Old Bruin". Commodore Matthew C. Perry, 1794–1858 . . . London, 1968. xxii, 482 pp. illus, maps.

Ch. 13: 'Commodore of the African squadron, 1843–1845.'

3474   WARD, William Ernest Frank
The Royal Navy and the slavers: the suppression of the Atlantic slave trade . . . London, 1969. 248 pp. illus, maps.

Account of the West African squadron 1811–69.

3475   TEAGUE, Michael *and* COWAN, Zélide
' "Nil disprandum".' (AH, vol. 20, no. 2, 1969, pp. 18–25: illus.)

On water colour paintings by Captain W. Buck of scenes from service in the British West African squadron 1846–49 and 1856–58.

T. TRIALS FOR ILLEGAL SLAVE TRADING

3476 'CIRCUMSTANCES attending the capture of some slave vessels.' (Philanthropist, London, vol. 2, 1812, pp. 44–55.)

> Official papers relating to three American slave ships brought to Sierra Leone 1810–11; one, the 'Amelia', had been taken over and returned to Africa by the Congolese slaves on board.

3477 The TRIALS of slave-traders, Samuel Samo, Joseph Peters, and William Tufft, tried in April and June, 1812, before the Hon. Robert Thorpe, L.L.D. Chief Justice of Sierra Leone, &c. &c. with two letters on the slave trade, from a gentleman resident at Sierra Leone to an advocate for the abolition, in London. Sherwood, Neeley, & Jones, London, 1813. 56 pp.

> This was the first case of foreigners tried under the anti-slave trade act of 1811; the accused were convicted. (Reviewed in: ER, vol. 21, 1813, pp. 72–93.)

3478 DODSON, John
A report of the case of the Louis, Forest, master; appealed from the Vice-Admiralty Court at Sierra Leone, and determined in the High Court of Admiralty; on the 15th of December 1817 . . . J. Butterworth & Son, London, 1817. 56 pp.

> Judgment reversed on a Martinique ship condemned at Sierra Leone in 1816 for suspected slaving.

3479 'ABOLITION of the slave trade.' (GM, vol. 89, Dec. 1819, pp. 518–20.)

> Trial of two Englishmen by the Vice Admiralty Court at Jamaica, July 1819, for the illegal introduction of slaves.

3480 'HIGH Court of Admiralty. The ship Dolores, Carbonel, master.' (AnR 1819, vol. 61, 1820, pp. 285–88.)

> The commander of the African station Sir George Cockburn, demands a share of the bounty for a slave ship condemned at Sierra Leone 1816.

3481 MASON, William Powell
A report of the case of the Jeune Eugénie, determined in the Circuit Court of the United States, for the first circuit, at Boston, December, 1821 . . . Wells & Lilly, Boston, 1822. 108 pp.

> Case of a French slave ship captured off Gallinas in May 1821.

3482 FIGANIÉRE E MORÃO, Joaquim César de
Descripção de Serra-Leôa e seus contornos. Escripta em doze cartas. Á qual se ajuntão os trabalhos da commissão-mixta portugueza e ingleza, estabelecida naquelha colonia . . . João Baptista Morando, Lisboa, 1822. 97 pp.

> Description of the Windward Coast by a former member of the mixed commission court at Sierra Leone, with a summary of the cases dealt with in its first year, 1820–21.

3483 UNITED STATES OF AMERICA: Supreme Court
'The Josefa Segunda, Carricabura et al. claimants.' In: WHEATON, H. Reports of cases argued and adjudged in the Supreme Court of the United States, vol. 5 (New York, 1820), pp. 338–59; vol. 10 (1825), pp. 312–32.

> Case heard Feb. 1820 of a Cuban slave ship captured by a Venezuelan privateer and seized near New Orleans 1818.

3484 UNITED STATES OF AMERICA: Supreme Court
'The Antelope. The vice-consuls of Spain and Portugal, libellants.' In: WHEATON, H. Reports of cases argued and adjudged in the Supreme Court of the United States, vol. 10 (New York, 1825), pp. 66–133.

> Case of a Spanish slave ship seized in U.S. waters, heard Feb. 1825. (Chief Justice Marshall's opinion is reprinted in: AR, vol. 1, 1826, pp. 353–63.) Other slaving cases are

reported in Wheaton, vol. 8–12 (1823–27).

3485 ENGLAND: High Court of Admiralty
Reports of cases argued and determined in the High Court of Admiralty . . . By John Haggard. (1822–38.) J. Butterworth & Son, London, 1825–40. 3 vol.

Includes various cases of illegal slave trading. See (3495.)

3486 The AFRICAN captives. Trial of the prisoners of the Amistad on the writ of habeas corpus, before the Circuit Court of the United States, for the district of Connecticut, at Hartford; judges Thompson and Judson. September term, 1839. American Anti-Slavery Society, New York, 1839. 47 pp.

By Lewis Tappan. First trial involving slaves from the Cuban ship 'Amistad' taken off Long Island in August 1839; the writ was refused.

3487 UNITED STATES OF AMERICA: Supreme Court
'The United States vs. Isaac Morris.' *In*: PETERS, R. Reports of cases argued and adjudged in the Supreme Court of the United States, vol. 14 (Philadelphia, 1840), pp. 464–77.

Prosecution of an American citizen (Jan. 1840) for participation in the Cuban slave trade.

3488 MOORE, Edmund Fitz
Reports of cases heard and determined by the Judicial Committee and the Lords of His Majesty's most honourable Privy Council. W. T. Clarke, London, [1840–67]. 15 vol.

Vol. 2, 4, 10 and 11 contain appeal cases involving slave ships 1836–66.

3489 ADAMS, John Quincy
Argument of John Quincy Adams, before the Supreme Court of the United States, in the case of the United States, appellants, vs. Cinque, and others, Africans, captured in the schooner Amistad, by Lieut. Gedney, delivered on the 24th of February and 1st of March, 1841. With a review of the case of the Antelope; reported in the 10th, 11th and 12th volumes of Wheaton's reports. S. W. Benedict, New York, 1841. 135 pp.

Speech for the defence of the 53 Africans who had seized the 'Amistad', arguing their right to freedom and

denying the validity of the case of the 'Antelope', captured off Florida 1820 and restored to Cuba 1826, as a precedent (3484).

3490 *BALDWIN, Roger Sherman
Argument of Roger S. Baldwin, of New Haven, before the Supreme Court of the United States, in the case of the United States, appellants, vs. Cinque, and others, Africans of the Amistad. S. W. Benedict, New York, 1841. 32 pp.

3491 UNITED STATES OF AMERICA: Supreme Court
'The United States, appellants, v. the libellants and claimants of the schooner Amistad, her tackle, apparel, and furniture, together with her cargo and the Africans mentioned and described in the several libels and claims, appellees.' *In*: PETERS, R. Reports of cases argued and adjudged in the Supreme Court of the United States, vol. 15 (Philadelphia, 1841), pp. 518–98.

Decision (Jan. 1841) upholding the judgment of the Connecticut district court, but declaring the Africans free.

3492 GILDEMEISTER, Johann Carl Friedrich
Verfahren und Erkenntniss des Bremischen Obergerichts in Untersuchungssachen wider den Capitain des Bremischen Schiffs Julius u. Eduard u. Cons. wegen Sklavenhandels. Nach den Acten dargestellt. Heyse, Bremen, 1842. 111 pp.

Case of a Bremen ship boarded by a British patrol and charged with carrying goods for the Cuban slave trade; the owners were acquitted.

3493 TRIAL of Pedro de Zulueta, jun., in the Central Criminal Court of the City of London, on the 27th, 28th, and 30th of October, 1843, on a charge of slave-trading. Reported by J. F. Johnson, short-hand writer. With introductory and concluding remarks, by the committee of the British and Foreign Anti-Slavery Society. Second edition. Ward & Co., London, 1844. viii, 95 pp.

Case against the owners of the 'Augusta' from Liverpool, taken off Gallinas 1841; verdict: not guilty.

3494 TRIAL of Pedro de Zulueta, jun., on a charge of slave trading, under the 5 Geo. IV, cap. 113, on Friday the 27th, Saturday the 28th, and Monday the

30th of October, 1843, at the Central Criminal Court, Old Bailey, London. A full report from the short-hand notes of W. B. Gurney, Esq. With an address to the merchants, manufacturers, and traders of Great Britain, by Pedro de Zulueta, jun., Esq. and documents illustrative of the case. C. Wood & Co., London, 1844. lxxiv, 410 pp.

Zulueta's speech in his own defence, evidence given to the 1842 committee on West Africa, other official papers, and the trial proceedings.

3495 ENGLAND: High Court of Admiralty
Reports of cases argued and determined in the High Court of Admiralty . . . By William Robinson. (1838–50.) Henry Butterworth, London, 1844–50. 3 vol.

Includes slave trade cases 1842–48; others appear in the reports for 1855–61. See (3485).

3496 HEWSON, William Basset
The case of the Queen, against Serva and others, inclusive of the trial, and the argument before the judges. William Benning & Co., London, 1846. xi, 160 pp.

Trial at Exeter of the crew of the Brazilian slaver 'Felicidade' 1845; the prisoners, who had killed a British prize crew, were discharged.

3497 HOCQUARD, Charles Phillippe
Before the Judicial Committee of Her Majesty's most honourable Privy Council: the "Newport," C. P. Hocquard, master: Charles Phillippe Hocquard, master, original appellant, and Messrs. Pinto, Perez, & Co., and Jose Maria Perez, respectively, interveners, against Our Sovereign Lady the Queen and John MacDonald Skene, Esquire, the commander, and the officers and crew, of Her Majesty's ship of war "Philomel", original respondents, on an appeal from the Vice Admiralty Court at St. Helena: further appendix. [London?] 1855. ii, 301 pp.

The 'Newport' was seized off Ambriz and condemned at St. Helena in 1854. (Appeal case, Dec. 1857, in: MOORE, E. F. Reports of cases heard and determined by the Judicial Committee, vol. 11, London, 1858, pp. 155–88.)

3498 *HAYNE, Isaac William
Argument before the United States Circuit Court by I. W. Hayne, Esq., on the motion to discharge the crew of the Echo. Delivered in Columbia, S.C., December, 1858. Reported by Douglass A. Levien. Albany, 1859. 24 pp.

3499 *ANDREW, John Albion and BROWNE, Albert Gallatin
Circuit Court of the United States, Massachusetts District, ss. In Admiralty. The United States, by Information, vs. the schooner Wanderer, and cargo, G. B. Lamar, claimant. John A. Andrew, A. G. Browne, Jr. proctors for the claimant. The claimant's points. Boston, 1860. 27 pp.

3500 *MAGRATH, Andrew Gordon
The slave trade not declared piracy by the act of 1820. United States vs. Wm. C. Corrie. Presentment for piracy. Opinion of the Hon. A. G. Magrath, District Judge in the Circuit Court of the United States for the District of South Carolina, upon a motion for leave to enter a nol. pros. in the case. S. G. Courtenay & Co., Charleston, 1860. 31 pp.

3501 *FERNANDEZ DE LA HOZ, José M.
Defensa del Sr. José A. Argüelles, en la causa de supuesto plagio de bozales pertenecientes a la gran expedición apresada por el mismo en la isla de Cuba. Madrid, 1867. 111 pp.

3502 *AZCUTIA, Manuel
Causa contra el Teniente Gobernador que fué de Colón, D. José Agustín Argüelles y consortes, por plagio de negros y falsedad. Acusación por D. M. Azcutia. Madrid, 1868.

3503 *MADRAZO, Fernando de
Defensa del Sr. D. Maximiliano Molino, secretario que fué del Ayuntamiento de Colón en la isla de Cuba (en la causa de supuesto plagio de bozales, procedientes de la expedición de la Agüica) . . . Madrid, 1868. 31 pp.

3504 *OLÓZAGA, José de
Defensa del Sr. D. Antonio Prats y Salas, comandante, en la causa de supuesto plagio de negros bozales . . . hecha por D. José de Olózaga. Madrid, 1868. 22 pp.

3505 *APARISI Y GUIJARRO, Antonio
Defensa del Sr. D. José del Toral, en causa de supuesto plagio de bozales, pertenecientes a la expedición Agüica, apresada el 12 de noviembre de 1863 en la isla de Cuba. Madrid, 1868. 58 pp.

3506 *JACKSON, Henry Rootes
The Wanderer case; the speech of

Hon. Henry R. Jackson of Savannah, Ga. . . . Biography of General Jackson, by Joseph M. Brown . . . Atlanta, Ga., 1891. 83 pp. port.

Jackson was government counsel in the unsuccessful prosecution of the slave ship 'Wanderer' in 1859.

3507 CATTERALL, Helen Honor Tunnicliff Judicial cases concerning American slavery and the negro . . . Washington, 1926–37. 5 vol.

Extracts from trial records, including slave ship cases.

U. MILITARY ACTION

3508 BAKER, *Sir* Samuel White
Ismailïa. A narrative of the expedition to central Africa for the suppression of the slave trade organized by Ismail Khedive of Egypt. London, 1874. 2 vol. maps.

> Account of the Egyptian expedition under Baker's command to the upper White Nile 1870–73.

3509 BAKER, *Sir* Samuel White
'La traite des esclaves sur le Nil Blanc.' (Revue Scientifique, Paris, ser. 2, vol. 3, 1874, pp. 933–37.)

> Describes Baker's antislavery efforts.

3510 'The SLAVE trade on the upper Nile.' (Canadian Monthly and National Review, Toronto, vol. 7, 1875, pp. 56–66.)

> On Baker's expedition 1870–73.

3511 GESSI, Romolo
'Gessi Pascha über den Sklavenhandel.' (ÖMO, vol. 6, Dec. 1880, pp. 196–97.)

> Letter on the suppression of the slave trade in the Egyptian Sudan.

3512 *'GESSI Bey's Erfolge in der Unterdrückung des sudanischen Sklavenhandels.' (Allgemeine Missions-Zeitschrift, Gütersloh, vol. 7, 1881, pp. 28–32.)

3513 GORDON, Charles George
Colonel Gordon in central Africa 1874–1879 . . . From original letters and documents. Edited by George Birkbeck Hill. London, 1881. xlii, 456 pp. map.

3514 FELKIN, Robert William
'Der Sklavenkrieg im ägyptischen Sudan während der Jahre 1878 und 1879.' (Ausland, Stuttgart, vol. 55, 1882, pp. 1021–28.)

> Description of Gessi's campaign against the slave traders of Bahr el Ghazal province. See (3519).

3515 'The JEDDA massacres and slavery in the Red Sea.' (Signed: P.) (McM, vol. 49, 1884, pp. 384–93.)

> By R. L. Playfair. Describes the revival of the Somali slave trade around 1858; the author, political officer at Aden, crossed by steamer and liberated 140 slave girls at Berbera.

3516 WYLDE, Augustus Blandy
'83 to '87 in the Soudan. With an account of Sir William Hewett's mission to King John of Abyssinia . . . London, 1888. 2 vol. map.

> Vol. 2, ch. 9: 'The slave trade in eastern Soudan'.

3517 LUGARD, Frederick John Dealtry
'The fight against slave-traders on Nyassa.' (CR, vol. 56, 1889, pp. 335–45.)

> Description of the fighting at Karonga 1888–89.

3518 LUGARD, Frederick John Dealtry
'Les Arabes au lac Nyassa.' (RFEC, vol. 9, 1889, pp. 534–36; map.)

> Letter to The Times reporting on the campaign against the slavers round Lake Nyasa and requesting government support.

3519a GESSI, Romolo
Sette anni nel Sudan egiziano. Esplorazioni, caccie e guerra contro i negrieri. Memorie . . . pubblicate da suo figlio Felice Gessi. Milano, 1891. xv, 489 pp. map.

Translated as:

3519b Seven years in Soudan. Being a record of explorations, adventures, and campaigns against the Arab slave hunters . . . Collected and edited by his son Felix Gessi. London, 1892. xxiv, 467 pp. illus, map.

> With chapters on the slave trade and its suppression on the Bahr el Ghazal about 1878–80.

3520 DETIERRE, E.
'Les progrès de l'œuvre antiesclavagiste belge en Afrique.' (MA, vol. 3, 1891, pp. 129–32; map.)

> On Belgian antislavery expeditions in the Katanga area.

3521 **BÉTHUNE, Léon,** *baron*
'Les Frères armés du Sahara.' (MA, vol. 3, 1891, pp. 132–41; illus.)

Describes the military Christian order recently founded by Cardinal Lavigerie to suppress the slave trade by establishing settlements for liberated slaves.

3522 **FOTHERINGHAM, L. Monteith**
Adventures in Nyassaland. A two years' struggle with Arab slave-dealers in central Africa. London, 1891. xiii, 304 pp.

Account of the Karonga war 1887–89.

3523 **DUCHESNE, Aug.**
'La lutte de Joubert contre les esclavagistes.' (MA, vol. 4, 1892, pp. 201–02.)

On antislavery operations in the eastern Congo. (See also: ibid., pp. 20–23.)

3524 'La LUTTE antiesclavagiste actuelle dans l'État Indépendant.' (Signed: Th. P.) (MA, vol. 4, 1892, pp. 222–28.)

3525 **URSEL, Hippolyte d',** *comte*
'Les Belges au Tanganika . . .' (Bulletin de la Société Royale Belge de Géographie, Bruxelles, vol. 16, 1893, pp. 75–96.)

On the expeditions of the Congo Free State forces against the Arabs 1891–93. (Reprinted separately, Bruxelles, 1893; 24 pp.—Articles on this subject in Mouvement Géographique, Bruxelles, 1891–93, are listed in: WALRAET, M. Bibliographie du Katanga, Bruxelles, 1954–56.)

3526 *SAINT-BERTHUIN, A. M. de
Alexis Vrithoff, compagnon des capitaines Jacques et Joubert au lac Tanganika (Afrique centrale), sa jeunesse, son "journal de voyage", sa mort glorieuse. [Lille,] 1893. 192 pp. illus, maps, port.

Biography of a young Belgian killed in action against the Congo Arabs in 1892.

3527 **LUGARD, Frederick John Dealtry**
The rise of our East African empire. Early efforts in Nyasaland and Uganda. Edinburgh & London, 1893. 2 vol. illus, maps.

With an account of the suppression of the Nyasaland slave trade from 1888.

3528 'ÉTAT Indépendant du Congo.—Succès sur les Arabes esclavagistes. (Lutte contre les Arabes.)' (Bulletin de la Société Royale Belge de Géographie Bruxelles, vol. 17, 1893, pp. 274–80, 478; vol. 18, 1894, pp. 87–93, 160–64, 260–64.)

Reports on the campaign against the Arabs on the upper Congo.

3529 **CHALTIN, Louis Napoléon**
'La question arabe au Congo.' (Bulletin de la Société d'Études Coloniales, Bruxelles, 1894, pp. 163–96; map.)

Account of the Arab penetration of the eastern Congo and the campaign against them by the Congo Free State forces 1892–93.

3530 **DESCAMPS, Édouard Eugène François,** *baron*
Les stations civilisatrices au Tanganika. Discours sur l'œuvre de la Société antiesclavagiste de Belgique prononcé le 4 juillet 1894 au Palais des Académies. Bruxelles, 1894. 15 pp.

Speech at celebrations for Capt. A. Jacques, describing the antislavery expeditions against the Congo Arabs 1890–93. (Reprinted from: MA, 1894, pp. 252–68.)

3531 'La CAMPAGNE arabe au Congo. Retour en Belgique du commandant Dhanis.' (Bulletin de la Société Royale Belge de Géographie, Bruxelles, vol. 18, 1894, pp. 369–99; map.)

Speech by J. Du Fief and reply by Dhanis at a ceremony in his honour after the Katanga campaign 1892–94.

3532 **WAUTERS, Alphonse Jules**
'La conquête du Manyema par le commandant Dhanis.' (Congo Illustré, Bruxelles, vol. 3, 1894, pp. 153–60; illus, maps, port.)

3533 **DHANIS, Francis,** *baron*
'La campagne arabe au Manyema. (Congo Illustré, Bruxelles, vol. 4, 1895, pp. 25–27, 33–35, 41–43, 53–55, 60–63, 68–70, 77–79; illus, map.)

Account of the campaign against the Arabs in southeastern Congo 1892–93.

3534 *ALEXIS, *Frère*
Soldats et missionnaires au Congo, de 1891 à 1894 . . . [Lille,] 1896. 240 pp. illus.

By J. B. Gochet.

3535 **GLAVE, E. J.**
'Glave in Nyassa land. British raids on the slave-traders. Glimpses of life in

Africa, from the journals of the late E. J. Glave.' (CIMM, vol. 52, 1896, pp. 589–606; illus, map.)

On the war with Arab slavers in Nyasaland 1893–94.

3536 HINDE, Sidney Langford
The fall of the Congo Arabs. London, 1897. viii, 308 pp. map.

On the Kasai-Lualaba campaign of 1892–94.

3537 BOULGER, Demetrius Charles
The Congo State, or the growth of civilisation in central Africa. London, 1898. viii, 418 pp. illus, map.

With an account of the anti-slave trade campaigns.

3538 VANDELEUR, Cecil Foster Seymour
Campaigning on the upper Nile and Niger. London, 1898. xxvii, 319 pp. maps.

Narrative of expeditions in Nigeria and Uganda 1894–95; with an introduction by G. T. Goldie stressing their antislavery purpose.

3539 JACQUES, Alphonse Jules Marie
'La lutte contre l'esclavagisme au Tanganika . . .' (MA, vol. 13, 1901, pp. 33–41, 57–70; illus, ports.)

Report presented to the antislavery conference in Paris 7 August 1900 on the Belgian expeditions in central Africa 1891–94. (Also printed in: Missions d'Afrique, Malines, vol. 22, 1901, pp. 149–54, 161–69, 193–200.)

3540 DESCAMPS, Édouard Eugène François, baron
L'Afrique nouvelle. Essai sur l'état civilisateur dans les pays neufs et sur la fondation, l'organisation et le gouvernement de l'État Indépendant du Congo. Paris; Bruxelles, 1903. xvi, 626 pp.

Pt. 2, ch. 2: 'La conférence de Bruxelles et la lutte contre l'insurrection des traitants arabes.'

3541 BOURNE, Henry Richard Fox
Civilisation in Congoland: a story of international wrong-doing . . . London, 1903. xvi, 311 pp. map.

Ch. 8: 'Antislavery crusade (1894–1897).'

3542 MAC DONNELL, John de Courcy
King Leopold II. His rule in Belgium and the Congo. London, (etc.), 1905. viii, 391 pp.

With chapters on the suppression of the slave trade in the Congo.

3543 DHANIS, Francis, baron
'La campagne arabe.' (Bulletin de la Société Royale de Géographie d'Anvers, vol. 30, 1906, pp. 58–64.)

Brief account of the Congo campaigns. (Biographical article on Dhanis: ibid., pp. 155–257; port.)

3544 JACQUES, Alphonse Jules Marie
'Expéditions de la Société antiesclavagiste de Belgique.' (Bulletin de la Société Royale de Géographie d'Anvers, vol. 30, 1906, pp. 79–92.)

On the Congo expedition 1891. (Biographical article on Jacques: ibid., pp. 261–91; port.)

3545 LEJEUNE-CHOQUET, Adolphe
Histoire militaire du Congo. Explorations, expéditions, opérations de guerre, combats et faits militaires. Bruxelles, 1906. viii, 254 pp. illus, maps.

Describes anti-slave trade operations 1886–94.

3546 *DUPONT, Henri
Préliminaire de la campagne arabe. Anvers, 1910. 32 pp. map.

3547 *Le BARON Francis Dhanis au Kwango et pendant la campagne arabe. Anvers, 1910. 30 pp. illus, map.

3548 SWANN, Alfred James
Fighting the slave-hunters in central Africa. A record of twenty-six years of travel & adventure round the great lakes and of the overthrow of Tip-pu-tib, Rumaliza and other great slave-traders. London, 1910. 358 pp. illus, maps.

The author was a missionary in central Africa 1882–1909. (Reissued with an introduction by N. R. Bennett, London, 1969.)

3549 *HEUSCH, Waldor de, baron
'Les Belges et la campagne arabe au Congo.' (Expansion Belge, [Bruxelles?] 1911, pp. 573–78.)

3550 *RENIER, Gustave Ferdinand Joseph
'La traite des nègres, les expéditions antiesclavagistes et la conférence de Bruxelles.' In his: L'œuvre civilisatrice au Congo (Gand, 1913), pp. 232–52; illus, maps.

3551 'La PACIFICATION de la Côte d'Ivoire et la répression de l'esclavagisme.' (Renseignements Coloniaux, Paris, 1913, no. 10, pp. 341–46.)

26,500 slaves were released after the defeat of Samori in 1898.

3552   MOIR, Frederick Lewis Maitland
After Livingstone. An African trade romance. London, [1923]. xx, 200 pp.

History of the African Lakes Company, including the Karonga war against slave traders in Nyasaland 1887–89.

3553   *VERHOEVEN, Joseph Ch. M.
Jacques de Dixmude l'Africain. Contribution à l'histoire de la Société anti-esclavagiste belge, 1888–1894. Bruxelles, 1929. 160 pp. map, port.

Biography of a Belgian officer who participated in the Tanganyika campaign against slave traders 1891–94.

3554   DIXMUDE, Jacques de
'La campagne antiesclavagiste belge racontée par les lettres de Jacques de Dixmude. Lettres réunies et annotées par le comte Hippolyte d'Ursel . . .' (Revue Belge, Bruxelles, vol. 6, 1929, pt. 1, pp. 481–500; pt. 2, pp. 25–42, 132–49.)

Letters from the Tanganyika expedition 1891–94.

3555   *HENRY, Josué
'Souvenirs de la guerre contre les Arabes.' In: FRANCK, L. Le Congo belge, vol. 1 (Bruxelles, 1930), pp. 91–101.

On the Congo campaigns in the 1890s.

3556   *RINCHON, Dieudonné
'La campagne arabe. La traite et l'esclavage des noirs par les Arabes. La croisade antiesclavagiste. La chute de la domination arabe.' (Expansion Belge, [Bruxelles?] 1930, pp. 447-51.)

3557   ALLEN, Bernard Meredith
Gordon and the Sudan. London, 1931. xii, 485 pp. maps.

Describes the struggle against the slave traders 1877-84.

3558   HIVES, Frank
Justice in the jungle. London, [1932]. x, 239 pp.

Describes the capture by the author of Aro slave-dealers in Southern Nigeria about 1901.

3559   SABRY, Moustapha
L'empire égyptien sous Ismaïl et l'ingérence anglo-française (1863–1879) . . . Paris, 1933. 570 pp. bibl. pp. 553–58.

On the anti-slave trade efforts of Baker and Gordon in the Sudan,

which concealed an increase of British influence.

3560   CRABITÈS, Pierre
Gordon, the Sudan and slavery. London, 1933. x, 334 pp.

3561   BUCK, Jean Marie de
Jacques de Dixmude . . . Bruxelles, 1933. 262 pp.

Ch. 3: 'La croisade antiesclavagiste.' See (3553).

3562   RUSSELL, Lilian Marian
General Rigby, Zanzibar and the slave trade. With journals, dispatches, etc. edited by his daughter Mrs. Charles E. B. Russell. London, 1935. 404 pp. illus, map.

On the role of Rigby in the suppression of the Zanzibar slave trade about 1855–70.

3563   MESSEDAGLIA, Luigi
Uomini d'Africa. Messedaglia Bey e gli altri collaboratori italiani di Gordon Pascia. Bologna, 1935. x, 345 pp. maps.

Includes material on the antislavery campaign in the Sudan about 1880.

3564   LYNE, Robert Nunez
An apostle of empire. Being the life of Sir Lloyd William Mathews, K.C.M.G., Lieutenant, Royal Navy; first minister of the Zanzibar government. London, 1936. 247 pp. maps.

With chapters on the suppression of the slave trade during Mathews' years of service in Zanzibar 1875–97.

3565   ZAVATTI, Silvio
Romolo Gessi, il Garibaldi dell'Africa. Forlì, 1937. 158 pp. illus, map.

Includes a report by Gessi on antislave trade activities in the Sudan 1882.

3566   SHUKRY, Muhammad Fuad
The Khedive Ismail and slavery in the Sudan (1863–1879). A history of the Sudan from the Egyptian conquest of 1820, to the outbreak of the Mahdiist rebellion in 1881, with special reference to British policy and the work of Sir Samuel Baker and Charles George Gordon. Cairo, 1938. x, 322, 64 pp.

Ph.D. thesis, Liverpool, 1935.

3567   COUPLAND, Sir Reginald
The exploitation of East Africa 1856–1890. The slave trade and the Scramble. London, 1939. ix, 507 pp. map.

Pt. 1: 'The end of the Arab slave trade.'

3568 ZAGHI, Carlo
Vita di Romolo Gessi. [Milano,] 1939.
383 pp. map. bibl. pp. 333–80.

Includes chapters on the campaigns against slave traders in the Sudan about 1880.

3569 HASTINGS, Archibald Charles Gardiner
'Thirty years ago.' (National Review, London, vol. 112, 1939, pp. 352–62.)

Describes the capture of a Fulani slave caravan in northern Nigeria.

3570 WALLIS, E. J. N.
'Aere perennius: S. S. Bordein, a public monument to Gordon at Khartoum.' (BM, vol. 247, 1940, pp. 677–93; vol. 248, 1940, pp. 1–19.)

On a river steamer brought to Khartum by Baker in 1871 and used against slave traders on the Nile by Gordon.

3571 *BAXTER, T. W.
'Slave-raiders in north-eastern Rhodesia.' (Northern Rhodesia Journal, Livingstone, vol. 1, 1950, pp. 7–17.)

On the anti-slave trade activities of the British South Africa Company 1890–95.

3572 *PETERS, C.
'Un chapitre de la campagne arabe: la campagne contre Rumaliza.' (Bulletin Militaire, Léopoldville, no. 40, 1950, pp. 139–55.)

3573 *DEVRESSE, L.
Le capitaine Joubert . . . Leverville-Kikwit, 1951. 36 pp. illus, maps, port.

Joubert served in the war against the Congo Arabs 1890–93.

3574 GORDON, Charles George
Equatoria under Egyptian rule. The unpublished correspondence of Col. (afterwards Major-Gen.) C. G. Gordon with Ismaïl Khedive of Egypt and the Sudan during the years 1874–1876. With introduction and notes by M. F. Shukry. Cairo, 1953. xvii, 478 pp. maps. bibl. pp. 457–67.

3575 GANN, Lewis Henry
'The end of the slave trade in British Central Africa: 1889–1912.' (Human Problems in British Central Africa, Manchester, no. 16, 1954, pp. 27–51; map.)

3576 HANNA, Alexander John
The beginnings of Nyasaland and north-eastern Rhodesia 1859–95. Oxford, 1956. viii, 281 pp. maps.

Pt. 1: 'Christianity, commerce, and civilization versus the slave-trade.'

3577 *MATTAGNE, Antoine
'Depuis deux générations le Congo est libéré des esclavagistes arabes.' (Revue Nationale, Bruxelles, vol. 28, no. 277, 1956, pp. 259–66.)

3578 VERBEKEN, Auguste
'La campagne contre le chef arabe Rumaliza. Textes inédits . . .' (Académie Royale des Sciences Coloniales, Bulletin des séances, Bruxelles, n.s., vol. 4, 1958, pp. 813–42.)

Letters relating to the Congolese campaign of 1893–94.

3579 CEULEMANS, P.
La question arabe et la Congo (1883–1892). Bruxelles, 1959. 396 pp. maps. bibl. pp. 368–80.

On the relations of the Congo Free State with the East African Arabs, the Brussels conference of 1889–90, and the war against the Arabs. (Reviewed in: Académie Royale des Sciences Coloniales, Bulletin des séances, Bruxelles, n.s., vol. 4, 1958, pp. 580–85, 640–42.)

3580 VILLERS, André
Nous les avons libéré de l'esclavage . . . Bruxelles, 1961. 237 pp. maps.

History of the war against Arab slavers in the eastern Congo 1890–97.

3581 *TERRY, P. T.
' "The Arab war on Lake Nyasa 1887–1895": an account of the campaign against the slaver Mlozi.' (Nyasaland Journal, Blantyre, vol. 18, 1965, pp. 55–77.)

3582 COOKEY, Silvanus John Sodienye
'Tippu Tib and the decline of the Congo Arabs.' (Tarikh, London, vol. 1, no. 2, 1966, pp. 58–69; map.)

3583 BOUCHE, Denise
Les villages de liberté en Afrique noire française 1887–1910. Paris, La Haye, 1968. 278 pp. illus, maps.

Villages for freed slaves were established during the French conquests in West Africa. (Ph.D. thesis, Dakar, 1965.)

U

V. HISTORY OF THE ABOLITION MOVEMENT

3584 CLARKSON, Thomas
The history of the rise, progress, and accomplishment of the abolition of the African slave-trade by the British Parliament. Longman, Hurst, Rees, & Orme, London, 1808. 2 vol.

> The basic account of the British abolition movement. (Reviews in: ER, vol. 12, 1808, pp. 355–79, by S. T. Coleridge; EclR, vol. 4, 1808, pp. 924–30, 1024–33; GM, vol. 79, 1809, pp. 445–49. 535–38; CO, vol. 66, 1866, pp. 481–88.)

3585 *NEDERMEYER VAN ROSENTHAL, Joannes Theodorus Henricus
Dissertatio historico-politica inauguralis de servorum Afrorum commercio eoque recte sublato nec non de Afrorum servitute penitus tollenda . . . L. Herdingh, Lugduni Batavorum, 1816. xii, 231 pp.

> See (3591).

3586 EDWARDS, Bryan
The history, civil and commercial, of the British West Indies . . . With a continuation to the present time. Fifth edition. G. & W. B. Whitaker (etc.), London, 1819. 5 vol. maps.

> Vol. 4 contains a 'History of the abolition of the slave trade'.

3587 BREVE resumo sobre a natureza do commercio de escravatura e das atrocidades que d'elle resultam: seguido de huma relação historica dos debates que terminaram a final abolição. Ellerton & Henderson, London, 1821. xii, 112 pp.

> History of the slave trade and its abolition to 1807.

3588 BRAND, Charles
'A visit to the island of Madagascar.' (USJ, 1829, II, pp. 529–40.)

> Account by a British naval officer of a visit in 1822, with the text of a proclamation by king Radama I against the slave trade.

3589 TIMPSON, Thomas
The negroes' jubilee: a memorial of negro emancipation, August 1, 1834: with a brief history of the slave trade and its abolition . . . Ward & Co., London, 1834. vi, 151 pp.

3590 COPLEY, Esther
A history of slavery, and its abolition. Sunday School Union, London, 1836. xi, 634 pp.

> Includes sections on the British abolition movement.

3591 NEUFVILLE, Jacobus de
Dissertatio historico-politica inauguralis, de iis, quae ad tollendum servorum Afrorum commercium, inde a congressu Viennensi, inter populos gesta sunt . . . D. Groebe, Amstelodami, 1840. x, 130 pp.

> Continuation of (3585), on the measures taken by the European nations to abolish the slave trade 1815–39.

3592 *FRIENDS, Society of
A brief statement of the rise and progress of the testimony of the religious Society of Friends against slavery and the slave trade . . . Joseph & William Kite, Philadelphia, 1843. 59 pp.

> Guide to Quaker antislavery ideas 1671–1787.

3593 'OVERZIGT van de verrigtingen der Engelschen, ten aanzien van slavernij en sklavenhandel.' (Signed: J. H. S.) (Bijdragen tot de Kennis der Nederlandsche en Vreemde Koloniën, Utrecht, 1844, pp. 1–17.)

> By J. Hora Siccama. Account of the English antislavery movement 1670–1840.

3594 'The CLAPHAM sect.' (ER, vol. 80, 1844, pp. 251–307.)

> By Sir James Stephen. Description of the group which included the abolitionists Sharp, Wilberforce, Macaulay and Clarkson. (Reprinted in the author's 'Essays in ecclesiastical biography', 1849.)

3595 COFFIN, Joshua
A sketch of the history of Newbury,

Newburyport, and West Newbury, from 1635 to 1845. S. G. Drake, Boston, 1845. 416 pp.

Appendix H (pp. 334–50) contains antislavery material 1641–1785, including letters written by Benjamin Colman 1774–83 attacking the African slave trade.

3596 NEEDLES, Edward
An historical memoir of the Pennsylvania Society, for promoting the abolition of slavery; the relief of free negroes unlawfully held in bondage, and for improving the condition of the African race . . . Merrihew & Thompson, Philadelphia, 1848. 116 pp.

History of antislavery activities in the United States from 1775 to about 1820.

3597 *MATLACK, Lucius C.
The history of American slavery and Methodism, from 1780 to 1849 . . . New York, 1849. 2 vol.

3598 BOWDEN, James
The history of the Society of Friends in America. London, 1850, 54. 2 vol.

With a chapter on the history of the Quaker antislavery movement.

3599 GOODELL, William
Slavery and anti-slavery; a history of the great struggle in both hemispheres; with a view of the slavery question in the United States. New-York, 1852. x, 604 pp.

On the development of American slavery and the abolition movement from the 17th century.

3600 KAPP, Friedrich
Die Sklavenfrage in den Vereinigten Staaten . . . Göttingen; New-York, 1854. vi, 185 pp.

History of the movement to abolish the slave trade in the United States 1778–1819.

3601 STEPHEN, Sir George
Anti-slavery recollections: in a series of letters, addressed to Mrs Beecher Stowe, written by Sir George Stephen, at her request. London, 1854. xii, 258 pp.

British antislavery history during the first half of the 19th century.

3602 NATIONAL AMERICAN PARTY
The record of George Wm. Gordon. The slave trade at Rio de Janeiro—seizure of slave vessels—conviction of slave dealers, personal liberation of slaves, &c. . . . Boston, 1856. 16 pp.

Election pamphlet, describing how, as consul at Rio de Janeiro 1844–46, Gordon arrested U.S. slave ships and sent their crews home for trial.

3603 'EARLY congressional discussions upon slavery.' (DBR, vol. 23, July 1857, pp. 35–47.)

Extracts from speeches in debates on slavery and the slave trade 1796–1800.

3604 GOODLOE, Daniel Reaves
The southern platform: or, manual of southern sentiment on the subject of slavery. Boston, 1858. 79 pp.

Compilation of writings on slavery by Benjamin Franklin and others 1774–1829.

3605 *DE FONTAINE, Felix Gregory
History of American abolitionism; its four great epochs, embracing narratives of the ordinance of 1787, compromise of 1820, annexation of Texas, Mexican war . . . &c., &c., &c. . . . New York, 1861. 66 pp.

3606a COCHIN, Augustin
L'abolition de l'esclavage. Paris, 1861. 2 vol.

Translated as:

3606b* The results of emancipation . . . Boston, 1863. xiv, 412 pp.

3606c The results of slavery . . . Boston, 1863. x, 413 pp.

Includes the history of the abolition of the African slave trade and Christian attitudes to slavery.

3607 SIMONENKO, Grigory Feodorovich
Abolitsionizm i abolitsionistui. Istorichesky ocherk unichtozheniya rabstva negrov. Sanktpeterburg, 1862. 194, 4 pp.

History of the European and North American antislavery movements.

3608 LIVERMOORE, George
An historical research respecting the opinions of the founders of the republic on negroes as slaves, as citizens, and as soldiers . . . Boston, 1862. xiv, 215 pp.

American views on slavery and the slave trade 1774–1808.

3609 DUMAS, Florent
'Le catholicisme et l'esclave noir.' (Études Réligieuses, Historiques et Littéraires, Paris, n.s. vol. 2, 1863, pp. 15–39, 357–85, 744–73.)

Study of the attitude of the Catholic church to African slavery and the slave trade; the second section, 'Les nègres et la traite', largely quotes Molina (1685).

3610 TAVARES BASTOS, Aureliano Candido
Cartas do Solitario. Estudios sobre reforma administrativa, ensino religioso, Africanos livres, trafico de escravos . . . Segunda edição. Rio de Janeiro, 1863. xiv, 433 pp.

Ch. 10–11: 'O trafico de negros'; its suppression was good for Africa and Brazil.

3611 'SIR James Hudson in Brazil. A chapter in the history of English relations with Brazil.' (Victoria Magazine, London, vol. 3, 1864, pp. 1–18.)

Account of the diplomatic pressure for the abolition of the Brazilian slave trade 1845–51.

3612 GREAT BRITAIN: Foreign Office (*Slave Trade Department*)
Slave trade suppression tables; or, a chronologically and an alphabetically arranged statement of the periods at which different nations have taken measures for the abolition of the slave trade. London, 1864. 33 pp.

List of events in abolition history 1776–1863, also arranged by country.

3613 MARGRAF, J.
Kirche und Sklaverei seit der Entdeckung Amerika's oder: Was hat die katholische Kirche seit der Entdeckung Amerika's theils zur Milderung theils zur Aufhebung der Sklaverei gethan? Tübingen, 1865. x, 230 pp.

Discusses the attitudes of the Roman Catholic church to slavery and the slave trade since the 16th century.

3614 LORD Palmerston. A opinião e os factos. Um brado a pró da verdade. Por C. T. Lisboa, 1865. 37 pp.

Attack on Britain's insolent anti-slave trade policy based on intimidation of Portugal since 1839.

3615 MOORE, George Henry
Notes on the history of slavery in Massachusetts. New-York, 1866. iv, 256 pp.

Includes material on the antislavery movements in New England during the 18th century. (Reviewed in: Historical Magazine, Boston, vol. 10, 1866, suppl. II, pp. 47–57.) See (1697–98).

3616 MOISTER, William
Memorials of missionary labours in western Africa, the West Indies, and at the Cape of Good Hope . . . Third edition, revised and enlarged . . . London, 1866. viii, 592 pp.

Ch. 3: 'African slavery and the slave trade.'

3617 'La RIVOLUZIONE e l'abolizione della tratta e della schiavitù.' (CC, ser. 6, vol. 7, 1866, pp. 549–65.)

By V. Steccanella. Account of the French abolition campaign 1789–94.

3618 'L'ABOLIZIONE della tratta e della schiavitù.' (CC, ser. 6, vol. 8, 1866, pp. 15–34.)

By V. Steccanella. On the abolition movement of the 18th and 19th century.

3619 FRANCO DE ALMEIDA, Tito
O Brazil e a Inglaterra ou o trafico de africanos . . . Rio de Janeiro, 1868. 32, 458 pp.

History of the abolition of the Portuguese slave trade to 1822; British pressure on Portugal was hypocritical and tyrannical.

3620 WILSON, Henry
History of the rise and fall of the slave power in America. Boston, 1872–77. 3 vol.

3621 LABRA Y CADRANA, Rafael María de
La abolición de la esclavitud en el orden económico. Madrid, 1873. xx, 458 pp.

Includes chapters on the British and American campaigns against the slave trade.

3622 POOLE, William Frederick
Anti-slavery opinions before the year 1800 . . . To which is appended a facsimile reprint of Dr. George Buchanan's Oration on the moral and political evil of slavery, delivered at . . . Baltimore, July 4, 1791. Cincinnati, 1873. 82, 20 pp.

History of the early abolition movement in the United States.

3623 DAVENPORT, J.
Memorandum on the slave trade. [London, 1874.] iii, 29 pp.

Brief history of the slave trade and its abolition (to 1845), prepared for E. Hertslet at the Foreign Office about 1858.

3624 'PROGRESS of anti-slavery among Friends.' (Signed: J. M. T.) (Friends' Intelligencer, Philadelphia, vol. 31, no. 6, 1874, pp. 91–93.)

Documents on slavery from Philadelphia Quaker meetings until 1712, including a 'paper about negroes' by Robert Pile (reprinted in: 3733).

3625 SEIDENSTICKER, Oswald
'The first anti-slavery protest.' (Penn Monthly, Philadelphia, vol. 5, July 1874, pp. 496–503.)

On the protest by Quakers of Germantown, Pennsylvania, against the slave trade and slavery in 1688. (First published in: The Friend, Philadelphia, vol. 17, 1844, pp. 125–26.)

3626 *'ABOLITION de la traite et l'esclavage à Madagascar.' (Missions Evangeliques au Dix-Neuvième Siècle, Neuchâtel, vol. 15, 1875, p. 64; vol. 17, 1877, pp. 317–18; vol. 18, 1878, pp. 76–82; vol. 23, 1883, pp. 285–87.)

3627 QUESTION cubaine. L'esclavage et la traite à Cuba. Paris, 1876. x, 30 pp.

Anonymous pieces (translated by R. E. Betancès) written to show that the Cubans had generally opposed the slave trade and that Spain was to blame for delaying its suppression and for maintaining slavery in Cuba.

3628 MATLACK, Lucius C.
The antislavery struggle and triumph in the Methodist Episcopal church . . . New York; Cincinnati, 1881. 379 pp.

On the Methodist antislavery movement from 1774.

3629 *DIÉNY, Jean
L'abolitionnisme de l'esclavage chez les chrétiens anglais du XVIIIᵉ siècle . . . Montauban, 1882. 46 pp.

B.Litt. thesis, Faculté de théologie protestante, Montauban.

3630 HOPKINS, Ellice
'Conquering and to conquer: or the triumphs of the moral sense.' (SuM, 1886, pp. 594–600.)

Account of the abolition of the English slave trade.

3631 *RODRÍGUEZ, Gabriel
La idea y el movimiento anti-esclavista en España en el siglo XIX. Madrid, 1887. 34 pp.

3632 ARANGO Y PARREÑO, Francisco de
Obras. Habana, 1888. 2 vol.

Contains a number of important documents relating to the Spanish slave trade and abolition controversy 1789–1832.

3633 SPONT, Alfred
L'abolition de l'esclavage au Brésil. Paris, 1888. 47 pp.

History of the abolition of the Brazilian slave trade and slavery. (Reprinted from: Revue du Monde Latin, Paris, vol. 15, 1888, pp. 273–92, 462–86.)

3634 *FONT Y DE BOTER, Joaquín de
L'esclavitud y la Iglesia. Barcelona, 1889. 30 pp.

3635 'Die EUROPÄISCHE Bewegung gegen den Sklavenhandel.' (Signed: P.) (Deutsche Rundschau für Geographie und Statistik, Wien, vol. 11, 1889, pp. 490–92.)

3636 KLEINSTÜCK, Gustav
'Ein deutscher Protest gegen die Sklaverei vor 200 Jahren.' (DKZ, n.s., vol. 2, 1889, pp. 53–55.)

Text of an antislavery document of 1688, with comments. See (3625).

3637 ABIGNENTE, Giovanni
La schiavitù nei suoi rapporti colla chiesa e col laicato. Studio storico giuridico pubblicato in occasione della conferenza antischiavista di Bruxelles. Torino, 1890. 333 pp.

History of the attitude of the Catholic church to slavery and the slave trade.

3638 BRECHT, Theodor
Kirche und Sklaverei. Ein Beitrag zur Lösung des Problems der Freiheit. Barmen, [1890]. iv, 227 pp.

Critical history of the attitude of the Catholic church to slavery and the slave trade.

3639 PINHEIRO CHAGAS, Manuel
As colonias portuguezas no seculo XIX (1811 a 1890). Lisboa, 1890. 228 pp.

Includes notes on the suppression of the slave trade in Angola and Mozambique.

3640 SCARSEZ DE LOCQUENEUILLE, A.
L'esclavage, ses promoteurs et ses adversaires. Notes et documents pour servir à l'histoire de l'esclavage dans ces rapports avec le catholicisme, le protestantisme et les principes de 89. Liège, 1890. 327 pp.

History of Protestant and Catholic antislavery movements.

3641 'La MISSION des Deux-Guinées et l'esclavage. Par un pére de la Congrégation du St-Esprit et du St-Cœur de Marie.' (Missions Catholiques, Lyon, vol. 23, 1891, pp. 543–45, 560–61, 569–72, 581–84, 594–96, 605–08, 615–16.)

By L. A. Lejeune. Account of the Catholic mission in Gabon since 1845 and its antislavery activities.

3642 APPLEGARTH, Albert Clayton
Quakers in Pennsylvania. Baltimore, 1892. 84 pp.

Ch. 4: 'Attitude of Quakers towards slavery.'

3643 STEINER, Bernard Christian
History of slavery in Connecticut. Baltimore, 1893. 84 pp.

With a section on the antislavery movement.

3644 BIANCHETTI, Carlo
L'antischiavismo alla fine del secolo XIX. Torino, 1893. viii, 407 pp.

Account of Catholic antislavery attitudes from the Middle Ages to the present day, with a chapter on Cardinal Lavigerie.

3645 JOHNSTON, William Dawson
Slavery in Rhode Island, 1755–1776. Providence, R.I., 1894. 56 pp.

Describes the development of the antislavery movement. (Reprinted from: Publications of the Rhode Island Historical Society, vol. 2, 1894, pp. 113–64.)

3646 BYRD, William
'Colonel William Byrd on slavery and indented servants, 1736, 1739.' (AHR, vol. 1, 1895, pp. 88–90.)

Two letters by a Virginian criticising the import of African slaves.

3647 BÅÅTH-HOLMBERG, Cecilia
Kampen för och emot negerslafveriet. Ett blad ur Förenta Staternas historia. Stockholm, 1896. 304 pp.

Includes material on the slave trade and early abolition movement in the United States.

3648 DU BOIS, William Edward Burghardt
The suppression of the African slave-trade to the United States of America 1638–1870. New York, 1896. xi, 335 pp. bibl. pp. 299–325. (Harvard historical studies, vol. 1.).

First general history of the American slave trade and abolition movement. M.A. thesis, Harvard, 1892. See (3934). (Reviewed in: AHR, vol. 2, 1897, pp. 555–59.)

3649 COOLEY, Henry Scofield
A study of slavery in New Jersey. Baltimore, 1896. 60 pp.

With sections on the slave trade and antislavery movement.

3650 WEEKS, Stephen Beauregard
Southern Quakers and slavery. A study in institutional history. Baltimore, 1896. xiv, 400 pp. bibl. pp. 345–62.

Includes a chapter on the 18th century abolition movement.

3651 *THOMAS, Allen Clapp
'The attitude of the Society of Friends towards slavery in the seventeenth and eighteenth centuries, particularly in relation to its own members . . .' (Papers of the American Society of Church History, New York, vol. 8, 1897, pp. 263–99.)

3652 BONET-MAURY, Gaston
'La France et le mouvement anti-esclavagiste au XIXᵉ siècle.' (RDM, vol. 160, 1900, pp. 132–66.)

Reprinted as ch. 4 in his: France, christianisme et civilisation (Paris, 1907).

3653 BRITISH AND FOREIGN ANTI-SLAVERY SOCIETY
Sixty years against slavery. A brief record of the work and aims of the British and Foreign Anti-Slavery Society 1839–1899 . . . London, [1900]. 15 pp.

3654 LOCKE, Mary Stoughton
Anti-slavery in America from the introduction of African slaves to the prohibition of the slave trade (1619–1808). Boston, 1901. xv, 255 pp. bibl. pp. 199–231.

Standard work on the early anti-slavery movement in the United States.

3655 *WISSMAN, Hermann von
'Der Anteil des deutschen Reichs an der Unterdrückung des afrikanischen Sklavenhandels.' (Die Deutschen Kolonien, Gütersloh, vol. 1, 1902, pp. 20–25.)

3656 *DURAND, Louis
Le mouvement anti-esclavagiste (1876–1900). Conférence faite . . . le 13 juin 1902 . . . Toulouse, [1902]. 39 pp.

3657 RODRIGO, Julián
'León XIII y la esclavitud africana.'
(Ciudad de Dios, Madrid, vol. 60,
1903, pp. 458–76.)

On the antislavery campaign led
by Cardinal Lavigerie.

3658 STEVENS, William
The slave in history. His sorrows and
his emancipation. London, 1904. 379 pp.
illus.

Popular history of slavery, the slave
trade and the British abolition
movement.

3659 HOCHSTETTER, Franz
Die wirtschaftlichen und politischen
Motive für die Abschaffung des britischen Sklavenhandels im Jahre 1806/
1807. Leipzig, 1905. x, 120 pp.

Study of the British abolition movement 1783–1807, relating it to the
economic crisis following the loss
of the American colonies.

3660 BOISSONNADE, Prosper
Sainte-Domingue à la veille de la révolution et la question de la réprésenta-
tion coloniale aux États généraux
(janvier 1788–7 juillet 1789).' (Bulletin
et mémoires de la Société des Antiquaires de l'Ouest, Poitiers, ser. 2,
vol. 29, 1906, pp. 283–579.)

Includes material on the beginning
of the French abolition campaign
and the emergence of a settler
opposition party.

3661 CAHEN, Léon
'La Société des Amis et Condorcet.'
(Révolution Française, Paris, vol. 50,
1906, pp. 481–511.)

Mainly the text of the society's
rules (3036) and some reports by
Condorcet.

3662 TELFORD, John
A sect that moved the world. Three
generations of Clapham saints and
philanthropists. London, [1907]. 246 pp.
illus.

Ch. 4: 'The abolition of the slave
trade.'

3663 *MACDONALD, Eugene Montague
A short history of the Inquisition . . .
to which is appended an account of . . .
the attitude of the American churches
toward African slavery . . . New York,
1907. 645 pp. illus.

3664 *SWANK, James Moore
'Protest against slavery.' (Pennsylvania-

German, Lititz, Pa., vol. 11, 1910,
pp. 746–48.)

On the Quaker protest of 1688, the
first public antislavery statement in
America. See (3625).

**3665 *PENNSYLVANIA SOCIETY FOR
PROMOTING THE ABOLITION OF
SLAVERY**
The oldest abolition society; being a
short story of the labors of the Pennsylvania society for the abolition of
slavery, the relief of free negroes unlawfully held in bondage, and for
improving the condition of the African
race. Philadelphia, 1911. 8ll.

3666 ROSE, John Holland
William Pitt and national revival.
London, 1911. xii, 655 pp. illus.

Ch. 20: 'The slave trade'; on the
abolition campaign 1787–1802.

3667 HOCHSTETTER, Franz
Die Abschaffung des britischen Sklavenhandels im Jahre 1806/07. Ein Kapitel
aus der britischen Schiffahrtspolitik.
Berlin, 1911. 38 pp. (Meereskunde,
vol. 5, no. 4.)

Economic motives were more important than moral ones for Britain's
abolition of the slave trade.

3668 TURNER, Edward Raymond
The negro in Pennsylvania. Slavery—
servitude—freedom, 1639–1861. Washington, 1911. xii, 314 pp. bibl. pp.
254–94.

Includes chapters on the abolition
movement 1682–1850.

3669 *WHITSON, Thomas
'The early abolitionists of Lancaster
County . . .' (Papers read before the
Lancaster County Historical Society,
Lancaster, Pa., vol. 15, no. 3, 1911,
pp. 69–89.)

3670 *SPINDLER, Adaline Bream
'The slavery question during the terms
of office of John Whitehill and Robert
Jenkins, congressmen from Lancaster
County from 1803 to 1807 and 1807 to
1811, respectively.' In: LANCASTER
COUNTY HISTORICAL SOCIETY,
Historical papers and addresses, vol.
15 (Lancaster, Pa., 1911), pp. 253–65.

3671a JORNS, Auguste
Studien über die Sozialpolitik der
Quäker. Karlsruhe, 1912. xii, 150 pp.

Translated as:

3671b The Quakers as pioneers in social work. New York, 1931. 269 pp.

> Ch. 6: 'Mitwirkung an der Aufhebung des Sklavenhandels und der Sklaverei'; on Quaker antislavery activities 1671–1909.

3672 TURNER, Edward Raymond
'The first abolition society in the United States.' (PMHB, vol. 36, 1912, pp. 92–109.)

> Describes the Pennsylvania antislavery society of 1775 and its background.

3673 TURNER, Edward Raymond
'The abolition of slavery in Pennsylvania.' (PMHB, vol. 36, 1912, pp. 129–42.)

> On the antislavery movement 1688–1780.

3674 DUTILLEUL, J.
'Esclavage.' In: VACANT, A. Dictionnaire de théologie catholique, vol. 5 (Paris, 1913), col. 457–549.

> Includes sections on the African slave trade to America and the attitude to it of Catholic churchmen from the 16th century onward.

3675 PERROUD, Claude
'La Société française des Amis des Noirs.' (Révolution Française, Paris, vol. 69, 1916, pp. 122–47.)

> History of the Amis des Noirs 1788–99.

3676 *MORAES Evaristo de
Extincção do trafico de escravos no Brasil (ensaio historico). [Rio de Janeiro,] 1916. 57 pp.

3677 ALVES, João Luiz
'A questão do elemento servil. A extincção do trafico e a lei de repressão de 1850. Liberdade dos nascituros.' (RIHGB, Tomo especial consagrado ao Primeiro Congresso de Historia Nacional, 1914, pt. 4, 1916, pp. 187–257.)

> Political history of the abolition of the Brazilian slave trade 1822–55.

3678 HERRON, Stella
'The African apprentice bill.' (Proceedings of the Mississippi Valley Historical Association, Cedar Rapids, Iowa, vol. 8, 1916, pp. 135–45.)

> On a Louisiana bill 1858 to import African labourers and the failure of Southern attempts to reopen the slave trade.

3679 SOUZA SÁ VIANNA, Manoel Alvaro de
'O trafico e a diplomacia brasileira.' (RIHGB, Tomo especial consagrado ao Primeiro Congresso de Historia Nacional, 1914, pt. 5, 1917, pp. 539–64.)

> History of the diplomatic pressures on Brazil to abolish the slave trade 1822–52.

3680 KLINGBERG, Frank Joseph
'A general survey of the anti-slavery movement in England.' (SAQ, vol. 17, 1918, pp. 1–9.)

> On the abolition movement 1772–1833.

3681 COHEN, Chapman
Christianity and slavery . . . London, [1918]. 95 pp.

> Ch. 4: 'The English trade'; refutes the claim that 'Christianity abolished the slave trade'.

3682 *DUQUE-ESTRADA, Osorio
A abolição (esbôço histórico) 1831–1888 . . . Rio de Janeiro, 1918. xii, 328 pp.

3683 CRUIKSHANK, J. Graham
'African immigrants after freedom.' (Timehri, Demerara, ser. 3, vol. 6, 1919, pp. 74–85; illus.)

> Account of the introduction of recaptured African slaves to British Guiana as labourers 1841–51.

3684 *HARDY, Charles Oscar
The negro question in the French revolution . . . Menasha, Wis., 1919. 91 pp. bibl. pp. 87–91.

> Ph.D. thesis, Chicago, 1916.

3685 FOX, Early Lee
The American Colonization Society 1817–1840. Baltimore, 1919. 231 pp.

> Ch. 5: 'Colonization and the African slave trade'; on Liberia's contribution to the suppression of the slave trade.

3686 SWINNY, Shapland Hugh
'The humanitarianism of the eighteenth century and its results.' In: MARVIN, F. S. The western races and the world (London, 1922), pp. 121–45.

> Includes an account of the English antislavery movement.

3687 'FIRST protest against slavery in the United States.' (JNH, vol. 8, 1923, p. 333.)

Text of a Virginia document of 1657 ordering that slaves be held for a maximum of ten years.

3688 LUGARD, *Sir* **Frederick John Dealtry**
'The passing of slavery in Africa.' *In*: WEINTHAL, L. The story of the Cape to Cairo railway and river route, vol. 1 (London, 1923), pp. 491–97.

On European suppression of the slave trade and slavery in Africa.

3689 SCHUYLER, Robert Livingston
'The constitutional claims of the British West Indies. The controversy over the slave registry bill of 1815.' (Political Science Quarterly, New York, vol. 40, 1925, pp. 1–36.)

On the reaction of the colonial legislatures to the registration bill.

3690 *PONTOPPIDAN, Morten Oxenbøll
Kampen mod Negerslaveriet i De forenede Stater. En historisk Skildring. København, 1925. 208 pp.

3691 *MARTIN, Thomas Powderley
'Some international aspects of the anti-slavery movement, 1820–1840.' (Proceedings of the sixth annual convention, Southwestern Political and Social Science Association, Austin, Texas, 1925, pp. 119–33.)

See (3699).

3692 *GALBREATH, Charles Burleigh
'Thomas Jefferson's views on slavery.' (Ohio Archaeological and Historical Quarterly, Columbus, vol. 34, 1925, pp. 184–202.)

3693 ADAMS, Jane Elizabeth
'The abolition of the Brazilian slave trade.' (JNH, vol. 10, 1925, pp. 607–37.)

Largely on Britain's efforts until 1852 to suppress the trade.

3694 KLINGBERG, Frank Joseph
The anti-slavery movement in England. A study in English humanitarianism. New Haven; London, 1926. xii, 390 pp. bibl. pp. 309–20.

Standard work on the British abolition movement to 1839.

3695 JACKSON, Emily Nevill
'Anti-slavery relics.' (Connoisseur, London, vol. 77, 1927, pp. 9–10, 13–17; illus.)

On English antiques with abolitionist motifs from the period 1785–1835.

3696 TREPP, Jean
'The Liverpool movement for the abolition of the English slave trade'. (JNH, vol. 13, 1928, pp. 265–85.)

Account of the antislavery writings of Roscoe and others 1777–1807.

3697 GREENE, Lorenzo Johnston
'Slave-holding New England and its awakening.' (JNH, vol. 13, 1928, pp. 492–533.)

On the slave trade and abolition movement in the 18th century.

3698 RAGATZ, Lowell Joseph
The fall of the planter class in the British Caribbean, 1763–1833. A study in social and economic history. New York, London, [1928]. xiv, 520 pp. bibl. pp. 461–90.

Ch. 8: 'The abolition movement'; ch. 11: 'The registration controversy.'

3699 MARTIN, Thomas Powderley
'Some international aspects of the anti-slavery movement, 1818–1823.' (Journal of Economic and Business History, Cambridge, Mass., vol. 1, 1928, pp. 137–48.)

On the economic rivalries underlying the abolition movement, particularly over Indian versus American cotton and sugar. See (3691).

3700 *MONHEIM, Christian
La croisade antiesclavagiste; Leopold II et le cardinal Lavigerie. Louvain, 1928. 32 pp.

3701 MATHIESON, William Law
Great Britain and the slave trade 1839–1865. London, 1929. xi, 203 pp. map.

History of British antislavery policy in the Atlantic and Indian Ocean.

3702 LOTZ, Adolf
Sklaverei, Staatskirche und Freikirche. Die englisshen Bekenntnisse im Kampf um die Aufhebung von Sklavenhandel und Sklaverei. Leipzig, 1929. 114 pp. map.

On the established church and dissenters in the British antislavery movement until 1838.

3703 GEWEHR, Wesley Marsh
The great awakening in Virginia, 1740–1790. Durham, N.C., 1930. viii, 292 pp.

Ch. 10: 'The evangelicals and slavery.'

3704 SAINTOYANT, Jules François
La colonisation française pendant la révolution (1789–1799). Paris, 1930. 2 vol. maps.

Deals with the controversy about the slave trade and slavery and their abolition in 1794.

3705 *HANSTEIN, Otfrid von
Elfenbeinjäger und Sklaventreiber. Geschichte der Entwicklung und Bekämpfung der Sklaverei auf der ganzen Erde vom frühesten Altertum bis zur Gegenwart. Leipzig, 1931. 249 pp. illus.

3706 HIRSCH, Leo H.
'The negro and New York, 1783 to 1865.' (JNH, vol. 16, 1931, pp. 382–473.)

With sections on the abolition movement and on the illegal slave trade from New York to 1860.

3707 DONNAN, Elizabeth
'Agitation against the slave trade in Rhode Island, 1784–1790.' *In*: PERSECUTION and liberty. Essays in honor of George Lincoln Burr (New York, 1931), pp. 473–82.

On Samuel Hopkins and Moses Brown.

3708 HILL, Lawrence Francis
'The abolition of the African slave trade to Brazil.' (HAHR, vol. 11, 1931, pp. 169–97.)

Diplomatic history of the suppression of the illegal slave trade 1826–53.

3709 MAZYCK, Walter H.
George Washington and the negro. Washington, [1932]. vii, 180 pp.

Study of Washington's attitude to slavery and the abolition movement.

3710 WESLEY, Charles Harris
'The neglected period of emancipation in Great Britain 1807–1823.' (JNH, vol. 17, 1932, pp. 156–79.)

Includes material on recaptured Africans and the slave registration controversy.

3711 'ANTI-SLAVERY papers of John Jay.' (JNH, vol. 17, 1932, pp. 481–96.)

Documents from the European abolition societies and correspondence of Jay 1785–96.

3712 *VOLKHARDT, H
Die Bekämpfung der Sklaverei und die internationale Abstellung von Missbräuchen in den Kolonien bis zum Vertrag von St. Germain sowie die Kolonialschuldlüge . . . Aschersleben, 1932. 62 pp.

3713 COUPLAND, Reginald
The British anti-slavery movement. London, 1933. 255 pp.

Lectures on the abolition and suppression of the African slave trade and slavery.

3714 CADBURY, Henry Joel
'Colonial Quaker antecedents to British abolition of slavery.' (Friends' Quarterly Examiner, London, 1933, pp. 260–75.)

On the American abolitionists in the period 1671–1783.

3715 GARLICK, Phyllis L.
Towards freedom. Evangelicals and slave emancipation. London, 1933. 31 pp.

Sketch of the slave trade and abolition movement.

3716 HARRIS, *Sir* John Hobbis
A centenary of emancipation. London, 1933. xvi, 287 pp. illus.

History of the abolition of the slave trade and slavery.

3717 WATTS, Maurice
"Liberty to the captives". A short account of the movement to abolish slavery . . . London, 1933. 94 pp.

Popular history of English abolitionism.

3718 MANCHESTER, Alan K.
British preëminence in Brazil. Its rise and decline. A study in European expansion. Chapel Hill, 1933. xi, 371 pp. bibl. pp. 343–54.

Ch. 7: 'England's attempt to abolish the Portuguese slave trade, 1808–1822.'

3719 MARTIN, Percy Alvin
'Slavery and abolition in Brazil.' (HAHR, vol. 13, 1933, pp. 151–96.)

On the abolition of the slave trade and emancipation.

3720 POSADA, Eduardo
La esclavitud en Colombia. Por Eduardo Posada. Leyes de manumision. Por Carlos Restrepo Canal. Bogotá, 1933, 38. 2 vol. illus.

The second part contains an account of the abolition of the slave trade and slavery in Colombia and the texts of abolition laws 1789–1851. See (1227).

3721 MELLON, Matthew Taylor
Early American views on negro

slavery. From the letters and papers of the founders of the Republic. Boston, 1934. 164 pp.

Deals with Franklin, Washington, John Adams, Jefferson and Madison.

3722   GILLARD, John Thomas
'Lafayette, friend of the negro.' (JNH, vol. 19, 1934, pp. 335–71.)

On Lafayette's part in the antislavery movement of the 1780s.

2723   SILBERSCHMIDT, Max
'Das britische Reich und die Abolition des Sklavenhandels.' (Archiv für Kulturgeschichte, Berlin, vol. 24, 1934, pp. 90–109.)

3724   *ALMEIDA CORREIA DE SÁ, José de, marquez de Lavradio
A abolição da escravatura e a ocupação do Ambriz . . . Lisboa, [1934]. 296 pp.

On the abolition of the Angolan slave trade.

3725   JENKINS, William Sumner
Pro-slavery in the Old South. Chapel Hill, N.C., 1935. xi, 381 pp. bibl. pp. 309–58.

Describes the abolition movement 1670–1860 and the opposition to it in the United States, including the proposed reopening of the slave trade in the 1850s.

3726   CICOGNANI, Dante
La questione della schiavitù coloniale dal congresso di Vienna a oggi. Firenze, 1935. 260 pp.

Diplomatic history of the abolition of the African slave trade 1815–1935.

3727   GHERSI, Emanuele
La schiavitù e l'evoluzione della politica coloniale. Padova, 1935. x, 273 pp.

History of the slave trade and international action to abolish it to the present day.

3728   KRAUS, Michael
'Slavery reform in the eighteenth century: an aspect of transatlantic intellectual cooperation.' (PMHB, vol. 60, 1936, pp. 53–66.)

On the pietistic and radical background to abolitionism in America, England and France until 1792.

3729   PIERSON, William Whatley
'Francisco de Arango y Parreño.' (HAHR, vol. 16, 1936, pp. 451–78.)

Arango opposed abolition of the slave trade 1811–14 but served as a judge of the mixed commission court in Havana 1819–21.

3730   ROSE, John Holland
'Palmerston and the suppression of the slave trade.' (Eagle, St. John's College, Cambridge, vol. 49, 1936, pp. 215–21.)

On British antislavery policy 1830–65.

3731   *MARTIN, Percy Alvin
La esclavitid y su abolición en el Brasil. Buenos Aires, 1936. 48 pp.

3732   *GARCÍA MAYO, Manuel
'Los abolicionistas del siglo XVI.' (Revista Bimestre Cubana, Habana, vol. 39, 1937, pp. 46–63.)

Mostly on Las Casas, with notes on Tomas de Mercado and Bartolomé de Albornoz.

3733   CADBURY, Henry Joel
'An early Quaker anti-slavery statement.' (JNH, vol. 22, 1937, pp. 488–93.)

On the Germantown protest 1688 (3625); with the antislavery paper by Robert Pile dated 1698 (3624).

3734   BREADY, John Wesley
England: before and after Wesley. The evangelical revival and social reform. London, 1938. 463 pp.

Includes an account of 'Wesley's attack on slavery'.

3735   'The SLAVE trade, slavery and Liberia.' (Tyler's Quarterly Historical and Genealogical Magazine, Richmond, Va., vol. 19, 1938, pp. 10–29.)

Southern view of the abolition movement.

3736   *CESARINO, Antônio Ferreira
'A intervenção da Inglaterra na supressão do tráfico de escravos africanos para o Brasil.' (Revista do Instituto Histórico e Geográfico de São Paulo, vol. 34, 1938, pp. 144–66.)

3737   *MONHEIM, Christian
'Afschaffing van den slavenhandel in Kongo.' (Nieuw Afrika, Antwerpen, vol. 54, 1938, pp. 525–39; illus.)

Reprinted separately: Antwerpen, 1938; 18 pp.

3738   *BREWSTER, Robert Wallace
'The rise of the anti-slavery movement in southwestern Pennsylvania.' (Western Pennsylvania Historical Magazine, Pittsburgh, vol. 22, 1939, pp. 1–18.)

3739   APTHEKER, Herbert
'The Quakers and negro slavery'. (JNH, vol. 25, 1940, pp. 331–62.)

On the development of Quaker anti-slavery opinion 1657–1858.

3740   COUPLAND, Reginald
'The abolition of the slave trade.' *In*: The CAMBRIDGE history of the British empire, vol. 2 (Cambridge, 1940), pp. 188–216. bibl. pp. 915–19; 922–36; 952–57.

History of the British antislavery movement 1783–1807.

3741   *MARTIN, Percy Alvin
'A escravatura e a sua abolição no Brasil.' *In*: CONGRESSO de Historia, e Geografia Sul Rio-Grandense, 1935, Anais, vol. 3 (Pôrto Alegre, 1940). pp. 1203–38.

3742   *KLINGBERG, Frank Joseph
Anglican humanitarianism in colonial New York . . . Philadelphia, [1940]. x, 295 pp. bibl. pp. 251–65.

Includes three S.P.G. sermons concerning negro slaves (pp. 197–249), by bishops William Fleetwood 1711 (2283), Thomas Secker 1741, and William Warburton 1766 (2287).

3743   BINDER-JOHNSON, Hildegard
'The Germantown protest of 1688 against negro slavery.' (PMHB, vol. 65, 1941, pp. 145–56.)

See (3625).

3744   *ERICKSEN, Nestor
'O negro no Rio Grande do Sul.' (Revista do Instituto Histórico e Geográfico do Rio Grande do Sul, Pôrto Alegre, vol. 21, no. 84, 1941, pp. 258–81.)

Includes material on the slave trade and abolition movement.

3745   BELL, Whitfield Jenks
'Washington County, Pennsylvania, in the eighteenth century antislavery movement.' (Western Pennsylvania Historical Magazine, Pittsburgh, vol. 25, 1942, pp. 135–42.)

On antislavery activities 1780–92.

3746   NUERMBERGER, Ruth Ketring
The free produce movement. A Quaker protest against slavery. Durham, N.C., 1942. ix, 147 pp. bibl. pp. 120–31.

Includes a brief account of slave produce boycott in the 18th century.

3747   *FELIÚ CRUZ, Guillermo
La abolición de la esclavitud en Chile: estudio histórico y social. [Santiago de Chile,] 1942. 368 pp. illus. bibl. pp. 307–50.

3748   NELSON, Bernard H.
'The slave trade as a factor in British foreign policy, 1815–1862.' (JNH, vol. 27, 1942, pp. 192–209.)

3749   WILLIAMS, Eric Eustace
'Laissez faire, sugar and slavery.' (Political Science Quarterly, New York, vol. 58, 1943, pp. 67–85.)

The antislavery movement was part of the general attack on monopoly characterizing the transition of the English economy from mercantilism to laissez faire.

3750   KING, James Ferguson
'The Latin-American republics and the suppression of the slave trade.' (HAHR, vol. 24, 1944, pp. 387–411.)

On British diplomatic pressure and developments 1810–50.

3751   MERRILL, Louis Taylor
'The English campaign for the abolition of the slave trade'. (JNH, vol. 30, 1945, pp. 382–99.)

The turning point of the abolitionist movement came in 1787.

3752   CERECEDA, Feliciano
'Un asiento de esclavos para América en el año 1553 y parecer de varios teólogos sobre su licitud.' (Missionalia Hispanica, Madrid, vol. 3, 1946, pp. 580–97.)

Includes the text of several opinions on the slave trade by Spanish theologians.

3753   DRAKE, Thomas Edward
Quakers and slavery in America. New Haven, 1950. viii, 245 pp. bibl. pp. 201–36.

History of the Quaker antislavery movement 1672–1865.

3754   MOSS, Simeon F.
'The persistence of slavery and involuntary servitude in a free state (1685–1866).' (JNH, vol. 35, 1950, pp. 289–314; map.)

On the abolition movement in New Jersey.

3755   SMITH, Robert Worthington
'The attempt of British humanitarianism to modify chattel slavery.' *In*: BRITISH humanitarianism. Essays honoring Frank J. Klingberg . . . Edited by Samuel Clyde McCulloch (Philadelphia, 1950), pp. 166–80.

On the antislavery movement 1787–1833.

3756 NABUCO, Joaquim
'A escravidão. Consideraçoes geraes.'
(RIGHB, vol. 204, 1951, pp. 10–106.)

Essay written 1870, including sections on the abolition of the Brazilian slave trade 1810–54.

3757 MELLOR, George Radcliffe
British imperial trusteeship 1783–1850 . . . London, 1951. 499 pp. bibl. pp. 457–79.

Ch. 1: 'The abolition of the British slave trade'.

3758 *VALLADÃO, Alfredo
Eusébio de Queiroz e os centenários do código comercial, do regulamento 737 e da supressão do tráfico africano . . . Rio de Janeiro, 1951. 56 pp.

Queiroz was the author of the Brazilian law abolishing the slave trade 1851.

3759 DEBIEN, Gabriel
Les colons de Saint-Domingue et la révolution. Essai sur le Club Massiac (août 1789–août 1792). Paris, 1952. 414 pp.

History of the resistance of colonial deputies in Paris to the abolitionist campaign of the Amis des Noirs.

3760 ORTIZ, Fernando
'La "leyenda negra" contra fray Bartolomé.' (Cuadernos Americanos, México, vol. 11, no. 5, 1952, pp. 146–84.)

Refutes the charge against Las Casas of having initiated the African slave trade to America; this began as early as 1501.

3761 HOWSE, Ernest Marshall
Saints in politics. The "Clapham sect" and the growth of freedom. [Toronto,] 1952. xv, 215 pp. bibl. pp. 191–208.

Account of the achievements of the Wilberforce group, including the abolition of the slave trade and slavery 1787–1833.

3762 MOTT, Lucretia Coffin
Slavery and "the woman question". Lucretia Mott's diary of her visit to Great Britain to attend the world's anti-slavery convention of 1840. Edited by Frederick B. Tolles. Haverford, Pa.; London, 1952. 86 pp. illus.

Describes the convention and abolitionists of the period.

3763 VIBÆK, Jens
'Dansk Vestindien 1755–1848.' *In*: BRØNDSTED, J. Vore gamle trope-

kolonier, vol. 2 (Copenhagen, 1953), pp. 161–350.

Includes a chapter on the abolition of the Danish slave trade.

3764 SOARES DE SOUZA, José Antônio
'Documentação para uma tese sôbre o tráfico de escravos.' (RIHGB, vol. 219, 1953, pp. 266–86.)

Critique of (3458).

3765 GREAT BRITAIN: Central Office of Information
Britain and the suppression of slavery. London, [1953]. 14 pp.

3766 MÁRQUEZ MIRANDA, Fernando
'El padre Las Casas y su "Historia de las Indias".' (RCHG, no. 122, 1953, pp. 5–63; no. 124, 1956, pp. 27–81.)

Includes a section on 'Las Casas y los negros'; Las Casas neither inspired nor approved of the African slave trade to Spanish America.

3767 REES, Alan Maxwell.
'Pitt and the achievement of abolition.' (JNH, vol. 39, 1954, pp. 167–84.)

On the parliamentary campaign for the abolition of the British slave trade 1787–1807.

3768 'FRIENDS and the slave trade. A Yorkshire election declaration, 1806.'
(Journal of the Friends' Historical Society, London, vol. 46, 1954, pp. 65–66.)

Evidence of Quaker support for abolition.

3769 COURSIER, Henri
'La lutte contre l'esclavage au XIXᵉ siècle.' (Revue Internationale de la Croix-Rouge, Genève, vol. 36, 1954, pp. 260–71.)

On the suppression of the African slave trade 1814–90. (Pt. 3 of a series of articles, 'Le problème de l'esclavage'.)

3770 DIKE, Kenneth Onwuka
Trade and politics in the Niger delta 1830–1885 . . . Oxford, 1956. vi, 250 pp.

Describes the transition from slave trade to palm oil trade and British antislavery policy.

3771 WEATHERFORD, Willis Dyke
American churches and the negro. An historical study from early slave days to the present. Boston, [1957]. 310 pp.

Mainly on the attitudes of the various Christian denominations to negro slavery.

3772 *McCLOY, Shelby Thomas
The humanitarian movement in eighteenth-century France. [Lexington, 1957.]
274 pp.

> Includes chapters on the antislavery
> movement.

3773 GREENIDGE, Charles Wilton Wood
Slavery. London, 1958. 235 pp.

> With chapters on the anti-slave trade
> movement 1673–1890 and the text
> of the Brussels act 1890 (3232–33).

3774 ALEXANDER, Stella
Quaker testimony against slavery and
racial discrimination. An anthology . . .
London, 1958. 63 pp.

> Extracts from Quaker writings, mainly
> American, from 1676 onwards.

3775 FURNAS, Joseph Chamberlain
The road to Harpers Ferry. New York,
1959. 477 pp. illus, bibl. pp. 437–57.

> Includes chapters on the African slave
> trade and the abolition movement,
> critical of the 'fanaticism' of the
> abolitionists.

3776 FRETZ, James Herbert
'The Germantown anti-slavery petition
of 1688.' (Mennonite Quarterly Review,
Goshen, Ind., vol. 33, 1959, pp. 42–59.)

> On the background and reaction
> to the first protest against slavery
> by German Quakers in Pennsylvania.
> See (3625).

3777 SHERRARD, Owen Aubrey
Freedom from fear. The slave and his
emancipation. London, 1959. 200 pp.

> Account of the slave trade to America
> and the British abolition movement
> to 1833.

3778 MAYNARD, Douglas H.
'The world's anti-slavery convention of
1840.' (MVHR, vol. 47, 1960, pp.
452–71.)

3779 APTHEKER, Herbert
And why not every man? The story
of the fight against negro slavery
assembled and edited by Herbert
Aptheker. Berlin, 1961. 278 pp.

> Anthology of writings by American
> abolitionists from the 17th to the
> 19th century.

3780 DUMOND, Dwight Lowell
Antislavery. The crusade for freedom
in America. Ann Arbor, [1961]. x,
422 pp. illus, maps.

> Includes chapters on the early anti-
> slavery movement in the United
> States.

3781 BOLLER, Paul F.
'Washington, the Quakers, and slavery.'
(JNH, vol. 46, 1961, pp. 83–88.)

> George Washington only changed
> his views on slavery as a result of
> the American revolution but remained
> a slave owner to his death.

3782 LANDRY, Harral E.
'Slavery and the slave trade in Atlantic
diplomacy, 1850–1861.' (JSH, vol. 27,
1961, pp. 184–207.)

> British diplomatic pressure served
> to unite the United States; relaxation
> of this pressure after 1858 had a
> direct relation to the outbreak of the
> civil war.

3783 *COLLISTER, Peter
The last days of slavery: England and
the East African slave trade, 1870–1900.
Nairobi, 1961. 150 pp. illus, maps.

3784 GAVIN, Robert James
'The Bartle Frere mission to Zanzibar,
1873.' (Historical Journal, London,
vol. 5, 1962, pp. 122–48.)

> On Britain's anti-slave trade policy
> in East Africa.

3785 DAVIS, David Brion
'The emergence of immediatism in
British and American antislavery
thought.' (MVHR, vol. 49, 1962, pp.
209–30.)

> Describes the 18th-century back-
> ground to abolitionism.

3786 FORTUNE, Armando
'Fray Bartolomé de las Casas y la
esclavitud del negro.' (Lotería, Panamá,
vol. 8, no. 91, 1963, pp. 72–76.)

> Absolves Las Casas from responsi-
> bility for suggesting the introduction
> of African slaves to America.

3787 LINDE, Jan Marinus van der
Heren, slaven, broeders. Momenten
uit de geschiedenis der slavernij. Nijkerk,
1963. 124 pp.

> Provides information on antislavery
> opinion from the 16th to the 19th
> century.

3788 *CALVERT, Monte Alan
'Abolition Society of Delaware, 1801–
1807.' (Delaware History, Wilmington,
1963, pp. 295–320.)

3789 *CRUZ MONCLOVA, Lidio
'La idea abolicionista: sus defensores.'

(Revista del Instituto de Cultura Puertorriqueña, San Juan, P.R., vol. 7, no. 22, 1964, pp. 32–34.)

3790 McCOLLEY, Robert
Slavery and Jeffersonian Virginia. Urbana, 1964. 227 pp. bibl. pp. 200–08.

The progress toward abolition was arrested in the 1780s by slave-holding interests.

3791 BOAHEN, Albert Adu
Britain, the Sahara, and the western Sudan 1788–1861. Oxford, 1964. ix, 268 pp. maps.

Ch. 6: 'The diplomatic attack on the trans-Saharan slave trade.'

3792 GISLER, Antoine
L'esclavage aux Antilles françaises (XVIIe-XIXe siècle). Contribution au problème de l'esclavage . . . Fribourg, 1965. xiv, 213 pp.

Describes attitudes to slavery in France.

3793 MATHEWS, Donald G.
Slavery and Methodism. A chapter in American morality 1780–1845. Princeton, N.J., 1965. xi, 329 pp. bibl. pp. 305–24.

Ch. 1: 'Compromise and conscience: the Church and slavery 1780–1816.' The leading Methodist abolitionist in this period was Bishop Francis Ashbury.

3794 NEWBURY, Colin Walter
British policy towards West Africa. Select documents 1786–1874. Oxford, 1965. xxviii, 656 pp. maps.

Includes a section on the suppression of the slave trade.

3795 *DURAM, J. C.
'A study of frustration: Britain, the USA, and the African slave trade, 1815–1870.' (Social Science, Winfield, Kan., vol. 40, 1965, pp. 220–25.)

3796 GOVEIA, Elsa Vesta
Slave society in the British Leeward Islands at the end of the eighteenth century. New Haven & London, 1965. ix, 370 pp. map.

The introduction contains an account of the parliamentary campaign to abolish the slave trade 1788–1807. (Ph.D. thesis, London, 1952.)

3797 CURTIN, Philip De Armond
The image of Africa. British ideas and action, 1780–1850. London, 1965. xvii, 526 pp. illus. maps.

Describes the theories behind British antislave trade policy in the 19th century.

3798 BETHELL, Leslie M.
'Britain, Portugal and the suppression of the Brazilian slave trade: the origins of Lord Palmerston's act of 1839.' (EHR, vol. 80, 1965, pp. 761–84.)

3799 DAVIS, David Brion
The problem of slavery in western culture. Ithaca, N.Y., 1966. xiv, 505 pp.

History of antislavery opinion to about 1770. (Reviewed in: JMH, vol. 40, 1968, pp. 279–82.)

3800 FLADELAND, Betty
'Abolitionist pressures on the Concert of Europe, 1814–1822.' (JMH, vol. 38, 1966, pp. 355–73.)

Wilberforce and Clarkson influenced British antislave trade policy at the congresses of Vienna, Aix-la Chapelle and Verona.

3801 VIOTTI DA COSTA, Emília
Da senzala à colônia. São Paulo, 1966. 497 pp. bibl. pp. 468–97. illus, map.

Includes chapters on the abolition of the Brazilian slave trade.

3802 *DAVIS, Robert Ralph
'James Buchanan and the suppression of the slave trade, 1858–1861.' (Pennsylvania History, Philadelphia, vol. 33, 1966, pp. 446–59.)

3803 SARAIVA, Antonio José
'Le père Antonio Vieira S.J. et la question de l'esclavage des noirs au XVIIe siecle.' (AESC, vol. 22, 1967, pp. 1289–1309.)

On Catholic views of slavery in the 16th and 17th century; Vieira, a missionary in Brazil, showed concern for the African slaves.

3804 ZILVERSMIT, Arthur
The first emancipation. The abolition of slavery in the North. Chicago, 1967. x, 262 pp.

History of the early campaigns against slavery and the slave trade in New England, 1688–1830.

3805 WOODS, John Aubin
'The correspondence of Benjamin Rush and Granville Sharp 1773–1809.' (Journal of American Studies, London, vol. 1, 1967, pp. 1–38.)

3806 LIPSCOMB, Patrick Cleburne
'William Pitt and the abolition question: a review of an historical controversy.'

(Proceedings of the Leeds Philosophical and Literary society, vol. 12, pt. 4, 1967, pp. 87–128.)

Account of the parliamentary campaign to abolish the slave trade 1787–1806, showing that Pitt failed because of strong opposition in the House of Lords.

3807 BEIGUELMAN, Paula
Formação politica do Brasil. São Paulo, 1967. 2 vol.

Vol. 1 includes the history of the abolition of the Brazilian slave trade.

3808 CORWIN, Arthur Francis
Spain and the abolition of slavery in Cuba, 1817–1886. Austin & London, [1967]. xviii, 373 pp. illus. bibl. pp. 315–29.

Ch. 1–7 on the slave trade and its abolition under pressure from Britain 1815–60.

3809 DUFFY, James
A question of slavery. Oxford, 1967. vi, 240 pp. maps.

History of British opposition to the Portuguese slave trade and labour contracting from Angola and Mozambique 1850–1920.

3810 MIERS, Suzanne
'The Brussels conference of 1889–1890: the place of the slave trade in the policies of Great Britain and Germany.' In: GIFFORD, P. and LOUIS, W. R. Britain and Germany in Africa (New Haven & London, 1967), pp. 83–118.

Describes the exploitation of the antislavery movement for imperial ends in Africa.

3811 DIAS TAVARES, Luís Henrique
'As soluções brasileiras na extinção do tráfico negreiro.' (Journal of Inter-American Studies, Coral Gables, Fla., vol. 9, 1967, pp. 367–82.)

On the abolition of the Brazilian slave trade 1815–54.

3812 GENOVESE, Eugene Dominick
'A Georgia slaveholder looks at Africa.' (GHQ, vol. 51, 1967, pp. 186–93.)

On the Southern controversy over reopening the slave trade in 1859.

3813 *STANGE, Douglas Charles
'Compassionate mother to her poor negro slaves: the Lutheran Church and negro slavery in early America.'

(Phylon, Atlanta, Ga., vol. 29, 1968, pp. 272–81.)

3814 *KATES, D. B.
'Abolition, deportation, integration: attitudes toward slavery in the early Republic.' (JNH, vol. 53, 1968, pp. 33–47.)

3815 MARSHALL, Peter
The anti-slave trade movement in Bristol. Bristol, 1968. 26 pp. illus.

Deals with the period 1783–1806.

3816 *La RÉVOLUTION française et l'abolition de l'esclavage. Paris, 1968. 12 vol.

Facsimile reprints of 89 tracts on the slave trade, slavery and their abolition published 1788–1801.

3817 REICH, Jerome
'The slave trade at the congress of Vienna—a study in English public opinion.' (JNH, vol. 53, 1968, pp. 129–43.)

Argues that abolition of the slave trade was motivated by humanitarian ideas, not solely by economic ones.

3818 LUNA, Luiz
O negro na luta contra a escravidão. Rio de Janeiro, 1968. 237 pp.

With chapters on the abolition of the Brazilian slave trade 1810–54.

3819 ASIEGBU, Johnson Uzoha Jonah
Slavery and the politics of liberation, 1787–1861. A study of liberated African emigration and British anti-slavery policy. London, 1969. xvi, 231 pp. bibl. pp. 215–24. illus.

On the relationship between British slave trade suppression and 'African emigration' to the West Indies 1840–60.

3820 BOLLINGER, Armin
Die Sklavenbefreiung in Brasilien . . . Zürich, 1969. 21 pp.

Ch. 2: 'Der Negerhandel.'

3821 BOLT, Christine
The anti-slavery movement and reconstruction. A study in Anglo-American co-operation 1833–77. London, 1969. 197 pp. bibl. pp. 171–83.

Ch. 1: 'The British anti-slavery movement, 1833–60.'

3822 HELLY, Dorothy O.
' "Informed" opinion on tropical Africa in Great Britain 1860–1890.' (African Affairs, London, vol. 68, 1969, pp. 195–217.)

Includes notes on H. Waller and the British and Foreign Anti-Slavery Society.

3823 COHEN, William
'Thomas Jefferson and the problem of slavery.' (Journal of American History, Bloomington, Ind., vol. 56, 1969, pp. 503–26.)

On the development of Jefferson's attitude, as a slave owner, to slavery 1774–1824.

3824 BITTERLI, Urs
Die Entdeckung des schwarzen Afrikaners. Versuch einer Geistesgeschichte der europäisch-afrikanischen Beziehungen an der Guineaküste im 17. und 18. Jahrhundert. Zürich & Freiburg i. Br., 1970. 247 pp. illus, maps. bibl. pp. 213–21.

Includes chapters on the antislavery controversy 1750–1807.

3825 *PORTER, Dale Herbert
The abolition of the slave trade in England, 1784–1807. [Hamden, Conn.,] 1970. xii, 162 pp. bibl. pp. 146–57.

3826 QUINNEY, Valerie
'Decisions on slavery, the slave-trade and civil rights for negroes in the early French revolution.' (JNH, vol. 55, 1970, pp. 117–30.)

Describes the lobbying on the slave trade in the National Assembly 1789–90.

3827 HANSEN, Thorkild
Slavernes øer . . . [Copenhagen,] 1970. 449 pp. illus, maps.

Ch. 7: 'De følsomme mænd'; on the background to the abolition of the Danish slave trade 1792–1802.

3828 DAVIS, David Brion
Was Thomas Jefferson an authentic enemy of slavery? . . . An inaugural lecture . . . Oxford, 1970. 29 pp.

3829 BETHELL, Leslie M.
The abolition of the Brazilian slave trade. Britain, Brazil and the slave trade question 1807–1869. Cambridge, 1970. xvi, 424 pp. maps. bibl. pp. 396–414.

Detailed history of British pressure for abolition; with an appendix: 'Estimates of slaves imported into Brazil, 1831–1855'.

3830 RICE, C. Duncan
' 'Humanity sold for sugar!' The British abolitionist response to free trade in slave-grown sugar.' (Historical Journal, London, vol. 13, 1970, pp. 402–18.)

Critique of Eric Williams' view of the abolitionists as free traders (1309); in the 1840s they opposed the removal of protective sugar duties. (Expanded version of paper in: 348.)

3831 BELLOT, Leland J.
'Evangelicals and the defense of slavery in Britain's old colonial empire.' (JSH, vol. 37, 1971, pp. 19–40.)

Religious Englishmen like James Habersham and William Knox, both connected with Georgia, actively defended slavery in the later 18th century.

3832 *ROBINSON, Donald Leonard
Slavery in the structure of American politics, 1765–1820. New York, [1971]. xii, 564 pp.

3833 RENAULT, François
Lavigerie, l'esclavage africain et l'Europe 1868–1892. Paris, 1971. 2 vol. maps. bibl. vol. 2, pp. 479–99.

Vol. 2: 'Campagne antiesclavagiste.'

W. HISTORY OF ABOLITION LITERATURE

3834 *LEFÈVRE-PONTALIS, Antonin
Rapport de M. Lefèvre-Pontalis . . . sur les mémoires envoyés au concours international institué par S. Ém. le cardinal Lavigerie, en faveur du meilleur ouvrage populaire propre à favoriser la cause de l'abolition de l'esclavage africain. Société Antiesclavagiste, Paris, 1893. 16 pp.

3835 GOODELL, Abner Cheney
'John Saffin and his slave Adam.' (Publications of the Colonial Society of Massachusetts, Boston, vol. 1, 1895, pp. 85–112; illus.)

Includes biographical information on Saffin and a fuller text of (1698) than reprinted in (3615), together with related material on the legal case between him and his slave Adam, 1694–1711.

3836 JAMESON, Russell Parsons
Montesquieu et l'esclavage. Étude sur les origines de l'opinion antiesclavagiste en France au XVIIIᵉ siècle. Paris, 1911. 371 pp.

On Montesquieu's antislavery views and their background.

3837 BERNBAUM, Ernest
'Mrs. Behn's Oroonoko.' In: ANNIVERSARY papers by colleagues and pupils of George Lyman Kittredge (Boston & London, 1913), pp. 419–33.

3838 BERNBAUM, Ernest
'Mrs. Behn's biography a fiction.' (PMLA, vol. 28. 1913, pp. 432–53.)

See (3852).

3839 ÉTIENNE, Servais
Les sources de "Bug-Jargal" . . . Bruxelles, 1923. 159 pp.

On antislavery fiction 1688–1820 as background to Victor Hugo's novel (4338).

3840 JOHNSON, Edwin D.
'Aphra Behn's "Oroonoko".' (JNH, vol. 10, 1925, pp. 334–42.)

Mrs Behn introduced a new genre with her novel about an African slave (4157).

3841 *COOPER, Anna Julia
L'attitude de la France à l'égard de l'esclavage pendant la Révolution. Paris, 1925. 172 pp.

3842 VIGNOLS, Léon
'Une version remaniée et inconnue du "Tamango" de Mérimée.' (Revue d'Histoire Littéraire de la France, Paris, vol. 34, 1927, pp. 207–27.)

Mérimée rewrote 'Tamango' (4345) as 'Un révolte sur un négrier' (4361) in 1837.

3843 VIGNOLS, Léon
'Les sources du "Tamango" de Mérimée et la littérature "négrière" à l'époque romantique.' (Mercure de France, Paris, vol. 200, 1927, pp. 542–57.)

On novels based on the slave trade 1829–59.

3844 SCUDDER, Harold H.
'Melville's Benito Cereno and Captain Delano's voyages.' (PMLA, vol. 43, 1928, pp. 502–32; illus, port.)

Shows Melville's source to be (735).

3845 TURNER, Lorenzo Dow
Anti-slavery sentiment in American literature prior to 1865. Washington, [1929]. viii, 188 pp. bibl. 153–82.

Ch. 1 deals with antislavery literature 1641–1808. See (1754). (Also published in: JNH, vol. 14, 1929, pp. 371–492.)

3846 *ANDREA, Raffaello d'
Le origini italiane dell'antischiavismo moderno. Appiano Bonafede e "le conquiste celebri". Tivoli, 1929. 15 pp.

On an Italian writer on natural law, 1763.

3847 LUCAS, E.
La littérature anti-esclavagiste au dix-neuvième siècle. Étude sur Madame Beecher Stowe et son influence en France. Paris, 1930. 281 pp.

The introduction deals with early antislavery literature.

3848 IRVINE, Dallas D.
'The Abbé Raynal and British humanitarianism.' (JNH, vol. 3, 1931, pp.
564–77.)

Raynal's 'Histoire philosophique'
(1753) influenced Clarkson, Romilly
and other abolitionists.

3849 FLETCHER, Frank Thomas Herbert
'Montesquieu's influence on anti-slavery
opinion in England.' (JNH, vol. 18
1933, pp. 414–26.)

Discusses the legal and philosophical
influence of the 'Esprit des lois' on
Sharp and others. See (1723).

3850 RICE, Howard Crosby
Le Cultivateur Américain. Étude sur
l'œuvre de Saint John de Crèvecœur.
Paris, 1933. 263 pp. illus.

Ch. 3: 'Crèvecœur, ami des noirs.'

3851 SEEBER, Edward Derbyshire
'Parny as an opponent of slavery.'
(Modern Language Notes, Baltimore,
vol. 49, 1934, pp. 360–66.)

On Évariste Parny and French anti-
slavery literature 1775–87.

3852 PLATT, Harrison Gray
'Astrea and Celadon: an untouched
portrait of Aphra Behn.' (PMLA,
vol. 49, 1934, pp. 544–59.)

Argues (against 3838) that Mrs Behn
did live in Surinam about 1660–63.

3853 WOODSON, Carter Godwin
'Some attitudes in English literature.'
(JNH, vol. 20, 1935, pp. 27–85.)

On the African in fiction, including
antislavery literature.

3854 SEEBER, Edward Derbyshire
'Anti-slavery opinion in the poems of
some early French followers of James
Thomson.' (Modern Language Notes,
Baltimore, vol. 50, 1935, pp. 427–34.)

On the abolitionist poetry in the
period 1769–1811.

3855 SEEBER, Edward Derbyshire
'Oroonoko in France in the XVIIIth
century.' (PMLA, vol. 51, 1936, pp.
953–59.)

Elaboration of (3839); 'Oroonoko',
one of the most read novels in
France after 1745, confronted the
French public with the question of
slavery.

3856 KAIN, Richard Morgan
'The problem of civilization in English
abolition literature, 1772–1808.' (Philo-

logical Quarterly, Iowa City, vol. 15,
1936, pp. 103–25.)

3857 COOK, Mercer
'Jean Jacques Rousseau and the negro.'
(JNH, vol. 21, 1936, pp. 294–303.)

Rousseau had an indirect influence
on the abolitionists.

3858 *CADBURY, Henry Joel
'Quaker bibliographical notes, II. Anti-
slavery writings.' (Bulletin of Friends
Historical Association, Philadelphia,
vol. 26, 1937, pp. 39–53.)

Essays on early American abolitionists.

3859 PRICE, Lawrence Marsden
Inkle and Yarico album. Selected and
arranged by Lawrence Marsden Price.
Berkeley, 1937. 171 pp.

Study of an antislavery theme in
European literature 1734–1830. See
(4159).

3860 JONES, Joseph
'The "distress'd" negro in English
magazine verse.' (Studies in English,
Austin, Texas, no. 17, 1937, pp. 88–
106.)

On the theme of the 'injur'd African'
in English verse 1749–1832.

3861 SEEBER, Edward Derbyshire
Anti-slavery opinion in France during
the second half of the eighteenth
century. Baltimore, 1937. 238 pp. bibl.
pp. 201–29.

History of French antislavery literature 1748–1802.

3862 SHELLEY, Philip Allison
'Crèvecoeur's contribution to Herder's
"Neger-Idyllen".' (Journal of English
and German Philology, Urbana, Ill.,
vol. 37, 1938, pp. 48–69.)

On antislavery themes in (4302).

3863 HARTLEY, Lodwick Charles
William Cowper, humanitarian. Chapel
Hill, 1938. ix, 277 pp.

Ch. 3: 'Pity for poor Africans: the
abolitionist poetry.'

3864 SYPHER, Wylie
'Hutcheson and the "classical" theory
of slavery.' (JNH, vol. 24, 1939, pp.
263–80.)

Describes theories of slavery from
Aristotle to Wesley; Hutcheson's
'Moral philosophy' (1728) was a
turning point of 'romantic' humanitarian ethics.

3865 SYPHER, Wylie
'The West-Indian as a "character" in the eighteenth century.' (Studies in Philology, Chapel Hill, N.C., vol. 36, 1939, pp. 503–20.)

3866 *CADBURY, Henry Joel
'Another early Quaker anti-slavery document.' (JNH, vol. 27, 1942, pp. 211–12.)

Antislavery letter from Philadelphia, 1698.

3867 SYPHER, Wylie
'A note on the realism of Mrs. Behn's Oroonoko.' (Modern Language Quarterly, Seattle, vol. 3, 1942, pp. 401–05.)

3868 SYPHER, Wylie
Guinea's captive kings: British antislavery literature of the XVIIIth century. Chapel Hill, N.C., 1942. x, 340 pp.

Conservative account of English literature on African themes, 1688–1807.

3869 DYKES, Eva Beatrice
The negro in English romantic thought, or a study of sympathy for the oppressed. Washington, 1942. 197 pp. bibl. pp. 157–66.

Deals largely with abolitionist literature.

3870 *WILLIAMS, Stanley Thomas
' "Follow your leader": Melville's Benito Cereno.' (Virginia Quarterly Review, Charlottesville, vol. 23, 1947, pp. 61–76.)

3871 *FELTENSTEIN, Rosalie
'Melville's Benito Cerano.' (AL, vol. 19, 1947, pp. 245–55.)

3872 SCHIFFMAN, Joseph
'Critical problems in Benito Cereno.' (Modern Language Quarterly, Seattle, vol. 11, 1950, pp. 317–24.)

3873 JADOT, Joseph Marie and COPPENS, Paul
'Le baron Édouard Descamps, écrivain antiesclavagiste et ministre d'état de l'É.I.C.' (Institut Royal Colonial Belge, Bulletin des séances, Bruxelles, vol. 25, no. 2, 1954, pp. 495–541; port.)

Includes a section on the antislavery literary competition of 1893.

3874 STEIN, William Bysshe
'The moral axis of "Benito Cereno".' (Accent, Urbana, Ill., vol. 15, 1955, pp. 221–33.)

3875 *CONNOLLY, Thomas Edmund
'A note on name symbolism in Benito Cereno.' (AL, vol. 25, 1956, pp. 489–90.)

3876 KAPLAN, Sidney
'Herman Melville and the American national sin: the meaning of Benito Cereno.' (JNH, vol. 41, 1956, pp. 311–38; vol. 42, 1957, pp. 11–37.)

3877 KLUTH, Käte
'Die Negerfrage in der englischen Literatur des 18. Jahrhunderts.' (Zeitschrift für Anglistik und Amerikanistik, Berlin, vol. 5, 1957, pp. 68–89.)

On English antislavery literature 1688–1807.

3878 HORCH, Hans Jürgen
Antônio de Castro Alves (1847–1871). Seine Sklavendichtung und ihre Beziehungen zur Abolition in Brasilien. Hamburg, 1958. 384 pp. illus. bibl. pp. 239–71.

See (4407).

3879 WAALDIJK, Eugenius Theodorus
Die Rolle der niederländischen Publizistik bei der Meinungsbildung hinsichtlich der Aufhebung der Sklaverei in den westindischen Kolonien . . . Münster/Westf., [1959]. iii, 229 pp.

Deals with criticism of slavery in Dutch literature from Hugo Grotius onward.

3880 RAMSARAN, John Ansuman
' "Oroonoko": a study of the factual elements.' (Notes and Queries, London, vol. 205, 1960, pp. 142–45.)

3881 *FOGLE, Richard Harter
'Benito Cereno.' In his: Melville's shorter tales (Norman, Okla., 1960), pp. 116–47.

3882 CASTELLANO, Juan Rodríguez
'El negro esclavo en el entremés del siglo de oro.' (Hispania, Storrs, Conn., vol. 44, 1961, pp. 55–65.)

On African slaves described in Spanish plays of the 16th and 17th century.

3883 DEBBASCH, Yvan
'Poésie et traite. L'opinion française sur le commerce négrier au debut du XIXᵉ siècle.' (RFHO, vol. 48, 1961, pp. 311–52.)

On French abolitionist literature 1814–23.

3884 FRANKLIN, Howard Bruce
' "Apparent symbol of despotic com-

mand"; Melville's Benito Cereno.'
(NEQ, vol. 34, 1961, pp. 462–77.)

3885 McCULLOUGH, Norman Verrle
The negro in English literature. A critical introduction. Ilfracombe, [1962]. 176 pp.

Includes a section on antislavery literature.

3886 SHEFFEY, Ruthe T.
'Some evidence for a new source of Aphra Behn's Oroonoko.' (Studies in Philology, Chapel Hill, N.C., vol. 59, 1962, pp. 52–63.)

Suggests influence on Mrs Behn from Tryon (1695).

3887 JORDAN, Winthrop Donaldson
'An antislavery proslavery document?' (JNH, vol. 47, 1962, pp. 54–56.)

On a letter in a Philadelphia newspaper 1773 quoting a bogus biblical passage to prove the inferiority of Africans.

3888 BERNSTEIN, John Albert
'Benito Cereno and the Spanish Inquisition.' (Nineteenth-Century Fiction, Berkeley, vol. 16, 1962, pp. 345–50.)

3889 *PUTZEL, Max
'The source and symbols of Melville's "Benito Cereno".' (AL, vol. 34, 1962, pp. 191–206.)

3890 CANTOR, Milton
'The image of the negro in colonial literature.' (NEQ, vol. 36, 1963, pp. 452–77.)

Includes notes on American abolitionist literature to about 1775.

3891 TOWNER, Lawrence W.
'The Sewall-Saffin dialogue on slavery.' (WMQ, ser. 3, vol. 21, 1963, pp. 40–52.)

3892 WALDMAN, Loren K.
'An unnoticed aspect of Archibald Dalzel's The history of Dahomey.' (JAH, vol. 6, 1965, pp. 185–92.)

Dalzel's work (170) was polemical, written to counter parliamentary action against the slave trade.

3893 CONSTANTINE, James Robert
'The ignoble savage, an eighteenth-century literary stereotype.' (Phylon, Atlanta, Ga., vol. 27, no. 1, 1966, pp. 171–79.)

The type was used in defence of slavery and the slave trade throughout the century.

3894 GENOVESE, Eugene Dominick
'A Georgia slaveholder looks at Africa.' (GHQ, vol. 51, 1967, pp. 186–93.)

On a controversy over reopening the African slave trade, 1859.

3895 JORDAN, Winthrop Donaldson
White over black. American attitudes toward the negro, 1550–1812. Chapel Hill, [N.C., 1968]. xx, 651 pp. bibl. pp. 610–14.

On the background to the 18th-century antislavery movement.

3896 *VANDERHAAR, M. M.
'Re-examination of Benito Cereno.' (AL, vol. 40, 1968, pp. 179–91.)

On the short story by Herman Melville (4382).

3897 MOORE, Jack B.
'Images of the negro in early American short fiction.' (Mississippi Quarterly, State College, Miss., Winter 1969, pp. 47–57.)

On 'slave-question literature' of the 1790s.

3898 SIMPSON, Eleanor E.
'Melville and the negro: from Typee to "Benito Cereno".' (AL, vol. 41, 1969, pp. 19–38.)

3899 GILMAN, Sander L.
'The image of slavery in two eighteenth century German dramas.' (Germanic Review, New York, vol. 45, no. 1, 1970, pp. 26–40.)

On 'Die Mohrinn zu Hamburg', 1775, by E. L. M. Rathlef and the anonymous comedy 'Die Negersklaven', 1779.

3900 MOSER, Arnulf
'Las Casas und die französische Revolution von 1789.' (Jahrbuch für Geschichte von Staat, Wirtschaft und Gesellschaft Lateinamerikas, Köln, vol. 7, 1970, pp. 225–38.)

Grégoire (3989) presented Las Casas as an early abolitionist, thus starting a debate that continued into the 19th century.

3901 YELLIN, Jean Fagan
'Black masters: Melville's Benito Cereno.' (American Quarterly, Philadelphia, vol. 22, 1970, pp. 678–89.)

X. LEGAL HISTORY

3902 GAYOT DE PITAVAL, François
'Liberté réclamée par un negre contre son maître, qui l'a amené en France.' *In his*: Causes célebres et intéresssantes, vol. 15 (Amsterdam, Liège, 1775), pp. 1–112.

> Account of the case of the slave Jean Boucaux, who successfully claimed his freedom at La Rochelle in 1738.

3903 ANTUNEZ Y ACEVEDO, Rafael
Memorias históricas sobre la legislacion, y gobierno del comercio de los Españoles con sus colonias en las Indias Occidentales. Sancha, Madrid, 1797. xv, 330, cv pp.

> Includes a section on the 'asientos' and laws regulating the Spanish slave trade 1530–1792.

3904 'NOTICE sur l'état de la législation relative à traite et à l'esclavage des nègres, dans les deux Amériques.' (Signed: T.) (RE, vol. 17, 1823, pp. 228–32.)

> Translated from the sixth report of the African Institution, London (3066).

3905 WEST INDIA COMMITTEE
British colonial slavery. [London, 1833.] 16 pp.

> List of British charters, acts and other legal documents on the slave trade 1662–1775.

3906 SPOONER, Lysander
The unconstitutionality of slavery. Bela Marsh, Boston, 1845. 156 pp.

> Discusses British, colonial and United States laws on the slave trade 1670–1787.

3907 'The BRAZILIAN slave traders.' (Signed: A.) (Law Magazine, London, vol. 35, 1846, pp. 251–63.)

> Analysis of the slave trade treaties 1815–26 and account of a trial for illegal slaving in 1845.

3908 'SLAVES in Britain.' (CJ, n.s., vol. 18, 1852, pp. 70–72.)

> On G. Sharp and the slavery cases of 1767–78.

3909 WASHBURN, Emory
'The extinction of slavery in Massachusetts . . .' (Collections of the Massachusetts Historical Society, Boston, ser. 4, vol. 4, 1858, pp. 333–46.)

> Account of cases 1769 and 1781 (Walker v. Jennison) which showed slavery to be illegal in Massachusetts.

3910 'U.S. laws on the subject of the slave trade.' (AR, vol. 34, 1858, pp. 240–43.)

> Explains the acts relating to the slave trade 1794–1818.

3911 *TOLEDANO, Eustaquio
Historia de los tratados, convenios y declaraciones de comercio entre España y las potencias. Madrid, 1858. 288 pp.

> Includes a chapter on the Anglo-Spanish slave trade conventions.

3912 WAYNE, James Moore
'Slave trade. Charge of Mr. Justice Wayne, of the U.S. Supreme Court, delivered on the 14th day of November, 1859, to the grand jury of the Sixth Circuit Court of the United States, for the Southern District of Georgia.' (AR, vol. 36, 1860, pp. 97–114.)

> Account of antislave trade legislation 1794–1820, for the jury in the 'Wanderer' case. (Reprinted in; GHQ, vol. 2, 1918, pp. 87–113.)

3913 'Le CAUSE influenti nella introduzione della tratta.' (CC, ser. 6, vol. 5, 1866, pp. 153–71.)

> By V. Steccanella. On the background in secular and ecclesiastical law to the beginning of the Iberian slave trade.

3914 *GAREIS, Karl von
Das heutige Völkerrecht und der Menschenhandel. Eine völkerrechtliche Abhandlung, zugleich Ausgabe des deutschen Textes der Verträge von 20. Dezember 1841 und 29. März 1879. Berlin, 1879. 54 pp.

> See (3206).

3915 GAREIS, Karl von
Der Sklavenhandel, das Völkerrecht und das deutsche Recht. Berlin, 1884. 40 pp.

On German laws against the slave trade and contract labour during the 19th century.

3916 MARTITZ, Ferdinand von
'Das internationale System zur Unterdrückung des afrikanischen Sklavenhandels in seinem heutigen Bestande.' (Archiv für Öffentliches Recht, Freiburg i.B., vol. 1, 1886, pp. 3–107.)

3917 FLEISCHMANN, Adolf
'Sclavenhandel und Strafgesetzgebung.' (Gegenwart, Berlin, vol. 34, 1888, pp. 401–04.)

Discusses the state of German law in relation to the slave trade.

3918 FULD, Ludwig
'Die Bestrafung des Sclavenhandels.' (Gerichtssaal, Stuttgart, vol. 42, 1889, pp. 35–42.)

On the German law of 1889 against the slave trade in East Africa.

3919 ROLIN-JAEQUEMYNS, Gustave
'Note sur la conférence antiesclavagiste de Bruxelles.' (RDILC, vol. 21, 1889, pp. 602–06.)

3920 NYS, Ernest
'L'esclavage noir devant les jurisconsultes et les cours de justice.' (RDILC, vol. 22, 1890, pp. 57–69, 138–51.)

History of European law relating to slavery from 1100 to 1800. (Reprinted separately, Bruxelles, 1890; 33 pp.)

3921 BARCLAY, Thomas
'Le droit de visite, le trafic des esclaves et la conférence anti-esclavagiste de Bruxelles.' (RDILC, vol. 22, 1890, pp. 316–35, 454–72.)

3922 'La CONFÉRENCE de Bruxelles 16 novembre 1889–2 juillet 1890.' (Correspondant, Paris, vol. 160, 1890, pp. 205–43.)

3923 BÉTHUNE, Léon, baron
'L'œuvre de la conférence de Bruxelles.' (MA, vol. 2, 1890, pp. 246–53, 393–402, 425–32.)

Analysis of the general act of 2 July 1890 for the suppression of the slave trade (3232). (Text of the act: pp. 229–46.)

3924 'La CONFÉRENCE anti-esclavagiste de Bruxelles.' (Afrique Explorée et Civili-

sée, Genève, vol. 11, 1890, pp. 253–61, 285–91, 315–23.)

On the antislavery movement since the Congress of Vienna.

3925 *BANNING, Émile
'La conférence de Bruxelles, son origine et ses actes.' (Bulletins de l'Académie Royale des Sciences, des Lettres et des Beaux-Arts, Bruxelles, ser. 3, vol. 20, 1890, pp. 375–97.)

Reprinted separately: Bruxelles, 1890; 26 pp.

3926 AVRIL, Adolphe, baron d'
'La traite des noirs et les conventions internationales.' (Revue d'Histoire Diplomatique, Paris, vol. 4, 1890, pp. 509–33.)

On legal measures against the slave trade 1814–1889.

3927 ENGELHARDT, Édouard Philippe
'La conférence de Bruxelles de 1890 et la traite maritime . . .' (RDILC, vol. 22, 1890, pp. 603–18.)

3928 AVRIL, Adolphe, baron d'
'La conférence anti-esclavagiste de Bruxelles.' (Revue d'Histoire Diplomatique, Paris, vol. 5, 1891, pp. 66–82, 176–91.)

3929 DESCAMPS, Édouard Eugène François, baron
'La législation pénale contre la traite des esclaves. Les obligations résultant, pour les puissances, de l'acte général de la conférence de Bruxelles.' (MA, vol. 3, 1891, pp. 293–303.)

3930 DESJARDINS, Arthur
'La traite maritime. Le droit de visite et la conférence de Bruxelles.' (MA, vol. 3, 1891, pp. 366–87.)

Address to the Cour de Cassation de France on the history of the antislavery movement and the right of search.

3931 REGELSPERGER, Gustave
'Conférence de Bruxelles pour l'abolition de la traite.' (RE, 1891, pp. 467–70; map.)

Explanation of the Brussels general act of 1890 (3232).

3932 ROLIN-JAEQUEMYNS, Gustave
'Quelques mots encore sur l'acte général de la conférence de Bruxelles et la répression de la traite.' (RDILC, vol. 23, 1891, pp. 560–76.)

3933 LENTNER, Ferdinand
Der schwarze Kodex (Code noir). Der

afrikanische Sklavenhandel und die Brüsseler General-Akte vom 2. Juli 1890 in ihren einheitlichen Massnahmen zur Bekämpfung der verbrecherischen Gewerbsmässigkeit . . . Innsbruck, 1891. 140, lvi pp. map.

3934 **DU BOIS, William Edward Burghardt**
'The enforcement of the slave-trade laws.' *In*: Annual report of the American Historical Association, 1891 (Washington, 1892), pp. 163–74.

Summary of M.A. thesis, Harvard, 1892. See (3648).

3935 **ENGELHARDT, Édouard Philippe**
'Rapport de M. Ed. Engelhardt sur les décisions de la conférence de Bruxelles de 1890, relatives à la traite maritime.' (Annuaire de l'Institut de Droit International, Paris, vol. 11, 1892, pp. 241–62.)

Explains the anti-slave trade act of 1890 (3232).

3936 **LE GHAIT, Alfred**
'The anti-slavery conference.' (NAR, vol. 154, 1892, pp. 287–96.)

On the Brussels conference 1889–90.

3937 **TREE, Lambert**
'The treaty of Brussels and our duty.' (Forum, New York, vol. 12, 1892, pp. 614–20.)

Describes the background to and results of the Brussels conference.

3938 'Die STAATLICHE Thätigkeit bei der Bekämpfung des Sclavenhandels.' (ÖMO, vol. 19, 1893, pp. 99–102.)

Report on action taken by various governments to implement the decisions of the Brussels conference.

3939 *****VISSER, H.**
De Brusselsche anti-slaverny conferentie 1889–1890. Leiden, 1893.

3940 *****LÉVY, Henri**
La traite des noirs et les puissances . . . Nancy, 1894. 195 pp.

Doctoral thesis.

3941 **FULD, Ludwig**
'Das Gesetz über die Bestrafung des Sklavenhandels.' (Archiv für Öffentliches Recht, Freiburg i.B., vol. 11, 1896, pp. 537–51.)

On the German anti-slave trade law of 1895.

3942 **SCHERLING, Emil**
Die Bekämpfung von Sklavenraub und Sklavenhandel seit Anfang dieses Jahrhunderts. Breslau, 1897. 83 pp.

3943 *****JUNG, Albert**
Die Bestrafung des Sklavenraubs und Sklavenhandels, systematische Darstellung des Reichsgesetzes vom 28. Juli 1895. Inaugural-Dissertation . . . Konstanz, 1897. 64 pp.

3944 **MONTARDY, Henry de**
La traite et le droit international . . . Paris, 1899. 203 pp.

Thesis on the slave trade and its suppression in international law.

3945 *****ZEYS, Ernst**
'Esclavage et guerre sainte. Consultation adressée aux gens du Touat par un érudit nègre, cadi de Timboctou au XVIIe siècle.' (Bulletin de la Réunion d'Études Algériennes, Paris, vol. 2, 1900, pp. 166–89.)

In 1615 the people of Tuat asked the kadi of Timbuktu, Ahmad Baba, if slavery was legitimate; his reply explained the permissibility in Muslim law of slave raids on pagans (Kitab al-kashf wa-'l-bayan li-asnaf majlub al-Sudan).

3946 *****BARTLETT, Ellen Strong**
'The Amistad captives.' (NEM, n.s., vol. 22, 1900, pp. 72–89.)

See (1481).

3947 **JOZON, Louis**
L'État indépendant du Congo . . . Paris, 1900. vii, 297 pp.

Pt. 4, ch. 1: 'La traite des nègres.– La conférence anti-esclavagiste de Bruxelles.'

3948 **KAYSEL, Paul**
Die Gesetzgebung der Kulturstaaten zur Unterdrückung des afrikanischen Sklavenhandels. Breslau, 1905. 108, 6 pp.

On the implementation of the Brussels act by Germany and other states.

3949 *****QUÉNEUIL, Henry**
De la traite des noirs et de l'esclavage. La conférence de Bruxelles et ses résultats . . . Paris, 1907. 292 pp.

3950 *****LIST, Waldemar**
Die Beteiligung Deutschlands an der Bekämpfung des Sklavenhandels und Sklavenraubes. Eine völkerrechtliche Studie . . . Würzburg, 1907. viii, 75 pp.

3951 **QUÉNEUIL, Henry**
'Conférence anti-esclavagiste de Bruxelles. Acte général du 2 juillet 1890.— Application et résultats.' (Revue Gén-

érale de Droit International Public, Paris, vol. 15, 1908, pp. 131–46.)

States that the slave trade has not yet been suppressed in parts of the Sudan.

3952 WINANDY, Ar.
'La répression internationale de la traite et de l'esclavage.' (Bulletin de la Société Belge d'Études Coloniales, Bruxelles, vol. 16, 1909, pp. 433–81.)

Account of measures taken against the slave trade since the Brussels conference 1890.

3953 RIDDELL, William Renwick
'Le code noir.' (JNH, vol. 10, 1925, pp. 321–29.)

On the laws and charters governing the French and English slave trade 1685–1770. See (922).

3954 SANDIFORD, Roberto
'La schiavitù e la tratta degli schiavi.' (Rivista Marittima, Roma, vol. 59, 1926, pp. 435–51; map.)

Account of anti-slave trade laws 1792–1890 in relation to the slavery issue in the League of Nations. (Published separately: Roma, 1926; 19 pp.)

3955 RIDDELL, William Renwick
'Encouragement of the slave-trade.' (JNH, vol. 12, 1927, pp. 22–32.)

On British legislation 1710–62 dealing with slave imports to the American and West Indian colonies.

3956 *ROSENBERG, Paul
Das Verbot des Negerhandels im Völkerrecht. Augsburg, 1927. 39 pp.

Thesis, Würzburg, 1927.

3957 RIDDELL, William Renwick
'Pre-revolutionary Pennsylvania and the slave trade.' (PMHB, vol. 52, 1928, pp. 1–28.)

On slave trade legislation 1700–1773.

3958 *RIDDELL, William Renwick
'Notable trial for slave-trading.' (Journal of the American Institute of Criminal Law, Chicago, vol. 20, 1930, pp. 572–77.)

3959 RIDDELL, William Renwick
'Observations on slavery and privateering.' (JNH, vol. 15, 1930, pp. 337–71.)

Includes sections on the Sommersett case (1759), on the capture of slave ships by privateers, and on the Zulueta case (3493).

3960 McCENDON, R. Earl
'The Amistad claims: inconsistencies of policy.' (Political Science Quarterly, New York, vol. 48, 1933, pp. 386–412.)

On diplomatic exchanges between the United States and Spain 1839–61 arising from the 'Amistad' case (1481).

3961 FIDDES, Edward
'Lord Mansfield and the Sommersett case.' (Law Quarterly Review, London, vol. 50, pp. 499–511.)

On the legal background to the famous case in 1772. See (1759).

3962 DODD, Dorothy
'The schooner Emperor. An incident of the illegal slave trade in Florida.' (FHQ, vol. 13, 1935, pp. 117–28.)

On a case, heard in the Florida supreme court, of a ship seized in May 1837 bringing slaves from Cuba.

3963 FISHER, Ruth Anna
'Granville Sharp and Lord Mansfield.' (JNH, vol. 28, 1943, pp. 381–89.)

On the Sommersett case of 1772. See (1759).

3964 VAN ALSTYNE, Richard Warner
'The African slave trade and the right of search.' In his: American diplomacy in action (Stanford, Cal., 1944), pp. 438–48.

On U.S.-British diplomacy 1807–61.

3965 FISCHER, Hugo
'The suppression of slavery in international law.' (International Law Quarterly, London, vol. 3, 1950, pp. 28–51, 503–22.)

Deals largely with the African slave trade in the 19th century.

3966 WILSON, Howard Hazen
'Some principal aspects of British efforts to crush the African slave trade, 1807–1929.' (AJIL, vol. 44, 1950, pp. 505–26.)

On the legal history of the suppression of the slave trade.

3967 DURENEVSKY, V. N. and FABRIKOV, E. M.
'O deistvuyushchikh konventsiyakh i dogovorakh po bor'be s rabstvom i rabotorgovlei.' (Vestnik Moskovskogo Universiteta, 1950, no. 11, pp. 141–51.)

Brief survey of international conventions against the slave trade 1814–1926.

3968 UNITED NATIONS: Economic and Social Council (*Ad Hoc Committee on Slavery*)
The suppression of slavery. (Memorandum submitted by the Secretary-General.) New York, 1951. iv, 83 pp.

Account of the international abolition treaties from 1814 onwards; with the text of the Brussels act of 1890 (3232).

3969 O'BRIEN, William
'Did the Jennison case outlaw slavery in Massachusetts?' (WMQ, ser. 3, vol. 17, 1960, pp. 219–41.)

Detailed account of a legal case 1781–83 involving African slaves; its significance has been exaggerated. See (3980).

3970 McMANUS, Edgar J.
'Antislavery legislation in New York.' (JNH, vol. 46, 1961, pp. 207–16.)

Deals mainly with the period 1771–1807.

3971 CUSHING, John D.
'The Cushing court and the abolition of slavery in Massachusetts: more on the "Quock Walker case".' (American Journal of Legal History, Philadelphia, vol. 5, 1961, pp. 118–44.)

The Walker case in 1783 did not end slavery in Massachusetts but it was a move in that direction. See (3980).

3972 SAMSON, Ph. A.
'Edward Shenley, lid van het Gemengd Geregtshof tot wering van de Slavenhandel.' (Nieuwe West-Indische Gids, 's-Gravenhage, vol. 41, 1961, pp. 52–55.)

Biographical notes on a British member of the mixed court of commission in Surinam 1838–43.

3973 HOLLANDER, Barnett
Slavery in America: its legal history. London, 1962. xx, 212 pp.

Compilation on slavery and the slave trade in British and U.S. law.

3974 *KUTLER, Stanley I.
'Pennsylvania courts, the abolition act, and negro rights.' (Pennsylvania History, Philadelphia, vol. 30, 1963, pp. 14–27.)

3975 HOWARD, Warren Starkie
American slavers and the federal law 1837–1862. Berkeley & Los Angeles, 1963. xii, 336 pp. bibl. pp. 315–24.

On the illegal slave trade and its

suppression by the U.S. government. (Based on: 4472.)

3976 BETHELL, Leslie M.
'The mixed commissions for the suppression of the transatlantic slave trade in the nineteenth century.' (JAH, vol. 7, 1966, pp. 79–93.)

Covers the period 1819–71.

3977 NADELHAFT, Jerome
'The Somersett case and slavery: myth, reality, and repercussions.' (JNH, vol. 51, 1966, pp. 193–208.)

The case has been misunderstood; it did not abolish slavery, which continued to exist in England after 1772. See (1759).

3978 STAFFORD, Frances J.
'Illegal importations: enforcement of the slave trade laws along the Florida coast, 1810–1828.' (FHQ, vol. 46, 1967, pp. 124–33.)

Florida became a base for slave smuggling while still under Spanish rule.

3979 SPECTOR, Robert Melvyn
'Quock Walker cases (1781–83)—slavery, abolition, and negro citizenship in early Massachusetts.' (JNH, vol. 53, 1968, pp. 12–32.)

3980 ZILVERSMIT, Arthur
'Quok Walker, Mumbet, and the abolition of slavery in Massachusetts.' (WMQ, ser. 3, vol. 25, 1968, pp. 614–24.)

The Walker-Jennison test case 1781–83 decided the unconstitutionality of slavery in Massachusetts.

3981 WEISBORD, Robert
'The case of the slave ship 'Zong' 1783.' (HT, vol. 19, 1969, pp. 561–67; illus.)

Account of the trials in 1783. See (3998).

3982 WILSON, Nan
'Legal attitudes to slavery in eighteenth-century Britain; English myth; Scottish social realism and their wider comparative context.' (Race, London, vol. 11, 1970, pp. 463–75.)

On the Sommersett and Wedderburn cases; the contribution of Scottish law to the repudiation of slavery in Britain has been underestimated. See (1759, 1787).

3983 MAC EACHEREN, Elaine
'Emancipation of slavery in Massa-

chusetts: a re-examination 1770–1790.'
(JNH, vol. 55, 1970, pp. 289–306.)

Study of manumissions in wills of
the period shows that slavery 'with-
ered away' after 1780.

3984   GREAT BRITAIN: Foreign Office
Law officers' opinions to the Foreign
Office 1793–1864. A reproduction of
the manuscript series with index and
commentaries prepared and edited
by Clive Parry. vol. 74–76. Farnbor-
ough, Hants., 1970.

The law officers' reports on slave
trade questions 1846–60.

Y. BIOGRAPHIES OF ABOLITIONISTS

3985a *FLEURIAU, Bertrand Gabriel
La vie du vénérable père Pierre Claver, de la Compagnie de Jésus, apôtre de Carthagene et des Indes occidentales . . . Bordelet, Paris, 1761. xxiv, 503 pp.

Translated as:

3985b The life of the venerable father Claver, S.J. apostle of the West Indies . . . Thomas Richardson & Son, London, 1849. xxiv, 421 pp.

Biography of St. Peter Claver, a 17th century Spanish missionary at Cartagena (Colombia), who dedicated himself to converting African slaves.

3986 'CURSORY remarks on the character of Anthony Benezett.—Read in the Franklinian Society, March 1791.' (AM, vol. 9, 1791, pp. 192–94.)

3987 RUSH, Benjamin
Essays, literary, moral and philosophical. Thomas & Samuel F. Bradford, Philadelphia, 1798. 378 pp.

Contains 'Biographical anecdotes of Anthony Benezet' and 'Biographical anecdotes of Benjamin Lay'.

3988a WILLIAMS, Helen Maria
'Lettre de la citoyenne Hélène-Maria Williams, au C. J.-B. Say, sur la mort du philantrope Wadstrom.' (Décade Philosophique, Littéraire et Politique, Paris, an VII [1799], pt. 3, pp. 229–35.)

Translated as:

3988b 'Memoirs of the life of Charles Berns Wadstrom.' (Monthly Magazine, London, vol. 7, 1799, pt. 1, pp. 462–65.)

Biographical notes on C. B. Wadström. (English version also in: AnR 1799, vol. 41, 1801, pp. 322–26.)

3989 GRÉGOIRE, Henri Baptiste
Apologie de Barthélemy de Las-Casas, évêque de Chiappa . . . Baudouin, [Paris, 1802]. 31 pp.

Las Casas was not responsible for the African slave trade to America; negro slaves were there before he arrived. (A letter written 1806 by the Mexican Dominican S.T. de Mier, supporting Grégoire, is printed in: Obras de Las Casas, Paris, 1822, vol. 2, pp. 403–37.)

3990 *EDMUNDS, Lucy
A short sketch of the life of our dear friend John Horn: with some of his expressions towards his close . . . Also, considerations on the African slave trade and the use of West India produce. First published by him in his last illness. G. Cooke, London, 1806. 35 pp.

See (2243).

3991 CECIL, Richard
Memoirs of the Rev. John Newton, late rector of the united parishes of St. Mary Woolnoth, and St. Mary Woolchurch Haw, Lombard Street; with general remarks on his life, connexions, and character. J. Hatchard, London, 1808. vii, 322 pp.

3992 'NOTICES respecting the late Mr. Granville Sharp.' (Philanthropist, London, vol. 3, 1813, pp. 383–96.)

3993 'MEMOIR of William Wilberforce, Esq., M.P.' (EMLR, vol. 66, 1814, pp. 287–88; port.)

3994 VAUX, Roberts
Memoirs of the lives of Benjamin Lay and Ralph Sandiford; two of the earliest public advocates for the emancipation of the enslaved Africans . . . Solomon W. Conrad, Philadelphia, 1815. 73 pp.

3995 'MEMOIR of Granville Sharp, Esq.' (Signed: H. G. W.) (EMLR, vol. 70, 1816, pp. 483–88; port.)

3996 VAUX, Roberts
Memoirs of the life of Anthony Benezet. James P. Parke, Philadelphia, 1817. 136 pp.

See (4039).

3997 TOOKE, William
'Memoir of the late Granville Sharp, Esq.' (GM, vol. 88, 1818, pp. 489–92; port.)

3998 HOARE, Prince
Memoirs of Granville Sharp, Esq. composed from his own manuscripts,

and other authentic documents . . .
Henry Colburn & Co., London, 1820.
xxxii, 524, xxxiii pp. port.

Biography and history of the abolition movement; the appendix includes Sharp's report of 1783 on
the case of the slave ship 'Zong'
(791, 3981) and other documents.
(Reviewed in: BR, vol. 16, 1820, pp.
1–36; AR, vol. 2, 1826, pp. 5–8, 33–
40, 65–71, 101–09, 133–42, 165–72,
197–211, 229–39.)

3999 FUNES, Gregorio
'Carta del doctor don Gregorio de
Funes, dean de Cordova del Tucuman
. . . al señor de Gregoire . . . sôbre si
el señor obispo de Chiapa tuvo ú no
algun influjo en que se hiciera por los
Españoles en América el comercio de
negros africanos.' [Buenos Aires, 1819.]
In: Obras de Las Casas, vol. 2 (Paris,
1822), pp. 365–402.

Las Casas influenced the Spanish
government to develop the slave
trade to America.

4000 'LAS CASAS and the slave trade.'
(Retrospective Review, London, vol. 6,
1822, pp. 261–71.)

The charge that Las Casas initiated
the slave trade to America is unfounded.

4001 VILLENAVE, Mathieu Guillaume Thérèse de
'Sur une dissertation, imprimée en
1780, dans le Journal de Monsieur, en
faveur de la liberté des noirs.' (Journal
de la Société de la Morale Chrétienne,
Paris, vol. 3, 1824, pp. 156–65.)

Madame d'Onnoy was the first
in France to propose a plan for
civilising and emancipating negro
slaves in her 'Dissertation sur l'esclavage des noirs'.

4002 NEWTON, John
Life of the Rev. John Newton, late
rector of St. Mary Woolnoth, Lombard
Street, in a series of letters written by
himself to the Rev. Dr. Hawies. To
which is added a short sketch of his
life and character. From the conclusion
of his own narrative, till his death in
1807. By the Rev. James Brewster . . .
Anderson & Bryce, Edinburgh, 1824.
2 pt.

Consists mainly of Newton's 'Authentic narrative' (714) and letters (727);
by a slave captain turned abolitionist.

4003 HAZLITT, William
'Lord Eldon and Mr. Wilberforce.'
In his: The spirit of the age (London,
1825), pp. 343–63.

Criticizes Wilberforce for 'moral
equivocation'.

4004 BRISSOT, Jacques Pierre
Mémoires de Brissot, membre de
l'Assemblée législative et de la Convention nationale, sur ses contemporains, et la révolution française. Publiés
par son fils, avec des notes et des
éclaircissements historiques par M.-F.
de Montrol. Ladvocat, Paris, 1830–32.
4 vol.

Edited by A. Brissot.

4005 *HUGHES, Benjamin F.
Eulogium on the life and character
of William Wilberforce, Esq . . . New
York, 1833. 16 pp.

4006 *WHIPPER, William
Eulogy on William Wilberforce, Esq.,
delivered at the request of the people
of colour of the city of Philadelphia . . .
on the sixth day of December, 1833.
W. P. Gibbons, Philadelphia, [1833?].
35 pp.

4007 ROSCOE, Henry
The life of William Roscoe . . . T. Cadell,
London; W. Blackwood, Edinburgh,
1833. 2 vol.

Reviewed in: NAR, vol. 41, 1835,
pp. 94–109.

4008 *BROWN, David Paul
Eulogium upon Wilberforce; with a
brief incidental review of the subject
of colonization . . . T. K. Collins &
Co., Philadelphia, 1834. 40 pp.

4009 ROBERTS, William
Memoirs of the life and correspondence
of Mrs. Hannah More . . . Second
edition. R. B. Seeley & W. Burnside,
London, 1834. 4 vol. port.

4010 *STUART, Charles
A memoir of Granville Sharp, to
which is added Sharp's "Law of passive
obedience" and an extract from his "Law
of retribution". American Anti-Slavery
Society, New-York, 1836. 156 pp.

4011 'THOMAS Clarkson, Esq.' (Christian
Keepsake and Missionary Annual,
London, 1837, pp. 42–61.)

Attributed to Elizabeth Shewell.

4012 GRÉGOIRE, Henri Baptiste
Mémoires de Grégoire, ancien évêque de
Blois . . . précédés d'une notice historique

sur l'auteur, par M. H. Carnot . . . Ambroise Dupont; E. Legrand & Descauriet, Paris, 1837. 2 vol.

4013 *GURNEY, Joseph John
Familiar sketch of the late William Wilberforce. Norwich, 1838. xv, 136 pp.

4014 'LIFE of William Wilberforce.' (ER, vol. 67, 1838, pp. 142–80.)

By Sir James Stephen.

4015 WILBERFORCE, Robert Isaac
The life of William Wilberforce. By his sons, Robert Isaac Wilberforce . . . and Samuel Wilberforce . . . John Murray, London, 1838. 5 vol.

Reviewed in: Tait's Edinburgh Magazine, n.s., vol. 5, 1838, pp. 339–54; QR, vol. 62, 1838, pp. 214–85. See (4016).

4016 CLARKSON, Thomas
Strictures on a life of William Wilberforce by the Rev. W. Wilberforce and the Rev. S. Wilberforce . . . Longman, Orme, Brown, Green, & Longmans, London, 1838. xv, 136 pp.

Defence of the author's account (3584) of the abolition of the slave trade against accusations by Wilberforce's biographers that Clarkson had exaggerated his own role in the campaign. See (4015).

4017 TAYLOR, Thomas
A biographical sketch of Thomas Clarkson, M.A. With occasional brief strictures on the misrepresentations of him contained in The life of William Wilberforce; and a concise historical outline of the abolition of slavery. John Rickerby, London, 1839. 152 pp. port.

4018 *A BRIEF sketch of the life of the late Zachary Macaulay, Esq., F.R.S., as connected with the subjects of the abolition of the slave trade and slavery. London, 1839.

4019 UHDEN, Hermann Ferdinand
Leben des William Wilberforce in seiner religiösen Entwicklung dargestellt nach "The life of Wm. Wilberforce by his sons . . ." Wilhelm Besser, Berlin, 1840. xi, 364 pp.

See (4015).

4020 ROMILLY, Sir Samuel
Memoirs of the life of Sir Samuel Romilly, written by himself; with a selection from his correspondence. Edited by his sons. John Murray, London, 1840. 3 vol.

4021 WILBERFORCE, William
The correspondence of William Wilberforce. Edited by his sons, Robert Isaac Wilberforce . . . and Samuel Wilberforce. John Murray, London, 1840. 2 vol.

Contains a number of letters on the slave trade and slavery.

4022 CHILD, Lydia Maria
Memoir of Benjamin Lay: compiled from various sources. American A. S. Society, New-York, 1842. 35 pp.

4023 ISAMBERT, Alfred
'Notice sur Clarkson'. (Abolitioniste Français, Paris, vol. 3, 1846, pp. 337–49.)

Obituary of Thomas Clarkson.

4024 CRUMMELL, Alexander
The man: the hero: the Christian! A eulogy on the life and character of Thomas Clarkson: delivered in the city of New-York; December, 1846 . . . Egbert, Hovey & King, New-York, 1847. 44 pp.

4025 *GURNEY, Joseph John
Brief memoirs of Thomas Fowell Buxton and Elizabeth Fry . . . J. Fletcher, Norwich; (etc.), 1848. 60 pp.

4026 BUXTON, Sir Thomas Fowell
Memoirs of Sir Thomas Fowell Buxton, Baronet. With selections from his correspondence. Edited by his son, Charles Buxton, Esq. John Murray, London, 1848. xvi, 600 pp.

4027 The SLAVE and the preacher; a history of the Rev. John Newton, written for children. London, 1851. 51 pp.

4028 L'APÔTRE des nègres, ou vie du b. Pierre Claver. Par M. F. Lille, 1852. 101 pp.

By Mathilde Lippens Froment.

4029 HOPKINS, Samuel
The works of Samuel Hopkins. Boston, 1852. 3 vol.

Vol. 1, prelim. pp. 1–266: 'Memoir' of Hopkins by Edwards Amasa Park.

4030 *RILLIET DE CONSTANT, Victorine
Vie de Buxton, précédée et suivie de deux notices sur l'esclavage et sur la colonie de Libéria, traduite par Mlle Rilliet de Constant. Paris, 1853. 340 pp.

Life of T. F. Buxton.

4031 MAUNDER, George
Eminent Christian philanthropists. Brief biographical sketches, designed especially for the young. London, 1853. 245 pp.

Includes chapters on Sharp, Clarkson, Wilberforce and Buxton.

4032 MAUNDER, George
Friends of the slave; and other philanthropists. London, [1854]. 141 pp.

See (4031).

4033 TRESKOW, A. von
Sir Thomas Fowell Buxton, Bart. Ein Bild des englischen Lebens . . . Entworfen nach "Memoirs of Sir Th. Fowell Buxton, Bart., edited by his son, Charles Buxton, Esq., B.A." Volks-Ausgabe. Berlin, 1854. xii, 297 pp.

See (4026).

4034 ELMES, James
Thomas Clarkson: a monograph. Being a contribution towards the history of the abolition of the slave-trade and slavery. London, 1854. xxx, 320 pp.

4035 HOLZWARTH, Friedrich Joseph
Petrus Claver, Sklave der Negersklaven. Bilder aus der Mission unter den Negern. Tübingen, 1855. viii, 282 pp.

4036 BRANDIS, Bernhard
Das Leben des Sir Thomas Fowell Buxton nach dem Englischen des Charles Buxton Esqr . . . Hamburg, 1855. viii, 381 pp.

See (4026).

4037 KAYSER, Friederich
Das Leben des englischen Staatsmannes und Sklavenfreundes William Wilberforce. Hamburg, 1856. viii, 178 pp.

Popular biographical sketch.

4038 The SLAVES' champion, or, a sketch of the life, deeds, and historical days of William Wilberforce . . . London, 1859. 168 pp. port.

By Henry M. Wheeler.

4039 VAUX, Roberts
Anthony Benezet. From the original memoir: revised, with additions, by Wilson Armistead. London, 1859. xv, 144 pp.

See (3996).

4040 *COLLIER, Mary A.
Memoir of Thomas Fowell Buxton: embracing a historical sketch of emancipation in the West Indies, and of the Niger expedition for the suppression of the slave trade . . . Boston, [1861]. 290 pp.

4041 HARFORD, John Scandrett
Recollections of William Wilberforce, Esq. M.P. for the county of York during nearly thirty years. With brief notices of some of his personal friends and contemporaries. London, 1864. xii, 326 pp.

4042 RICHARD, Henry
Memoirs of Joseph Sturge. London, 1864. xix, 622 pp.

Biography of one of the founders of the British and Foreign Anti-Slavery Society.

4043 MUDGE, Zachariah Atwell
The Christian statesman; a portraiture of Sir Thomas Fowell Buxton: with sketches of British antislavery reform. New York, [1865]. 268 pp.

4044 COLQUHOUN, John Campbell
William Wilberforce: his friends and his times. London, 1866. vii, 448 pp.

4045 PETER Claver: a sketch of his life and labors in behalf of the African slave. Boston, 1868. 117 pp.

4046 NEWTON, John
John Newton of Olney and St. Mary Woolnoth. An autobiography and narrative, compiled chiefly from his diary and other unpublished documents by the Rev. Josiah Bull. London, [1868]. 378 pp.

4047 FÉLICE, Guillaume de
Biographie de William Allen, membre de la société des Amis, ou Quakers. Paris; Toulouse, 1869. 276 pp.

Includes chapters on Allen's abolitionist efforts.

4048 BERNARDI, Jacopo
Nicolò Olivieri e il riscatto delle fanciulle arabe. Cenni storici. Torino, 1870. 142 pp.

Olivieri founded a society in 1853 for the redemption of slave girls in Egypt; with separate chapters on three of them: Zoava, Amna and Faldacarim.

4049 SKETCH of the life of Thomas Clarkson. London, 1876. 40 pp.

4050 PITTO, Antonio
Della vita del servo di Dio Sac. Niccolò G. B. Olivieri di Voltaggio nella Liguria fondatore della pia Opera del Riscatto delle Fanciulle More . . . Genova, 1877. 104 pp.

4051 STOUGHTON, John
William Wilberforce. London, 1880. 213 pp.

Ch. 3: 'Anti-slavery crusade.'

4052 *VILLEFRANCHE, Jacques Melchior
Vie de Nicolas-J.-B. Olivieri prêtre
génois fondateur de l'Oeuvre du Rachat
des jeunes Négresses. Bourg, 1880.
100 pp.

4053 NICOLL, Henry James
Great movements and those who
achieved them. London, 1881. iv, 456 pp.
ports.

> Ch. 2: 'The abolition of the slave
> trade: William Wilberforce.'

4054 *CAPECELATRO, Alfonso, *Cardinal*
La vita del P. Lodovico da Casoria . . .
Napoli, 1887. 671 pp.

> Includes chapters dealing with Cas-
> oria's Opere dei Moretti and delle
> Morette for the redemption of slave
> children in the Sudan.

4055 *FERNANDEZ, José
Vida de san Pedro Claver de la Com-
pañia de Jesus apóstol de los negros . . .
Refundida y acrescentada por el P.
Juan Maria Solá . . . Barcelona, 1888.
621 pp.

4056 BRIOSCHI, Pedro A.
Vida de san Pedro Claver, heroico
apóstol de los negros. Paris, 1889.
xii, 544 pp.

4057 CLARKE, Richard Frederick
Cardinal Lavigerie and the African
slave trade. Edited by Richard F.
Clarke. London, 1889. viii, 379 pp.

> Describes Lavigerie's efforts to stop
> the Muslim slave trade in Africa.

4058 BROWNE, Granville
'Granville Sharp and the slave-trade.'
(McM, vol. 61, 1890, pp. 205–13.)

4059 KLEIN, Félix
Le cardinal Lavigerie et ses œuvres
d'Afrique. Paris, 1890. iv, 418 pp.

> Ch. 7: 'L'antiesclavagisme.'

4060 MICHAEL, Charles D.
The slave and his champions. Granville
Sharp, Thomas Clarkson, William
Wilberforce, and Sir Thomas Fowell
Buxton. London, [1891]. 160 pp. illus.

4061 CARTUYVELS, Jules
Oraison funèbre de S.É. le cardinal
Lavigerie prononcée au service funèbre
célébré à Sainte-Gudule le 15 décembre
1892. Bruxelles, 1892. 40 pp. port.

> Reprinted in: MA, vol. 5, 1893, pp.
> 1–40.

4062 *SLATTERY, John Richard
The life of St. Peter Claver, S.J., the

apostle of the negroes . . . Philadelphia,
[1893]. 265 pp.

4063 BOURNAND, François
Son Éminence le cardinal Lavigerie . . .
Paris, [1893]. 329 pp.

> With an appendix on the antislavery
> crusade.

4064 'SIR T. Fowell Buxton.' (Friends'
Quarterly Examiner, London, vol. 28,
1894, pp. 457–66.)

> By Richard Westlake. Account of
> Buxton's antislavery activities 1821–
> 38.

4065 WESTLAKE, Richard
Sir Thomas Fowell Buxton, Bart., and
the slave trade . . . London, 1894.
10 pp.

> Reprinted from: 4064.

4066 PETRE, Maude Dominica Mary
"Aethiopum servus." A study in Christian altruism. London, 1896. vi, 226 pp.

> Biography of St. Peter Claver, with a
> chapter on the attitude of the Church
> to the slave trade.

4067 BAUNARD, Louis Pierre André
Le cardinal Lavigerie. Paris, 1896. 2 vol.

> With chapters on the antislavery
> campaigns of 1888–89.

4068 ROBINSON, Wilfrid C.
'Cardinal Lavigerie.' (American Catholic Quarterly Review, Philadelphia,
vol. 22, 1897, pp. 1–17.)

4069 'OPINIÃO de um frade capuxinho
sôbre a escravidão no Brasil em 1794.'
(RIHGB, vol. 60, pt. 2, 1897, pp. 155–
57.)

> Official report on an Italian priest at
> Bahia, Jozé de Bolonha, suspended
> for his dangerous belief that slavery
> was 'illegitima e contraria á religião'.
> (See also: Annaes da Bibliotheca
> Nacional do Rio de Janeiro, vol.
> 34, 1914, pp. 317–18.)

4070 GUILLELMO Wilberforce, gran liber-
tador de los negros. Madrid, 1900.
40 pp.

4071 HOLLAND, Margaret Jean *Viscountess
Knutsford*
Life and letters of Zachary Macaulay.
London, 1900. 496 pp. port.

> Includes chapters on Sierra Leone in
> the 1790s and the abolition of the
> slave trade.

4072 BUXTON, Travers
William Wilberforce. The story of a great crusade. London, [1903]. 187 pp.

Short popular biography.

4073 *JUSTICE, Hilda
Life and ancestry of Warner Mifflin, Friend—philanthropist—patriot . . . Philadelphia, 1905. 240 pp. map.

4074 COLLEVILLE, Ludovic, *comte* de
Le cardinal Lavigerie. Paris, 1905. 229 pp.

Ch. 10: 'L'esclavage.—Croisade anti-esclavagiste.'

4075 AXON, William Edward Armitage
'Cobden, civilisation and commerce.' (WR, vol. 166, 1906, pp. 265–71.)

On Cobden's antislavery activities in 1840.

4076 *'La TRAITE des nègres et William Wilberforce.' (Signed: A.J.W.) (Mouvement Géographique, Bruxelles, 1907, no. 14, col. 163–65.)

By A. J. Wauters?

4077 CALLIS, John
John Newton, sailor, preacher, pastor and poet. Centenary memorials . . . Compiled and edited by Rev. John Callis . . . London, [1908]. 132 pp.

Sermons and addresses by various authors.

4078 SHORE, William Teignmouth
John Woolman, his life and our times. Being a study in applied Christianity. London, 1913. ix, 273 pp. map.

4079 DAHLGREN, Erik Wilhelm
'Carl Bernhard Wadström. Hans verksamhet för slafhandelns bekämpande och de samtida kolonisationsplanerna i Västafrika. Bibliografisk sammanställning.' (Nordisk Tidskrift för Bok- och Biblioteksväsen, Uppsala & Stockholm, vol. 2, 1915, pp. 1–52; illus, port.)

On the activities of Wadström in the abolition movement 1788–98.

4080 ELLERY, Eloise
Brissot de Warville. A study in the history of the French revolution. Boston & New York, 1915. xix, 528 pp. bibl. pp. 455–508.

Biography of one of the leading 'amis des noirs'.

4081 BÅÅTH-HOLMBERG, Cecilia
'Svensk och afrikan.' *In her*: Från gammal tid och ny (Stockholm, 1916), pp. 197–270.

On C. B. Wadström and Sweden's contribution to the antislavery movement.

4082 TRAVERSO, Luigi
Niccolò Olivieri e il riscatto delle schiave africane. (Storia d'un eroe della carità.) . . . Firenze, 1916. vii, 304 pp.

Describes Olivieri's work for the redemption of slave children from 1838 onward.

4083 WOODSON, Carter Godwin
'Anthony Benezet.' (JNH, vol. 2, 1917, pp. 37–50.)

4084 HOUSTON, Gordon David
'John Woolman's efforts in behalf of freedom.' (JNH, vol. 2, 1917, pp. 126–38.)

4085 WOOLMAN, John
The journal and essays of John Woolman, edited from the original manuscripts with a biographical introduction by Amelia Mott Gummere. London, 1922. xxii, 643 pp.

Biographical introduction: pp. 1–150. (J. G. Whittier contributed an 'appreciation' of Woolman to the edition published in Boston, 1871.) See (1784, 1797).

4086 COUPLAND, *Sir* Reginald
Wilberforce. A narrative. Oxford, 1923. vi, 528 pp.

Standard modern biography.

4087 DE MONTMORENCY, James Edward Geoffrey
Francis William Fox. A biography. [London,] 1923. 141 pp.

Life of a Quaker, including an account of his antislavery activities in the Sudan and eastern Africa 1876–97.

4088 *PANNIER, Jacques
Antoine Bénezet (de Saint-Quentin) un quaker français en Amérique. Toulouse, 1925. 44 pp.

4089 GOYAU, Georges
Un grand missionnaire. Le cardinal Lavigerie . . . Paris, [1925]. 271 pp. ports.

Ch. 4: 'La croisade contre l'esclavage . . .' (Reprinted from: RDM, ser. 7, vol. 26, 1925, pp. 310–43, 579–609, 775–807; vol. 27, 1925, pp. 149–86.)

4090 LASCELLES, Edward Charles Ponsonby
Granville Sharp and the freedom of the

Y

slaves in England. London, 1928. viii, 151 pp.

> Popular account of the abolition movement.

4091 ROSS, A. H.
'John Newton, slaver of Plantain Island and vicar of Olney.' (Sierra Leone Studies, Freetown, no. 14, 1929, pp. 53–61.)

> Newton lived as a slave-dealer in the Sierra Leone area 1744–48 and returned as captain of a slave ship in the following years. See (714).

4092 *ORTIZ, Fernando
José Antonio Saco y sus ideas cubanas. La Habana, 1929. 248 pp. illus, port.

4093 MATHEWS, Godfrey William
William Roscoe. A memoir. London, [1931]. 55 pp. port.

4094 JENKINS, Wilfrid John
William Wilberforce. A champion of freedom. London, 1932. 128 pp.

> Ch. 3: 'The slave trade.'

4095 *NARDI, Gennaro
Il Ven. Ludovico da Casoria e i collegi dei moretti. Milano, 1932. 104 pp.

> See (4054).

4096 BROWNE, Arthur Bevil
'G♯, crusader.' (NC, vol. 114, 1933, pp. 360–73.)

> On Granville Sharp.

4097 BRUCE, Eleanor
'The vested interests and the slave trade.' (Millgate, Manchester, vol. 28, 1933, pp. 588–90.)

> On William Wilberforce.

4098 GRAY, William Forbes
'Wilberforce and the anti-slavery movement.' (QR, vol. 261, 1933, pp. 67–84.)

4099 LAW, Alice
'The achievement of Wilberforce.' (FR, n.s., vol. 133, 1933, pp. 749–58.)

4100 BOOTH, Charles
Zachary Macaulay. His part in the movement for the abolition of the slave trade and of slavery. An appreciation. London, 1934. 119 pp.

> Ch. 2: 'The slave trade.'

4101 LUNN, Arnold Henry Moore
A saint in the slave trade, Peter Claver (1581–1654.). London, 1935. vii, 256 pp.

> On the missionary work of Claver and the attitude to slavery of the Catholic church in Latin America.

4102 LEAHY, Ellen Mary Agnes
Light in darkest Africa. Charles Cardinal Lavigerie, 1825–92. Dublin, 1935. 127 pp.

> Ch. 11: 'Anti-slavery crusade.'

4103 GRIGGS, Earl Leslie
Thomas Clarkson, the friend of slaves. London, 1936. 210 pp. illus, bibl. pp. 199–204.

4104 *CAMINADA, Costantino
Il missionario degli schiavi. Don Biagio Verri. 2a edizione. Como, 1936. 364 pp.

> Verri continued Olivieri's work of redeeming African slaves. See (4048).

4105 Der VATER der Neger. Der hl. Petrus Claver S.J. [Salzburg, 1937.] 96 pp.

4106 BROOKES, George Sprague
Friend Anthony Benezet. Philadelphia, 1937. ix, 516 pp. bibl. pp. 179–203, 501–02.

> Biography and collection of letters and writings of the American Quaker abolitionist.

4107 SHEPPARD, Thomas
William Wilberforce, emancipator of slaves. 1759–1833. Exeter, 1937. 60 pp. illus.

4108 *CAMINADA, Costantino
Don Biagio Verri . . . Torino, 1937. 140 pp.

4109 COOK, Orator Fuller
'Aublet the botanist, a pioneer against slavery . . .' (Journal of the Washington Academy of Sciences, vol. 30, 1940, pp. 294–99; illus.)

> Aublet, author of a work on the flora of French Guyana, 1775, condemned slavery as injurious to the settlers themselves.

4110 DRAKE, Thomas Edward
'Cadwalader Morgan, antislavery Quaker of the Welsh tract.' (Friends Intelligencer, Philadelphia, vol. 98, no. 36, 1941, pp. 575–76.)

> Includes the text of an antislavery paper presented by Morgan to the Pennsylvania yearly meeting 1696.

4111 *WHITNEY, Janet
John Woolman, American Quaker . . . Boston, 1942. x, 490 pp. illus.

4112 HANLEY, James
'A religious slaver.' (Life and Letters To-day, London, vol. 37, 1943, pp. 69–74).

On John Newton.

4113 *ZAVALA, Silvio
'Las Casas esclavista?' (Cuadernos Americanos, México, vol. 3, 1944, pp. 149–54.)

Las Casas proposed bringing Spanish-born negroes to America but changed his mind when he learned about the African slave trade.

4114 LASK, John S.
'John Woolman: crusader for freedom.' (Phylon, Atlanta, vol. 5, 1944, pp. 30–40.)

4115 HAGEN, Ellen Helga Louise
En frihetstidens son. Carl Bernhard Wadström. Bergsvetenskapsman. Forskningsresande. Filantrop. Stockholm, 1946. 203 pp.

Biography of a Swedish abolitionist active in London and Paris 1789–99.

4116 MOTTRAM, Ralph Hale
Buxton the liberator. London, [1946]. 142 pp.

4117 HENNELL, Michael Murray
William Wilberforce. London & Redhill, 1947. 32 pp.

4118 PARSONS, Albert William
John Newton 1725–1807. Slaver and singer, profligate and preacher. London, [1948]. 31 pp.

4119 *HARBECK, Hans
William Wilberforce: der Befreier der Sklaven. Hamburg, 1948. 71 pp.

4120 *GRUNEBAUM-BALLIN, Paul Frédéric Jean
Henri Grégoire, l'ami des hommes de toutes les couleurs. La lutte pour la suppression de la traite et l'abolition de l'esclavage 1789–1831. Paris, 1948. 278 pp.

4121 *PICÓN-SALAS, Mariano
Pedro Claver, el santo de los esclavos. México, 1949. 212 pp.

4122 CADBURY, Henry Joel
'John Hepburn and his book against slavery, 1715.' (PAAS, vol. 59, 1949, pp. 89–160.)

Includes a facsimile of a large part of (1704).

4123 *PICÓN-SALAS, Mariano
'Sandoval the unsung.' (Americas, Washington, vol. 2, 1950, pp. 13–15.)

On the missionary Sandoval and the slave trade in Colombia.

4124 MARTIN, Bernard Davis
John Newton. A biography. London, 1950. viii, 372 pp. illus.

Revised edition published 1960 as 'An ancient mariner'.

4125 SCHUTZ, John Adolphe
'James Ramsay, essayist: aggressive humanitarian.' In: BRITISH humanitarianism. Essays honoring Frank J. Klingberg . . . Edited by Samuel Clyde McCulloch (Philadelphia, 1950), pp. 145–65.

Analysis of Ramsay's 'Essay' (1819) and the controversy it provoked.

4126 *KENNEDY, Melvin Dow
Lafayette and slavery; from his letters to Thomas Clarkson and Granville Sharp . . . Easton, Pa., 1950. 44 pp. ports.

4127 HENNELL, Michael Murray
William Wilberforce 1789–1833. The liberator of the slave. London, [1950]. 31 pp.

4128 GALLAGHER, John
'Fowell Buxton and the new African policy, 1838–1842.' (Cambridge Historical Journal, London & Cambridge, vol. 10, 1950, pp. 36–58.)

Britain's 'forward' policy against the slave trade, including the Niger expedition of 1841, showed the political influence of the humanitarians.

4129 DELLICOUR, Fernand
'Deux témoignages.' (Institut Royal Colonial Belge, Bulletin des séances, Bruxelles, vol. 23, 1952, pp. 113–32.)

The first section deals with the anti-slavery campaign launched by Cardinal Lavigerie in 1888.

4130 McCORMICK, Elsie
'Pioneer in the fight against slavery.' (Readers Digest, London, vol. 63, no. 380, Dec. 1953, pp. 17–20.)

On William Wilberforce.

4131 HALL, Helena
William Allen, 1770–1843. Member of the Society of Friends . . . Howards Heath, 1953. 175 pp. illus, ports.

4132 CHORLEY, Katherine
'St. Peter Claver.' (Month, London, n.s., vol. 13, 1955, pp. 325–41.)

4133 CROPPER, Margaret Beatrice
Sparks among the stubble. London, 1955. xiii, 226 pp.

Studies of evangelical 'saints', including John Newton, Hannah More and William Wilberforce.

4134 *NEIVA, Venâncio de Figueiredo
José Bonifacio; conferencia . . . Rio de Janeiro, 1955. 28 pp.

On J. B. d'Andrada e Silva, the Brazilian abolitionist.

4135 PRICE, Thomas
'Portuguese relations with David Livingstone.' (Scottish Geographical Magazine, Edinburgh, vol. 71, 1955, pp. 138–46.)

Livingstone's anger at Portuguese slave trading in the 1860s led him to deny their territorial claims in the interior of southern Africa.

4136 'L'ABBÉ Grégoire. "L'ami des hommes de toutes les couleurs".' (Europe, Paris, vol. 34, 1956, pp. 1–158; illus, port; bibl. pp. 157–58.)

Special issue, with fifteen articles including: LA GRAVIÈRE, E. 'Grégoire et l'esclavage' (pp. 26–46).

4137 KREBS, Albert
'La Fayette et l'abolition de l'esclavage.' (Cahiers Français, Paris, 1957, no. 24, pp. 24–29; illus, port.)

On La Fayette's antislavery opinions 1783–1834.

4138 HERNÁNDEZ Y SÁNCHEZ-BARBA, Mario
'David Turnbull y el problema de la esclavitud en Cuba.' (Anuario de Estudios Americanos, Sevilla, vol. 14, 1957, pp. 241–99.)

On Turnbull's period as consul at Havana 1840–44.

4139 FIELD, James A.
'A scheme in regard to Cyrenaica.' (MVHR, vol. 44, 1957, pp. 445–68.)

On M. Vidal, U.S. consul at Tripoli 1870–76, and his anti-slave trade activities.

4140 PERRAUDIN, Jean
'Le cardinal Lavigerie et Léopold II.' (Zaïre, Bruxelles, vol. 11, 1957, pp. 901–32; vol. 12, 1958, pp. 37–64, 165–77, 275–91, 393–408.)

Includes an account of the antislavery campaign 1888–92.

4141 KREBS, Albert
'La Fayette et le problème de l'esclavage.' (Annuaire-bulletin de la Société de l'Histoire de France, Paris, vol. 1956/57, 1958, pp. 49–60.)

4142 VALTIERRA, Angel
Peter Claver. Saint of the slaves. London, [1960]. viii, 328 pp.

Biography of the missionary, with much incidental information on the slave trade 1610–50. (Translation of: El Santo que libertó una raza, Bogotá, 1954.)

4143 DAVIS, David Brion
'James Cropper and the British antislavery movement, 1821–1823.' (JNH, vol. 45, 1960, pp. 241–58.)

Cropper, a Quaker, believed in free trade as the solution to slavery and the slave trade.

4144 MARTIN, Bernard Davis
John Newton and the slave trade. London, 1961. 89 pp. illus.

Written for children.

4145 CHRISTIANI, Léon
Le cardinal Lavigerie. Un grand bienfaiteur de l'Afrique (1825–1892). Paris, [1961]. 334 pp.

Ch. 14: 'La croisade antiesclavagiste.'

4146 LAWSON, Audrey and LAWSON, Herbert
The man who freed the slaves. The story of William Wilberforce. London, 1962. 141 pp.

Popular account.

4147 WARNER, Oliver
William Wilberforce and his times. London, 1962. 174 pp. illus, ports.

Based on Coupland's biography (4086).

4148 *SIQUEIRA, Sônia Aparecida
'A escravidão negra no pensamiento do bispo Azeredo Coutinho. Contribuição ao estudo da mentalidade do último inquisidor geral.' (Revista de História, São Paulo, vol. 27, 1963, pp. 349–65; vol. 28, 1964, pp. 141–76.)

4149 BOAHEN, Albert Adu
'James Richardson: the forgotten philanthropist and explorer.' (JHSN, vol. 3, 1964, pp. 61–71.)

Richardson was a passionate opponent of the Saharan slave trade, worthy of comparison with Clarkson and Livingstone.

4150 CARROLL, Kenneth L.
'William Southeby, early Quaker anti-

slavery writer.' (PMBH, vol. 89, 1965, pp. 416–27.)

On the antislavery activities of Southeby in Pennsylvania 1695–1715.

4151 MOULTON, Phillips
'John Woolman's approach to social action—as exemplified in relation to slavery.' (Church History, New York, 1966, pp. 399–410.)

4152 WILBERFORCE, Yvette
William Wilberforce. An essay. [London,] 1967. viii, 26 pp. illus.

4153 *LOVEJOY, David Sherman
'Samuel Hopkins: religion, slavery, and the revolution.' (NEQ, vol. 40, 1967, pp. 227–43.)

4154 D'ELIA, Donald J.
'Dr. Benjamin Rush and the negro.'
(Journal of the History of Ideas, Ephrata, Pa., vol. 30, 1969. pp. 413–22.)

On the abolitionist activities of Rush 1773–97.

4155 BAKER, William
'William Wilberforce on the idea of negro inferiority.' (Journal of the History of Ideas, Ephrata, Pa., vol. 31, 1970, pp. 433–40.)

4156 Ó BROIN, Leon
An Maidíneach. Staraí nÉireannach aontaithe. Baile Átha Cliath, 1971. 376 pp. illus, ports.

Biography of R. R. Madden, with chapters on his antislavery work in Jamaica, Cuba and the Gold Coast (1833–43).

Z. IMAGINATIVE LITERATURE

4157 BEHN, Aphra
Oroonoko: or, the royal slave. A true history. Will. Canning, London, 1688. 239 pp.

Romantic novel about a 'Coromantien' taken as a slave to Surinam where he is killed after organizing a revolt; 'the first work in English literature since Othello with a black man for its hero' (Coupland). See (4158).

4158 SOUTHERNE, Thomas
Oroonoko: a tragedy as it was acted at the Theatre-Royal, by His Majesty's Servants. H. Playford; (etc.), London, 1696. 84 pp.

Based on (4157), with the hero as an Angolan prince.

4159 'The STORY of Inkle and Yarico. From the 11th Spectator.' (London Magazine, vol. 3, May 1734, pp. 257–58.)

Poetical version of Richard Steele's tale of an American Indian girl enslaved by an Englishman in Barbados (Spectator, no. 11, 1712, pp. 62–65); the girl is here a 'negro virgin'. For the development of the theme see: 3859.

4160 SAVAGE, Richard
Of public spirit in regard to public works . . . R. Dodsley, London, 1737. 18 pp.

Verse epistle, including censure of the trade in African slaves 'tho' form'd by Nature free'.

4161 INCLE and Yarico: a tragedy, of three acts. As it was intended to have been performed at the Theatre-Royal, in Covent-Garden. By the author of The city farce, The voyage up the Thames, &c. T. Cooper, London, 1742. 69 pp.

Attributed to — Wedderburn. The story (4159) has been transferred to Africa.

4162 BEHN, Aphra
Oronoko, traduit de l'anglais. Amsterdam, 1745. xv, 168 pp.

Translation of (4157) by 'D. L. ****' (P. A. de La Place), providing a happy ending with the return to Africa of the hero and his family.

4163 'The AFRICAN prince, now in England, to Zara at his father's court.' (GM, vol. 19, July 1749, pp. 323–25.)

By William Dodd. Lament in verse of a liberated slave (see 1458). Reprinted in: Dodd, W. Poems (London, 1767), pp. 8–14. See (4164).

4164 ZARA, at the court of Annamaboe, to the African prince, now in England. J. Payne & J. Bouquet, London, 1749. 15 pp.

By William Dodd. Reply in verse to (4163). First printed in: GM, vol. 19, Aug. 1749, pp. 372–73; reprinted in: Dodd, W. Poems (London, 1767), pp. 15–20.

4165 BARKER, Robert
The unfortunate shipwright & cruel captain. [London? 1756.] (2 pp.)

Account in verse of a slaving voyage to West Africa. See (712).

4166 GENTLEMAN, Francis
Oroonoko: or the royal slave. A tragedy. Altered from Southerne . . . Robert & Andrew Foulis, Glasgow, 1760. 87 pp.

Verse play based on (4158).

4167 SEDAINE, Michel Jean
'Inkle et Iarico.' In: Recueil de poesies de M. Sedaine (London, 1760), pt. 1, pp. 121–26.

Poem, set in Africa and Mexico. See (4159).

4168 Le PHILOSOPHE nègre, et les secrets des Grecs . . . Londres, 1764. 2 pt.

By G. Mailhol. Includes the narrative (pt. 1, ch. 3–8) of 'Tintillo', an African prince captured and sold to the French.

4169 SHENSTONE, William
'Elegy XX. He compares his humble fortune with the distress of others;

and his subjection to Delia, with the miserable servitude of an African slave.' *In*: The works in verse and prose of William Shenstone (London, 1764), vol. 1, pp. 73–76.

Condemns the slave trade.

4170 GRAINGER, James
The sugar-cane: a poem . . . R. & J. Dodsley, London, 1764. vii, 167 pp.

Bk. 4 advises on the purchase of slaves, describing the characteristics of various African nations.

4171 The SABLE Venus. An ode. Inscribed to Bryan Edwards, Esq. Bennett & Woolhead, Kingston, Jamaica, 1765. 12 pp.

By Isaac Teale. Romantic allegory of the slave trade. (Reprinted in: 1603, vol. 2, pp. 27–33.)

4172 YARICO to Inkle, an epistle. By the author of the elegy written among the ruins of an abbey. J. Dodsley, London, 1766. 19 pp.

Poem by Edward Jerningham. Yarico is a 'Nubian' princess sold to Barbados. See (4159).

4173a 'ZIMEO. Par George Filmer, né primitif.' *In*: Les SAISONS, poème (Amsterdam, 1769), pp. 226–59.

Translated as:

4173b ZIMAO, the African. Translated by the Rev. Weeden Butler . . . Vernor & Hood, London, 1800. xi, 105 pp.

Short story by J. F. de Saint-Lambert, ending with an appeal for the abolition of slavery; the hero, abducted from Benin to Jamaica, leads a slave revolt. (The English version contains an appendix on the slave trade.) See (1757).

4174 *BUTINI, Jean François
Lettres africaines, ou histoire de Phédime et d'Abensar. Londres; Fétil, Paris, 1771. 245 pp.

Novel by a Swiss author about two lovers enslaved but reunited in the West Indies. (Reviewed in: Ephémérides du Citoyen, Paris, vol. 8, 1771, pp. 68–118.)

4175 The DYING negro, a poetical epistle, supposed to be written by a black, (who lately shot himself on board a vessel in the river Thames;) to his intended wife. W. Flexney, London, 1773. 19 pp.

Anti-slave trade poem by Thomas Day and John Bicknell, dedicated to Rousseau. See: The Poetical register and repository of fugitive poetry, for 1810–1811 (London, 1814), pp. 353–67.

4176 HAWKESWORTH, John
Oroonoko, a tragedy, as it is now acted at the Theatre Royal in Drury-Lane. By Thomas Southern. With alterations by John Hawkesworth. C. Bathurst; (etc.), London, 1775. 64 pp.

See (4158).

4177 *DOIGNY DU PONCEAU, ——
Discours d'un nègre à un Européen, pièce qui a concouru pour le prix de l'Académie françoise, en 1775. Demonville, Paris, 1775. 15 pp.

Antislavery poem.

4178 LE MONNIER, Guillaume Antoine
'Discours d'un nègre marron, qui a été repris, & qui va subir le dernier supplice.' *In his*: Fêtes des bonnes-gens de canon et des rosières de Briquebec (Avignon; Paris, 1777); 7 pp.

Speech of a slave to his white captors, denouncing the slave trade. See (4217).

4179 MOUNT Pleasant. A descriptive poem . . . W. Eyre, Warrington, 1777. 49 pp.

By William Roscoe. Description of Liverpool, with an attack on the slave trade.

4180 'The NEGRO's dying speech on his being executed for rebellion in the island of Jamaica; by B. E. Esq.' (UM, vol. 61, Nov. 1777, pp. 270–71.)

Poem by Bryan Edwards. An African slave hopes that death will restore him to his 'native skies'.

4181 *GUDIN DE LA BRENELLERIE, Paul Philippe
Discours en vers sur l'abolition de la servitude dans les domaines du roi. Demonville, Paris, 1781. 12 pp.

4182 'MORNING; or the complaint. (By a gentleman of Liverpool.)' (GM, Dec. 1783, pp. 1043–44.)

By Hugh Mulligan. Antislavery poem, headed: 'American eclogues. Eclogue I.' An African slave in Pennsylvania curses his oppressors.

4183 'EVENING; or the fugitive. By the Rev. Mr. Gregory.' (GM, Jan. 1784, pp. 45–46.)

By Hugh Mulligan. 'American eclogues. Eclogue II.'

4184 'The LOVERS, an African eclogue.' (Signed: H. M.) (GM, March 1784, pp. 199–200.)

By Hugh Mulligan. Two slaves escape from a slave ship on the Guinea coast.

4185 'A NEGRO's address on the apparition of slavery.' (Signed: T. N.) (EMLR, vol. 5, June 1784, pp. 455–56.)

Antislavery poem.

4186 *FAUSTIN; oder, das philosophische Jahrhundert . . . [Zürich?] 1784. 332 pp.

By Johann Pezzl. Ch. 34, 'Europäische Bestialitäten', describes a voyage on a slave ship from the Gold Coast to Jamaica. (First published 1783.)

4187 'NEGRO trade.—A fragment.' (AM, vol. 1, Jan. 1787, pp. 45–46.)

Discussion between a slave ship captain and an American crowd, showing the cruelties of the slave trade.

4188 'The PARADISE of negro-slaves.—a dream.' (Columbian Magazine, Philadelphia, vol. 1, no. 5, Jan. 1787, pp. 235–38.)

By Benjamin Rush. The author dreams that he meets the spirits of African slaves and among them Benezet.

4189 KNIPE, Eliza
'Atomboka and Omaza; an African story.' In her: Six narrative poems (London, 1787), pp. 51–60.

A chief and his mistress are captured in battle and sold but throw themselves overboard from a slave ship.

4190 'ADDRESS to the heart, on the subject of American slavery.' (AM, vol. 1, June 1787, pp. 540–44.)

Tragic story of the African slave trade.

4191 WEST-INDIAN eclogues. W. Lowndes; J. Philips, London, 1787. 32 pp.

By Edward Rushton. Antislavery poems in the form of dialogues between African slaves.

4192 The WRONGS of Africa, a poem. R. Faulder, London, 1787, 88. 2 pt.

By William Roscoe. Critical account

of the slave trade in Africa and the passage to the West Indies.

4193 The PRINCE of Angola, a tragedy, altered from the play of Oroonoko. And adapted to the circumstances of the present times. J. Harrop, Manchester, 1788. ix, 2, 52 pp.

By John Ferriar. Written as an abolitionist work. See (4158.)

4194 HUMANITY, or the rights of nature, a poem; in two books. By the author of Sympathy. T. Cadell, London, 1788. iv, 114 pp.

By S. J. Pratt. Attacks the African slave trade and slavery. (Reviewed in: CrR, vol. 66, 1788, pp. 51–56.)

4195 *PUDDICOMBE, John Newell
Poem to the Rev. Messrs. Ramsay and Clarkson, Granville Sharp, Esq., Captain Smith, and the respectable Society of Quakers, on their benevolent exertions for the suppression of the slave trade. Richardson (etc.), London, 1788.

Extract in: UM, vol. 82, 1788, pp. 265–66.

4196 BREWSTER, John
Ardra and Abala: an African tale in verse with a preface on the slave trade . . . R. Christopher, Stockton upon Tees, 1788. 16 pp.

4197 YEARSLEY, Ann
A poem on the inhumanity of the slave-trade . . . G. G. J. & J. Robinson, London, [1788]. 30 pp.

Addressed to the city of Bristol.

4198 MORE, Hannah
Slavery, a poem. T. Cadell, London, 1788. 20 pp.

Attacks the slave trade and slavery. Reprinted in her Works (London, 1801) as 'The slave trade: a poem'.

4199 STREET, Thomas George
Aura; or The slave. A poem. In two cantos . . . G. Kearsley, London, 1788. 36 pp.

Romantic story of African lovers kidnapped by slave traders.

4200 WATERS, Edward Pye
'On the slave trade.' (UM, 1788, vol. 2, pp. 149, 205–06, 318–19, 433.)

Laborious antislavery poem.

4201 *The AFRICAN. Liverpool, [1788].

By William Roscoe and James Currie. Abolitionist poem. Reprinted in: Carlton House Magazine, London, vol. 2, 1793, p. 131; also in: Metrical miscellany (London, 1802), pp. 23–25.

4202 The WRONGS of Almoona, or the African's revenge. A narrative poem, founded on historical facts. By a friend to all mankind. H. Hodgson, Liverpool; (etc.), [1788]. viii, 66 pp.

Based on an incident during the English conquest of Jamaica 1655.

4203 FALCONAR, Maria
Poems on slavery: by Maria Falconar, aged 17, and Harriet Falconar, aged 14. Egertons; (etc.), London, 1788. vii, 25 pp.

4204 MULLIGAN, Hugh
Poems chiefly on slavery and oppression, with notes and illustrations. W. Lowndes, London, 1788. iii, 90 [99] pp.

Includes several poems critical of the African slave trade.

4205 'The SLAVES. An elegy.' (Signed: Della Crusca.) (EMLR, vol. 13, March 1788, pp. 219–20.)

By Robert Merry. Describes the sugar cane as manured with blood. (Reprinted in: SM, vol. 50, April 1788, pp. 199–200.)

4206 GOUGES, Olympe de
Zamore et Mirza, ou l'heureux naufrage, drame indien, en trois actes, et en prose. Auteur; Cailleau, Paris, 1788. 99 pp.

Play written 1783 about a slave revolt, reissued with an appendix: 'Réflexions sur les hommes nègres'. See (4230).

4207 WILLIAMS, Helen Maria
A poem on the bill lately passed for regulating the slave trade. T. Cadell, London, 1788. 23 pp.

Welcomes the new law. For a critique by Robert Burns, see: 'A few strictures on Miss Williams' poem on the slave trade' (SM, n.s., vol. 1, 1817, pp. 109–11.)

4208 JAMIESON, John
The sorrows of slavery, a poem. Containing a faithful statement of facts concerning the African slave trade. J. Murray, London, 1789. 80 pp.

Describes the slave trade in Africa, the middle passage and West Indian slavery.

4209 STANFIELD, James Field
The Guinea voyage. A poem. In three

books. James Phillips, London, 1789. vi, 37 pp.

Depicts the slave trade from personal experience and advocates its abolition. See (717).

4210 *ERZÄHLUNGEN von den Sitten und Schicksalen der Negersklaven. . . Haller, Bern, 1789.

By J. E. Kolb. Antislavery stories including 'Quaschi' and 'Zameo'.

4211 'ORONOOKO, ein Trauerspiel in fünf Aufzügen.' In: Deutsche Schaubühne, vol. 7 (Augsburg, 1789), pp. 201–330.

Adaptation by von Eisenthal of W. H. von Dalberg's play 'Oronocko' (Mannheim, 1786), based on (4158).

4212 *NICHOLLS, F.
Sable victims. A Barbadoes narration; inscribed to the promoters of the slave trade, and addressed to J. Hargrave, Esq. a friend to natural liberty. Richardson (etc.), London, 1789. 41 pp.

Antislavery poem. (Reviewed in: CrR, vol. 68, July 1789, p. 74; MR, vol. 81, Aug. 1789, p. 180; GM, Sept. 1789, p. 827.)

4213 CRAWFORD, Charles
Liberty: a Pindaric ode. Jasper Sprange, Tunbridge-Wells, [1789]. iii, 12 pp.

'Fourth strophe' deals with the African slave trade.

4214 PLUM, Frederik
'Brev i Anledning af Hr. Capitaine Iserts Død i Guinea.' (Minerva, Kiøbenhavn, Aug, 1789, pp. 264–68.)

Poem describing the slave trade as Europe's shame and praising Isert as a humanitarian.

4215 WILKINSON, Thomas
An appeal to England, on behalf of the abused Africans, a poem. James Phillips, London, 1789. 34 pp.

Urges abolition of the slave trade.

4216a *Le NÈGRE comme il y à peu de blancs, par l'auteur de Cécile, fille d'Achmet III. empereur des Turcs. Madras; Buisson, Paris, 1789. 3 vol.

Translated as:

4216b The negro equalled by few Europeans . . . G. G. J. & J. Robinson, London, 1790. 2 vol.

By Joseph La Vallée. Sentimental novel about Itanoko, a Senegalese carried as a slave to St. Domingue. Reissued 1799 in: Nouvelle bibliothèque des romans, Paris, ser. 1, vol. 16; 210 pp. (English translation, by Phillis Wheatley, reprinted in: AM, vol. 9, 1791, pp. 53–60, 99–107, 145–53, 205–13, 257–65, 313–24; vol. 10, 1791, pp. 29–40, 77–88, 129–44, 185–200, 241–56, 285–303.)

4217 **CAMUS, Nicolas René**
Le songe, suivi du Discours d'un nègre, conduit au supplice. Desenne, Paris, 1790. 56 pp.

The 'Discours' is an antislavery poem based on (4178).

4218 *A POETICAL epistle to the enslaved Africans, in the character of an ancient negro, born a slave in Pennsylvania; but liberated some years since, and instructed in useful learning, and the great truths of Christianity. With a brief historical introduction, and biographical notices of some of the earliest advocates for that oppressed class of our fellow-creatures. Joseph Crukshank, Philadelphia, 1790. 24 pp.

By Joseph Sansom.

4219 'The AFRICAN boy.' (Signed: The Bard.) *In*: The British album, vol. 2 (London, 1790), pp. 103–05.

Poem attributed to Edward Jerningham.

4220 'A RHAPSODICAL execration of the slave trade.' *In*: WESLEY, John *and* WHITEFIELD, G. The triumph of divine mercy (London, *c*. 1790), pp. 43–48.

Abolitionist poem, 'by a lover of peace and liberty'.

4221 NO abolition of slavery; or the universal empire of love: a poem. R. Faulder, London, 1791. 24 pp.

By James Boswell. Sarcastic attack on the abolitionists, dedicated to the West Indian planters.

4222 *The DICTATES of indignation. A poem on the African slave trade. By an undergraduate, Oxford. Rivingtons, London, 1791. 28 pp.

Reviewed in: MR, n.s., vol. 4, 1791, pp. 469–70.

4223 **BARBAULD, Anna Letitia**
Epistle to William Wilberforce, Esq. on the rejection of the bill for abolishing the slave trade. J. Johnson, London, 1791. 14 pp.

Poem deploring the failure of Parliament to pass an abolition bill.

4224 *An ADDRESS to every Briton, on the slave trade; being an effectual plan to abolish this disgrace to our country. Robinson, London, 1791. 19 pp.

Antislavery poem. Reviewed in: MR, n.s., vol. 6, 1791, pp. 228–29.

4225 'The DYING African.' (Signed: S. S.) (GM, vol. 61, Nov. 1791, pp. 1046–47.)

By Frank Sayer. Death song of a slave.

4226 **COWPER, William**
'The negro's complaint.' (SM, vol. 54, Jan. 1792, p. 32.)

One of the best known antislavery poems. (Reprinted in: TCM, vol. 24, 1792, p. 185; GM, Dec. 1793, p. 1133; also as 'The slave' in: BrM, vol. 4, 1796, pp. 26–27.) See (2104, 3048).

4227 An EPISTLE to Will. Wilberforce, Esq. written during the disturbances in the West Indies. Darton & Harvey, London, 1792. xi, 31 pp.

Attack on the slave trade in verse.

4228 **MARJORIBANKS, John**
Slavery: an essay in verse . . . Humbly inscribed to planters, merchants, and others concerned in the management or sale of negro slaves. J. Robertson, Edinburgh, 1792. 31 pp.

Opposes the African slave trade and West Indian slavery.

4229 **BIRKETT, M.**
A poem on the African slave trade. Addressed to her own sex by M. Birket. J. Jones, Dublin, 1792. 19; 25 pp.

Abolitionist.

4230 **GOUGES, Olympe de**
L'esclavage des noirs, ou l'heureux naufrage, drame en trois actes, en prose . . . Veuve Duchesne, Paris, 1792. 90 pp.

New edition of (4206).

4231 **HOLDER, Henry Evans**
Fragments of a poem, intended to have been written in consequence of reading Major Majoribanks's Slavery. R. Cruttwell, Bath, 1792. 20 pp.

4232 A MONITORY address to Great Britain; a poem in six parts . . . (Signed: Britannicus.) J. Guthrie, Edinburgh, 1792. xxxvii, 344 pp.

By Niel Douglas. Includes a section

opposing the slave trade; with an appendix of notes.

4233 The PRINCESS of Zanfara; a dramatic poem. A new edition. B. Law & Son, London, 1792. 64 pp.

By William Hutchinson. Five act play on African slavery in Latin America.

4234 *HALL, Thomas
Achmet to Selim; or, the dying negro; a poem. Liverpool, 1792.

'Verses against the slave trade' (Watt).

4235 TEA and sugar, or the nabob and the creole; a poem, in two cantos, by Timothy Touchstone, Gent. J. Ridgway, London, 1792. 18 pp.

Canto II, 'The creole', denounces the cruelty of the West Indian economy based on the African slave trade.

4236 A WEST Indian converted, and slave grateful. John Elder, Edinburgh, 1792. 8 pp.

Dialogue in verse between an African slave and his master on the rights and wrongs of slavery.

4237 ADNEY, Thomas
'The slave, an ode.' (EMLR, vol. 22, Oct. 1792, pp. 304–06.)

Lament of a slave for his Gambian homeland.

4238 FLORIAN, Jean Pierre Claris de
'Sélico, nouvelle africaine.' *In his*: Nouvelles nouvelles (Londres, 1792), pp. 64–90.

Short story; the hero, Selico, sells himself to save his family but is released by the king of Dahomey. See (4245–46).

4239 'ON slavery and the slave trade.' (BrM, vol. 1, 1793, p. 90.)

Antislavery poem.

4240 'MUNGO's address.' (Signed: P. P.) *In*: ANDERSON, J. The Bee, vol. 13 (Edinburgh, 1793), pp. 215–16.

Antislavery epilogue written for a popular 'West Indian' comedy.

4241 'The AFRICAN's complaint on-board a slave ship.' (Signed: J. C.) (GM, vol. 63, Aug. 1793, pp. 749.)

Poem in 'pidgin' English.

4242 CASSAN, ——
La liberté des noirs, décrétée par la Convention nationale. Hymne patriotique, présenté à la société populaire des Gardes-Françaises. Pellier, [Paris, 1794]. 4 pp.

Poem celebrating the French law abolishing slavery and the slave trade.

4243 *EEREZANG voor het fransche volk by gelegenheid dat het den slaven-handel afgeschaft heeft. [Holland,] 1794. 36 pp.

Antislavery poem.

4244 LARIVALLIÈRE, ——
Les Africains ou le triomphe de l'humanité, comédie en un acte et en prose, représentée sur les principaux théâtres de la République. Meurant, Paris, an troisième [1794]. 48 pp.

Play set in Whydah when the slave trade is abolished.

4245 *GASSIER, J. M.
La liberté des nègres, pantomime patriotique mêlée de danses et à grand spectacle . . . Toubon, Paris, 1794. 8 pp.

Play based on (4238).

4246 *SELICO, an African tale, translated into English verse, from the French prose of Monsieur de Florian. R. Trewman & Son, Exeter, 1794. viii, 31 pp.

See (4238). Sold for the benefit of the abolition committee.

4247 'ODE on seeing a negro-funeral.' (UM, vol. 95, Sept. 1794, p. 203.)

Poem by Bryan Edwards, contrasting life in Africa with slavery. (Also in: GM, Dec. 1809, p. 1149.)

4248 REITZENSTEIN, Carl, Freiherr von
'Die Negersklaven. Ein Trauerspiel in fünf Aufzügen.' *In*: Deutsche Schau-bühne, vol. 61 (Augsburg, 1794); 176 pp.

Antislavery play set in the West Indies; dedicated to Wilberforce.

4249 BOWLES, William Lisle
'The African.' *In his*: Sonnets (Bath; London, 1794), pp. 93–95.

Reprinted as 'The dying slave' in his Poetical works (Edinburgh, 1855), vol. 1, pp. 58–60.

4250 The SORROWS of Yamba; or, the negro woman's lamentation. J. Marshall; R. White, London; S. Hazard, Bath, [1795]. 12 pp.

By Hannah More. Poem about an African woman taken as a slave to the West Indies.

4251 COWPER, William
'On slavery.' *In*: The Bee, a selection
of poetry (London, 1795), pp. 9–10.

Antislavery poem.

4252 BUTLER, Weeden
'The slave.' *In his*: Bagatelles (London,
1795), pp. 1–6.

Poem. An African remembers his
native home.

4253 LLOYD, Charles
'The slave.—An ode.' *In his*: Poems on
various subjects (Carlisle, 1795), pp.
62–64.

Abolitionist.

4254 PINDAR, Peter, *pseud*.
'Azid, or the song of the captive negro.'
(SM, vol. 57, Aug. 1795, pp. 517–18.)

By John Wolcot. Lament in verse of
an African slave for his homeland.

**4255 *PIGAULT-LEBRUN, Guillaume
Charles Antoine**
Le blanc et le noir, drame en quatre
actes et en prose . . . Mayeur, Paris,
an IV [1795]. xii, 92 pp.

Antislavery play about the revolt in
St. Domingue.

4256 PARNY, Évariste Désiré de, *chevalier*
'A Madagascar song.' (SM, vol. 57,
1795, p. 846.)

Translation of no. IX of his 'Chansons madécasses' (Londres, 1787);
a mother sells her daughter into
slavery. (Also in: Monthly Mirror,
London, vol. 1, Dec. 1795, p. 89.)

4257 'The NEGRO boy.' (BrM, vol. 3, 1795,
p. 57.)

An African prince regrets having
bartered a boy for a watch. (Also
printed, signed 'Anti-Doulos', in:
MoM, vol. 2, Dec. 1796, p. 890;
signed 'W. M.' in: UM, n.s., vol. 8,
1807, p. 240.)

**4258a KOTZEBUE, August Friedrich Ferdi-
nand von**
Die Negersklaven. Ein historisch-drama-
tisches Gemählde in drey Akten. Paul
Gotthelf Kummer, Leipzig, 1796. 139
pp.

Translated as:

4258b The negro slaves, a dramatic-historical
piece, in three acts . . . T. Cadell &
W. Davies; J. Edwards, London,
1796. x, 142 pp.

Prose drama set in Jamaica, with
discussions of the slave trade and
slavery.

4259 *MORRIS, Thomas
Quashy, or the coal-black maid. A
tale. J. Ridgway, London, 1796. 26 pp.

Antislavery poem set in Martinique.

4260 'LINES written on seeing a negro
boy begging, in great distress.' (Signed:
L. G. Z.) (Monthly Mirror, London,
vol. 2, Dec. 1796, p. 498.)

Verse spoken by an African boy,
sole survivor of a wrecked slave ship.

4261 ENORT, T.
'Alico and Maila; or, the injured
Africans. An original tale.' (EMLR,
vol. 31, Feb. 1797, p. 99.)

Tragic story of a raid by European
slave traders.

4262 TRIBUTES of affection: with The
slave; and other poems. By a lady;
and her brother. T. N. Longman;
C. Dilly, London, 1797. 143 pp.

Includes 'The slave', by Sophia
Tomlins (written 1787), and 'To the
House of Commons, on their vote
for the abolition of the slave-trade,
April 2, 1792', by E. Tomlins.

4263 GORTON, John
Tubal to Seba. The negro suicide. A
poem . . . W. Kemmish, London;
(etc.), 1797. 41 pp.

Death song of an African slave,
cursing Europe's slave traders.

4264 'The AFRICAN's appeal to the Britons
for the abolition of the slave trade.'
(Signed: I. H. C.) (Monthly Mirror,
London, vol. 3, June 1797, pp. 367–69.)

A poem.

4265 *'The SORROWS of Yamba.' (Signed:
E. S. J.) (UM, vol. 101, July 1797, pp.
43–44.)

4266 HAWKINS, Joseph
A history of a voyage to the coast of
Africa, and travels into the interior of
that country; containing particular
descriptions of the climate and inhabitants, and interesting particulars concerning the slave trade . . . S. C. Ustick
& Co., Philadelphia, 1797. 179 pp.

Account of a purported slaving
voyage from Charleston to West
Africa in 1795; the description of the
interior is patently fictitious.

4267 The ALGERINE captive; or, the
life and adventures of Doctor Updike

Underhill: six years a prisoner among the Algerines. David Carlisle, Jun., Walpole, N.H., 1797. 2 vol.

> By Royall Tyler. Novel, including an account of a slaving voyage to the Congo and Benin in 1788 which ends in capture by Algerian corsairs.

4268 HOLCROFT, Fanny
'The negro.' (MoM, vol. 4, Oct. 1797, p. 286.)

> Poem. A dying African slave curses his Christian masters.

4269 *KONGEN af Dahomet, en virkelig Tildragelse strax efter den amerikansk-engelske Krig. Interessant for Konger og Folket. Christian Frederik Holm, Kiøbenhavn, 1797. 32 pp.

> By Baron F. C. Wedel-Jarlsberg.

4270 SOUTHEY, Robert
'Poems on the slave trade.' *In his*: Poems (Bristol; London, 1797), pp. 29–43.

> Six sonnets (1794) and 'To the genius of Africa' (1795). The second edition (1799) includes 'The sailor, who had served in the slave trade' (1798): vol. 2, pp. 103–14. See (4311).

4271 *MOENS, Petronella
'Bij het afschaffen van den slavenhandel door de fransche natie.' *In her*: Vruchten der eenzamheid (Amsterdam, 1798), pp. 24–27.

> Poem on the abolition of slavery by France 1794.

4272 *PIQUENARD, J. B.
Adonis, ou le bon nègre, anecdote coloniale. Didot le jeune, Paris, an VI [1798].

4273 'The AFRICAN.' (Signed: I. M.) (EMLR, vol. 34, Oct. 1798, p. 259.)

> Poem describing a slave about to be carried to the West Indies.

4274 McLAREN, Archibald
The negro slaves, a dramatic piece, of one act, with songs . . . London, 1799. 24 pp.

> Antislavery comedy set in the West Indies.

4275 ROBINSON, Mary
'The negro girl.' *In her*: Lyrical tales (London, 1800), pp. 107–14.

> Zelma mourns her enslaved lover Draco; the slave ship is wrecked and both drown.

4276 'The NEGRO's imprecation.' (Signed: W. C.) (Meteors, London, vol. 2, 1800, pp. 53–56.)

> Antislavery poem.

4277 'BOKO, or the African.' (Signed: R. H.) (MoM, vol. 11, Feb. 1801, pp. 45–46.)

> A slave curses his condition and commits suicide. (Also in: SM, vol. 63, March 1801, p. 204.)

4278 FRANCES, Henry
'The slave; a plaintive ballad. Written and inscribed to the Honourable Mr. Wilberforce, M.P.' (Lady's Magazine, London, vol. 32, March 1801, p. 159.)

4279 BURDETT, William
The life and exploits of Three-finger'd Jack, the terror of Jamaica; with a particular account of the Obi; being the only true one of that celebrated and fascinating mischief, so prevalent in the West Indies . . . On this history is founded the popular pantomimical drama of Obi; or, Three-finger'd Jack; performed at the Theatre-Royal, Haymarket; an accurate account of which . . . is also added. A. Neil, Sommers Town, 1801. 64 pp.

> Antislavery story, adding material from Mungo Park's account of Bambara to the story of a Jamaican rebel. Headed: 'Fourth edition, with additions.' First published anonymously as: The LIFE and exploits of Mansony. Commonly called Three-finger'd Jack, the terror of Jamaica (Somers Town, 1800).

4280 BAILLIE, R.
'On the slave trade. Inscribed to P. Butler Esq. of South Carolina . . .' (GM, March 1802, p. 255.)

> Abolitionist poem.

4281 'The SLAVE.' (Signed: J. W., Glasgow.) (SM, vol. 64, Oct. 1802, p. 847.)

> Slaves at sea welcome a storm as their deliverer.

4282 COWPER, William
Poems. London, 1803. 2 vol.

> Contains three antislavery poems written in 1788 (vol. 1, pp. 311–19): 'The negro's complaint', 'Pity for poor Africans' and 'The morning dream'. ('Sweet meat has sour sauce: or, the slave-trader in the dumps', also from 1788, was printed in his Works, vol. 10, London, 1837, pp. 10–11.)

4283 BRANAGAN, Thomas
Avenia: or, a tragical poem, on the oppression of the human species, and infringement of the rights of man. In six books, with notes explanatory and miscellaneous . . . Silas Engles, Philadelphia; Samuel Wood, New York, 1805. 358 pp.

Epic poem on the African slave trade and West Indian slavery.

4284 *MARRIOTT, John
'Mialma; or a description of some of the miseries resulting to the inhabitants of Africa, from the traffic in men carried on by the Europeans.' In his: Poems (New-Bradford, 1805), pp. 70–83.

4285 SOUTHEY, Robert
'The dancing bear. Recommended to the advocates for the slave trade.' In his: Metrical tales and other poems (London, 1805), pp. 135–37.

4286 The TONGUE; or, essays on the uses and abuses of speech . . . including a description of the sufferings of the negroes in Africa and the West-Indies . . . J. White, Wisbech; (etc.), [c. 1805]. 203 pp.

By Richard Wright. 'Essay II' includes a 'digression' (pp. 52–79) consisting of a poem and prose pieces attacking the slave trade.

4287 GRAHAME, James
'To England on the slave trade.' In his: The birds of Scotland (Edinburgh, 1806), pp. 167–69.

Poem, bitterly critical of England for rejecting Wilberforce's abolition bill in 1795.

4288 The HISTORY and adventures of that famous negro robber 3 Finger'd Jack, the terror of Jamaica. C. Randall, Stirling, 1806. 24 pp.

See (4279).

4289 'SONG, on the wreck of a slave ship.' (Signed: Marcius.) (Monthly Mirror, London, vol. 22, Oct. 1806, p. 272.)

4290 *BRANAGAN, Thomas
The penitential tyrant; or, slave trader reformed: a pathetic poem, in four cantos . . . The second edition, enlarged. Samuel Wood, New-York, 1807. xii, 290 pp. illus.

The appendix includes: 'Buying stolen goods synonymous with stealing; or, the immorality of using the products of slavery demonstrated' (pp. 219–39).

4291 STANFIELD, James Field
The Guinea voyage, a poem, in three books . . . To which are added, Observations on a voyage to the coast of Africa, in a series of letters to Thomas Clarkson, A.M.   J. Robertson, Edinburgh; (etc.), 1807. vi, 77 pp.

Joint reissue of (4209) and (717).

4292 MANT, Richard
The slave, and other poetical pieces . . . University Press, Oxford; (etc.), 1807. 63 pp.

The title poem (pp. 9–30) describes the slave trade and its effects on Africa.

4293 THELWALL, John
'The negro's prayer.' (MoM, vol. 23, April 1807, pp. 252–53.)

Verse; an African slave prays for the abolition of the slave trade.

4294 *JONES, Jenkin
'The white man's gratitude, a negro tale; written when the abolition of the slave trade was first brought forward in the House of Commons.' In his: Pros and cons (London, 1807), pp. 162–64.

A tribute to Wilberforce.

4295 'The NEGRO: a poem. Written on the island of St. Croix.' (Signed: L. S.) (MoM, vol. 25, Feb. 1808, pp. 44–45.)

Describes the longing of an African slave for his homeland.

4296 STEPHENSON, Benjamin
'Negroes fettered, and conducted to the vessel which conveys them from their native land. A fragment.' (Lady's Magazine, London, vol. 39, Feb. 1808, p. 79.)

4297 SANSOM, Francis
A poetical epistle on the abolition of the slave trade; addressed to W. Wilberforce, Esq. M.P. Longman, Hurst, Rees & Orme, & H. D. Symonds; J. Hatchard, London, 1808. 46 pp.

4298 'POEMS on the anniversary of the abolition of the slave trade.' (CO, vol. 7, 1808, pp. 304–05, 367–69; vol. 9, 1810, pp. 220–21.)

4299 'The CAPTIVE.' (Signed: W. M. T.) (MoM, vol. 27, July 1809, p. 587.)

Sonnet about an African chief on a slave ship.

4300 POEMS on the abolition of the slave trade; written by James Montgomery, James Grahame, and E. Benger . . . R. Bowyer, London, 1809. ii, 141 pp.

Contains: 'The West Indies', by Montgomery (1807); 'Africa delivered; or, the slave trade abolished', by Grahame; 'A poem occasioned by the abolition of the slave trade in 1806', by Elizabeth Benger. (Reviewed in: CO, vol. 9, 1810, pp. 103–17; EcR, vol. 6, pt. 1, 1810, pp. 289–306, 440–50.)

4301 MONTGOMERY, James
The West-Indies, and other poems . . . The third edition. Longman, Hurst, Rees, Orme & Brown, London, 1810. ii, 160 pp.

'The West Indies. A poem, in four parts. Written in honour of the abolition of the African slave trade by the British legislature, in 1807' (pp. 1–79). (Reviewed in: The Philanthropist, London, vol. 1, 1811, pp. 93–100, 196–200.)

4302 HERDER, Johann Gottfried von
'Neger-Idyllen.' *In his*: Sämmtliche Werke, vol. 11 (Tübingen, 1810), pp. 248–59.

Antislavery poems, part of 'Briefe zur Beförderung der Humanität', first published 1797.

4303 *The AFRICANS; or, war, love, and duty; a play in three acts . . . M. Carey, Philadelphia, 1811. 169 pp.

By George Colman. (Adapted version by William Dunlap.) Set in Senegal where European slave merchants exploit local wars; first performed in London 1808. Based on (4238), with material from Mungo Park (172).

4304 WILSON, John
'On reading Mr Clarkson's History of the abolition of the slave trade.' *In his*: The isle of palms, and other poems (Edinburgh, 1812), pp. 357–61.

Vision of a better future for Africa.

4305 'STANZAS on the anniversary of the abolition of the slave trade.' *In*: METRICAL effusions (Woodbridge, 1812), pp. 114–18.

By Bernard Barton.

4306 'The HORRORS of slavery. A poem. Addressed to W. Wilberforce, Esq. M.P.' *In*: MY hookah; or, the stranger in Calcutta . . . By an officer (Calcutta, 1812), pp. 1–6.

By Joseph Stewart.

4307 The ADVENTURES of Mr. Thomas Freeman, who was shipwrecked on the coast of St. Domingo, in the year 1806; and received into the family of Orizo, an African . . . W. Nicholson, London, [*c.* 1812]. 28 pp.

Includes Orizo's account of his enslavement (pp. 12–22).

4308 CAPP, Mary Elizabeth
The African princess, and other poems. J. Keymer, Yarmouth, 1813. 188 pp.

'The African princess, or The slave's tale. An eclogue' (pp. 1–36).

4309 JENNINGS, John
The prospects of Africa, with other poems. T. Lester; Sherwood, Neely & Jones, London, 1814. 120 pp.

The title poem (pp. 1–61) describes the miseries of the slave trade and a utopian future.

4310 MONTGOMERY, James
The abolition of the slave trade, a poem, in four parts. R. Bowyer, London, 1814. 53 pp.

With portraits of abolitionists, plates illustrating the slave trade, and notes.

4311 SOUTHEY, Robert
The minor poems of Robert Southey . . . Longman, Hurst, Rees, Orme & Brown, London, 1815. 3 vol.

'Poems concerning the slave trade' (vol. 1, pp. 31–62); 'The dancing bear' (vol. 2, pp. 101–03). See (4270, 4285).

4312 WORDSWORTH, William
'To Thomas Clarkson, on the final passing of the bill for the abolition of the slave trade, March, 1807.' *In his*: Poems (London, 1815), vol. 2, pp. 229.

A sonnet.

4313 'ODE on the abolition of the slave trade.' (Signed: G. T.) (MoM, vol. 47, June 1819, p. 431.)

4314 STAËL-HOLSTEIN, Anne Louise Germaine, *baronne de*
'Mirza, ou lettre d'un voyageur.' *In her*: Oeuvres complètes, vol. 2 (Paris, 1820), pp. 221–44.

Short story written 1795; the Wolof hero, Ximéo, is saved from slavery by the French governor of Goree.

4315 SHERWOOD, Mary Martha
The re-captured negro . . . Second edition. F. Houlston & Son, Wellington, Salop., 1821. 72 pp.

Story of an African boy released from a slave ship at Sierra Leone. Also published as: Dazee, or the recaptured negro (Newburyport [Mass.], 1822; 47 pp.).

4316 MORE, Hannah
The sorrows of Yamba, or the negro woman's lamentation, by Hannah More. The negro's complaint, by William Cowper. Etc. Newcastle Religious Tract Society, Newcastle, 1823. 12 pp.

See (4250) and (4226).

4317 SAMBOE; or, the African boy . . . Harvey & Darton, London, 1823. viii, 175 pp.

By Mary Ann Hedge. Novel for children about the slave trade from Whydah to Jamaica.

4318 CHAUVET, Joseph Joachim Victor
L'abolition de la traite des noirs . . . Firmin Didot père & fils, Paris, 1823. 10 pp.

Poem awarded first prize in Académie Française competition. Also published as: Néali, ou la traite des nègres. (Reviewed in: RE, vol. 19, 1823, pp. 496–501.)

4319 *CORBIÈRE, Édouard
Élégies brésiliennes, suivies de poésies diverses et une notice sur la traite des noirs . . . Plancher, Paris, 1823. 97 pp.

4320 *BIGNAN, Anne
L'abolition de la traite des noirs. Epître aux souverains de l'Europe rassemblés au Congrès de Vienne, qui a obtenu la première mention honorable au jugement de l'Académie française, à la séance publique du 25 août 1823. F. Didot, Paris, 1823. 26 pp.

A poem.

4321 *ALLETZ, Èdouard
L'abolition de la traite des noirs, poème . . . Delaunay, Paris, 1823. 12 pp.

4322 *L'ESCLAVAGE, poème, par M.D. . . . Firmin Didot, Paris, 1823. 36 pp.

By A. B. Marie Du Mesnil. Written for the Académie Française competition.

4323 MORTON, Sarah Wentworth Apthorp
'The African chief.' In her: My mind and its thoughts (Boston, 1823), pp. 201–03.

Poem on the capture and murder of a Gambian chief by slave traders.

4324 The KOROMANTYN slaves; or, West Indian sketches . . . J. Hatchard & Son, London, 1823. viii, 278 pp.

Novel about the African slave trade and colonial slavery.

4325 COLERIDGE, Samuel Taylor
'The negro's euthanasia. Translated from the introductory stanzas to a Greek prize ode of Mr. Coleridge.' (London Magazine, vol. 8, Oct. 1823, p. 356.)

Translation by 'Olen' (Sir Charles Elton) of four stanzas of the 'Greek prize ode on the slave trade' (written at Cambridge 1792), printed in: The poetical works of Samuel Taylor Coleridge (London, 1893), pp. 46–47, with the Latin title 'Sors misera servorum in insulis Indiae Occidentalis'.

4326 *PICARD, Espérance
L'abolition de la traite des noirs, poème. Chalopin fils, Caen, 1824. 16 pp.

4327 RUSHTON, Edward
'The Coromantees.' In his: Poems and other writings (London, 1824), pp. 72–76.

Slaves defend a British ship against a French attacker.

4328 OPIE, Amelia Alderson
The negro boy's tale, a poem, addressed to children. Harvey & Darton, London; S. Wilkin, Norwich, 1824. viii, 16 pp.

Antislavery story of Zambo, an African slave in Jamaica.

4329 *GUNIMA, nouvelle africaine du dix-huitième siècle, imitée de l'allemand par M. Hippolyte C..... J.-N.Barba, Paris, 1824. iv, 191 pp.

By Hippolyte Carnot. Antislavery novel, with Hottentot heroes, based on a story by K. F. van der Velde.

4330 RADAMA; or, the enlightened African. With sketches of Madagascar . . . Harvey & Darton, London, 1824. 172 pp.

By Mary Ann Hedge. Novel about the suppression of the illegal slave trade from East Africa.

4331 FAIRBURN's edition of The wonderful life and adventures of Three Fingered Jack, the terror of Jamaica! Giving an account of his persevering courage and gallant heroism in revenging the cause of his injured parents . . . J. Fairburn, London, [1825]. 24 pp. illus.

Story of the capture by European slavers of a Gambian family and the son's vengeance in Jamaica (4288).

4332 *DOIN, Sophie
La famille noire, ou la traite et l'esclavage. H. Servier, Paris, 1825. viii, 148 pp. illus.

Novel about Africans sold to St. Domingue. (Reviewed in: RE, vol. 28, 1825, pp. 274–75.)

4333 *PABAN, Gabrielle de
Le nègre et la créole, ou mémoires d'Eulalie D***. Boulland & Cie, Paris, 1825. 3 vol.

Novel set in West Africa; the hero, Zambo, dies in a revolt on a slave ship.

4334 OPIE, Amelia
The black man's lament; or, how to make sugar. Harvey & Darton, London, 1826. 25 pp. illus.

Antislavery poem for children describing the slave trade and sugar cultivation.

4335 The NEGRO's friend, or, the Sheffield anti-slavery album. J. Blackwell; Miss Gales, Sheffield; (etc.), 1826. xii, 204 pp.

Includes 'Zangara, or the negro slave', by Samuel Roberts, and 'The voyage of the blind' (based on the case of the slave ship 'Rodeur').

4336 COWPER, William
The negro's complaint: a poem. To which is added, Pity for poor Africans. Harvey & Darton, London, 1826. 22 pp. illus.

Edition for children. See (4226).

4337 *EVANS, Ann
Africa. A poem. Flagg & Gould, Andover, Mass., 1826. 20 pp.

On the slave trade.

**4338a*BUG-JARGAL, par l'auteur de Han d'Islande. Urbain Canel, Paris, 1826. 386 pp.

Translated as:

4338b The slave-king. From the Bug-Jargal of Victor Hugo. Smith, Elder & Co., London, 1833. viii, 319 pp.

Novel by Victor Hugo on the slave revolt in St. Domingue 1791. Also translated as: The noble rival; or, the prince of Congo (London, [1845]).

4339 'The AFRICAN chief.' (Signed: B.) (United States Review and Literary Gazette, Boston, vol. 1, Dec. 1826, pp. 219–20.)

By William Cullen Bryant. Poem, based on a story published in: AR, vol. 1, 1825, p. 61.

4340 BOWDICH, Sarah
'The Booroom slave.' (Forget Me Not, London, 1828, pp. 37–77; illus.)

Short story about the slave trade in the hinterland of the Gold Coast. (Reprinted in: AR, vol. 5, 1829, pp. 65–85.)

4341 The ANTI-SLAVERY album: selections in verse from Cowper, Hannah More, Montgomery, Pringle, and others. Howlett & Brimmer, London, 1828. (12 ll.)

4342 The POOR black man . . . Written before the abolition of the slave-trade, while the subject occupied the attention of Parliament, about twenty years ago . . . J. Flamank, Jun., Wallingford, 1828. (2 pp.)

Poem for children.

4343 MILMAN, Henry Hart
'The slave ship.' *In*: The poetical works of Milman, Bowles, Wilson, and Barry Cornwall (Paris, 1829), pt. 1, pp. 187–88.

Poem based on the 'Rodeur' case (QR, vol. 26, 1821, p. 71). See (868).

4344 MOORE, Dugald
'Sambo.' *In his*: The African, a tale; and other poems (Glasgow, 1829), pp. 201–03.

Sambo jumps overboard from a slave ship and drowns.

4345a MÉRIMÉE, Prosper
'Tamango.' (Revue de Paris, vol. 7, Oct, 1829, pp. 43–64.)

Translated as:

4345b 'Tamango.' *In*: Tales from Mérimée (London, 1929), pp. 49–74.

The hero, a Senegalese trader, is kidnapped by a French slaver, leads a successful revolt at sea, is rescued by a British warship and brought to Jamaica. Also translated as: The slave ship . . . A tragedy in black and white (Evanston, Ill., 1934; 46 pp., illus.). See (4361).

4346a*SUE, Eugène
Atar-Gull . . . 3e édition. C. Vimont, Paris, 1831. xvi, 400 pp.

z

Abridged version translated as:

4346b The negro's revenge; or, Brulart, the
black pirate . . . J. Clements, London,
[1842]. iv, 49 pp.

Novel about a Namaqua slave taken
to Jamaica, where he avenges the
death of his father.

4347 *JAL, Auguste
'Un négrier.' *In his:* Scènes de la vie
maritime (Paris, 1831), vol. 3.

Short story, in imitation of (4345).

4348 'The SLAVE ship.' (Signed: B.) (New
Monthly Magazine, London, vol. 32,
1831, pt. 2, p. 312.)

4349 BOURGEOIS, Anicet *and* MASSON,
Michel
Atar-Gull, mélodrame en trois actes et
six tableaux, imité du roman de M.
Eugène Sue . . . Représenté, pour la
première fois, sur le Théâtre de l'Am-
bigu-Comique, le 26 avril 1832. Marchant, Paris, 1832. 68 pp.

Adaptation of (4346), set in Haiti.

4350 *CORBIÈRE Édouard
Le négrier. Denain & Delamarre,
Paris, 1832. 2 vol.

Realistic novel about the West
African slave trade 1814–18, in the
style of Mérimée. (An illustrated
edition, Paris, 1936, has a biographical introduction by Charles de la
Morandière.)

4351a BÉRANGER, Pierre Jean de
'Les nègres et les marionettes. Fable.'
In: Chansons de De Béranger, vol. 3
(Bruxelles, 1832), pp. 106–07.

Translated as:

4351b 'The negroes and the puppet-show. A
fable.' *In:* Béranger: two hundred of
his lyrical poems (New-York, 1850),
pp. 249–50.

Slaves are entertained with puppets
on a slave ship.

4352 WOOD, Hamlet
The negro: an historical poem, in the
shape of dialogue, describing the unchristian and wicked principle and
practices of slavery, as exhibited, thro'
different periods of time, in Africa, and
the West Indies. R. Timmis, Burslem,
1833. xiii, 100 pp.

Mungo, an African chief, is captured
and taken as a slave to Cuba.

4353 TOM Cringle's log . . . Second edition.

William Blackwood, Edinburgh; T.
Cadell, London, 1834. 2 vol.

By Michael Scott. Sea novel, with an
account of antislavery cruising. (Originally published as a serial in:
BM, vol. 26, 1829, pp. 317–19, 728–
30; vol. 27, 1830, pp. 861–63; vol.
28, 1830, pp. 65–67, 350, 687–89;
vol. 29, 1831, pp. 45–47, 977–79;
vol. 30, 1831, pp. 795–801; vol. 31,
1832, pp. 195–200, 884–906; vol. 32,
1832, pp. 22–31, 145–64, 300–12,
456–79, 751–66, 912–30; vol. 33,
1833, pp. 26–42, 170–87, 298–320,
451–75, 737–63; vol. 34, 1833, pp.
71–94, 141–71.)

4354 ROSCOE, William Stanley
'Ode to May, written in 1807, on the
abolition of the African slave trade.'
In his: Poems (London, 1834), pp. 96–
101.

Describes Africa's joy at abolition.

4355 The BOW in the cloud; or, the negro's
memorial. A collection of original
contributions, in prose and verse,
illustrative of the evils of slavery and
commemorative of its abolition in
the British colonies. Jackson & Wal-
ford, London, 1834. xv, 408 pp.

By various authors, including tributes
to Clarkson, Sharp, Wilberforce and
Grégoire.

4356 'The CRUISE of the Midge . . .'
(BM, vol. 35, 1834, pp. 311–30, 459–80,
587–608, 899–921; vol. 36, 1834, pp.
29–47, 190–208, 300–22, 471–93, 642–51,
812–28; vol. 37, 1835, pp. 319–35, 447–
66, 579–94, 767–91, 893–906.)

By Michael Scott. Novel about the
West African antislavery squadron.
Republished in 2 vol. by W. Black-
wood & Sons, Edinburgh, 1836.

4357 *DESNOYERS, Charles *and* ALBOIZE
DU PUJOL, Jules Édouard
La traite des noirs, drame en cinq
actes . . . Représenté pour la première
fois, à Paris, sur le Théâtre National
du Cirque, le 24 avril 1835. Neirinckx &
Laruel, Bruxelles, 1835. 90 pp.

Play based on (4350).

4358 CHANDLER, Elizabeth Margaret
The poetical works of Elizabeth Margaret Chandler . . . L. Howell, Philadelphia, 1836. 180 pp.

Includes 'The Afric's dream', 'The
slave ship' and other antislavery
poems.

4359 *A NARRATIVE of the travels, etc. of John Ismael Augustus James, an African of the Mandingo tribe, who was captured, sold into slavery, and subsequently liberated by a benevolent English gentleman. Truro, 1836.

'Pious hoax in the antislavery cause' (P. D. Curtin).

4360 WHITTIER, John Greenleaf
'The slave ships.' In his: Poems written during the progress of the abolition question in the United States (Boston, 1837), pp. 29–34.

Based on the 'Rodeur' story.

4361 *MÉRIMÉE, Prosper
'Une révolte sur un négrier.' (France Maritime, Paris, 1837, vol. 2, pp. 321–36.)

Another version of (4345).

4362 'The AMERICAN slave-ship.' (Signed: C. E. N.) In: TUCKEY, Mary B. The wrongs of Africa (Glasgow, 1838), pp. 17–18.

4363 LANDON, Letitia Elizabeth
'The African prince.' In: The Zenana and minor poems of L. E. L. (London, 1839), pp. 78–82.

The hero is carried away in a slave ship and pines to death in the West Indies.

4364 ELLIOTT, Ebenezer
'Famine in a slave ship.' In: The poetical works of Ebenezer Elliott (Edinburgh, 1840), pp. 127–28.

4365 MADDEN, Richard Robert
Poems by a slave in the island of Cuba, recently liberated; translated from the Spanish by R. R. Madden . . . to which are prefixed two pieces descriptive of Cuban slavery and the slave-traffic, by R. R. M. Thomas Ward & Co., London, 1840. 188 pp.

'The slave-trade merchant, a poem descriptive of the Cuban speculators in stolen men' by Madden (pp. 9–19) is based on first-hand information. (Reviewed in: CO, vol. 41, 1841, pp. 43–61.)

4366 STEINMETZ, Andrew
A voice in Ramah; or, lament of the poor African, a fettered exile, afar from his fatherland. A poem, in five cantos. Harvey & Darton, London, 1842. xxx, 340 pp.

Antislavery poem, with extensive notes.

4367 LONGFELLOW, Henry Wadsworth
'The slave's dream.' In his: Poems on slavery (Cambridge, Mass., 1842), pp. 11–14.

A slave in America dies dreaming of Africa.

4368 POLLOK; Robert
'The African maid.' In: POLLOK, D. The life of Robert Pollok (Edinburgh, 1843), pp. 432–34.

Poem about a Gambian girl who mourns her lover sold overseas.

4369 *GREEN, Charles C.
The Nubian slave. Bela Marsh, Boston, 1845. 8 ll. illus.

A poem.

4370 LANDOR, Walter Savage
'Romilly and Wilberforce.' In: The works of Walter Savage Landor (London, 1846), vol. 2, pp. 197–202.

One of his 'Imaginary conversations'; Romilly accuses the abolitionists of diverting attention from pauperism in Britain.

4371 *WHITTIER, John Greenleaf
Voices of freedom . . . 7th and complete edition. T. S. Cavender, Philadelphia; (etc.), 1846. 192 pp.

Includes the poems 'The slave ships' and 'The world's convention of the friends of emancipation, held in London, 1840'.

4372 SCHULTS, Adolf
'Das Negerschiff.' In his: Gedichte (Magdeburg, [1847]), pp. 135–38.

Poem (1843) describing the mass suicide of slaves on a Spanish slave ship.

4373 NEILSON, Peter
The life and adventures of Zamba, an African negro king; and his experience of slavery in South Carolina. Written by himself. Corrected and arranged by Peter Neilson. Smith, Elder & Co., London, 1847. xx, 258 pp.

Supposed autobiography of a Congolese slave transported to America in 1800; written by Neilson.

4374 DIGNAN, John
The slave captain; a legend of Liverpool. T. G. Newby, London, 1847. 288 pp.

Novel, including a short account of the slave trade in the 1790s.

4375 *OELSNER-MONMERQUÉ, G.
Schwarze und Weisse. Skizzen aus
Bourbon. Schlodtmann, Bremen, 1848.
x, 291 pp.

Novel about the slave trade and slavery in Réunion.

4376 'The AFRICAN cruiser.' (USM, 1848,
II, pp. 523–33; III, pp. 277–90; 1849,
I, pp. 200–18.)

Account of naval life in the West
African antislavery blockade.

4377 MAYO, William Starbuck
Kaloolah, or, journeyings to the Djébel
Kumri: an autobiography of Jonathan
Romer. Edited by W. S. Mayo. G. P.
Putnam, New-York; D. Bogue, Lon-
don, 1849. 514 pp.

Novel written by Mayo. An American
becomes involved with Cuban slave
traders but escapes and marries a
princess in the interior of Africa.

4378 MARCH, L.
'The slaver. A story of the French slave
trade.' (USM, 1852, I, pp. 218–29.)

Unacknowledged adaptation of Mérimée's 'Tamango' (4345).

4379 *MICHIELS, Alfred
Le capitaine Firmin, ou la vie des
nègres en Afrique. Paris, 1853. 359 pp.

Also published as: La traite des
nègres en Afrique.

4380 POEMS on slavery, by Longfellow,
Whittier, Southey, H. B. Stowe, &c.
London, 1853. iv, 13–232 pp.

Includes poems on the African slave
trade by Longfellow, Whittier, Chandler, Southey, C. Mackay, D. Mallock,
B. Barton, J. Harnard and A. B.
Reach.

4381a HEINE, Heinrich
'Das Sclavenschiff.' In his: Vermischte
Schriften (Hamburg, 1854), vol. 1,
pp. 136–43.

Translated as:

4381b 'The slave ship.' In: The poems of
Heine (London, 1859), pp. 514–17.

A slave trader prays God to spare
at least half his cargo or he will be
ruined.

4382 MELVILLE, Herman
'Benito Cereno.' (Putnam's Monthly
Magazine, New York, vol. 6, 1855,
pp. 353–67, 459–73, 633–44.)

Short story based on (735). Reprinted

in his: The piazza tales (New York,
1856), pp. 109–270.

4383 WHITTIER, John Greenleaf
'Song of slaves in the desert.' In his:
The panorama, and other poems
(Boston, 1856), pp. 104–07.

On the Saharan slave trade, written
1847.

4384 GREENHALGH, Thomas
Kennee-voo; or, the sacking of Allar-
oonah: an incident of the African
slave trade. London, 1856. 429 pp.

Novel about a West African slave
who returns home after the Haitian
revolution 1791.

4385 KINGSTON, William Henry Giles
Salt water: or, the sea life and adventures of Neil D'Arcy, the midshipman . . . London, 1857. viii, 407 pp.

Novel dealing with the British anti-
slavery squadron.

4386 BURNS, Robert
'The slave's lament.' In: The poetical
works and letters of Robert Burns
(Edinburgh, 1859), pp. 320–21.

Short poem (written 1792) about
a slave carried from Senegal to
Virginia.

4387 The SLAVE ship. London, [1860?]
(1 p.)

Broadsheet poem about the voyage
of the 'Rodeur' in 1819. See (868).

4388 WARNEFORD, Robert, pseud.
Tales of the slave squadron. London,
[1860]. 353 pp.

A novel, set in West Africa.

4389 PONT-JEST, René de
Bolino le négrier. Souvenirs de l'Océan
Indien. Paris, [1862]. 322 pp.

Novel about the illegal slave trade
from East Africa.

4390 PICKERING, C. L.
'Daouda, the warrior chief. A recol-
lection of a stay on the West Indies'
station.' (USM, 1863, I, pp. 209–19.)

Unacknowledged adaptation of a
story by Mérimée (4361).

4391 The PRINCE of Kashna: a West
Indian story . . . With an editorial
introduction by Richard B. Kimball.
New York, 1866. ix, 450 pp.

Supposed autobiography of a Hausa
slave in Jamaica.

4392 HORN, W. O., *pseud.*
Die letzte Ghazwah oder Sklavenjagd im Sudan unter der Regierung
Mehemed Ali's von Egypten. Erzählung . . . Wiesbaden, [1867]. 104 pp.
illus.

By Wilhelm Oertel. Novel about the
Sudanese slave trade.

4393 *ENDURAN, Lodoïx
La traite des nègres, ou deux marins au
Sénégal. Lille, 1868. 139 pp.

4394 CREMONY, John C.
'A cruise on a slaver.' (Overland
Monthly, San Francisco, vol. 1, 1868,
pp. 398–408.)

Purported account of a passage on a
slave ship from Bonny to Puerto
Rico.

4395 *THOMES, William Henry
A slaver's adventures on land and sea
. . . Boston; New York, [1872]. 406 pp.
illus.

4396 SADLER, Samuel Whitchurch
The African cruiser. A midshipman's
adventures on the west coast. London,
1873. 197 pp.

Novel on the antislavery squadron in
the 1840s.

4397 BALLANTYNE, Robert Michael
Black ivory. A tale of adventure among
the slavers of East Africa. London,
1873. vi, 416 pp.

Novel for juveniles about the Arab
slave trade.

4398 KINGSTON, William Henry Giles
The three midshipmen . . . New edition.
London, [1873]. xiii, 416 pp. illus.

Novel, dealing largely with anti-
slavery patrolling off West Africa
about 1850.

4399 STANLEY, Henry Morton
My Kalulu, prince, king, and slave: a
story of central Africa. London, 1873.
xiv, 432 pp.

Sentimental novel for boys about
the friendship between an Arab
slaver's son and an African prince.

4400 KINGSTON, William Henry Giles
The African trader; or, the adventures of
Harry Bayford. London, [1873]. 128 pp.
illus.

Novel for children about the Spanish
slave trade in the 1840s.

4401 SADLER, Samuel Whitchurch
The slave-dealer of the Coanza. A
naval story. London, [1874]. 127 pp.

4402 *JACOLLIOT, Louis
La côte d'ébène. Le dernier des négriers. Paris, 1876. 329 pp.

A novel.

4403 The ETHIOP's plaint: by Osiris . . .
Westminster, 1877. 39 pp.

Poems lamenting the Muslim slave
trade in Africa.

4404 SADLER, Samuel Whitchurch
The flag-lieutenant. A story of the slave
squadron. London, 1877. 318 pp.
illus.

4405 *KINGSTON, William Henry Giles
Ned Garth; or, made prisoner in
Africa. A tale of the slave trade.
London, [1878].

4406a VERNE, Jules
Un capitaine de quinze ans . . . Paris,
[1878]. 373 pp. illus, map.

Translated as:

4406b Dick Sands, the boy captain . . .
London, 1879. viii, 486 pp. illus, map.

Novel, the second part of which
describes the Angolan slave trade in
the 1870s.

4407 CASTRO ALVES, Antônio de
Vozes d'Africa. Navio negreiro (Tragé-
dia no mar). Rio de Janeiro, 1880. 28 pp.

The second poem, written 1868, is
a moving evocation of the 'middle
passage'. (Translated as 'The slave
ship' in a four-language edition,
Bahia, 1959.)

4408 REID, Mayne
Ran away to sea. An autobiography
for boys. New York, 1881. 359 pp.

Novel about a slaving voyage which
ends in disaster.

4409 SADLER, Samuel Whitchurch
Slavers and cruisers. A tale of the west
coast. London, [1881]. 384 pp.

4410 *CAUMEL-DECAZIS, Roseline
La traite des esclaves dans l'Afrique
centrale, poème en vers. Paris, 1881.
31 pp.

4411 COLLINGWOOD, Harry, *pseud.*
The Congo rovers: a story of the slave
squadron. London, 1886. 352 pp.

By W. J. C. Lancaster. A novel.

4412 JACOLLIOT, Louis
Les chasseurs d'esclaves. Paris, [1888].
316 pp.

Novel about the Sudanese slave
trade.

4413 *MARIENBERG, Maria
Suema, die kleine afrikanische Negerin.
Drama in 5 Aufzügen frei nach dem
Französischen bearbeitet. Mainz, 1889.
60 pp.

Antislavery play.

4414 DRUMAUX, Arthur
'La voix des esclaves. Cantate.' (MA,
vol. 1, 1889, pp. 168–70.)

Poem about the Saharan slave
trade.

4415 *HALKA, Alexander, pseud.
Zaïda das Negermädchen. Volksdrama
in fünf Aufzügen . . . Salzburg, [1889].
87 pp.

By M.T.F. Halka-Ledóchowska. Anti-
slavery play.

4416 JOHNSTON, Harry Hamilton
The history of a slave. London, 1889.
xii, 168 pp.

Novel in the form of a narrative
by an African enslaved by Adamawa
Fulani.

4417 *NEY, Chr.
Der Sklavenjäger. Dramatische Szenen
aus Ostafrika in 1 Akte. Paderborn,
1889. 37 pp.

4418 DELMER, Louis
L'esclave. Drame antiesclavagiste et
national. (Pièce en quatre actes.)
Bruxelles; Paris, 1890. viii, 140 pp.

The author was secretary of the
Comité Antiesclavagiste de Bruxelles.

4419 'CANTATE sur l'esclavage africain.'
(Signed: L. R.) (MA, vol. 2, 1890, pp.
386–87.)

Exhortation to an antislavery crusade.

4420 BOUHOURS, Fl.
Les trois vierges noires de l'Afrique
équatoriale. Paris, 1891. 189 pp.

Story of three African girls rescued
by the Belgian antislavery expedition
in Burundi, 1888. (Also published
in Spanish and Italian.)

4421 *DU CAMPFRANC, M., pseud.
Sœur Louise. Paris, 1891. 288 pp.

By M. S. Coutance. Antislavery
novel.

4422 DESCAMPS, Édouard Eugène François,
baron
Africa. Drame en cinq actes, en vers . . .
Paris, 1893. 132 pp.

Play about the struggle between
Arab slavers and Christians in
Uganda; awarded a prize by Lavig-
erie.

4423 *SEVERUS, Justus, pseud.
Africus, ou le génie récompensé, drame
nègre en un acte et en vers. Bruxelles,
1893. 39 pp.

By Hector Hoornaert?

4424 MAY, Karl
Die Sklavenkarawane. Stuttgart, 1893.
v, 493 pp. illus.

Novel about the Sudanese slave
trade in the 1870s.

4425 *CARL, Sébastien
Les rédempteurs. Scènes de la lutte
anti-esclavagiste. Liège, 1893. 107 pp.

4426 VIGNERON, Lucien
Sang noir. Scènes de la vie esclavagiste
dans l'Afrique équatoriale. Paris, 1893.
xiv, 293 pp.

Novel based on the Manyema slave
trade.

4427 *VALENTIN, Émile
Rédemption, poème antiesclavagiste
en six chants. 2e édition. Liège, 1894.
66 pp.

4428 *COLLINGWOOD, Harry, pseud.
The pirate slaver. A story of the West
African coast . . . London, [1895].
384 pp.

By W. J. C. Lancaster.

4429 *JAMES, Alexander MacGregor
Virginie: a tale of the slave-trade, and
other poems. Kingston [Jamaica], 1895.
53 pp.

4430 *TRESS, Gebh.
Losgekauft. Schauspiel aus der afrikan-
ischen Sklaverei in fünf Aufzügen.
Trier, 1895. 22 pp.

4431 MAY, Karl
Im Lande des Mahdi. Reiseerlebnisse.
Freiburg i/B., 1896. 3 vol.

Trilogy (Menschenjäger; Der Mahdi;
Im Sudan) describing campaigns
against Sudanese slave traders in the
1870s.

4432 OLIVER, W. F.
'Wag Benton, the black-birder. A tale
of African slave-stealing.' (Overland
Monthly, San Francisco, ser. 2, vol.
30, 1897, pp. 49–55.)

Story of a sailor who participated in a

slaving expedition to the Congo about 1850.

4433 SPEARS, John Randolph
The fugitive. A tale of adventure in the days of clipper ships and slavers. London, 1899. 325 pp. illus.

Includes accounts of the West African slave trade about 1860.

4434 *SCHULER, G. M.
Der Sklavenjäger von Sansibar. Poetische Erzählung aus Afrika. Würzburg, 1900. 92 pp.

APPENDIX I: UNPUBLISHED THESES

4435 AIMES, Hubert Hillary Suffern
The Cuban slave trade: a study in the history of Cuba. [New Haven, Conn.,] 1905. (Yale)

4436 KLINGBERG, Frank Joseph
The parliamentary history of the abolition of slavery and the slave trade in the British colonies. [New Haven, Conn.,] 1911. (Ph.D., Yale)

4437 SMALLPAGE, Eric
The slave-trade in European diplomacy, 1814–1818. Liverpool, 1922. (M.A.)

4438 HERRINGTON, Elsie Irene
British measures for the suppression of the slave trade from the west coast of Africa. 1807–1833. London, 1923. iii, 228 ll. bibl. (M.A.)

Summary: 3442.

4439 RICHARDS, A. M.
The connection of Bristol with the African slave trade. Bristol, 1923. (M.A.)

4440 HEYN, Heinrich
Die Bekämpfung des Sklavenhandels und Sklavenraubes in ihrer rechts-geschichtlichen Entwicklung. Erlangen, 1924. iii, 90 pp.

4441 CHILD, Alfred Thurston
Gentle Benezet, schoolmaster, abolitionist and Friend. [New York,] 1928. (M.S., Columbia)

4442 HICKMAN, Elizabeth L.
Antislavery agitation in France during the latter half of the eighteenth century. [Ithaca, N.Y.,] 1930. (Cornell)

4443 MILNE, Alexander Taylor
The slave trade and Anglo-American relations, 1807–1862. London, 1930, 200 ll. (M.A.)

Summary: 3445.

4444 HARSHBARGER, Emmett L.
The African slave trade in Anglo-American diplomacy. [Columbus, Ohio,] 1933. (Ph.D., Ohio State)

4445 SCOTTER, William Henry
International rivalry in the Bights of Benin and Biafra, 1815–85. London, 1933. vi, 364 ll. (Ph.D.)

Ch. 2: 'Slave trade suppression and intervention ashore, 1837–61.' Summary: 3448.

4446 CAWTE, Lawrence Henry
Great Britain and the suppression of the Cuban slave trade, 1817–1865. London, 1934. 277 ll. maps. (M.A.)

4447 JONES, Mary Katherine
The slave trade at Mauritius, 1810–29. Oxford, 1936. (B.Litt.)

4448 SYPHER, Wylie
The anti-slavery movement to 1800 in English literature, exclusive of the periodical. [Cambridge, Mass.,] 1937. (Harvard)

4449 WILLIAMS, Eric Eustace
The economic aspect of the abolition of the British West Indian slave trade and slavery. Oxford, 1938. 408 pp. (Ph.D.)

See (1309).

4450 KING, James Ferguson
Negro slavery in the viceroyalty of New Granada. Berkeley, 1939. (M.S., California)

4451 LASHLEY, Leonard C.
Anthony Benezet and his anti-slavery activities. [New York,] 1939. (Ph.D., Fordham)

4452 SCHULTZ, Harold Seessel
The movement to revive the foreign slave trade, 1853–1861. [Durham, N.C.,] 1940. (M.A., Duke)

4453 RADICE, C.
Il contributo italiano all' azione anti-schiavista nei secoli XIX–XX. Roma, 1940. 267 pp.

4454 WILSON, Howard Hazen
Devices employed by Great Britain to suppress the African slave trade. Chicago, 1941. (Ph.D.)

4455 MURRAY, Weston L.
The international control of the slave trade from 1855 to 1937. [Chapel

Hill, N.C.,] 1942. (Ph.D., North Carolina)

4456 BROWN, Genevieve
The illicit slave trade to Cuba and the other islands of the Caribbean. [Columbus, Ohio,] 1944. (Ph.D., Ohio State)

4457 MANICE, Edward A.
George Fox, Quakers, negroes, and slavery on Barbados, 1671–1675. [New Haven, Conn.,] 1946. (Senior history essay, Yale)

4458 KENNEDY, Melvin Dow
The suppression of the African slave trade to the French colonies and its aftermath, 1814–1848. Chicago, 1947. (Ph.D.)

4459 MECKLING, Frank E.
The Pious Party, 1785–1833. [Los Angeles,] 1950. (UCLA)

On the antislavery movement.

4460 REES, Alan Maxwell
The campaign for the abolition of the British slave trade and its place in British politics, 1783–1807. Oxford, 1952. (B. Litt.)

4461 CONSTANTINE, James Robert
The African slave trade: a study of eighteenth century propaganda and public controversy. Bloomington, Ind., 1953. 386 pp. (Ph.D., Indiana)

Summary: DA, vol. 14, 1954, p. 97.

4462 MACKENZIE, Kenneth
Great Britain and the abolition of the slave trade by the other powers (1812–22), with special reference to the efforts of Castlereagh. Oxford, 1953. (B.Litt.)

4463 PILGRIM, Elsie Isalie
The anti-slavery sentiment in Great Britain, 1841–1854; its nature and its decline, with special reference to its influence upon British policy towards the former slave colonies. Cambridge, 1953. (Ph.D.)

4464 PUTNEY, Martha Settle
The slave trade in French diplomacy, 1814–1865. Philadelphia, 1955. xiv, 303 ll. bibl. ll. vii–xiv. (Ph.D., Pennsylvania)

Summary: DA, vol. 16, 1956, pp. 110–11.

4465 KELLY, John Barrett
British policy in the Persian Gulf, 1813–1843. London, 1956. v, 590 ll. maps. (Ph.D.)

Ch. 7: 'The Arab slave trade and British policy 1813–35'; ch. 10: 'The attack on the Arab slave trade, 1835–42.'

4466 DALLAS, George Mifflin
The African squadron, 1843–1861. Cambridge, Mass., 1956. (Honors thesis, Harvard)

4467 GAVIN, Robert James
Palmerston's policy towards East and West Africa 1830–1865. Cambridge, 1958. (Ph.D.)

4468 LIPSCOMBE, Patrick Cleburne
The Church of England and the negro slaves in the West Indies, 1783–1833. Austin, Tex., 1956. 106 ll. bibl. ll. 100–04. (M.A., Texas)

4469 HUNT, Edward Martin
The influence of the French revolution on the British anti-slavery movement. [Manchester, 1958.] 57 pp. (B.A.)

4470 SMITH, Arthur Francis
Spain and the problem of slavery in Cuba, 1817–1883. Chicago, 1958. 416 ll.

4471 HARWOOD, Thomas Franklin
Great Britain and American antislavery. [Austin, Tex.,] 1959. v, 838 ll. bibl. ll. 804–38. (Texas)

Summary: DA, vol. 20, 1959, pp. 2251–52.

4472 HOWARD, Warren Starkie
The United States government and the African slave trade, 1837–1862. Los Angeles, 1959. (Ph.D., UCLA)

See (3975).

4473 McDANIEL-TEABEAU, Hazel
Wilberforce's speeches on the abolition of the slave trade. [Columbia, Mo.,] 1959. 383 pp. (Ph.D., Missouri)

4474 MERRITT, James E.
The Liverpool slave trade, 1789–1792: an analytical study of the returns to the Committee of Enquiry into the Slave Trade, 1788, 1790, 1791, with special reference to the profitability of the slave trade and the nature of the triangular trade. Nottingham, 1959. (M.A.)

4475 HUNT, Edward Martin
The North of England agitation for the abolition of the slave trade, 1780–1800. Manchester, 1959. (M.A.)

4476 LIPSCOMB, Patrick Cleburne
William Pitt and the abolition of the slave trade. [Austin, Tex.,] 1960. 624 pp. (Ph.D., Texas)

Summary: DA, vol. 20, 1960, p. 4642.

4477 TEMPERLEY, Howard
The British and Foreign Anti-Slavery Society, 1839–1868. [New Haven, Conn.,] 1960. (Ph.D., Yale)

See (4640).

4478 WAX, Darold Duane
The negro slave trade in colonial Pennsylvania. Seattle, 1962. 418 pp. (Ph.D., Washington)

Summary: DA, vol. 24, 1963, pp. 272–73.

4479 ASPINWALL, Bernard
William Smith, M.P., 1756–1835, and his importance in the movements for parliamentary reform, religious toleration, and the abolition of the slave trade. Manchester, 1962. (M.A.)

4480 ZILVERSMIT, Arthur
Slavery and its abolition in the Northern states. Berkeley, 1962. 383 pp. (Ph.D., California)

Summary: DA, vol. 24, 1963, p. 2455. See (3804).

4481 M'BAYE, Guèye
La traite négrière au moyen âge en Afrique occidentale. [Dakar,] 1963.

4482 CARLSON, Donald Arthur
Great Britain and the abolition of the slave trade to Latin America. [Minneapolis, Minn.,] 1964. 336 pp. (Ph.D., Minnesota)

4483 TENKORANG, Sammy
British slave trading activities on the Gold and Slave Coasts in the eighteenth century and their effect on African society. London, 1964, 279 ll. maps. (M.A.)

4484 WEISE, Günter
Das Erzählwerk Aphra Behns (1640–1689) . . . Halle (Saale), 1964 [1965]. iii, 243 ll.

Ch. 10: 'Die Gestalt des "edlen Wilden": "Oroonoko; or, the royal slave".'

4485 ALPERS, Edward Alter
The role of the Yao in the development of trade in East-Central Africa, 1698–c. 1850. London, 1966. 321 ll. maps. (Ph.D.)

Ch. 5: 'The growing influence of the slave trade, 1785–1810.' See (4529).

4486 ROBINSON, Donald Leonard
Slavery and sectionalism in the founding of the United States, 1787–1808. [Ithaca, N.Y.,] 1966. viii, 570 ll. (Ph.D., Cornell)

Summary: DA, vol. 28, 1966, p. 1882.

4487 CONRAD, Robert Edgar
The struggle for the abolition of the Brazilian slave trade, 1808–1853. [New York,] 1967. 392 pp. (Ph.D., Columbia)

Summary: DA, vol. 28, 1967, p. 1757.

4488 KARASCH, Mary
The Brazilian slavers and the illegal slave trade, 1836–1851. [Madison, Wis.,] 1967. (M.A., Wisconsin)

4489 KATZ, Naomi
The kingdom of Dahomey: political organization and ecological relations in a slave trading state. [Los Angeles,] 1967. vii, 149 ll. map. (Ph.D., UCLA)

Summary: DA, vol. 28, 1968, p. 2702.

4490 HIGGINS, William Robert
The South Carolina negro duty law, 1703–1775. [Columbia, S.C.,] 1967. (M.A., South Carolina)

4491 ZIMMERMANN, Matilde
The French slave trade at Moçambique, 1770–1794. [Madison, Wis.,] 1967. (M.A., Wisconsin)

4492 MURRAY, D. R.
Britain, Spain and the slave trade to Cuba, 1807–1845. Cambridge, 1967. (Ph.D.)

4493 PORTER, Dale Herbert
The defense of the British slave trade, 1784–1807. [Eugene, Oreg.,] 1967. 243 ll. bibl. ll. 224–41. (Ph.D., Oregon)

Summary: DA, vol. 28, 1967, pp. 2183–84.

4494 STETSON, Kenneth Winslow
A quantitative approach to Britain's American slave trade, 1700–1773. [Madison, Wis.,] 1967. (M.A., Wisconsin)

4495 TAKAKI, Ronald Toshiyuki
A pro-slavery crusade: the movement to reopen the African slave trade. Berkeley, 1967. 249 pp. (Ph.D., California)

Summary: DA, vol. 28, 1967, p. 3127.

4496 BOWSER, Frederick Park
Negro slavery in colonial Perú, 1529–1650. Berkeley, 1967. 525 pp. (Ph.D., California)

Summary: DA, vol. 29, 1968, pp. 205–06.

4497 MAC MASTER, Richard Kerwin
The United States, Great Britain and the suppression of the Cuban slave trade 1835–1860. [Washington, D.C.,] 1968. (Ph.D., Georgetown)

Summary: DA, vol. 29, 1969, p. 2645.

4498 HILTY, Hiram Horace
North Carolina Quakers and slavery. [Durham, N.C.,] 1969. 381 pp. (Ph.D., Duke)

Summary: DA, vol. 30, 1969, p. 1500.

4499 MIERS, Suzanne
Great Britain and the Brussels anti-slave trade act of 1890. London, 1969. 451 ll. maps. (Ph.D.)

4500 POSTMA, Johannes
The Dutch participation in the African slave trade: slaving on the Guinea coast, 1675–1795. [East Lansing, Mich.,] 1970. 301 pp. (Ph.D., Michigan State)

Summary: DA, vol. 31, 1971, p. 4068.

APPENDIX II: ADDENDA

SECTION A

4501 *GREAT BRITAIN: House of Lords
Minutes of evidence taken on the second reading of the bill, intituled, "An act to prohibit the trading for slaves on the coast of Africa, within certain limits.' [London, 1799.] 346 [i.e. 355] pp.

SECTION B(b)

4502 JOHNSTON, James Hugo
'The Mohammedan slave trade.' (JNH, vol. 13, 1928, pp. 478–91.)

On the medieval trade in African and European slaves.

4503a OLBERT, Ernst A., *pseud.*
England als Sklavenhändler und Sklavenhalter. Berlin, 1940. 55 pp. illus.

Translated as:

4503b*The slave business, by George W. Booker. Scotch Plains, N. J., [1941]. 53 pp. illus.

By Konrad Oehlrich. Anti-British propaganda; also issued in French, Portuguese and Spanish.

4504 *DIGGS, Irene
Chronology of notable events and dates in the history of the African and his descendants during the period of slavery and the slave trade. Association for the Study of Negro Life and History, Washington, 1970. ii, 71 pp.

4505 *GUSTAVSSON, Rolf
'Afrika — från slavhandel till nykolonialism.' (Zenit, Stockholm, vol. 14, no. 16, 1970, pp. 12–30, 54.)

4506 *MRVALJEVIĆ, Jakov
Tropska Afrika; uticaj kolonijalizma na razvitak stanovništva. Beograd, 1970. 139 pp. map.

4507 CURTIN, Philip De Armond
'The Atlantic slave trade 1600–1800.' *In*: AJAYI, J. F. A. *and* CROWDER, M. History of West Africa, vol. 1 (London, 1971), pp. 240–68.

4508 *OFOSU-APPIAH, Lawrence Henry
People in bondage; African slavery in the modern era. Minneapolis, 1971. 131 pp. illus, maps.

For schools.

4509 DESCHAMPS, Hubert Jules
Histoire de la traite des noirs de l'antiquité à nos jours. Paris, [1971]. 338 pp. maps. bibl. pp. 319–30.

Good general history of the African slave trade.

4510 *PIERCE, Milfred C.
'The Atlantic slave trade: a case for reparations.' (Negro History Bulletin, Washington, vol. 35, 1972, pp. 44–47; illus.)

4510/1 HOWARD, Richard
Black cargo. London; New York, [1972]. 128 pp. illus.

Popular account of the slave trade and slavery.

SECTION C(b)

4511 *KRAUSE, Gottlob Adolf
Einige Stimmen über den Sklavenhandel in Togo. Berlin, 1899. 32 pp.

Reprinted from: Export, Berlin, vol. 21, 1899, pp. 92–94, 106–08, 120–21, 133–35, 148–49, 161–63.

4512 *A ESCRAVATURA em Mossamedes: carta aberta dirigida a S.Exª o Presidente da Republica por um grupo de agricultores, industriaes e commerciantes de Mossamedes. Lisboa, [1912]. 39 pp.

On slavery and labour conditions in Angola.

SECTION C(c)

4513 WYNDHAM, Hugh Archibald
The Atlantic and slavery. London, 1935. vii, 310 pp. maps.

Pt. 1 describes the slave trade on the west coast of Africa.

4514 DESCHAMPS, Hubert Jules
'Quinze ans de Gabon. Les débuts de l'établissement français 1839–1853.' (RFHO, vol. 50, 1963, pp. 283–345; vol. 52, 1965, pp. 92–126; maps.)

Contains sections on the Gabon slave trade and its suppression.

4515 *RODNEY, Walter
'Gold and slaves on the Gold Coast.' (Transactions of the Historical Society of Ghana, Achimota, vol. 10, 1969, pp. 13–28.)

The slave trade surpassed that in gold by 1740.

4516 *MANNING, Patrick
'Slaves, palm oil, and political power on the West African coast; a historical hypothesis.' (African Historical Studies, Boston, vol. 2, 1969, pp. 279–88.)

Coastal states changed without disruption from slave to palm oil trade in the 19th century.

4517 ANJOS DA SILVA REBELO, Manuel dos
Relações entre Angola e Brasil (1808–1830). Lisboa, 1970. 452 pp. map. bibl. pp. 445–52.

Includes sections on the slave trade.

4518 *AGUESSY, Honorat
'Le Dan-Homê du XIXᵉ siècle était-il une société esclavagiste?' (Mois en Afrique, Dakar, no. 50, 1970, pp. 71–91.)

4519 *AUSTEN, Ralph Albert
'The abolition of the overseas slave trade: a distorted theme in West African history.' (JHSN, vol. 5, no. 2, 1970, pp. 254–74.)

4520 RONEN, Dov
'On the African role in the trans-Atlantic slave trade in Dahomey.' (CEA, vol. 11, 1971, pp. 5–13.)

The Dahomean state sold slaves as 'surplus' from human sacrifice.

4521 WRIGLEY, Christopher Crompton
'Historicism in Africa. Slavery and state formation.' (African Affairs, London, vol. 70, 1971, pp. 113–24.)

Reply to (366): the slave trade did great harm to West African societies.

SECTION D(c)

4522 KÜRCHHOFF, Detmar
'Alte und neue Handelsstrassen und Handelsmittelpunkte in Nordwest-Afrika.' (Geographische Zeitschrift, Leipzig, vol. 13, 1907, pp. 126–42, 174–85.)

Includes notes on the slave trade of the western Sahara and Sudan.

4523 VALENSI, Lucette
'Esclaves chrétiens et esclaves noirs à Tunis au XVIIIᵉ siècle.' (AESC, vol. 22, 1967, pp. 1267–88; map.)

With a section on the trans-Saharan slave trade.

4524 AYANDELE, Emmanuel Ayankanmi
'Observations on some social and economic aspects of slavery in pre-colonial Northern Nigeria.' (Nigerian Journal of Economic and Social Studies, Ibadan, vol. 9, 1967, pp. 329–38.)

Includes notes on the 19th-century Muslim slave trade.

4525 *OLIVER DE SARDAN, Jean Pierre
Les voleurs d'hommes. (Notes sur l'histoire des Kurtey.) Paris; Niamey, 1969. 68 pp. map.

On a slave raiding Fulani group.

4526 MEILLASSOUX, Claude
'Le commerce pré-colonial et le développement de l'esclavage à Gūbu du Sahel (Mali).' (Homme et la Société, Paris, no. 15, 1970, pp. 147–57.)

Commerce was a means to obtain servile labour for local production.

4527 KALCK, Pierre
'The slave trade.' In his: Central African Republic (London, 1971), pp. 32–43.

Notes on slave trading in the Ubangi region.

SECTION E(c)

4528 *CORNEVIN, Robert
'Les "bienfaits" de l'esclavage arabe en Afrique orientale et centrale par le capitaine Jérôme Becker, en 1887.' (France-Eurafrique, Paris, vol. 19, no. 184, 1967, pp. 36–41.)

4529 ALPERS, Edward Alter
'The French slave trade in East Africa (1721–1810).' (CEA, vol. 10, 1970, pp. 80–124.)

The trade reached its peak 1785–94. See (4485).

SECTION F(b)

4530 *BIE, Lorentz
'Paa Togt med en dansk Slave-Fregat.' (Verden og Vi, København, vol. 21, 1931.)

4531 NØRREGÅRD, Georg Pedersen
'Slaveoprøret pa „Patientia" 1753.' (Handels- og Søfartsmuseet, Helsingør, Årbog 1950, pp. 23–44; illus.)

Account of a slave revolt on a Danish ship off the Gold Coast.

4532 NØRREGÅRD, Georg Pedersen
'Vandmangelen på ,,Haabet Galley" 1724.' (Handels- og Søfartsmuseet, Helsingør, Årbog 1953, pp. 41–55; illus.)

On a Danish slaving voyage from the Gold Coast to St. Thomas.

4533 *GAUTIER, Georges
'Capitaines de négriers.' (Cahiers des Salorges, Nantes, no. 3, 1961, [3 pp].)

4534 *VIAUD, Charles
'Le senau La Marie séraphique, négrier nantais.' (Cahiers des Salorges, Nantes, no. 4, 1962, [4 pp].)

4535 *HOWARD, Thomas, editor
Black voyage: eyewitness accounts of the Atlantic slave trade. Boston, [1971]. x, 243 pp. map.

4536 *OLSEN, Peter
'The negro and the sea; black resistance to slavery.' (Negro History Bulletin, Washington, vol. 35, 1972, pp. 40–44.)

SECTION H

4537 GREAT BRITAIN: Laws
'An act for better regulating the manner of carrying slaves, in British vessels, from the coast of Africa.' In: The STATUTES at large, vol. 42 (Cambridge, 1799), pp. 326–41.

The act (39 Geo. III. c. 80; 12 July 1799) lays down operating conditions for English slave ships.

4538 PORTUGAL: Laws
'Alvará sobre o trato da Guiné (24–10–1512).' In: BRÁSIO, A. Monumenta missionaria africana, ser. 2, vol. 2 (Lisboa, 1963), pp. 51–52.

All West African slaves must be brought to Lisbon for sale. (Other regulations 1514–20 are reprinted in the same volume.)

SECTION J

4539 *BELLEGARDE, Dantès
Pages d'histoire: I. L'esclavage et le trafic des noirs dans l'île d'Haïti; II. La société française de Saint-Domingue en 1789; III. Pétion et Bolivar. Port-au-Prince, 1925. 67 pp.

4540 *'The FIRST cargo of African slaves for Louisiana, 1718. Introduction by Henry P. Dart.' (Louisiana Historical Quar-terly, New Orleans, vol. 14, 1931, pp. 163–77.)

4541 ALDRIDGE, Harold Richard
'Slave trade economics.' (British Museum Quarterly, London, vol. 9, 1935, pp. 119–21.)

On the account book of the Liverpool slaver 'Mongovo George' 1785–87. See (785).

4542 TOBAR CRUZ, Pedro
'La esclavitud del negro en Guatemala.' (Antropología e Historia de Guatemala, vol. 17, no. 1, 1965, pp. 3–14.)

On the slave trade in the 16th century.

4543 LE RIVEREND BRUSONE, Julio
'Afroamérica.' (Cuadernos Americanos, vol. 24, no. 2, 1965, pp. 232–42.)

Includes notes on the slave trade.

4544 MEYER, Jean
'Du nouveau sur le commerce négrier nantais du XVIIIᵉ siècle.' (Annales de Bretagne, Rennes, vol. 73, 1966, pp. 229–39.)

Review of (1420).

4545 FRANCO, Franklin J.
La aportación de los negros . . . Santo Domingo, 1967. 29 pp.

Discusses the early slave trade to Spanish America.

4546 BUSSON, Jean Pierre
'La correspondance du négociant Luc Magon de La Balue. Trois négriers en traite (1741–1743).' (Actes du quatre-vingt-onzième Congrès National des Sociétés Savantes, Rennes, 1966, Section d'histoire moderne et contemporaine, vol. 1, Paris, 1969, pp. 155–68.)

On slave traders of St. Malo.

4547 VIDALENC, Jean
'La traite négrière en France sous la Restauration 1814–1830.' (Actes du quatre-vingt-onzième Congrès National des Sociétés Savantes, Rennes, 1966, Section d'histoire moderne et contemporaine, vol. 1, Paris, 1969, pp. 197–229.)

Describes slaving cases involving ships from Nantes and other ports.

4548 NARDIN, Jean Claude
'Encore des chiffres: la traite négrière française pendant la première moitié du XVIIIᵉ siècle.' (RFHO, vol. 57, 1970, pp. 421–26.)

Criticizes Curtin's figures (1448) for the French slave trade 1721–40.

4549 *RINCHON, Dieudonné
'Comment travaillaient les négriers qui ont assis la fortune de l'Europe.' (Terre Entière, [Bruxelles?], vol. 39, 1970, pp. 22–61.)

4550 CRAVEN, Wesley Frank
'Twenty negroes to Jamestown in 1619?' (Virginia Quarterly Review, Charlottesville, vol. 47, 1971, pp. 416–20.)

4551 KLEM, Knud
'Det kgl. oktr. Østersøisk-Guineiske Handelsselskab.' (Handels- og Søfarts-museet, Helsingør, Årbog 1970, 1971, pp. 7–66; illus.)

See (946).

4552 TAKAKI, Ronald Toshiyuki
A pro-slavery crusade. The agitation to reopen the African slave trade. New York; London, [1971]. x, 276 pp. bibl. pp. 245–67.

The pressure to resume the slave trade in the 1850s was a response to internal social tensions in the southern United States. See (4495).

4553 DAVIS, Robert Ralph, *editor*
'Buchanian espionage: a report on illegal slave trading in the South in 1859.' (JSH, vol. 37, 1971, pp. 271–78.)

Report from secret agent B. F. Slocumb that only a few hundred Africans have been landed in the United States during 1859.

4554 SHERIDAN, Richard Bert
'Africa and the Caribbean in the Atlantic slave trade.' (AHR, vol. 77, 1972, pp. 15–35; illus.)

On the demographic aspects of Afro-Caribbean slavery.

SECTION K

4555 CASTAING, Alphonse
'Souvenirs d'un indigène de la Nigritie.' (Revue Orientale et Américaine, Paris, vol. 3, 1860, pp. 141–55.)

Saïd Abd-Allah, of the Mayek tribe south of Darfur, was captured about 1827, taken via Sennar to Cairo and bought by an Italian.

4556 FÉRAUD, Laurent Charles
'Délivrance d'esclaves nègres dans le sud de la province de Constantine.' (Revue Africaine, Constantine, vol. 16, 1872, pp. 167–79.)

Contains the narrative of Atman, a Hausa slave recently brought to Algeria. See (1516).

4557 *KRÄMER, August
Koba Michael. Eine Erstlingsfrucht auf dem ostafrikanischen Missionsfelde. Berlin, 1894.

On a Shambala slave boy baptised at the Tanga mission in 1892.

4558 *LATINI, Silvestro
Fed-el-Kerim, ovvero l'orfanella di Téghelé vittima della tratta dei negri. Torino, 1896. 80 pp.

See (1512).

4559 *LATINI, Silvestro
Suema ovvero una vittima della tratta dei negri. 2ª edizione. Cuneo, 1897. 68 pp.

See (1513).

4560 BALDOCK, W. F.
'The story of Rashid bin Hassani of the Bisa tribe, Northern Rhodesia, recorded by W. F. Baldock.' *In*: PERHAM, M. F. Ten Africans (London, 1936), pp. 81–119.

Rashid (Kibuli bin Mchubiri) was enslaved by Angoni raiders about 1882 and sold via Kilwa to Zanzibar.

4561 WELLENKAMP, Dieter
Der Mohr von Berlin. Afrikaforscher Rohlfs und Sklave Noël. Darmstadt, [1970]. 190 pp. illus, ports.

The Baghirmi boy Abd el Faradj accompanied Rohlfs from Murzuk to Lagos 1865–66 and in Egypt 1873; he spent the last 52 years of his life in a mental hospital at Ancona.

4562 *BONTEMPS, Arna Wendell, *editor*
Five black lives; the autobiographies of Venture Smith, James Mars, William Grimes, the Rev. G. W. Offley, James L. Smith . . . Middletown, Conn., [1971]. x, 240 pp.

For Venture Smith, see (1464).

SECTION L

4563 *BARBERENA, Santiago Ignacio
'Respecto a los esclavos africanos importados en el Nueva Mundo.' *In his*: Historia de El Salvador, vol. 2 (San Salvador, 1917), pp. 296–323.

4564 *ACOSTA SAIGNES, Miguel
'Gentilicios africanos en Venezuela.' (Archivos Venezolanos de Folklore, Caracas, vol. 3, no. 4, 1956, pp. 9–30.)

4565 BOYD-BOWMAN, Peter
'Negro slaves in early colonial Mexico.'

(The Americas, Washington, vol. 26, 1969, pp. 134–51; illus, map.)

Evidence for ethnic origins in documents 1527–85.

4566 *SURET-CANALE, Jean
'Les origines ethniques des anciens captifs au Fouta-Djalon.' (Notes Africaines, Dakar, no. 123, 1969, pp. 91–92.)

SECTION M

4567 AUBLET, Jean Baptiste Christophe Fusée
'Observations sur les négres esclaves.' *In his*: Histoire des plantes de la Guiane Françoise (Londres & Paris, 1775), vol. 2, app. pp. 111–22.

Emancipation would turn the colonial negro population into more productive workers. See (4109).

4568 *FRIENDS, Society of
To the General Assembly of the State of Rhode-Island, next to be holden at Providence. The petition and memorial of the representatives of the people called Quakers, in New-England, being met together in capacity of a meeting for sufferings . . . [Bennett Wheeler, Providence,] 1788. (1 p.)

On the slave trade. Dated Feb. 1788.

4569 *PORPHIRE, ——
Tableau précis de la malheureuse condition des nègres dans les colonies d'Amérique . . . Traduit de l'anglais. Londres; Regnault, Paris, 1788.

4570 *ADRESSE à l'Assemblée nationale par les propriétaires de St-Domingue résidans à Paris. [Paris? 1789?] 7 pp.

Protest against plans to abolish slavery.

4571 *LEGAL, G.
Observations sur tout ce qui concerne les colonies d'Amérique, notamment celle de Saint-Domingue. [Paris? 1789?] 64 pp.

Reply to (1978), on the French colonial slave trade.

4572 *LETTRE d'un habitant de la Martinique à tous les amis des noirs ou négromanes de France. [Paris? 1789.]

By ——Ducuré.

4573 CLARKSON, Thomas
Essai sur les désavantages politiques de la traite des nègres . . . Précédé de l'extrait de l'Essai sur le commerce

de l'espèce humaine, par le même auteur. Traduit de l'anglois par M. Gramagnac . . . Neufchatel, 1789. xxviii, 320 pp.

Translation of part of (1836) and of (1864).

4574 *ADRESSE à l'Assemblée nationale par les négocians de Bordeaux. [Bordeaux? 1789.] 5 pp.

Dated 28 Nov. 1789. See (1974).

4575 *ADRESSE de l'armée patriotique bordelaise à l'Assemblée nationale. Bordeaux, [1790]. 27 pp.

Opposes abolition of slavery or the slave trade.

4576 *ABEILLE, Jean Joseph André
Aperçu rapide sur les colonies. [Paris? 1790.] 7 pp.

Defends slavery. Dated 1 March 1790.

4577 *COURNAND, Antoine de
Réponse aux Observations d'un habitant des colonies sur le Mémoire en faveur des gens de couleur, ou sang-mêlés, de Saint-Domingue, & des autres isles françoises de l'Amérique, adressé à l'Assemblée nationale par M. Grégoire . . . [Paris? 1790.] 37 pp.

See (1986).

4578 *MÉMOIRES sur les nègres, pour servir de matériaux aux cahiers des colonies. (Signed: Un propriétaire à Saint-Domingue, député suppléant.) Clouzier, Paris, 1790. 41 pp.

4579 *SUITE de la Découverte d'une conspiration contre les intérêts de la France. [Paris? 1790?]

See (2031).

4580 *ÉVANGILE du jour. [Paris? 1791.] 4 pp.

Opposes a decree of the National Assembly on slavery. See (3163).

4581 'NOGLE Efterretninger om Neger-slaverne paa Guinea, og om deres Tilstand paa Europæernes americanske Colonier.' (Signed: M.F.L-g.) (Borger-Vennen, Kiøbenhavn, vol. 4, 1792, pp. 207–12, 215–20, 225–28.)

By M. F. Liebenberg. Hostile account of the slave trade and slavery.

4582 'BREV fra Landet.' (Signed: R-d G-e.) (Borger-Vennen, Kiøbenhavn, vol. 4, 1792, pp. 331–37.)

By J. P. Rosenstand-Goiske. Defends the Danish abolition decree (3165).

2A

4583 *CORBIN, Marie Thérèse Lucidor
Discours de la citoyenne Lucidor F. Corbin créole républicaine, prononcé par elle-même au Temple de la Raison, l'an 2ᵉ de la liberté. Coutubrier, Paris, [1794]. 2 pp.

Celebrates the French emancipation decree (3169).

4584 PRADT, Dominique Georges Frédéric Dufour de
'Des nègres et de l'esclavage aux colonies.' *In his*: Les trois âges des colonies, vol. 2 (Paris, 1801), pp. 54–134.

Colonial slavery must be reestablished.

4585 'OM Negerhandelens Ophævelse i Hensyn til de danske vestindiske Øer.' (Minerva, Kiøbenhavn, Feb. 1805, pp. 189–240.)

By J. P. Rosenstand-Goiske. Answers objections to the abolition of the Danish slave trade. See (2257).

4586 'An ADDRESS to the good sense of the people of the United Kingdom.' (Signed: Senex.) (Cobbett's Political Register, London, vol. 9, 1806, col. 66–79.)

Political and economic defence of the African slave trade, quoting Malthus in its favour.

4587 'NOGET mere om Negerhandelen i Anledning af Hr. Generalmajor Oxholms Anmærkninger &c.' (Ny Minerva, Kiøbenhavn, Julii 1806, pp. 1–39.)

By J. P. Rosenstand-Goiske. Reply to (2257). The editor, K. L. Rahbek, added an account of the slave trade debates in the British House of Commons: ibid., pp. 39–71, 142–78 (Aug.), 259–70 (Sept.); Oct. 1806, pp. 1–17.

4588 NELSON, Horatio, *Viscount Nelson*
'Slave trade. Copy of a letter from Lord Nelson to Mr. Simon Taylor of Jamaica, dated, Victory off Martinico, June 10, 1805.' (Cobbett's Political Register, London, vol. 11, 1807, col. 295–96.)

Vows opposition to the 'cursed doctrine' of the abolitionists.

SECTION N

4589 *EDWARDS, Jonathan
The injustice and impolicy of the slave trade, and of the slavery of the Africans: illustrated in a sermon . . . To which

is added, A short sketch of the evidence for the abolition of the slave trade, delivered before a committee of the British House of Commons. (Signed: W.B.C.) John Carter, Providence, [R.I.,] 1792. 60 pp.

See (2308) and 2144).

4590 GRIFFIN, Edward Dorr
A plea for Africa. A sermon preached October 26, 1817, in the First Presbyterian Church in the city of New-York, before the Synod of New-York and New-Jersey . . . Gould, New-York, 1817. 76 pp.

Includes notes on the slave trade and on some former slaves.

SECTION P

4591 *SIDNEY, Joseph
An oration, commemorative of the abolition of the slave trade in the United States; delivered in the African Asbury Church, in the city of New-York, on the first of January, 1814. J. S. Pudney, New-York, 1814. 15 pp.

4592 *HAMILTON, William
An oration, on the abolition of the slave trade. Delivered in the Episcopal Asbury African Church, in Elizabeth-St. New-York, January 2, 1815. By William Hamilton: a descendant of Africa. N.Y. African Society, New-York, 1815. 12 pp.

4593 'COMMERCIO da escravatura.' (Correio Braziliense, Londres, vol. 15, dez. 1815, pp. 735–39.)

The slave trade to Brazil should be abolished and replaced by mechanisation or European immigration.

4594 *GRÉGOIRE, Henri Baptiste
Observations préliminaires sur une nouvelle édition d'un ouvrage intitulé: Histoire du commerce homicide appelé traite des noirs. [Paris, 1822.] 4 pp.

Preface to the French translation of (2569).

4595 *FORSTER, Josiah
Adresse aux habitants de la ville de Nantes, par Josiah Forster, membre de la Société des amis communément appelés quakers. Lachevardière, Paris, [1824]. 3 pp.

On the slave trade.

4596 *FORSTER, Josiah
Quelques observations sur la traite des noirs. Lachevardière, Paris, [1824]. 4 pp.

4597 *DISCURSO historico-refutatorio-politico sobre a carta do Leitor Effectivo ... por um viajante de paizes coloniaes. Rio de Janeiro, 1825. 74 pp.

> Reply to an article by an opponent of abolition in Brazil.

4598 *BUXTON, *Sir* Thomas Fowell
Letter on the slave trade, to the Lord Viscount Melbourne, and the other members of Her Majesty's Cabinet Council. J. W. Parker, London, 1838. xv, 215 pp.

> See (2645).

4599 *MELLO MORAES, Alexandre José de
A Inglaterra e seus tratados ou o governo inglez perante o mundo. Bahia, 1844.

4600 *VELLOSO DE OLIVEIRA, Henrique
A substituição do trabalho dos escravos pelo trabalho livre no Brasil por um meio suave e sem difficuldade. Obra offerecida á nação brasileira e precedida de uma allocução á assembléa geral legislativa. Rio de Janeiro, 1845.

4601 *HORRORS of the slave trade. [London? 1848.] 16 pp.

4602 FITZHUGH, George
'The Conservative principle; or, social evils and their remedies. Part II.—Slave trade.' (DBR, vol. 22, May 1857, pp. 449–62.)

> Urges resumption of the African slave trade by the United States.

4603 *The CHARLESTON Courier and the slave trade, By Las Casas. [n.p., 1858.] 16 pp.

> By Alexander Mazyck.

4604 *COXE, Richard Smith
The present state of the African slave trade: an exposition of some of the causes of its continuance and prosperity, with suggestions as to the most effectual means of repressing and extinguishing it. Washington [D.C.], 1858. 36pp.

> Also printed as: 3410.

4605 FRIENDS, Society of
Addresses and papers illustrative of Christian principle or testimony, issued within the last fifty years, by or on behalf of the yearly meeting of the religious society of Friends. London, 1863. viii, 248 pp.

> Edited by J. Forster. Includes publications on the slave trade and slavery 1822–54 (pp. 95–175). See (2573, 2759, 2788).

4606 CAMERON, Verney Lovett
'Colonisation of central Africa.' (Proceedings of the Royal Colonial Institute, London, vol. 7, 1876, pp. 274–96.)

> Lecture given 13 June 1876, and discussion; only colonisation can put an end to the slave trade in Africa.

4607 A POLICY for the eastern Soudan and central Africa. (Signed: Index.) Biarritz, 1885. 37 pp.

> By T.H.B. The conquest of the upper Nile and East Africa will solve Britain's economic problems and avert God's wrath from Europe for not suppressing the slave trade.

4608 *BORTOLUCCI, Giovanni
Il cardinale Lavigerie e la sua propaganda per l'abolizione della schiavitù: lettera. Bologna, 1889. 13 pp.

4609 *DEUTSCHE KOLONIALGESELL-SCHAFT
Gegen den Sklavenhandel! [Berlin, 1891.] 25 pp.

> By Bertha von Suttner. See (616).

4610 *GOBBI, *Mons.* G. B.
La schiavitù, appello alla carità cristiana: brevi parole dette il 6 gennaio 1897. Bassano, 1897. 11 pp.

4611 *SCIALDONI, Luigi
I villaggi di libertà: discorso. S. Vito al Tagliamento, 1908. 16 pp.

> Reprinted from (4616), pp. 48–62.

4612 *GENOCCHI, Giovanni
Il cristianesimo e la schiavitù: discorso. S. Vito al Tagliamento, 1908. 9 pp.

> Reprinted from (4616), pp. 63–70.

SECTION Q (a)

4613 *SOCIÉTÉ DES AMIS DES NOIRS
Lettre aux bailliages de France. [Paris, 1789.] 6 pp.

> By Condorcet. Urges abolition of the slave trade. See (2339, 3039).

4614 *NORTH OF ENGLAND ANTI-SLAVERY LEAGUE
Report of the proceedings of the anti-slavery conference and public meeting, held at Manchester, on the 1st August, 1854, in commemoration of West India emancipation. London & Manchester, 1854. 40 pp.

4615 *BRITISH AND FOREIGN ANTI-SLAVERY SOCIETY
London anti-slavery conference. Papers

read and statements made on the principal subjects submitted to the anti-slavery conference, held at the London Tavern on the 29th and 30th of November 1854. London, [1854]. 36 pp.

Also reported in: Anti-Slavery Reporter, London, ser. 3, vol. 3, 1855, pp. 12–15.

4616 *CONGRESSO ANTISCHIAVISTA ITALIANO
Atti del secondo Congresso antischiavista italiano tenuto in Roma nei giorni 3–4–5 decembre 1907. S. Vito al Tagliamento, 1908. 90 pp.

Issued as: Bollettino della Società Antischiavista Italiana, vol. 21, 1908, no. 1. See (4611–12).

4617 *AMERICAN CONVENTION FOR PROMOTING THE ABOLITION OF SLAVERY

Minutes, constitution, addresses, memorials, resolutions, reports, committees and anti-slavery tracts. 1794–1829. New York, [1969]. 3 vol.

SECTION R

4618 GREAT BRITAIN: Foreign Office
'Negociaçoens no Congresso de Vienna, sobre o commercio de escravatura.' (Correio Braziliense, Londres, vol. 14, abril 1815, pp. 409–17.)

Letters written by Castlereagh from Vienna, Oct. 1814–Jan. 1815.

4619 EARNSHAW, William
A digest of the laws (from 12 Charles II. to 58 George III. inclusive) relating to shipping, navigation, commerce, and revenue, in the British colonies in America and the West Indies, including the laws abolishing the slave trade. A. Strahan, London, 1818. xx, 424 pp.

Contains laws on the slave trade 1805–18 and the abolition treaties with Spain and Portugal 1817. (A new edition 1819 adds the Dutch treaty of 1818 and the British slave registry laws of 1819.)

4620 UNITED STATES OF AMERICA: House of Representatives, (*Committee on Commerce*)
Report of Mr. Kennedy, of Maryland, from the Committee on commerce of the House of Representatives of the United States, on the memorial of the friends of African colonization, assembled in convention in the city of Washington, May, 1842. To which is appended

. . . all the diplomatic correspondence between the United States and Great Britain, on the subject of the African slave trade. February 28, 1843 . . . Gales & Seaton, Washington, 1843. xiv, 1088 pp. map. (27th Cong., 3d sess. House. Rep. 382.)

Headed: 'African colonization — slave trade — commerce.' Official correspondence on the slave trade about 1817–43.

4621 UNITED STATES OF AMERICA Department of State
African slave trade. Message from the President of the United States, transmitting, in compliance with a resolution of the House, a report from the Secretary of State in reference to the African slave trade, December 6, 1860 . . . [Washington, 1860.] 648 pp. (36th Congress, 2d session. House of Representatives. Ex. doc. no. 7.)

Official correspondence on the slave trade 1855–60.

4622 *PEREIRA PINTO, Antônio
Apontamentos para o direito internacional ou collecção completa dos tratados celebrados pelo Brazil com differentes nações estrangeiras . . . Rio de Janeiro, 1864–68. 4 vol.

Vol. 1 contains Portuguese and Brazilian slave trade treaties 1810–27.

SECTION S(b)

4623 *BAILEY, John Crawshay
First commission of H.M.S. "Sharpshooter." [London? 1893?] 264 pp. illus.

On antislavery patrolling off Brazil in 1851. See (3454).

SECTION S(d)

**4624 *The CREOLE case and Mr. Webster's despatch; with the comments of the N.Y. American. New-York American, New-York, 1842. 39 pp.

By William Jay.

4625 *TOWNSEND, Henry
Letter to Capt. Trotter, R. N. on the African coast blockade. London, 1849.
See (3387).

SECTION S(e)

4626 GRAHAM, Gerald Sandford
Great Britain in the Indian Ocean. A study of maritime enterprise 1810–1850. Oxford, 1967. xii, 479 pp. maps.

Includes chapters on the East African slave trade and its suppression by the British navy.

SECTION U

4627 *CAMBIER, René
Carte des campagnes antiesclavagistes. (Kaart van de veldtochten tegen de slavenhandel.) Bruxelles, 1952. 8 pp. map. (Atlas général du Congo belge.)

Map of the antislavery expeditions in the Congo Free State, with notes.

SECTION V

4628 'CARTA do bispo de Cabo Verde a el-Rei (século XVI).' In: BRÁSIO, A. Monumenta missionaria africana, ser. 2, vol. 3 (Lisboa, 1964), pp. 442–45.

Letter, probably from Bishop Pedro Brandão c. 1598, urging legislation to emancipate all baptized African slaves, most of whom were unjustly enslaved. See (1683–84).

4629 HAUBERT, Maxime
L'Église et la défense des "sauvages". Le père Antoine Vieira au Brésil. Bruxelles, 1964. 280 pp. map, port.

Pt. 2, ch. 3: 'La servitude des hommes de couleur'; Vieira accepted 'just' slavery. See (3803).

4630 *CASTAÑEDA, Humberto
'El caso de Dr. David Turnbull, el cónsul inglés.' (Universidad de La Habana, La Habana, no. 168–69, 1964, pp. 127–53.)

See (4138).

4631 *LA GAYE, Jacques
'L'Église et l'esclavage des Indes de 1537 à 1708.' (Travaux de l'Institut d'Études Latino-Américaines de l'Université de Strasbourg, vol. 5, 1965, pp. 91–101.)

Papal antislavery policy was contradicted by the complicity of some churchmen in American slavery.

4632 *AUSTEN, Ralph Albert and SMITH, Woodruff Donald
'Images of Africa and British slave-trade abolition: the transition to an imperialist ideology, 1787–1807.' (African Historical Studies, Boston, vol. 2, 1969, pp. 69–84.)

4633 *DAGET, Serge
'J. E. Morenas à Paris, l'action abolitionniste, 1819–1821.' (BIFAN, ser. B, vol. 31, 1969, pp. 875–85.)

See (2554).

4634 TENÓRIO D'ALBUQUERQUE, Alcir
A maçonaria e a libertação dos escravos. A abolição da escravatura, uma grandiosa vitória da maçonaria . . . Rio de Janeiro, 1970. 373 pp. illus.

On the antislavery movement in Brazil, with special reference to freemasonry.

4635 *LUWEL, Marcel
'Un plan d'action contre les esclavagistes dressé par l'explorateur Hermann von Wissmann.' (Africa, Tervuren, vol. 16, 1970, pp. 85–106; illus.)

See (641).

4636 DAGET, Serge
'L'abolition de la traite des noirs en France de 1814 à 1831.' (CEA, vol. 11, 1971, pp. 14–58.)

The abolition issue was political, lacking 'un humanitarisme essentiel'.

4637 DUCHET, Michèle
'La critique du système esclavagiste.' In her: Anthropologie et histoire au siècle des lumières (Paris, 1971), pp. 137–93; bibl.

On French antislavery ideas in the period 1750–89. See (4641).

4638 *DE JONG, Gerald Francis
'The Dutch Reformed Church and negro slavery in colonial America.' (Church History, New York, vol. 40, 1971, pp. 423–36.)

4639 MAC MASTER, Richard Kerwin
'Anti-slavery and the American Revolution. A crack in the liberty bell.' (HT, vol. 21, 1971, pp. 715–23; illus.)

On the antislavery movement 1770–90.

4640 TEMPERLEY, Howard
British antislavery 1833–1870. London, 1972. xvii, 298 pp. bibl. pp. 277–84.

Ch. 9: 'The abolitionists and the slave trade 1839–1853.' See (4477).

SECTION W

4641 DUCHET, Michèle
'Esclavage et humanisme en 1787. Un mémoire inédit de Saint-Lambert sur les gens de couleur.' (Annales Historiques de la Révolution Française, Paris, vol. 37, 1965, pp. 344–60.)

With the text of Saint-Lambert's 'Réflexions sur les moyens de rendre meilleur l'état des nègres ou des affranchis de nos colonies' (pp. 349–60). Reprinted in (4637), pp. 177–93.

4642 DAVIS, David Brion
'New sidelights on early antislavery radicalism.' (WMQ, ser. 3, vol. 28, 1971, pp. 585–94.)

On George Wallace and other abolitionist writers 1760–62.

SECTION X

4643 THAARUP, Frederik
'Den afskaffede Negerhandel.' *In his*: Udførlig Vejledning til det danske Monarkies Statistik, vol. 6 (Kjøbenhavn, 1819), pp. 659–98.

Account of the abolition of the Danish slave trade, 1791–1805.

4644 *BUZZATI, Giulio Cesare
La schiavitù e la tratta; discorso letto il giorno 8 novembre 1891 per l'inaugurazione dell'anno accademico nella R. Università di Macerata. Macerata, 1891. 40 pp.

4645 VELLA, Oreste da
'La Francia e la conferenza antischiavista di Bruxelles.' (Rassegna Nazionale, Firenze, vol. 66, 1892, pp. 3–24.)

On anti-slave trade agreements 1814–90. (Reprinted separately: Firenze, 1892; 24 pp.)

4646 TRIER, Carl Aage
'Det dansk-vestindiske Negerindførselsforbud af 1792.' (Historisk Tidsskrift, Kjøbenhavn, ser. 7, vol. 5, 1905, pp. 405–508.)

On the background to the Danish abolition decree (3165) and its implementation 1792–1807.

4647 *LEWIS, Alonzo N.
'Recollections of the Amistad slave case: first revelation of a plot to force the slave question to an issue more than twenty years before its final outbreak in the civil war . . .' (Connecticut Magazine, Hartford, vol. 11, 1907, pp. 125 ff.)

4648 *TAMBORRA, T.
'Un decreto di Ferdinando II sull'abolizione della schiavitù.' (Africa, Napoli, no. 1, 1939, pp. 9–12.)

See (3198).

4649 WYATT-BROWN, Bertram
'The Mendi Africans.' *In his*: Lewis Tappan and the evangelical war against slavery (Cleveland, 1969), pp. 205–25.

Describes Tappan's role in releasing the 'Amistad' captives. See (3486).

4650 FINAZZO, Giuseppina
'Il granducato di Toscana e l'abolizione della tratta.' (Africa, Roma, vol. 25, 1970, pp. 413–36; vol. 26, 1971, pp. 59–84.)

Though Tuscany acceded to anti-slave trade treaties in 1837 her citizens were involved in slaving cases until at least 1845.

SECTION Y

4651 BRUNS, Roger
'Anthony Benezet's assertion of negro equality.' (JNH, vol. 56, 1971, pp. 230–38.)

From 1762 Benezet added human equality to the theological arguments against slavery.

4652 SEBALD, Peter
Malam Musa — Gottlob Adolf Krause, 1850–1938. Forscher — Wissenschaftler — Humanist. Leben und Lebenswerk eines antikolonial gesinnten Afrika-Wissenschaftlers unter den Bedingungen des Kolonialismus. Berlin, 1972. 291 pp. map. bibl. pp. 265–91.

Krause agitated against the slave trade in Togo during the 1890s.

SECTION Z

4653 *'INTREPIDITY of a negro woman.'
(Massachusetts Magazine, Boston, vol. 3, Dec. 1791, p. 228.)

A slave gives birth on a ship and throws her child overboard.

4654 *'TAILLAH.' (Massachusetts Magazine, Boston, vol. 4, April 1792, pp. 250–51.)

An American, rescued from a shipwreck by an African woman, sells her and her family into slavery.

4655 *CORBIN, Marie Thérèse Lucidor
Hymne des citoyens de couleurs, par la citoyenne Corbin, créole et républicaine. Coutubrier, Paris, [1794]. 2 pp.

See (4583).

4656 RUSHTON, Edward
'Briton, and negro slave.' *In his*: Poems (London, 1806), pp. 84–88.

4657 RUSHTON, Edward
Poems and other writings . . . To which is added, a sketch of the life of the author, by the Rev. William Shepherd. Effingham Wilson, London, 1824. xxviii, 212, 10 pp.

Includes 'The Coromantees', a poem

about a slaving voyage (pp. 72–76), and other antislavery pieces.

4658 *WAAL, Anton de
Tim, der Negerknabe. Schauspiel in drei Aufzügen . . . Paderborn, 1889. 44 pp.

> Based on the story of Allagábo (Lebbe), a Bongo boy captured by Dinka about 1870 and brought to Germany by G. Schweinfurth.

APPENDIX I

4659 WHALLEY, Wilfred
Slavery and its abolition, particularly with regard to England's efforts for its extinction to the year 1846, and with especial reference to the West Indies. Manchester, 1926. (M.A.)

4660 McCONNELL, Roland Calhoun
The reopening of the African slave-trade to the United States of America, 1850–1860. [Washington,] 1933. (M.A., Howard)

4661 BELLEGARDE, Auguste Dantès
Évariste-Désiré Parny, poète et philanthrope. [Québec,] 1948. 246 pp. (Ph.D., Laval)

> See (3851).

4662 OWEN, Gwynne Evan
Welsh anti-slavery sentiments 1790–1865: a survey of public opinion. Aberystwyth, 1964. (M.A.)

4663 M'BAYE, Guèye
L'esclavage au Sénégal de la fin du XVIIᵉ siècle au début du XXᵉ siècle. Nantes, 1969. 445 pp. (3e cycle)

> Ch. 1–2 on the slave trade and its suppression.

4664 BROHOVICI, Liviu Sorel
L'hygiène et l'état sanitaire au temps de la navigation à voiles—navires négriers et galères. Paris, 1969. 55 pp. (Doctorat, médecine)

4665 DAGET, Serge
La France et l'abolition de la traite des noirs de 1814 à 1831. Introduction à l'étude de la répression française de la traite des noirs au XIXᵉ siècle. Paris, 1969. 357 pp. (3e cycle)

4666 DANTZIG, Albert van
Les Hollandais et l'essor de l'Ashanti et du Dahomey. Paris, 1970. (3e cycle)

4667 MARISSAL, Jacques
La traite orientale à Zanzibar. Paris, 1970. (Maîtrise, Sorbonne)

4668 FILLIOT, Jean Michel
La traite des esclaves vers les Mascareignes au XVIIIᵉ siècle. Paris, 1970. (3e cycle, Sorbonne)

4669 BOULANGER, Alain
Deux négriers nantais d'après leurs journaux, 1741–1744. Nantes, 1970. (Maîtrise)

4670 BLANC, Patricia
Le sucre et la traite des noirs à Cuba. Paris, 1970. (Maîtrise, Sorbonne)

4671 TSIMANGA, Zacharie
Le rôle de la France à la conférence anti-esclavagiste de Bruxelles de 1889 et 1890. Toulouse, 1970. (3e cycle)

4672 METGE, Anne-Marie
La conférence de Bruxelles de 1890 sur la traite africaine. Paris, 1970. (Maîtrise, Sorbonne)

4673 KAPLAN, Richard Paul
Daniel Defoe's views on slavery and racial prejudice. [New York,] 1970. 220 pp. (Ph.D., New York)

> Summary: DA, vol. 31, 1971, p. 6556.

4674 BEAN, Richard Nelson
The British trans-Atlantic slave trade, 1650–1775. [Seattle,] 1971. 298 pp. (Ph.D., Washington)

> Summary: DA, vol. 32, 1972, pp. 4221–22.

4675 DAGET, Serge
La répression française de la traite des noirs de 1817 à 1885. Paris, 1971. (Doctorat, Sorbonne)

AUTHOR INDEX

A., J. S. *See* Suárez Argudín, J.
A., W. (1792). *See* Allen, W. (1770–1843)
A., W. (1849), 1493
Abbadie, Antoine Thompson d' (1810–97), 590, 2951, 3017
Abdel-Malek, A., 125
Abdulbaki, *Sarkin Burmi*, 1592
Abeille, Jean Joseph André (1756–1842), 4576
Abeken, Hermann (1820–54), 2737
Aberdeen, *Lord. See* Hamilton-Gordon, G.
Abignente, Giovanni (1854–1915), 3637
Abingdon, *4th Earl of. See* Bertie, W.
Abir, Mordechai, 689
Aborigines' Protection Society, 3146
Abou Bekir Sadiki. *See* Abū Bakr al-Siddīq
Abramova, Svetlana Yur'evna, 352
Abreu de Brito, Domingos de, 217
Abreu y Bertodano, Joseph Antonio de, 931
Abū Bakr al-Siddīq (*c.* 1790–   ), 1477, 1479, 1568, 1593
Acosta Saignes, Miguel, 1391, 1436, 4564
Adair, James Makittrick (1728–1802), 2024
Adam, William, 496
Adams, Ephraim Douglass (1865–1930), 3436
Adams, Henry Gardiner, 1502
Adams, James Hopkins (1812–61), 3215
Adams, Jane Elizabeth, 3693
Adams, John (d. 1866), 739
Adams, John Quincy (1767–1848), 2409, 3489
Adams, Robert, 379
Adams, Thomas Maxwell, 1865
Adee, Augustus Alvey (1802–44), 3462
Adger, John Bailey (1810–99), 2808
Adjuah (Marie Adélaïde; *c.* 1886–   ), 1541
Adney, Thomas, 4237
African Civilization Society, 3076–77, 3080, 3083, 3085, 3143
African Institution, 43, 45, 2499, 2503, 2536, 2551, 3066, 3171
Africanus, *pseud.*, 1858, 1929
Afrika-Verein deutscher Katholiken, 3152
Agostini, Domenico, *Cardinal*, 2949
Aguessy, Honorat, 4518
Aguilera, Francisco Vicente (d. 1877), 1150
Aguirre Beltrán, Gonzalo, 1312–13, 1646–7
Agutter, William, 2294
Ahuma, Samuel Richard Brew Attoh (1863–1921), 1543
Aimes, Hubert Hillary Suffern, 1193, 4435
Aiton, Arthur Scott, 1232
Akinjógbìn, Isaac Adéagbo, 342
Akinola, G. A., 691
Alamandini, Fortunato, 142
Albert, James. *See* Gronniosaw, U.
Alberti, Christian Carl (1814–90), 1137
Albionicus, *pseud.*, 2213
Alboize du Pujol, Jules Édouard (1805–54), 4357
Albuquerque Felner, Alfredo de, 217
Alden, Carroll Storrs, 3439

Aldridge, Harold Richard, 4541
Alexander, Ann (1767–1849), 2249
Alexander, George William (1802–90), 2659, 2691, 2697
Alexander, *Sir* James Edward (1803–85), 3263
Alexander, Jorge G. *See* Alexander, G. W.
Alexander, Joseph Gundry, 3130
Alexander, Stella, 3774
Alexander, William, 2646
Alexis, *Frère. See* Gochet, J. B.
Alfred, *pseud.* (1793), 2157
Alfred, *pseud.* (1811, 14), 222, 2459
Ali Effendi Gifoon (1836–91), 1533
Ali Eisami Gazirmabe (*c.* 1786–   ), 1499, 1593
Allemand-Lavigerie, Charles Martial, *Cardinal* (1825–92), 465, 619, 2332, 2888, 2900–1, 2906, 2908–9, 2912, 2916, 2923, 2932–3, 2953, 2958–9, 2974, 2976–7, 2984, 2986–8, 2992, 3000, 3003, 3100, 3102–3, 3105–6
Allen, Bernard Meredith (1864–   ), 3557
Allen, Charles Harris, 463, 2898, 3015
Allen, James, 1939
Allen, William (1770–1843), 2095
Allen, William (1793–1864), 3274, 3362
Alletz, Édouard, 4321
Allinson, William J. (1810–74), 1496
Almeida Correia de Sá, José de, *marquez de Lavradio* (1874–   ), 3724
Almeida e Araujo Corrêa de Lacerda, José de (1803–77), 565
Almeida Prado, João Fernando de (1898–   ), 1335, 1361
Alpers, Edward Alter (1941–   ), 687, 4485, 4529
Álvares d'Almada, André, 149, 188
Alves, João Luiz, 3677
Alves Branco Moniz Barreto, D. *See* Moniz Barreto, D. A. B.
Amaral, Braz Hermenegildo do, 1616, 1621
American Anti-Slavery Society, 2642, 2815, 3073–5, 3139
American Colonization Society, 2550, 2790, 3068, 3135
American Convention for promoting the Abolition of Slavery, 3057–8, 3065, 4617
American Missionary Association, 2832
American Society for Colonizing the Free People of Colour in the United States. *See* American Colonization Society
American Tract Society, 2725, 2844
Americanus, *pseud.*, 3339
Amicus, *pseud.*, 1138, 2146
Amon, *chevalier* d'. *See* Damon
Amsterdam: *Stad*, 1094
Amunátegui Solar, Domingo (1860–   ), 1248
Amyntor, *pseud. See* Belknap, J.
Andel, Martinus Antonie van (1878–1941), 904
Anderson, James (1739–1808), 1932
Anderson-Morshead, Anne Elizabeth Mary, 659

Boutillier, Jean Louis, 361
Boutwell, George Sewall, 783
Bouveignes, Olivier de, 320
Bowden, James, 3598
Bowdich, Sarah, 4340
Bowles, William Lisle (1762–1850), 4249
Bowring, Sir John (1792–1872), 384, 2559
Bowser, Frederick Park, 4496
Boxer, Charles Ralph (1904–), 1341, 1742
Boyd, Willis D. (1924–), 3470
Boyd-Bowman, Peter, 4565
Boyle, James, 875
Bradburn, Samuel (1751–1816), 2137
Bradshaw, Thomas, 2296
Brady, Cyrus Townsend (1887–), 673
Brakel, Simon van (1879——), 1203, 1206, 1212
Bramley, W. E. J. See Jennings Bramley, W. E.
Branagan, Thomas (1774–), 2239, 2245, 4283, 4290
Brand, Charles, 3588
Brandão, Pedro, Bishop of Cabo Verde (d. 1608), 4628
Brandis, Bernhard, 4036
Brandt, L., 1178
Brasahemeco, Ananias Dortano, pseud. See Barão de Mascarenhas, A.
Brásio, António, 188, 776, 4628
Brazil: Laws, 3212
Brazil: Treaties, 4622
Brazil, Etienne I. de. See Étienne, I.
Bready, John Wesley (1887–), 3734
Bréard, Charles (1839–), 1170
Brecht, Theodor, 3638
Breckinridge, Robert Jefferson (1800–71), 2671
Brent, John Carroll, 3275
Bressi, Salvatore Maria Brunone, Archbishop of Otranto, 2952
Bretagne, Christian, 118
Brewster, James, 4002
Brewster, John (1753–1842), 4196
Brewster, Robert Wallace, 3738
Bridge, Horatio (1806–93), 3269
Bridges, George Wilson, 1606
Brie-Serrant, Clément Alexandre, marquis (1748–1814), 2087
Briggs, Thomas V., 787
Brioschi, Pedro A., 4056
Brisson, Pierre Raymond de, 724
Brissot, Anacharsis, 4004
Brissot, Jacques Pierre (1754–93), 1859, 1892, 1954, 1985, 2043, 2050, 4004
Britannicus, pseud. (1773), 1780
Britannicus, pseud. (1792), 4232
Britannicus, pseud. (1804), 2240, 2274
Britannus, pseud., 1933
British and Foreign Anti-Slavery Society, 30, 278, 456, 458, 463, 499, 550, 604, 656, 761, 897, 2678, 2698–9, 2707, 2712, 2801, 2853–4, 3079, 3081–2, 3084, 3086–9, 3091–5, 3141, 3493, 3653, 4615
British and Foreign Society for the Universal Abolition of Negro Slavery and the Slave Trade, 3138
Brito, Figueroa, Federico, 1140, 1406, 1413
Brock, Robert Alonzo (1839–1914), 1162
Brode, Heinrich, 552
Brodie, William, 3386
Broglie, Achille Léonce Victor Charles, duc de (1785–1870), 2391–3
Brohovici, Liviu Sorel, 4664
Brøndsted, Johannes (1890–1965), 321, 3763

Brooke, Henry K., 747
Brookes, George Sprague, 4106
Brougham, Henry Peter, Baron Brougham and Vaux (1778–1868), 2228, 2231–2, 2236, 2393, 2402–6, 2410, 2412, 2419
Brown, David Paul (1795–1872), 4008
Brown, Genevieve, 4456
Brown, Godfrey Norman, 133
Brown, Joseph M., 3506
Brown, Robert (1842–95), 96
Brown, Vera Lee (1890–), 1223
Brown, William Keer, 3407
Browne, Albert Gallatin (1835–91), 3499
Browne, Arthur Bevil, 4096
Browne, Granville, 4058
Browne, John Hutton Balfour (1845–1921), 583
Browne, William George (1768–1813), 376
Browning, James Blackwell, 1242
Bruce, Charles, 540
Bruce, Eleanor, 4097
Brue, André (1654–1738), 147
Brulez, Wilfrid, 833
Bruns, Roger, 4651
Brunschwig, Henri (1904–), 128
Brussels Slave Trade Conference, 31, 3104, 3112, 3114, 3118, 3229, 3232
Bryan, Edward B., 2814
Bryant, William Cullen (1794–1878), 4339
Bryson, Alexander (1802–69), 884, 888
Buchanan, George (1763–1808), 2154, 3622
Buchanan, James (1791–1868), 2420, 4621
Buchner, Max, 534
Buck, Jean Marie de, 3561
Buenos Aires: Municipalidad, 1208
Buffet, Henri François, 1265
Buhões, M. de, 2884
Bull, Josiah, 4046
Burckhardt, John Lewis (1784–1817), 380
Burdett, William, 4279
Burdo, Alphonse, 597
Burgess, Thomas (1756–1837), 1931
Burgess, Wilson, 2780
Burke, Edmund (?1729–97), 2279, 2335, 2388, 2539
Burlamaqui, Frederico Leopoldo Cesar (1803–66), 2629
Burn, Andrew (1742–1814), 2093, 2116
Burnett, Sir William (1779–1861), 884
Burns, Robert (1759–96), 4207, 4386
Burton, Richard Francis (1821–90), 202, 508
Burton, William Frederick Padwick (1886–), 667
Burtt, Joseph, 278
Busson, Jean Pierre, 4546
Butini, Jean François, 4174
Butler, Weeden (1742–1828), 4173, 4252
Butterworth, William, pseud. See Schroeder, H.
Büttner, Carl Gotthilf, 2915
Buxton, Charles (1822–71), 4026
Buxton, Sydney Charles, 2430
Buxton, Sir Thomas Fowell (1786–1845), 55, 240, 562, 2644–5, 2656, 3080, 3095, 4026, 4598
Buxton, Travers, 4072
Buyacost, A., 412
Buzzati, Giulio Cesare (1862–1920), 4644
Byam, Edward Samuel, 2447
Byers, Samuel Hawkins Marshall (1838–1933), 785
Byrd, William (1674–1744), 3646

2B

Marshall, John (1755–1835), 3484
Marshall, Peter, 3815
Martens, Fedor Fedorovich, 3425
Martens, Georg Friedrich von (1756–1821), 3181
Martens, Karl, *Freiherr* von (1790–1863), 3210
Martin, Bernard Davis (1897–), 774, 828, 4124, 4144
Martin, Christopher, *pseud. See* Hoyt, E. P.
Martin, Eveline Christiana, 216, 1238
Martin, Gaston, 1244, 1260, 1324
Martin, James (1738–1810), 2335, 2539
Martin, Percy Alvin (1879–1942), 3719, 3731, 3741
Martin, Phyllis, 372
Martin, Samuel, 1780
Martin, Thomas Powderley (1887–), 3691, 3699
Martínez Montero, Homero, 1293
Martitz, Ferdinand von (1839–1921), 3916
Maryland Society for promoting the Abolition of Slavery, 3043
Mason, George Champlin (1820–94), 1151
Mason, Michael, 370, 374
Mason, William (1725–97), 2293
Mason, William Powell (1791–1867), 3481
Massachusetts: *Laws*, 3042
Massachusetts: *Senate*, 3200
Massie, James William, 2728
Massio, R., 1662
Masson, Michel (1800–83), 4349
Mather, Cotton (1663–1728), 1702
Mathews, Donald G., 3793
Mathews, Godfrey William, 4093
Mathieson, William Law (1868–), 3701
Mathison, Gilbert Farquhar, 2509, 2511
Matip, Benjamin, 1379
Matlack, Lucius C., 3597, 3628
Matson, Henry James (1810–), 3356
Mattagne, Antoine, 3577
Matthews, John, 161
Maugat, Émile, 1358
Maunder, George, 4031–2
Mauny, Raymond, 776
Maupassant, Jean de, 3438
Mauri, Egidio, *Bishop of Osimo* (1828–96), 2902
Mauro, Frédéric, 1383
May, Karl (1842–1912), 4424, 4431
May, Philip S., 1316
Mayer, Brantz (1809–79), 754
Maynard, Douglas H., 3778
Mayo, William Starbuck, 4377
Mazères, F., 2495
Mazois, Marc, 1988
Mazyck, Alexander, 4603
Mazyck, Walter H., 3709
M'Baye, Guèye, 4481, 4663
Mbotela, James Juma, 1581
Meadley, George Wilson (1774–1818), 2278
Meaux, Marie Camille Alfred de, *vicomte*, 2945
Meckling, Frank E., 4459
Meerveldhoven, Paschasius van, 102
Meillassoux, Claude, 4526
Meiners, Christoph (1747–1810), 1602, 1906, 2017, 2034
Mejía, Antonio, 2562
Meléndez, Ch. Carlos, 1674
Mellafe, Rolando, 1380, 1412
Mello, Miguel Antonio de, 971
Mello Moraes, Alexandre José de (1816–82), 4599

Mellon, Matthew Taylor (1897–), 3721
Mellor, George Radcliffe, 3757
Melville, Herman (1819–91), 4382
Mendes, M. M. *See* Maia Mendes, M.
Mendes Castello Branco, Garcia, 206
Mendiburu, Manuel de, 1142
Mendoça Corte-Real, Diogo de (1658–1736), 1044, 1046
Mendonça, Renato, 1626, 1648
Mends, Herbert, 2305
Menges, Josef, 615
Menkman, W. R., 1264, 1291, 1300, 1306, 1320, 1347
Mentor, Étienne Victor, 2365
Mercado, Thomas de (d. 1575), 1783
Mercator, *pseud.* (1772), 1103
Mercator, *pseud.* (1807). *See* Gladstone, J.
Mercator, *pseud.* (1811), 2450
Mercator Honestus, *pseud.*, 1717
Mercer, Charles Fenton (1778–1858), 2790
Merensky, Alexander, 2946
Mérimée, Prosper (1803–70), 823, 4345, 4361
Merlin, Mercédes, *condesa* de (1788–1852), 2677, 2718
Merrien, Jean, *pseud. See* Fréminville, R. M. L. de
Merrill, Louis Taylor, 3751
Merriman-Labor, A. B. C., 98
Merritt, James E., 4474
Merry, Robert, 4205
Merse and Teviotdale, *Synod of*, 2053
Messedaglia, Luigi (1874–), 3563
Metcalfe, George Edgar, 2645
Metcalfe, James Stetson (1858–1927), 100, 782
Metge, Anne-Marie, 4672
Meyer, Jean, 1386, 4544
Meyer-Heiselberg, Richard, 3472
Meynadier, Jacques, 1727
Michael, Charles D., 4060
Michelsen, A., 527
Michiels, Alfred (1813–92), 4379
Middleton, Arthur Pierce, 1576
Mier Noriega y Guerra, Servando Teresa de (1763–1827), 3989
Miers, Suzanne, 3810, 4499
Mifflin, Warner (1745–98), 2153, 2192
Mignard, Jacques, 2184
Miles, Victor, 3422
Millant, Richard, 474
Millar, John (1735–1801), 1756
Miller, C. W., 2802
Miller, Samuel, 2196
Miller, William, 2324
Millin, Samuel Shannon, 1224
Millingen, Frederick, 401
Milly, Louis Lezin de, 1996
Milman, Henry Hart, 4343
Milne, Alexander Taylor, 3445, 3447, 4443
Milton, *Lord. See* Fitzwilliam, C. W. W.
Mims, Stewart Lea (1880–), 1200
Minchinton, Walter Edward, 820
Mirabeau, *comte de. See* Riquetti, H. G.
Mirabeau, *vicomte de. See* Riquetti, A. B. L.
Miramón, Alberto, 1307
Mockler-Ferryman, Augustus Ferryman (1856–1930), 468
Moens, Petronella, 4271
Moir, Frederick Lewis Maitland (1852–), 3552
Moister, William, 3616
Molina, Luis de, 1685

PERSONAL NAME INDEX

GEOGRAPHICAL NAME INDEX

ANONYMOUS TITLE INDEX